IMPOSSIBLE DREAM

IMPOSSIBLE DREAM

THE MARCOSES, THE AQUINOS, AND THE UNFINISHED REVOLUTION

SANDRA BURTON

WARNER BOOKS

A Warner Communications Company

Copyright © 1989 by Sandra Burton
All rights reserved.

Warner Books, Inc., 666 Fifth Avenue, New York, NY 10103
W A Warner Communications Company

Printed in the United States of America
First printing: March 1989
10 9 8 7 6 5 4 3 2 1

Library of Congress Cataloging-in-Publication Data

Burton, Sandra.
  Impossible dream : the Marcoses, the Aquinos and the unfinished
revolution / Sandra Burton.
      p.   cm.
  1. Philippines—Politics and government—1973– 2. Marcos,
Ferdinand E. (Ferdinand Edralin), 1917– 3. Marcos, Imelda
Romualdez, 1929– 4. Aquino, Benigno S. 5. Aquino, Corazon
Cojuangco. I. Title.
DS686.5.B79 1988
959.9'046—dc19
88-4090
CIP
ISBN 0-446-51398-9

Book design: H. Roberts

In memory of Ninoy, who,
as Cory says,
"got us all into this."

Contents

Acknowledgments

This book depended upon access to Filipinos at both extremes of the political spectrum, and it is a tribute to their political sophistication that everyone I met—from Communists in the hills to the colonels leading squads against them, from *Coryistas* to Marcos loyalists—tolerated my efforts to get to know their opponents. In that regard, I am particularly grateful to President Corazon Aquino, who remained generous with her precious time, even after she began writing her own book; to members of the Aquino and Cojuangco families, who were immensely helpful from August 21, 1983, on; to Vice-President Salvador Laurel and his wife, Celia; to Senator Juan Ponce Enrile; to the honorable military officers in various factions of the armed forces who were my main sources; to the Communist party cadres who never asked me for anything but a fair hearing; and to the lawyers, citizen board members, and prosecutors who were not afraid to let the truth about the Aquino assassination come out. I would also like to acknowledge the willingness of ex-President Ferdinand Marcos and his wife, Imelda, to entertain my questions, both while they were in power and afterward.

In addition to the people quoted in the text and cited in the reference notes, and those people who are cited without attribution, at their own request, I would like to express my general appreciation to a long list of others who helped me in various ways:

To my editors at TIME magazine: Henry Grunwald and Henry Muller, who granted me a sabbatical in which to write the book; to Chief of Correspondents John Stacks and his deputy William Mader, for their tolerance of the time the book took after that; to Karsten Prager for persuading me to move to Asia in the first place, and for his inspired editing of TIME's Philippine coverage, together with Muller, Don Morrison, and their teams. To the TIME colleagues, all of them friends, with whom I worked in the Philippines: most notably to Nelly Sindayen, TIME's Manila reporter, with whom I shared most of my bylines and four years of unforgettable experiences; to Photographers Robin Moyer and Sandro Tucci, who not only did a fine job of illustrating the evolving revolution, but who helped with my reporting and were fine company on the road as well. To Carl Mydans, who is in a category all by himself, with whom I was privileged to work on several occasions. To Attorney Enrique Belo, for his wise counsel. To my colleagues Helen Huang, Yuman Wong, and Virginia Lau, who kept the Hong Kong bureau running during all the months I spent in the Philippines and provided essential logistical support; and to William Stewart, my successor as Hong Kong Bureau Chief, for his cooperation. To Susan Lynd and Eileen Harkin at the Time-Life News Service in New York for helping facilitate shipment of the manuscript and galleys to Beijing, after I took up my current post there.

To the Filipino journalists with whom I discussed the stories behind their stories: Amando Doronilla, Melinda De Jesus, Letty Jimenez-Magsanoc, Tony Lopez, Marites Vitug, Ninez Cacho-Olivares, Julie Yap Daza, Alice Villadolid, Monica Feria, Barbara Dacanay, Gerry Zaragosa, and others. To fellow foreign correspondents Rodney Tasker, Guy Sacerdoti, Kiyotaka Yamamoto, Lewis Simons, Matt Miller, James Laurie, Seth Mydans, William Branigan, Lin Neumann, Gwen Robinson, Mark Fineman, Melinda Liu, Robert Secter, Jonathan Broder, Steve Lohr, Catherine Manegold, and Luisita Lopez-Torregrosa, with whom I shared many a meal and much colorful debate about how it would all turn out.

To the many other people who cannot be so easily catalogued by profession or association, but whose information and assistance were essential: General Mariano Adalem, the late Leandro Alejandro, Felix Bautista, Amante Bigornia, John Bresnan, Miguel Campos, Antonio Carag, Gregorio Cendaña, Edith Coliver, Carlos and Cynthia Dominguez, Ramon Farolan, Marcelo Fernan, Filemon Fernandez, Jose Flores, Manuel Herrera, Carlos Garcia, Antonio Gatmaitan, Richard Gordon, Eva Kalaw, Donald Klein, Noor Lucman, Michael and Lourdes Mastura, Roberto

Millena, Felipe Miranda, Benjamin Muego, Joan Orendain, Sally Perez, Marilyn Robles, David Rosenberg, Roy Rowan, Antonio Zumel.

To the Council on Foreign Relations for awarding me its 1986–87 Edward R. Murrow Fellowship, which not only allowed me to take a year off, but introduced me to the world of American foreign policy-making, which I had previously only viewed from my posts abroad. Special thanks are due to Murrow Program Director Margaret Osmer McQuade and Research Assistant Merle d'Alziel.

Finally, personal thanks to those who offered me professional assistance and moral support during the writing of the book. To Stanley Karnow, whose own book on the Philippines will be the definitive foreign work, for his criticism and camaraderie. To Raymond Bonner for his good advice and the generous loan of his many cartons of Freedom of Information Act documents, which helped fill the void created by the FOIA bureaucracy's inability to process a single one of my requests for information, which I filed more than two years ago. To Scott Armstrong and Craig Nelson of the nongovernment, nonprofit National Security Archives, and to Attorney Ronald Plesser, who supported me in my vain effort to speed up the processing of the FOIA documents. To Gwen Davis, who encouraged me from the start. To Nansey Neiman of Warner Books, who helped me talk it out. To Regina Guillermo, who kept my life and my Philippine files in order for five years; to Socorro Mendoza, who sent me weekly clippings from the Philippine press after I left Manila, and who checked scores of facts and figures for me there. To Jimi and Ana FlorCruz, my TIME colleagues in Beijing, who, being Filipinos, were willing sources of information in the final checking and editing of the manuscript. To my friends at the Midtown Manila Hotel, who made me feel secure during those first anxious months after the assassination, and to my other friends, at the Manila Hotel, which became my home away from home for four years. To my parents, Charles and Helen Burton, and my sister, Stephanie Zimmerman, for their encouragement and everlasting humor. To Robert for being such a good audience for my stories, and for putting up with me while I was writing them.

Beijing, 1988

Prologue

My memories should be mournful, even macabre, considering that my initiation into the often violent world of Philippine politics took place there at the airport when Ninoy Aquino was assassinated. Instead, they are warm, smiling, sunny—like the archipelago and the people, who tolerated a dictator for a decade of what some called "smiling martial law" and then overthrew him in a four-day rebellion that felt more like a fiesta.

Just below the surface of my subconscious, however, is an awareness, born of the suddenness with which a happy landing became a nightmare, that a tropical tragedy such as I had witnessed, is all the more treacherous for its deceitful camouflage. Had the killing occurred in the spare setting of the classics, there might have been a sense of foreboding. As it was, neither the clear, blue sky and gently swaying reeds outside the plane, nor the hesitant manner of the soldiers who entered the cabin to fetch Ninoy hinted of the plot that would be executed seconds later.

Now, in the sober light of retrospect, I realize that the sudden death which, in one way or another, claimed both Aquino and Marcos is very much a part of Filipino life and the Filipino character. Located astride the so-called "rim of fire," the island chain is a product of its volcanic origins. The conical mountains which lend beauty to the landscape and fertility to the soil erupt periodically without warning, smothering the surroundings in fire and ash. The grinding of tectonic plates deep below the surface of white sands and azure seas triggers earthquakes and tidal waves with awful randomness.

Even the skies can exact a terrible revenge. The typhoons which well up in mid-Pacific each year between June and November attain lethal velocity as they approach the serene coral lagoons of the Philippine islands. Some veer away at the last minute, others do not. The advances of modern meteorological science have not enabled the experts to forecast with complete reliability which will be the killers.

Filipinos and those who study them have coined terms to describe the human behavior which has evolved in such an environment. *Ningas cogon*, the flame of the fast-burning cogon grass, is the peasant metaphor for the flash of emotion which typically arouses individuals and masses to action, only to consume itself in a surfeit of words.

"Optimistic fatalism" is sociological jargon for the attitude of a people who, having had no control over the natural disasters, epidemics, and outside invasions which have plagued them over the centuries, have traditionally greeted their fate, not with anger or mass defiance, but with superstition, prayer, black humor, and inspired improvisation.

Marcos the dictator, Ninoy the martyr, Imelda the First Lady, who wanted to be president, and Cory the backstage wife, who did not, were all creatures of this world and therefore shared this peculiar mind-set, which distinguishes Filipinos from other peoples. Although intellectually equipped to analyze problems in the rational, Western manner taught by their colonizers, they instinctively factored elements of the irrational into their decision making.

Before acting, Marcos routinely consulted numerologists, faith healers, and astrologers, and he invariably scheduled important events on dates divisible by his lucky number seven, while Cory retreated to a convent to fast and pray, hoping for divine guidance. When plans went awry, Ninoy turned momentary setbacks into victories through the use of humor and hyperbole, in contrast to Imelda, who frenetically scribbled equations based on geometric symbols representing concepts like love and power, then searched in vain for answers in the resulting socio-mathematical product.

However, none of the four was comfortable with the passivity that such habits reinforced in the population at large—a passivity which, reduced to its most simplistic origins, was bred by generations of islanders conditioned to wait for the coconuts to fall from the trees. All were driven by their vastly different family histories but similar ambitions toward the same goal: power to shape the future of a promising, young republic.

Their story began for me as an ordinary assignment. In 1983, from my base in Hong Kong, I had proposed to cover the return from exile of President Ferdinand Marcos's chief political opponent, former Senator Benigno ("Ninoy") Aquino. By accompanying him on his flight to Manila, I would have a chance to interview him before he was, presumably, jailed. Ross Munro, a Washington bureau colleague with a pipeline to Aquino, had communicated my request to him, and had forwarded me his itinerary. My editors at TIME magazine in New York had scheduled a page-long article with a "could grow" clause, which was dependent on events.

Aquino's trip had been conceived as a major media event, opening with a press conference in Tokyo and climaxing with a giant airport welcome in Manila, where he was scheduled to arrive aboard a Japan Airlines 747. However, it had quickly turned clandestine when the Marcos regime refused to grant him a passport and publicly warned of a plot to assassinate him upon his return. In defiance of the warnings, Aquino left Boston on August 13 and disappeared from public view. Discreetly, before his departure, he notified a few trusted sources of his now secret travel plans. On August 15, Munro telexed them to the Hong Kong bureau:

> By the time you receive this, Aquino should already be in
> Southeast Asia. His plan is to hop around for a few days, trying to
> keep Marcos confused while simultaneously meeting with some
> political friends. The sensitive part is that he will end up in Taipei,
> perhaps after making feints at entering Manila via Hong Kong and/
> or Seoul. His plan is to board China Airlines flight 811 from
> Taipei to Manila at eleven ayem Sunday August 21. He will be in
> economy class. He suggests you fly to Taipei Saturday and check
> in at the Grand Hotel.

I arrived in Taipei on the evening of August 20, in a state of suspense. Although it had never been said, I accepted as a given that I had been "invited" to accompany Aquino because my presence and that of the other fourteen journalists, who joined him there, would serve as a deterrent to those who might try to harm him and would guarantee that, no matter what happened, the whole world would be watching.

It is a sad reality, which we bemoan each time we see one another, that our presence was no deterrent to his enemies. All we were able to do was record what we saw and heard. I switched on my minitape recorder as uniformed soldiers escorted him from our plane, which had just landed in Manila. Ten seconds after he passed through the door and out of my sight, he was shot. The tiny cassette caught the sounds of his murder and became a vital piece of evidence in the investigation and trial which followed.

For the next three years I covered the search for Ninoy's assassins as it broadened into a search by Filipinos for a new national identity and a leader who would personify this new spirit. By the time Marcos called a snap election, the Philippine story had become more than an assignment for me. It had become a quest for answers to questions that went beyond the scope of my weekly reporting of events: questions about the metabolism of revolution and how far the U.S. should go in propagating democracy in the Third World. It had also become an obsession. My brief association with Ninoy had sucked me into the vortex of the Philippine story, and had made me look at it through his eyes—the eyes of an optimist. Once he was suddenly gone, it mattered deeply to me that his brutal death have meaning, and that the vision of a peaceful transition from dictatorship to democracy with which he had imbued his favorite song, "The Impossible Dream," be realized.

This book is the product of my quest for a better understanding of the unfolding Philippine revolution and the reflection of my obsession with the extraordinary Filipinos whom I have come to know. It is primarily the story of the Marcoses and the Aquinos, told as much as possible in their voices, during conversations and interviews over a four-year period, because I could not have said it better.

In a more general sense, it is the story of an archipelago of 7,100 islands, separated not only by deep ethnic and cultural divides, but also by a gulf between rich and poor that is wider than in neighboring developing countries. Unhappily, neither its first quarter century of democracy, nor the decade of martial law which followed, nor even the democratic space secured by the Aquino government during its first two years in power has been conducive to the bridging of those gaps. As a result, the revolution that began with Ninoy's assassination has yet to play itself out.

It is also the story of two peoples, the Yanks and the Pinoys, who have been involved in a love-hate relationship for nearly a century. There have been moments that have highlighted our closeness, such as February 1986, when Filipinos resorted to the ballot rather than the bullet to replace a leader and a system of government. We saw in them then our own idealistic beliefs, and we wanted them to triumph. We also knew that elections, even in a luxuriously stable society like ours, do not in themselves solve problems. They are but a first step taken by those who consent to accept their outcome.

Whether or not the unfinished revolution in the Philippines will draw to a redemptive conclusion depends, not only on the ability and inspiration of Ninoy's widow, but on the will of the Filipino people to finally come together as a nation to correct the blatant economic inequality that continues to fuel the Communist insurgency. Whether the fall of Marcos will, in retrospect, be seen to have ushered in an era of peaceful political change, economic growth, and moral rebirth, or will prove but a temporary victory for the forces of moderation and nonviolence is a question with vital consequences for other societies that aspire to democracy, and for the American government, which encourages them to do so.

1

Meeting Ninoy

"Call Mr. Boston, Room 514." The message was waiting for me in the rosewood cubbyhole behind the registration desk at the Grand Hotel in Taipei. I was paranoid enough to think that the desk clerk committed it to memory as she handed it to me with my room key. The alias seemed a bit transparent for a fugitive as recently identified with the city of Boston as Filipino opposition leader Benigno S. Aquino, Jr. At this moment Aquino, the most popular political opponent of Ferdinand Marcos, was being hunted in at least three countries by several private planeloads of the president's henchmen, and his whereabouts was the subject of front-page speculation on both sides of the Pacific.

On reaching my room, I dialed 514, as instructed, and asked for "Mr. Boston." The friendly voice that answered was the same one that had greeted me the previous day when he had called my home from the transit lounge of Hong Kong's Kai Tak airport en route to Taiwan. I had ended that conversation abruptly, to prevent him from blurting out the time and place of our planned rendezvous in Taipei over a public phone which was, in all likelihood, tapped. His carelessness had surprised me. This evening he was more circumspect. He simply set the appointment for the interview I had requested at 8 P.M., one hour hence.

I used the interim to finish reading the news clippings, which I had brought along as background material for the story I would file. The chronology of Aquino's actions over the past two months raised more questions than it provided answers. In mid-June he had announced his intention to go home. In mid-July he had received a telex from Manila, informing him that Philippine intelligence had uncovered a plot to assassinate him. It advised him to stay away until the plotters had been "neutralized." He and his supporters in Manila had paid it little heed, setting the date of his arrival for August 7 and scheduling a welcome rally at Manila International Airport.

On July 31, a progovernment newspaper reported, ominously, that the death sentence originally imposed on Aquino in 1977 for subversion, murder, and possession of firearms had been upheld by a military court, despite a pending appeal before the Supreme Court. The following day another telex, this one signed by Marcos's minister of national defense, Juan Ponce Enrile, urged Aquino to delay his return "for at least one month."

Taking seriously the advice of Enrile, whom he knew to be locked in a bitter struggle with First Lady Imelda Marcos and armed forces Chief of Staff General Fabian C. Ver for influence over Marcos, Aquino pressed his fellow opposition leaders to compromise with the regime and reset his arrival in Manila for August 21. That date had malicious significance that would not be lost on Marcos. It was the twelfth anniversary of the Plaza Miranda bombing, an infamous hand-grenade attack on an opposition political rally that had become a milestone of the anti-Marcos movement. It was also divisible by seven, the lucky number of the superstitious president.

Several days later the presidential palace made a bizarre announcement: Marcos was going into seclusion for three weeks to write two books. So out of character was the disappearance of the highly visible president from public view that rumors quickly swept Manila's morning coffee-shop circuit that the president was dead or dying. The last public word on the government's intentions had come from the widely feared General Ver, who had warned that if Aquino tried to enter the country by air, he would be sent back aboard the same plane to his point of embarkation.

By the time I headed downstairs to meet Aquino, I had convinced myself that, given all the previous attempts by Marcos to block his homecoming, getting out of Taiwan, a country with a longer history of martial law than the Philippines, would not be easy. What I saw when the elevator door opened on the fifth floor added to my apprehension. Aquino's pseudonym had clearly fooled no one, for the long corridor leading to his suite was bristling with more uniformed bellboys and room-service waiters than even the most demanding guests would require, and they were clearly monitoring his guests.

It was immediately apparent, however, that the animated man in the rimless glasses who flung open the door did not feel threatened by their presence. Nor did he seem to be considering a retreat or even a detour from the travel agenda which had been relayed to me. He radiated confidence, impatience, faith that everything was proceeding satisfactorily. Speaking in the automatic, rapid-fire manner that was his political trademark, his hands in constant motion, he seemed metabolically incapable of remaining in place one moment longer than called for in his secret itinerary. Smiling an effervescent smile, he greeted me, repeated an earlier request to "call me Ninoy," thanked me for coming, and swept me into his confidence in one breath.

In typical Filipino fashion no business could begin until the guest was made comfortable and refreshments were served. Meanwhile, my concern that the men in the hall outside were spies was brushed off with a cackle of laughter. His nonchalant attitude in such a situation brought to my mind the words of an American businessman who had recently made his first trip to the Philippines. "What a tutti-frutti country," he exclaimed. His head was still spinning from the anarchy of the traffic, the cacophony of conflicting points of view, the use of nicknames like Ting-Ting and Ding-Dong by people of substance. He found it difficult to accept the proclivity of even top cabinet members, opposition leaders, military officers, and the First Family itself to sing away their cares at home, at state dinners, or in sing-along bars, seemingly oblivious to the economic and political problems, which outsiders routinely predicted would lead to imminent revolution.

Western diplomats and journalists would often similarly shake their heads at what they regarded as the too lighthearted response by one Filipino official or another to a situation that to a Westerner was no laughing matter. "They are not serious," the Westerners would chide.

There was no question, when Ninoy began to talk, however, that he was serious. He had, he insisted, taken safety precautions, which I would come to understand later. Meanwhile, he had other priorities. There was background to impart, skepticism to quell, actions and motives to explain, logistics to arrange. He seemed eager to answer questions about where he had come from and to outline where he was headed, both literally and figuratively. There was a sense of urgency in his apparent need to record small details as well as sweeping conclusions. He was, I thought later, like the survivor left at the end of the fifth act of a Shakespearean tragedy, whose role it is to pass on to posterity the lessons about where the king went wrong.

Yet he did not look or act like a tragic figure. He was intense, perplexed, even anguished during our interview and later on during the seven and one-half hours I spent with him that evening and the next day. But he was, at the same time, full of levity and optimism, and always entertaining. All Filipinos are performers, but Ninoy was celebrated for having raised political drama in the islands to a fine art. He had conducted the first nationwide electoral campaign by helicopter throughout the archipelago and, some years later, the first campaign waged from a prison cell. Here in Taipei he was poised to play the most important role of his life.

Watching and listening to Ninoy for the first time, I found it easy to understand why the Marcoses wished to prevent his return only six months prior to the opening of the campaign for the first regular parliamentary election since the imposition of martial law in 1972. He was, quite simply, a spellbinding personality, who possessed all of the dangerous faculties which that implies. He was a born orator with an ability to convince an audience of the correctness of his vision. And he had an appetite for direct physical contact, which made him seem of the people, when in fact he was a member of the landed elite.

Despite claims by his friends that a spiritual rebirth during his prison years had transformed him from a ruthless, Marcos-style politician into a veritable Gandhi, he retained that old pol affinity for smoke-filled rooms, raucous anecdotes, gossip, and intrigue. He was as cocky and self-assured as a rock star or a French diplomat. His critique of the deteriorating Philippine political and economic situation under Marcos was more prophetic than anything written before or since by the political scientists and risk analysts who make the Philippines their business. Most threatening of all for the strongman he opposed, there was, underneath Ninoy's bravado, the deep caring and what can only be called the madness that drive all the world's dissidents, refuseniks, and prisoners of conscience into unarmed confrontation with oppressors far more powerful than they.

As he talked about his past life and why he was returning to the Philippines, he acted out the parts of all the key characters in the unfolding drama. He could have begun his narrative much earlier in his personal history, but perhaps because she was at the heart of it, he began with Imelda.

*   *   *

On May 21, 1983, Ninoy recounted, Philippine First Lady Imelda Romualdez Marcos had summoned him to meet with her at the Philippine Center in New York City. The periodic reunions of these two longtime adversaries titillated and upset their respective friends and relatives. Ninoy portrayed Imelda as a manipulator with designs on the presidency herself, once Marcos was gone. As such, she was to be feared in her own right, as well as in tandem with her husband. And yet, he could not escape the bonds of a friendship dating back to adolescence and a more recent debt of gratitude, which obliged him to inform her of his plans.

They had not seen each other in more than a year. They greeted each other with a mixture of sentimentality and suspicion. Filipinos are not confrontational people, so even opposites like Ninoy and Imelda sparred in a surprisingly civilized manner.

Ever professing innocence, the wide-eyed Imelda had made her invitation to Ninoy sound spontaneous and personal. He knew otherwise. After she had postponed the initial appointment they had set, he had learned from his numerous sources inside the Philippine foreign affairs bureaucracy in the United States that she had been obliged to await further instructions from Marcos in Manila before meeting him. Nonetheless, if only for old time's sake, he was straightforward in revealing his plans to her.

"Since you were the one who got me out of prison," he began, "I want to tell you that I am coming back."

Claiming to speak as "mother and wife, not as First Lady," she beseeched him to wait.

"My fellowship is about to end, and I never expected to seek political asylum in the U.S.," replied Aquino. He reminded her how, to the contrary, he had promised the Marcoses that he would return to the Philippines as soon as he had recovered from heart bypass surgery.

Always emotional, Imelda nonetheless startled Ninoy by voicing an implicit threat. "You realize that if there is a conflict of interest between you and Marcos, he would be stupid to let yours prevail," she stated baldly, referring to her spouse by his last name, as she generally did to outsiders, although he was "Andy" in private.

Aquino, for once, was reduced to a one syllable retort, "Yes."

Impetuously she continued, "If you go home, you must be jailed."

"Why?"

"Because the interests of Marcos would be hurt if you were harmed."

"Who would kill me?" Aquino asked, indignant.

"Many people," she replied. "You are very controversial. Our people might think they are doing a favor." She added, "You have many enemies . . ." Then, always the bottom line in any conversation with either the president or the First Lady, she reminded Aquino: "The Communists are always looking for a target. They kill you and blame it on my husband."

Aquino did not flinch. "Those are some of the hazards of the game," he said with a shrug.

The conversation lasted for three and one-half hours. When threats did not work, Imelda tried bribes, offering him money and the services of such eminent financiers as David Rockefeller and Felix Rohatyn to invest and shelter it. Finally forced to admit failure in reaching an agreement,

Imelda asked Ninoy to postpone making a firm decision on his return until her next trip to the U.S., following the celebration of her birthday in the Philippines.

Imelda later told an investigative board that she had extracted a promise from Aquino not to return home until they had met again. He claimed no such commitment. In fact, there was no point to another meeting, since she had already done all that she could to prevent his homecoming. Back in April 1982, when they had last met, he had been planning a trip to Saudi Arabia to meet with dissident Filipino Muslim leaders. However, his passport had expired, and the Foreign Ministry would not issue him a new one. "Give it to me," she had said, as if offering to do a favor.

She had never returned the passport, and no new one was ever authorized. "She later apologized to me," recalled Aquino. "She said she got a real shellacking from her husband" for even entertaining the notion of furnishing his chief enemy such a valuable weapon as a renewed travel document.

Imelda's failure to consummate a deal to prevent Ninoy's return to the Philippines had undoubtedly caused her a loss of face, not only with Marcos, who had entrusted that mission to her, but with his cousin and protector, General Ver, as well. Likewise, some of Ninoy's friends and relatives feared that he had further provoked her by using his appearance on June 23, 1983, before a subcommittee chaired by a well-known critic of the Marcos regime, U.S. Democratic Congressman Stephen Solarz, to publicly confirm reports that he was going home.

Ninoy did not appear to regard his rebuff of the vindictive First Lady as likely to have dire consequences. He acted as if his pointedly timed testimony had been just another speaking engagement. "Steve Solarz found out about my plans," he explained, matter-of-factly, "and he scheduled a hearing on the Philippines. I saw it as a chance to unload."

* * *

Ninoy's portrait of Marcos was surprisingly sympathetic. "Marcos. . . ," he said, exhaling loudly, then pausing to flash back on more than thirty years of shared history. Smiling, he reached into the past and selected what appeared to be his favorite recollection of the man who had aborted his political career, decimated his family's fortunes, and virtually silenced a nation. It was an anecdote festooned with the surreal digressions and absurd asides which so often are the real substance of Filipino conversation.

"I will never forget that day he had me in the palace before they gave me the death sentence. Both times he asked me, 'Brod . . .' "

Here Ninoy digressed to explain the intimate manner in which they addressed each other as blood brothers in Upsilon Sigma Phi, the number-one fraternity at the University of Philippines Law School. After he came to power, Marcos had tended to favor Upsilonians with cabinet appointments and business deals. Ninoy, having remained in opposition to Marcos, was a rare exception. Still, they had continued to address each other as "Brod."

Ninoy returned to his interrupted narrative, picking up where he had left off, with the question posed by Marcos:

". . . 'What would you do if I release you tomorrow?'

"I said, 'I don't know, because you've got me in the dark. I've not received any newspapers in five years.' "

Here again, the conversation went off on a tangent, as Marcos, disbelieving, asked his chief of army intelligence General Josephus Ramas, "General, how come he does not get any newspapers?"

The general snapped, "He'll get them tomorrow, sir."

Once more Ninoy picked up the thread of his recollections:

I said, "So I don't know what's happening. If people are happy, I'll just go home to my province and retire there. But if they are unhappy, you can bet your neck I'll be mounting a soapbox. So if you think you have done well, release me, but if you don't, don't release me, because it will only exacerbate the situation."

He repeated the question four times. He was looking for a deal. He wanted me to give my word, "Okay, I've had it." He was waiting for me to shake hands and say I was throwing in the towel.

Finally, he said, "Well, the law will have to take its course."

I said, "Suit yourself," and he gave me the death sentence. But they never carried it out.

Ninoy spoke of the man who had denied him the presidency of the republic with the grudging admiration of one who measures his own abilities in terms of the skills demonstrated by his opponent. He recalled proudly how a former senate president had once told him, "We were with the president, and he was so angry with us, because we were attacking some of his bills and pestering him with appointments, and out of the blue, he said, 'You know, I hate the guts of that Aquino, but if I had just three of him, I would not need any of you.' "

To my astonishment, the image of Marcos which gradually filled the room was not the cold, cynical figure invoked so often in the past by oppositionists like himself. Rather, as he talked, Ninoy conjured the apparition of a man grown old and tired, aware of his failures, and ready to compromise. In another cameo from his prison days, Ninoy recalled,

He said, "I envy you, because now you have the luxury of communing with the gods and the writers, unmolested by anybody.

You can go and pick your book and be talking to Plato one minute and Toynbee another minute. But me, I have to talk to all of these jokers."

Ninoy told Marcos about another unexpected blessing derived from his imprisonment:

If you admit that friends are priceless, thanks to you, I now know my friends. Out of ten thousand, five have remained loyal—friends who would go through the gauntlet at the prison to see me and risk their own businesses in doing so. I have discovered my five, but I don't think you have discovered yours yet.

"That's the kind of dialogue we were having," said Ninoy wistfully. They seldom met personally during the years of his imprisonment, but Ninoy was a prolific letter writer. "I would write and tell him what my notions were. He would call me presumptuous, but then he received and acknowledged them, and all of a sudden I would hear that he was implementing some bits and pieces."

If Ninoy was almost mawkishly sentimental toward Marcos the man, he was appropriately harsh in his appraisal of Marcos the president. His analysis of Marcos's failures was all the more damning, rendered as it was in sadness rather than in spite.

Marcos, I think, had a grand design, but somewhere along the line he got sidetracked. If he had pulled off the economic miracle, I think he could have gone down as one of the great presidents, like Park Chung Hee [of South Korea]. You can be authoritarian in Asia, provided there is an economic tradeoff. But if you go from bikes to barefoot and take away their rights at the same time, the whole place goes bust. Unfortunately, he had no notion of the economic pitfalls, and he overborrowed. He relied too much on his technocrats. It's a great tragedy.

Ninoy had correctly fingered the economy as Marcos's fatal weakness. Furthermore, he was preparing to exploit that weakness, he intimated, by rallying the moribund opposition political parties to challenge Marcos's candidates in elections for the National Assembly, scheduled nine months from now in May 1984. The way Ninoy saw it, if Marcos allowed fair elections as the first step in restoring the democratic process that he had sabotaged by imposing martial law, he could still rescue his reputation and save the nation from otherwise inevitable ruin. If, on the other hand, Marcos resisted reform and engaged in the massive election fraud for which he was notorious, the opposition could make victory so costly for him that the economy would collapse and his own political demise would be hastened.

Ninoy, like most Filipinos, not only believed in but loved elections. The introduction of the electoral process in the Philippines was a rare example of the successful grafting of a foreign institution onto an indigenous culture. Frequent political campaigns offered the archipelago's seventy different ethnic and linguistic groups a way to settle their scores with a maximum of the verbal pyrotechnics at which they excelled and a minimum of the tribal violence, which the Roman Catholic Church had been trying to eliminate since it began converting the pagan islanders more than four hundred years ago. Vote buying was standard practice in Philippine elections, and it was this practice that Ninoy intended to exploit in order to bring down an uncooperative Marcos.

When Ninoy's political elders traveled to the U.S. in 1983 to consult him there about whether the opposition should boycott the 1984 elections, as it had all the others called by Marcos since martial law, he told them, "We will not win as long as Marcos is doing the counting, so we should not participate to win." But, he added, "I think we should participate, because this is one way to bleed him." His reasoning was perversely simple:

> If you rig an election and don't pay people off, you are in trouble. So every six years he must spend money for an election. But if there is no enemy, he can cut the costs. This time Marcos is caught on the horns of a dilemma: The technocrats are under pressure from the World Bank to hold down the deficit, and yet you have Imelda and the politicians urging him to spend more. Marcos can no longer buy the votes. He ain't got the money. Our strategy is to force this contradiction to explode.

Ninoy's forecast for the post-Marcos era into which the country was now heading was entirely pragmatic. There were no demagogic flourishes about democratic ideals, only cold, hard calculations about how the military would behave, when the time came, without Marcos or one of its own as commander in chief. "I happen to believe that Marcos is the only man who can return democracy peacefully," stated the president's leading critic, "because if he dies tomorrow, there is no one who can control that military."

While at Harvard University and Massachusetts Institute of Technology, where he held fellowships in international affairs during his exile, Ninoy had worked, he explained, to construct "a model on the four stages of a military takeover." What he had learned from studying takeovers in countries like Argentina and Chile appeared to apply in the Philippines as well. "In the first stage," he said, "the military merely dictates policy." In the second stage, "they start participating in government." To illustrate his point, he noted: "Before martial law, the military was out of it. With martial law, Marcos made them partners. They are now ambassadors and judges. They no longer discharge just military functions. There were twenty-seven generals before martial law, now there are one hundred and seven. There were fifty-seven thousand soldiers in 1952, now there are two hundred and fifty thousand."

His voice grew ominous as he warned, "As long as Marcos is alive, it's okay. They are loyal to him." However, he was grimly prophetic about who and what would follow. No civilian besides Marcos, he feared, would be able to secure the military's blessing. Mrs. Marcos would almost surely try, and she would probably be accepted as a figurehead at the start, but even she would most likely be "retired," following the Isabel Peron precedent, giving way to a full military takeover by General Ver. If that should happen, Ninoy reasoned, the country would quickly be sucked into the fatal downward spiral of right-wing juntas, replaced by left-wing revolutions, that is common to banana republics.

The only alternative, he believed, was to pressure the president, while he was still alive, to preside over the transition from dictatorship to democracy. This could be done by allowing honest legislative elections to determine the relative popularity of a number of potential successors. His words were eerily relevant to the problems that his widow would one day face upon her improbable ascension to the presidency. "The military still recognizes the dominance of the civilian government," he said, "but under martial law it has tasted power and tasted blood. That presents a problem. But if we can restore our democratic political institutions, then any attempt by the army to take over after Marcos would be seen for what it was: a naked grab for power."

As if rehearsing for the larger audience he would have in Manila, Ninoy explained: "The rationale for my going back, against the advice of all my political mentors and my colleagues, who think I am crazy, is that I still know, deep in my heart, that if I can only talk to him and appeal to his sense of patriotism, his sense of humanity, I can open up a little window. If Marcos destroyed democracy in the first place, then could he not recreate it now?"

Aquino had been careful while in the U.S. not to discuss publicly one additional factor affecting the timing of his return. That was his alienation from the administration of President Ronald Reagan. Jimmy Carter had been in office when Aquino arrived in the U.S. for heart surgery in May 1980. There had been a natural affinity between the Filipino opposition leader and the human rights activists within the Carter administration. Shortly after Aquino had recuperated and begun his fellowship at Harvard, however, Reagan defeated Carter in the 1980 election. Doors that had been open to Aquino in Washington suddenly slammed shut.

Now, three years later in Taipei he was more forthcoming. "It is my frustration," he admitted, "that is sending me home. I have decided Reagan will be president for another term, so for me there is no hope. When Carter was in the White House, I could walk into the office of Dick Holbrooke and put my feet up on the desk. Since Reagan won, they have really distanced themselves from me. Now I'm treated like the mistress well removed."

The alternative to his timely intervention now, he feared, was the continued impotence of the moderate, non-Communist opposition, to which he belonged, and accelerated growth for the Communist insurgency. "I really feel the country is heading toward a crisis," he said, "being pulled by two tendencies: toward the right and a military junta, toward the left and a Communist takeover."

He was concerned that what he perceived as "a deterioration of the superpower relationship" between the U.S. and the Soviet Union could result in Russian intervention in the insurgency, which had taken root all across the geostrategically important archipelago, where America's two largest overseas military bases were located. Already, he noted, the guerrillas of the Communist-led New People's Army were moving in battalion strength in areas of the embattled southern island of Mindanao. "If this drift continues," he predicted, "in five years the left will be a factor in the Philippines, and it will have to be involved in some kind of coalition."

The only way to avoid a bloody civil war between the military right and the Communist left, he believed, was to strengthen the center, which had been rendered impotent by years of martial law. "My point is," he said, "that if the moderates want to be relevant to the situation, we must move now. Otherwise there will be a Nicaragua or an El Salvador situation."

✻ ✻ ✻

Some two hours after it began, my interview with Ninoy was gradually transformed into a press conference as, one by one, the fourteen other reporters, photographers, and TV camera and sound men who had made arrangements to travel with him quietly checked into the Grand Hotel. With their arrival, what had seemed a somewhat tenuous plan for returning to Manila was on the verge of becoming a bona fide media event. Only the cameras and lights were missing, out of deference to Ninoy's ever-thinning cover. "No cameras until we are airborne," he had instructed.

Each new arrival brought with him rumors that Marcos was dying, for which we sought Aquino's confirmation. Was it true that he had had a kidney operation? Or was he too sick to have one? As always, when the source was Filipino, the more outrageous the rumor, the more detailed and specific it would be. One report was so specific as to be irresistible: The donor of the transplanted kidney was Manny Ortega, widely believed to be Marcos's illegitimate son by Carmen Ortega, a lover who predated Imelda.

Not surprisingly, Ninoy added the most interesting information. On the basis of conversations he had had with his most trusted State Department contact before leaving the U.S., he had concluded that Washington was "petrified" about the prospect of Imelda running the show. "They think that would lead to chaos," he said. "They believe the situation is unraveling." He was impressively up-to-date. His sources in Manila had told him further that U.S. Ambassador Michael Armacost and Congressman Solarz, who was now in the Philippines, had met briefly with Marcos yesterday. He was not in the palace, but in the guest house, where the palace hospital also was. "They only spent about fifteen minutes there," reported Ninoy. "According to Solarz, Marcos's hand was limp, he was visibly tiring, and he had a hard time sitting down." Others had told him that "a major government reshuffle has gone on," but he had been unable to gather any details.

Today's wire services were reporting an announcement by General Ver that if Aquino got as far as Manila, he would be sent back on the same plane that brought him. What was Senator Aquino's reaction? "There is no way they can put me back on that plane," he replied, physically contorting himself to underline his point. "I'll be an international cause. I'll be a Flying Dutchman. I'll be a political Ping-Pong ball. Marcos will look silly."

A clamor erupted. We were all talking at the same time, all expressing confusion over the crossed signals emanating from Manila, all wondering which city we would be filing our stories from tomorrow. We besieged him with queries about the time and logistics of tomorrow's homecoming, as well as skeptical comments about his safety and the central question of whether the Marcos regime would allow him to return alive. The master performer now had an international audience, and he led us on a memorable *tour d'horizon* of the various possibilities he had been pondering. Arms folded, brow furrowed, he voiced his own puzzlement over the apparent goings-on in Manila.

"I cannot understand why he let it escalate into an international thing," he said. "They have escalated my value a thousand times." Then squinting, as if into the brain of his foe, he talked about the reaction he had expected to his announced homecoming. "If Marcos were still sane and normal," he ventured, "he would send me the presidential limo, and the next day the headlines would say, 'Marcos-Aquino hit a deal.' " He laughed heartily at the notion. "They can kill me that way," he observed, still chortling.

"Or," he added, seized by sudden inspiration, "if Imelda showed up there and gave me a kiss and said, 'The car is waiting,' I would be compromised to some extent. People would say, 'Oh my God, big sellout.' "

Still inside the mind of Marcos, Aquino came up with another likely ploy to sabotage his homecoming that would take account of his death sentence and the recent reports that it had been upheld by the military courts.

They would completely black me out from the press, and maybe there would be only four thousand to five thousand people [to welcome him]. After that an officer will say, "Mr. Aquino, you can go home and pack your bags, but tomorrow we will pick you up and you go back in detention. The law is the law, and you are a convicted man." And Marcos would say nothing, and if the correspondents will ask him, "What are you going to do with Aquino?" he will say, "It's out of my hands." You know, make it a nonevent and treat me like a nuisance.

As a matter of fact, he noted, "For my colleagues, the greatest worry was that my homecoming might be a dud."

The merriment dissipated quickly, however, because Aquino was forced to conclude that the "old Marcos" mentality, on which he was such an authority, did not seem to be evident in the handling of this affair. As he continued to weigh the evidence of recent days, it seemed to be dawning on him that the astonishingly benign portrait of Marcos which he had earlier painted for me was an anachronism. Somberly, he stated, "My friend Marcos is no longer the vintage Marcos that I once knew."

Then Ninoy rendered the only conceivable explanation one could expect from someone with as much respect for Marcos's prowess as he had previously expressed. "The pros are no longer in charge. I think a group with very narrow vision has taken over Marcos." He paused and then identified it: "Ver and his men." With a somewhat cryptic reference to his relationship with the First Lady and his refusal to accept her deal, he added, "Imelda is running the shop. She is so naive. She can do it out of emotion. She is a woman scorned."

Since he could no longer count on Marcos's logic, which he trusted because it had proven akin to his own in the past, Ninoy was forced to speculate about what would happen at the airport. He began by reeling off a perfunctory list of possibilities: "The plane will not be able to land. Or it will land and they will off-load me. Or they will allow me to meet the press and then we go to jail. Or I just go home and go under house arrest."

Gradually, however, his scenarios grew more sinister. Oddly enough,

Aquino's first mention of assassination involved, not the Marcos military, but the Communists. "It is possible that our allies on the extreme left could knock me off, because they will see me as a potential rival who will set them back thirty years." But he quickly added, "You cannot think about that or you become really scared." He maintained that, contrary to the accusations made against him at his trial, he had refused to cooperate with the Communists. "The left in the Philippines has never succeeded in getting me to denounce the U.S. bases," he said, "and they have always held that against me."

At around eleven o'clock, the phone rang for the second time that evening, and Ninoy excused himself to take it in the bedroom. When he returned to the sitting room after about fifteen minutes, a noticeable change had come over him. His energy was drained, his mood sullen.

Speaking in their native Pampangan dialect to frustrate telephone tappers, his sister Teresa ("Tessie") Oreta in Manila had just given him an update on the situation. Referring to the military, he said, "They are raising the barricades at the airport. Ver is taking full control. Imelda refused to talk to Doy." This last development seemed to upset him the most. All evening he had been counting on some word from Imelda to the organizer of his homecoming, his childhood friend and fellow op-position leader Salvador ("Doy") Laurel, that would allow him to judge who was really running the show. Now it was late, and Ninoy could only conclude that "Imelda hid from Doy and would not see him."

His voice choked as he searched for an analogy to what might be going on. "Something could be happening like in Sri Lanka," he said, referring to the recent bloody rioting by the Sinhalese population against an increasingly threatening Tamil minority. "I think that is one of Marcos's fears—that a little spark can get such a thing going. There have been no crowds in the Philippines for a long time. Marcos cannot afford to have any blood in our streets."

His mind raced ahead, making deductions about his own entry into such a new equation. "It's a bad sign . . . they take me off to jail and don't let me talk to anyone." Now he was revising his thinking about the whole trip. "The scenario of talking to Marcos," he stated flatly, "you can forget that."

As he mused, his thoughts came back to roost on the bald head of the man who would, in the aftermath, become the center of suspicion. "I've always been scared of Ver," he said. Ver's name did not come up in a vacuum. Off and on all evening, Ninoy had discussed the divisions within the military between the men loyal to Ver and those loyal to his vice-chief of staff, General Fidel Ramos. He had already painted a com-posite portrait of the Ramos faction. "He is West Point, scholarly, contemplative," said Aquino. "The good guys are behind him." "However," he feared, "I don't think Ramos will prevail. He has no instinct for infighting. He plays the game according to Hoyle." "Even worse," he added, "Ramos asks 'Why?' about the orders he is given."

"On the other hand," said Aquino, "Ver never asks 'Why?' when Marcos orders him to jump out the window. He salutes and answers, 'From which floor, sir?' " Jolted out of his gloom by the hilarious image of the jut-jawed Ver, upholstered in braid, preparing to jump, Aquino stood and impersonated his messy landing, to the laughter of all. Playing to his audience, he went on to tell two anecdotes that painted the highest-ranking Philippine military officer as a philanderer, a murderer, a thief, and a fool.

One was told him by a retired general close to Defense Minister Enrile, who had visited Ninoy at Harvard en route to the fiftieth reunion of his West Point class. He related how Ver, already rich, in his sixties, and bucking for his fourth star, had taken a mistress. When she had subsequently betrayed him with a younger man, Ver, overcome by jealousy, had had the young lover shot. What had impressed both the general and Ninoy about the story was not so much that Ver had allegedly masterminded a murder, but that he had given so little thought to the possibility that such behavior might jeopardize his military career. So secure was he in the service of Marcos that he had lost all discretion. To them this represented the height of arrogance.

The second was the well-known story of the extravagant wedding thrown by Ver for his eldest son, Irwin, head of the elite Presidential Security Command. What had scandalized Manilans was that Ver, a soldier without any known family inheritance or legitimate outside sources of income, had so publicly flaunted his questionable wealth. "Would a calculating guy do that?" questioned Ninoy. The portrait of Ver with which Ninoy left us that night was one which likened him to the Greek Colonel Ioannides. "He was the colonel who overreached himself by getting Archbishop Makarios overthrown and in the process brought the junta tumbling down," said Ninoy, with more prescience than he could know.

With Ver apparently in charge, there was no telling what might happen tomorrow. Demonstrating a showman's sense of timing, Ninoy then reached into a piece of hand luggage to show us the preparations he had made for the trip. He pointed to a pair of briefs and a tube of toothpaste, in the event he was immediately taken into custody and sent back to prison. He passed around the fake Philippines passport he had gotten from Filipino Muslim rebel leader Nur Misuari, whom he had visited in exile in Saudi Arabia. It looked like the real thing except for the name he had chosen to use on it: Marcial Bonifacio. Ninoy was gleeful about this alias. "Marcial for martial law," he explained, "and Bonifacio for the camp where I was imprisoned." Then, playfully, he pulled out a bulletproof vest, which he agreed to model before the cameras tomorrow on the plane.

As we made plans to meet him at ten minutes after nine the next morning in the hotel lobby, Ninoy gave the impression of feeling that whatever doom awaited him was further in the future. He confided,

> One of my other fears was that Marcos would allow me in
> tomorrow and send someone to tell me, "You're under house
> arrest, you can go home, just keep it low-key." After that they
> would allow me to go out on speaking engagements, and on one of
> my sorties to the provinces, they would hit me and say, "Well, he
> was a nice guy, and we warned him about it, but he was
> bullheaded and insisted on coming back." It would be clean and
> surgical. People would cry for two weeks, and then it's over.

It was clear, however, by the time we bade him goodnight, that he realized the old rules of the game no longer applied. "I did not expect this heavy-handedness at the start," he said. Then, so as not to end the evening on a down note, he added spiritedly, "My only consolation is that I won't be staying three more years in prison. The regime won't last that long."

As we filed out, he stood in the doorway to his suite, smiling his effervescent smile. "I'll say my prayers tonight," he promised.

2

"He would be lonely without me"

Ninoy was late for our rendezvous on the morning of August 21, 1983, because, as he explained, he had been on the phone to his wife, Cory, in Boston. As was her habit, she had opened the Bible at random and read him a verse to start his day. This one, Colossians 4:10, foretold a joyous welcome. He considered it auspicious.

His mood swings had been acute these last several days, according to his travel companions. On the afternoon before I met him, one of them confided later, Ninoy's confidence in a safe return had been shaken by his realization that his presence in Taiwan was known to certain Filipinos. While his friends washed out their socks in a bathroom basin in the suite, Ninoy questioned them about what he should do.

"Do you think Marcos would kill me?" he asked for the first time.

"If I were Marcos, I would," said one.

As Ninoy paced the room, they tried to convince him it was not too late to change his mind and call the whole thing off.

Their fears got to him. He decided to call San Francisco. If his brother-in-law ABC television correspondent Ken Kashiwahara had not yet left, maybe he would advise him to delay his trip to Taiwan. He was too late. Ken was already en route.

"We can still do something," said one of the men in the room, searching for a face-saving way out of this for Ninoy. "We can start a fight and then call hotel security and say Marcos's goons beat him up."

But Ninoy would have none of it. The die was cast. There was no turning back now. He would proceed as planned. His friends were troubled, but they said no more. For the rest of that day, as they observed him finalizing arrangements, and later that night, as they watched his performance before us journalists, they marveled at how, in the words of one companion, "He seemed to have forgotten all his anxiety."

After the eleven o'clock phone call from his sister Tessie, he had returned to his brooding. But this morning, his state of mind seemed to have brightened considerably, as he contemplated the final leg of his trip home. His appetite was hearty, according to his companions, who winced as they watched Ninoy pour catsup all over the eggs on his room-service tray. Afterward, as he greeted the small group of journalists who would travel with him to Manila, Ninoy noted, with just a touch of vanity, that the white safari suit he was wearing, with his initials embroidered on the shirt pocket, was the same one in which he had left the Philippines three years before to seek medical treatment in the U.S. Obese throughout his political career until he was imprisoned and went on a hunger strike, Ninoy was proud that he had not gained weight since undergoing heart surgery in 1980.

As we gathered around him in the hotel lobby, Ninoy pulled a pair of sunglasses from his pocket and announced with mock seriousness that he would travel incognito, disguised as a tourist bound for Manila with his girlfriend. To my surprise, I had been designated the night before as girlfriend and decoy. I would ride with him to the airport in the car loaned to him by a Chinese friend in Taipei, wait with him in the passport line, and board the plane with him.

Dismayed once again at his casual attitude toward his own security, but delighted to be guaranteed another several hours of his time, I had put a fresh tape in my minicassette recorder. As we pulled out of the winding drive of the Grand Hotel and entered the access road to the airport autoroute, the Chinese driver and Ninoy's brother-in-law Antolin ("Len") Oreta looked back to make sure we were not being followed.

Again Ninoy expressed puzzlement about what was going on in Manila. "It's gotten so out of hand this time," he said, referring to the highly publicized palace warnings to stay away, "that it is overkill. People are saying, 'The only guy who is going to kill him at this point is one of their own men.'" Using his heaviest American slang to underline his point, Ninoy reiterated, "That is why I am saying that my friend ain't the guy I knew before. He's allowed a few jokers to issue his press releases, which are shot through with contradictions."

Intrigued by his previous remarks about his chilly relations with the Reagan administration, I pressed him about his views on the future status of the U.S. bases in the Philippines. Ninoy said candidly:

> I am realistic enough to know that you cannot demand the removal of those bases without encountering the ire of the U.S.A, and at this stage of the game, that's where our bread is buttered. A small country does not have the luxury of independence, and I've been telling my colleagues, "Look, even Castro with the backing of the USSR could not close Guantanamo for pete's sake. Now, I'm not going to have the CIA undermining me and causing me so many problems. Let's face the realities and negotiate with the guys."

His long-term plan for the bases, after the 1991 expiration date of the agreement under which the U.S. controls the military facilities, was to set a deadline of five years for the Americans to give them up. Meanwhile, he would spend the interim economic support funds to develop the base sites as industrial zones and lease those facilities to the U.S. or other interested parties.

"I have been harsh in my criticism of the U.S. where I found fault, but I am reasonable," said Ninoy. "You can argue with me." What bugged him about some American bureaucrats, he went on, was that "they have not gotten over the notion that we are their little brown brothers in a colony. They think we are still incompetent and cannot run our own shop." Irreverently, he declared, "I don't belong to the generation of Marcos that sheds crocodile tears every time they start playing 'The Star-Spangled Banner.' "

"The Americans look at me as a kind of Dennis the Menace," he mused. "I am a product of their system. I know the jokers across the table. They are not going to put one over on me. But at the same time, while I may be a hard bargainer, they would much rather have me than the Commies. I am not ideologically dangerous. They may not love me, but they are stuck with me."

As we neared the airport, I returned to the subject of Marcos and the curious relationship which Ninoy seemed to enjoy with his adversary. I related to him what an old Asia hand had told me—that, contrary to their very different images, Aquino and Marcos were actually alter egos. As president, he ventured, Aquino would probably not prove to be significantly less ruthless than Marcos. With fascination I listened as Ninoy responded affirmatively to that observation.

"Some people have said I can be as ruthless as Marcos and even more dictatorial," he acknowledged. "I don't deny that. I believe in a strong president." There, however, he separated himself from Marcos. ". . . But a strong president with the checks: a free judiciary and a free press."

Aquino continued:

I admit you cannot run that country with a weak leadership.
You've got to have a strong hand, and you've got to mean it. I
could be ruthless when I say, "By George, you're going to jail."
And when I tell the Commies, "You are going to be legalized, you
are going to have your chance to speak out, but you pick up the
gun, brother, and I'm going to chase you. As long as you don't
pick up the gun, I won't pick it up either. But don't forget: I pick
up the gun legitimately. You don't. I can shoot you like a dog, so
don't force my hand."

*　　　*　　　*

We arrived at Taipei's Chiang Kai-shek International Airport at about 10 A.M. One of Ninoy's Filipino friends, Noy Brizuela, who had traveled with him from Los Angeles, had gone to the airport earlier that morning to check in Ninoy's five suitcases and pick up his boarding pass. The prearranged drill was for Noy to await our car at the arrivals entrance.

He was not there as we drove up, so we circled the airport and passed by again. Still no Noy. This time Len got out. Ninoy kept talking. Finally, he confided why he had remained unconcerned about the spies in the corridor outside his hotel room—because he had worked out a deal with Taiwan authorities to assure his safe passage out of the country.

According to Ninoy, when he arrived in Taiwan, he had dined with the wife of an old and influential Chinese friend, Han Lih-wu, a former ambassador to the Philippines, who was traveling abroad at the time. The next morning, Mrs. Han had called him to report having received queries from acquaintances at China Airlines, who had heard rumors that Aquino would fly to Manila aboard a CAL plane, and who seemed to be fishing for information as to his whereabouts. Fifteen minutes later she phoned him back to report another mysterious call—this one from Manila.

This had unnerved Ninoy. "I hit the panic button," he confessed. He decided that it was imperative for him "to go aboveground and call the chief of staff" to Taiwan President Chiang Ching-kuo. Weighing heavily on his mind was the fact that Narciso Ramos, the father of Marcos's armed forces vice-chief of staff, Lieutenant General Fidel Ramos, had recently emerged from retirement and returned to Taipei as the Marcos government's official trade representative. In the interest of protecting Ramos, whom he did not consider an adversary, Ninoy stressed to his friends his desire that "with Ramos here, no incident should occur."

That afternoon, a ranking Taiwan official had paid a call on Ninoy in his suite. Ninoy refused to divulge his name, saying only that he had "gone to the highest leadership and told them I am here." His brothers-in-law later revealed the official to be Congressman Lu Ching-shih. Animatedly, Ninoy recreated the argument he had put to this elderly official:

> The Chinese Nationalist Government can refuse to board me tomorrow, but I am a hot potato, so what do you do to me? The best thing is to ignore me and send me off to Manila. I did not forge a Chinese document, I did not break a Chinese law. I will show a travel document to protect China Airlines. You can cable that you did not catch me here.

One member of Ninoy's party, Japanese freelance photojournalist Kiyoshi Wakamiya, later described the visit of the "Taiwan bigshot" to the hotel. "I was in the same room," said Wakamiya, "and Ninoy was crying, 'Let me go, I am under the name of Marcial Bonifacio.'" After that encounter Ninoy expressed confidence that he would be assured government protection and facilitation of his departure.

By the time we drove past the passenger terminal entrance again, Len was outside motioning that the coast was clear. As the car drew up to the curb, Ninoy paused before responding to one last question about Marcos's intentions toward him. Everything that he had told me about his former relationship with Marcos and his plans for challenging his candidates in the coming elections indicated that Ninoy remained a serious political threat to the president. Why, I asked, had Marcos, who was after all a dictator, tolerated Aquino, even to the point that he had? Why would he do so now?

His answer haunts me to this day. "At the back of my mind," said Ninoy, "I've always felt that he may not like me, but that I was a sparring mate for him, and he would be lonely without me."

*　　　*　　　*

The airport was crowded with weekend travelers, and the lines at the China Airlines counter were long and slow. To avoid exposing Ninoy to possible surveillance, the men went on ahead, up the escalator to the departure area, while I checked in. I joined them just outside the roped-off immigration hall about ten minutes later. I had no trouble locating them. In his white safari suit and shades, Ninoy stood out among the more formally dressed Chinese passengers and the few Caucasians.

It was there that Len and Noy were forced to take leave of Ninoy. Both men, longtime Marcos opponents, were barred from entering the Philippines. Len liked to joke that his crime against the state was marriage to Ninoy's sister Tessie, or "illegal possession of brother-in-law." They hugged each other hard and went their separate ways. Ninoy and I passed through the ropes, into a large gallery with glass walls and six long passport lines. Everyone in this room was under surveillance from four sides. "Just keep talking," said Ninoy, who had, uncharacteristically for him, fallen rather silent.

I put on a big smile and did my best to look both infatuated and on vacation. Soon we were laughing about this weird "honeymoon" on which we were embarked. We spotted some of our party in line nearby, but following Ninoy's instructions, we did not acknowledge each other, lest Marcos's presumed spies associate the journalists with the fugitive. Likewise, we had agreed not to take pictures or notes openly until we were safely airborne.

Suddenly a voice behind us boomed, "Are there any Filipinos here?" I continued to smile and chat, pretending not to hear the question.

"Turn around and keep talking," Ninoy instructed me under his breath.

As I did so, I noticed that he had maneuvered himself to one side of me, so that I now blocked the questioner's view of him. I smiled at the official in the white uniform, who continued past us and on down the line, inquiring about the presence of Filipinos. Almost swooning with relief, I looked at Ninoy. His back was still turned to me, and he was staring at the window wall to his far right, behind which a man in a beige uniform stood staring back at him.

"There's my guardian angel," he whispered, excitedly.

Indeed, the Taiwan security connection on whom Ninoy had been counting appeared to be in place. The security man's eyes met his again for a split second. Then he turned away and strolled slowly in the direction of the immigration desks, which we were approaching. By now the agent, who just seconds ago had been searching for Filipinos, was nowhere to be seen, while the "guardian angel" appeared to be positioning himself to help Ninoy through the passport checkpoint, should there be any question about his papers. When finally it was his turn in line, he stepped up to the desk, assuring me that he would wait for me just beyond.

I watched as he handed his passport up to the woman behind the elevated counter. She punched some information into her Wang computer and waited for clearance. The man in beige was by now standing almost behind her, his eyes on Ninoy. Quickly, she stamped the passport and handed it back to him. He passed behind the glass, where he was greeted cordially by his contact. When I reached them a few moments later, they were engaged in conversation. We were given full VIP treatment through the line for the hand luggage check.

Just as we caught sight of our departure gate, number 6, the guardian angel halted in response to the crackle on his walkie-talkie. He held the device to his ear, then spoke into it in Mandarin. "Wait one moment," he said to Ninoy. "My boss wants to meet you." Ninoy froze, and no wonder. We had gotten to within yards of our plane without incident, only to be stopped in the stretch. Observing our discomfort, our escort smiled. "Don't worry," he said.

The uniformed personnel near the luggage scanner stepped back and bowed, as a thin Chinese man, dressed in a Western suit and obviously well known to them, strode in our direction. Our escort also bowed, then introduced Ninoy. The thin man pumped Ninoy's hand energetically, then pulled him aside to say a few words. They shook hands again, and I heard the gentleman wish him "Good luck." He and the guardian angel then turned and walked away, while Ninoy and I went on to the gate.

"Who was that?" I asked Ninoy.

"The head of the Taiwan Garrison Command," he answered. I reached for my notebook to write down his name, but Ninoy added, "I don't remember it. All Chinese names sound alike." Later Ninoy confided to Ken that the officer had "made a very curious comment that he was called by Philippine Airlines that morning, and they told him to take good care of me."

Ninoy was almost giddy with delight at the way he had been received by the government of Taiwan. "That's the beauty of a dictatorship," cackled the man who had so often opposed it from podiums in his own country. "They will shut up here."

*　　　　　*　　　　　*

The ground hostesses at Gate 6 greeted Ninoy as if they had been expecting him. "Since nine forty-five A.M., in Manila they already know you are on board," one volunteered. He had lapsed back into a tense silence as we entered the Boeing 767.

The stewardess, who did not seem to recognize him, showed Ninoy to seat 14E on the left aisle. I found my own seat, 15G, in the row behind him in the midsection of the tourist cabin. Two Filipino women were already seated to my left, and directly behind Ninoy. One leaned over and asked discreetly, "Is that man Senator Aquino?"

Remembering our pact not to give ourselves away until the plane was in the air, I played dumb. "I don't know Senator Aquino," I said.

The plane was due to depart at 11 A.M. At 11:10, it was still sitting at the gate with its doors open. Ninoy leafed through the in-flight magazine. I tried not to act concerned. Ken Kashiwahara, seated across the aisle from Ninoy, was ashen-faced. At 11:15, ABC-TV producer Bill Stewart entered the plane, panting. He had received the wrong boarding pass and had had to return to the check-in desk to exchange it. Congestion in the immigration area had then delayed him and other passengers. Now, however, they were all aboard. The stewardess secured the heavy door. Strains of "That Special Feeling" piped forth from the cabin sound system, rich with irony.

Minutes later we were in the air. When the No Smoking sign went off, we allowed ourselves to acknowledge each other. When the seat belt sign went off about ten minutes into the flight, a cheer went up, and the photographers and TV crews began taking out their equipment. Ninoy was ebullient. I apologized to the two Filipinos for not confirming his identity, and explained why I had been unable to do so. Expressing their longtime admiration for him, they thrust their boarding passes forward for autographs.

Ninoy was quickly surrounded by well-wishers, as Ken led him and the two TV crews, from the U.S. and Japan, to the nearly empty aft cabin for a midair press conference. As I followed them back, several Asian and European passengers and a bewildered steward asked me who he was. Most were not familiar with Aquino's name, but they immediately nodded and grinned when reference was made to his being an adversary of Marcos.

Ninoy answered, on camera, some of the same questions we had posed to him in the hotel last night. He was going back, he repeated, to try to persuade Marcos to make some essential reforms to assure a peaceful succession later on. He spoke of the Philippines' grave economic problems, the yawning gap between rich and poor, the growing Communist insurgency, the threat represented by a bloated military. He acknowledged that he was putting his life in danger by returning and voiced the possibility that he could be shot or sent back to prison. But spirits were high, and he spoke animatedly about the future.

We returned to the forward cabin when lunch was served, and I sat down beside him in a vacant window seat for a few more minutes of talk. I began eating. He did not touch his tray. "I can't eat or I'll throw up," he said. His worries over what awaited him in Manila had recurred. "I told Doy to see Imelda," he repeated. "They were supposed to see her, but the fact that she hid from them and refused to see them . . ." His voice trailed off. "The thing that scares me," he continued, "is how they keep repeating that intelligence report about assassins."

I tried to say something reassuring, but before I could, he had snapped out of his pensiveness, and a strange serenity, which I had not perceived earlier, settled over him. He spoke with particular poignance about his wife and children. He had written letters to each of them last night while all the rest of us were sleeping.

"You see, Sandra," he began, without explanation, "I have lived with this for so long that I really feel this is a bonus." I guessed from the faraway look in his eyes that he was speaking of living with death, and that the bonus was the reprieve he had enjoyed in recent years. Now the memories came pouring out of him. He explained how in 1975, the third year of his imprisonment, he had gone on a hunger strike to protest his trial by a military court whose jurisdiction he refused to acknowledge. "I gave many reasons for the hunger strike," he said, "but the real reason was that I had had it. I was in solitary, and before I cracked up, I thought my wife was still young, and she could get married again. Her family was getting harassed, my father-in-law had lost his fortune because I married into the family. It was not fair. So I went on a hunger strike for forty days and forty nights, and I lost sixty pounds, and believe me, I literally died in 1975, so this now is all fun."

This statement was in such contrast to the consternation he had expressed only seconds before, that I had to ask if anything at all frightened him. "The only thing that frightens me is that people might get hurt," he answered, "that because of my coming somebody might get hurt. There are so many imponderables here, so many actors. One little thing can go awry . . ."

His gaze had turned to the window, where the lush green landscape of the northern Philippine island of Luzon suddenly hove into view beneath the clouds. Ninoy was ecstatic.

"I'm home. All I have to do is kiss Philippine soil, and that will be enough, don't you think?" he asked.

For the first time during our short acquaintance, I voiced a personal opinion about what he was telling me. "No," I said impulsively, "that's not enough. You have so much more to do."

He had been through so much, and he spoke with such clarity about what his country needed. He was the underdog, and he was full of such passion. I was the American, and I believed that people like him made a difference. What had seemed to me a fruitless mission only yesterday now appeared to be a rare convergence of the right leader at the right time. I wanted him to succeed, which, in my terms, meant putting his words into action. I was embarrassed by the strength of my emotion. I apologized for presuming to tell him what he should do.

With touching sensitivity, he picked up the thread of my thoughts and began reformulating them in Asian terms. The backroom politician was gone. In his place was a more spiritual person. The transformation was dramatic and totally unself-conscious.

"I have never attracted this size following from the Japanese press," he said, gesturing toward the Japanese photographers and cameramen who were filming our conversation. "It's because of the kamikaze. The concept of dying for one's country is very Asian. Hara-kiri. These things have not been done in Japan since the war, but now all the articles about me tend to say, 'Here is a leader of the old mold.' This really attracts the attention of the Asians more than anything."

Earnestly, he beckoned me to discard my Western skepticism and look at him through the eyes of an Asian. "Western people might think I am crazy," he acknowledged. "They say the guy is stupid to go home. He can do more by staying outside. They don't understand the value of self-sacrifice. Gandhi kneeling down and getting bashed. The vanquished is the victor. If you can get at the bad thing within your enemy, you unmask him. Here you are, pure, coming in in white. In Japan when you commit hara-kiri, you come in in white. In my country you cannot qualify for leadership without courage, so you must be ready to lay down your life."

I did not want to hear what he was saying. I was afraid I might cry. What had attracted me to him from the start was his positive thinking and his humor. That was what had initially drawn me to Filipinos in general. There was a tragic inevitability about the problems which plagued their country, but they rarely let it defeat them. Ninoy epitomized their resilience.

Sensing my resistance to his way of seeing things, he tried harder to explain. "Maybe they are not that sentimental in the West," he ventured. "In Asia unless a movie can evoke tears from the audience, it does not sell." Intuitively, he lightened his tone and retreated once again behind his comic mask. "They gotta cry. That's why the mass magazines are all writing about me. It has become the biggest guessing game: Will he come? They don't talk of anything else. Will he come? Will he outsmart them? Wait for the next chapter. Marcos has played along with me, and that's my lucky star. It takes two to tango, and he obliged me, so I love the guy."

At 12:40 P.M. the seat belt sign flashed back on, and the captain advised that we were beginning our descent into Manila. "Don't forget me," said Ninoy.

"Forget you?" I answered in disbelief. Before we parted, I asked him to autograph my boarding pass, and I elicited from him several phone numbers of family members, who could inform me which jail he was in.

"At twelve-forty-five P.M., it is eighty-eight degrees Fahrenheit in Manila," reported the stewardess. "We hope you have enjoyed your flight and will fly again soon with China Airlines." The cabin crew, by now aware that it was party to a historic event, came by to wish Ninoy well. A photogenic Filipino woman, who had watched him from afar until now, came forward to kiss him. Recognizing a good picture, the photographers flocked to the couple and snapped several different poses.

"My wife better not see this," Aquino joked, playing to his audience. But his mind was clearly elsewhere, and as soon as they returned to their seats, he bowed his head and fingered his rosary beads.

The air was turbulent as we passed over the sprawl of metropolitan

Manila and caught the sea breeze. We banked sharply over the harbor, then headed back inland, over the geometric patterns of fish pens resembling those built by the pre-Hispanic Malay fishermen who once plied these shores, lower over the palm-frond roofs of the squatter huts, lower still over the rusting, corrugated tin roofs of the urban slum dwellers, then down onto a runway bordered by vivid green grass and tall reeds bending in the wind of our exhaust.

"1:04 P.M., touchdown," I wrote in my notebook. "Machine guns and tanks near the terminal."

Ever the politician, Ninoy was interested in whether any of the reporters seated near the windows on the left-hand side of the plane could see the size of the crowd on hand to welcome him. Unfortunately, the terminal blocked our view of the airport entrance and parking lots, where his supporters would presumably have gathered. What was highly visible everywhere was the military presence. "I expected fighter planes," said Ninoy without explanation.

Fearful of missing something as I prepared to follow Ninoy down an aisle which would soon be crowded, I removed the minirecorder from my briefcase. On the audiotape I recorded that day, the action is much quicker and more to the point than in the slow motion of my memory, which I am forever replaying, even now, five years later. The taped event is only two minutes and forty seconds long, the portions which interest the courts only ten seconds and seventeen seconds respectively. The tiny cassette carries the sounds of a murder, isolated from the agony of a nation. In my mind they are one, and that is the story.

*   *   *

As the plane taxied to its berth at Gate 8 of Manila International Airport, the rolling tape caught the strains of the on-board Muzak and the chattering of passengers already preparing to disembark. The pilot broke in with an announcement: "Please remain in your seats for ten minutes." Ninoy, who expected to be arrested, heeded the instructions. We journalists, not sure where events were leading us, posted ourselves near windows and in the aisles. Our voices, forever captured on that little band, I realize now, were the first in what would become a global chorus to the tragedy.

> *ABC-TV correspondent*. . . . Remain on board.
> *Aquino*. Everybody remains on board.
> *TIME correspondent*. There's that van and what else?
> *UPI correspondent*. That's it.
> *Aquino*. There's a car waiting for us?
> *Aquino's brother-in-law*. Yeah, there's a car . . .

We watched, fascinated, as a blue van backed up to the service stairs of the movable passenger tube, which had by now been coupled to the door of our plane. Military men in blue jumpsuits, armed with automatic rifles, fanned out around the plane. Sharpshooters appeared on the roof of the terminal. At about the same time three uniformed soldiers entered the economy-class section. As they moved down the aisle, they surveyed the rows of passengers, obviously looking for Ninoy. The TV crews trained their cameras on them. I turned off my recorder and began taking notes. The first two passed by without identifying him. The third, shielded behind sunglasses, recognized him and stopped. Naturally affable and trusting, Ninoy reached out and shook his hand. The soldiers helped him to his feet, picked up his carry-on luggage, and escorted him toward the door.

I rushed to follow. As Ninoy began to disappear out the door, I switched my recorder back on and thrust it into the crowd which separated us, hoping to catch the voices of those who waited outside to greet him. The press of newsmen confronting plainclothes security people, as I followed him through the door of the plane into the movable passenger tube, became audible. Urgent voices hurried him along, out the service door, onto the exterior service stairs. More urgent voices, speaking Pilipino, drowned the others out. Security men in white shirts barred us from exiting behind him. They shoved some of us back against the cold, stainless-steel body of the plane, causing the metal floor of the passenger tube to shake wildly. We gathered our strength and lunged forward again, pushing the door open and jabbing cameras and microphones blindly through:

Voice 1. *Ako na, ako na* [I'll do it]!
Voice 2. *Kanila na, kanila na* [They can have it]!
Woman's voice. *Manong magigiba ito—magigiba ito* [It (the metal floor) will collapse]!
Voice 3. Get down, get down!
[*As the metal structure continued to vibrate dangerously from all the motion, a single shot sounded just outside the door to the service stairs.*]
TIME correspondent. What happened? What was that?
[*Three more pops and a crescendo of wails and sobs from a female passenger attested to the dawning horror of what was taking place outside. A fifth shot.*]

Desperate to see but still blocked from reaching the outside stairs, I pushed my way back inside the plane, stepping over terrified passengers, who had dived for cover, to the nearest window. Ninoy lay dead on the tarmac, blood spurting from a hole in the back of his head. The lifeless body of another man, this one dressed in blue, lay near him. None of the khaki-suited escorts was anywhere to be seen. Nothing moved for what seemed like a long interval.

> *TIME correspondent.* Wait. What happened? Oh no, he's . . .
> *Female passenger.* Oh no [*wails*].

The tape rolled on, recording the half-formed questions about the deceased and picking up gasps, screams, and curses, as another volley of gunfire was inexplicably pumped into the torso of the dead man in blue.

> *TIME correspondent.* Oh, the soldiers are . . .
> *ABC-TV correspondent.* What happened?
> *TIME correspondent.* The soldiers . . . they put about sixteen shots in him. They shot Ninoy. He's dead out there. Christ almighty, they . . . oh, he's dead, he's dead. I can't believe it.
> *Japanese reporter.* I saw that . . .

As we stood there trying to comprehend, the SWAT commandos, who had previously emptied their Armalites into the man in blue, turned their attention back to Ninoy. While a number of them aimed their guns menacingly at potential witnesses inside the plane and at the windows of the passenger terminal, others picked up his limp body and heaved it into the van. Then they all jumped in, and the vehicle sped off, leaving behind only the mysterious man in blue, a small pool of blood, a larger puddle of water, and several objects strewn on the tarmac as evidence of a crime.

The tape continued, picking up our dazed attempts to make sense of what we had just seen:

> *TIME correspondent.* Does anybody know what those uniforms were?
> *Japanese reporter.* They pretend that this guy killed him. . . . Goddamn Philippines.
> *TIME correspondent.* The whole place is gonna go. It's gonna pop like a cork.

3

Ferdinand and Imelda, Ninoy and Cory

In the scant interval of less than two minutes that elapsed from the time the soldier escorts helped Ninoy from his seat until SWAT commandos heaved his lifeless body into a military van, a political rivalry, which had shaped more than a decade and a half of Philippine history, ended. The impertinent voice that had challenged Marcos's authority since the early months of his presidency was silenced, the bluff and swagger that had mocked his own was stilled. "Marcos will be lonely without me," Ninoy had said just before boarding his last flight. Perhaps that was too sentimental a statement to apply to as Machiavellian a man as Marcos. Perhaps the word *unrestrained* better characterized the prospect of Marcos the dictator, suddenly free of the last hostile claimant to his power in a succession struggle that had been under way since he set out to defy the two-term constitutional limit on the presidency.

Theirs had been the symbiotic relationship of two instinctive politicians who knowingly enhanced their reputations by opposing each other. Although their differences were real, they stemmed less from ideology than from age and degree of cynicism. Both were the sons of fathers whose honor they sought to avenge. Both were products of the same system, political pragmatists, who built grass-roots organizations, set their sights early in life on the presidency, and chose wives who could advance their careers. Since both held a strongman's view of democracy, neither was a stranger to backroom deals or violence. Perhaps because fate was kinder to Ninoy in his youth, he was an optimist, an idealist, for whom everything seemed possible, while Marcos saw life as a hard struggle to stay one step ahead of unkind destiny. Years of political rivalry had made each perversely dependent on the other to define his own goals, gauge his own performance, and check his own worst impulses.

President Ferdinand Edralin Marcos was the most brilliant politician produced by a young republic that thrilled to stirring rhetoric and tales of political intrigue. The way Filipinos had learned it from their American mentors during the era of Tammany Hall and the capitalist robber barons, it mattered not how the game was played, only that it be won. Marcos had played dirty from the beginning, but his victories had been spectacular, and that was what counted in the eyes of voters, who prized courage and cunning above all other qualities.

It was a central fact of Marcos's political legend that his career had begun, as it would end, with a murder. The story of the murder of his father's political opponent circulated through Manila's political coffee shops much like the oral history which had linked the chain of ethnically varied Philippine islands in their tribal past. In fact, as a young law student, he had been convicted of shooting the man who defeated his father for a seat in the new Commonwealth Congress. Much of the mystique that would later surround Marcos emanated from that incident. To his opponents he would always be a man not only capable of calculating a murder but also of crafting a deft legal defense of his own innocence. To his supporters he remained to the last a fighter, who had the guts and brains to argue his own case before the Supreme Court and the good fortune to draw a sympathetic justice who acquitted him.

The part of the country in which the crime was committed was a clannish little world unto itself: the rugged coastal province of Ilocos Norte, in the far northwest corner of the main island of Luzon. Cursed with a harsher environment than that inhabited by most of the other peoples who occupy the archipelago, Ilocanos found it difficult to prosper on their own soil, and many had migrated southward to more fertile lands. Even then, no matter where they settled, they remained something of an alien breed: hardworking, miserly, fiercely loyal to each other, but prone to violence as a means of settling family feuds and affirming their honor.

Ferdinand's father, Mariano Marcos, was a two-term congressman who had hit a losing streak. A stirring orator in three languages, he drifted naturally into politics from his position as a traveling public-school supervisor. However, his decision to quit his job and enter law school in Manila, as a precursor to running for Congress, had put a strain on his wife, Josefa, who supported the family of four children by teaching school. Their financial situation hardly improved after Mariano became a congressman in 1924, as his earnings were poured into his campaigns or drained away by needy supporters and hangers-on. Still, because politics was the only thing that engaged her husband, Josefa deferred to his ambitions and even drew from her modest inheritance to tide them over in lean seasons. When he suddenly lost his seat in a close three-way race in 1932, the family lost its focus.

Mariano was plunged into a depression so deep that he was unable to practice law for a year. Only a fortuitously timed appointment by President Manuel Quezon to the governorship of the province of Davao, on the far southern island of Mindanao, prevented a profound crisis. For the first time, far from home and far from the vortex of politics, parents and children experienced the closeness of normal family life.

Ferdinand Marcos's fondest memories dated from that period of respite in the south, where his father taught him and his brother to box, wrestle, and shoot and instilled in the boy a lesson he would later repeat and live by: "Don't start a fight until you know you can win it." It was, however, his mother's influence that had long since molded his character, causing him to scorn gambling, drinking, and tobacco, and instilling in him the drive to excel in his studies, lest he lose his state scholarships and with them the possibility of one day enjoying the financial security she had never known as a married woman.

A landmark election in 1935, the year the colony became a commonwealth, lured Mariano back home to run for his old seat. His loss, to incumbent Congressman Julio Nalundasan, was gleefully celebrated by the winner's followers, who paraded a casket labeled Marcos before the defeated candidate's house, chanting, "Marcos is dead, long live Nalundasan." Such provocation was not uncommon in the wake of a bitter election. Nor was retaliation by the aggrieved party considered unreasonable. Thus, when Nalundasan was shot dead by a single bullet three days later, while engaged in his evening ritual of brushing his teeth before a lighted window, the likeliest suspects were Mariano Marcos and his kin.

Particularly under a shadow was son Ferdinand, a marksman at the University of the Philippines, who would later brag that he was "one of the best shots in the country." However, he was not charged with the crime until four years later, after another man had been tried and acquitted. On December 7, 1938, after a UP target pistol was identified as the murder weapon, a constabulary officer interrupted the young Marcos during a night class in law at the university and arrested him.

Marcos was released on bail from prison in time for his law school graduation in April 1940. Accompanied by two constabulary guards, he accepted his diploma from President Quezon in a heavily reported commencement ceremony, then crammed for the bar exams under the watchful eyes of two uniformed police escorts.

In the trial that followed, Marcos's attorney rejected in its entirety the testimony of the state's star witness, a clerk who claimed that he was privy to the unfolding plot by the Marcos family to kill Nalundasan in the event he won the election. After the defense attorney finished his summation, his twenty-two-year-old client made his courtroom debut, arguing emotionally in his own behalf.

Pointing his finger, gunlike, at the chief constabulary investigator, Marcos questioned why, after the lawman had publicly branded the UP target pistol as the murder weapon, he had presented no ballistics evidence to prove that the bullet that killed Nalundasan had been fired from that gun. He ridiculed the state's notion that he and his relatives, all well versed in the law, would have confided their alleged murder plot to a man who was a stranger to all but one of them.

The trial lasted two months and climaxed with the same bizarre confluence of events that had marked the whole history of the case. Early on November 29, 1940, Marcos learned that he had earned the highest score in the history of the Philippine bar. As he was accepting the congratulations of his fellow students and professors, a siren sounded, a police vehicle approached, and two agents informed him that he was once again under arrest.

Found guilty of murder and sentenced to seventeen years in jail, he was recommended for a pardon as "one of the most intelligent of our youth." Stubbornly, Marcos declared that he would settle for nothing less than an acquittal. With his family's political influence lost, his mother's inheritance exhausted by lawyer's fees, and his own career as a lawyer at least temporarily aborted, his only recourse was to carry his appeal to the Supreme Court himself.

According to an account in the *Lawyer's Journal*, at the time, Marcos's plea for provisional liberty to allow him to prepare his brief "was so impassioned that all spectators, court employees and even the judge himself found themselves in tears." Today, given the hindsight afforded by nearly a decade of martial law, his soaring tribute to the law and his stinging indictment of false testimony seem laden more with irony than with passion. Marcos declared, in an oration not dissimilar to that which his premier prisoner Ninoy Aquino would deliver thirty-five years later before a military tribunal:

> . . . if within his heart he knows that he has been ordained to this death of a million deaths by the single falsehood of a lying tongue, then the rebellion of his soul is unquenchable. . . . And even if acquittal should follow, the wrong cannot be undone.

Marcos was not freed, but he was granted permission to defend himself and extended special treatment. Provincial authorities supplied him with a study table, volumes of legal reference books, and a Ping-Pong table for exercise. After months of work, Marcos submitted an 830-page brief.

On October 12, 1940, dressed for dramatic effect in the white of innocence and arguing eloquently without notes, he asked the justices to set aside the verdicts for murder and contempt, which he claimed were based on illogical and erroneous testimony and assumptions. Two weeks later a unanimous decision, penned by presiding Justice Jose P. Laurel, found the testimony of the key state's witness to be "inherently improbable and full of contradictions in important details." On that basis, Laurel acquitted Marcos. For the rest of his life, Marcos would feel in the personal debt of the Laurel family to the point that he would not threaten its fortunes, even after its scions turned against him.

In the meantime, Marcos's notoriety was quickly transformed into celebrity. The weekly *Philippines Free Press* named him "Lawyer of the Year" even before he had begun to practice. His law fraternity feted him with a banquet attended by the most important lawyers in Manila. The justices of the Supreme Court convoked a special ceremony to swear him in as a member of the bar. President Quezon summoned him to Malacañang Palace, the graceful riverside structure which has served as the seat of government since the days of the Spanish viceroys, to offer him a position as chief prosecutor in the Department of Investigation.

Marcos's official campaign biographer, Hartzell Spence, sketched a revealing scene in which Marcos icily rejected Quezon's offer, prompting the president to confide that he himself had committed murder as a young man. Said Quezon:

> When I was young, I killed the man who murdered my father. I understand how a young man may avenge a family insult. The point is now to rehabilitate yourself and make this count for you and not against you. You must uproot your bitterness. Your defense prevented anyone from destroying you—why do you now destroy yourself?

*   *   *

The Japanese air attack on an American military base in the Philippines four hours after the attack on Pearl Harbor interrupted the lives of Marcos and his generation, and marked the end of innocence for the six-year-old commonwealth by exploding its assumptions about the power of the U.S. to protect it. Summoned out of retirement to become senior U.S. commander in the Far East, former army Chief of Staff Douglas MacArthur found himself with only 22,000 U.S. soldiers and Philippine scouts plus a commonwealth army of 80,000 mostly raw recruits to face

Japan's 6-million-man military. Among the better trained of those newly mobilized Filipino troops was Ferdinand Marcos, a reserve officer with a law degree, who had been called up three weeks earlier and assigned as an intelligence officer to an infantry division that was being positioned in the path of an expected Japanese naval invasion.

On December 8, 1941, the Japanese launched an air attack on Clark Field, fifty miles northwest of Manila, virtually destroying the entire U.S. Air Force in the islands. To spare the capital from a similar fate in the days which followed, MacArthur declared it an open city and hurriedly withdrew its defenses westward to the mountainous Bataan peninsula, off the shore of which lay Corregidor. The island redoubt had been fortified against attack from land and sea, but not from the air.

Marcos's division was diverted to Bataan, where it was immediately engaged in fierce combat. Gradually, it dawned on the Filipino soldiers fighting there that the reinforcements they had awaited would not arrive, that the master planners in Washington were pursuing a "Europe-first" policy, which would leave them and their archipelago defenseless. In March, MacArthur left to set up Pacific headquarters in Australia. He took with him both President Quezon and Vice-President Sergio Osmeña, leaving the rest of the cabinet to deal with the Japanese.

Lieutenant Marcos helped smuggle Yankee and Filipino volunteers out of Bataan to other islands in the archipelago, where they had been ordered to organize networks of guerrillas and spies to prepare for MacArthur's return. When the Japanese began their bombardment of Corregidor, Marcos was severely wounded by shrapnel and sniper fire while leading a group of fleeing Filipino and American soldiers toward a new line of resistance, inland at Mount Samat, where, as president, he would later inaugurate a seven-story cross as a monument to the 5,000 men who died there.

The inevitable surrender of Corregidor on April 10, 1942, resulted in the forced evacuation of Filipino and American soldiers from Bataan to a Japanese prison camp in Tarlac. Marcos was among the 70,000 men who made the infamous Bataan Death March. Ten thousand of them died from starvation, disease, and injuries in the course of the fifty-five-mile trek. More than half the remainder died during their first three months in the camp. Marcos's biographer wrote:

> He did not survive entirely. Something of him was drained away. It was not his youth: He had lost that in the ordeal of the murder trial. Somewhere on the Death March, in the torment and from the shock, annealed the man Ferdinand Marcos would become.

An objective evaluation of the Marcos war record is difficult, not only because of the heated emotions he still provokes, but also because the records are incomplete and confusing, and because American and Filipino views as to who were the true guerrillas differ so widely. Marcos's carefully cultivated image as "the most decorated Filipino soldier of World War II" was central to his political success. Yet the thirty or so medals on which his reputation was built were based on affidavits filed years after the fact, which were either unsubstantiated or disputed by others. While most citations for bravery in action are awarded within weeks of the battle, almost half of Marcos's medals were issued two decades later in 1963 by former President Diosdado Macapagal. The president did so, according to an aide, in an attempt to persuade Senator Marcos not to challenge his nomination for a second term. Only one medal was awarded while Marcos was still in the army.

Even more clouded by doubts and counterclaims than his medals is the legend, which he relived throughout his presidency in televised reunions with his former comrades in arms, of his exploits with the guerrilla unit he founded, *Ang Mga Maharlika* (The Free Men). On the eve of the Philippine election which ended with Marcos's ouster, an American professor, who had sifted through previously unreleased files, led reporters to army documents that pronounced the president's claims to leadership of Maharlika "fraudulent" and the insertion of his name on its roster "a malicious criminal act."

Reexamined in the more neutral postelection environment, the documents lead to the less sensational conclusion that the American military officials who had the authority to recognize and award back pay and decorations to guerrilla units organized during the war rejected Marcos's inflated claims to a force of 8,300 men and a quarterly budget of 1.3 million pesos for personnel, intelligence, and dynamite. The documents do not, however, successfully refute Marcos's claim to leadership of a parent organization known as Maharlika, under which a special intelligence branch of Maharlika, which was officially recognized by the U.S. military, operated.

Contained in the same U.S. National Archives files is an affidavit by Narciso Ramos, the late foreign minister and highly respected father of Philippine Defense Secretary Fidel Ramos. The senior Ramos was wartime chief of the special intelligence section of Maharlika. According to his account, Marcos had failed to meet the American filing deadline for a roster of members of the parent organization, because he was thrown in the brig by an American captain acting on information fed to him by "unsympathetic" rival guerrilla groups. Lacking that central roster, U.S. military authorities granted sole accreditation to the Maharlika intelligence branch, on the basis of a more limited membership roster submitted by Ramos, who was acting as commanding officer in Marcos's absence.

Undaunted by American officials' initial rejection of his claims, Marcos flooded them with corroborating data. In response, the American commanding general denied accreditation a second time on different grounds. Among other things, he argued, Marcos's group did not "contribute materially to the eventual defeat of the enemy," and operated "on a part-time basis only." Marcos retorted with a curt, point-by-point refutation of the American commander's objections and a profusion of affidavits, including that of Ramos, which listed twenty-one instances in which Marcos's Maharlika had in fact contributed to defeating the Japanese. Most noteworthy was Ramos's affirmation that in 1944 Maharlika's sabotage sections sank two ships in Manila Bay and "became so active in the destruction of enemy telephone and electric lines that it is presumed this was the reason for the announcement of severe penalties for anyone caught tampering."

The irony of Marcos's failure to win recognition for his own war claims is that it was he who, as judge advocate general of the U.S.– Philippine command in his region at the end of the war, endeared himself to thousands of Filipino veterans by winning American recognition for their claims. Over 1 million Filipinos claimed guerrilla status after the war, whereas the U.S. estimated that only about 250,000 had actually fought the Japanese. Exaggeration and complete fabrication were commonplace. There was even a phrase for those who faked their claims: "Escolta guerrillas," named for the main street of Manila, where the under-the-table deals with American claims processors took place.

After two unsuccessful tries, Marcos submitted a dubious claim for cattle allegedly commandeered by the U.S. army. It too was rejected. He appealed no further. However, Marcos would not forget the way the American military command had humiliated him. He began practicing law and joined the new Liberal party founded by Manuel Roxas, the Filipino official who had secured his release from the American brig. Thanks to his friendship with General MacArthur, Roxas was on his way to becoming the first president of the Philippine Republic.

In 1949, Marcos ran for Congress in his father's old bailiwick. His first promise to voters was that, if elected, he would find a cash crop to lift the standard of living in the agriculturally poor region. He is better remembered for his second promise:

> Elect me a congressman now, and I pledge you an Ilocano
> president in twenty years . . .

*   *   *

In order to win the presidency by 1969, Congressman Marcos knew that he would have to broaden his base of popular support beyond the confines of the north. In a predominantly Roman Catholic country, where economic and political power is in the hands of an oligarchy of sixty families, making the right marriage is one way of doing that. Rated one of the country's most eligible bachelors, Marcos had courted many women, and had fathered children by a beautiful mestiza who could not, however, further his career, as she was from his own region.

Late one night in April 1954, quite by coincidence, Marcos, at the age of thirty-six, finally met his match. Following a speech attacking the programs of popular President Ramon Magsaysay, the cocky minority party congressman from Ilocos Norte strode into the House cafeteria. Most of the faces he saw there were the familiar ones of fellow legislators, exhausted from the annual filibuster over the budget. One, however, was fresh, fair, and female. "Who is she?" he asked a colleague. Marcos thrilled to the answer: the twenty-four-year-old cousin of House Speaker pro tempore Daniel Romualdez, the man who had just presided over the budget debate.

Instantly smitten by her beauty, the influence of her family name, and her southern origins—support in the south was demographically essential to any northerner aiming for the presidency—Marcos solicited an introduction.

"Would you mind standing up?" he asked Imelda Remedios Romualdez. Puzzled but intrigued, she got up from the table where she was seated with her aunt. Marcos took a position back-to-back with her and drew his hand over the top of his head toward hers. "Fine," he said, when his hand passed a few millimeters above hers. "Everything else is okay."

Tall for a Filipino woman, Imelda had left the Romualdez house that evening wearing slippers instead of her usual pumps, her hair spilling over her shoulders rather than piled atop her head. Thus, Marcos, who was extremely self-conscious about his short height and was wearing his usual elevator shoes, had been able to convince himself that he was taller than she. It was not out of character that his perception differed from the facts: at five feet eight inches, Imelda is one inch taller than he.

Marcos fell in love with a fantasy of Imelda which would one day destroy them both. Although he did not fully realize it at the time, her origins were humbler than his. Since moving from the southern province of Leyte to Manila two years earlier, she had exploited the influential Romualdez family connection and her stunning looks to make a name for herself in a society where wealth and position were everything. Afire with the same ambition that fueled Marcos to escape obscurity, she had embarked on a well-calculated climb up the social ladder.

First, she had entered the "Miss Manila" beauty contest, boldly enlisting the influential mayor of Manila to back her candidacy, even at the risk of sparking rumors of an illicit romance between herself and the married but flirtatious politician. "In those days the winner was the girl who sold the most tickets," recalls Jorge Araneta, scion of a wealthy family of sugar planters and Liberal party leaders. "I remember a birthday luncheon for my father to which Mayor Arsenio Lacson came with this pretty young girl in tow. Before they sat down to eat, he sold a big wad of tickets to my father and the other politicians."

Imelda's title was ultimately contested by a runner-up, who refused to accept the verdict of a mayoral committee that the mayor's candidate was the winner. By then, however, she was on her way, reveling in job offers as a model, invitations to the best parties in cliquish Manila, and a romance with a handsome, Harvard-educated aristocrat named Ariston Nakpil. There was only one cloud on her horizon. Nakpil was married, and divorce was not sanctioned in the heavily Catholic Philippines. In the eyes of her family, that relationship thus had little future.

It would have made no difference if it had. Once Marcos saw her, he was determined to win her and, characteristically, willing to do so shamelessly, using whatever means were necessary. He insisted on driving her to the mountain resort of Baguio, where she was obliged to spend the Holy Week tending to the Romualdez children. There Marcos began a campaign as relentless as any he had waged to clinch a financial deal or win an election. Armed with a signed marriage license in his briefcase, he dogged her at home, in church, and at a tea dance, which was heavily covered by local society columnists. Finally, on Good Friday she agreed to countersign.

On Holy Saturday, just eleven days after their midnight introduction in the congressional cafeteria, Ferdinand and Imelda were married by a justice of the peace. To get her to agree to the civil ceremony then and there, Marcos, who had been raised as an Aglipayan, a breakaway Catholic sect, promised her that he would be baptized as a Catholic and would stage a proper church wedding for the benefit of her family afterward. Deeply superstitious about the power of numbers, Marcos gave his bride a ring set with eleven diamonds—the length of their courtship and the date of his birth.

The official wedding, which he choreographed for her two weeks later on May 1, 1954, exceeded in ostentatiousness anything to which Manila society was accustomed. He commissioned the country's leading couturier to design her jewel-encrusted wedding gown, and a fancy bakery to produce a one-meter-square, pastry replica of the Congress building. He furnished society editors with press releases that magnified her relationship to Daniel Romualdez to the point of transforming her into a political blueblood, yet barely mentioned her own father, the Speaker's unsuccessful cousin. He invited President Magsaysay to stand as the principal sponsor of the bride, while he was attended by a bipartisan lineup of the country's leading politicians.

The president threw a wedding breakfast for the couple on the grounds of Malacañang Palace, to which he invited the entire Senate, House of Representatives, and Supreme Court. After slipping an eight-carat diamond on her finger, Marcos swept Imelda off on a round-the-world honeymoon. "Wedding of the year," swooned the Philippine press. "Marcos's debut as a presidential contender," commented a more cynical observer.

Not until Marcos visited Imelda's family in Leyte some time later did he begin to understand the gulf that separated the affluent and influential branch of the Romualdez family from the poor, obscure one to which his bride truly belonged. Only in 1970, when an unauthorized biography, titled *The Untold Story of Imelda Marcos*, was published, would Marcos learn the full extent to which Imelda had repressed her troubled childhood and invented a more enviable one. Embarrassed by the contents of the book, which he accused his political rivals of financing, he attempted to stop publication, discredit the author, Carmen Navarro Pedrosa, and bribe and threaten her key sources to retract the information they had provided on Imelda's life.

In fact, the untold story of her grotesque, impoverished childhood provided a far more sympathetic view of Imelda than the fairy tale which she and her own publicists had conjured up. In its portraits of her female forebears, one could see the warring facets of Imelda's own personality. Her indomitable grandmother Trinidad Lopez de Romualdez, the daughter of a Spanish friar, had given up her plans to enter a nunnery in order to marry and nurse back to health a tubercular husband. Years later the old woman searched the local convents to find a stepmother for the five children of her least successful son, the widowed Vicente Orestes.

Her candidate, Remedios Trinidad, had a cheerful disposition and a pleasant singing voice. However, she was no match for her husband's brood, which remained hostile to the arranged marriage. Naively, Remedios hoped that her first child would somehow bridge the gap between herself and Vicente Orestes' first family. The baby on whom that impossible burden fell, Imelda Remedios Visitacion Romualdez, was born July 2, 1929, in Manila. One year later Imelda gained a potential ally in the increasingly divided household with the birth of her brother Benjamin ("Kokoy"), to whom she would always remain close. By then economic problems had begun to aggravate the domestic rifts.

After repeated fights between husband, wife, and stepchildren, in which Vicente Orestes inevitably sided with his own flesh and blood, Remedios walked out, taking Imelda and baby Benjamin with her. Lacking the resources to raise her children alone, however, she let Vicente Orestes talk her into a reconciliation, during which she bore him three more children. When relations did not improve, Remedios, pathetic and defeated, gave up trying to keep peace within the warring household, and moved with her own children into the dank family garage, which had been vacant since the car was sold to cover debts. There she used a table as her bed, while her children and the maid slept on boards placed atop milk boxes. Each morning pretty little Imelda, her favorite, was dispatched to the main house to ask for the family's meager daily allowance.

It was reportedly this depressing chapter of Imelda's family history in Pedrosa's book that enraged the president. He felt, Pedrosa wrote, that the biography implied "that his wife and the First Lady of the land had been conceived on top of boxes. Aristocratic Imelda was his creature, and the book had torn his fiction to pieces."

In 1938, shortly after the birth of her sixth and last child, Remedios contracted double pneumonia and died. Seven months later Vicente Orestes sold the Manila residence and moved his eleven children back to his home province of Leyte. War and occupation forced the family to live a hand-to-mouth existence in a series of ramshackle houses. The children were continually embarrassed by their father's inability to meet their school payments on time.

"Meldy" grew to adolescence in a Quonset hut. When the Americans landed in Leyte in 1944, she and her father were able to solicit surplus building materials to improve the place. Despite the hardship of those years, she emerged as a young beauty with a clear soprano voice, who became a popular homegrown entertainer of the U.S. liberation forces. With the return of elections after the war and the declaration of independence in 1946, she was kept busy at fiestas, parades, and rallies, presenting the ritual flowered lei to visiting dignitaries.

It was during the 1946 election season that she caught the eye of her cousin Daniel Romualdez, who returned home to Leyte to campaign for Congress on the Nacionalista ticket. He initiated her into politics by engaging her to sing at his provincial rallies and taking her with him to visit political leaders. With his daughter Loreto, he planted in Imelda's mind the idea of moving to Manila after college to study singing. Vicente Orestes agreed to let her go in 1952, largely because he viewed the move as a way to distance his alluring daughter from an unwanted provincial suitor.

*   *   *

Among the first young people to befriend Imelda after she moved north were the children of the late prewar Senate majority leader and cabinet member during the Japanese occupation, Benigno Aquino, Sr. Not unusual in the Philippines, where family groups are intricately linked through intermarriage and a system of *compadres* and *commadres* or godparents, the Aquinos and the Romualdezes were distantly related.

"Pacing Gueco, the wife of Daniel Romualdez, was a first cousin of Ninoy's father," explains Mrs. Aurora Aquino, Ninoy's mother. "That's how Ninoy met Imelda." When the Aquinos visited the Romualdezes, she continues, "it was Imelda who would serve him and my other children Coca-Cola." By the time twenty-two-year-old Imelda moved to Manila to board with the Romualdezes in 1952, Ninoy had already gained a degree of fame as a foreign correspondent covering the Korean War for the *Manila Times*. Three years her junior, he had been promoted to diplomatic editor of the *Times*, and was also studying law at the University of the Philippines.

On at least two occasions when the Romualdez family traveled to the province of Tarlac, where Pacing owned a house near the Aquino ancestral home in Concepcion, Ninoy escorted Imelda to dances at the local auditorium. Doña Aurora denies that there was any more to the relationship than that. "She was pretty, but too tall," she says. "When he brought her there on New Year's Eve, no one else would dance with her." One of Ninoy's sisters remembers that Imelda, not yet having learned how to dress, wore the dowdy, hand-me-down clothes of her shorter and older aunt.

However, Ninoy and Imelda had in common their extroverted personalities. Imelda liked to perform, and she often sang at the parties given by her aunt. "Pacing would say, 'Meldy, why don't you sing for us?' " recalls Doña Aurora. "Imelda was not the shy type. She would mimic and dance as well as sing." Ninoy, on the other hand, was a born organizer of people, who made it his business to know everyone, and Meldy was the new girl in town.

In the summer of 1952 Ninoy encountered Corazon Cojuangco for the first time since adolescence. He had spent much of that particular summer interviewing political leaders in Southeast Asia for a *Times* series of articles about a proposed "Pacific Pact" against communism. One of eight children of Tarlac's other leading political and landowning family, Cory had spent her formative years in Catholic girls' schools in Manila and the U.S. Shy but smart, she found Ninoy more interesting than other young men her age. They corresponded throughout the 1952–53 school year, after she returned to New York for her last year at the College of Mount St. Vincent in Riverdale.

Meanwhile, Ninoy was often seen with Meldy, who was beginning to earn her own notoriety as a beauty queen. "Ninoy was quite talkative, and he enjoyed Meldy's company," says his friend from childhood Doy Laurel. "He had a Buick, and he would pick her up and take her to her job. He liked to be seen with a good-looking girl." After she was named "Muse of Manila," Imelda was besieged with suitors from families as prominent as Aquino's. One of them was Cory's brother Pedro ("Pete") Cojuangco. Ninoy's eldest sister, Maria Aurora ("Maur") Lichauco, once overheard him on the phone brokering a date with Imelda for Pete.

When she protested that Pete was too short for her, Ninoy deployed his celebrated persuasive powers. "After all, it's only a foursome," he sputtered.

Imelda finally consented. "At least he's rich," she said.

"The Cojuangco family did not like her, so Ninoy would fetch Imelda from her house, while Pete would bring Cory, and then they would switch," says business tycoon Enrique Zobel, who had been a friend of all four. By the time Imelda became involved with Nakpil, Ninoy was serious about Cory. "Ninoy always called her Corazon," says Pitoy Moreno, a fraternity brother who would later become Manila's top couturier and a charter member of First Lady Imelda Marcos's entourage. "He would tell us, 'I cannot go with you because of Corazon.'"

Having viewed Ninoy's relationship with Imelda as no more than a casual one at that time, Celia Laurel was shocked during the heated senatorial election campaign in 1967 when the First Lady confided strongly emotional feelings about Ninoy. Imelda was passing along some political advice to Celia, whose husband, Doy, was a first-time senatorial candidate on the Marcos ticket that year, running against a slate of oppositionists, which included his friend Aquino. "She told us not to dress up too well when we campaigned in the provinces, to know exactly to whom to give the money, and to look him straight in the eye and hold his hand when you give it out, and to wear strong perfume so everyone is aware that you have entered the room. Last but not least, she told me, 'You must squash Ninoy Aquino.'"

In order to underline the last point, Imelda made a pulverizing gesture, grinding her forefinger into the arm of her chair. "I was taken aback," says Celia. "I said, 'I cannot do that because Ninoy is very close to us. He is like a brother to me, or a son.' Imelda said, 'I think you must learn that in politics there are no brothers, sons, or friends.'"

On a later occasion Imelda explained herself further to Celia. "You know why I hated Ninoy?" she asked. "Because he used to court me, and then he just dropped me like a hot potato the minute he met this rich girl."

✳   ✳   ✳

Ninoy and Cory grew up in the world to which Marcos and Imelda aspired. They did not have to waste youthful energy clawing their way to the top. They started there. They could afford to look beyond the horizon, to be idealistic. Their families were members of the landed elite, which controlled most of the wealth and brokered most of the political deals that predetermined the outcome of elections in the unlikely American-style democracy that had been superimposed atop a feudalistic Spanish system of royal land grants.

Their parents, however, were sensitive to the postwar winds of change, and particularly to the peasant insurgency waged in the central Luzon rice-basket region, where their haciendas were located. They had prudently instilled in their children a sense of obligation to society and to others less blessed than they. As a result, the social consciences of Ninoy and Cory were at odds with the mentality of their own class, not to mention that of eager young men on the make like Marcos, who rushed in after independence to claim a share of the power and affluence they felt was due them.

Benigno Simeon Aquino, Jr., was the grandson of a revolutionary general, who had fought for Philippine independence against Spain and the United States. General Servillano Aquino had spent three years as a prisoner of the Americans before returning to the life of a planter and breeder of fighting cocks on the large haciendas he had amassed in Tarlac. The general's son, Ninoy's father, Benigno Servillano Aquino, had gone into politics at the age of twenty-four, and had served seven terms in the various legislative bodies established by the American government and the Japanese occupation forces by the time the Philippines was granted independence in 1946.

Both Aquino ancestors were strong critics of the way the U.S. had betrayed the Philippine revolution by initially enlisting the help of Filipinos in the fight against Spain and then, once the Spaniards had been defeated, annexing the islands as an American colony. The general proudly displayed a photo of himself dressed in his black-and-white, striped prison uniform. Although he lived to be eighty-five, he refused to learn English, which had become the common language of the country.

His son the congressman and senator was coauthor of a bill to create an "Independence Commission" to lobby the U.S. Congress for immediate Philippine sovereignty. For years before the war, he had argued vainly the nationalists' case for "absolute and immediate independence in the shortest time possible." During the Japanese occupation, he had deceived himself into believing that collaboration with the enemy would hasten the attainment of Philippine independence. His service in mobilizing a pro-Japanese nationalist political movement known as Kalibapi drew him the sobriquet "Judas Aquino."

In 1943 a puppet assembly elected Jose Laurel president and Benigno Aquino speaker of the occupied Philippines. However, neither their new status nor the fact that they were flown to Japan and decorated by the emperor brought them closer to the independence they sought. In 1944 events passed them by. As MacArthur returned to liberate the archipelago, and the Americans advanced toward Manila, the collaborationist government was withdrawn to Baguio. Laurel and Aquino were eventually spirited out by the retreating Japanese to Taiwan and finally Tokyo, where, in an ironic footnote to history, they sat out the long-awaited celebration of Philippine independence on July 4, 1946, in their cells in Sugamo Prison. Two months later they were flown home in a U.S. army plane and imprisoned for three weeks, after which they were released on bail to await trial for treason in a special People's Court.

Hoping for a popular victory before the court rendered its verdict,

Aquino took his case to voters in the district which he had long represented in Tarlac. There he campaigned in the 1947 elections for a congressional candidate who was widely identified with him. His son Ninoy, grateful finally to have the opportunity to become close to his well-known father, accompanied him on the hustings. For the first time in his career, the veteran politician was rebuffed at the polls. A few months later on December 20, 1947, he died in the arms of fifteen-year-old Ninoy, as a taxi rushed him to the hospital following his collapse at a title boxing match.

The day before Christmas, the case against him was dismissed by the People's Court. In its final tribute to Aquino, the Congress of the Philippines credited him with having been "instrumental in the success of the people's fight for independence." That citation could not, however, remove the psychological scars which the war had left on the Aquino family. "When we went to school, we each had a Japanese with us in the classroom," says Maur Lichauco. "Our classmates used to say nasty things to us." Ninoy's friendship with puppet President Laurel's children Doy and Dodjie dated back to that period, when the three sons of collaborators took comfort in each other's company inside the walls of Malacañang.

Although Ninoy worshipped his father, his conflicting emotions about the elder Aquino's decision to collaborate with the Japanese strongly influenced his behavior when his own moment of truth arrived with the imposition of martial law.

"I was nine years old when the war broke out," Ninoy explained to Marcos during a 1977 conversation in the palace, while he was still a prisoner. According to a still-secret transcript of their dialogue, Ninoy expressed his admiration for the Socialist peasant organizer Abad Santos, who, unlike his father, had refused to cooperate with the enemy. "When confronted by the Japanese, Abad Santos said, 'Shoot me.' To him there was no doubt." Ninoy had weighed the responses of both men, and he told Marcos, "When confronted with martial law, maybe where my father erred, I am opting for the Abad Santos formula."

When Benigno, Sr., died, he left his thirty-seven-year-old second wife, Aurora, with their five children, plus four older stepchildren from his first marriage. In order to get by, she was forced to sell what remained of her husband's land and to live off the income from her own rice lands. Devastated by the loss of the father he worshipped, restless in school, and mindful of the family's sinking fortunes, Ninoy transferred from the prestigious Catholic Ateneo de Manila to the cheaper University of the Philippines and traded on his name to get a job with the *Manila Times*, whose publisher, Joaquin ("Chino") Roces, had been a friend of his father. Thus began a first career as a journalist, which would stand him in good stead later on when he switched to politics.

Ninoy's insatiable curiosity and outgoing personality made him a natural reporter. When he was a child, his family had nicknamed him "T V T" after the chief newspaper chain of the day, because he always had the latest neighborhood news. At the *Times* he moved quickly from copyboy to reporter, then volunteered to accompany a Filipino battalion sent to fight with the Americans in Korea at the outbreak of war there in 1950. His experience as a foreign correspondent toughened his body, sharpened his mind, and caused him to question the unswervingly anti-Communist philosophy with which the Americans had infused the Philippine educational system. "When I came home, it couldn't be to an elite world," Ninoy said after it was all over.

One week after he returned from eleven months in Korea, he was awarded the Philippine Legion of Honor for meritorious service. More important to Ninoy than the medal itself was the sweet vindication of the words uttered by President Quirino in the presence of ranking diplomats and cabinet officials. "You bear a great name. You have made a good name for yourself. Be sure to keep it great."

For the next three years Ninoy juggled his studies at UP Law School, his job at the *Manila Times*, and a busy social life, while working on a campaign to draft the popular defense minister, Ramon Magsaysay, for president. By the time Magsaysay was elected in 1953, Ninoy had become a valued junior advisor. Shortly after Magsaysay's inauguration, Ninoy promoted himself as an intermediary between the government and Luis Taruc, leader of the *Hukbalahap* (People's Anti-Japanese Army) guerrillas.

Taruc's peasant forces had been waging an insurgency against landowners in Aquino's home province since the war. A split had developed within the Huk leadership over whether to continue fighting or to negotiate with the popular, new, reform-minded government of President Magsaysay. Taruc, who favored negotiation, was looking for a way to avoid being liquidated by the hard-core Communist faction. Ninoy, with the help of his older stepbrother Tony, who had organized the Huks in Tarlac to fight the Japanese and had served as a liaison between them and the U.S. military, arranged a clandestine rendezvous.

When they met on a remote peak beyond the confines of Clark Air Base early in 1954, Ninoy was surprised to find Taruc anything but the atheistic Communist he was portrayed as in the press. "He opened my eyes to the iniquities in my own hometown: how the peasants there would borrow ten pesos from the landlords and come back to find that a zero had been slipped in to make their debt a hundred pesos," Ninoy reported. The story he published about the encounter raised hopes for an end to the Huk insurgency and exposed divisions within the government about how to handle the rebels. Not unlike the situation that had plagued past governments and would continue to trouble future ones, the president was eager to open peace negotiations. However, the military and its U.S.

counterinsurgency advisor, Edward Lansdale, pressed for a raid on Taruc's hideout.

Magsaysay signaled Ninoy his willingness to accept Taruc's terms that he be turned over to the president himself, not the military. "The army will be given orders not to interfere," he had told Ninoy in a phone call the night before. Accompanied by his publisher, and armed only with a walkie-talkie, Ninoy drove to the site of the meeting, which had been set for dawn on May 17. After lengthy wrangling with the troops patrolling that area, he headed down a narrow country road toward the small barrio where Taruc was hidden. Just before 8 A.M. he returned to the main highway with the rebel leader beside him in the front seat.

Ninoy's instructions from Magsaysay had been to deliver the Huk *supremo* to him aboard the presidential yacht *Apo*. But before reaching Manila, Ninoy's car was stopped by soldiers, and he was informed that Taruc was to be turned over to armed forces Chief of Staff General Jesus Vargas at a military camp. Ninoy was anguished that Magsaysay, one of his heroes, had broken his word, under pressure from both the military and the Americans, and double-crossed his new hero, Taruc. "It was the beginning of my differences with the army," Ninoy would say years later.

Magsaysay would try to make amends by awarding the young reporter a second Legion of Honor for his role in weakening the insurgency. To help assuage her son's guilt, Doña Aurora would visit the detained Taruc regularly during the years of his incarceration and would finance his son's education.

In the end, Magsaysay proposed that Ninoy take a trip to the U.S. to study the CIA, and recommend ways to restructure the Philippine intelligence community along American lines. The timing was propitious. Ninoy had been going steady with Cory Cojuangco for the past year, following her graduation from college and her return to Manila. If they married soon, they could honeymoon in the U.S.

On October 11, 1954, six months after the Marcoses' "wedding of the year," President Magsaysay stood as sponsor for another prominent young couple. Although fifteen years Marcos's junior and not yet a candidate for any office, Ninoy was, no less than Marcos before him, cementing an alliance between two political families, as well as marrying his sweetheart.

*   *   *

The Cojuangco family had ruled the northern half of the province of Tarlac, while the Aquinos had held sway in the south. By tradition the two families had united behind a common candidate for the Congress, competing against each other only for local offices. But the war had drastically altered the political landscape for all the landed families. With independence in 1946, they had found it difficult to impose their political will on the masses. Even when they had backed a common candidate in one election, he had been defeated. "The candidate who won was from the grass roots," says Ninoy's mother, Doña Aurora. "The people turned against the elite."

Three generations ago the Cojuangcos came from the grass roots themselves. The suffix *co* added to the family name is derived from polite Hokkien Chinese usage and connotes the holder's entry into the Chinese *mestizo* class, which rose to prominence in the late eighteenth century and has monopolized power in the Philippines since the revolution of 1898.

The family patriarch Jose Cojuangco had come to the Philippines from Fukien province in 1836. Hardworking and frugal, he used the money he made as a junk dealer to acquire land in the town of Paniqui, on which he built a small rice mill. It prospered, and soon he expanded his business interests to include a small-scale money-lending operation. Eventually he was allocated freight cars on the rail line that was being expanded northward from Manila, and he shipped rice and other produce to Manila in exchange for dry goods to be distributed in the provinces. The house which Jose built for his family still stands today, marked by a bust of the founding father with a Chinese inscription on it.

But for a strong woman, the Cojuangco family could have lost its momentum when Jose's heir Melecio, the only male of his generation, died before his four sons were mature enough to take over his affairs. Into the void stepped his formidable spinster sister, Ysidra. Under the stern management of herself and her father, the family businesses prospered. So large were their agricultural holdings, mostly planted in rice, that they effectively set the price for that commodity throughout the island of Luzon.

By the time Melecio's sons reached adulthood, the Cojuangco family was firmly established. It was welcomed into the embrace of the oligarchy, when eldest son, Jose, Jr., Cory's father, married Demetria Sumulong, a graduate in pharmacy, who was the daughter of another politically prominent family. Demetria's father, the brilliant attorney Juan Sumulong, was known as "the brains of the opposition." As a minority member of the U.S.-appointed Philippine Commission, which ran the colonial government in the years after the revolution, and later as a member of the Commonwealth Congress, Sumulong spoke out loudly against the domination of the elite, to which he belonged, in Philippine politics. In contrast to the ruling Nacionalistas, who favored immediate independence, the opposition under Sumulong argued for gradual independence, in the belief that education and economic development were necessary prerequisites for the growth of real democracy.

The Cojuangco family fortune was amassed during the 1920s, when Jose, Jr. persuaded his wealthy aunt Ysidra to build a new sugar mill, which he managed. Profiting from the protected status on the U.S. market of the colony's sugar during the Great Depression, the so-called "sugar bloc," to which the Cojuangcos belonged, became one of the most powerful groups in society. Shortly before World War II, the Cojuangcos, along with two other families, had amassed assets sufficient to set up the first fully Filipino-owned bank, the Philippine Bank of Commerce, of which Jose became president.

The prewar years were a time of rapid population growth and significant social and economic change in central Luzon. As a consequence of the expansion of large hacienda owners like the Cojuangcos into agribusiness, the close, paternalistic ties, which landlords had previously had with their tenants, were loosening. As peasants began to be treated less like family and more like workers, they were becoming increasingly aggressive in seeking a share of the wealth.

Maria Corazon Cojuangco was born January 25, 1933, the sixth of Demetria and Jose's eight children. She and her brothers and sisters grew up in Manila, where they attended private schools and their father sat in the legislature. They spent summers and weekends in Paniqui, and it was there that they were initiated into politics. Cory remembers the politics of that era as far more refined than the flesh-pressing, marathon campaigning to which she was exposed later on as Ninoy's wife.

She met Ninoy for the first time when they were both nine years old at a birthday party for his father, who was her father's colleague in the prewar Congress. "Ninoy kept bragging he was a year ahead of me in school, so I didn't even bother to talk to him," she recounted. War had already come to the Philippines, and the Japanese occupation forces were in control. Cory stayed close to her sisters and to her books during those years, except when it came to games of "warball" (a kind of volleyball minus the net), in which she excelled.

Just before the liberation of Manila, Cory graduated from sixth grade as class valedictorian. Because Saint Scholastica's had sustained severe damage in the final days of the war, it did not reopen the next year. She therefore changed schools, taking her leave of the strict German nuns, who placed great influence on religion, and moving to the more refined, French-run Assumption Convent, which stressed social consciousness and the importance of being a lady. She remained there only one year, before moving with her parents to the U.S. The elder Cojuangcos returned to the war-torn Philippines after enrolling their daughters in exclusive Catholic schools and furnishing them with credit cards billed direct to Manila.

In the aftermath of the war, the Cojuangco family had found itself with more land than cash since tenants who had owed money or portions of their crop had paid off their debts in worthless Japanese currency. In order to recoup its losses, it resorted to less savory businesses. Distilling alcohol was one. From molasses made with their own sugar, the Cojuangco brothers and sisters brewed cheap rum that was eagerly bought by U.S. soldiers and poor Filipinos.

Like other young ladies of her class, Cory made her debut at the age of eighteen in the Fiesta Pavilion of the stately Manila Hotel, which had served as MacArthur's headquarters in the early days of the war. A year later, while home for vacation as a college junior, she encountered Ninoy again. "I was impressed because he had been to the war in Korea," she said. Each found in the other something his or her own privileged world lacked.

"What impressed Ninoy about Cory was the civilized and very refined breeding this lady had," says his friend journalist Napoleon ("Nap') Rama. "She was really different from the girls Ninoy got to see. Cory was like a princess in Tarlac."

Cory in turn was attracted by Ninoy's involvement in events like war and politics of which she had only a peripheral knowledge. Aside from the election day fiestas she had attended in Paniqui, her primary exposure to politics had been in New York in the 1948 American presidential campaign. "I was a Junior Republican," said Cory, arching her eyebrows with wonder over her early conservatism. "I went to Governor Dewey's rallies to see the movie stars, but to get in, you had to join." She is still impressed by the excitement that campaign evoked and the lesson it taught. "One thing I remember is that all the lights were turned off, and we lit matches. Everyone was so sure Dewey was going to win . . ."

The relationship continued by mail during her senior year. After she graduated, Cory returned to Manila and enrolled in law at Far Eastern University, a private institution which was owned by her brother-in-law and sister Josephine. "I was interested in law, not as a profession, but as a discipline," she said. It also served as a holding action while she got to know the man whom she would soon marry.

Their American honeymoon was a happy and productive experience. In Washington the newlyweds stayed with Ninoy's half-sister and her husband, who was the Philippine military attaché to the U.S. With his help Ninoy was able to gain access to the schools where American spies were trained and thus complete the study President Magsaysay had assigned him. That experience would come back to haunt Ninoy later on, when he would be accused by Marcos and Enrile of being not only a Communist, but also a CIA operative.

By the time they returned to Manila four months later, Ninoy had developed a taste for white chocolate, which had already begun to transform the boyish figure in the wedding photos into the stocky profile that would soon grace campaign posters across the archipelago. Cory was pregnant with their first child.

Being an Aquino married to a Cojuangco presented a bright young man with numerous options. First, Ninoy decided to farm, and he bought some land in his hometown at an auction by the Development Bank of the Philippines, which was run by Cory's father. Deep inside Huk territory, the acreage not only needed to be cleared of stumps before planting could begin, it also needed to be pacified. He consulted his grandfather, the general, daily, about everything from irrigation to handling the local folk, and he called on his half-brother to help him deal with the Huks.

He had barely finished clearing his land and planting it in rice, when a delegation of landowners, friendly with his family, began pressuring him to run for mayor of the town against the ruling Feliciano family on the Nacionalista party ticket of his mentor Magsaysay. Although Ninoy had not been planning to run for office so soon—he was, in fact, below the minimum age (twenty-five) for candidates—the prospect of turning the Felicianos out of office appealed to him. It was they who, only two years after the death of his father, had delivered the Aquino family a humiliating defeat in the presidential election of 1949 by seeing to it that the Aquino-backed candidate, ex-President Laurel, received only thirty-three votes in Concepcion: the precise number of registered Aquino family voters.

After consulting his family and surveying the situation, Ninoy entered what became a three-sided race: the incumbent mayor, Nicolas Feliciano, on the right, the Huk mayor whom he had displaced in a previous election on the left, and Ninoy in the center. It was the heyday of the private armies, and both Ninoy's opponents had their own. His hope was that he, with only a minimum of force behind him and a maximum of Magsaysay-style populism, could rally the defenseless masses that found themselves caught between the two armed camps. He therefore plotted a campaign for himself not unlike the man-of-the-people presidential campaign he had helped organize for Magsaysay in 1953.

His major hurdle was to convince the locals that he was one of them. The Huks had made the people aware of the oppressive nature of the landlord-tenant role and, in some cases, had persuaded them that revolution was the only way to attain justice. In this equation, Ninoy was the enemy. On the other hand, his contact with the Huks, his admiration for Taruc, his youth, and his personality were working for him. He exuded affection for the farmers. He reached out to them, and he mobilized his entire family to help him.

Cory, having just given birth to a daughter, Maria Elena (nicknamed "Ballsy" for a face deemed round as a jai alai ball), had a good excuse for not spending all her time on the hustings. Still, her life was shaped by Ninoy's political career. "My husband wanted to be one of the people," she said. When campaigning, that meant riding in a cart pulled by a water buffalo, the mode of transportation of most villagers living in Concepcion.

During the rest of the year it meant living without electricity, except at night, and opening her home to Ninoy's constituents at all hours. The adjustment was difficult for someone as cosmopolitan as Cory. Lack of privacy in the small town bothered her most. "Everyone knew what we had for lunch," she complained. She was frequently bored. "Thank God for transistor radios," she said, looking back on the early days of her marriage. "It was the only thing to keep me company. Suddenly I became such a homebody, knitting while listening to soap operas."

Ninoy's remarkable mother, Doña Aurora, did most of the surrogate stumping for Ninoy during that first campaign. She traveled the district, making speeches in the people's native Pampangan dialect, extolling her son, and explaining how he could help them, if elected. Realizing how times had changed, she sensed that Ninoy had the potential for bridging the yawning gap between the elite, into which he had been born, and the poor, who were finally demanding some of the fruits that democracy had promised, but so far had failed to deliver. "My husband was of the aristocrats," she says. "Ninoy was of the people. He had that ability to talk to the masses."

4

Into the Vortex of Martial Law

Had Marcos not intended to stay in power beyond the constitutional limit of two terms in the presidency, he could have afforded an ambitious rival like Aquino. He would not have had to make an enemy and then a martyr of him. After all, the fifteen-year age gap between them gave Marcos an insurmountable head start in the race to the top of the political hierarchy. However, it became clear to a number of his close advisors early on that Marcos had more permanent designs on the office. "From the outset, Marcos's plan was to stay in power forever," states his former information secretary, Francisco ("Kit") Tatad, without equivocation.

A student of Napoleon, de Gaulle, and the Filipino character, Marcos had begun, while still in law school, to develop a blueprint for a hybrid form of government, which he euphemistically called "constitutional authoritarianism." It would, he calculated, foster the stability necessary for economic takeoff in a poor country like the Philippines. Marcos's concept of power was more in keeping with the permanence of the Asian strongmen who were his neighbors in the region, than with the transience of presidents produced by the Philippines' American-style democratic system. He had observed the way postindependence Filipino leaders had been paralyzed by unruly congresses and a licentious press. None had been able to make a dent in the country's enormous problems before being voted out of office. He was determined to reverse that trend.

According to revelations made by the First Lady shortly after arriving in Malacañang, Marcos had also worked methodically to amass the funds it would take to win and sustain himself in power. "I remember Mrs. Marcos telling me a story about how, shortly after they were married, she found boxes of pesos hidden under the bed and in the closets of his house," says Tatad. Unable to resist, she had dipped into them, incurring the wrath of her husband when he discovered their absence later on.

"That was for my presidential campaign!" he wailed, a full decade before he would actually run.

Clever Imelda had redeemed herself in Marcos's eyes, however, she confided to Tatad. "I had invested the money in garlic," she said proudly, "and made a windfall."

In the beginning Ninoy had not been excluded from Marcos's career plans. Far from it. Marcos was happy to take advantage of his fraternity brother's social and political connections, and Ninoy was generous in his introductions to people who might further Marcos's interests. Enrique Zobel recalls lunching at the elite Polo Club with Mayor Aquino, who introduced him to Congressman Marcos. "Ninoy told me, 'This guy is going places. You will probably need to use him. Please give him a retainer.'"

Philippine society, more than Western societies, operates on the basis of favors, paid and unpaid, and modern-day politicians have carried the pre-Hispanic tradition of *utang na loob* (debt of gratitude) to its grossest extreme. As it had been practiced at the family level since the early tribal era, the system of mutual favors and reciprocal obligations fostered the warmth and hospitality for which Filipinos are famous. When extended beyond blood relatives through the ritual kinships of the *compadre* system, which the Spaniards introduced, *utang na loob* had helped to strengthen the social fabric of the island society. When, however, the Americans superimposed their system of free-market economics and democratic elections over the existing webs of patronage and favors, officials were immediately placed in the debt of a proliferation of special interest groups seeking political favors in return for money, and also of hordes of relatives, godchildren, and friends seeking favors from an otherwise unresponsive bureaucracy.

Marcos was not unique in offering his services as an elected official for profit. What distinguished him from all other practitioners of the old-fashioned ward style of politics, which was the norm in the Philippines, was the magnitude of his take. But Marcos also gave.

He had vowed during his first congressional campaign to provide his underdeveloped region with a cash crop, and he had delivered on that promise, introducing tobacco and garlic among others. That he had personally prospered in the process, receiving a cut of the profits of the tobacco monopoly, which was soon controlled by his cronies, was to be expected. The other major sources of revenue for his political war chest were the import licenses he granted on protected products.

"Marcos was the lord tong collector of every sizable import license approved by the Central Bank," wrote Primitivo Mijares, a Marcos spokesman who quit the regime and exposed Marcos's financial and political wheeling and dealing to a U.S. House subcommittee in 1975.

To Marcos every piece of legislation was a potential source of payola. Retired editor Teodoro Locsin recalls one petty scam whereby Senator Marcos himself made the rounds of Manila movie theaters, shaking down their owners for protection from a bill before the Congress that would ban foreign films. "That's not enough," Marcos told one owner. "Look how much money you are making from the James Bond films." The owner coughed up $5,000 to stay in business. After Marcos became president and launched a massive campaign of international borrowing to finance major development projects, the "percentages" and "commissions" that he and his cronies commanded made a quantum leap.

In 1966 Senator Jovito Salonga, who had headed a congressional investigation into public graft, received a confidential letter accompanied by a Chase Manhattan Bank statement in the name of Ferdinand Marcos. "It was a handsome amount—in the hundreds of thousands," says Salonga.

He wanted to expose the new president's foreign bank statement, but instead he took the advice of a political elder who told him, "It is too early. Give President Marcos a chance. You might tear the political unity of this country apart."

Looking back at the damage done by two decades of Marcos rule, Salonga, who subsequently became a leading member of the anti-Marcos opposition and was appointed by President Aquino to chair the probe into Marcos's hidden wealth, worries that he was too fair-minded. "I thought there was no evidence that this money was ill-gotten wealth, so I stopped," he says.

Those who played fair against Marcos would live to regret it. He was a man without a moral compass. He was a brilliant tactician, who, better than any of his peers, had mastered the mathematics of democracy—assembling majorities, trading and buying votes. But he understood nothing of its ethics. An American embassy report transmitted to Washington during the 1965 election campaign described him as "a consummate scoundrel."

The man who would be president-for-life of the Philippines expected a lot from his wife, and Imelda went through a painful period of adjustment to married life. While marriage to Marcos provided her the financial security she had so desperately craved, it magnified old, gnawing fears of inadequacy and rejection. "Becoming the wife of Marcos was too big a change for Imelda," ventures a member of the Aquino family, who had observed her since her arrival in Manila with a biased but astute eye. "Suddenly she had servants and money and people fawning all over her, but she still did not belong."

Indeed, her sense of not belonging was palpable on several levels, beginning at home. She was not allowed to redecorate Marcos's bachelor residence, although she was obliged to play hostess there, serving an average 60 breakfasts, 250 lunches, and 30 dinners each day to the favor-seeking constituents who called on the congressman. Although she much preferred spending time with her own friends, her social calendar was dominated by official engagements, many of them related to the maintenance of the 400 ritual kinships that Marcos, as an influential politician, acquired through the old, Spanish *compadre* system.

Besides learning to live without privacy or social freedom, Imelda was also expected to be conversant with the issues in which her husband was involved and worldly enough to charm the constituencies that were yet to be conquered, beyond the narrow one that he represented. "Marcos expected Imelda to be his bridge to Manila society," says a Marcos opponent. "He did not realize when he married her that she did not belong either. Nor did he realize how naive she was about public affairs. So he had to bring in tutors to teach her the things he thought she should know." Although she was an avid pupil, her self-esteem plummeted.

She began to suffer recurring headaches and bouts of melancholy, following the death of her father and the birth of her first child in 1955. One night Marcos, who was minority floor leader of the House, returned home to find her lying cold, pale, and hardly breathing. He panicked. When Filipino doctors could not diagnose her problem, she was flown to New York for examination and several months of treatment by migraine specialists and psychiatrists.

During the two years of therapy that followed on both sides of the Pacific, she made little progress. When, in 1959, Marcos finished first in the Senate election, she realized she had reached a crossroads. "Everybody knew then that he was on his way," she says. "So the doctor told Marcos, 'If you want her well, you should know that it is really your public life that she does not like. She is very sensitive, and she finds it really negative. She is depressed by it.' "

"What the doctor was saying," continues Imelda, "was that the only way for him was to get out of politics." Marcos was silent as he digested the cruel diagnosis. Politics was his life. All his past actions had been motivated by his desire to become president. Now he was being asked to give it all up. Imelda recalls vividly her shock at his response. "When he said, 'If that is what will make her well, then I will give up my politics,' I thought, 'That would not be fair.' So I concluded, if he loved me that much, to give up his politics, his lifelong ambition, and his great potential, then I can change my attitude. I can give up my privacy for him." She adds, "I had to get the bug. I had to love what he loved."

Typically, Imelda overdid it. Thinking to set things right, she forced herself to learn to love politics. The Imelda who emerged from therapy in 1959 was an immediate hit on the Senate campaign trail. Appearing at Marcos's side, impeccably coiffed and wearing a different *terno* (traditional gown with butterfly sleeves) on each rickety stage, she helped catapult both of them beyond the confines of their pasts and into national prominence. As the leading vote-getter in a field of thirty-two candidates for eight Senate seats, Marcos became the "man to watch" in Philippine politics.

Rarely did he disappoint his audience. In 1963, when President Diosdado Macapagal, a fellow Liberal party member, threatened to delay Marcos's presidential timetable for the second time, by reneging on a pledge that he would serve only one term in Malacañang, Marcos bolted the party and led a ruthless seven-month campaign to win the nomination of the rival Nacionalista party. In order to buttonhole personally every NP delegate at least once before the nominating convention, Marcos used Imelda as his surrogate. "I knew every delegate, because I talked with each of them and visited them in their homes," she related candidly. "Then the next time I came around, I had the new window, the new roof, or whatever was needed in each house."

By the time the nominating convention got under way, the couple's arm-twisting had become downright shameless. While Marcos worked the floor between ballots, Imelda, heedless of the innuendos to which her behavior subjected her, visited key delegates in the privacy of their hotel rooms. When balloting resumed, it was clear to all that she had made the desired impression. On the second ballot, 777 delegates—a strong majority—declared themselves for her husband. Thereafter, the superstitious Marcos would invest the number 7 with the same mystical function as his lucky number 11.

A central issue of the year-long presidential campaign was the perennial one in Philippine politics—corruption. There, Macapagal, who was an honest, if uncharismatic politician, had the advantage, while Marcos was highly vulnerable. All of the charges that would be used against him throughout his reign were trumpeted during the 1965 campaign. He was constantly vilified in the freewheeling Philippine press and in rallies as a murderer, briber, land grabber, smuggler, thief, and liar. He was accused of using his influence as a powerful legislator to pressure the armed forces to award him World War II medals. The Nalundasan murder was dredged up from the past, and the dead politician's son Cesar was enlisted by the Liberal party to personally accuse Marcos of having fired the fatal shot.

Marcos worked to counter what he called the "black propaganda" by portraying himself as a wartime hero determined to drive out the rascals under whom the country had "retrogressed." A Marcos loyalist recalls wistfully that the American film *The Audie Murphy Story* was playing in the Philippines at the time, and people who came from his rallies were calling him "the Audie Murphy of the Philippines." As the campaign climaxed without a clear winner, Imelda, whose looks and love songs had already benefited his candidacy enormously, rendered what was probably her most valuable service to her husband's career. She confronted the accusations against him head-on.

Her ingenuous comments, many believe, saved the day for Marcos. "They say that my husband is a forger, a murderer, a land grabber," she said in one of many interviews. "Look at me," she continued, tears glistening in her large, dark eyes. "Do you think I would have married this man if he was that bad? Do you think I would have stayed with him and campaigned for him, if the charges were true? He is the best, the tenderest husband in the world."

The voters believed her, electing Marcos by a margin of over half a million votes. Marcos proudly referred to her as "my secret weapon" and credited her with putting him in Malacañang. Political analysts agreed. Nap Rama, one of the country's most astute commentators, wrote, "It was Imelda who provided the Nacionalistas with the armor that shielded Marcos from political destruction."

*   *   *

Once he was in office, Marcos moved more aggressively than his predecessors to consolidate his control over the institutions that would be essential to his success in governing—and in extending the duration of his presidency. In so doing, he inevitably came into conflict with Ninoy, who was governor of one of the few provinces that Marcos had not won.

No president since Magsaysay had made any progress toward overriding the narrow interests of the landowning families, some of whom exercised greater power than the chief of state. Marcos was determined to tame the oligarchy by destroying or co-opting the old political warlords and centralizing power over their former fiefdoms in the hands of one family—his—and one army, loyal to him. Ninoy presented a particular challenge to him. He had become a formidable warlord during nearly a decade in office. He not only possessed wealth and a substantial private army, but, more important in terms of Marcos's own plans, growing political appeal among the increasingly radicalized masses.

Ninoy had the ability to sway crowds like a snake charmer with his rhetoric. He made them laugh with his exaggerated truths, and for that they called him *sarsa,* a man given to white lies. Yet he also boosted their spirits by painting a vision of a better future and practicing at least some of what he preached. Persuaded that "the rich families are too greedy," he had cajoled his mother and some of his wealthy friends into deeding portions of their land to their tenants as a step toward preempting an eventual revolution. He had warned his in-laws that if he ran for president, he would like to turn their vast sugarlands, the Hacienda Luisita, into a model for nationwide land reform. By virtue of the fact that his power base was located in the heart of the central Luzon "rice basket," where the Huk insurgency still fed on the poverty of landless peasants, Aquino had been forced to work out a modus vivendi with the Huks. Were he to seek national office, his ties to the guerrillas and the mass base which supported them would make him a formidable opponent. Marcos opted to stop him before he got that far.

"As soon as Marcos took over, he changed the whole setup in Tarlac," complained Aquino. Marcos cut off the flow of national funds to his "enemy governor," and replaced Ninoy's key appointees with members of his own Nacionalista party. It was standard practice for incoming presidents to strengthen their grip on the levers of political power by forcing those who remained in the opposition after the election to switch parties or suffer the consequences. But Marcos went well beyond anything his predecessors had dared. He struck at the very heart of Ninoy's power by installing his own cousin as commander of the constabulary in Tarlac, an appointment that was designed to check the influence of Governor Aquino's private army, which Marcos wryly described as "bigger than the Philippine army."

The violent side of Philippine politics was not something the great families liked to acknowledge in polite society. Ninoy in particular sheltered his wife and children from some of the harsh truths about how he ran Tarlac. "He never discussed such things in Cory's presence," says a friend. His family knew that Ninoy had a huge gun collection in the basements of his homes in Tarlac and Quezon City, and that he was fond of presenting friends and allies with guns from this private arsenal.

"I personally did not like those guns," says Cory, "and I would say, 'Why on earth would you buy something like this?' But for him it was a hobby and for use for our own defense, especially if traveling at night." Referring to the charges which Marcos would later lodge against her husband, she adds, "I have yet to hear someone say my husband actually shot somebody."

While there was never any convincing proof that Ninoy shot the barrio captain whom he was accused of killing by martial law military authorities, he did, by his own admission, do more with guns than simply collect them, give them as gifts, and use them in self-defense. He and his henchmen openly brandished, frequently confiscated, and sometimes used them against their enemies.

He bragged to reporters about the imaginative scheme of weapons confiscation and threats that he had invented to settle landlord-tenant disputes. If a landlord refused to increase the tenant's share of the harvest or to lend money at a less extortionate rate, according to guidelines laid down by the governor, Ninoy would be obliged to "verify" the landlord's arms. His men would then confiscate the landlord's weapons and, once he was disarmed, harass him with anonymous threats. "Inevitably I would see the landlord in my office again. He would ask for his guns, but I would give them back only if he agreed to the terms I had set," Ninoy recounted, adding, "he usually agreed."

He acknowledged that his henchmen had killed twelve men one night while carrying out his directive to thwart a band of water-buffalo rustlers that had broken a tacit agreement not to touch any animals inside the boundaries of Tarlac. The governor's guns were used most often, however, as a deterrent against the heavily armed Huks. "The Huks would just shoot down someone and disappear into the hills," he said. Aware that they left their families behind when they fled, Ninoy recounted how on one occasion, after a Huk commander had gone on a shooting spree, he had tracked down the families of the commander and his men. "I took them all and put them on an island. I told the commander what I would do unless he came to terms with me. He did." Once having established his authority, Ninoy was willing to soften his approach. "I returned their families, with gifts yet: sewing machines and so on."

Columnist Luis Beltran, an old friend of Ninoy's, defends his carrot-and-stick approach to dealing with the insurgents in his province. "In terms of ideological sympathy," he says, "I don't think Ninoy had even a drop of it in his veins. But if you were governor of Tarlac or a mayor in Tarlac, you had to be a Communist sympathizer if you wanted to stay alive, because the central government at that particular point was unable to do anything about the old Hukbalahap army or, later on, the New People's Army."

Although the peasant insurgency had been broken as a revolutionary force during the Magsaysay era, when key guerrilla leaders like Taruc had been captured and the pro-Soviet Communist party with which it was linked lost its relevance, the Huks retained popularity among the poor peasants of central Luzon. Thus, the Huk leaders—although they were little more than hoodlums—remained forces with whom national politicians had to cut deals.

Shrewd tactician that Marcos was, he conceived a way of shattering the fragile truce that Ninoy had forged with the Huks to keep life civil in Tarlac. He simply co-opted one faction of Huks to work for him against a rival faction which backed Aquino. The cycle of violence which this policy generated resulted in a highly publicized incident known as the "Culatingan Massacre," which publicly pitted Aquino against Marcos for the first time in the press and in the deliberations of a Senate investigative committee.

Soldiers who announced they had killed five Huks in a barrio in Aquino's hometown were promptly promoted by Marcos. Governor Aquino and the townspeople, on the other hand, insisted that the victims were not Huks, but merely poor farmers, who had been wrongly accused of being subversives. A Senate investigation into the case confirmed Aquino's findings. However, civilian pleas for an end to such military abuse went unheeded. In order to divide the Huks and to discredit Aquino as soft on Communism and incapable of maintaining the peace, Marcos's military escalated such activities.

According to Nick Joaquin, author of *The Aquinos of Tarlac*, "Culatingan marked the start of the terrorist campaign that would culminate with the group known by pop-conscious Filipinos as the Monkees: hired hoodlums posing as Huks and sicked on the peasantry. Their actions would provoke a counter-gang of Huk terrorists who were quickly dubbed the Beatles. The province of Tarlac was fast becoming the primary battleground for Marcos's rhetorical war against subversives. In the process, the "enemy governor" was being pressured out of office.

Hoping to buy peace with the military, the Huks informed Ninoy they would not back him for another term as governor. He was thus forced to bow out of the 1967 race. Accepting the realpolitik of the situation, Ninoy advised his mayors to switch parties and back a gubernatorial candidate who would be acceptable to both Marcos and the Huks. Ironically, the figure chosen was Cory's cousin Eduardo ("Danding") Cojuangco, who won handily with the backing of the dominant Huk factions and went on to become President Marcos's chief business crony and an outspoken anti-Communist.

For a brief time, Marcos could take pleasure in having rid himself of a troublesome governor. But Ninoy did not disappear for long from politics. He decided to run for the Senate in the upcoming midterm elections, which Marcos had turned into a referendum on the first two years of his presidency. Fully aware that he was several weeks short of the required age minimum of thirty-five, Ninoy nonetheless entered the race after Liberal party legal expert Jovy Salonga promised to defend him, if he was challenged.

Marcos's Nacionalistas raised no objection when Aquino filed his candidacy. He was, after all, virtually unknown nationwide and thus no threat to the ruling party candidates. However, the newcomer spent big and traveled widely, appealing to the 72 percent of the population that was under thirty by using his nickname "Ninoy" and the campaign slogan

"Yeh!" (for Youth, Experience, Hope) from the popular Beatles refrain. The first candidate to barnstorm by helicopter, Ninoy made an immediate impact on voters. Midway through the three-month campaign, his name recognition had soared from an initial 6.3 percent to over 50 percent.

By then the anti-Marcos *bombas* about corruption, which Ninoy was tossing into his audiences, had begun to draw angry retorts from the president. Both politicians reaped publicity from the exercise, and thus the cross fire intensified. A classic exchange, which would be long-remembered by veterans of the 1967 campaign, was Marcos's colorful accusation that Ninoy was a "Huk-coddler" and Ninoy's blunt retort that the president was "a liar."

On October 29, just when Ninoy's private polls showed him to have advanced into the ranks of the top eight candidates, he picked up the morning newspapers in the southern Mindanao port of Zamboanga City and read: "Age Case Filed vs. Aquino." Angry, but full of perverse admiration for Marcos's pursuit of victory at any cost, Ninoy feared he would lose votes due to confusion over his eligibility. With so little time left before election day, Ninoy's only recourse was to keep his name—and therefore his candidacy—before the public. His efforts paid off. As news of Marcos's suit spread, Ninoy's crowds swelled. This, he knew, was what Filipino politics was all about. Like cockfighting, the sport was in watching the first blood drawn and in anticipating the kill. He knew, too, that he was uniquely capable of turning this craven public interest to his advantage, for no matter how much Filipinos might admire the skills of the champion, their hearts inevitably went out to the underdog.

While Salonga successfully argued his case before the Commission on Elections and then the Supreme Court, Ninoy orchestrated his press coverage. Having been a reporter himself, Ninoy knew the power of the press, and, says Salonga, "He courted it and spent a lot of money on it." Largely as a result of the publicity which the age case reaped, Salonga observes, "The picture that was created was of a president of the Philippines using a sledgehammer against this young Senate candidate."

Although Marcos's popularity carried a majority of his candidates into office, it failed to give him the eight-seat victory he needed to assure passage of his programs in the Senate. His heavy-handed attempt to challenge Aquino's age, only when he threatened Marcos's candidates, had made the oppositionist a winner. Marcos would see to it that that was Ninoy's last electoral victory. Meanwhile, however, the president had set in motion political forces that he would ultimately prove unable to control.

*   *   *

Ninoy had been elevated by Marcos's own hand to the status of the president's most outspoken adversary, and no one was better equipped than he to exploit the opportunity. With his age-disqualification case pending before the Senate Electoral Tribunal, Ninoy played each day in the chamber as if it were his last, wringing maximum publicity from the public perception of his rivalry with Marcos. "He became a very aggressive legislator, not in the legislature itself," explains fellow Senator Raul Manglapus, "but in what we called the privilege hour, where you could speak on anything with impunity and immunity. It was he who conducted the exposés and he to whom the victims went to get things exposed. In the process, he began to emerge as the peskiest thorn in Marcos's side."

"Marcos did not choose Ninoy as a target, Ninoy chose himself," says Salonga. "Ninoy had the ability to translate words into living fire, and he pointed his finger at Marcos, unlike most other politicians, who were a little subtler." Speculation as to Ninoy's motives made lively fare in the press and the political coffee shops.

"It is the observation of many," wrote the *Nation*, after viewing the opening volleys of Senator Aquino against President Marcos in the Senate "that Aquino is waging his current fight not so much to keep his Senate post as to expose himself to the widest publicity in preparation for his ultimate goal of running for the presidency of the Philippines in 1973."

The senator's brother-in-law Ricardo ("Baby") Lopa, concedes the truth of such assertions. "When Ninoy got to the Senate," says Lopa, "he very definitely had the presidency in mind, and I think his strategy of how to be noticed was to attack the president."

Ninoy's entry into the unofficial ranks of future presidential contenders was not greeted with the sense of impending salvation that many accounts written after his death imply. Far from perceiving him as the selfless patriot he would become following his martyrdom, many of Ninoy's own party mates and friends viewed Ninoy and Marcos as two sides of the same coin.

A political ally, who was Ninoy's contemporary in the Senate, counts the ways in which they resembled each other:

> There was that same romance with the gun. Ninoy always had the latest models. He would come to the Senate, and you would think his briefcase was stuffed with papers, but he would pull out an automatic machine gun. In some violent parts of the country where he campaigned, it was important to appeal to the voters as a tough guy, so he would stand up at rallies and brag about how as governor of his province he had ordered so many guerrilla commanders killed. The same man who recruited starlets for Marcos did it later for Ninoy. There was an absence of substance. We always said, if you sat around him long enough, you would catch him lying.

A mutual friend of both politicians attests to the shared sense of Filipino-style power politics that linked them, even after they became enemies. "Ninoy and Marcos would meet at my residence," he recounts, "and the conversations those two would have! 'You kill this guy, you kill that guy.' I would volunteer to leave the room, but they would say, 'You stay and be our witness.' "

An American political analyst casts the two adversaries in an equally decadent light. "They understood each other," he says. As the verbal warfare between the two escalated prior to martial law, he adds, "it was as if they were saying, 'Don't deprive me of this game. Besides womanizing, what else is there to do but play politics?' "

The refreshing thing about Ninoy was that he did not pretend to sainthood during his lifetime. The rhetorical question he had asked himself on entering the Senate, he told writer Nick Joaquin candidly, was "Where could we hit this guy [Marcos] hardest?" Ninoy's response was a paragon of analytical clarity. "Looking over the landscape," he said, "I saw where his main weakness lay: militarization. The Culatingan Massacre had proved that to me."

Ninoy's maiden speech before the Senate, delivered on February 5, 1968, a full four years before martial law, set the tone for a political assault on Marcos that was to be every bit as calculated as that of Marcos on Aquino. Titled "A Garrison State in the Make," it charged the president with using militaristic means "to condition the mass mind and build up the Marcos cult" in order to "transform our democratic society clandestinely into a garrison state."

Little more than a month later, a wounded Muslim who was rescued from the sea off the island of Corregidor and taken into protective custody by a sympathetic politician told a true tale far more chilling than Aquino's speculative "Garrison State" scenario. A palace-directed covert operation to train a secret Filipino Muslim army for missions inside territory claimed jointly by the Philippines and Malaysia had gone terribly awry, resulting in a bloody mutiny.

The ensuing scandal that broke over what came to be known as the "Jabidah Massacre" fanned fears already harbored by many Filipinos that the Armed Forces of the Philippines had been transformed into an armed forces of President Marcos. Even more damaging, it aggravated relations with neighboring Malaysia and helped escalate the sporadic warfare between Filipino Muslims and government troops into a full-fledged civil war in the southern islands.

Ninoy, who had been tipped to the operation, code-named "Jabidah" (the Muslim Helen of Troy), by his military intelligence sources, conducted his own investigation into the affair. His findings provided insight into the paranoia, the craziness, and the intrigues that had permeated the Marcos military from the beginning and would become the deposed president's unsettling legacy to Ninoy's widow years later.

The Jabidah affair made enemies of Marcos and Aquino, who had hitherto been only rivals. Ninoy and his informants saw Jabidah as a threat to national security. In the mind of Marcos, however, it was Ninoy's exposé of the clandestine operation that posed the threat. "Jabidah was what turned Ninoy into an enemy of the state," concludes Tatad.

With the 1969 presidential campaign looming, the cross fire between Aquino and Marcos grew hotter. Senator Aquino ushered in the election year by breaking a longstanding Filipino social and political taboo. He attacked a woman—the wife of the president—in public. The direct target of his attack was the pet project of the First Lady, construction of a lavish Philippine Cultural Center, which he dubbed "Imelda's Pantheon."

However, Ninoy was actually stalking bigger game. As the Liberal party's point man, he was setting the tenor for the 1969 campaign against Marcos's reelection. Beyond that, he was staking his own claim to the presidential nomination four years hence. In so doing, he was taking a first potshot at the woman who was emerging as Marcos's partner in office. Imelda was expected to play as essential a role in the upcoming presidential campaign as she had in the last one, and already speculation had been voiced about a possible race between herself and Ninoy for the presidency in 1973.

In a Senate privilege speech on February 10, 1969, Ninoy listed numerous projects, in a country too poor to properly house or feed a majority of its people, that were more deserving of subsidy. "But no," he raged, "a fifty million peso cultural center must be constructed so the bejeweled elite, the nation's first one hundred families, can enjoy the Bernsteins and the Bolshoi . . . Imelda must have her Pantheon."

Like the other denizens of the capital's coffeehouses, where political gossip is exchanged and public opinion molded, Ninoy had witnessed the transformation of an always impetuous Imelda into an extravagant and imperious First Lady. Before Marcos became president and Imelda the mistress of Malacañang, she had lacked the means to implement her every whim, and the sycophants to treat her every flight of fancy as worthy of praise or emulation. Now she was adored by the public, pampered by servants, and worst of all, heeded by a vast bureaucracy, regardless of the zaniness of her demands.

Already cabinet members and businessmen, whom she was hitting regularly for favors and contributions to further her myriad projects, were beginning to realize that, unchecked, Imelda was a potential menace. However, most knew better than to criticize her or to call for controls on some of her activities. "Marcos once said to me, 'If you are a leader, you should never allow anyone to complain to your face about your wife,' " recounts former presidential spokesman Adrian Cristobal. "I took it as a word to the wise." Only Ninoy was foolhardy enough to take her on.

From the moment she entered Malacañang Palace, the First Lady had poured her insomniac, almost maniacal energy into a project to build a world-class performing arts complex on waterfront property reclaimed from the sea. It had begun modestly enough as a privately financed enterprise designed to restore a sense of Filipino identity to a culturally and ethnically diverse people, who had lived for centuries under Spanish and American rule. The idea originated with Marcos, who told his wife that she must change her image from a politician's wife into something more after he was in office. He wanted her to have a project. "In my administration," he said, "I'll build a strong foundation and house for the Filipino people, you make it a home."

"I reflected on what makes a home," says Imelda, earnestly. Then she lapses into one of the flaky abstractions which characterize her thought process:

> The answer was love. What is love when made real? Beauty. What is beauty through the centuries? The culture and spirit of our race. So my first program was the cultural center, because it was the spirit of the Filipino people after four hundred years as a colonized people.

With the embarrassing candor of the nouvelle arrivée that she was at the time, she bragged, even before the foundation was laid, that she had invited John D. Rockefeller to its opening. Years later, full of the same naive enthusiasm with which she oversaw the center's construction, she retells the story:

> When I became First Lady, John D. Rockefeller was here. I showed him around Manila, but there was very little to see. I said, "There will rise the Cultural Center of the Philippines." He said, "There, my dear girl, is only water." He must have thought I was Don Quixote de la Mancha. I said, "The first two years we will cover it with soil. The third year the building will rise. The fourth year the curtain will rise." I said to him, "Please come to be our guest of honor on the eve of Marcos's birthday in 1969."

She set about hustling funds from the private business community and had amassed enough to launch the project in March 1966. Plagued by rising costs, however, the price tag had jumped to $12.5 million. It was Ninoy who revealed that, contrary to Malacañang propaganda, public money had been diverted in order to complete construction on time.

Ninoy's blast caused a sensation. Marcos's cabinet members and party leaders were prodded to defend the boss's wife. Unable to stand on the sidelines and simply let the pros argue her case, Imelda leaped to her own defense and ended up, as was her wont, protesting too much. "I became a beggar," she said, bragging about having personally solicited a contribution from President Lyndon Johnson during the Marcoses' 1966 state visit to the U.S. LBJ had responded with a pledge from a forgotten fund for educational projects.

Imelda's response to Aquino's assertion that the country was, at this stage of its development, too young and too poor to support a cultural center perfectly illustrated her skewed priorities, which inevitably invited charges of insensitivity and hauteur. "There will always be poor people," she said. "But my project is like this: I have helped the mentally retarded, the idiots, the morons, the unwed mothers, the orphans, the nontalented poor. The more reason we should be helping the talented poor, like the writers, the painters, the sculptors."

Aquino was widely chastised for expanding his offensive against the president to include the First Lady. He denied trying to make his old friend look bad. "No amount of effort on my part could deglamorize Imelda," he said patronizingly. "I consider her the prettiest Filipina of our generation." But, he argued, "Ferdie is hiding behind the skirts of a woman. He uses Imelda as a shield." In a remark which, in retrospect, appears fraught with irony, Ninoy added, "I think politics should not be for women. But if a woman indulges in politics, then she should share in the brickbats."

True to Imelda's boast, the curtain went up on September 10, 1969. It was hardly a serene opening. The exhausted architect took to his sick bed before the last chandelier had been hung. The political opposition, which had failed to obtain a court order to restrain Mrs. Marcos from further construction, petitioned for a similar order to prevent performances. When that was not granted, demonstrators picketed the site chanting: "Bread, yes, circuses, no."

The evening was nonetheless a stunning success for the Marcoses, with California Governor Ronald Reagan, who represented President Nixon at the gala inaugural performance, clearly stealing the show from the small corps of demonstrators protesting out front. Rockefeller could not make the premiere, but telexed Imelda from Rome: "I would not be able to bring enough hats to take off to you."

As a campaign event, the three-day Cultural Center gala was in keeping with the increasing extravagance of Imelda's life. The race for a second presidential term was turning into the most expensive in history, and her style on the hustings almost regal. Filipino poet Jose Lacaba, who was assigned by the *Philippines Free Press* to cover one of Mrs. Marcos's campaign swings, painted a scene more reminiscent of court life than democratic vote-getting:

> She came out of the helicopter, a dea ex machina, and walked into the school grounds, regal and tall, the hem of her white silk terno billowing in the wind, a parasol carried by a uniformed aide shielding her from the sun: the picture she made, walking beneath a dainty parasol brought to mind paintings of great Victorian ladies promenading on the beach.

Perhaps the most outrageous display of campaign whimsy was Marcos's attempt to play the "Catholic card" by dispatching Imelda to Rome as head of a giant 250-person official delegation for the investiture of a new Filipino cardinal. The fact that Monsignor Julio Rosales was the Archbishop of Cebu, the ancestral home of Marcos's opponent Sergio Osmeña, was no small factor in the Marcoses' decision to shanghai the religious event for their own obvious political purpose. Imelda's behavior during this trip betrayed her growing craving for publicity and obsession with the international jet set. She turned the voyage to the Vatican into a serialized photo opportunity by flying there via Mindanao, where she campaigned, and Bangkok, where she arranged to be greeted by the queen's sister. On her return she overnighted in an Iranian palace, where she dined on gold caviar.

She hit the front pages of all the Roman dailies by defying tradition and the chill spring air to show up at the official nomination ceremony of the cardinals wearing a saffron *terno*. Her décolletage was especially apparent, given that all the other women in attendance were properly cloaked in black for the solemn occasion. She explained to her hosts and to the paparazzi that her function was to project the Philippines, and the best way to do that was to wear the national dress. She was correct. By the next day the crowds that gathered along the route traveled by the visiting prelates were chanting, "Philippines, Philippines," and waiting to ogle the exotic Asian who appeared at each function dressed in a different gown.

Since no Filipino president had ever won a second term, the biggest challenge facing Marcos was to break the one-term jinx, which was rooted in the Filipino belief that frequent change in administrations was a necessary means of creating new jobs and distributing money to new groups. A parallel assumption, which was always fed by the party out of power, was that the incumbent had already spent, borrowed, and stolen all the money left in the state coffers and would therefore not be able to offer his supporters as much during a second term. Marcos succeeded in dispelling both beliefs by spending an estimated $50 million in public and private funds, plus countless IOUs, to appeal to special interest groups and to make good on his pledge to deliver the 239 irrigation projects and 3,400 kilometers of paved roads targeted in his "rice and roads" program.

So severe was the drain on the economy of this costliest campaign in Philippine history that the peso weakened dramatically, dangerously escalating the cost of the government construction projects, which Marcos had ordered completed by election day. Even before the last returns were counted, a balance of payments crisis had forced the government to seek an emergency loan from the International Monetary Fund to be able to meet its payroll. Before it would bail him out, the IMF ordered Marcos to float the peso. The result was a final destabilizing plunge in its value by nearly half, which drove the cost of imported flour so high that bakeries stopped producing Filipinos' daily bread, *pan de sol*. Over the years voters had become inured to a high level of electoral fraud and corruption, but never before had the aftershock of a campaign played such havoc with their pocketbooks.

*   *   *

The decade of the 1960s ended as traumatically for the Philippines as it had for the U.S. In the midst of the crisis of confidence brought on by the economic debacle at home and by the demoralizing course of the American war in Vietnam, to which Marcos had contributed a much-criticized Filipino contingent, President Marcos took his second oath of office. One month later, on the evening of January 26, 1970, a seismic event, seemingly out of proportion in its intensity to what had come before, shook the very foundations of his administration.

As the First Couple emerged from the marble lobby of the Congress building, following the president's State of the Nation address, they were greeted by a hostile crowd of students and other protesters, which had assembled to demand a nonpartisan convention to draft a new Philippine constitution. Suddenly, a mock coffin made of cardboard and symbolizing "the death of democracy" was hurled in their direction. A rain of rocks, gravel, bottles, and a papier-mâché crocodile with a dollar sign on its back followed. Marcos's security chief, Colonel Fabian Ver, shoved his boss inside the waiting limousine and shielded him with his body as the car sped off, leaving behind a raging riot between police and demonstrators.

From inside the heavily guarded walls of Malacañang, Marcos issued a statement blaming the rioting on "nonstudent provocateurs." Meanwhile, academics and clergymen, who were outraged over the police brutality, rallied to the support of the wounded, while radical groups began mobilizing to march on the palace. Those activist segments of the population were not alone in their condemnation of the regime. Disillusionment was rampant. The bottom had fallen out of President Marcos's landslide after only two months.

Most of the blame would land on Marcos. The economic chaos that followed the 1969 election had lent immediate and widespread credence to the opposition's charges of unprecedented vote-buying and overspending. Marcos had added to his problems when, so as not to be perceived as a lame duck, he had early in 1970 deliberately encouraged speculation that he might impose martial law to extend his rule until necessary reforms could be implemented.

Such sudden and drastic shifts in the political and economic weather in Manila acted as storm warnings on the highly suggestive minds of Filipinos, who as a people are unusually prone to rumor, intrigue, and paranoia. Individuals and groups interpreted the signals according to their own biases, which were magnified by a press known as the freest in Asia. Without a central clearing house or a trusted national leader to set the record straight, everyone believed what he chose to believe about the perceived crisis. Both Marcos and the predominantly youthful protesters saw themselves as victims of a dark conspiracy. To Marcos it was the Communists. To the students it was American imperialism. To complicate matters further, both sides employed provocateurs. Former Marcos spokesman Adrian Cristobal observes, "We had our students, and our rivals had their students, and it became impossible to keep track of who was doing what. In the end the left was able to capitalize on the confusion."

Four days after the riots, explosions resounded outside the palace walls near Mendiola bridge, where a demonstration led by the radical *Kabataang Makabayan* (Patriotic Youth) had been building all day. Homemade "pillboxes" (packets of foil filled with gunpowder and nails) and Molotov cocktails were hurled over the gates into the palace grounds, as a crowd, which had grown to some 5,000 people, surged toward the high, iron gates. Some protesters set fire to cars and lampposts outside the compound, while others commandeered a fire truck and rammed it through gate number 4. As the demonstrators stormed the palace grounds, security troops inside the walls fired on them.

What would go down in contemporary Philippine history as "The First Quarter Storm" had begun. The so-called "Mendiola Massacre" claimed the lives of six people—the first casualties of the political demonstrations that would sweep the islands during the early 1970s. Out of the rallies and protest marches that followed, a "parliament of the streets" emerged to declare war, not just on the Marcos administration, but on the democratic system itself. The corrupt politicians, who had monopolized the system of government since the founding of the republic but had failed to narrow the yawning gap between rich and poor, appeared increasingly irrelevant to the needs of this newly assertive group of disenfranchised students, laborers, and peasants.

Throughout the crisis, the president remained strangely incommunicado inside palace gates that were now welded shut. Troops patrolled the surrounding streets, which would be closed to traffic for the rest of the Marcos era. The president had appealed to the opposition Liberals not to exploit the tense situation for political purposes, and for once, Ninoy remained silent.

His preliminary analysis of the situation told him that the traditional opposition, to which he belonged, had ceased to be regarded as an alternative to Marcos in a rapidly polarizing situation, where extremists on the left and the right were fast removing the ground from under the democratic center. "Disenchanted with the two political parties, many of our young people looked to the students as the new force or third force," he told a journalist. He agonized over how to react, knowing that anything he said would appear to be politically motivated. Finally on February 2, he rose in the Senate to side with the students against the administration, which he denounced as "a factory of privilege" and "a police state." In defending the lawless behavior of the protesters as a moral alternative to the actions of the chief of state, Aquino moved inexorably closer to an open clash with Marcos.

The revolution did not come. In time, nervous residents of the affluent, walled enclaves, which were home to Manila's elite, uncrated the antiques and artwork they had readied for shipment to the U.S. and put them back on display. What came in its place was only more confusion and a vague but widespread fear of an unknown enemy that lurked on the other side of wherever the beholder was. Such an environment was ripe for manipulation by a clever ruler.

In the analysis of Ninoy and his fellow Liberals, Marcos was not vulnerable to a revolution from the left in the aftermath of the "Mendiola Massacre." Quite the reverse, it was they, themselves, in the moderate opposition who were more likely to fall victim to a crackdown from the right-wing Marcos military. In order to survive, they had to preempt such a move, while at the same time making the Liberal party more responsive to the changing political currents.

As the Liberals' point man, Ninoy was hardly less reckless than Marcos in blasting his opponents, airing wild charges against them, and exploiting every possible opportunity to discredit them in the eyes of the voters. In allowing their political battles to take precedence over attempts to solve the critical problems plaguing the nation, both men were playing with fire. As Marcos's political fortunes continued to sour, his opponents grew bolder. Intransigence hardened into immovability on all fronts. There followed an inevitable drift toward martial law.

Long-simmering discord between Marcos and the Lopez family, the mightiest of the Philippine oligarchs, erupted into outright political warfare. Vice-President Fernando Lopez resigned from his cabinet post, and the Lopez-owned *Manila Chronicle* used its editorial page to express a public lack of confidence in Marcos. Then, as the president prepared to deliver an important TV speech announcing cutbacks in unpopular fuel price increases—a policy which the Lopezes opposed—the Lopez-owned electricity company pulled the plug on Marcos, blacking his address off the air.

More humiliation was heaped upon the president when radical students declared the University of the Philippines a "liberated area" occupied by "guerrilla fighters of the revolution," and commandeered a local radio station. Among the more provocative pieces of programming they aired was the tape of a much-publicized bedroom encounter between a sexy B-movie actress, named Dovie Beams, and President Marcos. Just before she was unceremoniously evicted from the country, after Mrs. Marcos learned of their affair, the buxom Miss Beams had played the tape for reporters. Now the students were playing it over the public airwaves.

That was too much for a proud chief of state to bear. He sent in troops to disperse the campus communards. As they approached the occupied area, the soldiers began to snigger. By the time they reached their quarry, they were convulsed with laughter, for blaring over the public address system was the familiar voice of their commander in chief singing Ilocano love songs, followed by heavy breathing, the creaking of mattress springs, and climactic cries of ecstasy, which the shameless starlet had identified as those of her "Fred."

A scandal nearly as colorful, but far more sinister, eclipsed all the others on April 5, 1971, when a sometime treasure hunter named Rogelio Roxas reported the confiscation of a priceless, jewel-encrusted statue from his home in the middle of the night. The mysterious disappearance of the Golden Buddha would become the quintessential Filipino crime: lacking in tangible evidence, subject to vicious rumors and wild intrigue, implicating numerous members of the First Family and various branches of the military, guided by no clear motive, and forever unsolved.

Before the case of the Golden Buddha was ever submitted to the objective examination of a court, it became the explosive centerpiece of the Liberal party's 1971 senatorial election campaign. Once again Marcos had turned the midterm senatorial and local races into a referendum on his presidency. The eight Nacionalista party Senate candidates had been handpicked by the president and First Lady. They were pitted against a Liberal party ticket dominated by respected opposition incumbents.

The climactic event of the opposition campaign was a nighttime rally in the Plaza Miranda on August 21, 1971. Long Manila's best-known forum for free discussion, the plaza fronting an ancient Spanish church had seen many a political rally and not a little violence. Rumors had swept Manila's coffee shops all week that the opposition candidates were planning to document onstage the graft and corruption which riddled the Marcos government. Senator Salonga would exhibit some of the 2 million fake ballots allegedly used by Marcos forces in the 1969 election. Sergio Osmeña would reveal new information about the case of the Golden Buddha, with personal testimony from its discoverer, Rogelio Roxas, whom he had bailed out of jail the previous Friday.

As the rally began, Roxas was sitting in Osmeña's car at the edge of the crowd, waiting to be introduced as a surprise speaker. Senator Aquino, who had not yet shown up, was scheduled for the finale: an exposé on the alleged "hidden wealth" of the Marcoses, complete with photographs of Imelda's jewels and Marcos mansions in Baguio, Metro-Manila, Bataan, Switzerland, and London.

At 9:13 P.M., just seconds after the party leader had introduced the eight candidates, an explosion rocked the apron of the stage. Three seconds later a second blast sent wooden chairs and people flying into the air above the stage, while the audience below stampeded a hysterical retreat. The Channel 4 cameraman switched on his camera ten minutes ahead of schedule at 9:20 and relayed a scene of carnage that was shocking even to violence-weary Filipinos. Nine spectators, including a news photographer, were dead, and ninety-eight others wounded. All of the opposition candidates were wounded, several of them critically. The only Liberal senator untouched by the bombing was Ninoy Aquino, who had been delayed at the wedding reception for his goddaughter Suzie Laurel.

Predictably, the opposition blamed the regime for the Plaza Miranda attack. Equally predictable, Marcos blamed the Communists. Three days later, claiming evidence that a group of Marxists had been plotting to "forcibly seize political power in this country," Marcos announced that he was suspending the writ of habeas corpus in order to facilitate the quick arrest of subversives responsible for the Plaza Miranda attack.

Before a nationally televised presidential press conference the following day, Marcos was more specific in his accusations. He revealed that "some politicians have joined together with the New People's Army. These politicians have become partners with them." When reporters pressed him to identify the politicians, Marcos dropped a bombshell. He named Aquino as the guilty party.

Marcos's accusation was not an impulsive one. He had come prepared to back up his charges with a chronology of Aquino's relationship with the subversives and photographs of the weapons he had allegedly passed to them.

Harking back to the period immediately preceding the Culatingan

Massacre, the president accused Aquino of presenting the late Huk commander Alibasbas with a carbine bearing a telescopic sight. He detailed meetings between Aquino and Commander Dante in 1968 and 1969, the period when Dante's faction of Huks united with University of the Philippines political science instructor Jose Maria Sison to form the new, Maoist Communist party of the Philippines and its armed branch, the New People's Army (NPA). Marcos cited intelligence reports that Aquino had armed the NPA with grenade launchers, M16 rifles, and walkie-talkies. For good measure, Marcos added that financing of the radicals was carried out by the family of his antagonistic vice-president, the Lopezes.

Ninoy took to the press to defend himself against the president's highly defamatory charges. His association with the Huks, he reiterated, dated back to his tenure as governor of Tarlac. "Before Marcos assumed office, Tarlac was peaceful," he reminded his interviewers. "When he came to power and changed our policy from coexistence to search-and-destroy, the massacres began." Now, Ninoy contended, he was being framed by bogus intelligence reports, cooked up by the president's men. Aquino mused prophetically, "What if they come up to a Huk surrenderee and say, 'You will go free if you agree to implicate Aquino.' If they do that, I'm finished."

An opinion poll published a few days after the suspension of the writ showed that a healthy 68 percent of Manilans refused to believe that Aquino was insidiously linked to the Communists. At the same time only 8 percent thought the president had anything to do with the Plaza Miranda bombing. A substantial 41 percent attributed the crime to unknown enemies of the Liberal party. Eighteen years later, those enemies have yet to be pinpointed and tried for the Plaza Miranda bombing.

When the campaign resumed, Marcos continued to hammer away at the unsubstantiated Communist threat. But his line that a vote for the Liberal party was a vote for the Maoists fizzled, as voters watched the injured opposition candidates earnestly addressing rallies from their wheelchairs.

The 1971 elections were yet more bloody than all the others, with 200 killed, and some 40,000 soldiers and 12,000 ROTC cadets called out to keep the peace on election day. Filipino voters were serving notice on Marcos that his time was up. All but one of Marcos's eight Senate candidates went down to defeat in what the press dubbed an "LP typhoon." As if to underline the message, the Constitutional Convention, which had begun meeting in June to draft a new constitution, had passed a resolution prohibiting Marcos from running for a third term, or any of his close relatives from succeeding him in 1973.

*　　　　*　　　　*

Marcos's enemies were closing in on him. When cornered, he was at his most dangerous. As the Intelligence and Research Bureau of the

U.S. State Department warned in a May 7, 1971, report on Marcos's intentions, it had become increasingly clear that his reelection to a second term "has not satisfied his ambitions, and that he has already decided to try to extend himself in office by one means or another after his present term expires in December 1973."

The means he planned to use was still in question, but Marcos was a master of squeezing options for himself out of seemingly optionless situations. This one presented him with four: (1) reconcile with the opposition and organize a coalition government; (2) engineer through the ongoing Constitutional Convention some legal means of extending his rule; (3) back Imelda as his successor; (4) invoke the martial law provisions in the present constitution, thereby canceling elections.

Aquino and his Liberal party confreres, smelling an electoral victory for themselves in 1973, had all but written off any possibility of reconciliation. Meanwhile, both Marcoses were already ardently wooing Constitutional Convention delegates, although apparently at cross-purposes. Signs of a marital spat were manifest in the designation of "his" delegates, who favored a parliamentary system that would permit Marcos to continue ruling as prime minister, and "hers," who favored retention of the presidential system, which would necessitate Imelda's candidacy as his successor. Few could dissociate this apparent domestic power struggle from Imelda's pique over the lurid disclosures made by Dovie Beams about her liaison with the president. In the years that followed, members of the First Couple's inner circle would frequently overhear "the ma'am" berate "the sir" with references about the Hollywood starlet and other Marcos dalliances, as a means of getting her way on political matters.

By early 1972 the Marcos forces had swung the responsible Constitutional Convention, or Con-Con, committees around to approving the adoption of the parliamentary system, in which the leader of the majority party, Marcos, would hold power as prime minister. On May 19, Delegate Eduardo Quintero, a conscience-stricken retired diplomat, would expose the truth about how delegates had been bribed to change their votes. He himself turned over eleven envelopes containing a total of 11,150 pesos (about $550) which he had received from Marcos operatives.

Despite the palace's success in winning approval of a parliamentary system, Marcos never ceased to cultivate his fourth option: martial law. He stepped up his campaign to publicize the growing Communist threat as a means of tarring his opponents and of justifying his efforts to strengthen the military. As if by clockwork, alleged secret documents, revealing leftist plans to intensify terrorism in order to create "a revolutionary situation," fell into the hands of the military. Then a string of violent incidents occurred, all serving to underline his claims.

By August, when a succession of devastating floods hit central Luzon, destroying crops and ultimately driving the price of commodities up by 25 percent, the country seemed to be careening toward martial law. Both Marcos and his opponents knew that the economic aftereffects of the floods were potentially more damaging to his already unpopular presidency than his exaggerated reports of a Communist threat. Thus he had all the more reason to regard an acceleration of apparently Communist-inspired violence as a welcome diversion of public attention from economic problems.

On September 12, Marcos sent shivers through the populace when he stated that with the rising tide of violence in the land, "the basis for the use of emergency powers exists." U.S. intelligence analysts, who had conducted their own studies on the size and operations of the new Maoist movement, which had sprung from the ashes of the old Huk insurgency, did not attribute the same importance to it that Marcos did. A U.S. National Security Study Memorandum, issued shortly after martial law was declared, concluded that "while the Communist insurgency, if left unchecked, might have been able to overthrow the Philippine government in another five years, it clearly does not have that capability at the present time."

As for the other violent incidents which Marcos cited as justification for his declaration of martial law, the State Department's Bureau of Intelligence and Research wrote: "It was widely believed in Manila that most of the bombings were the work of Marcos's own hirelings trying to create an atmosphere of crisis in which martial law would be more acceptable."

The same day that Marcos broached the subject of martial law, Senator Aquino paid a call on the U.S. embassy. He had an explosive document to show the diplomats. Code-named "Operation Plan Sagittarius," it was a secret military plan ordered by Marcos to place the capital region under the control of the Philippine Constabulary as a prelude to martial law. In discussing the prospect of martial law with embassy officers, Aquino surprised them by commenting that if he were president, he would declare martial law in order to take strong enforcement and reform measures to correct worsening subversive and socioeconomic problems. In a cable to Washington, Ambassador Byroade pointed to the obvious danger to Aquino in such a situation: Aquino would "have little choice in the short run, since he would be one of the president's prime targets, were he to oppose Marcos actively."

The following day Ninoy delivered a riveting exposé of "Oplan Sagittarius" in the Senate. It was a stunning sequel to his maiden speech nearly three years before. There he had speculated that Marcos was laying the foundation for a future "Garrison State." Now he was presenting confirmation, supplied to him, he said, by the military planners themselves.

Marcos could not let him go unchallenged. He invited Ninoy's rival for the 1973 presidential nomination, Liberal party president Gerry Roxas to discuss with him evidence that had come into the possession of the administration that certain LP leaders were engaged in a plot to overthrow the government. Roxas, who saw through Marcos's move to divide the opposition, declined the invitation on grounds that such an accusation was so grave that it should not be reviewed in secret; the Filipino people and the courts deserved to know about it, as well. So Marcos went public with his charges.

On September 16, he declassified a confidential report submitted to him by Secretary of Defense Enrile, claiming that Ninoy had met secretly with the alleged leader of the Communist party of the Philippines, Jose Maria Sison. Marcos told journalists that after Ninoy's meeting with Sison on September 7, the oppositionist had confided details of their discussion to Enrile, who had once served as the Cojuangco family's lawyer.

According to the president, the information which Aquino had given Enrile indicated a possible "linkup" between the Communist party of the Philippines and the Liberal party in terms of political action and propaganda, in the event that Marcos decided to use his emergency powers. Ninoy denied Marcos's charges, but berated the president for failing to prosecute him immediately after his meeting with Sison, if he had the evidence, rather than waiting until after his exposure of "Oplan Sagittarius." Then Ninoy dared Marcos, "If he has any bill against me, I say to him: 'Mr. President, go to court. Charge me.' "

Ninoy's performance contained a good deal of bluster. He was more worried about Marcos's charges than he originally let on, as his public comments on the subject during the next few days indicated. On September 20, he made another privilege speech in which he puzzled aloud over Marcos's motivations in accusing him of confiding information about the Communists to the Marcos regime. His conclusion served as an eerie preview to the circumstances surrounding his death in 1983.

Marcos, he deduced, had, godfather style, planted two fatal kisses on him by portraying him, not simply as an enemy of the state, but also as a man who had betrayed his Communist allies to the regime. "Should I be assassinated," he said, "Mr. Marcos and the defense establishment would have a ready alibi: The NPAs killed Aquino because he betrayed them." Playing to the galleries, Ninoy uttered the last prophetic line of his Senate career. "I would now like to enter these words into our records: Should I be assassinated, my blood would be on the hands of those who set me up for the kill."

Events were rushing toward a climax, and Ninoy knew it. He had, after all, sounded the earliest warnings about martial law, hoping to deter it by exposing the president's plans. He had been warned in recent weeks by friends in high places in both the Philippine military and the Marcos administration that his exposés had failed to deter the inevitable, and that he should protect himself and his family by leaving the country.

Ninoy's sister Guadalupe ("Lupita") Kashiwahara tells how "an American dressed in white came up to Ninoy after a premartial-law speech and told him, 'I have a helicopter waiting.' Ninoy never knew the guy, who volunteered to take him out of the country."

In response, Ninoy told his friends and family, "I pulled myself up to my full height and said, 'If Marcos is going to declare martial law, my place is with my people.' " Later, when he retold that story in jail, he would add, self-deprecatingly, "How dumb I am!" As a result of the American offer to spirit Ninoy to safety, the Aquino family concluded, says Lupita, that U.S. Ambassador Henry Byroade "knew about martial law and wanted an anti-Communist regime without any blood on its hands."

Too late, Ninoy had realized the subtle brilliance of Marcos's machinations to use him as a prime justification for imposing emergency rule. Summing up Ninoy's rude awakening, the *Free Press* wrote: "Ninoy felt he was finally seeing through the maze to the administration's intention."

On Thursday, September 21, thirty anti-Marcos organizations held a rally at Plaza Miranda to denounce the pattern of fear and repression which pointed toward the impending imposition of martial law. For the second day in a row, Marcos huddled with members of his inner circle. Unknown to even his own cabinet, a proclamation of martial law had been prepared for his signature, and a last scenario of violence awaited enactment.

On Friday night, September 22, that scenario began to roll. Defense Secretary Enrile's car was ambushed as he was being driven home to his fortresslike home in Dasmariñas Village. Enrile himself was not wounded because he was riding in the escort vehicle, but his car was badly damaged by explosives. Seasoned observers believed from the start that the attack had been staged. Years later, as he was in the midst of his own revolt from the Marcos regime, Enrile would confirm those suspicions.

Using the ambush as a pretext, Marcos signed Proclamation No. 1081 and the executive order which implemented it. Although the date was September 22, the documents were antedated September 21. Within two hours of the signing, the military had sealed all newspaper offices and broadcasting stations. By 4 A.M. September 23, 100 of the 400 citizens listed as subversives had been rounded up and detained at Camp Crame. The public would not begin to learn what had happened until after daybreak. Even then, its understanding of what was going on would be confused. "If the charges and countercharges did anything, they certainly did not prove that Marcos was a liar and Aquino not, or vice versa," editorialized the *Free Press*. "They simply cast a heavier shroud on the mystery the nation ached to unravel, the mystery of who's terrorizing the people."

The nation was not alone in its confusion. Subsequent revelations by both Marcos and Aquino indicate that neither of them had an altogether clear understanding of the other's actions and motivations or of who was behind the terror. In trying to bluff each other, they had unwittingly created a climate of severe instability, in which public anxiety over the escalating violence was intensified and the personal paranoia of the two chief antagonists magnified.

Six years after he declared martial law, President Marcos published a ghostwritten account of what was going on in his mind as he made that fateful decision. Although the book, *Revolution from the Center*, was clearly a piece of propaganda written to dispel the widespread belief that Marcos had manufactured the violent incidents used to justify martial law, it was nonetheless valuable for its revelations of the convoluted thinking of a president who had become a prisoner of fears fueled by his own intrigues.

As he examined documents, both real and counterfeit, about all manner of plots and counterplots against the regime, Marcos wrote, he could suddenly see the outlines of a Communist masterplan to turn his own military against him. "Clearly what they wanted was to blame the anarchy and disorder on the President, to have him dragged out of office and then killed," he wrote. "In the confusion Communist supporters in the Armed Forces would help them in a coup d'etat." So, Marcos concluded, "on the long night of Sunday, September 17, 1972, I saw clearly that the rightist conspiracy and the leftist rebellion had almost won. At the end of that September vigil, I found my duty clear to me. My mind and spirit calm at last, I set out to do it."

Later, the transcript of the June 1977 meeting between Marcos and Aquino would similarly reveal great uncertainty and suspicion in Aquino's mind about the president's intentions on the eve of martial law. Aquino admitted to Marcos that he had confided intelligence about Communist activities to Enrile and Ramos, as charged, because he had come to realize the newly emerging NPA's capacity to be infinitely more treacherous than the old, mafia-style Huks of his day. Yet, when it came to publicly cooperating with Marcos to form a common front against the Communists, Aquino had remained unconvinced about the gravity of the threat and distrustful of the president's motives.

"There was a tremendous lack of communication," Aquino admitted to Marcos, attributing most of the blame to the president. He explained that he believed at the time that the army was still capable of containing the rebels, so he was left to conclude that Marcos's anti-Communist diatribes were primarily political in nature. He told Marcos that he therefore rejected the president's invitations to meet in the palace to discuss the crisis. The Liberals had quite simply feared that Marcos would use such talks to frame them. It was not the first time that paranoia and petty politics would so inflame a situation that could have been brought under control, had both sides been mindful of the consequences and had the will to compromise. "Politics was in our minds in those days," Ninoy admitted to Marcos, "because we were nearing 1973, and within the party, we were jockeying for position."

5

The Willing Sacrifice

"**M**artial law has been imposed. Please restrain your security." It was the voice of Colonel Romeo Gatan, a former provincial commander in Ninoy's home province of Tarlac, calling on the house phone from the lobby of the Manila Hilton. At one o'clock on Saturday morning, September 23, 1972, he had come on orders to deliver an important letter from Defense Minister Enrile to Senator Aquino. So as to discourage the senator from acting rashly, he noted that 200 of his men were surrounding the hotel where he and other legislators were closeted while writing the final text of a tariff bill. Ninoy did not resist.

Ninoy summoned his car and driver, asking Gatan's permission to phone his wife on the car's radio-phone. "Listen carefully," he told Cory. "Martial law has been declared. I have been arrested. I'm being taken to Camp Crame." She had dreaded such a call since he had asked her, several weeks ago, to take the children abroad. He had even contacted three embassies for visas. He would not accompany them, he told her, but would stay in Manila to "face the music."

Cory balked at leaving without him. "I said, 'If you are going to die, let's all die together.'" She quickly explains, "It wasn't because I wanted to be some kind of heroine here, but I had little Kris, who was one year old, and I was not about to live in some strange country with five children."

Years later, she feels sure that "it was the right decision." "Suppose I had left with my children," she says. "Then Ninoy would have gone to the hills to escape arrest, and that would have been the most convenient alibi for Marcos to impose martial law." She explains that "in order for any movement to succeed, you need a popular leader, and the Communists did not have that." But, she adds, "If Ninoy had been with them, that would have justified Marcos's imposition of martial law." Instead, Marcos would be stuck with a political prisoner who, in refusing to resist arrest or defend himself before military prosecutors, would become an international symbol of the injustice of martial law.

Ninoy was the first of some 50,000 martial law detainees to be arrested. He was booked into Philippine Constabulary headquarters at Camp Crame, and fingerprinted, prior to incarceration inside Fort Bonifacio. In charges filed against him later, he would be called an enemy of the state. However, the coffee shop consensus later that morning, when the news began to circulate, was that Aquino's major crime was his opposition to Marcos, and that declaring martial law was a way for the president to do what everyone had long expected: prolong his tenure beyond the constitutional limit of two terms.

At 2 A.M., while Ninoy was being interviewed by the constabulary chief, General Fidel ("Eddie") Ramos, who was in charge of rounding up the initial, high-visibility list of 400 alleged "subversives," the phone rang in Ramos's office. It was journalist Maximo ("Max") Soliven. "Eddie, there's a squad of Metrocom in front of my house. Are they yours?" he asked.

The mild-mannered Ramos informed him about martial law and confirmed that his men were there to arrest him. He offered his fellow Ilocano some friendly advice, "Max, don't go over the wall. Surrender, and I promise you will come under no physical harm. I will see you when you are brought to Crame, and I will allow your wife." Then, mindful of the arsenal that Max had in his home following a bloody campaign against a provincial warlord who was finally gunned down in church, Ramos added, "If you surrender now, it will give your guys some time to sanitize your house."

Across town the officers who were sent to fetch Senator Jose "Pepe" Diokno agreed to join him for a cup of coffee while his wife, Nena, packed a few things for him to take. By dawn the constabulary gymnasium was crowded with moderate opposition leaders, editors, TV newscasters, labor leaders, radical activists, and anti-Marcos delegates to the Constitutional Convention. "Welcome to the club," said Ninoy, as he greeted old friends. "So they got you too." It was, at least at the start, martial law Filipino-style: no tanks, no barbed wire, repression with a cheerful face. Ferdinand Marcos knew the Filipino psyche better than any other politician, and he had tailored a hybrid form of dictatorship, his longheld notion of "constitutional authoritarianism," to suit it.

Not until 7:30 that evening did Marcos finally appear on government radio and television to explain what had taken place. "My countrymen," he began, cloaking his every action under the mantle of the law. "I have proclaimed martial law in accordance with powers vested in the president by the constitution of the Philippines," he said. He quickly added, "This is not a military takeover of civil government functions." What it was, he explained, was an assumption by him of extraordinary powers in order to "eliminate the threat of a violent overthrow of our republic." He used those powers immediately to close schools, place all media and public utilities under government control, establish military tribunals to try certain cases, forbid the carrying of firearms and prohibit rallies, demonstrations, and strikes.

Once peace and order had been reestablished, he assured his audience, programs to remove the inequities of society, clean up government corruption, and develop the economy would be implemented, in order to build a "New Society." In the days and months that followed, the regime moved to eliminate certain of the excesses that democracy and loose law enforcement had spawned. Political warlords were arrested or co-opted and their private armies disarmed. A program of confiscation of private firearms netted more than half a million of the weapons which macho males routinely packed in their belts, giving the Philippines its reputation as an Asian "Wild West." After he closed Congress, Marcos decreed a land reform law far more comprehensive than any the elite-dominated legislature could have passed.

As an air of stability returned to the countryside and calm to the cities between 1972 and 1975, economic growth climbed to an average 7 percent annually, and foreign investment more than doubled. American businessmen were among the most enthusiastic supporters of Marcos, whom many regarded as their best shield against a growing sense of Philippine nationalism, which had threatened to manifest itself one month before martial law, when the Supreme Court ruled that past land acquisitions by Americans were illegal and would revert to the government in 1974.

It would take time for most Filipinos to realize the high price in civil liberties and political and economic accountability that was being exacted for the temporary peace and order and the initial increase in prosperity offered by the "New Society." It would take even more time for them to realize that Marcos's chief justification for martial law—to curb the subversive activities of the Communists—had in fact had the opposite effect. Most of the party cadres in Manila had managed to escape the crackdown and flee to the hills, where they worked underground through-out the next decade, emerging vastly strengthened by the time martial law was lifted.

The bottom line was that the Filipino people, out of apathy, fear, and hope for relief from economic hardship and physical violence, which democracy had not alleviated, bowed silently to martial law. They were not alone. The American government, which had prided itself on trans-forming its former Pacific colony into a "showcase for democracy," reacted passively to the news. The Nixon White House, preoccupied with a divisive reelection campaign and the war in Vietnam, learned about Marcos's plan before it was implemented, but raised no objections. Marcos was a staunch anti-Communist in a part of the world that was viewed as vulnerable to the "domino effect" of Communism in Southeast Asia.

Before the declaration of martial law, everything had seemed to go Ninoy's way. "Ninoy felt his political machine was in fine shape," says Cory. "He was ready for the presidential elections of 1973." Even she was ready. Although she had no intention of playing anything but the back-ground role that had been hers from the start, she had begun preparing for the transition to First Lady.

"I told her, 'If you are going to be First Lady, you need your teeth fixed,' " says her dentist, Primo Gonzales. "So we did it, but then martial law came. Years later she told me, 'The only thing I was First Lady of was Fort Bonifacio.' "

In a single night, Ninoy and most of the leaders and sympathetic journalists who would have supported his campaign were in prison. Ninoy's cellmate, journalist Max Soliven, observes, "It was then that I realized that Ninoy Aquino, for all his wit, his air of bright cynicism, and his veneer of tough political pragmatism, was an incurable romantic."

One day Ninoy said to him, "Don't worry, Max, within six months we'll both be out of here. The Filipino people are used to democracy—they love liberty. You just can't take it away from them."

Soliven scoffed at his "cockeyed optimism," reminding him that "Marcos is the greatest group-dynamics expert in this neck of the woods, and he's studied the Filipino's weaknesses. He knows that a few voices may be raised in protest, but almost everyone else will sit back and do nothing."

In January 1973, in an attempt to rally public opinion outside the Philippines to the plight of the Filipino people, Ninoy began smuggling letters from his cell to members of the foreign press. "There was a mirror on the wall in the visitors' house," explains daughter Ballsy. "He would go to the bathroom and leave it there. When we would arrive, we would pretend that Kris [the youngest Aquino child] needed to go, and I would take her in and get it." They would insert the thin, folded sheets of paper inside candy wrappers, in the space between the vacuum bottle and the shell of thermos jugs full of juice, or between the layers of gauze in their sanitary napkins.

One of the letters which Ballsy carried out in a pocketful of wrapped candies in February 1973 was headlined in the *Bangkok Post* a few days later. Its brutal analysis of the regime was widely quoted elsewhere in the world press. Not long afterward a military officer appeared at the door of the Aquinos' ranch-style home on Times Street in Quezon City, and handed Cory Ninoy's prison clothes, watch, glasses, and wedding ring, saying only, "He won't need these anymore." For the next forty-one days no one would tell her where her husband was or whether he was dead or alive.

Unbeknownst to their wives, Ninoy and Pepe Diokno had been hustled out of their detention cells and flown by presidential helicopter, blindfolded and handcuffed, to Fort Magsaysay in the central Luzon town of Laur. There, they were stripped of their clothes and personal effects and locked inside stifling cells, lit day and night by neon lights. Without a watch Ninoy told time by the shadows. After the guards removed his glasses, he began to suffer terrible headaches, disorientation, and paranoia. Suspecting his keepers to be members of "the dreaded Monkees," he feared he would be quickly liquidated or slowly poisoned. Refusing to eat anything except crackers, which were rationed, six per day, his weight fell dangerously.

For the first time in his hyperkinetic life, Ninoy was forced to reflect in solitude on his life and his beliefs. In the course of his month of solitary confinement in Laur, he underwent a profound religious experience that would clarify his thinking and transform him from a traditional politician into a crusader with an agenda for the restoration of civil liberties and democratic institutions, which Filipinos had taken for granted since independence.

In a long letter smuggled out later to former Senator Francisco ("Soc") Rodrigo, a deeply religious family friend, Ninoy described his "conversion." The sudden shift of fate that had left him naked and alone had also made him resentful. "At this point of my desperation and desolation, I questioned the justice of God. I felt he was having a very good siesta, and I was afraid when he finally woke up, I would have been gone!" Unable to sleep one night, he had begun to meditate on the life of Christ, when "suddenly Jesus became a live human being." He scolded Ninoy for feeling sorry for himself and made him aware that, as he had approached the pinnacle of political success, he had adopted more and more of the tactics and ethics of his opponent Marcos. Ninoy concluded:

> In the loneliness of my solitary confinement in Laur, in the depths of my solitude and desolation, during those long hours of

meditation, I found my inner peace. He stood me face to face with myself and forced me to look at my emptiness and nothingness. . . .

While Ninoy was experiencing his epiphany, his wife was undergoing a crash course in realpolitik. Martial law had forced shy, sheltered Cory to shed the comfortable anonymity of housewife and mother and assume the sensitive role of liaison between her jailed husband and the outside world. For the first time since their marriage, she had become an integral part of the political milieu he inhabited. As she and Nena Diokno canvased the military bureaucracy for news of their husbands and petitioned the Supreme Court to produce them, she encountered firsthand the arbitrary power wielded by those who administered the vast martial law apparatus. For weeks the women's search was in vain.

One day while Ninoy's sister Tessie Oreta was visiting her detained husband, Len, a sergeant nudged her and told her where Ninoy had been taken. The sergeant had been contacted by a lieutenant from Tarlac, whom Ninoy had recognized among the guards at Laur and had begged to inform Cory of his whereabouts. Thirteen years later, immediately after her inauguration, Cory would send for that lieutenant, Voltaire Gazmin, who had risked his life by helping her husband. She would name him chief of her palace security force.

Cory's search seemed to near an end, when she was told to report once more to Fort Bonifacio. Inside the gates, she was met by the deputy commander, an army colonel, who invited her to his office to talk. "I thought he was going to ask me how I smuggled out the *Bangkok Post* article," says Cory. Instead, she recalls, he began to taunt her with stories of Ninoy's womanizing:

> I am in this highly nervous state. They have sent me Ninoy's things, and I have not seen him for forty-one days, and he asks, "Mrs. Aquino, have you been writing to your husband?" I said, "Yes, three times." Then he said, "You know, Filipino men are not to be trusted. There is this woman who has been writing to your husband for a long time. Would you like to see the letters? I also have letters from your husband to this woman." I cut him short, saying, "Things like this I only discuss with my husband." He must have expected a strong reaction, but I was calm. I said, "If you have nothing else to tell me, we have nothing else to talk about."

That encounter was as torturous for Cory as Ninoy's solitary confinement was for him, since she knew about his womanizing, but had kept her knowledge to herself. Being confronted with it again by his captor, at a time when she felt so abandoned and vulnerable, was a form of mental cruelty not categorized by the human rights organizations that would later intercede for her husband. However, she recognized their game. "If they could not get Ninoy, they made a concerted effort to get to me, so that I would finally tell my husband, 'I cannot take anymore of this, so please do as you are told.' " Like him, she held fast and did not crack under the pressure.

That afternoon permission was granted for both women and their families to visit Laur. "After three hours' ride, we were allowed to visit across barbed wire for one-half hour," Cory recalled. "When Ninoy saw us, he and the children started to cry. It was heartbreaking." She was the only one who did not cry; she just stood there holding baby Kris. She later realized why. "You see, by mistake, they gave me a librium of ten milligrams. The next day when it wore off, the tears kept flowing and flowing; flowing without end, it seemed."

*   *   *

Although Ninoy was returned to the less-threatening environment of Fort Bonifacio, the Aquinos' long martial law nightmare was far from over. The regime, in trying to build a case against him, put the heat on many of his former associates and domestic employees to testify against him. As Ninoy's hordes of supporters and hangers-on scattered, and social invitations stopped coming, Cory learned a painful lesson about who their friends really were. Later she would name those who had been closest to Ninoy to key posts in her government. At the same time, she developed compassion for the helpless victims of political wars, those caught in the middle.

Their servants became the first such victims. "Ninoy and I had agreed that to save them from any further suffering, they should sign whatever papers they were asked to sign," recounts Cory. Those who signed were eventually released, although one driver was beaten half-deaf and a maid, who was three months pregnant, was pressured to tell the military who had visited the house. Ros Cawigan, Ninoy's chief of security, had secretly turned government informant and had sneaked back to the house in an attempt to intimidate the remaining domestics into testifying for the prosecution. When Cory realized what was going on, she surrendered the guns he had left there and warned him, "Don't ever come to this house again!" Cory says, "In the beginning I could not tell my husband all these terrible things that were happening, because he would have gotten so depressed."

Still emotional, years later, about Cawigan's betrayal of Ninoy, she digresses briefly. "It takes me a long time to get angry and a long time to forget." Cory showed herself to be similarly unforgiving of the colonel who had broached the subject of Ninoy's love letters. On New Year's Eve in 1973, eight months later, he knocked on the door of Ninoy's detention cell. It was one of the nights when Cory had conjugal visiting privileges there. "I had told Ninoy about that conversation, and now here was this colonel bringing us a bottle of light liquor, knowing we don't drink. It was a peace offering."

Ninoy, who was quick to anger, but also quick to forget, thanked him and returned the officer's wish for a "blessed Christmas season" with one of his own for a happy New Year. Cory stared at the television and said nothing. "Mrs. Aquino, I hope you have gotten over the anger you had the last time we met," interjected the colonel. Ninoy nudged her to respond to the man, who had gone out of his way to apologize. "I hope time will make me forget," she said coldly.

On August 27, 1973, eleven months after he was detained, Ninoy was brought before Military Commission No. 2 in Fort Bonifacio and charged with violating the antisubversion law by giving guns, bulletproof vests, walkie-talkies, and money to NPA Commander Dante; conspiring with Dante to kill a local barrio captain suspected of being a police informer; and illegal possession of sixteen firearms, 4,474 rounds of ammunition, and assorted grenades and mines.

When asked how he pleaded, Ninoy launched into a scathing denunciation of his trial as "an unconscionable mockery." Over the objections of the prosecutor, he insisted that he could not expect to receive justice from a panel of military officers whose commander in chief, President Marcos, had publicly declared him guilty, following the Plaza Miranda bombing two years before, of the same charges. At that time Ninoy had dared Marcos to arrest him, in which case he would have been tried in a civil court. "But he did not," Ninoy pointed out. "He waited for his own brand of martial law and ordered the creation of military tribunals."

Declaring that, as "an act of protest," he would not participate in the tribunal's proceedings, he delivered a moving speech, one line of which would live on as his unofficial epitaph, printed on the T-shirts of thousands of mourners who marched in protest against his assassination: "I would rather die on my feet with honor than live on bended knees in shame." When he finished, the audience, which he had held in rapt silence, broke into cheers. His military guards, incapable of enforcing order, simply stopped trying. An exuberant Ninoy whispered to his lawyer, Jovy Salonga, "Prof, I can die now after that speech."

He had frustrated whatever plans Marcos may have had for his speedy trial. His defiance led to the suspension of hearings for a year and a half, while the charges against him were reinvestigated. Meanwhile, Enrile gradually expanded family visiting privileges. Eventually close relatives were permitted to see him on Wednesdays, and Cory was granted weekend rights from Saturday afternoon to Sunday morning, when the children would join them. "I cannot remember an occasion where I was alone with

Ninoy for twenty-one uninterrupted hours before his imprisonment," wrote Cory in an account of the prison years. "In his desire to be current on what was happening to each of us, Ninoy would ask me to give him a detailed report of everything that had transpired the week previous. We had no distractions, and we really opened up to each other."

She worried about Malacañang's eavesdropping during those conjugal visits, even going so far as to drape the video camera and the mirror in his room with sheets, to his considerable amusement. "Look, we're married, so what do you have to be worried about?" he asked. "I still want this to be private," she replied. Of greater interest than Ninoy and Cory's sex life to the military men who monitored the cell were their conversations. To thwart the electronic surveillance, Ninoy wrote sensitive messages and assignments out for her on an erasable "magic slate." She would commit them to memory and relay them to supporters outside, then report their responses back to him in the same manner.

Still, Marcos's men were able to pick up enough bugged conversations and purloined letters during Ninoy's confinement to intensify their paranoia about his impressive network of contacts, which reached as far afield as the Communist underground, on the one hand, and the Philippine and U.S. intelligence communities, on the other. Colonel Josephus Ramas, the army intelligence chief who was in charge of a cell-monitoring program known as "the Alpha Project," had assigned Ninoy the code name "Sierra Bravo," while Cory was "Mrs. Sierra Bravo," and Enrile was "Aquarius."

Ramas became disturbed about a possible "tie-up of Sierra Bravo with the CIA" when he read the transcript of an August 1974 visit by two Americans, whom he described as "CIA agents," to Ninoy's cell. The topic of conversation among diplomat Paul Kattenburg, Rand Corporation analyst Guy Pauker, and Ninoy was the succession to Marcos, about which Pauker was preparing a classified report. Marcos had already ruled out Enrile as "mediocre" and without a national following, they told Ninoy, according to Ramas's transcript. Marcos had considered the First Lady, but had "come to the conclusion that she cannot hold the country." On the other hand, the visitors reported, the CIA was considering Aquino, Marcos's executive secretary, Alejandro Melchor, constabulary chief General Fidel Ramos, and a nationalist, code-named "Delta." Because of his political acumen and large popular following, they told him, Aquino was "the strongest contender."

Ninoy greeted the news with excitement. "I can wait it out here." He reminded the analysts, "Karamanlis of Greece stayed in France as an exile to come back to power after ten years."

Although he was denied daily newspapers, and his family was allowed to visit him only twice a week, Ninoy learned of a military raid on a

Catholic convent "with remarkable speed," in Ramas's view. This led the colonel to suspect that Ninoy was being fed by informants within the military itself. Indeed, Ninoy explained in one bugged conversation that keeping his "net" intact was "a necessity for one who might be called upon to serve the country. . . . I have to keep abreast of what is going on beyond this cubicle."

Frequently, the transcripts show, Ninoy would refer members of his private intelligence network to Cory. "Cory will answer for all your expenses," he told his longtime political ally Bren Guiao, in a 1974 message asking Guiao to survey the mayors in their region for a status report on the NPA insurgents in central Luzon. In July 1974, Ninoy was monitored telling a colonel that an agent who had penetrated the Philippine Communist party "got in touch again with my wife" and passed along, among other tidbits, the information that Enrile was putting together dossiers on Imelda Marcos and her brothers, and that arms shipments from sympathetic Arab countries, bound for the Muslim guerrillas, were being landed on the shores of Mindanao.

By the time his trial resumed on March 31, 1975, even Ninoy had begun to admit to himself that the Filipino people were not going to rise up against Marcos. Worse, he felt responsible for loosing a plague on his loved ones. His imprisonment had brought personal hardship and anguish to his wife and children and financial ruin to his in-laws, whom the regime had forced out of the bus and banking businesses and continually threatened with confiscation of their hacienda sugar lands. When the military tribunal brushed aside his original objections to standing trial before a military court and recalled the same discredited witnesses who had previously incriminated him, he decided to unsheathe the only weapon left to him: a hunger strike.

Marcos responded with cold brilliance by ignoring him. His trial continued, and he was forcibly carried into the courtroom each morning and obliged to stay there throughout each day's proceedings. As he grew visibly weaker, no mention of his fast was allowed in the Philippine press. Only in the foreign media did news of his lonely resistance to martial law appear.

The hunger strike was a heavier burden than all the others for Cory to bear. In a letter to "Cory, my dearly beloved wife," he apologized for the "immeasurable anguish and sorrow" he had caused, but begged her to understand "there comes a time in a man's life when he must prefer a meaningful death to a meaningless life." She agonized, prayed, and consulted theologians about whether or not to support his attempt to starve himself to death. Then she did his bidding, acting as his public voice and communicating regular bulletins to the reporters who covered him. His fasting, she explained, had broadened from a protest against his own situation to a protest against martial law. It would end when Marcos began a return to normalcy.

Her stand drew criticism from some of Ninoy's supporters, who correctly reckoned that public opinion was not strong enough to force Marcos to bend. Each day, they pointed out, Ninoy's jailers delivered to his cell —and photographed—three meal trays. One angry foreign journalist and drinking buddy of the old, preprison Ninoy confronted her cruelly, "You are encouraging him to become a martyr, because that is the only way you can have him all to yourself."

One month after Ninoy's fast had begun, the palace was forced to take notice, if only to spare itself liability for his death. The military secretly transferred him from his detention quarters to Veterans Memorial Hospital. It was Cory who conveyed the news to the outside world by releasing an affidavit in which she reported that he had lost forty pounds and was dehydrated to the point that a finger touched to his flesh would leave a dent. Human rights organizations immediately rushed their observers to the Philippines. In the course of a meeting with William Butler, a representative of the International Commission of Jurists, Marcos advised him, with stunning irreverence, "Get your ass over to that hospital, that guy may be serious."

Butler recalls, "It was as if the two of them were playing a game."

Because the military doctors were not force-feeding him yet, the Aquino family began to fear that, instead of allowing Ninoy to die the meaningful death he had willed himself, the government would step in to save him—but only after damage to his brain and vital organs had become irreversible. A mass held for him drew only about a hundred people. His ordeal seemed more and more in vain to those who loved him.

On the thirty-seventh day of Ninoy's fast, a small group of family members and close friends had dinner at the home of his eldest sister, Maur, and her businessman husband, Ernesto Lichauco. Serious family matters were frequently debated over Maur's gourmet meals. Early in the evening the group took a vote on whether Ninoy should be allowed to go on. Most seemed resigned to letting him continue the hunger strike until death. Whereupon Teodoro M. Locsin, publisher of the suspended *Philippines Free Press* and one of Ninoy's closest friends in journalism, objected. "Those of us who eat three times a day plus *merienda* should have no business telling somebody not to eat until he dies." Warning that in a few more days Ninoy would become a vegetable, he registered a defiant no. The majority turned and followed.

Ninoy was forced to listen to his wife, his mother, and his confessor, who argued that by continuing his fast, he was sentencing himself to a "meaningless life." On May 13, his fortieth day without nourishment, he made a pact with the Lord: "I want to die today, but if You do not allow me to die, I'll take it You want me to continue my work. Your will be done." He did not die, so he ended his fast.

*   *   *

Two years later the unresolved fate of Ninoy Aquino and other political prisoners hung heavy on the regime. In Washington the Carter administration was paying greater lip service to human rights in the policy-making process than had its predecessors. In Manila the regime was still smarting from an Amnesty International report on torture in Philippine prisons. Reporters regularly grilled Marcos on his country's human rights record. One of his responses—that he was planning to phase out military courts in the near future—inspired Ninoy to write and seek an appointment with the president.

Marcos agreed to see Aquino for the first time since his arrest. On June 21, 1977, a presidential helicopter picked him up during his daily outdoor-exercise period and took him to Malacañang. Like Ninoy's memory of that conversation, as he related it to me in Taiwan, the military's transcript of their meeting is remarkable for the cordiality of the conversation and the like-mindedness of the two men as they talked politics and tested each other's limits. Marcos, laughing, complimented Ninoy on the slim profile he had assumed since his hunger strike. They got down to business immediately, with Ninoy asking Marcos for transferral of his case from the military court system into the civilian courts, where he would be more likely to receive a fair hearing.

As the conversation meandered onto other subjects, it was always Marcos who briskly returned it to its original point. "What did you expect, let us say, from this meeting?" he asked Aquino bluntly. "What were your minimum and your maximum expectations?" For the next half hour they kicked around possible deals like the two political horsetraders they were. Shrewdly noncommittal throughout, Marcos from time to time consulted his solicitor general or defense secretary on details. He expressed himself willing to talk with Aquino, "not as a prisoner or even an accuser, but as Ninoy Aquino, who used to be my fraternity brother." And yet every proposed solution raised another problem for him as a strongman. If he ordered Aquino's trial switched from a military to a civilian court, he noted, the Supreme Court "would probably say, 'What's happening? You've lost faith in the military tribunals.' "

Gloating over the underdog status he had achieved by virtue of his long imprisonment, Ninoy noted in passing, "I'm beginning to be the hero—I'm the Indian—and you are the Cavalry." His remark did not go unnoticed.

Stubbornly, the president protested, "You know damn well that if you had been in my place, you would have arrested you. There's no other way." Ninoy did not dispute him.

By the end of their discussion, it sounded as if Marcos and Aquino might have the makings of a bargain, whereby the murder charge would be dropped and the remaining charges transferred to civil courts. Marcos's advisors would contact Ninoy's lawyer, they agreed, to inform him of their decision. Yet like a dog with a flea, Marcos continued to scratch, searching for options that would rid him of his insolent adversary without having to continue this no-win trial.

"What would you do if I release you tomorrow?" he queried.

Ninoy was rambling and ambiguous, deferring in the end to Cory, whom he indicated was "asking maybe I should go to a university and try to polish what I have written."

If, on the other hand, the judicial process were to proceed on its present course and Ninoy were convicted, Marcos asked, "Will you be willing to ask for a pardon?"

Here Ninoy was unequivocal. "No sir, I will not ask for a pardon for the simple reason that I feel that I have not committed the charges against me."

Marcos posed another alternative, "If you are convicted, would you like to appeal to a civil court?"

Again Ninoy was firm in his response, "Yes!"

Six days later Marcos wrote to tell Aquino that his request for a civil trial was being denied because of the complexity of procedural and legal constraints. However, he offered his rival a means of appeal. He had, he said, promulgated a decree that would permit Aquino to appeal the decision of the military tribunal to the civilian Supreme Court.

The legal proceedings, so long stalled, now began to speed up. After several preliminary hearings, Ninoy was taken on the morning of November 25, 1977, to the hall inside Fort Bonifacio, where Military Commission No. 2 would hear his case. He was asked once again if he would defend himself. Continuing his strategy of waging a "holding battle," he asked the tribunal to defer the hearing until two petitions pending before the Supreme Court had been decided. This time the commissioners refused, stating their intention to rule on the pending motions of the defense. The hearing was abruptly recessed, and Ninoy, sensing that "it was all over," turned his thoughts to the closing statement that he had spent two years composing.

During the long recess which followed, Ninoy waited, full of premonitions that his case was secretly under deliberation without any presentation by his court-appointed counsel, and that he would not be given a chance to make his closing statement. "Every minute was agonizing," he recalled later in a letter to the Supreme Court, describing his last day before the tribunal. At 7 P.M. he received a message to "be ready and stand by on call." By 9:30, when no further word had arrived, he put on the charcoal-gray denim suit that he had ordered specially for his conviction and sentencing. His request to consult his lawyer remained unanswered.

At 10:10 P.M. he was finally led, in the dark, from his cottage back into the hall and told to stand before the commission. It took less than ten minutes for the presiding general to deliver convictions and death sentences to Aquino and his codefendants Bernabe Buscayno, alias NPA Commander Dante, and Victor Corpus, a former colonel who had defected to the NPA. "Death by firing squad," snapped the presiding general. With a single tap of his gavel he declared the hearings adjourned. The seven commissioners filed out.

At 11 P.M. Ninoy sat down at the desk in his security unit and addressed a letter to the Supreme Court: "Your Honors: I am writing you this letter alone in my lonely cell. I have been sentenced to die by firing squad because I refused to participate in a proceeding which I consider a conscienceless mockery of justice."

He noted that he had mistrusted military commissions ever since he had learned that his own grandfather, General Servillano Aquino, had been convicted by an American military tribunal and sentenced to death by musketry for alleged war crimes during the Phil-American war. He reminded the justices that Philippine national hero Jose Rizal had been sentenced by a previous one set up by the Spanish. It was his burden now to be sentenced to die by a military commission made up of his own countrymen.

"Why the indecent and immoral rush to judgment?" he asked, appealing to the Supreme Court to "assert the independence of the judiciary if our Republic is to be saved." Still believing that he was in some way expressing the will of a silent Filipino majority, he concluded: "If I have obstinately refused to yield to the tyranny of Mr. Marcos all these long years, it is because I have not lost hope that sooner than later the Filipino's love for freedom will ultimately assert itself above the demands of temporary security and convenience."

National and international reaction to news of his death sentence finally began to bear him out. Newspaper editorials and human rights organizations registered protests. Many wondered aloud why the pragmatic president, who surely knew that he could never win by executing Ninoy, had allowed the trial to proceed to such an unseemly end, under cover of darkness. Four days later, the pressure of public opinion forced Marcos to intervene. Reacting, he said, to Aquino's letter to the Supreme Court justices, Marcos ordered the trial reopened.

On December 5, Aquino was granted the opportunity that had been denied him the previous week to make a closing statement in his defense. This time the room was full of friends, supporters, and journalists, some of them wearing "Ninoy Is My Hero" T-shirts. Two observers from the International Commission of Jurists were present. Those who watched Ninoy taking advantage of his first real public forum since his arrest felt they were witnessing a performance that was at once the best of the old and the new politics. His Machiavellian analysis of Marcos's motives in allowing his charade of a trial to continue was that of the veteran opposition politician. Yet his references to Gandhi and his belated, public acknowledgment of the role played by his wife, whom he had so deliberately relegated to the sidelines in the past, foreshadowed the emergence of a new politics of conscience, born out of his experience in prison and his country's experience under martial rule.

"Where lies my duty?" he asked. In response he articulated a still-evolving ideology of Christian Democratic Socialism and a strategy of nonviolent activism that would one day launch a revolution:

What can a helpless detainee do to fight an entrenched tyranny? In my search for the right option, I came across the teachings of Gandhi . . . who dramatically first employed the strategy of fasting and nonviolent resistance. My duty, as I see it, is to tell our people that we must not only dream of a good and just society. We must resolve to make this dream come true. We must encourage the young to rise above a society that has been apathetic and indifferent and where justice has long been ignored.

He had tried to set an example, he said. "I pray that the seeds of thought that germinated in me—which I tried to nurture in my several statements—will eventually find fertile soil and bear fruit in the hearts and minds of my beloved countrymen."

His closing words were to and about Cory. Although neither could know it at the time, they would bind her to the task of creating a climate for the growth of such seeds after he was gone:

Hopefully, with the end of these proceedings, the woman who is the hope and light of my life's dark night will be delivered from her anxiety and anguish. She has stood by me with an unshakable faith, unruffled and undeterred by the endless humiliations, the abandonment of friends and the heavy burdens of having to be a teacher, father, mother and provider of my children. She has been the healing oasis in the desert of my prison.

The martial-law years had served as a test of the strength of Ninoy and Cory Aquino. Those years were not yet over, but at the moment when his death sentence was pronounced and all seemed lost, both of them realized that they had won. "You are really strongest when you are weakest," Cory would muse aloud to me in 1985, as she stood on the threshold of her own political career. "Ninoy was strongest when he was in Fort Bonifacio."

*　　　*　　　*

In April 1978 Ninoy chose to test that strength by running for a seat in the new interim National Assembly that Marcos had, under pressure from Washington, decided to constitute. The time seemed ripe. Ninoy's death sentence had added to his moral stature at home and abroad, at the same time that it had raised serious questions about the direction in which Marcos's "New Society" was headed. Five years of martial law had brought neither economic recovery nor political stability. Corruption was rampant, and a civil war between Christians and Muslims was raging in the southernmost islands. Filipinos were finally beginning to question the price they were paying for the surrender of their political freedom.

At the same time, the Carter administration was pressuring Marcos to make good on past promises to move toward political normalization. At issue was not only the Carter administration's commitment to human rights in the making of its foreign policy, but, more important, the Pentagon's wariness of negotiating a five-year renewal of the military bases agreement on the word of one man alone—Marcos. The election of a legislature would satisfy a variety of needs.

Ninoy's subsequent entry into the race at the head of a new party known as *Lakas ng Bayan* (People's Power), which was formed to put up a token fight against Mrs. Marcos's handpicked slate of candidates in Metro-Manila, sparked controversy within the opposition. Welcomed by the president, because it legitimized the exercise, Ninoy's candidacy was criticized as divisive by some of his own Liberal party colleagues, who had previously announced an election boycott.

Although Ninoy was free to run, he was not free to campaign. Using the same argument that the regime would make against Aquino's return from exile in 1983, Enrile maintained that the government's decision not to release him from prison was for his own protection. Should his enemies try to kill him, said Enrile, "the government would be blamed for his assassination." Accordingly, the campaign logo of Lakas ng Bayan, Laban (Fight) for short, was a pair of chained fists. Ninoy's surrogate campaigners were Cory and seven-year-old Kris, whose slogan "Help My Daddy Come Home" was so effective that the military, in a perverse attempt to counter it, distributed anonymous handbills depicting a child whose father could never come home, because he had been killed by Ninoy.

Unseen inside his cell, Ninoy did not go unheard. So powerful was his impact on voters, palace polls showed, that he looked as though he might win a seat. "An effort was therefore mounted to help divert public attention," reveals a military intelligence officer, whose agency was called on to provide the necessary documentation. In early March, Defense Minister Enrile appeared as a guest on the weekly "Face the Nation" and let fly charges that were said to come from dossiers that had been declassified two years earlier, allegedly showing that Ninoy continued to be a national security risk, due to his connections with both the Communist New People's Army and the U.S. Central Intelligence Agency.

The broadcast caused a sensation. While the NPA charges were the same old ones that had been used against him since the Plaza Miranda bombings, the accusation that he worked for the CIA was new to the public, if not to the monitors of "Project Alpha." Ninoy demanded equal time, and one week later, on March 10, the streets of Manila were practically deserted for the duration of his ninety-minute television appearance on the same show. The people were not disappointed. The Ninoy they saw on their screens was the same fast-talking, nimble-witted politician they had last seen accusing the regime of plotting martial law the day before his arrest. By the time the broadcast was over, he had turned some of Enrile's contentions to his own advantage and made a mockery of others.

"Am I a CIA agent?" asked Ninoy rhetorically. "Most emphatically, I deny that." Yet, sensitive to the importance attributed by Filipino voters to politicians who appeared to enjoy the approval of Washington, Aquino added some qualifiers. Enrile had said he worked "for" the CIA. In fact, he stated, "I worked with the CIA on three occasions," which he described straightforwardly as missions undertaken with the full knowledge of both the Phillippine and U.S. governments.

The public loved it. People would still be quoting Ninoy's pungent replies to the charges made against him years later. His final statement was a fervent defense of his innocence of the subversion and murder charges that had drawn him the death penalty. "I am not a Communist, I have never been a Communist, I have never even been a member of a front organization," he said.

Precisely at 7 P.M. on the eve of the election, April 6, 1978, opposition supporters created a din the likes of which Metro-Manila had never heard. Through word of mouth, citizens had been instructed to honk horns, clatter pots and pans, blow whistles, and bang doors to show their opposition to Marcos. The volume of the pro-Aquino "noise barrage"—an anonymous and distinctly Filipino form of protest—led opposition supporters to expect victory on election day. But when the counting had been completed, all twenty-one of Imelda's candidates in Metro-Manila—including one person who was a total unknown—had won, while the entire

Laban ticket had gone down to defeat. Outrage over the known examples of fraud on the part of the ruling party was intense, inside the Philippines and abroad.

More than any other confrontation with the regime, the outcome of the 1978 Assembly race in Manila caused oppositionists to despair of continuing on a moderate, nonviolent course to reform. In growing numbers they moved further left, many of them joining or lending support to groups advocating violence.

Ninoy would remain in jail for two more years, during which time he would try to foster reconciliation between Marcos and the moderate opposition in order to prevent the erosion of the political center. Increasingly, however, such efforts would be regarded by his peers, and eventually by himself, as reactionary and irrelevant.

*　　　*　　　*

"Before the 1978 election, I could not even say the word *exile*," says Cory, "but after his defeat, when it was so clear he had won, we agreed it was time to leave the country." Accordingly, the idea was indirectly broached to Marcos. With surprising accord, representatives of the opposition and the palace moved to break the stalemate that had blocked Aquino's release for so long. They worked together to draft an amendment to the existing amnesty provisions, which promised to eliminate the necessity for him to plead guilty to the charges against him before receiving a pardon.

"On June 8," Cory relates, "I was called to Fort Bonifacio to meet Johnny Ponce Enrile, who was representing the government, and Senator Tañada, who was representing Ninoy. It was such a high feeling. I thought things would finally really happen then." Enrile told her to plan on departing for the U.S. by the end of the month.

She was never sure what happened, she says, but the process suddenly stalled. My examination of private correspondence between parties in both camps indicates that in the two-year period between the first promising talks on his release and his actual departure for the U.S., both Marcos and Aquino and their respective representatives had stubbornly played politics with the issue, neither side willing to lose face. Further complicating the situation was the fact that the military base negotiations between the U.S. and the Philippine government were still under way in 1978, and Ninoy had become a pawn on that larger chessboard.

After five months of silence in the wake of the administration's first promising effort to approve the new amnesty clause, Tañada wrote Marcos to ask, "What is to happen to Senator Aquino?"

The handwritten reply he received reflected presidential pique over "the story being spread by interested parties that the release of Sen. Aquino is part of a deal with the Americans, or that the American government is demanding his release or else." He would not, Marcos wrote, allow himself to look as though he was being "coerced into the exercise of presidential discretion."

In fact, no further discussion of Aquino's release took place until after the bases agreement had been signed in January 1979 and Marcos was free to act on his own without leaving the impression that his superpower ally dictated Philippine policy. By then, however, the opposition had already begun organizing its own campaign to win Ninoy's release by mounting a petition drive in his behalf.

After conferring with Marcos, Doy Laurel conveyed a new offer from the president. If Ninoy would agree to defer the petition drive and would pledge "no publicity during negotiations, until full implementation of the agreement," Marcos would grant Ninoy's request for "indefinite exile" and amnesty under the no-guilt clause. On March 8, Ninoy agreed to all Marcos's points, and even added two more: "Will not attack RP government, will not attack government officials." Laurel returned Ninoy's initialed list to Marcos. Once again, however, the process simply hit a roadblock. Before Laurel heard anything more from Marcos, the anti-Marcos forces, playing to the human rights lobby in Washington, went ahead with their petition drive to gather 1 million signatures in favor of Aquino's release.

On June 30, 1979, businessman Antonio ("Tony") Gonzalez received a confidential message from his friend Ninoy, updating him on opposition strategy. Recent gains by the NPA had alarmed the moderate opposition leaders, he said, and they had decided to use Ninoy as "a rallying point for moderates in the event of a showdown with REDS." Accordingly, he reported, "all anti-Marcos opposition groups—radicals excluded" had met recently to form a united coalition to "prevent a Sandinista type of anti-Marcos campaign from developing." Ninoy concluded, "For the present, 'tis consensus I should remain in jail to preempt REDS from martyrdom role [and continue to act as] point man for united opposition and symbol of continuing anti-Marcos effort."

"Does he want release or to fight the government?" snapped Marcos when pressed by reporters about Ninoy's continued detention at that time. Nonetheless, foreign governments and even the Pope continued to bring pressure on Marcos to release Aquino. On January 7, 1980, Aquino wrote his friend Enrique Zobel that "Cardinal Sin informed me that Pope John Paul II made it a condition for his visit that he be allowed to visit me in jail, as a symbolic affirmation of his commitment to human rights—and Malacañang was forced to accept the condition. To get out of the pickle I would either be 'exiled' or be allowed to extend my pass until after the papal visit." The papal visit would not take place until February 1981. Meanwhile, an act of God intervened.

On the morning of May 6, 1980, Ninoy was escorted under heavy guard to the Philippine Heart Center for Asia for tests. He had suffered recurrent pains in his chest and shortness of breath over the past several weeks. Army doctors feared he might have suffered a mild heart attack while working out. Not wishing to be responsible, should the state's most notorious prisoner die on their watch, they had arranged for a more sophisticated diagnosis to be made elsewhere. When his mother was notified that Ninoy had been taken to the Heart Center, she dropped to her knees in a prayer of thanksgiving.

"I had always been praying for a situation in which Marcos could release Ninoy from prison without a loss of face for either of them," she explained. When she thanked the Lord for his deliverance, she said, "I thought You would give him something more glorious than a heart attack. I thought You would make him a good leader, purging him of his ambitions. Why a heart attack?" But she already knew the answer. "That was the key to his freedom."

Among the first visitors to Ninoy's bedside was Assistant Minister of National Defense Carmelo ("Mike") Barbero, a longtime friend and godfather to one of his children, who had served as a liaison between the president and his prisoner since the start of martial law. Ninoy expressed to Barbero a desire to undergo the coronary bypass surgery his doctors were recommending in the U.S., and Barbero communicated it to the palace that night.

Although Marcos was reluctant to let Aquino leave the country, Imelda was quick to see the advantage of the proposal. "If he is operated on here and he dies, everyone will think there was monkey business," she remarked. On the other hand, if he were flown to the U.S., the Marcoses could wash their hands of the troublesome prisoner. She won the argument, as she often did. She then swung into action to facilitate the speedy granting of Philippine passports and American visas for Aquino and his family, and the concurrence of the Supreme Court, before which his 1977 petition for habeas corpus was still pending.

Imelda being Imelda, she extracted two "covenants" from Ninoy in return for her help. He later summarized the conditions to reporters: "That I would return to my cell after my surgery and recovery; that I would not comment on partisan Philippine politics while abroad." Both were promises made to be broken. During a two-hour visit which she paid to the hospital room of her former escort and critic, the two talked politics and gossiped as if there had never been any animosity between them. Before Aquino left for the airport, he made the emotional gesture of removing from around his neck a gold crucifix, given to him by Enrique Zobel, which he had worn throughout his seven years and seven months in prison as an *anting-anting* (protective amulet), and handing it to Imelda as a gift for the president. In confiding it to the First Lady, he said he was taking back his earlier criticisms of her and her extravagant projects, including the heart hospital in which he lay.

His family was appalled by Ninoy's generosity. "I myself did not like it," admits Doña Aurora. "I thought it was a surrender." After he died, however, she found consolation in her son's act. "The spontaneity of it indicated that there was no bitterness in his heart," she says, renewed in her belief that Ninoy's years in prison had in fact purified him.

Imelda's personal role in arranging for Ninoy's release had left his friend Doy Laurel full of foreboding. "When Imelda interceded to win Ninoy's release from prison, as far as she was concerned, she had saved his life, so he owed her his life," says Laurel. When she met Ninoy in New York in May 1983, he reasons, "she was trying to collect that debt." Imelda had translated Ninoy's refusal to agree to postpone his return to the Philippines as "a breach of promise." Once the military tribunal had reaffirmed Aquino's 1977 death sentence, Laurel believes that Imelda, in her own twisted mind, could justify his murder "as but the execution of a legal death sentence."

*   *   *

While Ninoy was recovering in Houston, influential friends were working to secure him a prestigious fellowship. Rand Corporation analyst Guy Pauker called Harvard political science professor Samuel Huntington, who was then administrative director of Harvard's Center for International Affairs, to pitch his good friend. Huntington, who retained close contacts with both the State Department and CIA, checked Aquino out and agreed "he was just the kind of fellow we wanted." He was enrolled as one of some twenty fellows at the center, paying the $7,500 annual tuition himself.

"I had the sense that he spent a good half of the day on the telephone," says Huntington, about Ninoy's two years at the center. Indeed, once he got to the U.S., his political commitments as the de facto leader of the Philippine opposition monopolized his attention, making it difficult for him to lead the settled life which Cory had envisioned.

Tony Gonzalez visited him in San Francisco, where he was recuperating from his surgery, and found half a dozen of his fellow opposition leaders already dividing the spoils that would be theirs once they defeated Marcos. Their attitude provoked Ninoy, who had changed his philosophy as well as his life-style during nearly eight years in prison. "He told them," says Gonzalez, who is now Cory's minister of tourism, " 'If we are going to go to all this effort simply to change the actors, only to continue operating in the same way Marcos did, I will be the first one to put you guys up against the wall and pull the trigger.' "

Ninoy's San Francisco visitors were not all traditional politicians.

Anti-Marcos groups that advocated violence also sought to link themselves with the most prominent opposition leader. Heherson ("Sonny") Alvarez, who was principal lobbyist for the democratic opposition in the U.S. at the time and is now a senator, explains, "He was the political cement that held the broad movement together."

Among the violent groups with which Ninoy was in contact at the time was a band of middle- and upper-class, anti-Communist, anti-Marcos Filipinos who called themselves "Social Democrats." They were training commando groups in Arizona and Baja, California, to carry out a series of bombings in Manila. "There were twelve two-man teams of people engaged in the bombings, at a cost of twenty-five thousand dollars per team," says Ernesto ("Ernie") Maceda, Ninoy's lawyer, who is now a senator. "They funded and trained themselves, but they asked his permission [to begin implementing their plan], and he reluctantly gave it."

As a preview of what was to come, Ninoy unveiled a new strategy of violence, which anti-Marcos activists were prepared to pursue. In a speech he delivered before the Asia Society in New York on August 4, 1980, he broke his agreement with Mrs. Marcos not to speak out against the Marcos government. "A pact with the devil is no pact at all," he began.

Stressing his own long years in solitary confinement as evidence of his commitment to nonviolence, he stated, nonetheless, that alternatives to the violence which many of his fellow oppositionists now advocated were fast running out. All opposition leaders, he said, were now unanimous in their demand that Marcos step down and dismantle his martial law regime. He then revealed that "a massive urban guerrilla warfare is being built up by young patriots to bring the Marcos regime to its knees. I am convinced they mean what they say and will do what they promise. This is no idle talk." Should Marcos fail to heed the message of the broad opposition, he warned, "the only alternative will be to remove him by force along the Iranian or Nicaraguan model."

It was in that speech that Ninoy coined the question that would become his other epitaph three years later. "Is the Filipino worth dying for?" he asked. Having weighed his people's virtues against such faults as their long silence under authoritarian rule, he was able to answer in the affirmative. "I have come to the conclusion he is worth dying for, because he is the nation's greatest resource."

Aquino's speech set off alarm signals in Manila and Washington. An election campaign was under way in the U.S., and Jimmy Carter was not helped by the apparent advocacy of violence by a recipient of his administration's support for human rights. Assistant Secretary of State Richard Holbrooke warned that the administration would not tolerate any attempt to destabilize an allied government through force. Several days later Aquino flew to Germany, where Cardinal Sin was traveling, to assure the prelate that he did not advocate the use of terror against Marcos, and to solicit his support for a nonviolent opposition effort to pressure Marcos to lift martial law.

When, however, bombs began exploding with frightening regularity in Manila, beginning on August 22, Aquino was inevitably suspect. The fact that the Social Democratic group that claimed credit for the blasts called itself the "April 6 Liberation Movement" (after the date of the pro-Aquino noise barrage in 1978) only confirmed Ninoy's involvement, as far as Marcos was concerned. The violence reached a bloody climax on October 19, when a powerful bomb exploded fifty feet away from President Marcos's seat on the podium at a convention of the American Society of Travel Agents (ASTA), which he was hosting in Manila. The April 6 Movement had previously warned the travel agents to boycott the convention. Eighteen delegates were wounded.

In correspondence to a friend in Manila, Ninoy praised the April 6 Movement for "pulling off its biggest coup at the ASTA convention." Wrote Ninoy, "That ASTA triumph is one in a thousand, and the leaders should start thinking of new scenarios." Those close to him insist that his interest was not to encourage more violence, but to exploit the paranoid situation which the bombings had created in Manila to force Marcos to negotiate a peaceful end to martial law and to call a presidential election.

"He saw the logic of the terrorist groups as being able to create an atmosphere of terror in the Philippines, as they had all over the world," says Teodoro ("Teddy") Benigno, a journalist and longtime friend of Ninoy, who would later become President Aquino's press secretary. "He probably went along, because he wanted to find out if the authors of that program were right in their tactical objectives, which were to scare off foreign investors, especially multinationals, and consequently erode U.S. government support for Marcos."

Whatever he might have concluded in October, when the ASTA bombing occurred, the international context changed in November, when Ronald Reagan was elected president. Imelda was among those who stressed this point to Ninoy, when she met with him at the Waldorf Astoria on December 16, 1980. She showed him videos of her meeting with ex-President Nixon, and she bragged about Marcos's close relationship with Ronald Reagan. She warned Ninoy against continuing the campaign of violence. "You must act differently, because this is a different government, and you could be picked up," she said.

Shortly after Reagan's inauguration, Ninoy witnessed the Marcos influence at work. "The FBI put the heat on him, and a lot of people were put in jail," says Tony Gonzalez. "Marcos really told the U.S. that he would not look very kindly on the whole relationship if these terrorists continued to find support in the U.S." By then, however, the violence had halted. Ninoy had dispatched Maceda, who had once belonged to the Marcos cabinet, to Manila to meet with the president in order to judge whether the violent action had made him any more amenable to a moderate course of action.

When Marcos announced the lifting of martial law on January 15, 1981, Maceda's analysis was that he did so, not to pacify the bombers, most of whom had by now been arrested, but to curry favor with the new Reagan administration, his international lenders, and Pope John Paul II, who was scheduled to visit the Philippines in February. It was a largely cosmetic action, in which Marcos lost almost none of his power, but one that was bound to ease Manila's strained relations with Washington.

Ninoy could see the handwriting on the wall. A more conservative, pro-Marcos administration in Washington would turn further violence on the part of anti-Marcos groups to its advantage, by increasing military and economic support to the Marcos regime to protect both Marcos and U.S. bases from a perceived Communist threat. For the present, violence was not a viable strategy. Yet he had given up any hope of bringing about fundamental change through the ballot. He could also see how vulnerable the democratic center would be once Marcos was dead, hit from the left side by armed Communists and from the right by General Ver.

"The one thing Ninoy did not have," says Teddy Benigno, "was the capability to link up with an armed contingent." The two other groups that would be competing for power after Marcos were heavily armed. Believing that as the leader of the moderates he must try to provide them a similar capability, Ninoy made two trips to Saudi Arabia in 1981, hoping to raise money for that purpose. Accompanied by Maceda, Ninoy met with Filipino Muslim guerrilla leader Nur Misuari, who lived in exile in Saudi Arabia, and with King Khaled.

The king, who enjoyed favorable relations with the Marcos government, could not help Aquino directly. He did, however, put him in touch with a crony, who agreed to allocate the Filipino opposition leader a 100,000-barrel oil quota, which could net his cause the $5 million per year needed to train and maintain an army. Back in the U.S. Ninoy's American contacts had, according to Maceda, found him a buyer, and a deal was in the process of being negotiated when the oil price plummeted. "The rug was literally pulled out from under us," says Maceda. When the deal fell through, the opposition was forced to abandon the idea of fighting its opponents with arms.

Immediately after his return from Saudi Arabia, in July 1981, Ninoy accepted an invitation from Nicaraguan President Daniel Ortega to be his guest at the second anniversary celebration of the Sandinista revolution. Again, Maceda accompanied him. He was treated like a head of state and given the opportunity to meet with top government officials, including the

Cuban ambassador, who offered to help him "in kind." There, obviously, lay one solution to the Philippine opposition's funding problems. However, Ninoy never even considered it. "Very sad, friend," he said to Maceda later. "After the revolution, the Russians are now the new lords of these people. If we'll be asked to choose between the Americans or the Russians, we'll go for the Americans."

As a witness to the political odyssey which her husband made in the course of his exile, Cory is very clear as to the final course he was charting. "At first Ninoy was of the opinion and the belief that no way could anyone defeat Marcos through the electoral process, and so he had to look into other alternatives," she says. "It was only after the Nicaraguan visit that he realized that violence was not the answer either. That's when he realized that the killers of today become the leaders of tomorrow."

If, in the course of his visits to Saudi Arabia and Nicaragua, Ninoy had eliminated violent revolution as an option for the non-Communist opposition, he lacked an attractive alternate strategy. Nearly a decade after the imposition of martial law, Ninoy was forced to admit that the democratic opposition, for which he had sacrificed so much, had registered almost no impact whatsoever on the situation in his country.

The armed groups were growing. Marcos had just won another six-year term, running virtually unopposed in an election that was boycotted by the democratic opposition on grounds that the president had refused to make true reforms. The U.S. continued to support him anyway. In fact, Vice-President George Bush, who had represented the U.S. at his recent inauguration, had dismayed moderates in both countries by publicly congratulating Marcos for "your adherence to democratic principles and to the democratic process." How, short of waging a violent revolution against the regime, Ninoy wondered, could freedom be restored to the Philippines?

That question obsessed Ninoy during his years at Harvard and Massachusetts Institute of Technology. Somehow, something had to be done to make the moderate alternative meaningful and relevant. The research conducted while at those institutions, as well as his travels to the Middle East and Central America, gave him a clearer notion of the parallels between the situation in the Philippines and those in other countries that had recently overthrown dictators. However, none provided the model he was looking for. More and more he looked inward for answers.

*　　　*　　　*

"The people on the left wanted to undo Marcos with violence," explains Sonny Alvarez. "Ninoy was above that. He sought to strip Marcos of his evil in order to analyze him and how he held on to power." After years of direct clashes and more years of observation, Ninoy had drawn the conclusions on which he would act. In his eyes, says Alvarez, "Marcos was no ordinary dictator. He did not ride in on a horse in front of an army. Rather, he grew out of the experience of our society, out of the rule of law and American-sponsored democracy, with all of its subtleties and intrigues and executive orders."

That being the case, Ninoy reasoned, Marcos's martial law had not been a simple, straightforward seizure of power or a coup, but an extension of the law. When he returned to Manila, says Alvarez, Ninoy's intention was "to use Marcos's own weapons of persuasion, logic, law, and elections to unravel the constitutional authoritarianism that Marcos had woven."

Once he had adopted a political strategy, Ninoy was finally able to reject the violent alternative that some of his allies still favored. In December 1982 a female courier for the New People's Army, who was from Ninoy's province, visited him in Boston and implicitly offered him Communist party support in a move against Marcos if he wished to return to Manila in 1985. By that time, she confided, the party's armed wing expected to reach the critical stage of "strategic stalemate" against the government. "The visit had the opposite effect on him," says Maceda. "It convinced Ninoy that the insurgency had become so bad that he must go home sooner."

On February 3, 1983, former Philippine Vice-President Emmanuel Pelaez, who was then serving as Marcos's minister of State for foreign affairs, encountered Aquino in Washington, D.C., at the annual congressional prayer breakfast. During the meeting Ninoy told the group that he was "going home and placing his entire faith in the hands of God." Said Pelaez, "He was in a period of transition from the old self to the new, from the combative man who lived the struggle to a man whose other side was taking over."

During the months that he debated with his family and friends whether and, then, when to return, he often invoked the example of Gandhi, the inspirational leader of Asia's other democracy, India. His favorite poker partner in Boston, Dr. Stephen Agular, recalls, "One day in the spring after he had seen the film *Gandhi*, he told me, 'Brod, that's it. Gandhi.'" He had studied the Indian leader's philosophy of nonviolence while in prison. In Boston he began trying to emulate his teachings. By the month of March, says Agular, "Everything he had studied, the long years of waiting, the maturation process at Harvard—all had contributed to his decision to go home. No one could dissuade him."

His appearance on June 23 before the Solarz committee "made his decision final," says Maceda. "Until then it had been a private decision, but when he publicly announced that he was going home, that was the point of no return."

The night before he left Boston, Ninoy typed his Manila airport arrival statement on the old Royal office manual in Steve Agular's study. "He used two fingers and he typed very fast, something he had learned as a reporter," says Agular, who is now chairman of the Ninoy Aquino Movement in the Boston area. When it was finished, the guests at his farewell party gathered around to hear him read it. The paragraph they remember best was one in the middle:

> According to Gandhi, the willing sacrifice of the innocent is the most powerful answer to insolent tyranny that has yet been conceived by God and man.

*   *   *

Ninoy asked Sonny Alvarez to inform the U.S. State Department of his date of departure. Alvarez knew no one at State, but he called on the head of the Philippine desk. "I told him Ninoy had left. He said, 'We know.' " Alvarez stresses, "They were tracking his movements."

So were Marcos's henchmen. Ninoy and his party were well protected on arrival in Singapore at two o'clock in the morning of August 16, where they were met by Prince Yem, son of the sultan of the Malaysian state of Johore, and his bodyguards. As a homesick student prince in Boston, Yem had become almost a part of the Aquino household. In his company Ninoy could cross the border from Singapore into Malaysia without an identity check. From Johore he could travel to the Malaysian capital of Kuala Lumpur, to meet secretly with Malaysian government officials and Filipino Muslim leaders.

Back in Singapore, however, Ninoy's brother-in-law Len Oreta spotted a former Aquino ally, turned enemy, whom he believed was tailing him. Chit Pineda had defected after martial law to the other side of the feuding Cojuangco family, the camp of Marcos's most influential crony, Danding Cojuangco.

On departure from Singapore, Ninoy's passport attracted the attention of immigration officials, who disappeared with it for several minutes, before stamping it and returning it to him. The Philippine Foreign Ministry later confirmed that it had received notice of Aquino's passage through Singapore from that country's internal security agency.

During a brief stopover in Hong Kong on August 19, Ninoy and his companions remained inside the drab transit lounge of Kai Tak Airport. Outside on the tarmac sat a private aircraft, which had been flown to Hong Kong by Danding Cojuangco's personal pilot. Among the passengers was Lieutenant Colonel Thompson Lantion, an officer of the Presidential Security Command, who was close to General Ver, and who would have been able to spot Ninoy from a distance, having been one of his security guards at Fort Bonifacio during martial law, and having served as military attaché at the Philippine Consulate in Los Angeles during the years of his exile. Ninoy boarded his flight from Hong Kong to Taipei, unaware that he was still being followed.

On August 20, at military headquarters in Manila the Daily Intelligence Operations Report (DIOR) carried a brief reference to the anticipated arrival the following day of former Senator Benigno Aquino, Jr., aboard China Airlines Flight 811. All copies of that document subsequently disappeared from the files of the Armed Forces of the Philippines (AFP). A key pillar of the regime's defense would be that the AFP command did not know which plane Aquino was on.

From Taipei that same day Ninoy, using code names, dictated to his sister Tessie in Manila a final message for Doy Laurel:

Dear Padre:

If all goes well, I should be in Manila on schedule. Tis important that you and Senator Tañada be inside the arrival area by noon so you can witness any government counter-moves. What is the latest bulletin on FM? Have you discussed my arrival with Imelda? Will she allow me to go under House Arrest? Please try to contact me not later than Saturday night. Tis important that I get the most accurate news bulletin before I enplane. My last contact should be 9 A.M. Sunday. After that my trip will be irreversible. Good luck . . .

Aguilar

$$6$$

The Cover–Up

"It's gonna pop like a cork." The logic that the assassination of Ninoy Aquino would precipitate an immediate political explosion in the Philippines had seemed inescapable to me a moment ago. But, as I was reminded on entering the Manila International Airport terminal, Western logic did not apply here. The scene inside the airy, glass-and-concrete building was surreal. Strains of music wafted over the sound system. Immigration officials joked with one another as they stamped passports. Baggage chutes coughed luggage onto carousels. Bribable customs inspectors looked for opportunity in the suitcases of passengers. It was as if none of these people knew, or cared, that two murders had just occurred in a blaze of gunfire outside Gate 8.

The brazen nature of the act—the virtual public execution of a man who had voluntarily delivered himself into the hands of the regime—revealed an arrogance of power that was as frightening as the crime itself. Whatever the affiliation of the assassin's squad, it was confident enough of official protection that it did its dirty business in front of scores of potential witnesses. My eyes, my ears, and my journalistic instincts told me that the Philippine military forces that had surrounded our plane, ostensibly to protect Ninoy, had engaged in a carefully choreographed plot to kill him instead.

By allowing himself to believe that the Marcos government might yet be susceptible to reform, Ninoy had walked into a trap. We had accompanied him there, without so much as a contingency plan to counter the assassination threats we had so blithely discussed but implicitly dismissed. What fools we were. How puny the forces of nonviolence looked in the face of the SWAT team, which had monopolized the action outside, and the indifferent bureaucracy, which was already at work on a cover-up inside this and dozens of other institutions. I was outraged at my own naiveté and embarrassed for Ninoy.

None among us had fallen for the charade, in which the unidentified man in blue was made to look like the assassin by soldiers who repeatedly fired at him after he was clearly dead. It made no sense. It looked phony. We were, nonetheless, bewildered by the sequence of events that had led to his death during the seconds when the security men in white shirts were barring our view through the door. My tape recorder, which I had neglected to turn off after the shooting stopped, captured a series of dazed remarks and disjointed questions by me and several others, as we filed off the plane, puzzling over where the alleged assassin came from. Suddenly, one voice on the tape, that of a male passenger, whom neither I nor the investigators who subpoenaed the cassette have been able to identify, told of seeing the man in blue while he was still on his feet.

"When I saw him, he was dancing backwards with the assassin and firing a forty-five," this passenger said. On hearing shots, he continued, "I ran to another window, and there was a security guard with a little burp gun—you know those short barrels—and he was firing. I saw shots coming from him . . . and I jumped back to my other window, and there was the guy I had seen firing the forty-five, dead." The stunning implication of this observation was that the man in blue had mistakenly believed his role was to kill Aquino's assassin, but before he could do so, he himself had been gunned down. The true assassin had then escaped, while soldiers had riddled the body of the man in blue with bullets, gangland style, and left it behind to serve as the scapegoat for a murder.

Important as such an observation was, it met with no reaction from any of us at the time. On my tape it was but one isolated remark bobbing in a sea of confusion. It was followed by a series of open questions about the uniforms worn by the various groups that participated in the plot. Which branch of the military did the SWAT commandos, dressed in the blue jumpsuits, represent? None of us knew. What had happened to the khaki-uniformed escorts? It was clear that they had not stuck around to protect Ninoy once the shooting began. "Who were the people in white?"

I kept asking, referring to the men who had prevented us from following Ninoy down the metal service stairs. No answers were forthcoming.

Before we had time to begin putting the pieces of the puzzle together, we were besieged by a group of local reporters who had made their way into the arrivals area after hearing rumors of a shooting. "What happened?" they cried, shoving microphones in our faces. "Was he able to get out of the plane?" The sudden responsibility of being the ones to tell them he was dead seemed too great.

"Why don't you just hold off?" suggested ABC-TV correspondent Jim Laurie.

"Yeah, I think we'd better wait and see what's happened," I said.

Yet, as journalists ourselves, we were not comfortable withholding information. Besides, it dawned on me, as we approached the immigration counters, that we were surrounded by authorities who could hold us here or confiscate our films and tapes. Better to spread the news as widely and quickly as we could before someone shut us up.

"I'm sure he's dead," I said.

"What's your name?" asked one of the reporters as the others ran for the telephones.

"I don't think this is the place to talk," I could hear myself saying, as I looked around an arrivals area swarming with white-shirted officials. "We've just seen two assassinations outside our window."

It was Laurie who waved them off. "I think I'd like to talk to my colleagues before I . . ."

With that, the ABC crew members surreptitiously ducked behind a pillar to make quick copies of the last video footage they had shot during the struggle with the security guards. They had no way of knowing what their lens had seen. "They were trying to keep us out, and we were fighting to get through, to at least get a camera up to the window to shoot," said the cameraman. "And we just held it up in the air and opened it wide."

Burying the unmarked video copies deep inside their hand luggage, Laurie confided, "I'm very worried about our tapes. The Filipinos are going to go absolutely berserk. They are going to confiscate everything under the sun."

To our relief, they did not.

❊   ❊   ❊

Filipino journalists and witnesses were not as fortunate as we that afternoon in the airport. The success of Marcos's peculiarly Filipino form of martial law was largely dependent on self-imposed silence by citizens and self-censorship by Filipino journalists. Fear and special privileges were the incentives that made the regime's control over the dissemination of information possible.

Accordingly, Filipino photographers and TV cameramen were given privileged access to Gate 8 just before the plane carrying Aquino taxied up to it. In return, they were asked to turn over their negatives to the government Office of Media Affairs several hours after the assassination. Meanwhile, in order to instill fear in any potentially dangerous Filipino eyewitnesses among the passengers on Aquino's plane, an obvious one was singled out as she stepped into the terminal. In front of many others, she was served a blunt warning about the consequences of talking to reporters. As Filipinos would say, she was "made a sample."

She was Rebecca ("Bec") Quijano, a comely thirty-one-year-old, who was known to the public only as the Crying Lady until she took the witness stand in the 1985 trial of General Ver and the twenty-five others accused of conspiring to kill Aquino. She had gone to Taipei on August 19 with a woman friend, named Arellina Santos, for a few days of family business and pleasure. Ten minutes before landing back in Manila on the afternoon of August 21, 1983, she had learned from a Japanese reporter that the celebrity on board Flight 811 was Senator Aquino. She was excited by the presence of the opposition leader, who had once been a houseguest of her late father, a local leader in Aquino's Liberal party before martial law. As soon as the plane landed, she crossed over to the other side of the plane, where he was seated, to wish him good luck and to take his picture.

As she stood near his seat, she heard a woman say, "They are here," and she watched as three uniformed soldiers headed down the aisle. Bec knew a lot about military uniforms. Her father had died while in military custody. The charges against him had been as unclear as the cause of his death, but the experience had left indelible memories of the military in her mind. She observed, for example, that the soldier who walked down the aisle of the plane past Aquino without recognizing him was wearing the uniform of a Metropolitan Command officer, while the two officers who followed him and who recognized their quarry wore uniforms bearing the markings of the Aviation Security Command.

After watching the three military men escort Aquino toward the first-class section of the plane and out the exit, Bec tried to follow, but was blocked by the same men in white shirts who had barred my way. Unlike me, however, she knew immediately who they were. She knew that the white *polo barong*, or short-sleeved shirt, is customary attire during working hours for plainclothes intelligence and security agents. "When I first saw a fellow in barong standing at the head of the aisle, I wondered why the military was in the plane," she told me, nearly two years later when we first met, just before she appeared in court as a fellow witness for the prosecution. She had seen this security officer leave the plane several steps ahead of Aquino and his uniformed escorts, presumably to join the other plainclothes agents, who barricaded the door to the service stairs.

Hoping to get a picture of Aquino's welcome, Bec had rushed back inside the plane, searching for a window with a view of the stairs. She stationed herself before one near the left wing. At that point, she said, Aquino and his escorts were about one quarter of the way down—two uniformed AVSECOM officers flanking Ninoy, followed by two uniformed METROCOM officers and a man in a white barong several steps above and behind.

Suddenly, she would testify later, "I saw a METROCOM man point a gun at the back of the head of Aquino, and at the same time a shot was fired." She saw Aquino's head slump down, and she began to wail. Terrified, she ran back to the other side of the plane, to tell her friend what she had seen.

"Bec, lie down, get down," cried Santos, as more shots rang out.

Quijano did not join the other passengers on the floor, but crossed the plane again to return to the window. Her keening is clearly audible on my tape throughout, indicating that we followed similar paths in search of a view.

This time she saw "a man in dark blue overalls with a long gun shooting toward the tarmac." By the time she exited the plane, after the shooting had stopped and the van full of soldiers had sped away, she was wracked with sobs.

Local photographers and TV cameramen waiting at Gate 8 rushed toward her, asking, "Are you sure it was Aquino?"

Looking through dark glasses into their lenses, she answered, "They already killed Aquino, why are you not crying yet?"

Before she could say more than that, a Filipino man in a T-shirt gripped her by the shoulders and pulled her backward, whispering in Tagalog, the national language, "Don't talk or you'll get hurt."

"I did not know he was a soldier from his dress," said Quijano later, "but from the way he was talking to me."

The Filipino journalists who watched and filmed the encounter knew him well and took his message to heart. He was Colonel Vicente Tigas, the Presidential Security Command's liaison with the media, and he had been assigned to supervise the local reporters who were accredited to wait for Aquino at Gate 8. He had completed that mission successfully, having managed to position the journalists inside a windowless portion of the passenger tube at the moment of the assassination so that they, like us foreign correspondents at the other end of it, would be unable to identify the killer.

Tigas steered Quijano into an empty departure lounge, away from the reporters, and offered her a glass of water. As she sipped it, slowly regaining her composure, she heard him say to his civilian companion, "It's all over."

Fearful of being left behind by Santos, who had taken one look at Tigas and walked in the other direction, Bec was anxious to follow the other passengers to immigration. Once in line she managed to get rid of Tigas by saying what Filipinos had learned to say in all such situations: "Leave me alone, I am all right. After all, I did not see anything."

As soon as they cleared customs, Quijano and Santos took a taxi to the Holiday Inn, where Bec placed two calls. "I was with Senator Aquino on the plane coming from Taipei, and he was shot by a soldier," she told her confidantes. She confided her fear of Tigas, and how he had warned her not to talk. Both begged her to go into hiding. Next she called her brother, who went to the hotel to keep her company. Together they watched the six o'clock press conference given by Generals Prospero Olivas and Luther Custodio, who had been assigned by General Ver shortly after the shootings to conduct an investigation. As she watched reporters putting their questions to the two officers, the camera caught a man in a T-shirt whispering in Olivas's ear. Quijano said, "That made me shout, 'That's the man in the T-shirt who threatened me and hurt me.' "

The fear instilled in her by Tigas, by frightened friends and relatives, and by later information that the military had been asking questions about her would be enough to silence her for two years.

*　　　　*　　　　*

By the time I found my luggage and passed through customs, it was mid-afternoon, and I was desperate to find a safe telephone from which to call my editors in New York. Outside the terminal, the only signs of the 20,000 Aquino supporters, who had come to the airport to welcome Ninoy home, were hundreds of yellow ribbons tied to lampposts and railings, and, swirling underfoot in the hot August breeze, dozens of leaflets bearing his homecoming speech: "I have returned to join the ranks of those struggling to restore our rights and freedom through nonviolence."

His kid brother, Agapito ("Butz") Aquino, working with opposition leader Doy Laurel had relayed news of the shooting over a portable microphone. Mistaking Butz for Ninoy, the crowd had begun to cheer and chant "Nee-noy, Nee-noy," as he climbed atop a truck to address them.

It was Doy who made the announcement. "Ninoy, our beloved, is back . . ." he said, his voice cracking with emotion. "But you might not be able to see him. Eyewitnesses say he has been shot." The demonstrators heaved a collective groan, which quickly dissipated into cries of disbelief, sobbing, and wailing. Instinctively, the organizers urged the stricken crowd to regroup at nearby Baclaran Church to pray for Ninoy.

Now, about an hour later, there were no taxis in sight. Despite my mounting paranoia, I agreed to the price quoted by one of the many gypsy drivers to take me into Manila. He was a Marcos supporter who wanted to talk about the radio report that Aquino had been shot. What he said during the fifteen-minute trip into town proved enormously valuable in the months ahead in helping me understand the grip Marcos had on his people. The driver's words paid chilling tribute to Marcos's successful manipulation of public opinion during nearly a decade of martial law and the three years of authoritarian rule since. "Among my codrivers, we have already accepted that this will happen," he said. "We were all brainwashed about this," he added, oblivious to the pejorative meaning of the term.

Incredulous, I asked if that meant that he thought Ninoy deserved to die, just for coming home in defiance of Marcos's warnings. "It was very daring to make the decision to come back, but it was very stupid," he said, avoiding a direct answer. Then he repeated practically verbatim the argument put forth by government spokesmen during the weeks when officials were trying to prevent Ninoy's return, "He knows that he has pending cases against him here, and that he can be assassinated." Somewhat defensively, he added, "The administration cannot be blamed for it, because he was given advance warning."

The driver's response to the question of who might have shot Aquino was similarly straightforward. "Personally, I think it would be a hired assassin." Conscious that in saying this, he was implicitly indicting the Marcos regime, he saw the need for further explanation. "We have been through so many presidents," he explained wearily, "but everyone who sits in that chair is the same. Maybe that's why we have just settled."

Settling for President Marcos had not been without its benefits, he allowed. The crime rate had been cut, making Manila a safer city in which to drive. Aquino, on the other hand, had not brought him any benefits. "I would not trust Aquino," he said, still parroting the government line. "He did not mellow over the years. He is still breathing fire. For me, he is very dangerous. I think he could plunge this country into something worse. He has affiliations with the NPA."

Fearful that I might have been followed, I chose and then rejected two hotels, before finally paying the driver, waiting until he was out of sight, and then walking to a third, carrying my heavy luggage. After checking into my room and calling TIME in New York, I unpacked my portable typewriter and prepared to write a story that would be inserted into the late editions of the magazine, which were already being printed. Just as I began to listen to my tape for the first time, the radio announced a press conference by General Olivas.

Five hours after the assassination, the government was finally confirming what had been clear since shortly after 1:00 P.M.: Aquino was dead. That was about the only fact to be broadcast by the government network. The so-called "findings" of the instant investigation sounded like pure fiction, compared to what I had seen and heard. The gunman, wearing blue denim pants and a blue shirt, reported General Olivas, had evidently breached the tight security cordon at the airport and "showed up as if from nowhere," close enough to Aquino to shoot him with a Smith & Wesson .357 Magnum revolver at "point-blank" range, as he was escorted across the pavement from the stairs to the waiting van.

I found that explanation preposterous. There were simply too many soldiers protecting too small an area for any unauthorized person to slip in. Nor were there any walls or solid objects behind which to hide under the plane. Furthermore, Ninoy had not had enough time to descend all nineteen stairs and start across the tarmac before the first shots sounded. At that instant—ten seconds after he had exited the aircraft on his way to the service stairs, according to my tape—I had been standing inside the movable passenger tube, to which the service stairs were connected. Such a struggle was going on outside on those stairs, as the firing began, that the tube was vibrating wildly. The shooting must have taken place on the stairs at the moment of greatest movement.

The airport military men escorting Aquino had subsequently fired at the gunman, "who died on the spot," continued Olivas. If that had been the case, I wondered why the SWAT team commando had continued to fire at him for so long afterward. Aquino was rushed to Fort Bonifacio army hospital in an effort "to save his life," said Olivas. I knew beyond a doubt that was not true. The impact of his landing inside the van, where the soldiers had heaved his limp body, headfirst, was surely enough to have killed him, had he not already been dead. Although I did not have enough eyewitness evidence to be able to state it unequivocally in print, it seemed clear to me by the time I had filed that first story that a government cover-up was underway.

*   *   *

The call to the Aquino family came late in the afternoon, after Ninoy's shocked brothers and sisters and his stoic mother had left the Baclaran Church prayer service and gathered at the Times Street house, which had remained Ninoy and Cory's legal address throughout their years in exile. There had been no official announcement confirming the shooting, much less his death. However, the family had steeled itself for the worst.

"Dead or alive?" questioned Ninoy's film director–sister, Lupita, who answered the phone. "Just come," said the soft-spoken military officer. Captain Theodore Grant was calling as a family friend, rather than a military official. He had been Ninoy's guard at the Fort Bonifacio Military Security Unit throughout his incarceration and was an unabashed admirer of his prisoner—just one example of the sometimes whimsical nature of martial law. "At first I saw to it that I maintained a warden/prisoner relationship," he would recall later. "But as time went by, I could not resist him. The family was so good, the man was so good, that I got to the point of asking myself, 'Why is this fellow here? He should be in Malacañang where he can help.' "

On reaching the gates of the military camp where Ninoy had been imprisoned for seven years and seven months of his life, the Aquinos found their entry barred by heavily armed military guards and antiriot police. "I am the mother, why can't I be allowed to see my son?" pleaded Doña Aurora to the young soldiers who were carrying out orders to let no one pass. Doy Laurel, who had accompanied them, pulled his weight as a former colonel in the air force, and asked to see the commanding officer, General Josephus Ramas. Eventually Ramas's aide appeared and granted them permission to enter—but only on foot. Disgusted with the contemptuous treatment that opposition members routinely received from the military, Laurel refused to let Ninoy's seventy-three-year-old mother walk the three miles from the gate to the hospital. Finally, after much wrangling, one car, carrying the women, was allowed to enter, while the rest had to walk.

Laurel observed, "The soldiers pointed their Armalites at us. You would have thought it was war."

When they finally got to the army hospital where Grant had instructed them to go, they were told, "No Senator Aquino here." Laurel's temper was fast fraying.

"You can shoot me, but I am not leaving until we see him," he told the officer in charge. Twenty minutes later they were shown to a second-floor room, where a body lay on a stretcher, covered by a sheet.

"I saw the feet sticking out from under the blanket, and I knew it was Ninoy," recalled his actor-brother, Butz. "When he was in office, I used to visit him in the mornings when he was still free—around 5:30 A.M.—before the crowds started coming to the house. He would be sitting in bed reading the papers and his feet would be sticking out."

Laurel asked the military authorities to release the body to the Aquino family. After lengthy consultation with the palace, a military officer told him they had been ordered to conduct an autopsy first. Laurel objected, expressing the family's fears that state-appointed doctors would skew the autopsy report to confirm the regime's version of how the assassination took place. At this point Defense Minister Juan ("Johnny") Ponce Enrile arrived, sent by Marcos to extend assistance to the family. Exuding authority, he quickly agreed to let the Aquinos take the body to a private mortuary of their choice, where an autopsy would be conducted by state doctors, with an Aquino-appointed doctor present.

"Johnny understood," said Laurel, who had remained on friendly terms with the defense minister after leaving the Marcos camp to found the opposition coalition known as UNIDO (United Nationalist Democratic

Organization). In fact, Enrile, who had been a leading tax and corporate lawyer before joining the government in 1966, had maintained surprisingly friendly relations with many of the moderate opposition leaders, despite the fact that it was he who had signed the warrants which landed most of them in jail during martial law. While Enrile's relationship with Cory Aquino had always been a formal one of granting or rejecting her requests for visiting privileges, he enjoyed a more casual acquaintance with her sister-in-law Lupita, who had, from time to time, delivered verbal messages to him from Ninoy. Their code word for the ruggedly handsome defense minister was "Crush."

After their interval alone with Ninoy, Mrs. Aquino made one request that would carry lasting symbolic significance. She asked that Ninoy be displayed in an open coffin, bloody and bruised, for all the world to see what the Marcos regime had done to him.

Maur maintained a vigil at the mortuary throughout the night. Staring into the dark sky above the atrium, where she sat waiting for the dawn, she said, "That's when God spoke to me."

Meanwhile, inside, the autopsy was being conducted in an atmosphere far less serene. A young photographer, who had been asked by the Laurel family to take pictures of the procedure, later confided his doubts to the Aquino family about the behavior of the government medico-legal officer and his findings. The official autopsy, he said, had falsely reported the existence of two bullet fragments in the brain, which had simply not been found there. It also referred to a third fragment in the chin, which the government doctor had refused to let him see or photograph in the place where it had purportedly lodged. He would later seek to expose those contradictions at the trial of General Ver, "because I knew that the military had used the autopsy to show that it was impossible for Ninoy to have been shot on the stairway." However, the prosecutor refused to introduce the evidence.

*   *   *

At about the time Ninoy's plane was beginning its descent into Manila International Airport, Imelda Marcos had made a highly visible entrance at Via Amare, a fancy Chinese seafood restaurant within the Cultural Center complex that she had built. In her luncheon entourage were such regulars as Jolie Benitez, the laid-back young deputy in her Ministry of Human Settlements, and J. V. Cruz, the glib Philippine ambassador to the Court of St. James, who seemed to spend as much time in Manila as in London. Generally seen in the company of beautiful women, Cruz was a favorite of the First Lady. He liked to tell how she had once asked him if he found her attractive, and he had answered, "Yes, but I would not risk my life for the president's wife."

The shark's-fin soup had just been served when one of her security aides came to the table with a message from General Ver to return to the palace. "I thought it was Marcos who had died," said Cruz some months later. Nervously, the whole party rode back to Malacañang in her limousine. According to Cruz, "She went off for fifteen minutes, then came back and told us Ninoy was dead."

A former journalist, Cruz had known Ninoy since the Magsaysay administration, when he served as press secretary and Ninoy as a political advisor. "I thought Ninoy was shallow. I never liked him," he said after his death, "but he was the only person capable of becoming president." The news that Ninoy had been shot at the airport filled Cruz with dread. "I knew immediately what we were in for. If it was our friends, it was the stupidest thing to have done. If it was our enemies, it was brilliant." Because he was popular with the foreign press and more adept at public relations than the information minister, Cruz would spend much of the next eighteen months in Manila presenting the administration's case.

*　　　*　　　*

Ver and Imelda both knew exactly where to find Marcos on the afternoon of August 21: in bed in the specially equipped guest house adjacent to the palace, recuperating from a kidney transplant, which had been performed secretly on August 7. It was too early to know whether or not his body would accept or reject the donated organ. The next several weeks would be critical. He was undergoing heavy drug therapy in order to fight rejection, and the chemicals had exacerbated old allergies, affecting his breathing, among other vital functions. Although mentally alert, he had been in an extremely weakened physical state for the past three weeks, during which time an inner circle consisting of his ambitious wife, his conniving brother-in-law Kokoy Romualdez, and General Ver had taken over the daily operation of government in his name.

The president had long been rumored to be suffering from a disease of the connective tissue known as lupus erythematosus. Even before Ninoy went into exile, he had confided to Agence France-Presse bureau chief Teddy Benigno that the CIA had confirmed to him that lupus was the source of Marcos's ailments. But this was the first time Marcos had ever been absent from public view for such a long time. His inner circle was sworn to secrecy not to reveal the seriousness of his illness, lest he lose his authority and invite a coup. Others, including important ministers, simply had not been told the truth about his condition.

On August 5, just after he had postponed his homecoming from August 7 to August 21, Ninoy sat in Boston's Logan International Airport, waiting for a friend to arrive from Saudi Arabia, and reading the *New York Times*. Tucked inside the news pages was a tickler, which noted that President Marcos had gone into seclusion for three weeks to write two books. On reading that, Ninoy recounted, "I said to myself, 'My God, this is it! I have been secretary to three presidents and never did I run across a three-week seclusion.' I thought I had hit the jackpot. The only reason could be a medical problem."

Ninoy began working the phones, both in the U.S. and abroad. By the time he reached Taiwan two weeks later, sources close to the Archbishop of Manila, Jaime, Cardinal Sin, a family friend, had furnished him information that Marcos had been tested for a possible kidney transplant. His impression on embarking for Manila had been that Marcos "had flunked the tests" and had therefore not undergone surgery.

That his impression was erroneous did not lessen the belief within the Marcos camp that Ninoy was being fed information on Marcos's illness by the American CIA. How else, they asked themselves, could one explain his decision to return home at precisely the period when Marcos would be most vulnerable? Ever since Marcos had singled out Ninoy as the chief threat to his prolonged stay in power, he had suspected that his rival might figure in American plans to replace him. Even more than he feared the reaction of his own men to knowledge of his declining health, Marcos feared U.S. reaction. He had observed at discomfortingly close hand American political machinations in Saigon before and during the Vietnam war. He was aware of the fate of rulers who were no longer perceived to serve U.S. interests.

The president had complained on at least one occasion to U.S. Ambassador Michael Armacost about an alleged CIA report on his poor health. He would flash similar anger at me during an interview in December 1985, when I began asking questions about the state of his relations with Ninoy at the time of his return. "Some members of Congress gave him documents," he claimed with obvious irritation. "One of those was supposed to be a medical report about lupus." He charged that Aquino was carrying those reports in his hand luggage when he arrived in Manila, and he challenged me to report that. "I am not sick of anything in the kidney," Marcos bellowed at me.

Given his paranoia about Ninoy, the Americans, and his illness, it is difficult to imagine that Marcos would not have communicated to his wife and his chief of staff his strong desire that Aquino be prevented from returning at such a vulnerable moment. If, as he insisted to me, he had remained alert in the days immediately preceding the assassination, he could have continued to communicate that desire through the morning of August 21.

Those who had seen Marcos during that period described an obviously ailing president who was trying to act as if nothing serious was wrong. When Enrile had been summoned to the guest house, he had been obliged to remove his shoes and don a pair of sterile "booties" before being received. Even then, he was not allowed near Marcos, who spoke to him as Juliet to Romeo, from a loggia one flight above the waiting room in which the minister was seated. No explanation was ever offered.

Several days later, on August 18, Ambassador Armacost and visiting Democratic Congressman Stephen Solarz had paid a call on the president in the same place. "He looked like death warmed over," Armacost recalled. The staff had gone to great lengths to arrange the furniture in the guest house waiting room to favor Marcos. His visitors were seated at a table without a view of the stairs.

"I'm sure he was probably helped down the stairs," said Armacost, who noted that once down, "he walked in a very infirm way, but was quite lucid and rather shrewd in the way he handled the meeting, which lasted for over an hour."

A banker friend told Solarz that that particular meeting had so exhausted Marcos that he had suffered a relapse. Most knowledgeable analysts believed that the decision to assassinate Aquino in such a brutal way could not be divorced from the reality of the president's critical physical condition at the time. "It was in that context that Imelda and Ver decided to do what they apparently did, because it looked like Marcos was on his last leg," Solarz opined. Indeed the prevailing view in Manila coffee shops since shortly after the assassination had been that it was the First Lady and the chief of staff—worried about maintaining their grip on power if Aquino was back in the Philippines when Marcos died—who had ordered military men close to them to keep him out at all costs.

Whether the burden of suspicion should rest more heavily on Marcos's likely successors than on himself is a question that may never be answered. The conventional wisdom is that Marcos was too shrewd to have ordered a killing to be carried out in a manner that would so obviously implicate his own administration. Such a view does not, however, take into account the bluffing that was such a part of his relationship with Aquino. When it had gotten out of hand in the past, it had led Marcos to declare martial law, rather than try to strike a compromise with the opposition. There were those people in the know who speculated that just such a thing had happened again.

"Those two had a love-hate relationship," observed former Vice-President Emmanuel Pelaez about the long rivalry between Marcos and Aquino. "They were the most able, intelligent pair of politicians in the country, and as often happens with contenders, they had a professional respect for each other." However, Pelaez continued, neither would give an inch. In the "contest of wills" that developed once Ninoy had announced his return, both men bluffed, neither dared to compromise nor allow himself to blink first. And no cooler head intervened on either side. The outcome was inevitably tragic.

"My feeling is that it got out of hand," concluded Pelaez. "It's similar to the nuclear arms race. No one thinks such a thing will happen, but all it takes is a miscalculation."

✻   ✻   ✻

Officials inside the white, colonial-style mansion which housed the U.S. embassy in Manila appeared to be looking neither in the direction of Marcos nor his inner circle for suspects, at least not in the days immediately following the Aquino assassination. Instead, embassy officers were eyeing the growing Communist revolutionary movement, the New People's Army. That was not surprising, given the closeness of the "special relationship" between the U.S. and its former colony, and the high priority put on continued U.S. use of its two largest overseas military facilities, which are housed on Philippine soil.

Not long after the Marcoses had received a red-carpet welcome from President Reagan in Washington in August 1982, a new five-year agreement on the bases had been satisfactorily negotiated by the two governments. As a result, Philippine-American relations were better in August 1983 than they had been in years. Moreover, American officials had reason to believe they were making progress in their efforts to prod Marcos to hold elections for a new National Assembly in 1984 which would be clean enough to induce the participation of the opposition. That would constitute a constructive next step toward a restoration of the democratic institutions that Marcos had destroyed by proclaiming martial law. Aquino's return home just nine months before those scheduled elections seemed like a good omen.

If Marcos's chief opponent agreed to run or to lead the opposition campaign, he would not only lend the exercise needed credibility, but would force Marcos to be more accountable for his actions. An assembly with a legitimate opposition could, it was believed, serve as a forum for debate on the shape of a post-Marcos government.

Aquino's death had sent shock waves throughout the Reagan administration, which had been tracking his journey from Boston to Taipei and on to Manila, and had a man waiting at the airport to report on the reception he received. At that time the intelligence flow between the U.S. and the Philippines was channeled exclusively through General Ver, to whom Marcos had granted virtual control over all military, police, and intelligence agencies, as well as Manila International Airport, only one month before. That action appeared to have climaxed a power struggle inside the military, in the process of which the civilian Defense Minister Enrile had been removed from the chain of command, and Vice-Chief of Staff Ramos had been passed over for the second time as a replacement to Ver. Enrile and Ramos, who were friends, had subsequently submitted their resignations to Marcos, who had not accepted them.

Despite the internal turmoil, the embassy had concluded that Marcos remained firmly in control. Ver was regarded as the epitome of a Marcos loyalist, a man whose devotion to his commander in chief was unswerving and total. Marcos, in turn, was understood to be prepared to treat Aquino leniently. A few days before Ninoy's arrival, Enrile had informed Ambassador Armacost that the opposition leader would be placed under house arrest of the same loose variety once accorded his cousin, former Senator Eva Kalaw, who had even been permitted to campaign for election.

Rumors that had found favor within the embassy had it that Marcos's strategy for getting Ninoy out of the way was characteristically Machiavellian —but well within the rules of the brutal game of Philippine politics. Marcos would welcome Ninoy's candidacy for an assembly seat from his native Tarlac. Then he would proceed to exacerbate old family rivalries by backing as Ninoy's opponent Cory Aquino's cousin Danding Cojuangco, Marcos's most powerful business crony. Given Danding's financial resources and his paid operatives within the Philippine Armed Forces, as well as his popularity among Ilocano-speaking voters in the province, Marcos believed that his man could "crush Ninoy at the start."

Congressman Solarz, who had left Manila only the day before Ninoy's return, received word of his death while in Bangkok. In Singapore, his next stop, he made arrangements to return to Manila to pay his condolences to the Aquino family. Once back there, he asked for a briefing from the CIA station chief. "He spent an hour giving me two dozen reasons why Marcos was not and could not have been involved," recalled Solarz.

"They knew absolutely nothing," complained the chairman of the House foreign affairs subcommittee on Asia and the Pacific. "Or if they did know, they were not telling me. They were only going on the logic of the situation."

Solarz could understand why. "They were obviously extremely reluctant to consider the possibility that Marcos might be involved, given the implications for Philippine-American relations. To even suggest it as a remote possibility could open the floodgates of criticism back home."

I was similarly dismayed at the way such logic governed the analysis of the situation that was presented to journalists during the U.S. embassy's first press briefing the week after the assassination. "Who stands to benefit most?" asked the background briefer, rhetorically. "The Communists, the extremists," he answered. "The act will most harm the Marcos people, the moderate opposition, and the general political order," he explained, thereby boosting the Communist effort to destabilize the country. Marcos himself, he added, "is very frustrated and angry about the killing."

Our questions about possible Philippine military involvement were practically dismissed out of hand, because "the top ranking military would not stand to gain much from such a destabilizing act. It would not help them consolidate power. It would make their problems more severe." As for any specific role in the conspiracy being ascribed to Ver, our briefer could not see what motive Ver would have. "Aquino was a long way from becoming president," he said.

Nothing in the briefing reflected the reality of the confrontation I had witnessed at the airport. I went back to the embassy later in the week to follow up on several of the questions posed in the initial briefing. I granted that logic favored the Communists as having the most to gain from the elimination of Aquino, the one political moderate who might have been able to unify the country after Marcos. Nonetheless, I confessed that I found it impossible to believe that a lone Communist could have gone unspotted in that small, exposed area so densely protected by military security.

The briefer spoke as if such penetration would be relatively simple. "The military is sloppy," he said. Even an elite command such as the Aviation Security Command (AVSECOM), which was in charge of protecting Aquino on his arrival, did not rate very high marks in his book. "I am not confident that those guys are competent to tie their own bootlaces without stringing them together," he said. On the other hand, U.S. intelligence indicated that there are "elements within the New People's Army [NPA] that are efficient and specialize in assassination." Underlining his point, he added: "There are urban assassinations here. Local mayors get knocked off, and the NPA could be behind some of those killings."

After closing my notebook and putting away my pen, I confided my strong suspicion that the men in white barongs inside the plane and the blue-suited AVSECOM commandos outside on the ground had very deliberately and quite skillfully coordinated their moves in order to kill Aquino with a minimum of witnesses in a very public place. The necessary element of surprise, which the sudden intrusion by a lone Communist gunman suggested, had not been evident in the actions of the security people I had seen.

Viewing the unedited ABC-TV videotapes shot from the plane had helped reinforce my initial suspicions, I said. They made it clear that the men in white had already positioned themselves inside the folding passenger tube before it made its umbilical connection with our plane. The moment the stewardesses opened the door of the plane, those men had moved deftly to prevent passengers and journalists alike from following Aquino and witnessing the crime that was about to be committed virtually in front of our eyes. Meanwhile, outside on the metal steps, where I reckoned the assassin would have had to be in order to shoot Aquino from behind so soon after he exited the plane, the TV footage confirmed the extent to which a lone Communist would have been greatly outnumbered. "It wasn't just a question of Ninoy and three men in khaki," I said. "Those steps were crowded with men in white shirts."

"Who wears white shirts like that?" I asked the embassy officer, as he punched the proper combination into the electronically locked door and ushered me out into the corridor. "Philippine military intelligence," he answered. Several days later the ambassador's secretary called, wanting to know where embassy officials could view the unedited ABC-TV video-tapes.

*   *   *

By the time Marcos appeared on television a full day after the assassination, the country was on the brink of hysteria. As he had literally monopolized the media for so long, his absence from the scene since early August was all the more suspicious. The added trauma of the Aquino assassination led many to conclude that a military coup had taken place. There were rumors that Enrile had been arrested, that Marcos had been flown to the U.S. for medical treatment, that martial law had been reimposed. A heavy buildup of troops around the presidential palace the night Ninoy was shot and a massive electric power failure, which blacked out most of the main island of Luzon the following day, seemed to confirm the direst scenarios. A taped audio message by the president, appealing for calm, only raised more questions about his health each time it was broadcast.

Meanwhile, bank runs and hoarding of food and gasoline reached such proportions that Metro-Manila Governor Imelda Marcos was obliged to pay a televised visit to local supermarkets and the city's main food terminal to reassure people that the government had sufficient food stocks to meet any artificial shortage. Although Imelda's appearance had a settling effect, it was no substitute for the sight of Marcos toughing out yet another crisis before the eyes of a citizenry that had become more dependent on an authoritarian leader than it liked to admit, during the decade since democracy died.

Pale, puffy, and apparently unable to stand for long periods or move his right arm, Marcos hardly cut a reassuring figure when he finally held a televised press conference one night after the assassination. Yet he did not appear as incapacitated as rumor had led me to believe. In order to belie whispers of a coup, he appeared flanked by his military commanders, the entire cabinet, and the chief justice of the Supreme Court. Although visibly weak, he had not lost his feistiness. At times, as he fielded softballs lobbed to him by the official palace press corps, he seemed impatient for more of a challenge. He bridled at the obsequious opening question.

"Mr. President, first, we would like to apologize for interrupting your writing routine," said the dean of the Filipino journalists who covered the palace. Then he asked: "By the way, sir, how is the book going?"

Marcos snapped, "That is all inconsequential now, because of this grievous tragedy, this barbaric act."

If his answers were more meandering than usual, his mental faculties had not been impaired. With customary duplicity, he managed to adopt the scenario already presented to the public by his military investigators, without at the same time closing the door to other possibilities, should the military case develop holes. The killer, who had managed to penetrate heavy government security, was clearly someone who wished to damage his administration as well as kill Ninoy. "No matter what explanation we make now, there will always be some kind of shadow over the entire government," he said.

However, Marcos was more careful than his military investigators in characterizing the assassin. He pointed a first finger of suspicion at the embittered clique of relatives and friends of witnesses who had incriminated Ninoy during his military trial and had subsequently been liquidated. Their motive, he suggested, would have been "revenge." On the other hand, he said, the NPA or the "Communist hierarchy, might have done it, as a means of shooting two birds with one stone. They would eliminate Aquino, who was responsible for some of the liquidations or killings, according to them, of some of their men whom he himself utilized. At the same time, they would embarrass the government and place us in the awkward position which they have."

Perhaps it was a Freudian slip, perhaps it was merely his understated way of acknowledging the barbarity of the crime. Whatever the case, he let drop an observation that night that would intrigue coffee shop pundits for months afterward. "We had hoped that the matter could be handled with a little more finesse," said Marcos.

7

Cory Sets the Tone

As Cory Aquino, with her five children and Ninoy's lawyer Ernie Maceda, settled into the long flight from Boston to Manila two days after the assassination, she was too exhausted from the shock of the event and the strain of sudden celebrity to either cry or sleep. Mingled with the personal pain of losing Ninoy, she was filled with bittersweet memories of the political struggle for which her husband had sacrificed everything, including, at times, the happiness of his family. The way she explained it to me later was that she had never believed that struggle to be as winnable as he did. Not only did she have less faith in Ferdinand Marcos's capacity for reform than he, but she also doubted the commitment of the Filipino people to unite in defiance of Marcos and in defense of their rights.

"When he was in prison, I had more contact with the people than he did, and I kept telling him, 'You know, Ninoy, the problem of Filipinos is they are such cowards, forgive me for saying so.' He would say, 'All it takes is a leader,' but I would tell him, 'Much as I believe in you, you don't know those countrymen of ours.' " She quickly qualified her remarks so as not to appear to condemn her own people. She made it clear that she was speaking, not as president, but as a wife who had been for nearly eight years "the victim of public apathy."

As she saw it, Ninoy's faith in the people's will to restore democracy had endured through a decade of martial law, in part, because he was spared full knowledge of his irrelevance to the lives of most Filipinos beyond the walls of Fort Bonifacio. She had been the one entrusted with carrying his messages to the outside world and raising money for the political campaign he waged behind bars. Thus, she knew better which people were too preoccupied with other news to give Ninoy priority, and how many refused to contribute for fear of reprisals from the regime.

When she stepped off the plane in Manila into a horde of reporters and cameramen, and more so, as her car inched through the crowd waiting outside her house to view Ninoy's body, the bitterness began to sweeten. Late into that night and throughout the numbing week ahead, her contact with Filipinos whose sense of loss seemed as profound as her own totally changed her outlook. "If people had not come to our house at Times Street after he died, I think I would have said 'good-bye,' " she confessed. "I would probably not have taken part in any action against Marcos. I would have said, 'Look, my husband has done his part. My role is to take care of my family.' " Laughing at the very notion of Cory, the shy house-wife, admitting such a truth about Ninoy, the ruthless politician, she added, "I was more of a cynic than Ninoy."

The Filipino people had indeed been passive for eleven years. With but a few exceptions, they had not rallied, protested, or allowed themselves to vent their political feelings in public since martial law was imposed in 1972. Even after emergency rule was lifted in 1981, many people continued to speak to each other in code over the telephone and to circumscribe their conversations to exchanges of petty gossip, never trading anything as dangerous as a heartfelt opinion or a thoughtful idea outside the close confines of the family.

Ninoy was one of the few who had continued to rationalize their silence, clinging to a deep-seated belief that at the right moment they would break it. "Ninoy compared the people's silence to a pregnant woman," recalls Cory. "When the fetus is only seven months old, no matter how much everyone wants it to come into the world, it won't. He said when the Filipino people are ready, they will act, but not before."

Now he was being proven right. The single bullet which silenced him had shattered their reserve and brought to term their long period of dormancy. By minding their own business and remaining uninvolved in politics, members of the Filipino middle class, in particular, had been able to block out much of the violence and injustice that had permeated society under martial law. Now those problems had come back to haunt them. This time the violence had broken out not in some dark street, the injustice perpetrated not against just another anonymous victim. The assault had been made in broad daylight in a public place, in a manner so blatant and to a man of such stature that they could no longer ignore it. It was an assault not just against Ninoy, but against anyone who had paid lip service to, much less believed in, democracy and human rights.

*   *   *

As the news sank in on the evening of August 21, a perceptual flip-flop of massive proportions occurred in the minds of Filipinos. It would take time for the impact of the change to become measurable. The government would insist until the end that the masses had been largely unmoved outside the traditionally oppositionist capital region. Foreigners, on the other hand, would mistake the absence of a major political explosion for lack of resolve on the part of the divided opposition. Such thinking overlooked the highly individualistic nature of Filipinos, the strength of their family ties, and their tendency to improvise rather than organize. Given the very nature of the place, change would take time.

The first stage of the process was readily visible the morning after the shooting in the outpouring of affection by hundreds of simple people, who traveled individually and in response to no call. They came to witness the predawn arrival of Ninoy's casket at his suburban, Quezon City home, and to weep for him and pray for the nation. They arrived on foot, in cars, or by jeepney—that garishly decorated Philippine contraption, half Jeep, half bus, which is at once the country's main mode of mass transit and its most authentic form of folk art.

By mid-morning, thousands more had found their way to the Times Street neighborhood. By afternoon, enterprising food and drink vendors had set up stalls in the neighborhood. By nightfall, 15,000 people, from well-known businessmen to simple laborers, had filed through the garage and into the living room of the modest, ranch-style house to circle the open coffin.

Among the first family friends to visit was Ninoy's fellow prisoner in Fort Bonifacio and Laur, former Senator Jose Diokno. The longtime oppositionist was heartened by the public reaction he witnessed. "Going to see him is one way people have of venting those years of repressed anger and outrage," said Diokno. As a respected human rights lawyer, he had represented dozens of little-known victims of martial law, and he drew an analogy between their own experiences and Ninoy's assassination. "People have identified with Ninoy because the moment he was put under arrest, he became one of them, and when he was shot while under custody the way they were shot, he symbolized what has happened to them."

Those people who followed his coffin on its journey from wake to burial would become the shock troops of a broad, new political movement. At the heart of it was the newly aroused middle class, including many members of the formerly apolitical private business community. Better than the politicians, the businessmen were able to analyze the dire economic crisis in which Marcos was trapped and to envision how the president could soon be forced by his international creditors to institute at least minimal reforms, as the price for receiving essential new loans. Accordingly, they came better prepared than the pols, with precise proposals.

Walking with them behind the funeral bier were people whom they might never otherwise have encountered: traditional politicians, left-of-center activists who campaigned for specific causes rather than for a particular party, left-wing militants, students, former political detainees, urban squatters, peasants. With varying degrees of fervor, all of these Filipinos had come to oppose Marcos. But their own different life-styles and goals had prevented them from uniting in the past. In Ninoy, the martyr, these disparate groups had found a common symbol.

Prominent among them were several individuals who aspired to succeed Ninoy as the de facto leader of the anti-Marcos opposition. The best-known and best-organized of them all was Doy Laurel. Because of his family's long relationship with Marcos, however, Laurel was unacceptable to both his fellow party leaders and to the left-of-center groups that advocated removal of U.S. bases and amnesty for political prisoners, and were also claiming Ninoy as one of their own.

The prime concern of moderates like himself, Laurel explained, was to "head off a bloody confrontation" between leftists, who would join the funeral procession, and the military which would be patrolling the streets. "At this point in time the situation is explosive, and all you have to do is throw a match," he warned. Rapid polarization was taking place within the opposition, between those intent on pursuing a nonviolent course and those who, he said, "think it is time for a revolution."

He proceeded to cite Saint Thomas Aquinas, whose thoughts on revolution would guide the moderate opposition in the ensuing years. "A revolution should be the last course, when all else has failed," he said, paraphrasing the Catholic thinker. "For a revolution there must be three justifications: (one) a very grievous matter, which we have; (two) a high chance of success; (three) no other recourse." He considered it his duty as an opposition leader "to try to hold people back until those three conditions concur."

As an alternative to revolution, Laurel proposed that Marcos and his government "step down and give way to a caretaker government acceptable to the people and composed of members who would not run for public office." However, his willingness to admit members of the Marcos cabinet, such as Prime Minister Cesar Virata and Vice-Chief of Staff General Fidel Ramos, was anathema to the issue-oriented groups.

"Laurel cannot lead the opposition, because he is a member of this

[Marcos] government," retorted Jose Diokno, a key organizer of a coalition of militant groups, known as "Justice for Aquino, Justice for All," that would dominate the early anti-Marcos protest demonstrations. Diokno was a pivotal opposition figure, standing between veterans of the traditional political parties, like Aquino and Laurel, and nontraditional practitioners of the "cause-oriented" protest politics of the early 1970s student, peasant, and labor groups.

Diokno's primary concern was in direct conflict with Laurel's. It would not be the left which would provoke a crisis, he insisted. Rather, Diokno's worst-case scenario was that the U.S., fearful of a leftist takeover, would step into the political vacuum at the center to help install a military government. "Of course, the Americans would pressure the military to accept a civilian head," he added, presciently.

Between Laurel and Diokno on the ideological spectrum were others who were likewise positioning themselves for the post-Marcos era, which seemed suddenly close at hand. "When Marcos killed Ninoy, he seemed to be killing the center," said Manuel ("Linggoy") Alcuaz, an activist of the non-Communist left, who was helping to organize the funeral procession. "But there is also the possibility that he will be seen to have built a new center, because before, the extremes on the right and the left were trying as hard as possible to organize, while the center remained passive. The people who have changed overnight are the silent majority."

Alcuaz's ideological characterization of the anticipated funeral procession provided an accurate snapshot of the opposition, which would apply throughout the struggle against Marcos. "There are two factions: those who believe in elections and those who prefer the protest movement," he said, drawing a distinction between the traditional party politicians and the so-called cause-oriented groups. Since the assassination, he ventured, the leftist proponents of protest had made great strides in convincing many newcomers to the struggle of the merits of their cause. "Those who before believed in election participation have turned a hundred and eighty degrees with the killing of Ninoy," he said. "Those who believed mainly in generating a protest movement and who were suspicious of Ninoy when he was alive have basically lost that suspicion now." For a time it would thus be easier for these two groups, with quite different agendas, to swallow their mutual suspicions and march together under Ninoy's banner.

*   *   *

Intuitively, Cory set the tone for the opposition confrontation with Marcos the moment she stepped off the plane and into an impromptu press conference on landing in Manila. "I don't want to point an accusing finger at anyone," she said demurely, "but I just want the government to answer certain questions that puzzled me." Her list was a scathing, if indirect, indictment of the military for failing to protect, if not deliberately murdering, her husband. Why, she asked, had soldiers who were unknown to him and junior in rank to those usually assigned to VIPs been assigned to meet him? And why only three close-in security escorts, when, during his years as a prisoner, truckloads of soldiers would accompany him on his rare furloughs home, for Christmas or to the office of his dentist?

She would remain the most outspoken critic of Marcos—the only one who dared accuse him personally of being responsible for the murder of her husband. Yet she would urge great restraint on the part of those who would fight him. The struggle must be nonviolent, the leadership incorruptible.

Although Cory quickly became the symbol of that struggle, no one in those early days thought of her as a potential leader. Nor did she envision such a role for herself. She was never the political neophyte that some of the pros took her for—at their peril. However, she lacked such leadership qualities as experience, ambition, and confidence, which other opposition personalities possessed in excess.

Not until much valuable time had been lost to petty feuding among rival politicians, of the sort which had paralyzed the moderate opposition in the past, would Cory begin to be perceived as the sole figure behind whom opposing factions would be willing to unite. Only then did it become apparent that the qualities that she had to offer were those which would be essential to winning this particular fight: courage; a contagious faith that victory was possible; and a profound understanding of the consequences of loss of freedom, which would serve as her ideological font.

Once home, her first priority was to carve out some time alone at Ninoy's coffin for herself and her children. Accordingly, visiting hours were suspended and the living room was cleared to give them the privacy they sought. "I made a pledge to my husband that I would carry on the struggle to restore our rights and freedoms," she later confided. Firm in that vow, she kissed his bruised face, ran her fingers through his hair for the last time, then put her grief on hold and immersed herself in a variety of activities aimed at achieving that goal.

First, there was a funeral to organize. Mindful that the silent majority looked to God and the Catholic Church more than to politicians for guidance, even on secular matters, Cory had strong opinions about how it should be handled. "The family is divided," said Linggoy Alcuaz, who was responsible for security and logistics for what was shaping up as a massive procession from the church to the cemetery. "The Aquino side of the family was working harder than the Cojuangco side on funeral arrangements until Cory arrived. Then her relatives began having more say."

Her friends and in-laws were abuzz with talk about how strong-minded the shy, backstage wife had suddenly become. Identified since her marriage only as Ninoy's wife, she was now reverting, some said, to her former identity as the well-traveled, convent-schooled daughter of the close-knit Cojuangco family. She was intent on preventing the funeral from becoming a circus. Like Jackie Kennedy, they intimated, she envisioned a dignified ceremony, rich in symbolism and more in keeping with her husband's new role as a martyr than his old role as a politician.

Next, there were discussions about opposition political strategy during and after the funeral. Of greatest importance to party leaders was maintaining the momentum of protest generated by the assassination and harnessing it to their own advantage. No one, not even her family, could predict what Cory's input into these discussions would be. "Suddenly, out of the blue, Cory quietly beckoned to my husband, Ken," recalled Ninoy's sister Lupita in describing the preliminary procession behind the coffin to Santo Domingo Church. "She consulted him, saying that Marcos was hinting at condolences through the media, but that she would refuse to accept them unless he released all political prisoners as proof of his sincerity." Lupita concluded, "She wanted to make a political statement. Her first. And from that moment on, we all knew that Cory would remain in the background no longer."

A key point of contention between Cory and some of Ninoy's political allies was the exploitation of Ninoy's body. It had already been booked for display in both Manila and Tarlac and would have been on tour for ten days in the torrid heat of the rainy season by the time it was laid to rest. She resented the way some politicians who had not been particularly supportive of Ninoy during his years in isolation had now jumped on the funeral train, hoping to profit from identification with the dead hero. She was also greatly concerned about the possibility of violence along the way. "The people want to take the body everywhere," said Alcuaz, "but the wife does not want to have on her conscience people dying or getting hurt."

Then, as now, nonviolence was the principle that would guide Cory's actions. Her concern for a peaceful burial was the top priority of Alcuaz and other organizers of the procession. The family was concerned that extremists from either the radical left or the right-wing military might attempt to provoke an incident to further their own ends. They were well aware that it could easily turn violent, particularly as it inched its way past such controversial landmarks as the U.S. embassy or Imelda's pet project, the Philippine Cultural Center. Worse yet, there was a great potential for bloodshed when the massive crowd dispersed after the burial and no longer felt constrained by respect for the dead.

Finally, there was her own personal agenda: to satisfy herself as to how Ninoy died and to seek justice from a future government. She set out on this quest almost immediately by arranging to meet Ninoy's confidant Captain Grant. Having hardly slept the night of her arrival, she arose before dawn and was driven to nearby Santo Domingo Church, where Ninoy's body would be put on view later in the day. For an hour she peppered the officer with questions. As preparations for Ninoy's trip home were being made, she had been shown a schedule which indicated that Captain Grant was to have been present to greet Ninoy on arrival at the airport. "I thought you would be the one to escort Ninoy," said Cory. "What happened?" Grant lacked an authoritative answer, but he told her everything he knew.

Grant had, in fact, been given instructions that he would once again be Ninoy's custodian at Fort Bonifacio. He had even gone so far as to prepare a room for him there. He was waiting to receive his old friend when the blue AVSECOM van pulled up to the gate outside the Military Security Command compound on the afternoon of August 21. "I asked the escort officer of the van, Captain Felipe Valerio, 'Where is the senator?'" says Grant. Valerio replied, "Sir, something wrong happened. Somebody shot the senator." Grant demanded, "Where is he now?" Said Valerio, "In the van."

At that point, Grant said, he rushed inside to inform his superiors, who asked him to verify that it was indeed Aquino. "I opened the van and saw it was Ninoy there, and I confirmed it was him." Only at that point —after a delay that could have meant the difference between life and death, had Ninoy still been alive when he was scooped up off the tarmac—did army commander General Josephus Ramas order that he be taken to Fort Bonifacio Hospital. It was then that Grant began calling members of the Aquino family to come to the camp.

His initial questioning of the men in the van had elicited some useful information, which he passed on to Cory. In addition to the man in blue and Aquino, a third person had been involved in the shooting, they had told him. "They mentioned another assassin—a man in white, who ran away," said Grant.

*   *   *

Seemingly oblivious to the turmoil that swirled all about her, Cory entered Santo Domingo Church with members of her family and took her place in a semicircle of chairs around the flag-draped coffin of her husband. Two uniformed private security guards stood conspicuously on either side of the bier, a reminder that the Armed Forces of the Philippines were not welcome here. Despite the presence of 800 people, including a platoon of foreign correspondents, several rows of Manila-based diplomats, and fifteen white-robed Roman Catholic priests and prelates officiating, the funeral carried the feeling of a family affair.

The mass began with a reading by the youngest of Ninoy's children. "I am twelve years old and now I will say good-bye to my Dad," was the way American-educated Kris began. Only a baby when her father was incarcerated, she had passed through much of her childhood seeing him but once or twice a week in prison. More than the others, who had known him earlier as a widely admired free man, she had therefore prized the family's three "superhappy years in Boston," highlighted by such new experiences as gathering autumn leaves, shoveling snow, and seeing *Return of the Jedi* with her father. Referring to Ninoy's observation that she was the child who most took after him in her desire to be "surrounded by many people," she concluded, "He liked my guts. Thanks for all the happiness you have given me."

Ninoy had told me that Asians "gotta cry." Already the entire congregation was weeping. The tears flowed more abundantly and the applause intensified as the service progressed. Each song, each reading swelled with meaning for Filipinos who were looking to this ritual for political guidance as well as spiritual solace. Ignored by state radio and TV, the funeral mass was broadcast and replayed throughout the day on Catholic Radio Veritas and received wide circulation through audio- and videocassettes distributed by opposition groups. Much was made of the presence of the six-foot-three-inch-tall U.S. ambassador, Michael Armacost, near the front of the church, seated with a dozen other diplomats who had ignored palace entreaties not to attend.

The homily delivered by the ironically named Archbishop of Manila, Jaime, Cardinal Sin, was appropriately political and theatrical. The jocular churchman, who was named head of the most important archdiocese in 1973, had guided a Church that was painfully divided over martial law from a position of noninvolvement in state politics to one of "critical collaboration" with Marcos. In the months prior to the assassination, the Church had been heading in the direction of more criticism and less collaboration with the recalcitrant president. The tone and content of the cardinal's message during the funeral of his friend Ninoy would be closely scrutinized for signs of the role the nation's second most powerful institution (after the Armed Forces of the Philippines) could be expected to play in the latest political crisis.

Sin had previewed his position several days earlier, when he turned down an already announced appointment to the presidential commission established to investigate the assassination. Implicit in that action was his determination not to lend the Church's credibility to an inquiry which few believed would be independent or objective.

Resplendent in his white robe and miter, his words echoing across the vast, domed nave and over a public address system to the crowds standing in the churchyard and boulevard beyond, Sin pleaded for a peaceful reconciliation of the hostile forces that threatened to plunge the country into civil war:

> Peace! May it come soon like gentle rain on you, my countrymen of the hills, who fight for a cause you believe in.

> Peace! May it also come soon for you, soldiers and officers, who, while recruited to protect our nation from invaders, must now suffer the anguish of knowing that your enemies are your own brother Filipinos.

> Peace! To our government officials and employees now struggling to preserve their humanity and integrity before the eyes of our people.

The cardinal's words brought the tearful crowd of mourners to its feet in a standing ovation—not an uncommon response by Philippine congregations to rousing rhetoric from the pulpit, even on solemn occasions like weddings and funerals. Although staunchly anti-Communist like most Filipinos, the prelate had been sensitized by an increasingly radicalized clergy to the sins that were being committed by the Marcos regime in the name of fighting Communism.

As the mass built to its emotional climax, a master of ceremonies, who had been announcing the hymns and readings, introduced the person everyone had been waiting to hear. "This outburst of love and sympathy should be answered," he said, in a tone not unlike that of a show biz impresario. "I present the better half of Ninoy Aquino—Mrs. Cory Aquino." The small, bespectacled woman, draped in black, received her standing ovation in advance as she walked to the podium.

We never suspected it then, but the brief address she gave that morning would become the centerpiece of two successive political campaigns, which would change the face of the Philippines. In the same singsong voice that would one day draw record crowds of voters to town plazas across the country, she spoke from the heart about what had happened to her husband. As she chronicled the events which followed her family's farewell to Ninoy in Boston, she began to emerge from the large shadows of her father and her husband. She became, for all who heard her that day, a personality in her own right, nationally identifiable without either of her surnames. Simply Cory.

"My dear friends and countrymen," she began, harking back to her last phone conversation with Ninoy, who had called from Taipei:

He told me he would soon be leaving for the airport. I told him I was informed that General Ver had warned any airline bringing him in that he would not be allowed to disembark, but would be flown back to the port of origin. Ninoy said they would not do that to him, because he is, was, and always will be a Filipino.

For the first of many times, she was interrupted by a burst of applause. There was not a sound in the church as she built toward the inevitable 2:30 A.M. phone call from a Japanese news agency, seeking confirmation of her husband's murder. Nuns, priests, and ambassadors wept unashamedly as she told of gathering her children around her to "pray the rosary and ask our Blessed Mother to help us."

Intuitively, masterfully, she segued from tragedy to redemption, expressing her initial disbelief at the "extraordinary display of love and devotion" manifested on her return to Manila by the countless mourners, "who did not even know Ninoy." Never overtly political, but proceeding from the assumption that the people were finally ready to exert their power, she thanked "all the Filipino men and women who have demonstrated to us that Ninoy did not die in vain." Almost muffled by applause was a personal postscript, "Ninoy, who loved you, the Filipino people, is now loved in return. I thank you."

Final prayers were said, and Ninoy's soul was committed to eternity. "May the martyrs come to welcome you," intoned the cardinal.

"Lord, save your people," responded the congregation in a last refrain.

As the pallbearers prepared to carry the casket out into the sunshine for its long march into history, Sin sounded a poignant farewell, "The mass has ended. Go in peace. Good-bye, my friend."

*   *   *

A national catharsis had begun. Leaving behind the dark mystery of religious ritual, the coffin was hoisted into place atop a bier of bright yellow chrysanthemums at the head of the first protest march permitted in the Philippines in more than a decade. As the cortege left the churchyard, the solid sea of people, who had flooded the main boulevards of Manila, parted just long enough to let pass the funeral truck and the caravan of vehicles carrying family members, opposition leaders, and press. Then it closed in behind and around them, a cheerful cacophony of hymns, chants, and banners reading Democracy, Freedom, Revolution; Marcos, Imelda, Ver—Wanted for Murder; and Ninoy, You Are Not Alone. It was an occasion marked by all of the glitz and circumstance with which Filipinos endowed their most solemn and their most festive occasions alike. "You can compare this to the death of JFK and Elvis," said one participant proudly.

He drew his references from an American culture that had so rooted itself in the Filipino psyche as to provoke a nationalist backlash. Indeed, many marchers expressed strong nationalist feeling, booing the presence of U.S. military bases and cursing American support for the Marcos regime as the procession passed before the U.S. embassy. They did not, however, attempt to crash the gates or trash the grounds, as some organizers had feared. The marchers recognized that this enormous demonstration, estimated to include 2 million people in the course of the day, was in itself a warning to the American government that the Marcos regime must go. There was an innate faith that the American people would understand them and help turn their government's policy of support for Marcos around. Even the most radical among them was appreciative of the fact that the American news media were covering every mile of the march, which their own official TV and press were ignoring.

Most marchers were somewhat timid at the start. Either too young to have ever participated in a mass action or old enough to remember the brutality with which police had stormed the 1970 student demonstrations, they were content to simply follow the coffin, singing hymns and patriotic songs, and waving to shopkeepers and apartment dwellers who greeted them from balconies and doorsteps along the way. Less than an hour into the procession, however, an air of excitement swept through the crowd. Through the raised windows of the air-conditioned press van, I could see expressions of astonishment on the faces of the people massed along the sidewalks. Their ears were cocked to catch a distant sound. Those who heard it first began relaying the message to others in the crowd. On opening the windows, a haunting melody wafted inside.

Sensing that something extraordinary was occurring, several of us left the van and joined the march. "What is the significance of that song?" I asked a young woman. As we walked along, she explained that it was a special song that was sung "during war or crisis." People had been forbidden to sing it during martial law, she said. That is why bystanders had reacted initially with fear when they heard the familiar strains. She took my pen and notebook in hand and wrote its Filipino name: "*Ang Bayan Ko*" (My Country). The anthem of Filipino nationalists in previous struggles for liberation, it would become the battle hymn of the anti-Marcos movement.

As the parade inched across the city, the marchers gathered courage from what appeared to be an almost universal outpouring of support by people along the route. Children waved yellow ribbons and pieces of cloth or showered confetti from upstairs windows on the marchers below. Outside the University of Santo Tomas spectators released cages full of white pigeons with yellow and black ribbons tied to their feet, as the cortege passed. As the coffin approached the historic Plaza Miranda, site of the bombing of an opposition rally twelve years earlier, the crowd assembled there let loose with a "noise barrage" of honking horns, clanking cans, firecrackers, and shouts.

A tropical downpour at midday soaked marchers and flooded streets along the procession route, but it did not dampen spirits. Spectators who raised their umbrellas were chided by student marchers, "That's Imelda's monopoly." The reference to the First Lady's penchant for protecting her delicate complexion under a parasol held over her by a uniformed aide drew laughter and more often than not shamed those who had sought protection from the rain into lowering their umbrellas.

As the clouds cleared, the fears of a decade lifted.

"We are not afraid," shouted a group of women, some holding children by the hand.

"I was warned by my mother and my boss not to join, but I ignored them," said one, buoyed by newfound courage. Members of the Federation of Free Workers unfurled a banner, which they had kept rolled up until they had tested the wind. All of them had walked off the job to pay their respects to Aquino.

"We lost the right to strike during martial law," they said. "We would like to restore it."

When darkness fell, a group of several thousand young people broke away from the procession, as organizers had feared they would, and drifted toward Mendiola Bridge, a political landmark of the 1970 student rioting, which had precipitated martial law. Security forces, which had remained in the background all day, were waiting for them there in anticipation of a reenactment of the 1970 Battle of Mendiola. At first the students hurled only insults and stones, which police lobbed back at them from behind their shoulder-high riot shields. Gradually, however, the confrontation escalated, with students tossing homemade "pillboxes," and antiriot police dispersing them by shooting into the air. When the confrontation was over, one student was dead and several police wounded.

Meanwhile, in an elite private cemetery on the outskirts of Manila, a trumpet played "Taps" and a single yellow balloon lofted over the floodlit burial site. Now teeming with mourners, the plot, owned by Cory's in-laws, was in ordinary times spacious and serene. It was not unusual for husbands to be buried with the families of their wives, and Cory had wanted it that way. But instead of being sealed inside the large, stone mausoleum housing the remains of members of the Cojuangco family, Ninoy's tomb would be situated on a grassy knoll, where his countrymen could go to pay their respects.

Separated from the near-hysterical crowd by only a rope and a ring of private security guards, the Aquino family took a last glimpse inside Ninoy's coffin, circling it to sprinkle water on his body and to thrust small bouquets of flowers into his hands. Then, as a priest led them in prayer, the pallbearers closed the lid. The family was hustled away into waiting limousines just seconds before the mourners broke through the ropes to see and touch the grave. As security guards struggled to hold them back, cemetery workers lowered the wooden casket into a cement vault and mortared it shut.

8

Intermezzo

As the Philippine marines at the palace gate checked my press card against their list of journalists scheduled for presidential interviews on the evening of September 22, 1983, I thought of the briefing I had received from the U.S. State Department officer on the Philippine desk just one year before, as I was preparing to move to Southeast Asia. "Don't make the mistake that most correspondents do and start thinking that you are the one who will be there to see Marcos fall," he had counseled. However, given what Marcos's opponents had been saying about the erosion of his political base, and the suspicions which I harbored about his role in the assassination, I entered the palace that evening prepared to believe that he was finished. I left two hours later persuaded that he would be around for some time to come.

Exactly one month had passed since the Aquino killing. Each day had brought with it fresh setbacks for Marcos and fiery rhetoric about his imminent ouster. He was unable to persuade creditable people to accept appointments to the commission to investigate the murder. New revelations, about ties between the alleged assassin, who had by now been identified as a convicted criminal named Rolando Galman, and the military, had given weight to speculation of official involvement in the plot.

The ailing president's silence on these and other issues had provoked even the more conservative opposition leaders like Doy Laurel to call for the president to "resign now."

Since the moderate opposition lacked the necessary leverage to extract concessions from the recalcitrant president, however, events remained stalemated. It was a situation begging for compromise but inviting violence. That violence had come last night, on the eleventh anniversary of martial law, and today Marcos had finally emerged from seclusion in an attempt to calm a nervous nation and reassure allies and creditors that he was still alive and in charge.

The interview, granted jointly to me and two other foreign correspondents, marked my first encounter with Marcos. Although he was sick, weak, and battered by the events of the past month, I had no doubt in my mind, after forty-five minutes of contentious questions and answers, that he was far from being the goner that his political enemies portrayed him to be. Sitting eyeball-to-eyeball with him, I felt I had glimpsed a caricature of the "old Marcos," whom Ninoy had conjured up for me in Taipei. He did not lack the legendary force of character with which he had been credited. It was, to be sure, a negative force. But it was strong, persuasive, even charismatic.

For the first time I could imagine what the Filipino voters, who had elected him twice and then tolerated his takeover, must have seen in him. He was a crusty, crafty, obstinate bastard. He was the kind of lawyer you would hire to get you off if you were really in trouble—particularly if you were guilty. He was the kind of maverick you would elect president when you deemed the system to be beyond the power of conventional leaders and remedies to repair. More to the point presently under debate, he seemed the kind of ruler who would stay until the bitter end. He was making clear by example now what he would later state baldly: Marcos was no Shah of Iran, ready to flee when challenged. He intended, in the words of an aide, to "die with his boots on."

"Don't be ridiculous!" bellowed the president, as if I were the only person on the planet to have conceived of such a dumb question. "You don't resign as president under these circumstances. You reestablish peace and order." Another reporter began to raise a follow-up, but Marcos wasn't finished. He continued, "Especially when you say that only a few hard-core radicals are exploiting and manipulating things." He paused, sized me up with his watery eyes, then administered a final, defiant blow. "If the party wants me, I'll run for reelection. This talk of resignation is ridiculous!"

In that one response, so laden with contempt, so resonant with mock disbelief, so outrageous, I had all the information I needed to forecast how far his political opponents' repeated demands for his resignation were likely to go in the weeks ahead. Marcos was utterly convincing that they would go nowhere. As long as his principal opponents clung to their old tactics of mouthing unobtainable political demands, like "resign now," at rallies and storming the gates of Malacañang, as they had attempted to do last night, with nothing more powerful than "pillboxes," the "old Marcos" was well equipped to keep them in their place. He, after all, still controlled the armed forces, while his opponents remained disunited and lacking in organization and disciplined supporters. He had defeated them before at the same game. Did they never learn from past mistakes?

The fatal flaw of the non-Communist political opposition, before and during martial law, had been its propensity to see Marcos as it wished he were, rather than as he was, and to thereby imagine him as a lesser foe than he turned out to be. For the nearly two decades that he had been in power, Marcos had succeeded in outlasting his democratic opponents, Ninoy included, because he was so much more the cold-eyed realist. He had understood the nature of raw power and the necessity for hard cash so much better than they. And he had had the stomach to use this power. Since the assassination, the regime had treated dissenters with "maximum tolerance," allowing them to demonstrate against him. But until they were able to back up their words with action, he would not be moved by their chants.

More than anything specific that Marcos said, the interview was fascinating as a study of the beleaguered president in the first stage of what would be a grueling fight for his physical and political survival. Former Vice-President Pelaez had described him to me as "a counterpuncher, who does not plan the future, but goes from situation to situation." That seemed an apt description. As I watched his mind in motion, it was clear that he would stop at nothing—bluffing, lying, unleashing the military, even implementing reforms—to stay in power. Unfortunately, for everyone involved, however, he was not looking very far beyond his own dulled reflexes and dated experience for guidance on how to proceed.

The veteran crisis manager seemed incapable of viewing this crisis except in terms of the past. "This is nothing, compared to nineteen seventy-two," he scoffed. "Then there were bombings, they ambushed Minister Enrile's car, they attempted to kidnap a general," he recalled, seeming to forget that his own people had staged some of the very incidents he was citing. As a reputed master of the Filipino psyche, Marcos was confident that old behavior patterns would repeat themselves. "The Filipino temperament is very volatile," he said. "It can swing back and forth. This is why a leader must know how to handle the situation. You cannot just counteract it violently. Let it cool off. Get everybody settled down and work out some kind of understanding." The president boasted, "I have this fund of experience."

His experience told him to employ the same tactics he had used successfully before: adopt an uncompromising pose, then divide and conquer the opposition by negotiating limited reforms with the moderate politicians, and reassert authority by cracking down on the more radical street protesters.

"Who are they?" Marcos asked, with customary disdain, spitting out the names of several lesser-known but legitimate opposition parties, which were calling for his resignation. There followed his eternal refrain: "Are the Communists in this?" Yet even as he was refusing to negotiate with those who were calling for his resignation, his politician's mind was busy converting their sweeping demands into several more easily negotiable ones and computing the minimum offer he would be prepared to put on the table. By the time the interview was over, he had convinced himself —and me—that the debate over resignation would eventually be reduced and played out over less-drastic election reforms. "I think what they are aiming at is winning the elections," said Marcos, who had shrewdly sized up the priorities of the traditional politicians, whose instincts he shared. "What they are working on is really more liberal terms for the elections of nineteen eighty-four."

He was, he intimated, prepared to be very reasonable on that issue. "We are ready to discuss that, so they can win a few seats in the National Assembly," he said, in a characteristically patronizing tone. With a gratuitous shrug of his shoulders and a flip of his good hand, Marcos asked, "What do they want? More participation in the counting of the ballots? Security of their candidates during the campaign? All of these we will talk about." When questioned about responding to other opposition demands, he expressed similar openness to the prospect of limited change. "I must go through the motions," he acknowledged, wearily. Then, acting like a beneficent potentate offering a gift to his subjects, Marcos announced that he would broaden the representation on the Aquino investigative panel to include the opposition. "I intend to authorize the parliament to nominate one person from the opposition and one from the majority party," he said.

＊　　　　＊　　　　＊

Had Marcos and the traditional political opposition been the only players on the board, and resignation versus election reform the central issue, the president might have been able to drive the sort of bargain he had previewed. However, the situation was far more complex than Marcos acknowledged, more complex, perhaps, than he even realized at the time. Marcos's reputation as his country's most celebrated practitioner of realpolitik was based on his unflinching acceptance of the hard facts about any given problem and the pragmatic solutions he conceived to dispose of them. No principle, no friend, no enemy was too cherished to escape sacrifice, should he deem the facts to warrant it.

During the approximately seven weeks that he remained confined to his bed and out of touch, however, a series of stunning changes, which fundamentally altered the political landscape and the assumptions of those fighting to reform the system, had taken place. Marcos, isolated by his illness and his *cordon sanitaire*, had missed them. As if lost in a time warp, he continued to compare the present crisis to the one he faced in 1972, mindless of several crucial differences between the two.

Unlike 1972, when much of the middle class had accepted martial law as a means of restoring order and reducing crime, today's middle class had become badly alienated from the government. It felt duped to have traded in its freedom and received nothing in return. Defying the cynical predictions of the Marcos loyalists, the white-collar workers and society matrons did not retreat behind the walls of their fashionable compounds after Ninoy's funeral was over. They mounted what would become a twice-weekly ritual of lunch-hour demonstrations on the main street of the Makati financial district.

In further contrast to 1972, the Roman Catholic Church was no longer neutral. Nor had its interest in seeing justice done in the Aquino assassination case faded after the funeral.

Perhaps the most important difference between 1972 and 1983, in terms of support for Marcos, was the fact that the private business community had lost confidence in the ability of the Marcos regime to guarantee the stability it thought it was buying when it had swallowed martial law. While it had not yet swung its weight behind the opposition, the private sector was no longer bullish on Marcos, as it had been a decade ago, or even neutral, as it had been during the years since then. With the killing of Aquino, it had come under pressure—much of it from wives and children, who had suddenly taken to sporting yellow ribbons and headbands—to choose sides. Because most businessmen were too prudent to jump ship until a better alternative presented itself, they were inclined to squeeze the economically hard-pressed president to agree to implement their priority reform: the election of a vice-president in order to assure a peaceful transition after Marcos.

Of all the changes which Marcos's once infallibly sensitive political antennae failed to detect, the loss of confidence of key U.S. officials in his ability to maintain stability in the geostrategically critical archipelago was the most important. Unlike 1972, when Washington tacitly accepted martial law, it now began pressing him for economic and political reforms, which, if granted, would undermine his authority.

"It all depends on him," said Scott Hallford, the U.S. embassy political officer, his pessimism showing. "If he can take the high ground for a change, instead of always taking the low ground, and if events have convinced him that he must rise above the tactical maneuvers for which he is known and act strategically, then there is hope." Among the fears of Hallford and his superiors was that Marcos would run out of time for compromise. "In a situation this fluid," said Hallford, "you are continually in the position of catching up. The danger is that the mood of the country could move beyond the point where actions could satisfy it."

Although official U.S. policy would continue formally to define Marcos as "part of the solution" until the day it offered him transportation out of the country and exile in the U.S., it quickly became clear to the professional policymakers in both the State Department and Pentagon that Marcos would not take the high road, and that preparation for a transition to a "post-Marcos era" must begin.

If the embassy had been slow to point the finger of blame for the assassination at the regime that first week, it had turned around quickly and with a discreet vengeance, acknowledged Ambassador Michael Armacost, "because of the way they handled the assassination investigation, the cover story they put out on it, and the lack of candor in their discussions with us."

Not only did Armacost ignore official diplomatic entreaties by Philippine officials not to attend Aquino's funeral, but he turned down an unseemly invitation to a party at Malacañang for visiting U.S. Senator Mark Hatfield that night. As soon as the official period of opposition mourning was over, he began reorienting embassy policy to broaden contacts with the opposition and the business community. He himself began inviting opposition politicians, businessmen, and journalists to his residence—something he had left to his subordinates in the past. He also began "speaking out in a way that the [Marcos] government did not like."

The change in tone was widely noted in Manila, where Armacost had been referred to by oppositionists behind his back as "Armaclose" because of his apparent closeness to the Marcoses. "I was never invited to the ambassador's residence until after the assassination," said a prominent businessman identified with the opposition. At a farewell party for Armacost in Manila, he confessed to the departing ambassador, "I used to think you were a Marcos *tuta* [lapdog]." Replied Armacost drily, "I had a bases treaty to renew."

Indeed, Armacost's brief, when he took over the embassy in March 1982, had been to negotiate a satisfactory second five-year renewal of the agreement governing continued U.S. access to Clark Air Base and Subic Naval Station. The Philippine flag had been raised over both bases for the first time as a result of the agreement reached during the previous round of negotiations under Presidents Ford and Carter, which had been bitter and long. Since then, following the election of Marcos's old friend Ronald Reagan, relations between the two governments had improved, but Washington had not wanted to take any chances.

Armacost had actively courted the First Couple from the time of his arrival in Manila. He had relayed Reagan's invitation to the Marcoses to make their first state visit to the U.S. in sixteen years, and he had subsequently suffered Marcos's threats to call off the trip, when an unflattering economic document, which the Philippine president chose to interpret as a piece of CIA disinformation, came to his attention.

After the August 1982 visit, which was regarded as a success by both governments, the Marcoses made a concerted effort to cultivate the Armacosts. In October they invited the ambassador and his wife, Bonnie, to accompany them and a small group of cronies to anniversary ceremonies marking the World War II landing of General MacArthur at Leyte. Although they had only packed clothes for a weekend aboard the presidential yacht, the Armacosts were induced to spend a week in the Marcoses' company, touring numerous development projects throughout the islands. The voyage received heavy coverage by state television and the rest of the Marcos-controlled media.

No sooner had they returned than another invitation—this one from Enrile—followed. The Armacosts accepted and arrived at inaugural ceremonies for a dam in the defense minister's home region of northern Luzon to find President and Mrs. Marcos among the guests. Again state television played up the friendly relations between the president and the diplomat. By the time a third invitation arrived, Armacost later related, "I began to sense that it suited their purpose to demonstrate great intimacy with the American ambassador." He did not fight the association with Marcos at that time, he explained, "because our purposes coincided; there was a bases agreement coming up, and we intended to get as good a deal as we could for the American government."

A deal, very much to Washington's liking, was concluded smoothly and in record time the following April. The Reagan administration promised to use its "best efforts" to obtain from Congress a total of $900 million in military and economic credits and assistance over the five-year life of the agreement, in return for continued "unhampered military operations" at the bases.

Once the negotiations were completed, the ambassador turned his attention to trying to prod the regime to hold "clean and honest elections" the following May. He suffered no illusions that reforms would be easily extracted from Marcos. It was difficult to imagine how Marcos, who, Armacost acknowledged, had declared martial law to perpetuate himself in power, would easily give up any significant degree of it in elections. "I would be surprised if he did not read Machiavelli once a week," commented Armacost.

Washington, however, was expecting a modicum of success in achieving what Armacost defined as America's policy goal in the Philippines: "to move the regime toward a broader popular base through legislative elections." The Aquino assassination had not altered that policy. Rather, it had made achievement of its objectives all the more urgent, since there was no obvious successor to Marcos in sight, and elections were regarded as the likeliest source of new leadership.

Based on a discussion he had had with Marcos not long after the assassination, Armacost doubted the validity of the administration's assumption that Marcos could somehow be compelled to change his ways.

"I related how I had come into government in nineteen sixty-nine when Nixon was a new president," said Armacost. He told Marcos of the respect he had had for Nixon's policies during his first term, but how the Watergate affair had changed all that. Then he made a thinly veiled reference to Marcos's deference to his discredited chief of staff, General Ver. "As I chose to characterize it to him," said Armacost, "Nixon had been ill served in his zeal to protect his subordinates. He had lied to protect them. At first they were little lies, but they eventually grew bigger."

Marcos saw where the story was leading, and before Armacost went further, he interrupted the ambassador. "It will never happen here," he vowed. "This will never be whitewashed. We will get to the bottom of this."

"It was the usual flimflam," commented Armacost, with considerable bitterness. "But it was one of those experiences that led me, perhaps more quickly than others, to relinquish any hope that he was capable at this stage of his life of any reform."

*   *   *

The degree to which the assassination had eroded Marcos's authority became glaringly apparent the week of September 21. For the past ten years, the anniversary of martial law had been officially marked as a "Day of National Thanksgiving," with the president presiding over a giant rally to commemorate the birth of his "New Society." In the immediate wake of the assassination, however, anti-Marcos forces announced their intention to commandeer the holiday to commemorate the slaying of Aquino. The regime made no effort to stop them. Nor did it try to prevent several loyalist politicians, who should have known better, from proceeding with their own plans to steal the opposition's thunder by scheduling a pro-Marcos rally in Makati one day before.

Before August 21, fear of the consequences of not joining such a rally and the inducements of free transportation, a box lunch, and a few pesos would have guaranteed a crowd of government employees numbering in the tens of thousands. This particular rally, however, on September 20, netted only 2,000 embarrassed marchers, who were greeted with hostility by twice their number of office workers, as they marched down Ayala Avenue, the Wall Street of the Philippines.

"The president is a marvelous politician," said Enrique Zobel with obvious regret, as he gazed down at the grim-faced demonstrators from his executive suite atop the Bank of the Philippine Islands building. "He must not know about this." Zobel was referring not only to the humiliating show of support for Marcos. He was also questioning whether Marcos or Imelda had approved the malicious positioning of the speaker's platform, bedecked with pro-Marcos banners, directly in front of his bank, or the vindictive anti-Zobel posters adorning walls along the marchers' route. A member of one of the country's most powerful families, Zobel, together with other business leaders, had tacitly sanctioned a pro-Aquino rally in normally apolitical Makati several days before. It had drawn some 10,000 office workers and executives.

Zobel stifled a laugh as he watched the pro-Marcos rally degenerate into a fiasco. Employees of the country's biggest banks and insurance companies, with the silent approval of their bosses, booed the marchers below, unfurled anti-Marcos banners from their windows, and finally let loose a barrage of water bombs, which drove the speakers off the platform and caused the marchers to drop their I Love Marcos signs and flee.

The Makati debacle was an omen of things to come. The next day, September 21, some 200,000 protesters marched on Post Office Square from four Roman Catholic churches to observe a "Day of National Sorrow" in memory of Aquino. Even the government-controlled media billed the gathering as the largest political rally held in the Philippines since martial law. Standing on the steps of the neo-Greek building under a Philippine flag at half-mast, representatives of the moderate political opposition parties, leftist student and labor groups, and the Aquino family called openly for Marcos's resignation.

The mood was militant. "The Filipinos are no longer afraid," said Doy Laurel, leader of the United Nationalist Democratic Organization (UNIDO), reflecting the views of many moderates, who only a short time ago had refrained from openly articulating their political opinions for fear of reprisals. For the first time, students sported T-shirts pointedly emblazoned with their names, universities, and class averages for the benefit of the plainclothes police posing as press photographers, who routinely monitored their campus assemblies.

The rally climaxed with a pledge by former Senator Diokno and Cory Aquino, her fist raised, to "end the Marcos regime and in its place establish a truly democratic, representative government, to halt the militarization of our country, and to assert the full sovereignty of our people and resist all forms of alien control or domination." Diokno declared, "This day marks the beginning of the end for Marcos."

Although the rally's organizers, both moderates and leftists, had called for the peaceful dispersal of the massive crowd, groups of radicals once again gravitated toward Mendiola Bridge. Much publicity had been given to police orders to exercise "maximum tolerance" toward demonstrators, and many police good-naturedly displayed empty holsters. However, trucks full of armed troops were parked nearby on barricaded side streets, and when violence inevitably broke out, eleven people were killed—a higher toll than in the 1970 "Mendiola Massacre"—most of them by gunfire.

At the height of the violence the clashes spread to nearby government merchandise centers established by Imelda Marcos's Metro-Manila Commission, which were pillaged. "This is Ninoy's gift to the people," shouted looters, as they carried off bags of rice and sugar, slabs of meat, and even ceiling fans. Elsewhere in the city a police van was "ambushed" and overturned, public buildings vandalized, and small stores bearing the "KKK" of Imelda's national livelihood movement, the *Kilusang Kabuhayan Sakaunlaran*, were put to the torch. Major streets in all four districts of Manila were barricaded by boulders and piles of tires, which had been systematically delivered earlier in the day and set afire after dusk. Only vehicles bearing yellow ribbons identifying them as pro-Aquino were allowed to pass.

The situation seemed headed toward a replay of 1970, as the president announced a military crackdown and threatened to reimpose martial law. Confrontation became inevitable when he removed the restraints he had placed on police shortly after the assassination. Under pressure from top generals, who complained that "maximum tolerance is interpreted as weakness" by demonstrators, Marcos announced that riot police would once again be armed, and permits would henceforth be required for all rallies.

The next day, masked Marcos "goons" (hoodlums working in league with law enforcement officials) terrorized a peaceful anti-Marcos demonstration in Makati by speeding down Ayala Avenue in Jeeps, their submachine guns aimed at confetti-throwing clerks and secretaries in the upper-story windows of corporate towers. Across Manila, protesters retaliated by setting fires and marching, only to be met by tear gas and truncheons.

Repeatedly, Marcos took to the airwaves to issue ever more belligerent warnings to the groups arrayed against him. The whipped-up emotions and the tide of confusion that swept the capital seemed reminiscent of 1972. He issued hate-filled threats to the same groups that had been the object of his paranoia then: the oligarchs, the students, and the Church. Addressing a host of unidentified enemies, he warned, irrationally, "To anyone seeking to seize the reins of government, even if you kill a hundred, a thousand men, you have no right to run the government."

"Marcos is a man beginning to panic," observed Jose Diokno, following the president's third television speech in a week. "He feels the power he has beginning to crumble. He is beginning to doubt even the loyalty of the men in government and is worried about the fact that the military may no longer be loyal to him."

Meanwhile, bankers reported that capital flight since the assassination had reached a staggering $500 million, nearly half of it in illegal black-market operations. Marcos had dispatched Prime Minister/Finance Minister Cesar Virata and Central Bank Governor Jaime Laya to Washington to seek a new package of standby credits from the International Monetary Fund (IMF), in an effort to avert a moratorium on repayment of their ballooning foreign debt. Added to those woes was the prospect that the White House might cancel President Reagan's scheduled November stop-over in Manila en route to China. Marcos had earlier warned that such a move would represent a "blow" to his presidency and would send a message which "the banks would translate into something more than a lack of sympathy and cooperation."

By the evening of September 29, events seemed to be escalating wildly out of control, as analysts of every political shade predicted an imminent explosion. I began to have serious doubts about my negative confidence in Marcos's stubborn will to hang tough. There no longer seemed to be any center of gravity to hold back the myriad, fractious forces. If Marcos's threats were not empty ones, then General Ver must be readying his troops. No civilian leader had emerged to point the way to a compromise. Trust was gone, and fact had totally given way to rumor. Such a gaping vacuum invited exploitation by extremists. If they were moving into place, why couldn't I see them or sense whether they were coming from the right or the left?

It was a Thursday, the day of the week when I should have been filing a story, but I couldn't distinguish what would set this story apart from the similarly pessimistic one I had filed the week before. There were no new casualties, no identifiable plot, not even any clear-cut action, just a sense of impending doom. At a loss for how to explain what was going on, I set out on my rounds of the day's demonstrations and press conferences. An unauthorized rally in Makati, which was disguised as a noon-hour mass, so as not to invite police intervention, ended peacefully with apparently sympathetic law enforcement officers even flashing the "L" sign (for *Laban*, meaning "fight") used by pro-Aquino forces. A check with officials at the still-inert commission named to investigate the assassination showed no date yet set for the opening of hearings. Marcos remained secluded inside Malacañang. No hot news from the wire services.

By evening, my notebook empty, my tape cassette blank, I sat with several other reporters outside the closed doors of Doy Laurel's dining room, waiting for a group of American human rights lawyers to emerge from a meeting with opposition leaders about the current political situation. The Americans were here, among other things, to gather opinion on which to base a recommendation to the White House as to whether the president should cancel his forthcoming Philippine trip. Their dinner meeting over, Laurel introduced the three members of the International Lawyers' Committee for Human Rights with appropriate drama. "This may be our last supper," he intoned. "Marcos is a virtual prisoner of General Ver inside Malacañang." Typically, however, no details or factual evidence followed.

We all trooped into Laurel's private study, where an informal press conference ensued. The lawyers expressed skepticism about the independence of the investigative panel named to probe the assassination, noted no improvement in the human rights situation since their last visit, and indicated they would recommend that President Reagan cancel his trip, because "Filipinos would tend to view a visit at this time as a show of support for their government, to which they would react."

Still no story. Ready to end another eighteen-hour day of ambiguity and foreboding, I closed my notebook and turned off my tape recorder. How much longer, I wondered, would it take for things to come to a head? With the stage so clearly set for a climactic confrontation, my Western metabolism called for a timely resolution, one way or the other.

Filipinos obviously had a higher threshold of tolerance for confusion and irresolution than we. Waiting and wondering when and how they would erupt was becoming a frustrating business. The rhythm of this struggle was very foreign to Westerners. We couldn't even sense when a Filipino dinner party was over. As we Americans, human rights lawyers and journalists, bid each other good-bye and prepared to leave, Doy's wife, Celia, came running after us, indicating that the main event of the evening was only now beginning. The serious agenda had been but a prologue to the upcoming entertainment.

With a flip of the switch, Celia, an accomplished actress and painter, summoned forth a disco beat from the electronic sing-along machine known as "One-Two-Three," with which every good, middle-class Filipino household is equipped. Swaying to the rhythm, she picked up the hand microphone and began her introduction of tonight's special program and performers. This was the fortieth night since Ninoy's death, she reminded us, and the end of the special period of prayers and novenas by means of which Filipino Catholics linger a bit longer with the spirit of their departed loved ones. While mourning for their hero would continue, tonight was a time for celebrating his life and his memory.

Addressing her remarks to his mother, Doña Aurora, his sister Maur, and brother Butz, who were present, as well as an array of opposition stalwarts, Celia recalled some of the happy moments she had spent with Ninoy, who had chaperoned her first dates with Doy, kept her company in the hospital as she waited to give birth to her first child, Suzie, and attended Suzie's wedding reception on the night of the deadly Plaza

Miranda bombing. Ninoy should have left earlier that night, so as not to be late for the rally, but Celia had insisted then, as she was insisting to us now, that he had to stay for the singing.

There followed an extraordinary program, the likes of which would be repeated in other living rooms at other times during my stay in the Philippines, but never with more relish. One after the other, and sometimes in duets and trios, the eight Laurel children sang a selection of American standards, each prefaced by a special dedication, "Philadelphia Bandstand" style, each accompanied by prerecorded orchestra music blaring from the "One-Two-Three" sound system. Ninoy's homecoming song: "Tie a Yellow Ribbon." The song Imelda banned during martial law: "Don't Cry for Me, Argentina." The song trilled by the mice in Walt Disney's *Cinderella*: "A Dream Is a Wish Your Heart Makes." And, to bring on the tears, Ninoy's favorite, which was fast becoming an opposition standard: "The Impossible Dream."

As the program reached its climax, with all of us rising to sing the haunting patriotic anthem "*Ang Bayan Ko*," the room was dripping with sentiment. Midway through the repertoire, one of the American lawyers had nudged me and asked me to surreptitiously turn on my tape recorder. I whispered that if I did, I would erase his press conference. "This is better," he whispered back. Now he checked to make sure the machine was still recording. "They will never believe this in New York," he exclaimed under his breath.

For me, the evening would become a metaphor for Filipino problem solving. Whenever, in the future, the suspense became unbearable and the prospects for resolution impossible, from my point of view, I would pause to wait for the unexpected compromise, the unimagined diversion —the intermezzo—that would avert confrontation, dissipate tension, lighten the mood, and refresh the spirits of would-be revolutionaries, as the Laurel family was doing now.

No sooner did the sing-along end than the "One-Two-Three" machine ripped into an instrumental encore of "Yellow Ribbon." Doy grabbed Ninoy's seventy-two-year-old mother and waltzed her around the living room, whereupon everyone else grabbed partners, startled New York attorneys included, and began to jitterbug.

"I bet when you woke up this morning, you did not think you would find yourself in a sing-along by nightfall," said Celia to Attorney Marvin Frankel.

His former inhibitions gone, Frankel beamed to the entire Filipino cast, "If being beautiful and talented would accomplish everything, you are all the way home."

Attorney Jack Greenberg joked, "How can you say you have no human rights, when you can sing like that?"

The final message of that serendipitous evening was pronounced by Butz Aquino. In its own zany way, it was a more appropriate precis of the critical events that had taken place over the last six weeks and the unknown future that lay ahead than any serious analysis I might have written that week. "Have you read the prediction of Jeane Dixon about the Philippines in the new *Playboy?*" asked Ninoy's kid brother. He then proceeded to recite it:

The South will turn red.
The North will collapse.
A man in white will fall.
Forty days later the President will die . . .

9

See No Evil

By the time I met Cory Aquino, one month after the assassination, I knew her as the brave widow, and she knew me as the woman reporter who had accompanied Ninoy on the final leg of his flight home from exile. I had watched her from the edges of crowds at the time of the funeral, hesitating to intrude. Only when my own emotions erupted on reentering that airport terminal for the first time after the murder did I find the words I wanted to say to her.

"Dear Mrs. Aquino," I wrote, "I am sitting in Manila International Airport two weeks later, waiting for a plane and thinking back over the circumstances that brought me to know your husband . . ." I asked for an appointment on my return.

When we met, one thing was immediately apparent. Though Cory was less flamboyant and more reserved than the charismatic, flesh-pressing politician in whose shadow she had lived for most of her adult life, her sense of rage over the course of events since Marcos imposed martial law was as strong as Ninoy's. The fact that hers was couched in personal terms and held in check by her devout religious faith did not diminish it. Like him, she had a fine sense of the absurd, and she loved to talk. After an hour, I felt I had known her for a long time.

I was intent on quoting the loving things Ninoy had said about her en route to Manila. She seemed touched to know that she was so vocally on his mind during those last hours, but as if to prevent the conversation from becoming overly sentimental, she deftly changed the subject to who killed him. I confided my near certainty that it was one of the security men in white barongs who had followed Ninoy through the service door.

She revealed that several witnesses had already contacted her, and that she and her younger brother Jose ("Peping") Cojuangco had slipped out in disguise to meet one of them. I did not push her to tell me more, because I thought it might be too painful for her to discuss. But she seemed to want to unburden herself. Her voice quavered a time or two, but she kept the tears at bay. She giggled at the notion of disguising her appearance, making light of the fact that until several weeks ago she never had to worry about anyone recognizing her. The young woman witness, who had made contact with her family through intermediaries, had said that she would talk only to Cory.

"They hit him on the head first with the butt of the gun," is the way Cory described the nub of this witness's account. She hoped this meant that Ninoy had been spared pain. "I asked her to put her story in writing, have it notarized by someone she trusts, then lock it up until Marcos is gone," said Cory. She made no attempt to persuade the witness to testify publicly before that time.

She remembered how Marcos's goons had terrorized her household staff to provide incriminating information about Ninoy, and how many of the key witnesses at his trial—witnesses who had testified for the state and against Ninoy—had died unnatural deaths not long afterward. Marcos charged that Ninoy's henchmen had eliminated them. She maintained that the regime had gotten rid of them, once they had served its purpose, because they knew too much to be trusted. She would not jeopardize an innocent passenger's life. Unambiguous in her conclusion that no objective inquiry could be made into the crime as long as Marcos was in the Philippines, Cory had already decided at that early date that the Aquino family would not cooperate with any investigative commission the president might establish.

She was just as straightforward in stating that she held Marcos personally responsible for the killing. Although she had no desire to defend Imelda, it rankled her, as a woman and a wife herself, that it was the First Lady, rather than the president, who was generally perceived to have ordered Ninoy's death. She disliked Marcos even more for allowing that perception to go unchallenged. While she might not have said it in so many words, I remember agreeing with one of her remarks to the effect that it was just like a man to stand by and let the woman take the heat.

Ninoy, she allowed, fondly, elsewhere during the conversation, had been something of a "male chauvinist" himself.

Other family members had been contacted by other witnesses about various aspects of the conspiracy that had resulted in Ninoy's death, and I set about methodically talking to each relative who appeared to have information, as well as to other Filipinos and foreigners thought to have direct evidence. Obsessed by a desire to know what my ears had heard but my eyes had failed to see, and compelled to pursue leads that the government was bound to ignore or cover up, I was presumptuous enough to think that I might find at least one eyewitness, out of the several dozen who had been in a position to see the shooting, who would talk in confidence to a foreign correspondent. That was before I properly understood the power of threat and intimidation that Marcos and Ver had so adeptly substituted for tanks and barbed wire as a way of cowing people into submission.

From the start there were many promising leads, but no witnesses courageous—or foolhardy—enough to come forward. Ninoy's mother, Doña Aurora, stoic in her grief, had revealed to Congressman Solarz that a mistress of General Ver had paid her a secret visit a month before. The woman had told Mrs. Aquino to warn her son that if he came back, Ver would kill him. However, as the woman's life would be endangered if her identity were revealed, there was no chance of learning more from her.

Whatever information I had any hope of getting would have to come from private citizens through the auspices of the opposition. Peping Cojuangco added a postscript to Cory's account of their conversation with the young woman whom they had sneaked out to meet. After seeing Ninoy hit with the gun by one of his khaki-uniformed military escorts, the woman told them that she had excitedly described what she had seen to the passenger who sat next to her during the flight. He, too, had been looking out the window at that point, but his account differed from hers. "No, they shot him," the man had said. With the help of his political operatives, Peping had traced the man, a Filipino, as far as southern California, where he had moved shortly after the assassination to live with a sister, who served in the U.S. Air Force. When a TIME correspondent sought him out there, however, the man professed to have seen nothing.

Similar tips from Doy Laurel and Butz Aquino, who claimed to be in contact with eleven eyewitnesses, led nowhere. Nor were we at that time able to contact two Philippine Airlines ground mechanics, who were widely rumored to have seen the killings. Not even a promise to shield their identities or help them obtain the necessary visas to escape to the U.S. persuaded any of these people to talk to me.

Foreign witnesses were no braver. Acting on information that the cockpit crew of a Royal Brunei Airlines plane had seen the shooting, I flew to the tiny Sultanate of Brunei on the northern coast of Borneo. Boarding a Royal Brunei flight from Hong Kong to the Brunei capital, Bandar Seri Begawan, I handed the steward a note for the pilot. After the dinner service had been completed, he responded with an invitation to visit the cockpit. He gave me the names and addresses of the two men who had been aboard the Manila flight that day. "The man who would have had the better view," he suggested, knowingly, "was the copilot."

The pilot, a former New Zealand Air Force flyer, was "hiking in New Zealand," I was told on arriving in Brunei. Copilot Ian McPherson did not return my calls. Finally, in answer to a note I had sent him, he replied brusquely in writing: "I actually work for British Airways, so would not be free to talk to the press even should I want to do so, which I do not. Sorry."

Unwilling to let him off so easily, I decided to confront McPherson directly by ticketing myself on the next return flight to Manila which he would be piloting. After landing, I waited until the other passengers had disembarked. Then I approached the open cockpit. The Royal Brunei plane was docked at Gate 7, exactly where it had been on August 21. Its view of Gate 8, the mobile passenger tube, or jetway, and the service stairs, which had been connected to the China Airlines flight that day, was breathtaking. The plane was perfectly angled and no farther away than the length of half a football field; every movement on the staircase would have been easily visible to both pilot and copilot. In fact, it would have taken an effort for people sitting in those two seats to avoid seeing what had occurred there.

Before I could introduce myself to McPherson, his copilot ordered me out of the cockpit, threatening to call the airport authorities if I did not leave the plane immediately. McPherson, who repeated his earlier refusals to comment, on grounds that he did not want to tangle with Philippine authorities, joined him in physically moving me out of the doorway into the hands of two Filipino ground officials. Aware that the airport remained a military preserve, I went quietly.

The fear which the Marcos regime was still able to inspire, even in its weakened condition, was impressive. Already the government of Taiwan had been subjected to Marcos's wrath for having permitted Aquino to travel on its state airline. Two days after the assassination, China Airlines' landing rights in Manila were suspended.

Meanwhile, the most important new evidence to point to a possible military role in the killing was coming from sources close to the second victim of the crime, who was finally identified a full nine days after the assassination, not by police, but by a columnist for the popular tabloid *Tempo*. Crime reporter Ruther Batuigas, a controversial character celebrated for his police connections and his own bullet-scarred torso, broke the story that the alleged assassin, Rolando Galman, was a provincial hit man with a pending warrant of arrest against him in connection with a 1981 shooting spree. Even more embarrassing for the regime was the information that Galman had once served time in a military prison under a Presidential Commitment Order signed by Marcos himself. How had Galman been freed, wondered the coffee shop pundits, mindful that only the president can lift that particular type of detention order?

Other publications subsequently revealed that Galman's girlfriend, who had stayed with him under heavy guard for three nights preceding the assassination in a small motel near the Manila airport, had disappeared a week later, along with her sister, never to be seen again. The depth of the military's connection to Galman was disclosed by *Newsweek*, which reported that Galman had enjoyed a close relationship with Colonel Arturo Custodio, an air force officer from his hometown, who was attached to Ver's headquarters.

Opening its proceedings against such a backdrop of fear, suspicion, and incriminating disclosures, the Marcos-appointed investigative body seemed all the more impotent, the testimony of government witnesses— the only witnesses there were—all the more contrived. From the start, the panel, known as the Fernando Commission, for its chairman, Supreme Court Chief Justice Enrique Fernando, had been dismissed by the opposition as hopelessly bound to Marcos by virtue of its members' long association with the regime. The public, which had strong memories of Chief Justice Fernando holding a parasol over Mrs. Marcos's head during outdoor public appearances, shared the opposition's skepticism.

After only two hearings, the five commission members bowed to public scorn and legal challenges by acting to "inhibit" themselves until the Supreme Court had ruled on the constitutionality of their endeavor. The commission would reconvene again twenty-four days later only to voluntarily dissolve itself in order to give the president a free hand in creating a new, more autonomous, panel of private citizens along lines proposed by Assemblyman Arturo Tolentino, a respected, ruling party legislator and constitutional expert.

The opposition was gleeful about having helped to sideline the commission, but, as usual, it was Marcos who profited. During the hiatus in the hearings, he unleashed his zealous propagandists to propagate the military version of the assassination through the government-controlled media. A video reenactment of the crime, based on the testimony of the soldiers, was aired repeatedly on government TV, and the witness whom the military claimed had first alerted its intelligence agents to a plot to assassinate Aquino was made available for press interviews.

Revelation of the witness's identity was greeted as black humor by the Aquino family and the political opposition. He was Rosendo ("Ros") Cawigan, the former Aquino bodyguard, who had terrified Cory's household staff after he turned state's witness against Ninoy at the start of martial law. Since then, Cawigan had been favored with government appointments, despite his self-proclaimed status as a commander in the outlawed Communist New People's Army. The fact that an informer as notorious as Cawigan had emerged as the government's star witness simply confirmed Cory's belief that the assassination had been an inside job.

Cawigan took full advantage of the managed interviews the government had set up for him to paint a portrait of Aquino as a Communist kingpin and himself as a dutiful double agent, informing the government of plots to destabilize it. He stated as fact the preposterous claim that Aquino's execution had been ordered by Philippine Communist party Central Committee Chairman Rodolfo Salas. When double agent Cawigan learned of the plot, well before August 21, 1983, he said, he turned his information over to associates of General Ver, who passed it along to the president.

Later, when he was submitted to rigorous questioning from the Fact-Finding Board, which took over the investigation of the assassination, Cawigan damaged the government's case by contradicting its central thesis that the military did not know the flight on which Aquino would return home. Cawigan told the board that two friends inside the Presidential Security Command had informed him one hour before its arrival that Aquino's plane would dock at Gate 8. Before the Fact-Finding Board issued its report, Cawigan was dead. He died while hospitalized, under government custody, of causes which were officially declared "natural."

*   *   *

Under strong pressure from the U.S. government and his international creditors to conduct a fair investigation of the assassination, the president had little choice but to appoint a more credible investigative body to replace the Fernando commission. However, as the actions of his aides and those of General Ver would later show, he had no intention of allowing an impartial investigation to proceed. Characteristically, Marcos had merely conceded what he felt he had to in order to survive for today. Tomorrow, when the world had lost interest in the investigation, he would find a way to intervene in the process to protect his men.

Such tactics had always worked for Marcos in the past. What he could not foresee were the dramatic changes that had occurred within the body politic as a result of the assassination. While the traditional political opposition remained essentially unchanged by the event, a moral opposition was emerging, composed of previously unrelated individuals, who were motivated to act on their own, without the impetus of organized politics to move them. It was these still relatively unknown and unorganized citizens, rather than the professional opposition politicians, who would ultimately turn the tide against him.

One such individual was Amadeo Seno, the deputy general counsel of the dissolved Fernando Commission, who started talking with dangerous candor about the government's investigation of the assassination, as soon as he was no longer serving in an official capacity. What Seno, a tough criminal lawyer from Cebu, said on the record, just after the last commission session, was so much more outspoken than anything said by any other public official over the past six weeks that the crowd of reporters around him began to grow, not only in size, but in protectiveness.

"The investigation by the person or party who was in charge of airport security violated the fundamental rules of criminal investigation," Seno said for starters. He questioned the investigators' presentation of the imported Smith & Wesson .357 Magnum at a press conference on August 21, before it had been dusted for fingerprints or submitted for ballistics tests. Where was the proof, he wanted to know, that the bullet fragments, said to have been removed from Aquino's head, had been fired from that gun? As private security guards moved into the room to clear it of people, Seno appeared to realize his exposure and decided he had said enough. Before he left the hall, however, I made an appointment to interview him the following morning.

The seedy office where we met belonged to a movie production company, which apparently specialized in *bomba* or skin flicks. Seated in the midst of a landscape of epidermis, we talked for several hours about the Aquino case, the available—and still-secret—evidence to which the Fernando Commission had been privy, and the conduct of the military investigation. I was heartened to hear Seno, the attorney named by the regime to lead the probe, drawing conclusions about the crime and the cover-up that were similar to mine. His evaluation of the military investigative report, which General Olivas had submitted to the commission, was scathing. I wondered how he could get away with such criticism of a report which had the president's blessing. One week later I would have my answer: Seno was forced to appear on government television to denounce the foreign correspondents who had "twisted" his words.

Meanwhile, Seno summarized for me the Olivas report, which had been submitted to the commission more than one month before, but was presently locked in a vault awaiting the convocation of a new commission. It confirmed that orders for securing Aquino had changed between August 20 and his arrival on August 21. On the day before Aquino's homecoming, METROCOM Commander Olivas had been informed in a phone call by AVSECOM Commander General Luther Custodio that should Aquino arrive, he must be taken to AVSECOM headquarters. "If he had no travel documents, he would be shipped back to his point of embarkation," said Olivas of that conversation. If Aquino had proper documentation, he would be returned to his former cell at Fort Bonifacio.

On the morning of August 21, however, General Ver "modified his previous order" to General Custodio to the effect that no matter what papers Aquino had, he would be arrested on landing in Manila and taken back to his former cell. The report indicated that the AVSECOM security plan code-named *Oplan Balikbayan* (Operational Plan Returnee) called for the Special Operations Squadron to set up a security ring around the aircraft and to provide "a boarding party to identify, secure and escort" Aquino from the plane to the SWAT van, which would carry him to Fort Bonifacio.

Great pains had been taken by Olivas in the writing of the report to stress that the military did not know with any certainty what time Aquino would arrive or on what aircraft from what destination. The boarding party therefore had to check every international flight that landed on that Sunday morning, the report claimed. Five men—not just the three who had entered the economy-class section—were identified by the report as having belonged to the boarding party that escorted Aquino from the plane.

Good, I thought, as Seno listed the names; that confirmed my observation that the stairway had been full of people. Boarding party leader Second Lieutenant Jesus Castro, dressed in khaki, had entered the plane and gone directly into the first-class cabin to look for Aquino, while three other men in khaki, Technical Sergeant Claro Lat, Constable Mario Lazaga, and Sergeant Arnulfo de Mesa had searched the economy cabin for their man. Constable Rogelio Moreno, also wearing khaki, was posted at the door of the aircraft.

What Seno said next came as more welcome news. A sixth man, Technical Sergeant Filomeno Miranda, a member of an intelligence unit, who was dressed in a white, short-sleeved barong, had been standing inside the mobile passenger tube or jetway. As the three men in khaki led Aquino out the door of the plane, into the jetway, then through the service door and down the steps, the khaki-clad Moreno joined them. Just before exiting the service door, Sergeant Lat passed Aquino's hand luggage to the intelligence officer in white, Sergeant Miranda, who followed the others down the stairs.

The Olivas report made no mention of any investigation by the military of what was inside the bag or what had become of it after the shooting. Here Seno interrupted his narrative to criticize the commission's procedure. "Any honest investigation should have looked into where the bag was and what was in it," said Seno. "Was there any inventory made of the contents of the bag, witnessed by official personnel?" he questioned. The claim that Marcos would later make to me—that the bag contained

CIA documents about his health, which had been turned over to investigators—was one which neither Seno nor the Fact-Finding Board that was set up to investigate the assassination had ever heard.

In addition to the white-shirted Miranda, six other intelligence agents had been assigned to provide covert security inside the jetway as Aquino disembarked, according to the report. When he was hustled out the door and down the service stairs, they had remained in place inside the tube. It was these men, I suddenly realized, who had moved into position to block us journalists from following him. "They were all dressed in plain clothes," confirmed Seno.

When Seno got to the point, in the Olivas report's narrative, where the lone assassin in blue darts from behind the stairs and shoots Aquino, he called on his cousin and law partner Erasmo Diola to help him demonstrate what he considered the gravitational fallacy in the testimony. "Everything about this report made me doubtful," said Seno.

Like the government's televised reenactment, the Olivas report chronicled Aquino's descent of the nineteen service stairs, flanked by Lat on his right, de Mesa on his left, Moreno, Miranda, and Lazaga following behind. According to the report, Aquino, Lat, and de Mesa had reached the tarmac and were striding toward the waiting van, which had backed up to the left of the stairs, when Galman suddenly darted from under the stairs and shot Aquino from behind. De Mesa, who was on Aquino's left, had told Olivas that he felt an object touch his shoulder at almost the precise moment that the first shot rang out. His reaction was to lift his arm to ward off the assassin. He claimed that in so doing he caused the gunman to lose his balance. Just then, according to the report, a volley of shots fired by his companions from the SWAT van hit the assassin, who dropped to the ground at a right angle to and in front of Aquino, who had fallen face first.

Here Seno and his cousin rose and proceeded to show what was wrong with the reenactment. "Logic and common sense and the law of probabilities will tell us that the assassin must have lost his balance backwards," said Seno. "He could not have been unbalanced forward." If that is true, continued Seno, "Galman would have fallen far behind Aquino rather than before him."

As for the report's claim that soldiers dressed in blue SWAT-team jumpsuits and standing inside the van had fired at Galman, again Seno and his cousin sprang into action. "If the shots were coming from the direction of the van, and the assassin had come from the direction of the stairway," said Seno, "then the assassin must have been hit in the front, and the natural tendency of a person hit with a hail of bullets from the front would be to fall on his back." Pausing dramatically for effect before climbing to his feet, after portraying the fallen assassin, Seno declared: "If that is what this story tells us, then how did that poor assassin sustain four shots in the back and one in the occipital region of the head?"

He had just played a scene worthy of Perry Mason, in order to point up the serious contradictions between the report and the likely reality. Too bad he could not have made such a demonstration in his official capacity as deputy general counsel before the commission. Seno's assumption was that Galman, who had already been singled out to be the fall guy, had been surrounded by soldiers and shot simultaneously from several directions by them. After he hit the ground, with several bullets already in him, the round of machine-gun fire had been pumped into his groin in the style of a gangland execution, for the benefit of spectators like me, who were supposed to conclude that Galman had been the assassin.

Having thus explained the murder of the alleged assassin, the key remaining question was whether Galman could have killed Aquino before being brought down himself? In answering this question, the elements of time and bullet trajectory became critically important. Analyses of the audiotapes—mine and those of the TV networks—would later indicate a lapse of only about ten seconds between the moment Aquino exited the door of the plane and the sound of the first shot, which was followed by four more in rapid succession. The man the military claimed shot Aquino was waiting for him on the ground. The military men, whom nearly everyone else suspected of the killing, were closer at hand, right behind him on the stairs.

Seno's performance built to a climax on this question of whether Aquino was shot on the steep stairs, as he conjectured, or on the flat tarmac, as the military claimed. He recounted how, during the hearing, the state medico-legal officer, who had conducted the Aquino autopsy, had clung tenaciously to the military's contention that Ninoy had been shot on level ground, despite evidence that the bullet had followed a downward trajectory from its entrance at the back of his head to its exit through his chin. In the end, however, he had admitted that the wound could have been inflicted by a gunman firing from several rungs above him on the stairway. Seno was thus able to lay the foundation for a case that would directly contradict the military thesis that the assassin was an outsider. If Aquino had been shot on the stairs, it followed that he could only have been shot by one of the military men who was descending behind him.

The other state's witness, whose testimony on this point was decisive, provided the colorful Seno with a classic anecdote, which came to stand for all that was wrong with the military's investigation of its own ranks. Dr. Nieto Salvador, the National Bureau of Investigation official who had autopsied Galman, testified before the commission that Galman, at five feet seven inches from heel to head, was a full two inches taller than the five-feet-five-inch Aquino, and therefore, implicitly, able to inflict a wound with a downward trajectory while standing on flat ground. Again, during the hearing, Seno got away with a few questions which sounded benign, but were nonetheless designed to trap the witness. "How did you arrive at this measurement?" he asked, matter-of-factly. The question hit pay dirt. Salvador had not measured Galman's corpse from head to heel with a conventional tape measure. Because he was in a rush to complete the autopsy, he had, he admitted, used "a wooden stick with notches."

Seno was still grappling with the issue of the two victims' relative heights. "This is what really begs my mind," said Seno. "I heard General Olivas on television during his first interview, and he mentioned that Galman was one hundred and sixty-three centimeters. I don't know if that was a slip of the tongue or based on some report given to him, but later on in another TV interview he mentioned his height to be one hundred and sixty-eight centimeters. Then finally in his report, which is submitted to the commission, the height is given as one hundred and seventy-five." In conclusion Seno joshed, "So you have a cadaver growing taller."

*   *   *

The new, more autonomous Fact-Finding Board, which replaced the discredited Fernando Commission, held its first hearing in the Philippine Constabulary morgue. Four weeks after the dissolution of the first investigative body and ten weeks after the Aquino assassination, the investigation of the crime had not gotten beyond the corpus delicti. The morbid venue was a matter of necessity, not choice. The body of Rolando Galman had been lying there since August 21. Although it had remained under refrigeration, it was deteriorating as fast as the level of national and international patience with what increasingly appeared to be a government cover-up of the Aquino assassination.

The five members of the new board and their attorneys were well aware that valuable momentum had been lost to the military during the months when no other entity was investigating the murder. To win public confidence, they would have to move quickly and boldly. More to the point, the Supreme Court had already begun proceedings to release Galman's body to his family for burial. If the board had any questions about how Galman died, it would have to speak now or hold its peace. "Obviously that was not the logical place to begin investigating the assassination of Aquino," acknowledged the board's general counsel, former law school dean Andres Narvasa, "but we had to decide almost immediately what more there was to say about the corpse of Galman."

The question the board chose to focus on was Amadeo Seno's lugubrious legacy: what he had called "the case of the growing cadaver." Constabulary crime lab officials confirmed to the board Dr. Salvador's admission that Galman's body had been measured with a wooden stick, which lacked legible numbers, instead of the more flexible and accurate tape measure. He offered no explanation for this departure from normal practice except that "confusion" had reigned following the double murder, and the tape measure had been missing the night the autopsy was performed. When the corpse was properly remeasured for the board, Galman's height was set at 170 centimeters (five feet six inches), compared to Aquino's 169 centimeters (five feet five and one-half inches)—not sufficient difference to account alone for the downward trajectory of the bullet. The strong implication of this more precise evidence was that Aquino's assailant had shot at him from the higher elevation of one or more stairs.

Shortly thereafter, the board heard the pitiful testimony of Galman's mother, Saturnina, and sister Marilyn, who told how they were picked up by soldiers on August 27, as they worked in their rice paddy, and taken to Villamor Air Force Base, headquarters for AVSECOM, in Manila. Informed that Galman had been identified as the unknown assassin of Aquino, they had been asked to confirm his identity. On the night of August 30, they had been driven to the crime lab to view the body. On seeing the corpse—bloated from having lain for more than five hours on the hot airport tarmac and riddled by as many as sixteen bullet wounds—Mrs. Galman was psychologically incapable of recognizing it as her son.

Not until the military sent two priests to calm her by promising to arrange for his burial was any progress made. After the priests appealed to her to remember any identifiable marks on the body, the mother confided to the soldiers that her son bore the scar of a small incision made on his testicle when he was a boy. With that, she was returned to the morgue. "I could not look at the face," she testified. "It was so swollen. . . . A pitiful sight, like it had gone through excruciating pain." However, she recalled quietly, "When I saw the mark, I screamed, 'Yes,' it was my Rolando."

Neither the military nor the priests kept their word to bury her son, and two months later Mrs. Galman and her daughter were still in detention. The military justified that detention on grounds that the women needed protection from Aquino supporters bent on avenging the assassination. Mrs. Galman now told the board that she had not believed the Aquino forces would harm her. As proof, she cited the presence of Ninoy's brother Butz Aquino beside the Galman family at the burial of her son. Under the protective wing of her lawyer, Lupiño Lazaro, a loud-dressing eccentric whose promotional abilities had helped transform Rolando Galman from a pariah into a folk hero, she used her appearance before the board to openly accuse the military of making her son its "fall guy."

Death was proving a strong adversary for Marcos. Two ghosts, not just one, now haunted him. He had thus far been able to defy the politicians calling for his resignation by deploying his considerable arsenal of political skills and wielding the threat of his acknowledged military power. But nothing in his experience had prepared him for banishing the spirits of martyrs.

The new Fact-Finding Board did not draw the number of brickbats that the old Fernando Commission had when it was announced. Nor did it, however, draw much praise from cynical Filipinos, who could not imagine that it would be permitted to act freely and impartially, no matter who its members were, as long as Marcos was in charge.

Board Chairman Corazon Juliano Agrava, an earnest, retired Appellate Court Justice, had been the consensus choice of the sectoral representatives who oversaw the selection process. Second in her class at the University of the Philippines law school, she had broken the sex barrier to become the first woman judge of the Court of First Instance and the first female bar examiner. She had built a reputation for fairness and compassion as presiding judge of the Juvenile and Domestic Relations Court of Manila, where she called her young defendants "my children" rather than "juvenile delinquents." Her lawyer-husband, Fred, was, said one of her colleagues on the board, "such a rich corporate lawyer that he would not need bribes." She was, therefore, despite the inevitable rumors to the contrary, generally believed able to afford impartiality in her deliberations.

The same held true for the representatives of the private business community and the legal profession. Dante Santos, the millionaire chairman of one of the country's leading manufacturers, was the only nonlawyer appointed to the board. As president of the Philippines Chamber of Commerce and Industry at the time of the assassination, he had written President Marcos to inform him of "the widely held perception that the commission charged with investigating the Aquino murder does not vest itself with adequate public credibility." Six weeks later Marcos asked him to accept a seat on the new Fact-Finding Board, which he had created by decree on October 14, 1983.

Luciano ("Sally") Salazar was pressured by the other partners in his prestigious law firm to retire, after agreeing to serve on the controversial panel. He did so on the day of his appointment, although he retained his seat on the boards of numerous local and multinational corporations. In an evident attempt to intimidate him, the regime planted articles in the Marcos-controlled press accusing him of being a dummy for American shareholders in several Philippine corporations.

The other two members, while not independently wealthy, were judged to be incorruptible by their peers and willing to work for the better part of a year without a salary and with only a modest expense account. Even so, the public remained skeptical. Ernesto ("Boy") Herrera, the young secretary-general of the country's largest confederation of moderate labor unions, the Trade Union Congress of the Philippines, was rumored, because of the regime's tight control over the labor movement, to be close to the palace. No one seemed to know what the bias of educator Amado Dizon was, but many of the spectators in the public gallery at the hearings were convinced that the quiet seventy-five-year-old professor and lawyer must have one.

In taking a leave from his modest law practice to become the board's general counsel, Andres Narvasa calculated that he would sacrifice six months of income. When the hearings and the preparation of his legal report dragged on for nearly a year, his wife was forced to sell two pieces of real estate that were part of her inheritance, to keep the family of seven intact.

A former law professor at the Dominican-run University of Santo Tomas, where he had gone on to become dean of the law school, Narvasa had taught a course on evidence. While he would continue to hope throughout the life of the board that a courageous and credible eyewitness would come forward to identify the killer or a photo of the actual murder would be unearthed, says Narvasa, "The sum and substance of my ambition at that time was to produce a report that would set down every doggone knowable fact, backed up by solid evidence."

"We had no fixed theory," stresses Narvasa. Nor was there any hard evidence to back up the individual suspicions of the various board members. Thus, their "game plan" was simply to put all possible witnesses on the stand, amass all possible concrete evidence, and then draw the appropriate conclusions. He adds with a guffaw, "It was a no-win situation. People were saying, 'If you come up with a verdict that the assassin was Galman, you are ruined, if you come up with another verdict, you'll be shot.' "

Narvasa assigned one of his deputies, Francisco ("Kit") Villa, to analyze and supplement the weak ballistics evidence turned over to the board by the previous commission. Villa, a lawyer, a former National Bureau of Investigation assistant director, state prosecutor, and police chief, had been trained at Scotland Yard and the FBI. His ties to the cops and the pro-Marcos politicians with whom they were allied would be helpful in opening doors for the otherwise suspect board. Narvasa himself would concentrate on gathering photographic, video, and audio documentation of the moments before, during, and immediately after the two shootings at the airport.

Late in 1984, after General Olivas had satisfied himself that none of the hundreds of airport negatives confiscated from Filipino photographers showed the actual assassination, he turned them over to the board. Narvasa hauled them home, laid them out on the long table on his porch, and enlisted the help of his wife, Janina ("Jani"), at night and on weekends, in constructing a photo chronology of the action in and around the China

Airlines plane. Meanwhile, the board engaged a popular record producer to synchronize copies of the original TV footage shot by the two camera crews on board into a composite video chronology of the same action. Those two chronologies, complemented by my audiotape, would become the objective evidence against which the testimony of the soldiers and the civilian witnesses would finally be weighed.

The board began its questioning with the soldiers, because they were the most readily available, having been confined to quarters since the assassination. It planned to work its way up to the man its members called the Big Guy, General Ver. Ver was the "biggest guy" they would invite to testify. They never seriously considered calling the president to take the witness stand, although they did hear from Mrs. Marcos.

First on the stand was AVSECOM commander General Luther Custodio, who was in charge of implementing *Oplan Balikbayan*. The military had prepared a slick slide show to illustrate the extensive security measures taken to protect Aquino. Confidently, Custodio began to read from his script. "Can we continue?" he asked perfunctorily, after showing the first slide. His response was a barrage of questions from the board.

"And then the fun began," recalled Narvasa. Instead of listening passively to his presentation, as Custodio had assumed they would, board members and lawyers questioned his every frame.

"The general began perspiring," related Mrs. Narvasa, who attended every hearing.

Midway through his testimony, Custodio was tripped up by an anonymous military artist, whose illustrations of the airport were entered into evidence. As Narvasa skimmed quickly through them, he spotted one that particularly interested him. "Does this indicate that the plane carrying Aquino would land at Gate Number Eight?" he asked.

Attorney Rodolfo ("Rudy") Jimenez, counsel for the AVSECOM soldiers, quickly interjected to remind Narvasa of the central tenet of the military's defense: that the soldiers did not know which plane would carry Aquino. In the cool, casual courtroom manner for which Narvasa would become famous in the course of the hearings, the general counsel pointed to one of the sketches of the arrival gate in Custodio's portfolio, which had been clearly labeled "Gate 8."

The hearing on November 24, 1983, was an important one, in that the witness, a soldier who purported to have seen Galman shoot Aquino, also claimed to have fired the first shots at the alleged assassin. Former deputy counsel Seno had already voiced his skepticism about the military report's improbable description of how Galman had been brought down. The Agrava Board would now have the opportunity to question the gunman himself.

The proceedings began, as all sessions did during the eight months of hearings, with the singing of the lilting Philippines national anthem. Following the lead of Board Chairman Corazon Agrava, the four board members and their legal staff stood up and turned their backs on the public gallery to face a large portrait of President Marcos. Agrava, in particular, sang fervently and with obvious reverence for the country's longtime leader. Seated again behind the long table marked by board members' nameplates, Agrava gaveled the hearing to order.

As Narvasa and his deputies arranged their papers on their desk to the left of the board, Sergeant Rolando de Guzman was sworn in as a witness. He was a certified sharpshooter and member of the Aviation Security Command's 805th Special Operations Squadron, the blue-suited SWAT team, which I had seen fanning out around the aircraft as it docked at Gate 8. Trained to combat hijackings, the SWAT team was tasked that day with securing the airport areas through which Aquino would pass after leaving the China Airlines plane.

Sergeant de Guzman had been a member of Team Alpha, one of four armed teams deployed around the aircraft. As the plane had taxied up to Gate 8, Bravo, Charlie, and Delta teams leaped out of the vans in which they had been traveling from gate to gate all morning and took up their positions around the plane. Team Alpha remained inside the closed, bulletproof AVSECOM van, parked near the foot of the service stairs, assigned, curiously enough, to protect Aquino only after he was inside the vehicle.

Until then, Aquino's close-in security consisted of the five-man boarding party, which had entered the plane to search for him and escort him to the van. It was comprised of men selected primarily for their size, in order to shield him with their bodies during the few moments between plane and van when he might be exposed to a crowd. They were said to have been unarmed. Additionally, four ramp guards had been prepositioned in the area at the foot of the stairs, although they had been instructed to move away as soon as Bravo, Charlie, and Delta were in place.

De Guzman testified that he did not see the man he was supposed to protect until another Team Alpha member opened the backdoor of the van, in which he was seated, to prepare to receive Aquino. At that point, he recounted, "When Sergeant Lat and Sergeant de Mesa with Senator Aquino in between them were nearing the van, I saw a person suddenly appear holding a gun, point it at the head of Senator Aquino, and fire." De Guzman, who had stood up and started toward the door "with the intention of meeting the senator and receiving him" as he was escorted into the van, was armed with a .45. "I drew my gun and fired at him," he said.

Chairman Agrava, who revealed a passion for theatrical direction in the course of the hearings, stopped attorney Villa's questioning of de Guzman and asked the sergeant to help reenact what he saw and did, with legal staffers playing the parts of the victims and the assailants. He claimed not to have seen most of Aquino's descent of the stairs, because the van door had been closed. Three times in quick succession in answer to her questions about who accompanied Aquino and his two escorts, de Guzman responded with what would become the standard refrain of a long line of military witnesses: "I did not notice, Ma'am."

When Agrava changed her tack and asked him if he had noticed whether Aquino and his escorts were talking to each other as they approached the van, de Guzman varied his refrain accordingly. "I did not hear, Ma'am," said the witness. This caused great hilarity in the public gallery, which, numbed by three weeks of soldiers' testimony, had begun to mock their statements with laughter, hisses, and catcalls.

Agrava, a stickler for decorum, pounded her gavel. The lack of spectator objectivity offended her. "Will the crowd please cooperate? This is not a *zarzuela*, nor an opera, nor a comedy," she exclaimed angrily. "My golly, we are dealing with something serious, and you just laugh and laugh." Silence having returned to the hall, she motioned to the bailiff, and added, "If you behave in this manner, I am going to clear this room."

Narvasa, who had been listening intently as Villa questioned the witness, now sprang into action, pressing de Guzman for greater detail about the two shootings. Cross-examination was not permitted by the Fact-Finding Board, but clarificatory questioning was. De Guzman was the first of nine military witnesses who alleged to have seen the shootings. Narvasa knew the importance of pinning him down on the fine points of a story, which the others would be bound to confirm in what the Olivas report had aptly called their "interlocking testimonies."

Wearing a sport coat and tie, rather than the more formal barong, Narvasa's manner was deceptively nonchalant, his voice sonorous with "nice guy" warmth. Slowly, studiously, artfully, the man whom the press had nicknamed the Gray Dean, for his graying crew cut and his academic background, led de Guzman through a seemingly harmless review of his initial testimony. Then he bore in on certain points.

"Did you see what happened after that man pointed the gun?" asked Narvasa, in reference to the alleged assassin Galman.

De Guzman answered the question with what sounded like well-coached precision. He saw Aquino's escort Sergeant de Mesa "swing his right arm upward" in an attempt to deflect the gunman's hand, he said. This caused the assailant to lose his balance. In falling, he explained, "the alleged gunman . . . , with the arm still holding the gun pointing upward, [made] a full one-hundred-and-eighty-degree turn or rotation." At that instant, de Guzman recounted, "I had the opportunity to shoot him, and so I fired at him." Standing on the bumper of the van, he hit Galman in the head with his first shot.

"Will you tell the board if you continued to fire at the gunman as he was falling down in the manner you have demonstrated?" Narvasa asked.

"Yes, sir, I continued firing," replied de Guzman.

"And where did you hit him?" continued the general counsel. Deeper and deeper, Narvasa beckoned the witness into what would turn out to be a thicket of contradictions. Arrogantly, ignorantly, de Guzman followed, trusting that the military alibi, which he had been coached to present, would hold up. He had shot a total of seven bullets at Galman, while standing on the bumper, he said. Some had hit him in the back, others in the front of the torso.

Minutes later, Narvasa gestured to Villa, who moved to adjourn the proceedings for lunch. During the two-hour break, the staff analyzed what de Guzman had told them. The lawyers had no concrete evidence to either confirm or reject it. "We were groping confidently," jokes Narvasa, simply trying to elicit as many details as possible from a soldier who claimed to have a vivid recollection of what happened. "We were still prepared to accept the military version if the evidence upheld it," he says.

When the session reopened, the lawyers bore down harder on de Guzman. Villa's questioning concentrated on the sequence of the sergeant's seven shots. De Guzman stated that there was a one-second interval between his first shot and the other six. In another slow-motion demonstration, de Guzman showed how the body of his victim, on being hit in the head, had rotated in a half circle. As Galman fell, "with his back toward me," de Guzman said he hit him three more times. By then, others were firing at Galman. De Guzman had turned around quickly to ascertain that the shots were coming from his teammates, then fired three final shots at Galman as he slumped onto the asphalt. De Guzman was asked to identify those teammates in photos shown to him by the board.

I was fascinated by de Guzman's testimony, which purported to describe those seconds of the drama that I had missed while I was battling the men in white shirts to let me out the door. Deftly, de Guzman had spoken to the point which had troubled attorney Seno, explaining that it was he who had put the bullets in Galman's head and back. He had even tried to duplicate the contortion he contended Galman had had to go through to expose his back to the van, while falling backward away from the van. He was not an unimpressive witness.

Yet most of what he said did not jibe with my recall of the sounds on my tape. Only five shots, very close together, had sounded while I was in the jetway. Then there had been a considerable interval of silence. The long volley of shots had begun only after I had run back inside the plane and positioned myself by a window. At that point, another soldier, armed with an automatic rifle, had proceeded to shoot the already fallen Galman.

In the weeks that followed, other members of the AVSECOM SWAT team echoed de Guzman's initial testimony. Instead of strengthening the case being built by the military, however, each new witness raised troublesome questions about the intent of the drafters of Operation Balikbayan and the behavior of the men charged with implementing it. The board members began to show their skepticism in questioning the soldiers.

The public, however, was paying little attention. Most Filipinos had dismissed the new board at the start with black humor. "Did you know there are still five Filipinos who don't know that Marcos killed Aquino?" went the popular joke. "The Agrava Board" was the punchline. Most of the media coverage of the hearings appeared in the crony press and on state television, which reported the soldiers' testimony exhaustively and in a credible light.

As soon as Sergeant Ernesto Mateo, a second Team Alpha member, testified on November 29 that he had been armed with an M-16 automatic rifle that afternoon at the airport, a chill came over me. He was slighter than he had appeared then, dressed in the blue antihijack-squad jumpsuit. He also had scared eyes that did not look as though they were hardened to the murders that had been committed there. He was about as far away from me in the witness box now as he had been from my vantage point inside the plane then. I watched his eyes with a gaze almost as riveted as that which I had at the time fastened on his elbow and upper arm, as they had recoiled with each shot pumped into Galman's groin.

Mateo, too, had been waiting inside the van for the arrival of the opposition leader, he told Deputy General Counsel Mario Ongkiko. When a teammate opened the backdoor of the vehicle to admit Aquino, Mateo caught a fleeting glimpse of the man he was assigned to protect. At the same instant a gun was fired. "When I heard a shot, I immediately jumped out of the van," said Mateo. The lawyer tried to pinpoint what Mateo saw that caused him to take that action, but to no avail. "That is part of our training," Mateo explained, with a certain pride. "As soon as you hear a shot, you jump out. You react immediately. I am the first one out of the van."

Mateo figured he was in midair when a second shot sounded, and he saw his teammate de Guzman shooting "somebody who fell backward." As soon as his feet were on the ground, Mateo did another thing that the board was left to conclude his training had taught him: He started shooting the same man. "When I saw Sergeant de Guzman firing at the gunman, I also fired, because I saw him still moving, and I was afraid he might shoot again, that he might harm Senator Aquino again or any one of us."

That line startled me. It was simply not true. He was lying. I had seen Galman's lifeless body sprawled on the pavement before anyone approached it. I had cried out in horror on seeing the man I now knew to be Sergeant Mateo shooting bullets into it for no apparent reason. There was no way Galman could have hurt anyone at that point, and certainly not poor Senator Aquino, who was beyond hurt by then. Until this moment I had thought that since I had not seen the actual murder of Aquino, I knew too little to be a useful witness. Suddenly I realized that I knew a lot. I knew enough to know that these soldiers were, one after the other, repeating a false story concocted by their superiors or their lawyers.

The board members, meanwhile, were asking the right questions. Although they acted with great prudence, they could not hide their skepticism about some of the answers they were hearing. I had recently met Narvasa, who had asked me to testify. My response had been politely ambiguous. I was not anxious to become involved in a controversial investigation, especially if it was to be a whitewash. However, as I watched the proceedings, I began to develop faith in the board. While the vast majority of Filipinos were paying no attention, something significant seemed to be happening in this hearing room. The fact-finding process that was unfolding here did not appear to be controlled by the government. The board members were not acting as if there were any constraints on their investigation. The soldiers were mouthing their inane refrain that they had seen no evil as if they believed it would strike the board as credible. A clash was inevitable.

As December wore on, the military testimony became harder and harder to sit through. Increasingly, the public gallery was not alone in its expressions of surprise, disgust, or mockery. If Team Alpha was exasperating in its blind-leading-the-blind behavior, Team Delta's conduct was downright pathological. Deployed around the nose of the plane, with orders to prevent the entry of unauthorized personnel into the area, Captain Llewelyn Kavinta's team had been facing outward toward the passenger terminal, rather than in the direction of the plane, as Aquino began his descent of the stairs. "What did you do when you heard the shot?" asked Justice Agrava, familiar with the drill by now. "I told my men to hit the deck," he said.

Kavinta sounded aggressive, compared to his laid-back superior, Captain Felipe Valerio, commander over all the teams and the boarding party as well. The way Valerio told it, he had arrived at Gate 8 in the cab of the AVSECOM van, and he had remained there throughout both shootings, monitoring the goings-on by radio, without ever even turning his head to see what was happening only a few feet away. He told board member Dante Santos that he had learned about the shooting "in the newspaper." He had even "shied away" from asking his own men about what he called "this affair that causes grief," he claimed.

I later learned that Valerio had found the official scenario so full of contradictions that he had balked at the notion of trying to stick to it under questioning on the witness stand. "I might as well tell the truth," he had said to his superiors. They convinced him to avoid sticky questions by simply testifying that he had seen nothing at all. Valerio, alone, of all the accused co-conspirators, disappeared not long after a Marcos court acquitted him, and before a new trial under a new government had opened. He has not been seen again. Some say he is hiding out in the U.S. Others say he is dead, a victim of foul play.

After eleven years of authoritarian rule, during which the Philippine Armed Forces had swelled from 60,000 to 250,000 men, and any critical examination of the consequences had been forbidden, the board had pried open the lid and caught a whiff of the incompetence and rot. It had found the chain of command in confusion, to the point that the minister of national defense and the manager of the airport had been cut out of the preparations for the Aquino arrival operation, and an intelligence agent had been able to join the special security operation to protect the opposition leader, without the knowledge of the officer in charge. It had observed an operation so full of holes that, as Narvasa would conclude in his final report, he had to wonder whether "the elaborate plans ostensibly geared towards protecting the life of Senator Aquino were in fact designed to camouflage the taking of that life."

In less than two months, the board's attitude and even its manner of dealing with military witnesses had changed. At the end of Sergeant Cordova Estelo's testimony, public coordinator attorney Bienvenido ("Benny") Tan had relayed a question from the public gallery that was straight out of the coffee-shop rumor mill, "Was Rolando Galman with you inside the SWAT van?" Everyone, including Estelo, knew that the question referred to the popular scenario, for which there was no concrete evidence, that the purpose of the van had been to transport the already dead body of Galman to the tarmac to be thrown onto the pavement, shot up by soldiers, and left behind as the scapegoat. Yet the board members not only tolerated the question, they ripped into Estelo when he balked at answering it.

"May I know, sir, who asked that question?" Estelo growled.

Narvasa jumped up and, glowering at the soldier, demanded, "And why do you want to know?"

His refusal to be bullied by a soldier was greeted with cheers, which Agrava made no effort to stop. In fact, she added her own caustic question: "And if you were told who it was, what would you do with that information?"

*　　　　*　　　　*

Three days after Christmas, the Fact-Finding Board, which most of the public had written off as harmless and ineffectual, suddenly asserted its autonomy, moved to protect a threatened witness, and found itself in the role of adversary to the regime. Overnight, board proceedings would be transformed from obscure hearings into the most popular show in town.

Just before lunchtime on December 28, the elfin figure of eighty-year-old attorney Juan David approached Chairman Agrava, as she listened to a soldier's testimony. He whispered to her that he had a witness "who will give an opposite story to the government's." She quickly called a recess, polled other board members for their reaction, and told David, a lawyer identified with the political opposition, who served as an independent legal observer for the All Asia Bar Association at the hearings, that they would stand by, ready to hear the witness and provide security for him if necessary. On being informed that the witness was waiting in a law office across town, they promptly slipped out a backdoor, in order to elude the press, and sped off in waiting cars.

It was four o'clock by the time the board members had set up their tape recorder and taken their places around a small coffee table in the second-floor law offices of attorney Isidro Hildawa and his wife, attorney Sinforosa Gomez, in a shabby neighborhood in Makati. The official board photographer recorded the watershed event in the short history of the Fact-Finding Board: the swearing-in of Ramon Balang, a twenty-eight-year-old Philippine Airlines ground engineer, who became the first eyewitness to give testimony under oath that was contrary to the military version of the events.

After forty-one witnesses, most of them soldiers assigned to protect Aquino, Balang's account marked a turning point, not only in terms of testimony received by the board, but also in its own initiative to pursue the truth about the assassination. In moving to extend the mantle of its protection over a witness against the government, board members would shock cynical Filipinos into a realization that decent people, working within tremendous constraints, could effect change.

Ironically, as the nervous, young mechanic told the board, it was the military that had unwittingly forced him to end his self-imposed silence and triggered this impromptu hearing. He had remained silent for four months and was planning to do so indefinitely. Then last evening, when he returned from basketball practice, he found a plainclothes agent of the Philippine Constabulary's Criminal Investigation Service (CIS) waiting for him in his mother's house. The man showed Balang a letter addressed to the general manager of Philippine Airlines by the commander of CIS, requesting that Balang report immediately to constabulary headquarters for "interview/investigation."

Startled at the abruptness of the invitation, Balang asked whether it had anything to do with the Agrava Board. "No," answered the officer, this would be an investigation preliminary to that which the board would make. Balang noticed a gun tucked into the officer's waist and hesitated. The officer upped the ante. "We might bring you to the president," he said. However, he betrayed uncertainty about whether Marcos was still in the mountain resort city of Baguio, or whether he had returned to Manila from his holiday there. Gathering his wits, Balang bought time by asking to consult his attorney.

When one of General Ver's men followed up on the first visit that same night, asking Balang to call the chief of staff, the shaken mechanic sought refuge in the home of his lawyer. The lawyer had already been approached by a Ver man, who had offered him a government position and his client a job and security in the U.S. if Balang would testify that he saw Galman shoot Aquino. Fearing the consequences of refusing to cooperate with the government, Balang and his attorney borrowed a video recorder and camera, summoned a friendly priest, and protectively taped his account of the events of August 21, which he was now relating directly to the board.

Balang told how he had helped guide the China Airlines plane into its bay at Gate 8. When told by his supervisor not to mount the service stairs to the cockpit to pick up the fuel charts on that particular day, he had begun his 360-degree, ocular inspection of the plane. As he made his way, counterclockwise, around the aircraft, he noticed one stranger among the fifteen to twenty uniformed service personnel, whom he had seen each day for the past two years under the plane. The stranger was dressed in a light blue PAL maintenance shirt over jeans, and was standing alone under the service stairs.

After completing his walk around, Balang headed for a concrete post on the other side of the Gate 8 jetway to fill in the aircraft registry number on a work sheet posted there. As he passed under the jetway, he glanced toward the service stairs to his left. There he saw a man dressed in white and wearing sunglasses being helped down the stairs by two uniformed soldiers. Descending right behind them were another man in khaki uniform and "at least three to five men in barong." Before logging in the time of arrival of the aircraft, Balang looked at his watch.

"As I was looking at the time, I heard a gunshot," said Balang. He looked back toward the stairs. "I saw the man in white falling down, and I saw blood spurting from the back of his head." The escorts, who had been holding him on either side, "just removed their hands and let the man in white fall face down."

Shifting his glance toward a patch of action just to the right of the stricken Aquino, Balang saw a scene that was so different from anything he had read about in the crony press, or seen in the official reenactment of the assassination, that it had been on his conscience ever since. "When I moved my eyes, I noticed a man in blue being surrounded by AVSECOM men in blue coveralls. I saw him smiling at them, as if he knows them already. He's gesturing like this [palms upraised]."

An instant later, said Balang, "I saw successive shots, and the man in blue fell down." Balang took cover as the several SWAT team members, who had a moment ago surrounded Galman, now began "firing successive shots," and the "soldiers cordoning the aircraft were pointing the guns anywhere—at the aircraft, the building, toward us."

Immediately afterward, Balang had told his Philippine Airlines superiors what he had seen, but by a peculiar twist of fate, his name had not been included on a work sheet that day, so he had never been questioned by government agents, as had other airport personnel. The only other people in whom he had confided were his lawyers. They told him to remain silent "until the right moment." He had had no intention of ever talking, he said, as his work brought him in daily contact with military men, and he feared both the loss of his job and retaliation against himself and his family if he spoke out.

Balang's revelations had a cathartic effect on everyone in the room. As he finished his account, they all realized that events—or some of them would later say fate, or divine circumstance—had bonded them together against the regime. Nonpolitical moderates all, none had known where the truth might lead. In accepting appointment to a body as controversial as the board, members and their counsels had given thought to what they would do in the event of an eventual conflict with the regime. But there had been no way of knowing where or when or in what form it would come. Most of them secretly hoped it never would. Suddenly this frightened young man had decided to entrust his life to them, and the board members had responded, attorney Juan David would later say, "with courage."

By the time we in the press corps had finally gotten wind of what was going on and made our way to the Hildawa-Gomez law office, a small crowd had gathered outside, attracted by the sight of so many large cars. As American and Japanese TV crews carried their cameras and lights into the modest two-story building, the excitement grew. In a matter of minutes, Balang was surrounded by a horde of reporters. Furniture was hastily rearranged to make room for the television equipment. Electric cords were threaded throughout the house in search of the few available sockets. The floor shook ominously under the weight of so many people.

Balang's remarks in the press conference that followed dealt the first death blow to the military version of the assassination by rejecting the soldiers' claim that Galman shot Aquino.

"Had Mr. Galman, in your opinion, the chance to fire a shot at Senator Aquino?" asked the first questioner.

Balang replied, "I don't think he had the opportunity to fire a shot."

As Dean Narvasa presented a summary of Balang's testimony, the lights suddenly blacked out. A collective shudder passed through the crowd. Those of us closest to the windows peered out, fully expecting to see the military surrounding the house. So powerful was the image of President Marcos, even in the weakened state in which he had been left by his illness and the assassination, that none of us believed at that moment that a citizen board and a mere mechanic would be allowed to threaten the credibility of his regime. Only when nothing happened did someone think to check the fuse box. Indeed, the overload of lighting equipment had caused a fuse to blow.

In several minutes the power was restored, and the press conference continued. Agrava brought the summary up-to-date by revealing that even as the board was questioning Balang, deputy counsel Ongkiko had been sent on a secret mission to the house where Balang lived with his mother and brother, to check out his brother's claim that CIS agents continued to hang around. Sure enough, Ongkiko reported back to Agrava, he had confirmed their presence.

Thereupon, she related proudly, she had called a brief recess in the makeshift hearing to telephone Defense Minister Enrile, requesting protection for the witness. She recounted how, in his own testimony just before Christmas, Enrile had assured the board that the military organization as a whole would not retaliate against the board if it were to find that military men had been implicated in the assassination conspiracy. He had offered the board the assistance of his ministry. She was now putting him to the test.

Without hesitation, she said, Enrile had offered to provide Balang with guards. He had also offered Agrava some advice, which she was heeding by holding this press conference. "As additional protection" for the witness, Enrile had suggested that the board make known the content of Balang's testimony as quickly as possible to the public.

As we filed down the stairs, I stopped to talk to the aged attorney David, the go-between in this affair. There was a look of satisfaction on his wizened face. After two decades of opposition to Marcos, including service as one of Ninoy's attorneys, he detected an auspicious turn in the course of events. "The government story is beginning to collapse," he said.

10

Hearing from the Big Guy

      "Now you're finished with your testimony, so they can't accuse you of being coached." Justice Agrava was in a festive mood, and she was ordering me to come to the birthday party she was throwing for board member Dante Santos. "If you don't stay, I will hold you in contempt!" she insisted.

I had spent the morning on the witness stand, answering questions about the minicassette tape recording of the assassination, now known as Exhibit 273, which I had turned over to the board the previous week. When Dean Narvasa "invited" me to testify, he did not know about the tape's existence. I did not believe it contained any sounds that had not already been very publicly aired on the sound tracks of the American and Japanese video footage, which had been taken aboard Flight 811. I had used it myself to corroborate several early stories I had filed about the assassination. Then I had locked it up in a filing cabinet in my Hong Kong apartment. The few times I played it for friends and family, they found it upsetting, as did I.

Not until one of Narvasa's junior lawyers questioned me before my first appearance on the stand had I made reference to it. When he asked me how I was able to recollect the number of shots I heard, I mentioned that I had refreshed my memory by listening to my tape. "You have a tape?" he exclaimed. "Can you bring it with you when you testify?"

The first time I testified, I spoke from memory, referring occasionally to the tape. I had been called back this morning to identify the voices and sounds recorded on both the original and an enhanced copy, which the board had made to play over the public address system in the courtroom. In his questioning, Narvasa had concentrated on the sequence of shots heard on the tape, which did not conform to the earlier testimony given by the AVSECOM sharpshooters in the van.

Months later he explained to me the role the audiocassette had played in the building of his case against the military men. The videotapes, which the board had reviewed numerous times, did in fact contain sound tracks that registered the same sequence of shots as my tape. But until he played the audiotape, he had never concentrated on the sounds. What he heard intrigued him. The night after I turned the tape over to the board, he had taken it home with him. Handing his stopwatch to his wife, Jani, he asked her to help him time the spaces between shots. That weekend he arranged all the photos in chronological order on the porch table, then asked the two priests who regularly dropped by for a beer and dinner on Saturday night to double-check the time sequence. "We played it over again and again," recounted Narvasa. While they looked at the stopwatch, he looked at the photos of de Guzman and the others emerging from the van to shoot Galman. Suddenly, as the inconsistencies between the soldiers' testimony and the audio evidence became clear, Narvasa shouted: "That son of a gun is lying!"

De Guzman had said under oath that immediately following the shot that killed Aquino, he had fired seven successive shots at Galman, whereas only five shots had sounded on my tape during the first round of fire, which killed both Aquino and Galman. The other soldiers who testified to having shot Galman purported to follow de Guzman's example, firing almost simultaneously at the alleged assassin. On my tape it is absolutely clear, both in elapsed time and in my emotional narration of the shooting of Galman, that 17.2 seconds of silence elapsed between the first burst of gunfire and the longer volley of automatic rifle fire. Narvasa would save that information for his final report, but the knowledge that at least eight soldiers had falsified their testimony about how Galman died gave him confidence that he would be able to crack the entire case before he was through.

What interested the people in the hearing room that morning, however, were not such details about the sequence of shots, but rather the dramatic reminder of the event which had brought us all here. Played now, seven months after the murder, before board members and reporters whose senses had been dulled by the mechanics of the crime and the repetition of facts and falsehoods, its impact on the professionals in the press pit and the spectators in the public gallery was devastating. For two minutes and forty seconds, people who had spent thousands of hours dissecting a conspiracy were forced to relive the event that was at the heart of it, to remember the human lives that had been lost and the national anguish that had been stirred by it.

By now, March 28, 1984, the board was basking in public popularity, and it showed in its members' high spirits and sense of camaraderie. No longer were they the butt of public ridicule. Filipinos lined up each morning and afternoon to get into the public gallery in the Social Security System Building in Quezon City, just to catch a glimpse of the citizen Davids doing battle daily with the military Goliath. Since the investigators had dared to hear Balang, they had become as celebrated as soap-opera characters.

Agrava was a bona fide folk heroine, who combined the lovable qualities of a favorite aunt with the strict demeanor of a schoolmarm. The Gray Dean, whose ingratiating style of interrogation had tripped up a number of witnesses thus far, was being touted as a political candidate, as were his fellow counsels and several board members. The mischievous antics of the Galman family's colorful counsel, Lupiño Lazaro, provided welcome comic relief. *Asiaweek* magazine had taken to calling the whole merry band "The Agravatars," a label which had stuck.

The Agravatars' birthday present to Santos, whose hardheaded pragmatism and risqué sense of humor had helped them over numerous hurdles, was a bottle of twelve-year-old Scotch, labeled "Black Dog." When I entered board headquarters atop the Social Security System Building in Quezon City, where the party was already under way, he was pouring liberal swigs of the stuff into tumblers and passing them around to his guests. As we sipped it, he took several of us outsiders on a quick tour of the twelfth-floor offices, the highlight of which was a bird's-eye view of an almost imperceptible line extending from National Bureau of Investigation headquarters to the rear, across a field to the SSS Building. "My friends in the business community think I'm joking when I tell them that everything we say is taped," said Santos. "I ask them 'What do you think that thing is, a clothesline?' "

After a typical Filipino lunch consisting of a dozen different dishes, from steamed shrimp and spareribs to pickled coconut and fresh mango, a singing telegram arrived: two young guitar players burst into the room singing "Happy Birthday" and stayed to play a few popular favorites. Eventually Santos, who is a millionaire, handed them a tip and dismissed them, noting puckishly that "songs other than 'Happy Birthday' cost extra." With that, Agrava herself sat down at the piano, which she had moved into her office for the duration of the proceedings, and accompanied the group in singing several more.

Over coffee the conversation turned back to the hearings. Chief of Staff General Fabian Ver, the Big Guy in board parlance, had been invited to testify and had indicated that he would do so without a subpoena in the near future. No one seemed to be able to forecast what kind of witness he would be. However Santos and company appeared to relish the prospect of grilling him. One lawyer had heard that "Ver is afraid of coming here—he called and asked Dean Narvasa what to wear." Great gales of laughter ensued, as the table joked about what kind of psy-war tactics to employ against the general once he took the stand.

Santos had the most imaginative idea. "The whole board should simply sit there staring skeptically at him for the first five minutes," he proposed, "then each one in turn should bare his fangs and bite and paw at the table."

*   *   *

To most of the board members, as to the public at large, Ver was a mysterious presence, who had long lurked in the shadows behind Marcos. Even the most well informed Filipinos seemed unsure whether to regard him as the president's loyal lackey or his *éminence grise*, as a simple oaf or a sinister mastermind. A native of the president's province of Ilocos Norte, Ver had been, as both cousin and friend, a Marcos confidant all his life. His identity had been linked to Marcos's from the moment he rose to prominence as a congressman, first as his driver, then as his bodyguard, informant, and fixer.

In 1965 when Marcos became president, he made the trusted Ver chief of presidential security. Ver's field of expertise from the start was intelligence, and he later became the first armed forces chief of staff to control all the intelligence agencies, both civilian and domestic, in the country. His appointment to the top military job in August 1982 was a controversial one, in that he edged out another Marcos cousin, General Fidel Ramos, for the job. West Pointer Ramos was the epitome of a professional soldier, who was widely admired for his honesty and field experience, while Ver's principal attribute was his close relationship to the president. It was but one of the ironies of Filipino political life that Aquino, while he was a senator, had blocked an early promotion of Ramos, although he had raised no objections to Ver's, thus contributing to Ver's seniority over Ramos in the competition for the top job.

Under Ver's leadership, the politicization of the military, which had begun when Marcos took office and intensified under martial law, became complete. He installed his three sons, Irwin, Rexor, and Wyrlo, all of them soldiers, in sensitive and important posts. As the Ver family's power grew, some cabinet members became alarmed at what they viewed as Marcos's growing dependence on the Vers for both security and information. In July 1983, just one month before the Aquino assassination, when Marcos was preparing to undergo kidney surgery, he had cut civilian Defense Minister Enrile out of the chain of command, vesting Ver with much of his power.

The finger of public suspicion for Aquino's murder was immediately pointed at Ver and Imelda, the two people who were believed to have the most to lose by Ninoy's return at a time when Marcos was reported near death. The longer Ver stayed on as chief of staff after the assassination, despite the obvious damage his continued presence did to the image and morale of the Armed Forces of the Philippines (AFP) and to the presidency, the more speculation grew that perhaps the tables had turned and Marcos's loyal minion had made the physically and politically weakened president a prisoner in his own palace. This was the image which Ver and his legal advisors hoped to counter when the general took the witness stand. If there was any message in the camera-shy Ver's agreement to cooperate with the board, it was, bluntly stated, that he did not intend to sacrifice himself to save Marcos and Imelda. He would defend them, but he would be looking out for himself as well.

Ver's supporters claimed it was only a matter of encouraging the general to act naturally and relate to the public as he would if he were not in uniform. Indeed, on meeting him, it was hard to square the image of sinister brutality with the overly deferential man who oozed flattery, cracked coarse jokes, and laughed so often as to appear almost silly. Only his nervous hyperventilating and an occasional answer that was too hard edged to have come from a nice guy gave him away.

The board, for its part, sought to expose the flimsiness of the alleged military intelligence on which the government claimed to have based its warnings to Aquino not to come home. It was bent on showing that, despite its denials, Philippine intelligence was monitoring Aquino's travels en route back to Manila, knew which plane he was on, and had designed a plan to secure him which was, at best, woefully inadequate, and at worst, murderous.

Despite their mutual suspicions, the board and the general were paragons of politesse when they confronted each other in Magsaysay Hall on the morning of April 6, 1984. Because of General Ver's closeness to the president and the widespread public perception that the military was involved in the assassination, his testimony had long been anticipated as a high point of the Fact-Finding Board's proceedings. It was widely believed on the coffee-shop circuit that Ver would never honor the board with his presence. In fact, he had already failed to show up for one scheduled appearance.

Nonetheless, a crowd of spectators three times the normal size turned up at the SSS Building before 8:30 A.M. on the morning of his rescheduled testimony to fight for access to the public gallery. The general did in fact arrive, but in order to avoid protesting members of the Galman family, who were expected to station themselves in front of the building, he made his entrance one hour early, in a phalanx of bodyguards.

When the hearing was gaveled to order by Chairman Agrava inside Magsaysay Hall, some 500 people were left outside, still pressing to get in. About an hour into the proceedings, their cacophony had become so intrusive that Agrava was forced to call a recess to allow technicians to install loudspeakers in the halls to pacify them. "General Ver is emerging as a superstar," she gushed.

Indeed, the sixty-four-year-old general had drawn the biggest following of any witness, and he seemed to be enjoying all the attention. He had quite obviously been coached on how best to dispel fears about his motives, because he fell all over himself to compliment the board on its "quest for truth and justice." Looking and acting more like a doting uncle than the monster which Dante Santos had jokingly prepared to greet with bared fangs, Ver managed to sandwich three "honorables" into his four-sentence opening statement. In it he expressed the hope that "my testimony, Madame, will somehow dispel any misconception, or any misinformation surrounding this tragic incident."

Ver's dissembling did not stop there. When advised by Justice Agrava of his right to counsel, Ver affected the manner of the kindly, trusting bumbler that he was not.

"I did not bring any counsel, Madame," he said, haltingly, "but if I need a counsel, Madame, I could probably call the Public Coordinator." Then, as if to underline the friendly relations he enjoyed with the popular Benny Tan, he added, "I was talking to Attorney Tan earlier to assist me, in the protection of my constitutional rights."

Agrava agreed to the bizarre proposal that Tan play counsel to the chief of staff, although directly behind him in the lawyer's box sat two colonels from the judge advocate general's office, who would in the course of the day be joined by three other lawyers who had been advising Ver. Tan's sister Christine, an activist nun, who visited the hearing hall that day, was quick to collect the debt that she felt the general owed her brother for agreeing to lend his name and reputation to such a hypocritical exercise. During the noon recess, she wrote out a pass for herself to visit a prominent political prisoner, then asked General Ver to validate it with his signature. He obliged with a smile and profuse praise for her brother.

Ver's nice-guy act did not deceive Narvasa. He was intent on playing the same role. He had intimated that he planned to affect a highly "un-aggressive" style in questioning the general, hoping to trap him by leading him gently but deliberately into incriminating himself and his government. Focusing on the Philippine military's warnings of a plot against Aquino's life, which had been relayed from Manila to the opposition leader by the consul general in New York, Narvasa posed a series of questions about the basis for those warnings. Ver related how as early as February 1983, the intelligence community began receiving reports of a plan to assassinate Aquino. As these reports proliferated, the chief of the Intelligence Service of the Armed Forces of the Philippines (ISAFP) decided to launch an intelligence project to collate and evaluate them and to recommend what action should be taken. On July 7, 1983, "Project Four Flowers" was born.

Narvasa, citing information from a briefing on intelligence gathering and the Communist insurgency, which the board had received from three colonels close to Ver, described the intelligence available in February as "hazy," having come from "some persons who had been overheard while eating and drinking in a restaurant, talking about a plot to kill Senator Aquino." Ver nodded in agreement. It was a pleasure to watch Narvasa building, ever so casually and humbly toward his point. The general counsel went on to relate that in July corroborating information had trickled in from an informant within the Communist New People's Army (NPA). But even with those new details, ISAFP had been unable to conclude with any precision what the plan was or who was involved. Again Ver agreed.

Then between August 15 and 17, less than a week before Aquino's announced return, Narvasa continued, the government's penetration agent inside the NPA "unaccountably disappeared," to resurface only some weeks after the assassination. There ensued, according to the briefing given the board, "a final desperate effort to see if the identity of any prospective assassin could be ascertained, but that failed." Ver confirmed that was so. He also acknowledged that he had kept the president informed about "Four Flowers" during the entire period.

Imprecise though the reports of a plot were, high military officials had prepared a wire, which was signed and relayed by Defense Minister Enrile, claiming that he was convinced "beyond reasonable doubt" that Aquino risked death if he returned to the Philippines, and urging him to postpone his arrival until details could be fleshed out and the conspiracy neutralized. The military rated the intelligence information it had received B-2: "source is usually reliable and the information itself is probably true." It surmised that likely suspects were the vengeful relatives of witnesses who had testified against Aquino during martial law and were subsequently killed.

Gently but calculatedly, Narvasa led Ver to admit that the military had monitored the relatives of these witnesses as part of its effort to protect Aquino. Deftly, he then attempted to draw the logical conclusion that as a complement to the monitoring of possible suspects inside the Philippines, the military would also have monitored the travels of the potential victim abroad "to try to find out the definite date of return to the Philippines, so that you will be better able to provide for ex-Senator Aquino's security?"

"No, Your Honor," said Ver firmly. "We did not monitor him."

Narvasa had scored a preliminary gain by creating a context in which Ver's predictable denial of foreknowledge looked as foolish as it in fact was. But Narvasa was just warming up. "If I were the government," he said, affecting the pose of a simple layman, "I would say, 'Now, I have to find out more closely the movements of the senator, so that I will be able to adequately protect him.' " Ver could not deny that logic, and he acknowledged receiving reports from embassies in the countries Aquino had traversed en route to Taiwan. That, however, was not a matter of government "monitoring," he argued, contesting Narvasa's choice of words. It was more a matter of "following up."

Narvasa proceeded to the next step of his postulate: that Ver must have communicated with those embassies, requesting them to remain on alert.

"No, Your Honor," replied Ver once again. Astonishingly, he claimed, he had chosen to rely instead on an August 18 letter to General Ramos, written by opposition Senator Doy Laurel, who was in charge of Ninoy's homecoming. Laurel's letter asked for protection for Aquino, who would be arriving, he said, aboard Japan Airlines from Tokyo at 1:30 P.M. August 21. On the basis of that information, Ver said he ordered General Custodio to prepare the security plan that would become known as "Operation Homecoming."

Narvasa was backing Ver further and further into a corner. It did not make sense that the chief of all Philippine intelligence would ignore information telexed from the regime's own operatives in Singapore on August 19 that Ninoy had entered and departed that country, traveling on a false passport, and was bound for Taiwan, in favor of the word of an opposition politician, who might be expected to deceive the military about Aquino's estimated time of arrival as a means of protecting Ninoy. And yet, Narvasa realized, the only way Ver could continue to argue the innocence of his own men in shooting Aquino was to deny that their commanders had tipped them off in advance about Aquino's arrival plans. How to trap him? Narvasa decided to press on, forcing Ver to trap himself.

"There was a possibility that, since [Aquino] and Senator Laurel were in the opposition," argued Narvasa, "and they were not exactly friendly to the government, they would try to deceive the government as to the time and even the date of the arrival of Senator Aquino. Was that not a possibility that occurred to you?"

Ver was effectively shamed into giving a positive reply. Nonetheless he continued to cling to the flimsy contention that the Laurel letter remained his best piece of intelligence as to Aquino's plans. However, he added a qualifier. "While we relied on [Laurel's] letter," he admitted, "we also considered the possibility of deception."

A few minutes later, Ver was hard-pressed to explain why, on the morning of August 21, he had revised the orders given earlier to General Custodio to return Aquino to his country of origin if he arrived without valid travel papers. Ver finally conceded: "We just relied on the information given by the head of mission [in Singapore] as part of the information then available." By that morning, said Ver, "we had reliable information that he was coming."

Convinced that Aquino was on his way, that he had travel documents which allowed him to move apparently freely from one country to another, and that nothing would discourage his coming, Ver had therefore ordered Custodio to drop the option of sending him back. Instead, he ordered the general to arrest Aquino on the basis of his 1977 death sentence for murder and subversion. To facilitate that move, Ver told the board, he turned over documents to Custodio—documents never seen by Aquino's lawyers, who said an appeal of his death sentence was still pending in the Supreme Court—that "affirmed" Aquino's death sentence.

Narvasa had succeeded in leading the general to water and had forced him to admit that he had relied on new information about Aquino's homecoming plans in making his decision to revise his instructions to Custodio. What was that new information? Narvasa now wanted to know, and, Did it not come from Philippine operatives abroad? Ver tried to backtrack, returning to the Laurel letter. He feigned absentmindedness. Finally, under persistent questioning from the coolly deliberate general counsel, Ver divulged his last-minute intelligence. His men had, he said, picked up some political flyers at the University of the Philippines, urging students to go to the airport at noontime. They had also, he added, observed an unusual amount of take-out breakfasts being sold to pro-Aquino demonstrators at a restaurant adjacent to the airport.

Those ridiculous answers provoked quiet jeers from the press and public galleries. If Ver had managed not to incriminate himself on the critical question of trying to ascertain when Aquino would arrive, he had bolstered the case of a government cover-up. It was impossible for anyone who knew anything at all about the domestic and international surveillance network over which Ver had presided for such a long time to believe that at the eleventh hour he resorted to polling customers at a restaurant take-out counter for his intelligence.

Ver's greatest success in the course of his three days of testimony was in portraying himself as a loyal follower, who was temperamentally incapable of taking initiatives of his own. He chronicled how he had learned of the Aquino killing and then notified the president. He had been in his office at Malacañang Park on the other side of the river from the palace, he said, when the first call came at about 1:30 P.M. Half an hour later General Custodio called to confirm that Aquino was dead. Custodio told Ver that "someone darted from behind and suddenly shot him" as he was being helped into the van.

Ver ordered Custodio to "protect the scene of the crime" and told him he was designating General Olivas to investigate it. At about 2:25 P.M. Ver telephoned Marcos. Under questioning as to whether it was he who gave Marcos the information that the gunman was a lone Communist, Ver stated, "I only informed the president at that time that Senator Aquino was shot. I did not tell him who shot him, because I did not even know."

"Can you remember how the president reacted when you gave him the news?" asked Chairman Agrava.

"He was shocked," said Ver. When pressed to elaborate, Ver added: "He said, 'Huh! I cannot believe it! I cannot believe why this tragic incident has to happen.' "

Toward the end of his three days of testimony, Ver was asked about rumors that even Marcos feared his chief of staff. The general looked stricken. "I am a loyal soldier," he declared. "My loyalty is my only asset in this world of the military." Playing on his humble background to the ordinary people in the gallery, he continued, "I am not as educated as the others, but I am loyal and I am dedicated. I am sworn to uphold the constitution at all cost, and I am loyal, especially to my commander in chief."

His dark eyes fairly glistening with devotion to his leader, Ver sketched a somewhat disjointed portrait of Marcos. "I am sure that my commander in chief has no reason to fear me. He is a very, very grateful man. I never knew him to hit anybody." Faster now, working himself almost into a frenzy, Ver continued to praise Marcos and protect himself. "The president is a very brave and gallant man, Your Honor. He would not be afraid of anybody, including me. But being brave is not being vindictive." Veering off on a tangent about how Marcos "is in constant communication with God," Ver ran through a generic list of the president's political enemies, ranging from the star witness in the Nalundasan murder case to the legions of people who had tried to assassinate him, and whom he had forgiven.

Delicately at first, then with greater determination, Attorney Ongkiko tried to calm Ver down and force him to conclude what had become a soliloquy on his relationship to Marcos, but the general appeared unused to taking direction from others.

I wanted to say that because of all these things that we have done
to save the president's life, I do not think there is any reason to fear

me. Everything that I have, all the authority that I have, they come from him, and I know that he has no reason to fear me. My long record of public service will show that I have not abused anybody. I may have the authority that I have as director general of the National Intelligence and Security Authority and, at the same time, chief of staff of all armed forces, but I never abused these powers. I execute the command functions of the president, and I do it in accordance with his authority.

When Ver finally rested his case, he apologized for his long-windedness. "Your Honor, I am sorry if I was rather enthused, Madame, with reference to the president. I hope you can forgive me, but I am a little bit touched by the question."

The Big Guy, whom some people close to Marcos had privately hoped might self-destruct on the witness stand, had survived three days of questioning—the longest of any witness. He had shown the public that, contrary to what his detractors had said about him, he was neither stupid nor incapable of speaking English. More important, he had convincingly portrayed himself as a man who only carried out orders from President Marcos. In so doing, he had made it clear that he was not prepared to serve as the regime's fall guy in the Aquino case. At the same time, since no evidence had been produced to suggest that Marcos had ordered him to kill Aquino, both men seemed likely to escape being charged as principal conspirators. However, Ver's answers had been so evasive, incredible, and in some cases false that it was obvious he was still engaged in a government effort to cover up the facts about the plot.

Later Narvasa would confide that many of Ver's answers were in such obvious conflict with the evidence at hand that he was easily indictable as an accessory to the cover-up of the conspiracy to kill Aquino. Some armchair critics believed Narvasa had let Ver off too easily. The Dean's off-the-record reply: "People asked me 'Why did you not chase him up a tree?' I said, 'Because I did not want to make him look like a monkey.' "

Ver himself seemed giddy with delight over his performance. I filed a story, which I considered to have been tough on him, raising as it did the question of "How could the nation's top military officer be so astonishingly ill-informed about the entire affair?" Thus I was surprised one week later to receive a hand-delivered letter from Ver, expressing "my deep sense of gratitude for your balanced and accurate reporting about my appearance . . ." Alluding to the questions TIME had raised about his testimony, Ver said that "The facts that I detailed before the Agrava Board are the best explanations that I can in conscience reveal to anyone." The general closed by praising the dedication of the board and encouraging me "to continue to carry on your noble task."

11

The Ballot Vs.
The Bullet

Watching Cory Aquino speak under a string of bare light bulbs on a provincial stage during the 1984 National Assembly election campaign, it was clear that Ninoy's widow had become the opposition's most effective weapon. Welcome Cory Aquino, said the hand-painted banner stretched across the main street of the town of Talavera in the rice-growing region of central Luzon. She was not a candidate, not a party leader, not even a member of any political party, as were the figures with whom she shared the stage, as she stumped the country. But it was Cory who brought out the crowds.

She had come to Talavera to endorse the opposition ticket for the province of Nueva Ecija. A photograph with Cory clasping a candidate's upraised hands in a "victory" pose was worth tens of thousands of votes. In districts where more than one opposition candidate had been fielded, getting the nod from Ninoy's widow could be decisive. Because of her popularity, she was scheduled as the last speaker on every program, which meant that she was not getting much sleep most nights.

On this particular evening, the crowd had sat in the packed plaza, some on portable sun chairs, some on their haunches, since sundown, listening raptly to the fiery anti-Marcos rhetoric of the candidates, who talked of recent political violence in the province, the loss of human rights, the poverty of the people, and Ninoy's vision of a better society. They had applauded a group of young entertainers, who serenaded them with such Western favorites as "Love Is a Many Splendored Thing," "The Way We Were," and of course Ninoy's song, the theme from the Broadway musical *Man of La Mancha*, "The Impossible Dream." They had laughed at the anti-Marcos jokes told by Ninoy's mother, Doña Aurora, a veteran campaigner, and they had cheered when she told them that a local boy, Rolando Galman, whom the government had accused of slaying Ninoy, could not possibly be guilty. Now, hours later, Cory was finally being introduced.

Dressed in black and white, eight months into her year of official mourning, she stepped up to the microphone, small, shy, radiating gratitude for the warm welcome. She clasped her hands in front of her and waited for the applause to subside. Then she began the narrative of Ninoy's imprisonment, exile, and return, which had become her standard campaign speech. She told how in 1973, after forty days of searching, she and Nena Diokno had finally been brought here to this province, to Fort Magsaysay, where their husbands were held in solitary confinement, and how Ninoy had later been sentenced to death by firing squad.

Her voice was even, almost monotonous in tone, as she spoke of Ninoy's heart attack, the move to Boston, the warnings not to return. Ninoy could have had an easier life, she said, if he had made a deal with Marcos, as so many others did. She hoped that people would now follow his example. There were none of the histrionics that Filipinos had come to expect from their politicians. Nor, by the time she was through, was there a dry eye. Speaking in Tagalog, she switched to English only once to quote the Japanese congressman who had broken the news to her in the middle of the night, Boston time: "Cory, I am very sorry to have to inform you that Ninoy is dead." By then the pain of her experience had touched them, opening hidden reservoirs of long-repressed memories of their own suffering, their own compromises, their own failure to fight back. Tears rolled down the cheeks of the faces looking up at her.

Fifteen minutes later she was on her way to a second rally. Her own analysis of her impact, which I pressed her to make later in the car, was as straightforward and concise as her speech. "It's very simple," she said. "I just tell them what Marcos has done to this country." As for the tears, she noted wryly, her son, Noynoy, had offered to supply her some jokes to cheer up her audiences, but she had realized they would be inappropriate. "I guess I am not meant to say anything funny," she observed about her widow's persona. "When it comes to me, people are prepared to bring out their handkerchiefs."

Not that she had any desire to introduce new material into her campaign at this late date. It had taken enough nerve for her to get up on stages and simply tell her story. She knew her limitations, she said. During the 1978 campaign, which Ninoy ran from his detention cell, she had been incapable of speaking in public at all. "I was just grateful that my youngest daughter enjoyed giving speeches," she said. "That saved me." While she was not as nervous now, public appearances still made her uneasy. Unlike all the politicians she knew, she found it difficult to remember people's names when she was in front of an audience. "After my first press conference, I needed a tranquilizer," she said.

However, Cory had learned a lot under the pressure of representing Ninoy before all of the competing constituencies that now claimed him as their own. Her most painful lesson had come earlier in the year, when she had joined twenty-nine other personalities representing the major groups of the democratic opposition in issuing a "Call for Meaningful Elections" in the form of an open letter to Marcos. Getting the fractious anti-Marcos forces to take a common stand on anything was rare, and this call for six major reforms had been hammered out at a particularly critical time, as scheduled elections were approaching and opposition sentiment for boycotting them was gaining strength.

On the premise that Marcos's international creditor banks and the U.S. government had put strong pressure on him to win a new mandate for his troubled government by holding fair elections, the more moderate signatories viewed the letter as a means of exacting concessions in return for their participation, which Marcos would need to legitimize the exercise. Those further to the left, on the other hand, certain that Marcos would never concede major reforms, saw the letter as a means of justifying their planned election boycott.

Cory had been persuaded by people in both camps to add her signature to the list of demands, which included amnesty for political prisoners, election reforms, and the abolition of the infamous Amendment Number 6, from whence Marcos derived his decree-making powers. If the demands were not met by February 14, 1984, said the letter, the signatories would boycott the elections.

Not surprisingly, Marcos denounced the letter as "childish," and refused to consider any further concessions, except the election reforms he was dangling in front of the opposition to entice its participation. Old pro that he was, he simply looked at his opponents' past record of unity in pressing for reforms and decided to sit back and wait until their fundamental ideological divisions once again drove them apart. He correctly calculated that no matter how he reacted to the letter, traditional politicians like Laurel, who were masters of compromise, would decide to participate, while issue-oriented leaders of the grass roots groups like Diokno and the aged, former Senator Lorenzo Tañada would boycott.

As he had predicted, once the opposition's February 14 deadline had passed, the signatories scrambled in opposite directions. As participators and boycotters castigated each other for their contradictory decisions, pressure mounted on private citizen Cory Aquino to state her intentions.

Demonstrating a pattern of behavior that would consistently apply to her future decision making, Cory agonized for weeks, listening to the arguments of one side and then the other. Even her own family was divided, with Ninoy's brother Butz promoting a boycott, and his mother, Doña Aurora, finding herself irresistibly drawn toward campaigning for those party politicians who had supported Ninoy. Prizing opposition unity above all else, Cory yearned to effect a compromise. "I said to Butz, 'Let's think of some way the boycotters and those who want to participate can have a joint position.'"

Compromise, however, was not what was called for at the moment. One of the penalties of her new prominence was that she was expected to take decisive stands on key issues. In an attempt to make up her mind, she sought more opinions, including those of friendly priests. One opinion that was increasingly given more weight than others in her deliberations was that of her younger brother, Peping. Since Ninoy's death, Peping had relieved his nonpolitician sister of many of the less savory responsibilities that had fallen on her shoulders, allowing her to concentrate on her mission to perpetuate Ninoy's legacy in a nonpartisan manner. Now Cory announced that she would reserve her decision on participation or boycott until after the convention of the newly formed PDP-Laban party—the product of a merger of the grass roots Pilipino Democratic Party and Ninoy's old Lakas ng Bayan, in which Peping had recently become a power.

Peping Cojuangco had been a congressman before martial law, but he preferred the role of kingmaker to king. He had tried to discourage Ninoy from returning home in August 1983, but when he realized that his brother-in-law was determined to be back in time to lead the May 1984 opposition campaign, Peping had begun contacting old allies and tapping potential campaign donors. Like Ninoy, he had been against a boycott from the start, because he believed it was incompatible with Filipinos' enthusiasm for elections and their gamblers' instincts to pick a winner. "When the people see a candidate as having a chance to win, they forget about the boycott and jump on the bandwagon," observed Peping. "When people are talking in the corner store after the election, they like to say who they voted for. They want to be a part of the victory." Peping, who raised fighting cocks and race horses, understood gamblers.

He had, therefore, pushed for participation in the elections. He was not under any illusions that the opposition could win a parliamentary majority in this election. On the other hand, he believed that even a thirty-member opposition group in the National Assembly could make waves. More important, in his opinion, than the 1984 elections were those that would follow. "If you get thirty this time, then people will believe it can be done, and in the next election that thirty will multiply," he said. Out of that core group of oppositionists, Peping believed, future "presidential timber" would emerge. Meanwhile, he stressed, a strong democratic opposition was the best way to prevent a military takeover. "Without that," he said, "if Marcos dies and the military wants to take over, it will find no resistance."

Peping's PDP-Laban party convention had split over the question of whether or not to endorse a boycott. In the end it adopted a proboycott position, but approved a clause allowing participation in those regions where party members wanted to mount slates. One week later, on March 6, Cory went on Church-run Radio Veritas to announce that she had changed her mind and that, despite her signature on the open letter, which committed her to boycott, she had decided to campaign for opposition candidates.

"At no time in my life have I felt more alone than I have been in these last few weeks as I grappled with the crucial questions of the appropriate opposition response," she told her listeners. In the end, she said, she had concluded that "the path of reconciliation and national unity through free, clean, and meaningful elections is the only means to avert violence." She still reserved the right to support a boycott if, by election week, the laws did not favor a fair contest. Meanwhile, though, she was urging the opposition "not to harden its position, but rather to keep its options open and to prepare to participate actively and vigorously in the May elections."

The reaction was swift and sharp. Boycotters accused her of betraying Ninoy's memory. The party politicians, on the other hand, were full of praise. "When Cory gave her statement in favor of participation," recounted Peping, referring to undecided members of his own PDP-Laban, "these people could not declare their candidacies fast enough." Eventually party participation would reach nearly 95 percent.

When I saw her shortly afterward, she expressed great relief that she had finally arrived at a decision, unpopular as it was in some quarters. "Ninoy, why have you gotten me into this?" she exclaimed, looking skyward and shaking her finger in mock anger at the spirit of the departed politician, who would have thrived on the controversy she had inadvertently created. She could laugh now at her speech, which, she noted apologetically, "used the word 'agonized' three times."

She was still bothered by the fact that she had broken a signed commitment, but she now understood why politics was defined as "the art of compromise." As if trying to speed the process of growing a thicker skin, she kept reminding herself, "I am not in a popularity contest. People have said uglier things about Ninoy and me."

What mattered in the end was that she had done the right thing by Ninoy. "It's difficult to accept that some people think they know Ninoy better than I did," she complained. "Even in those dark days, Ninoy was for participation, so why should I give up this excellent opportunity now, when so many are supporting us?" If clean elections could not be held now, with so much attention focused on the Philippines, then she might have to drop the democratic option. In the meantime, she said, "it all boils down to this: I want to give it one last try."

As Marcos and Imelda staged splashy rallies, flooded the airwaves with slick commercials, and announced a 10 percent preelection pay raise for public employees and soldiers, the opposition struggled to overcome the triple handicap of meager funds, a jerry-built machine that was rusty from thirteen years of disuse, and a determined boycott campaign aimed at its natural constituents. In Manila the coffee-shop forecast for the opposition's likely performance was grim. Out in the countryside where the vast majority of Filipinos lived, however, the prospects looked brighter. "There is no talk in the provinces about quitting this race," insisted Doy Laurel, president and campaign manager of the United Nationalist Democratic Organization (UNIDO), a coalition of a dozen opposition parties. Laurel spent almost all his time outside the capital, working with local party leaders.

The more time Cory spent on the road, the higher her own hopes rose that perhaps the people's long passivity was finally ending. She noticed several encouraging trends. "Before, you had to provide transportation for people and professional entertainment. Now they understand that the opposition has no money, so they don't expect it," she said. Neither were opposition candidates under the same pressure they once were to buy votes. "Especially when I campaigned with Ninoy for the Senate, there would not be a day when people would not come up and say they needed money for their children or for medicine," she recalled. "It was always money, money, money." Today people in droves were volunteering their services free.

She hoped that such changes in attitude signified that Filipinos had finally matured to the point where they might be able to assume responsibility for governing themselves again, rather than allowing themselves to be ruled. "People shake hands and tell me they are with me," she recounted. "I tell them, 'You have to be the leaders now. . . . I can only do so much, and the candidates can only do so much.'" Her instincts told her that they understood and accepted her reasoning. Like her, she believed, they innately distrusted any leader who pretended to have all the answers. "Before, people just left everything to their leaders," she said. "Now it is different." If that were the case, Cory concluded, then this election could indeed signify the first stage in the restoration of democracy.

After watching her in action and listening to her insightful analysis of what was stirring under the facades of the multitudes she addressed, I could not help but observe, only partly in jest, that she had a natural instinct for politics and appeared to have been bitten by the political bug. She bridled at the notion. "Heaven help me if I go nuts and decide to run for something!" she exclaimed.

*   *   *

As Ferdinand Marcos rose to address the crowd of 50,000 supporters bused to the official kickoff of his *Kilusang Bagong Lipunan* (KBL), or New Society Movement's campaign for the National Assembly, on March 27, 1984, he did not act like a ruler plagued by the worst political and economic crisis in his country's postwar history. He appeared fit as he strode to the podium from the pair of overstuffed red chairs, where he had been seated with the First Lady at the center of a glittering outdoor proscenium. He sounded feisty as he led members of the cabinet, the twenty-one KBL candidates from Metro-Manila, three male actors in drag, and a gaggle of other show biz supporters in a throbbing chorus of the new ruling party song:

> *Under the New Society*
> *Everybody is equal.*
> *Because of the "Self-Reliance" program*
> *Dreams are now attainable*
> *Everywhere in the Philippines.*
> *So pin your hopes*
> *On the KBL.*
> *For the future of the nation*
> *Remember, KBL.*
> *One nation, one thought—KBL.*

Much like the regime of "constitutional authoritarianism," which Marcos had imposed on the nation in 1972, the song was a well-packaged set of illusions. Its centerpiece, the "Self-Reliance" program, had been initiated only six weeks before, hardly time to make dreams attainable, especially in the notoriously sluggish Philippines. Moreover, the program was itself but a repackaging of other now-forgotten plans and projects, which had also sounded good at the time, but had made hardly a dent in the poverty in which 70 percent of Filipinos lived.

As the last strains of disco music faded on the breeze, and the blaze of fireworks over Manila Bay trailed off into a smoky haze, Marcos began his speech by looking backward over the record of his nineteen years in office. As always, he took the offensive, pugnaciously accusing the opposition of having joined forces with subversive organizations to foment rebellion against the government. Now, Marcos boasted, he was prepared to submit himself "to the people's judgment" by pitting his party's candidates against those with other beliefs and other agendas in the May 14 elections.

"This election is not only a matter of choosing men and women to sit in the National Assembly," said Marcos, "but choosing the alternate forms that government will take." In his most stentorian voice, he challenged his opponents, "We have a platform! We have a program! We have an ideology! We ask the opposition: Where is its platform? Where is its program? Where is its ideology?" After an appropriate pause, he sounded the appropriate answer: "None!"

For the next ninety minutes, the president's speech followed the tried and true course of his past campaign oratory in invoking his opponents' misdeeds. Still high on his list, in death as in life, was the man Marcos referred to as Aquino. Even as the opposition was keeping alive the memory of Ninoy in its rallies, Marcos was still struggling to bury it. Reporters began to count his negative references to Aquino. Four times Marcos repeated his name.

As in the past, Marcos dismissed his opponents as victims of "impotent democratic deadlock." Unfortunately, there he had a point. Despite the convergence of events since the assassination, which should have favored the anti-Marcos forces, their split over the issue of whether or not to boycott an election that might "legitimize" the regime had handed him an advantage. A master at exploiting the inherent divisions in the opposition, he had known just what to do with it. "Marcos has given us enough concessions to divide us," admitted PDP-Laban official Linggoy Alcuaz.

The boycotters' stand—principled as it was—frustrated many friends of the opposition. The influential Archbishop of Manila expressed dismay over "the bickering." Marcos and his supporters, said Cardinal Sin, "must be having the time of their lives." Sin made it clear in press conferences and in background chats with reporters that he favored participation. "This will be the last chance," he said. "If this election is not clean and honest, then democracy is over. If change does not come through the ballot, so it will come through the gun."

While the boycott would help Marcos, he was not one to leave his fate in the hands of his opponents. His greatest asset was the national political machine he had built, through a combination of recruiting fresh talent and co-opting regional warlords to his cause. It had never faced as great a challenge as this election, and he would make certain that it had all the resources it needed to deliver a decisive margin to the KBL. In addition to new money—he and his cronies would bring an estimated $1 billion in private funds back into the Philippines from foreign and offshore bank accounts—that meant candidates with proven records of past delivery from the KBL political pork barrel.

Throughout the archipelago during the forty-five-day campaign period, billboards crediting KBL candidates with this beneficence were as ubiquitous as jeepneys. In addition to what had been appropriated to these projects in past budgets, an estimated total of $28.5 million in public funds had been poured into an array of vote-getting projects, which were being rushed to completion just before election day.

*   *   *

At high noon on April 18, 1984, the hour of maximum visibility in the mountains of western Mindanao, a line of armed guerrillas filed across a ridge high above us. Moving at a fast clip, two dozen men, toting new M-16s and vintage Garands and dressed in army-surplus bullet belts and camouflage, headed down a steep incline, using the freshly tilled furrows as steps. A farmer following his water buffalo noted their passing. But so familiar and so unthreatening was the sight of the Communist New People's Army (NPA) in this part of the Philippines that he did not even interrupt his plowing to watch their descent.

When the barefoot fighters reached the bamboo hut on stilts, they received a worshipful welcome from a group of "white area" student sympathizers, who had trekked up into the hills for a programmed, week-long "exposure" to the revolution as it is waged in "red areas" like this one. "This is progress," exclaimed Tiban, a handsome member of an NPA militia unit from a nearby barrio, as we were introduced. "Before, we could not carry arms during the daytime here," he said. "The fact that now we can, without anyone reporting us, means that the people are sympathetic to us."

Indeed, TIME photographer Sandro Tucci and I, accompanied by three unarmed guides, had walked for a day and a half on our way here through what appeared to be areas sympathetic to the movement. Wherever we stopped along the narrow trails through the steep, treeless hills, peasant families willingly shared their meager meals of rice, salt fish, vegetables, and water with us. "The NPAs used to be thin," joshed one of our guides, "because there was no way for them to get much food in the hills. Now everyone is happy to feed them." We stopped for the night in the bamboo hut of a sympathetic farmer on whose land local NPAs helped cultivate a "communal rice paddy." As we unrolled the straw mats which our hostess had given us to sleep on, she took a pillow covered with a fresh, white pillowcase from a wooden chest and insisted that I lay my head on it.

We had seen many other signs of the growing self-reliance of the Communist insurgents along the way from the southern Mindanao city where we had entered the area to our final destination. The hotel where we had been instructed to stay by our Manila contact was evidently protective of the movement. The tricycle which picked us up at the hotel and the jeepney which delivered us to the airport at the end of our trip likewise appeared to be owned and operated by friends of the left. On the first morning of our trek, we stopped for lunch at a *nipa* hut (constructed of bamboo and woven palm fronds), where an NPA guerrilla named Robert was recuperating from a bullet wound in his foot. Our guides delivered the antibiotics he needed. As soon as he was able to walk, they told us, he would be helped down the mountain by other comrades (*kasamas*) to a doctor, who would surgically remove additional bullet shards without informing the authorities.

The riskiest part of our trip had been getting through the military checkpoints at the airport and along the main road into town without raising suspicions about what we were doing there. Having testified as a witness before the Agrava Board only a few weeks earlier, my photograph had been splashed across a number of front pages. Were the military to identify me as a reporter and follow us, we could endanger our guides and our sources. I had therefore changed my hairstyle and dressed like a tourist bound for the beach, wearing rubber thongs, a straw hat, and a gaily colored skirt and blouse. My hiking boots, jeans, dark T-shirts, and tape recorder, as well as the packets of pharmaceuticals and cigarettes I was delivering to the NPA, were buried in my backpack. Sandro, a tall Italian, had deliberately dressed in stylish sports clothes, carrying his cameras openly, as would a tourist. The fact that our destination was not on any tourist's itinerary was a detail we had decided to ignore.

My cover seemed as good as blown the moment we saw soldiers demanding identification documents from disembarking passengers. However, Sandro calmly gestured to me to stand back and leave the talking to him. He presented his Italian passport, then explained that "his wife" had forgotten to bring hers. The macho soldier, seeing no need for a wife to have a passport of her own, stepped aside and let us pass.

We were picked up by two men on a tricycle and transported through the military roadblocks to a rural intersection. In a clump of trees about a quarter of a mile away, we were greeted by a soft-spoken young man, who introduced himself as "Plam," and two of his comrades. Well-educated and fluent in English, Plam would lead us physically to the site of our encounter with the NPA and intellectually through the political evolution of one of the most dynamic Communist insurgencies in the developing world.

The major ingredients for a successful insurgency had been present in the Philippines before August 21, 1983: a grossly unequal distribution of wealth, a corrupt and abusive military, and an authoritarian government unresponsive to the needs of the people. Although many Filipinos believed that Marxism was too alien an ideology to thrive in their Catholic country, it had found its niche within the local revolutionary tradition as early as the 1920s.

Before and after World War II, it had fired the passions of peasants in central Luzon, a rice-growing region with the highest rate of tenant farming in the country. When the Japanese occupied the islands in 1941, members of the clandestine *Partido Komunista ng Pilipinas* (PKP) and the peasant-based Socialist Party, with which it had merged, founded a resistance movement known as the *Hukbalahap* or "People's Anti-Japanese Army," which had come out of the war armed, 10,000-men strong, and anxious to work within the legal system to improve the lot of the peasantry. The newly independent Philippine government, under pressure from large landowners and the U.S., manipulated Congress to refuse to seat the six victorious Huk candidates. With that, the peasant leadership turned against the government, and the Huk rebellion was born.

The Huk insurgency, spurred by the PKP, had made the mistake of pushing too early for revolution, rather than the reforms for which most peasants would have settled. As a result, it had collapsed under a counteroffensive mounted by the Philippine Armed Forces, with the help of American counterinsurgency advisors. Simultaneous with the military action against the guerrillas, a social and economic offensive had been launched by Defense Secretary Ramon Magsaysay, who rode the successful counterinsurgency campaign from there to the presidency in 1953.

In the mid-1960s a group of eleven Marxist students, who were inspired by the Cultural Revolution of Mao Zedong in China, briefly joined the weak and discredited PKP, challenged its Soviet theory, and were expelled. On December 26, 1968, the seventy-fifth birthday of Chairman Mao, they held a Congress of Re-establishment, during which the new Communist Party of the Philippines (CPP) was born. According to its chief theoretician and leader, Jose Maria Sison, writing under the alias of Amado Guerrero, the party's purpose was to bring about "the overthrow of U.S. imperialism, feudalism, and bureaucratic capitalism." Living by Chairman Mao's teaching that "political power grows out of the barrel of a gun," Sison and his fellow intellectuals linked up with the legendary Huk Commander Dante in 1969 to give the party an armed wing, known as the New People's Army.

Since then the CPP/NPA had built an entirely indigenous armed movement, estimated by American experts at 7,000-to-12,000-members strong, which had coped imaginatively with the geographical handicap of waging a guerrilla war throughout a chain of islands, without benefit of a Ho Chi Minh Trail for the infusion of foreign supplies.

Indeed, the movement's peculiarly Filipino character had distinguished it from its Huk antecedent and had guaranteed its survival and continued growth, even after the capture of top leaders like Sison and Dante. Individual guerrilla commanders and their largely self-sufficient units enjoyed tactical autonomy on their respective fronts. A superb interisland courier system linked them to the NPA military commission, which set strategy for the entire country. Meanwhile, a vigorous revolutionary underground, operating behind democratic or semilegal political front groups, which were seeded with members of the Communist-dominated National Democratic Front (NDF), worked at developing the sort of friendly "right of way" between protected mountain bases and coastal population centers, which we were enjoying, as we continued our uphill trek.

Now, one month before the May elections, the NDF—its influence and membership significantly expanded since the Aquino assassination had sent much of the nation into the streets—was spearheading the election boycott movement. A corresponding intensification of NPA activities in the weeks prior to the election had alarmed the Pentagon. Not only were the guerrillas striking military targets more frequently, from more fronts (45), and with larger, company size units (60-to-100-men), but Marcos's military was demonstrating a glaring inability to counter them. Meanwhile, Democratic Congressman Stephen Solarz was pressing the House to cut U.S. military assistance to the Philippines if political reforms were not forthcoming, a move which the Pentagon feared would favor the growth of the insurgency.

Plam had been working since 1978 to politicize this corner of the Communist-targeted southern island of Mindanao. In order to gain quick and easy access to the small and isolated peasant communities, the party had sent in priests and nuns to lay the groundwork for organizing a shadow government. Once they had gained a foothold, Plam and other political operatives followed. Contrary to the popular image of the NPA as a strictly military entity, Plam stressed that it was also very much a political and propaganda organization. Guerrillas thus spent a majority of their time, not in combat, but in pursuit of community action and new recruits. "The NPA carries out house-to-house propaganda," Plam related, educating residents about the national condition, until the people "accept us." At that point the "politicized" adults become willing to let their children join the NPA units as young fighters.

The guerrilla movement had no trouble finding able-bodied recruits. Membership was soaring these days, due to increased unemployment, political turmoil, and the aura of glamour associated with the NPA in dissident areas, particularly those in which abusive units of the armed forces were stationed. All an NPA commander had to do when he went home to his native barrio was pass around a few photos of himself and his comrades in their fatigues. By the time he was ready to return to the hills, three or four young men would be asking to accompany him.

The NPA had skillfully exploited the abuses committed by the AFP troops, which had been deployed in infiltrated areas and which now virtually occupied certain regions of Mindanao. According to Plam, many an NPA "tactical operation" was designed to provoke a response inside the barrios, which the military would be forced to address with inevitably negative consequences. "They respond to our tactical operations," he explained, with cynical understatement, "but when they come after us, all they find are civilians, whom they then proceed to abuse."

It was such action by the military that had driven Robert, the wounded NPA commander, to become a guerrilla. "Before the military began to harass my family, they were not sympathizers," he said. But the military had suspected them anyway and begun spying on them, picking them up for questioning, and making false accusations against them. In the end he and his six brothers had joined the NPA. He had received one week of initial training in "how to use a rifle and everything about the actual combat situation—including retreating if the enemy is too strong." The object of the NPA's style of guerrilla warfare was not necessarily to win military victories, but to maintain an aura of invincibility, while weakening the image of the armed forces.

In the afternoon, as we were making our way through a ravine covered with thick jungle foliage, it began to rain. The narrow trails became treacherously slippery and the air steamy. In order to help us "gringos" up and down the muddiest inclines, Plam improved his own traction by removing his shoes. It was a most revealing gesture, in that it showed that he was not only the articulate, urban political activist he appeared to be, but a calloused fighter as well, trained, like the NPA, to walk barefoot all night. "That's why they call the NPA *way sapatos* (without shoes)," he said.

Eventually we sought refuge from the downpour in a hut in which twenty-four people had gathered to say prayers on the death anniversary of a relative. Although the owners of the dwelling were Communist sympathizers, they were also practicing Catholics. This was another of the adaptations of conventional Marxist dogma to local realities that Filipino Communists had made to render their insurgency viable. "Religion is very strong in the barrios," Plam acknowledged later. "We could not force the people to give it up." The party's response to the thorny question of how it would deal with the apparent incompatibility between Philippine Catholicism and Marxist atheism was to leave it to the eventual revolutionary government. "The CPP is only a small group compared to the whole Filipino people," explained Plam. "It is only helping to shape the government to be established, and the government would support the practice of religion as it is now."

As we were preparing to resume our journey, after the rain had stopped, a stranger passed by the house, leading a pig to market. Suspicious of his sudden appearance there, our hosts urged us to wait until he had disappeared into the valley, lest he spot the presence of foreigners and report them to the authorities. As remote as this place looked, Plam explained, it was not far from a highway with a military checkpoint that had been established in the wake of two recent NPA ambushes of military troops, which had taken heavy casualties. "We have already killed almost one hundred soldiers from the Thirtieth Infantry Battalion since September 1983," boasted Khalid, one of our other two heretofore-silent guides.

The only other military presence in this area was the Civilian Home Defense Force (CHDF), which reported to the AFP. Its members had, however, been "disarmed" by the NPA in a recent "mock battle." Employing a common means of obtaining badly needed arms for its growing ranks, the NPA had staged operations against the hapless CHDF. Rather than fight to the death to defend themselves, the CHDF had surrendered their weapons to the NPA, then reported to the military that they had lost the weapons in battle.

Were a large unit of AFP soldiers to pass through a barrio in this area, NPA militiamen would not fire on them. They would simply pose as farmers and let them pass. The reason, said Plam, was a lack of arms. Every liberated barrio of fifty families had a militia numbering between seven and twelve men, only half of whom were generally armed. Militiamen did not, therefore, engage themselves lightly in combat. Rather, tactical operations were planned in advance, with militiamen and regular NPA units working together to achieve maximum political impact and to retrieve as many enemy weapons while incurring as few casualties as possible.

It was several hours after dark by the time we reached the farm where we were to spend our second night and meet the guerrilla leaders who would "secure" us en route to our final destination. The conversation over a modest dinner of rice, dried fish, and fresh eggplant was the coming election. Rumor had it that the government would send fourteen battalions to Mindanao to secure the area against attempts to steal ballot boxes and harass voters. NPA policy was to enforce the boycott. "We will confiscate ballot boxes in those barrios where people are forced by the military to vote," said Plam. However, he stressed, "We have a policy not to harm candidates, especially those from the opposition, because after the election, if the opposition will lose, we could perhaps win them over." He did not expect opposition candidates to win in this region against the heavily entrenched ruling party candidates. "Here in the city when the KBL has rallies, they are guarded by the military," said Plam.

By contrast, the opposition candidates lacked money or media, and were, in the eyes of the left, merely running at the behest of Marcos or the CIA in order to legitimize the exercise and keep the dictator in power. "The opposition running in these elections are only opportunists," charged Khalid. "The real opposition are the boycotters."

The current crisis was not just about getting rid of Marcos, said Plam politely, it was also about getting rid of the remnants of American imperialism. "The problem is not Marcos, but the system," he said. "Even with Marcos dead, the U.S. government can always replace him." Our guides reasoned that once the U.S. no longer had control over the Philippine government, then it would be possible for the sovereign Republic of the Philippines to enjoy friendly relations with the sovereign United States of America. The likelihood that the Soviet Union would step gingerly into any vacuum left by the withdrawal of U.S. bases from the Philippines was something its members glossed over, stressing that they were no more anxious to see Soviet interference in their internal affairs than American interference. This discussion ended the way of all others on the subject between American liberals and Filipino leftists, with a naive plea on the part of the Filipinos to "let us be neutral."

Around 10 P.M., three NPA guerrillas, dressed in camouflage and carrying World War II-era Garand rifles, entered the house. In contrast to our guides, they spoke no English, and their manner was surly, even hostile. After they had finished their dinner, Sandro and I offered them some of the Marlboros we had already passed to the others. "Those are the cigarettes of millionaires," scoffed the leader, refusing to touch the pack. He lectured us that in 1978 his comrades had adopted a policy of refusing gifts from outsiders in order to curb corruption. "Well-to-do people were giving the NPA liquors and cigarettes in return for their favor," he said, according to Plam, who translated his remarks and later apologized for his rudeness. After the guerrilla leader had said his piece, he pulled some tobacco from his pocket, tapped a little pile out onto a leaf, and rolled his own. The rest of the evening was spent in conversation about NPA strategy, which was shaped by its chronic arms shortage and its primarily rural base.

Because the guerrillas refused to accept "aid with strings attached," they were forced to obtain nearly all their weapons without outside help. That meant buying them "through Muslim smugglers" or grabbing them from the bodies of enemies killed in encounters. The NPA had had limited success raiding military arsenals, said Plam, because the supply depots were generally located in populated areas, where "most of our fighters are from the country, and are not good at city operations."

Since urban operations were becoming increasingly necessary, however, Plam added, special training was now being given to NPAs who volunteered for service in urban "sparrow units," named for their quick, darting attacks in crowded areas. Sparrows used .45-caliber weapons to liquidate "abusive" public officials, including, in particular, armed policemen.

Early the next morning, we hiked the last several miles uphill to the bamboo hut on stilts, where a dozen students from universities all over the Philippines were spending the first week of their summer vacation attending a ten-hour-a-day "basic party course." From a bench on the shady front porch, I listened to a lecture being conducted inside in Tagalog by a twice-detained party member. Using a brown wall as a blackboard, she outlined her initial lesson on *imperismo*.

Pointing to wall charts depicting the capitalist relationship between *industriya*, *bangko*, and *oligarkiya*, she decried the "collusion" of international organizations like the World Bank and the International Monetary Fund with Chase Manhattan and multinationals, such as Dole, Dupont, and Toyota, which operate in the Philippines. At the bottom of her graph, dancing like puppets on a string, were members of the Philippine political and economic "oligarchy," including such Marcos cronies as coconut tycoon Eduardo Cojuangco, sugar mogul Roberto Benedicto, and Prime Minister Cesar ("Viratax") Virata. Hovering over the whole equation was the omnipresent "U.S.-Marcos dictatorship."

During rap sessions over coffee and self-rolled cigarettes later on the porch, the May 14 elections were uppermost in the minds of students and instructors. Many of them had participated in the planning of a week-long "People's March" in support of the election boycott that was now going on in Mindanao. Such political initiatives were at the heart of Communist party strategy, which sought to harvest the discontent provoked by the Aquino assassination within the newly politicized middle class.

So crucial was the political battle of the Communist Party of the Philippines for the hearts and minds of these people, explained Plam, that the CPP's political arm, the National Democratic Front, had recently achieved "equal status" with the party itself, and was considered "the site of future leadership of the party." He added that the NDF was being positioned to take over the leadership of the anti-Marcos forces, if and when the traditional democratic opposition parties lost their credibility. It was the assumption of many of the students assembled here—the future leaders of the Communists' parliamentary struggle—that that moment might occur as early as May 14, when they foresaw another defeat for the moderate opposition at the hands of Marcos.

When the students went back inside the hut to resume their political lessons, I began interviewing the NPA fighters, who remained outside. Differences of class and education very clearly set them apart from the more sophisticated city kids in the other room. There had not been much real mixing of the two groups. It was easy to understand why, given the preoccupation of the NPA with matters of basic survival, rather than the esoterica of ballots or boycotts.

Lito, a twenty-three-year-old peasant with a fifth-grade education, leaned on his automatic rifle as he talked about the poverty that drove him to join the NPA. His father, he said, had been unable to sustain his family of nine children on the three hectares of land he owned. So father and sons had worked the lands of others for 8 pesos (50 cents) a day, plus free milk and meals. Lito was still young when he grasped the powerlessness of men in his father's situation and began listening to the NPA organizers who came to the barrio. "I am fighting for my children," he said.

His comrade in arms Tiban, thirty-three, was also a farmer, who realized he had no future under the feudal system of land ownership that still prevailed in the Philippines. As a tenant farmer, he was forced to give two thirds of his crop to an absentee landlord, who lived in the city. Finding this system grossly "unfair," he joined the NPA in 1982 as a part-time fighter, going full-time a year later. Although he had not engaged in a single tactical operation against the military, his gun and his membership in the movement had given him the clout he lacked before in dealing with community problems. His landlord, for instance, had agreed to a new sharecropping formula. "Instead of giving two thirds to him," said Tiban, "the farmer now keeps three fourths and gives one fourth to the landlord." "How did he convince the landlord to make such a drastic change?" I asked. "We politicized him," replied Tiban with a grin.

By the time the class took another coffee break, the students were engaged in setting a timetable for the revolution. "We are involved in a protracted peoples' war to transform the society," said Anwar, a Muslim student who was working to bring Muslim secessionists into the struggle with the Communists. "Our ideal would be to have a democratic state run by a people's coalition government made up of farmers, workers, professionals, and even those politicians who are with us, like Diokno, Tañada, and Butz Aquino. To get there, we have stages during which we conduct antifeudal actions in the countryside and antifascist and anti-imperialist actions in the cities.

"We are still young," said Anwar, "but even we cannot say that we can reach the final stage in our lifetime. Maybe that will be for our sons and daughters." Plam added, "Much depends on circumstances." Only time and the outcome of events like the approaching elections would tell whether "circumstances" would ultimately favor the revolutionary transformation of the society they envisioned. As we huddled around a transistor radio to listen to the evening news broadcast, today's "circumstances" sounded auspicious. The military had uncovered a "Communist plot" to sabotage the election, reported the progovernment station. General Ver had announced that documents to this effect had been seized in a series of raids on "underground houses" in Davao City, and he had issued a directive calling for the intensification of the military's drive against the CPP-NPA.

The group reacted with the knowing amusement of people who recognized the rhetoric of combat, because they spoke it themselves. "It's the same old thing they always say," said Plam. "They are saying it now to try and scare off the newly influenced groups from joining us." They laughed off the reports, while at the same time taking unspoken pride in their ability to keep the military on the defensive.

Out on the grass under the starry sky, a "white-area worker" plucked the melody of the Communist anthem, "The International," on her guitar. Tired of talking shop, the student activists and the NPA fighters on the porch drifted out to join her in song.

*   *   *

Among the more avid followers of the "circumstances" that might serve to accelerate or decelerate the progress of the insurgency was a small team of political officers on the second floor of the U.S. embassy. One of them combed military intelligence documents and newspapers for reports of rebel operations and marked each new encounter by sticking a colored pin in the appropriate geographical location on a large wall map in his office. By mid-March 1984, his map was sprouting colored pinheads, not only in the traditional NPA strongholds, but in new areas as well.

Another had just returned from a preelection fact-finding trip to Mindanao. What he had learned from Philippine military officers, politicians, and businessmen there had brought back bitter memories of past insurgencies he had witnessed during a long diplomatic career. "People laughed at the Algerian rebels who challenged mighty France," he recalled. "But eight years later Algeria became independent and forced France to do the unthinkable."

The grim situation, which he had outlined in a background interview conducted before my trip, had been largely borne out by what I had witnessed in southwestern Mindanao. "The Philippine government is not actively pursuing the guerrillas," he complained. He said he had asked one Filipino general whether his men had lots of engagements with the NPA. The general had replied, "No, only about two per month." The embassy officer reasoned, "That does not indicate that the insurgents are quiet. What he was really saying was that his troops are in a passive mode."

This was a dangerous trend, warned the American, because "the NPA is a political organization, which wants to go into a *barangay* (a unit of local government established during martial law to consolidate Marcos' grass-roots control) and proselytize, grab arms, look for good propaganda opportunities. It is not looking for big engagements, because the firepower advantage is on the military side." A passive military gave the insurgents more time for political organizing.

The American official was concerned about the increased deployment of NPA "sparrow units" in urban areas. "The AFP is stumped in urban guerrilla warfare," he explained, "because it realizes it cannot work in an area that is too crowded without harming too many innocent people." In just a two-month period, however, the NPA had liquidated eleven policemen, whom it charged were corrupt, in the streets of Davao City. Not a single sparrow had been apprehended.

With the economy on the skids and an estimated 300,000 Filipinos threatened with job layoffs, which would force them to return to their home provinces, the guerrilla war could only get worse, as far as this diplomat could see. For every NPA leader captured by the Philippine military, another young, well-educated Filipino was ready and willing to go to the hills to replace him. Meanwhile, the base of support for the insurgency was mushrooming. "Whole tracts of this country are already written off to the NPA!" he exclaimed. "Most of the country is active. It is spreading. There are surrogate governments in some places."

For all its anti-Communist rhetoric, the Marcos government was proving impotent in terms of countering the insurgency. "I do not feel that the central government has any real control over the situation or any strategy to overcome it," he said. Neither Marcos nor his minister of national defense had set foot on the island of Mindanao in years. Soldiers were poorly trained, poorly equipped, poorly paid, and improperly clothed. It was no wonder some of them committed abuses. "If his commanding officer is ripping off his food rations, or he's not getting paid regularly, he simply sets up a checkpoint and takes money from someone else," observed the diplomat.

More often than not, it was civilians who suffered as a result, from abusive soldiers on the one hand and abusive insurgents on the other. "The business community in a place like Davao is very disheartened," he reported. "They are squeezed between the NPA and the military. Most big businesses, particularly agribusiness, have to pay off the NPA to stay in operation, while some military commanders are on the take. Unless you are a Marcos crony who gets the necessary protection, the cost of doing business is too high there."

The only thing that had prevented the insurgents from gaining the upper hand was their shortage of weapons. "I'm worried that some day the people in the Kremlin are going to wake up," he said. Had the rebels been receiving weapons from external sources and had their forces been as large on August 21, 1983, as they were now, U.S. interests in the Philippines, most notably its two largest overseas bases at Clark Field and Subic Bay, would have been seriously threatened. "The Aquino assassination came two to three years too early for them," he said, expressing relief. "They were not ready to capitalize on it." Nonetheless, the turmoil stirred up by the killing had already benefited the Communists, and would continue to do so in the future.

This official felt he had seen it all before. "People say, 'This has been going on for a long time.' It's true that insurgencies can bubble along for a long time, but they can also become successful very quickly. They reach a point where the trend becomes irreversible." The solution would not be found in military action alone, he stressed, although he deplored threats from the U.S. Congress to cut military assistance unless the Marcos government instituted certain reforms. It was imperative for the regime to deliver jobs, goods, and services to the countryside. It needed to elect and select honest public officials and bureaucrats to administer government programs in the Communist-influenced areas. It needed to institute military reforms. Most of all, it needed to "wake up to the threat and get serious."

*   *   *

Before the polls opened at seven o'clock on the morning of May 14, a large crowd had already gathered outside the schoolhouse where President Marcos was registered to vote in his hometown of Batac. The face and name of the unquestioned winner of one of the two National Assembly seats from the province of Ilocos Norte, Imee Marcos Manotoc, was plastered on walls, lampposts, cars, and billboards all over town. A brass band stood ready to welcome Marcos and his daughters, who were flying up from Manila to cast their ballots.

At 9:30 a white van pulled up to the school entrance carrying Marcos, General Ver, daughter Imee, and her husband, basketball coach Tommy Manotoc, younger daughter Irene Marcos Araneta, and son Ferdinand, Jr. ("Bong Bong"), the provincial governor. Immediately mobbed by a friendly throng of well-wishers, Marcos entered the schoolroom, which had been set aside for the First Family's use.

In accordance with the new election rules, Marcos deposited his ballot in the square, metal ballot box, then held out his forefinger to be dabbed with the violet-colored indelible ink that was being used for the first time to help deter multiple or "flying" voters. After listening to a serenade by schoolchildren, the party climbed back into the van for a short visit to the president's northern residence. An Ilocano voter, his eyes ablaze with fierce loyalty to the region's favorite son, commented, "The vote will be one hundred percent for the KBL in this town, as it should all over the Philippines today."

Thanks to the changed attitudes of Filipino voters and to election reforms, which Marcos had conceded, that was not to be the case this year. After fourteen years of farcical martial-law elections, a new election code, passed in March, had provided for a number of reforms, including the resuscitation of the citizen, watchdog organization NAMFREL, the National Movement for Free Elections. Conceived and funded by the CIA during its first incarnation in 1953, the original NAMFREL had helped to counter cheating by the corrupt regime of that day, enabling the popular defense secretary Ramon Magsaysay to win the presidency. This year the opposition had made the establishment of a second-generation NAMFREL a condition of its participation. The Catholic Church, working with a group of progressive Makati businessmen, had secured contributions from both private sources and American foundations to train and deploy some 150,000 NAMFREL volunteers to monitor the vote-counting in about three fourths of the nation's 83,284 polling places. Just as important, NAMFREL had mounted "Operation Quick Count" to tabulate and broadcast over Catholic Radio Veritas its own set of election results to serve as a check on the figures reported by the Marcos-dominated Commission on Elections (COMELEC).

Two hundred miles down the China Sea coast from Marcos's hometown, NAMFREL would face one of its toughest challenges. If dirty elections were the norm in the Philippines, the city of Vigan was notable for its exceptionally lurid history. Family vendettas had long bloodied local election campaigns, leaving whole villages destroyed in their wake. When the violence of the ruling Crisologo dynasty had finally become too much for citizens to bear in 1971, they had thrown their votes to the competing Singson family, which promised reforms. In power ever since, the Singson dynasty had brought a change of style rather than substance. "Today they have refined the tactics so that instead of goons pulling guns, they can commit anomalies in a bloodless manner," said Father Loreto Villoria, NAMFREL provincial chairman.

It was those anomalies that NAMFREL was designed to expose and contest. However, the local political warlords were not about to willingly surrender their power to a group of reform-minded citizens. They used threats of violence to prevent a group of local laymen from establishing a NAMFREL branch in Vigan. They could not, however, prevent a courageous group of Benedictine nuns, who had played an unofficial, watchdog role in previous elections, from doing so again under the auspices of NAMFREL. "In the beginning we were only about twenty sisters involved with NAMFREL," said Sister Frideswida Pulido, "but as the lay people were told to get out, we became more determined." A total of eighty-eight nuns answered the call for help, promptly dubbing themselves "Nunfrels."

For the Nunfrels, election day began with a special mass at 4:30 A.M. in which they were administered the last rites of the Church. Then they were transported by jeepney to polling centers throughout the district. All day, they looked over the shoulders of the official poll watchers, periodically ducking outside to scribble details of polling violations and cries for help on pieces of blue paper, which were passed to waiting couriers and relayed to NAMFREL headquarters in the old, Spanish-era archbishop's palace.

Accompanying NAMFREL troubleshooter Dr. Antonio Lahaz on his rounds, I was heartened by the powerful impact which a small group of volunteers could have. Suddenly, the ruling party, which had for so long enjoyed an unquestioned monopoly on power, was being held accountable for its actions. In the *barangay* of San Julien, four sisters were driven out of a schoolhouse polling place by the *barangay* captain. One of them, Sister Teresita Felicitas, slipped a blue note pleading for reinforcements to a courier. The nun who arrived to check out her complaint found Sister Teresita accomplishing more outside than she had inside the classroom. While waiting for the troubleshooters to arrive, she had seen three jeepneys full of "flying voters" and batches of false ballots enter the schoolyard, accompanied by the mayor. Intent on thwarting their efforts to pad the count, the Nunfrel intercepted them on their way to the door. In his report on the day's events the troubleshooter later noted, "Sister Teresita talked lovingly to the mayor until he left."

A second complaint told of "open voting" in the village of San Ildefonso, where voters were obliged to show the presiding poll watchers the names of the candidates they had written in on the ballots. We went to the home of Mayor Azucena Punissima to check it out. To my astonishment, the mayor admitted cheerfully that "open voting" was common practice in the area. "There is no law against it," she said with conviction. Unfortunately, she was correct. The concept of the secrecy of the ballot was not one that had penetrated all levels of the Philippine electorate.

In this area, like so many others, the old ethic of *utang na loob* (debt of gratitude) governed the conduct of the voting, and it would take more than new laws to change the age-old behavior patterns which it had produced. The mayor unapologetically explained, "I have to be sure that the ballots are for my candidates, and I have told the voters I will be the one to repay them."

Her husband, a Manila judge, added, "The concept of voting here is predicated on kinship, loyalty, the expectation that you become part of the group. People here do not vote on issues, but on personalities and favors paid them." This bald admission of what we Americans would describe as voting fraud was especially useful information, coming as it did early in the process of the restoration of democratic institutions in the Philippines. It made me aware of the basic cultural differences that would limit the degree of real democracy that could be expected to take root in this, the third-world country that was considered to have the most suitable soil for its growth.

At sunset Nunfrels bearing ballot boxes began arriving at the provincial capital in tricycles, jeepneys, cars, and even the famous horse-drawn *calesas* that were still in use in Vigan. "This was the best election since 1971," said Sister Mary Bede enthusiastically, as she delivered her box to the county treasurer and watched as he stowed it inside a dank and cluttered vault in his office. There Dr. Lahaz congratulated the sisters. "Your presence in all the voting centers prevented party men from intimidating voters and gave voters the moral strength to resist any pressure against voting their conscience," he said.

It was well after midnight by the time the car in which I was traveling with two foreign photographers began to pick up radio news broadcasts from Manila, which carried the results of the experimental "Operation Quick Count," NAMFREL's computerized vote projection. First reports showed cabinet ministers trailing opposition candidates in a number of areas, and the opposition ahead in practically every race in Metro-Manila. The boycott appeared to have had little impact on the size of the opposition vote. We had been professional all day long, betraying no preference for either party, as we watched the voting and dealt with sources on both sides. But now we opened the car windows and shouted for joy that the opposition was leading. It was unheard of. It was difficult to imagine that Marcos could allow the opposition to control nearly half the elected seats, as the early projections were suggesting.

Of course he did not. As the week wore on, that total shrank, due to the influx of returns from the rural areas, which were a traditional source of support for Marcos, and due to padding of the ruling party vote in provinces where KBL ministers were threatened with defeat. Official protests lodged with the government-controlled COMELEC would keep the counts in limbo for months in certain areas, before ending in defeat for most of the opposition plaintiffs. But the ultimate victory of sixty-three non-KBL candidates—more than one third of the elective seats at issue —reflected a desire for change on the part of the Filipino people that no one could deny.

The most prominent loser was noncandidate Imelda Marcos, governor of Metro-Manila and KBL campaign manager for the capital region. Only one member of her slate won—maverick KBL Assemblyman Arturo Tolentino. Another loser was the left, which had wagered that the democratic opposition would regret its participation and prove ripe for recruitment. Neophyte Cory Aquino, on the other hand, had emerged a star, with coattails long enough to have pulled a majority of the candidates for whom she campaigned into office. The big winner, however, was the democratic system. "Despite determined attempts to thwart the popular will," said NAMFREL chairman, businessman Jose ("Joe") Concepcion, "the Filipino people have proved that democracy is alive in this country."

12

The Military Alternative

T he campaign trail was not the only front on which the battle to succeed Marcos was being fought. Several weeks after the National Assembly elections, Defense Minister Juan Ponce Enrile, a civilian, carried the succession struggle into the military arena by paying an official visit to the embattled island of Mindanao, where fully half the country's armed forces battalions were deployed against Communist and Muslim rebels. Under the guise of a fact-finding tour—his first official visit to the region in seven years—Enrile was reasserting his claim to lost influence over a highly politicized military that was not the monolith it seemed to outsiders. He was also testing the waters for a possible Magsaysay-style campaign for the presidency in 1987.

I had spent several days covering his successful National Assembly campaign in northern Luzon. During the long hours of travel from rally to rally in his van or over meals in the homes of his supporters, the voluble lawyer-politician had vented discreet frustration and even anguish to me and the several other foreign correspondents accompanying him about the crisis in the country. "You see what I am up against," he would sigh on occasion, when talking about one or another obstacle thrown up by Marcos to prevent change or reform. In speeches to his constituents Enrile made no secret of the fact that he was already running for president.

While Enrile had friends in Washington, he also had plenty of detractors who considered him too tainted by his association with Marcos and not sufficiently concerned about the growth of the Communist insurgency to take seriously as a candidate. "You've got to have a Magsaysay come on the scene to galvanize people to fight the cancer," said a U.S. embassy official in June 1984. He made it clear, however, that Enrile was not the embassy's choice for the role. "There must be reform," he said. "This country has got to have a 'white revolution.' " Citing Enrile's questionable acquisitions of land, logging concessions, and other sources of wealth during his long years in government, he added, "I cannot see him projecting himself as the leader of a reform regime."

Enrile had been with Marcos since the start of his presidency. He owed Marcos a debt, which he acknowledged often, for conferring on him and his family the status they enjoyed. While he continually reaffirmed his loyalty to Marcos in private conversations, it was readily apparent that it did not extend to such pretenders to the throne as Imelda and General Ver. Nor did the loyalty appear to flow indefinitely to Marcos, whom Enrile hoped would retire gracefully at the end of his term in 1987.

Born on Valentine's Day, the bastard son of a distinguished, American-educated lawyer and a washerwoman from the northern province of Cagayan, Enrile grew up as Juan Furagganan, scrappy, ambitious, and hungry for recognition. As an adolescent, he was attacked and stabbed by a group of boys from the better side of town for paying attention to the prettiest girl in the class. "I was tutoring her in math," Enrile explains today, "but they thought I was dating her."

Despite the fact that he was the victim, it was he, not his attackers, who was expelled from school. "Their parents were trustees of the school," says Enrile bitterly, "and I was punished because I had no lawyer." Instead of completing high school, he was forced to go to work for the Department of Public Works as a common laborer. When war broke out, he joined the Philippine resistance as a guerrilla in the north. It was during the Japanese occupation that he learned the identity of his father from his half sisters, who had been evacuated from Manila to his hometown of Aparri. After the war his father sent for him.

Clearly intelligent, though unschooled in English, he was able, with the help of tutoring from the Maryknoll sisters and an American GI, to complete his high school studies in two and one-half years at the exclusive Ateneo de Manila and go on to earn law degrees at the University of the Philippines and Harvard. On his return from the U.S., he joined his father's firm as a specialist in corporate tax law, with a string of multinational firms as clients.

Defense minister since 1970 and a coarchitect of martial law, Enrile was the only civilian politician besides Imelda Marcos with a following in the military. He thus seemed positioned to play as pivotal a role in the post-Marcos period as he had in the Marcos regime. I had been intrigued at the way Ninoy had bestowed more credibility on the telexed message of warning signed by the defense minister than he had on the others he had received. Since then I had become aware of what Ninoy knew at the time: that Enrile had lost much of his power to General Ver in recent years, and that he had tried to resign from the cabinet in July 1983, after having been effectively removed from the chain of command.

He had kept a relatively low profile since then, but now he was preparing to reemerge, challenging both the intelligence information and the policies of the chief of staff on the growth of the Communist insurgency, and making himself known to the young officers in the field, who would be tomorrow's commanders. He had come to doubt the figures on the strength of the New People's Army that were being fed to the president by Ver. He wanted to hear for himself the opinions of commanders, community leaders, and newly elected assemblymen, who lived in the eye of the Communist insurgency, on the extent of the problem and how to fight it.

On the surface, Enrile's Mindanao inspection tour was an educational five days of talks with the people who were most knowledgeable about the Muslim and Communist insurgencies that had wracked the resource-rich southern islands for nearly a decade. On the rubber- and copra-producing island of Basilan, which had been a center of conflict during the government's war against Muslim secessionists during the 1970s, Enrile accepted the surrender of the last, major rebel commander of the Moro National Liberation Front (MNLF) and his 1,300 armed men.

In a state of perpetual unrest since the arrival of the Spanish conquistadores in the sixteenth century, the Muslims of the southern Philippines, who comprise about one third of that region's 12 million inhabitants, had long dreamed of their own separate state. Some 50,000 Filipinos had died in the Muslim separatist rebellion against the Marcos regime. Eventually the government had succeeded in killing, capturing, or co-opting the major rebel leaders. With the surrender to Enrile of MNLF Commander Jerry Salapuddin, government military forces in the area could now turn their full attention to the Communist rebels, who had eclipsed the Muslims as the key security threat in the region.

As the defense minister's Fokker F-28, named after his glamorous wife, Cristina, carried us closer to the center of the insurgency, military briefers and citizens in each area we visited spoke with growing urgency about the increase in new NPA fronts in the countryside and the escalating sparrow activity in the cities. A city councillor in the coastal city of Cotabato complained that "the military commanders say there is nothing wrong with this place." But city dwellers like himself knew otherwise. "The violence suddenly sprouts like a mushroom and then goes away, and we never know truly whether the threat is still present or not," he exclaimed.

By the time we reached Davao City, the size of the caravan escorting the minister into town from the airport and the number of armed troops sweeping the shoulders of the road and patrolling major intersections bore silent testimony to the deterioration of public security. Enrile listened carefully as regional unified commander Brigadier General Jaime Echeverria underlined the problem by pointing to "at least eight guerrilla fronts" on a giant wall map marked "secret." So far, he observed, his men had been able to keep the guerrillas on the run.

"I don't think the NPA is ready to face us yet," said the general.

"We must not wait until they are ready," the minister interjected brusquely.

Concerned citizens lined up before the microphones to vent their fears in the community dialogues hosted by Enrile on each leg of his tour.

"One to two people a day being liquidated has become a normal rate here in a city of one million," reported a housewife.

"It would make me a liar to say there are no NPAs," said a *barangay* captain. "They go in and out, and we are tense, because any mistake we commit against them could land us in the funeral parlor."

Sitting around the hotel late in the evening, listening to Enrile, the young officers in his entourage, and the men fighting the counterinsurgency, I began to appreciate the strong undercurrent of discontent that lay just below the surface of a military organization that was popularly perceived to be at one with its chief of staff and commander in chief. Although restrained in the presence of reporters, it was not difficult to read between the lines of their comments anger about their men's low pay and their own infrequent promotions, and frustration at finding themselves abandoned by the politicians in the middle of an insurgency that they knew could not be solved by military means alone.

Colonel Rodolfo Biazon, a popular and progressive-minded young marine commander in the Davao City area, who had dropped by to see Enrile and his fellow officers inside the minister's omnipresent security group, expressed satisfaction that the local population and politicians trusted his men and sought their protection against the growing insurgency. In the past some of these same politicians had charged other units with "military abuses." But he was straightforward in stating that the work his men were doing in the region was not a proper mission for marines. "We would not like to be tied down here," he said. "We would like to be out there looking for the NPA." The problem was political. "The mayors want us to be physically occupying every *barangay*," said Biazon. But, he added plaintively, "It's impossible. If we want that, the budget would have to jump a hundredfold." He did not have to remind his friends that the country was bordering on bankruptcy, making such an expenditure out of the question.

After several beers, the subject was far from exhausted, but the group broke up to get some sleep. "Killing is not the answer," said Biazon, as he walked to his car. "It's a battle of the minds. Every time I see someone killed, I look at my skin and realize these are my brothers. Many of the NPAs do not know what they are killing for. They want a change, but they are confused."

In besieged Butuan City, the area of the NPA's most recent expansion of activity, an armored personnel carrier patrolled the building in which Enrile was being briefed by the regional commander. General Madriño Muñoz reported the steady growth of the NPA from three to four revolutionary provincial committees in his region. But what alarmed him more than the military escalation was the insurgents' political dynamism. The May 14 election boycott had enjoyed relative success in two of the provinces under his command, where the Communist front's "middle forces" had multiplied since the Aquino assassination. He predicted "continuous disturbances," including demonstrations and strikes, as long as the economic disparities which fueled the insurgency remained. "Hoarding in anticipation of devaluation has already occurred," stated the general, "and we have experienced a nine percent increase in crime, partly as a result of the economy."

When we reached the northern coastal city of Cagayan de Oro, one of the few in the country governed by an opposition mayor, Enrile's security group became visibly more active. While the minister fielded questions from a group of civilian officials and citizens on the parade ground of the Regional Unified Command headquarters there, the young officers in his entourage, whom he referred to in a fatherly way as his "boys," held private meetings with their classmates from the elite Philippine Military Academy (PMA). The depth of discontent harbored by the soldiers serving in Region 10 became a topic of conversation at the minister's dinner table that evening and on the flight back to Manila. Complaints of corruption inside command headquarters were widespread. An even greater irritant was Marcos's practice of extending the service of loyalist generals who had reached retirement age—a practice which blocked the advancement of younger officers and lowered morale, especially in areas where men were risking their lives daily in a guerrilla war they were not winning.

During the meal, Enrile aired some complaints of his own. If he were president, he allowed, off the record, he would reorganize the military to institute a system similar to the American one, in which the military would be headed by "joint chiefs of staff," comprised of the commander of each service branch, under the president. That way, he said, targeting General Ver, "all the power is not vested in one chief of staff, with the president being his only check and balance." Implicit in his remark was the notion that under the present system the chief of staff could virtually hold the president—and the military organization—hostage to his own ends.

Buoyed by the attentions of the statuesque songstress who had been engaged to entertain him and by the general camaraderie, Enrile grew expansive. He mused about how the counterinsurgency had been fought in Magsaysay's day. "Magsaysay didn't solve the Huk problem," he said, "rather it was the Philippine military with the help of the Americans." Enrile sought to distinguish himself from his predecessor in certain ways without, however, discouraging identification with the late defense secretary who had become so popular as a Huk fighter that he had ridden his antiguerrilla campaign to Malacañang.

"He would have pictures taken in a room in the ministry, where soldiers would lie on the floor and tomato soup would be poured over them, so it would look like he was in the center of the battle," said Enrile disapprovingly. While Magsaysay was playing hero, real soldiers were shedding real blood in central Luzon. "The operations against the Huks were big and bloody, and there were plenty of human rights violations," he said. "We don't want to do it that way anymore."

Left unspoken by Enrile was a sentiment he had expressed before: The army alone could not do the job; a credible civilian government was essential. He was clearly positioning himself to head such a government one day.

As Enrile prepared to return to Manila to report to the president, he was voicing a notably harder line than he had before he visited Mindanao. Six weeks before, he had concluded an interview with me by arguing that no matter what American officials might say, no more than 5,000 NPA guerrillas were at large in the land, and many of them were not armed. "If there were twelve thousand armed men loose in this country," he declared, "I would have a war on my hands every day, which I do not. I have been minister of national defense for more than fourteen years, and I can tell you that we don't have that kind of problem."

Today he was citing substantially higher figures, which indicated steady NPA growth, and telling his audiences, "This is not a problem of government or the military establishment all alone. It is a problem of the entire nation, because the purpose of the Communists is to supplant our system." He would later attribute the change in his rhetoric to the changed view of the situation that his trip had afforded him. He had confirmed to his satisfaction that "the president was getting wrong readings from General Ver" on the Communist threat. Ailing and often isolated from his cabinet ministers by Imelda and her brother Kokoy, Marcos had not been given bad news. "They wanted to underplay the seriousness of the problem," said Enrile, "because they were restructuring our foreign loans, and they did not want to create fears among Filipino investors."

For a time Enrile, too, had refrained from public comment on the subject, so as not to complicate negotiations with the country's foreign creditors. Eventually Marcos had begun receiving reports from other sources confirming what his defense minister had been telling him. Even then, however, "he could not publicly admit this," explained Enrile, "because Mrs. Marcos and the others were against it. It indicated a failure of the past policies."

As the man assigned to brief the stream of visiting American officials about the insurgency and to lead the debate for increased defense spending in the budget, which was before the new, two-party National Assembly, Enrile found himself at the center of a vicious circle—taking the heat for the failures of the military, while being denied the power to correct them.

Meanwhile, Marcos, who had built his entire career on opposing the spread of Communism, continued to direct his fire at the moderate political opposition, which represented the greater short-term threat to his hold on er. The president, to Enrile's dismay, refused to admit that, far from eliminating the longer-term threat of the NPA, martial law had only exacerbated it. Enrile was determined to force him to face the facts. "We could not contradict the reality of the insurgency any longer," Enrile argued. Yet when he brought the issue up in cabinet meetings, Enrile recounted, "I collided with the president."

In September 1984, when Enrile presented his findings and recommendations to President Marcos, prior to the opening of hearings in the National Assembly on the 1985 defense budget, he set off a fierce internal debate over how to react to the growing Communist threat. Little of that debate became public until months later, when Marcos, under pressure from both Enrile and American officials, grudgingly admitted that the NPA threat was serious, and gave the nod to new counterinsurgency measures.

Eventually Marcos was persuaded to unveil a $50-million military "Civic Action Program" to construct new roads, schools, and wells in communities that were either infiltrated or targeted by the NPA. However, Enrile admitted later, "That was all window dressing, because nothing was happening."

*   *   *

Enrile had a hidden, secondary agenda for his trip, which I would come to know only after Marcos's ouster. It was to afford his boys the opportunity to recruit their former PMA classmates, who were now commanding units throughout Mindanao, to join them in a coup to prevent General Ver and his clique of corrupt loyalist generals from grabbing power after Marcos's death. "The cover for the trip was to give the minister a chance to find out about the progress of the insurgency," admitted one officer later.

As long ago as 1977 the purposes of the minister had converged with those of the young officers who would one day found the Reform the Armed Forces Movement (RAM). "I had been coasting since 1977," Enrile revealed, shortly after Marcos's departure from the Philippines. "They started stripping me of all kinds of powers." In the early days of martial law there had been confrontations with Imelda Marcos. As chief administrator of the vast authoritarian bureaucracy, Enrile had prevented the First Lady from favoring a friend with an exemption from the harsh travel restrictions imposed by the regime. Relations between the two hot-headed cabinet members had remained glacial ever after.

In 1975, as public confidence in the martial law regime declined, Enrile had survived a power struggle within the administration over a purge of corrupt military and civilian officials. Three years later, however, his move to relieve a navy contingent, which citizens on the island of Samar had accused of provocative acts, triggered Marcos's growing paranoia about plots against him. The president accused Enrile of exceeding his authority, and with the flourish of a pen, arrogated unto himself the power previously shared by the minister of national defense and the armed forces chief of staff to assign or promote senior military officers.

Still the combative loner of his fatherless youth, Enrile had forced and won a showdown with Marcos in 1980 over preelection attempts by Imelda and her brother to intervene in the local politics of his home region. However, the minister's troubles were far from over, for he had attracted the enmity of Marcos's hatchet man, General Ver, as well. No area of the bureaucracy was as mired in intrigue as the intelligence network controlled by General Ver. Following a shoot-out in the driveway of Makati's plush Mandarin Hotel, Enrile was sucked into the swamp.

The intended victim, it seemed, was the new boyfriend of General Ver's longtime mistress. Enrile ordered an investigation of the possible involvement of General Ver in the crime. When a second attempt was made against the boyfriend's life a few months later, he appealed directly to Enrile for protection from Ver's men and was secreted out of the country under an assumed name. Not, however, before Ver, chief of the National Intelligence and Security Authority (NISA), had placed Enrile under surveillance. "I could be the only defense minister in the entire world who is under surveillance by his own government," commented Enrile wryly at the time.

Ver's suspicions toward Enrile were not, however, without grounds. As early as 1979, rumors were circulating that Marcos was suffering from a serious kidney disease. The question of succession became a contentious issue of debate over the coffee cups. Few politicians within or without the ruling party believed that the fifteen-person Executive Committee, which was designated to serve as a transition mechanism in the event of Marcos's death, would ever succeed in holding elections. The general assumption was that well before that, Imelda, backed by Marcos loyalists in the military, would make a grab for power. A corresponding assumption was that the person best poised to counter such a move would be Enrile.

In a meeting in Houston shortly after he had undergone heart bypass surgery in 1980, Ninoy informed a close friend, who made notes of the conversation, that he had received feelers, transmitted through his brother-in-law Baby Lopa, from representatives of Enrile. They wanted to know, according to Ninoy, "how much contribution" they could make to Ninoy's "cause." Ninoy told his visitor that he interpreted this inquiry as a pledge of "insurance" money by Enrile. In his reply to Enrile's representative, Ninoy promised to reciprocate in kind: "If JPE can eliminate Marcos, compadre [Ninoy] commits to round up support of the opposition to back up a regime under JPE." Enrile vehemently denies being the source of the feeler to which Aquino responded, although Aquino intimates do not find the notion of a potential pact between the two ambitious politicians to topple Marcos out of character for either man.

The level of palace intrigue rose dramatically after General Ver was chosen over Enrile's friend and ally General Ramos as the new chief of staff in 1981. By then the officers who made up Enrile's intelligence group had decided to arm and train themselves to protect the minister from what they perceived to be not only a vendetta against him on the part of Ver, but the start of the struggle for succession to Marcos.

The military, which had become highly politicized during its eight years as a partner in power, would be the likely arbiter of the succession. The selection of a "political general" like Ver for the top AFP post, over a "professional general" like Ramos, held strong implications for determining the outcome of the struggle. The controversial choice drove a wedge between the large corps of officers whom Marcos had elevated, based on loyalty to himself and the First Lady, and those who had risen —or not risen—in the ranks, based on their service and merit.

When Enrile's boys approached him with their plan, he readily agreed to foot the bill. "We were basically concerned with protection," said Colonel Gregorio Honasan, the young officer who led Enrile's security group at the time and would later spearhead the aborted February 1986 coup by reformist officers against Marcos and Ver. The boys were also concerned with the deteriorating image of the AFP. "What was also happening was that the Ministry of National Defense was becoming the depository of complaints about the armed forces, and we were becoming sensitized to what people thought of us," said Honasan. "We saw it was not an ordinary problem anymore. The system was beginning to crack."

"Their concerns were political as well as military," explained Enrile. "They wanted reform in government, and they wanted to establish a group to counterbalance the Ver group. Their interest in protecting me and the emerging disillusionment of these idealistic officers as a result of all the reported corrupt practices fused together." In an effort to give them the best training possible, Enrile underwrote the fees for two retired instructors of the elite British Special Air Service (SAS) regiment, whom Honasan had engaged.

Greg Honasan, known as "Gringo," for his mestizo good looks, had been a natural leader in the class of 1971 at the Philippine Military Academy, the West Point of the Philippines. At the time, that meant that he —like his contemporaries in the universities—was a protester. The two years prior to martial law had been marked in the Philippines, as elsewhere, by street protests and political violence, from which not even PMA cadets were exempt.

The class of '71 had protested everything from the placement of a living room suite donated by an alumnus to what it perceived as "an act of disrespect" on the part of the Quezon City police force. So exercised had the cadets become over the latter that they were preparing to attack the police station, when, a class member recalled, "President Marcos came and talked to us to cool us off." Their class advisor was the notorious Lieutenant Victor Corpus, a PMA political science instructor who defected to the NPA in 1971, taking with him a cache of arms which he had helped to steal from the school armory.

Their dissidence did not stop with graduation. In July 1972, Honasan and fellow officer-training candidates refused to stand up during their graduation ceremony in protest against the academy's failure to punish cheating. "This was a group of officers who stood on principles," said Lieutenant Colonel Marcelino ("Jake") Malajacan, a member of both the PMA class of 1971 and 1972 officer training school.

No sooner had its members taken up duty at their newly assigned posts than martial law was declared. Overnight they found themselves in a situation for which the PMA, with its high ideals of civilian supremacy and allegiance to flag and constitution, had not prepared them. Instead of soldiers protecting the welfare of the Filipino people, they were members of a new ruling class, which answered to one man.

Whatever reservations they may have had about enforcing martial law, these young officers were soon engaged in one of the bloodiest wars in Philippine history, between separatist Muslims and the AFP. It was marked by widespread abuses on both sides, the soldiers counting casualties by the ears they cut off their victims, the rebels slicing the soles off the feet of theirs. As a combat officer, Honasan became known for his splashy exploits, most notably jumping from planes with his pet cobra, Tiffany, around his neck. When they returned to Manila, the officers were greeted by many civilians, not as heroes, but as brutes.

The treatment they received from their superiors was hardly better. At the top of the hierarchy was a wall of senior officers whose duty had been extended by Marcos on the basis of their loyalty, rather than their ability. Many of them ran drug and black-market syndicates with the blessing of Malacañang. As martial law wore on and the regime's paranoia grew, these "overstaying generals" became its life insurance policy. Enjoying pay and perks out of proportion to that of the civilian population, they could be counted on to continue doing the dirty work that was necessary to keep an increasingly unpopular government in power.

There was no room in such a system for aggressive and idealistic colonels and captains. With their upward mobility blocked, they faced a stark set of choices: settle for the easy money available to obliging officers through extracurricular work, protecting or promoting the businesses and rackets of political warlords, large landowners, and the president's business cronies, or resist. "These are soldiers who graduated with all the glory and then found themselves being spit at," said General Hermilio Ahorro, a Philippine constabulary officer who was supportive of the young reformists. They decided to found a movement to unite the alienated, younger officers around what Honasan described as "the old values which we seemed to have forgotten."

One of the primary old values was promotion based on merit. Support for Honasan's group was bolstered when, in 1980, one of General Ver's three soldier sons was promoted to colonel in advance of his class and others more senior. In making Irwin Ver, PMA class of '70, a colonel, President Marcos caused him to leapfrog over a legion of deserving officers from the classes of '68 and '69, who were next in line. "It is no coincidence that the reform movement started when General Ver became chief of staff, and it surfaced after he was relieved," said retired General Manuel Salientes, a friend and former deputy to Enrile, who was fired by Marcos. "It was a reaction to the fact that promotions and assignments were given because of the right connections, because of the right *padrino*, or godfather, as a function of how close you were to the president."

Another value held high by the reform-minded officers was the democratic tradition. The young officers were particularly wary of being used, as they had been during martial law, to rig elections. "We stole ballot boxes during the plebiscites under martial law," confessed one lieutenant. "My mission was just to fly ballot boxes from place to place, but I realize now that I was flying votes: ballots filled out, not by the people, but by men in army camps." He did not balk at his orders at the time. "I just looked at the flight schedule to see where I was going each day, and I just went. I didn't ask questions." Now, years later, he was asking questions, not only about the military, but about the society as a whole. The answer he was getting was that "our people are capable of deciding for themselves who shall be their leaders."

The questioning had begun for a number of the officers while trying to counter the Communist insurgency. "The people were not giving us information," said Colonel Victor ("Vic") Batac, a constabulary intelligence officer. "They were letting our troops get ambushed. They made mocked-up charges against us, when we were supposed to be protecting them. We had to start asking ourselves why we should protect a people who are against us."

A staunch anti-Communist, like most of his peers, Batac was heartened by the progress of the special operations teams of intelligence officers which had begun working in Communist-influenced *barangays* to dismantle by means of psychological warfare, rather than bullets, the shadow governments erected by the NPA. He had grown quickly discouraged, however, by the lack of an attractive political substitute for the NPA in the hearts and minds of the people. "If you knock out the [Communist] linchpins, you must offer something in return," he explained. "So you sell them the government. But if the government does not deliver, then the next time around they will not believe you." Batac concluded, "To us soldiers, government credibility is very important."

In 1982, Ver increased his power within the AFP by creating a Regional Unified Command system, which was administered by thirteen hand-picked generals, who reported directly to him. Meanwhile tensions, which had been building between the young colonels around Enrile and the men of Colonel Ver, came to a head in July 1983, when the younger Ver, who was chief of staff of the Presidential Security Command, purported to receive an intelligence report indicating that Enrile's security group was preparing to kidnap or assassinate the president. Colonel Ver and his father took the report seriously, according to navy Captain Rex Robles, Enrile's chief of policy review, "because our units were among the few that were well trained, and we were not under their control." They carried the report to the president, who confronted Enrile and Ramos with it. Denying it as a fabrication by Ver, the two offered their resignations on the spot.

"Both Ramos and Enrile tried to convince the president that General Ver was taking charge of things in a way that was not good for either the military or the country," said Robles. "The minister told him, 'You are being held prisoner by one man in your palace.' The president corrected him. 'I am being held prisoner by one family in my own palace, and you must help me,' " he said. The meeting broke up, as had all others of the sort over the years, with no decisive action taken. Marcos did not accept the resignations; Enrile and Ramos stayed on, but neither side trusted the other, and each was more wary than before.

On August 1, 1983, Marcos gave more power to Ver by wresting operational control over the Integrated National Police from General Ramos and transferring it to the chief of staff and by effectively removing Enrile from the military chain of command. Twenty days later Aquino was assassinated while in the custody of a military, which was entirely under the authority of Ver. "Some military people were already unhappy with the image of the AFP before August 1983," said University of the Philippines political science professor Dr. Caroline Hernandez, "but it became even more compelling after the Aquino assassination, which crystallized the reform movement."

As Enrile viewed the body of Ninoy Aquino in the Fort Bonifacio Hospital, he told me, "I said to myself, 'This is no longer a safe country for anyone.' I felt that I was myself in mortal danger." Indeed, the assassination confirmed to Enrile and his security group the necessity for the protective action they had taken. "We knew that from a military viewpoint it is tactically impossible for an assassin to get inside a cordon of two thousand men, so there had to be some other explanation," said Honasan.

Not long afterward, an intelligence report carrying the same B-2 rating as the one which had warned of assassination threats against Aquino was delivered to Enrile's office. It revealed, he said, "that a team of five men had infiltrated Manila during the funeral of Senator Aquino, with plans to assassinate me." The messenger who had deposited the National Intelligence and Security Authority document with the ministry's receiving clerk had left no identification. Enrile, at once rattled and infuriated, wrote to NISA chief Ver to request that he make available the asset who had supplied the information. He never received an answer.

Meanwhile, Enrile told his boys, the convalescing president had taken him aside the first time he saw him after the assassination and whispered, "Please be careful, Johnny, you are one of those whom these people don't like. They are eyeing you." Enrile considered Marcos's words "a friendly warning." The interpretation of his security group was less benign.

"We immediately pulled him out of his residence and put him where he could not be found," said Robles.

In the turbulent weeks after the slaying, psychological warfare between the Ver and Enrile camps flared dangerously. Enrile's men viewed the anonymous intelligence report as "a test of the minister's defenses" by Ver. The assassin who was allegedly after Enrile appeared to be, like Galman, a criminal released from jail to serve as a hit man. "Within forty-eight hours, we were able to get this guy," said one of Enrile's officers. "We killed him." The fact that Ver's intelligence unit made no effort to protest the man's death confirmed to Enrile's men that Ver had been behind the plot.

"Now the war was on," said Robles. The British mercenaries were engaged once more to train two groups of fifty men each. Beginning in December 1983 and continuing for three months, this round of training was anything but secret. "This was propaganda," said Robles. "If you show them force, they recoil right away." For three months men in full battle gear ran from Defense Ministry headquarters at Camp Aguinaldo to the luxury residential neighborhood of Dasmariñas Village, where Enrile lived, in full view of residents and passing motorists. When they weren't running, they were rapelling buildings or practicing on the firing range. "We had to play the game the way they understand it," said Robles. "In running these people, the minister was saying in effect, 'I know you are trying to kill me. If you do, exceedingly great damage will result.' "

*   *   *

It was the middle of 1984 when Colonel Jake Malajacan attended his first meeting of what would become variously known among military reformists as "the Fourth Classmen" (the plebe, or freshman, class in PMA lingo) and "the Core Group" of the military reform movement. He had been invited by a 1971 classmate, who had driven a circuitous route to the house inside a semiresidential business compound in Metro-Manila, which served as the group's secret headquarters. Some of those in the room had been meeting regularly since shortly after the Aquino assassination. They wanted to expand their group to include representatives of a broad cross-section of the military. They also wanted to include men with troops behind them. Jake Malajacan was such a man. He was commander of the Sixteenth Infantry Battalion of the Second Infantry Division in Metro-Manila.

The main subject of discussion that night was the likely successor to General Ver as chief of staff, should Ver eventually be relieved of command, due to pressure from the U.S. and the Agrava Board investigation, which was nearing its climax. "Our assessment was that Marcos would not give the job to General Ramos," said Malajacan. That meant that the top job would probably go to the next most senior general, Josephus Ramas, Ninoy's former jailer, who was now commander of the army. Malajacan was an army man, and his classmates knew how he felt about Ramas. "If Ramas would become chief of staff," Malajacan said, "that is the end of the republic. He is too ambitious. He will not be satisfied with being chief of staff. The next step will be the presidency." Should that day ever come, Malajacan believed, the country would turn Communist out of spite. An avid anti-Communist, he nonetheless vowed to lead the stampede to the hills at such a time.

The group's preoccupation with Ramas was not entirely emotional. Although those who knew him and served under him truly despised the man, their concern was largely pragmatic. Ramas was in the process of training a countercoup force inside army headquarters at Fort Bonifacio, where Malajacan was based. He had been monitoring it for some time, and he had concluded that while Ramas was telling Ver and Marcos that his 1,500-man force was designed to counter a coup of younger officers, it was in fact a vehicle by which he could eventually take power himself. "Our assessment was that this was a post-Marcos move," said Malajacan. "After Marcos died, when there was a grab for power by various forces, Ramas would initially side with Ver, but afterward, he would use it to take over himself."

Even more than Ver, Ramas represented to the assembled group everything that had gone wrong with the armed forces. His loyalties were only to those who could further his ambitions. A Visayan, like the First Lady, he openly courted Imelda's favor. Those officials whom he didn't court, he threatened. "He was the J. Edgar Hoover of the Philippines," said Malajacan. "He kept dossiers on everyone, and they were afraid of him." Finally, he was, in the words of another of his battalion commanders, Colonel Pedro ("Sonny") Atienza, "filthy rich." His money was said to come from the infamous "intelligence fund," which Marcos had cleverly built into all his budgets as a slush fund to keep his top commanders happy.

"Our priority that night," Malajacan recalled, "was not a coup against Marcos. Initially, we were more afraid of the post-Marcos scenario, so Marcos was not our object. Our conclusion was that Marcos would die at any time, or someone like Ver or his wife would force him to retire." Believing that Ramas would use such an opportunity to strike, the Core Group made him its target. "We thought of ways to get rid of him," said Malajacan, "conducting a smear campaign against him or even getting rid of him physically. That's how naughty we were at the time."

Because the Fourth Classmen had decided to require unanimous approval of any major decision, their progress over the next months in recruiting members and settling on a precise course of action was slow. By the time it had adopted a plan, about a year later, the Core Group numbered some fifty officers, with an active membership of about twenty officers, who attended the weekly meetings in Manila and relayed information on the proceedings to their classmates in the field. All were PMA graduates. Each had been chosen on the basis of trust, dedication, and the resources he could contribute to the plan from his branch of service or region. About 50 percent of the men were assigned to Enrile, about 6 percent to General Ramos. The rest were like-minded professionals. In late 1984 each Core-Group member was presented with an Israeli-made

Galil assault rifle, paid for by Enrile and chosen by Honasan for its quality and efficiency.

The clandestine nature of their mission to rid the military of its corrupt leadership shaped the daily lives of the Fourth Classmen from that moment on. "I could not confide in anyone, not even my family," recalled Malajacan. "Every time I attended a meeting of our Core Group, I had to act like James Bond, taking a car to a place where I would catch a taxi to another place, before finally going to the place where we met. I was doing that for eighteen months."

13

The "Special Relationship"

In 1979 the U.S. "lost" Iran. In 1980 it "lost" Nicaragua. In late 1984 U.S. government officials began sounding alarms about the possible "loss" of the Philippines. I had never covered a country that had slipped into the foreign policy "loss" column, and I wondered what to expect from Washington. More aid? Less aid? Gentle pressure? Extreme pressure? Military intervention? Overthrow? I was prepared for almost anything except the politically popular and deftly subtle policy which the Reagan administration pursued.

In off-the-record briefings with journalists before the May 1984 elections, political and military officials at the U.S. embassy had begun to question President Marcos's ability to retain control over the increasingly volatile situation. Among the first expressions of such concern was a staff report prepared for the Republican-dominated U.S. Senate Committee on Foreign Relations in September 1984 and reprinted for distribution by the embassy. It warned: "Unlike other non-Communist Asian countries, the Philippines is experiencing deep social and political turmoil, plus a Communist insurgency which could within three to five years—and perhaps sooner—threaten the central government's stability."

Similar fears were shaped by Democratic legislators. Congressman

Stephen Solarz opened hearings of his Subcommittee on Asian and Pacific Affairs on September 20 with a stern reminder that "a Communist victory would end any chance of a return to democracy and would mean that the U.S. would lose its access to Subic Bay and Clark Field, which greatly facilitate our ability to preserve the peace and maintain a balance of power in Asia."

Richard Armitage, assistant secretary of defense for international security affairs, carried such logic to its negative end—a U.S. withdrawal from the bases—and informed the same Solarz subcommittee, on October 4, that the Pentagon had leased 18,000 acres on the Pacific islands of Saipan and Tinian as "an important fallback basing area for a redeployment from the Philippines."

Initially, American diplomats in Manila were more discreet, simply distributing transcripts of the hearings to interested journalists. Eventually, however, they too began to give similarly candid appraisals of the situation. The crisis which all of those officials described, and the worst-case scenarios they conjured, had an ominous familiarity. In the wake of the lost war in Vietnam, the losses of Iran and Nicaragua had been heavy for the U.S. in terms of prestige and geostrategic advantage. The loss of the Philippines, although far from the center of Americans' consciousness at the time, threatened to be even more grave.

Security issues had long dominated relations between the two countries, and it was in terms of security advantage that the cost of a potential "loss" of the Philippines would be calculated. Strategically situated astride the major shipping lanes between the oil-producing Persian Gulf and the dynamic economies of the so-called "Pacific Rim," the Philippines was the site of America's largest overseas air base and the world's largest naval supply depot. It was from Clark Air Base and Subic Bay Naval Station that U.S. force was projected westward into the Indian Ocean and the Persian Gulf. With the Soviet occupation of the former American bases at nearby Cam Ranh Bay and Danang in Vietnam, Clark and Subic had become even more vital as guardians of the South China Sea channels, through which the Soviet navy would resupply its ships in the event of another Pacific war.

However, there was an extra dimension to the Philippine-American relationship that was less easily quantifiable, if all the more devastating to contemplate losing. It was the intangible "special relationship" that existed between the United States and her ex-colony. Derived from a shared past, a shared system of government, a shared language, and a shared set of aspirations, this "special relationship" had bound two very different peoples with entirely different heritages together, for better or for worse, through three bloody Pacific wars and the long cold war.

Unlike the more alien states of Nicaragua and Iran, the Philippines had become a part of us, and to their often considerable frustration, we a part of them. A "loss" of the Philippines would be taken personally by both partners, as had every other element of the relationship over its eighty-five-year existence.

Robert Pringle, a Foreign Service officer and author, who had been posted in the Philippines, defined the "special relationship" as "an amalgam of security connections, historical ties, and emotional hang-ups." It was the latter that had most vividly colored relations between individuals of both nationalities and between mother country and ex-colony from the moment independence—with very definite strings attached—was granted on July 4, 1946.

For me, the emotional hang-ups involved feelings of kinship to people whose manner was charmingly familiar, but whose beliefs were sometimes exasperatingly foreign. There was the Marcos general who disarmed me by confiding that he too had spent his adolescence reading "Archie" and "Veronica" comic books. I was dashed to hear later from reformist officers that he was considered one of the most corrupt of commanders. In contrast, there was the Communist party leader who saw no inconsistency in railing against American policy over dinner, then repairing to the piano for a round of his favorite songs from hit Broadway musicals. Hooked on Filipinos' passion for political debate, I found myself disappointed that their rousing rhetoric often masked a lack of commitment to any particular principle or platform. Attracted by their warmth and openness toward strangers, I could not help but judge harshly their lack of discretion and inability to keep a confidence.

Such hang-ups, magnified from the individual to the national level, resulted in a love-hate relationship between the two countries that was alternately rewarding and frustrating for both partners. In order to cope with the acute sensitivities of Filipinos, who both craved the attention of their superpower ally and chafed at its counsel, the officials responsible for fulfilling America's commitments to the Philippine government had had to adopt a Filipino-like attitude of fatalism. "Either we 'meddle' in their affairs, or we neglect to 'meddle,' " observed a diplomat in Manila. "It is not possible to be right. It is only possible to pursue our interests and hope they are well enough chosen that they are in the mutual interests of both countries."

For nearly two decades American policymakers in five administrations had concluded that those interests were well served by Ferdinand Marcos. "Marcos was as good for the U.S. as he was bad for the Philippines," acknowledged Armitage, who would play an important role in shaping the policy that would lead to his eventual ouster. Yet Marcos's inability one year after the Aquino assassination to satisfy the demands of the formerly passive Filipino middle class for reform raised the specter of the fall of another friendly dictator.

The professionals who would be called upon to manage the transition to a post-Marcos era had been burned by Vietnam, Iran, and Nicaragua. They were determined not to allow the U.S. to repeat its mistakes in a country that was, by affinity, if not by distance, much closer to home. That meant, contradictorily, not propping Marcos up too long, yet not provoking widespread destabilization by withdrawing support from his regime too soon. It also meant trying to balance the overriding U.S. security concerns with an appreciation of Filipino aspirations.

Fortunately, there were in this group of policymakers a number of people whose experience in the Philippines had sensitized them to the less tangible elements of the special relationship, which, they correctly believed, could help them achieve such a delicate balance. Ambassador Stephen Bosworth, for one, while acknowledging that "the strategic interest the U.S. has in the Philippines does dominate the discussion," argued that "our interests are substantially broader."

> This is a people with a collective memory of a political system that resembles our own. That is a fundamental difference between the Philippines and Central America and the Philippines and Iran. What was absent in those countries were any viable institutions which could serve as a buffer for transition. This country has the remnants of those institutions and a strong urge to reestablish them.

The restoration of the Philippines' democratic institutions was viewed in Washington as a policy goal that was highly compatible with the strengthening of U.S. security interests in the archipelago. The conclusion of principal policymakers that neither America's security concerns nor the restoration of Philippine democracy could be seriously addressed until Marcos had vanished from the scene was reached more than a year before President Reagan was finally forced to specify how and when he should leave. By then, a series of policy decisions and the inexorable course of events that had flowed from them—plus a dose of good luck, or, as the Filipinos called it, a "miracle"—had left the president little choice but to offer refuge in the U.S. to his friend Marcos.

Among those responsible for helping to turn the inevitable transition of power in the Philippines into a major U.S. foreign policy success story in a season of setbacks for the Reagan administration were a crusty admiral, two soft-spoken U.S. ambassadors, a gung ho former marine, an articulate assistant secretary, and a number of knowledgeable aides, who did much to guide the thinking of their "seniors."

*   *   *

As U.S. ambassador to the Philippines at the time of the Aquino assassination, Michael Armacost presided over the shift in American policy from full support for Marcos to escalating pressure on him to reform or retire. Known as a "long-term thinker," Armacost was praised by embassy officials who worked under him for having made such a dramatic turn-around in his own role and for having set the tone for the transition. "As a professional," said one officer, "he thinks about things from the point of view of the outsider."

Armacost had arrived at the U.S. embassy in Manila in 1982 by way of academia, followed by a dozen years of government service in the State Department, National Security Council, and Pentagon, before landing back at State as deputy assistant secretary for East Asia in 1980. He had spent the first year of his Philippine tour tightly focused on his brief to conduct a successful renegotiation of the military bases agreement.

The Aquino assassination had forced American policymakers, most notably Armacost, to reexamine the skewing of the "special relationship" toward Marcos and to redefine what it signified and between whom it existed. As long as Filipino protest against the martial law regime had remained muted, U.S. policymakers had been able to overlook the destruction of democracy in the Philippines in favor of the perceived stability which Marcos brought to the archipelago. The security aspect had been allowed to totally eclipse the other elements of the relationship.

With Filipinos in the streets demanding the resignation of Marcos and the restoration of democracy, however, that complacency was no longer acceptable—or wise. Change became inevitable. However, Marcos had been a friendly ally and guarantor of U.S. interests for eighteen years. He had made it clear from the start that he was not going to be chased from office. He remained in control of the military and every other arm of government. And he had deliberately prevented any potential successors, other than his wife, from developing.

Marcos's strongest card was his own well-known special relationship with President Ronald Reagan. He and Imelda bragged about their closeness to the American president, and coffee-shop gossip had it that their personal friendship had been cemented by Marcos's contributions to the Reagan-Bush campaign of undeclared funds that had reportedly passed through a bank in Texas for laundering.

It fell largely to Ambassador Armacost in Manila and Assistant Secretary of State for East Asia Paul Wolfowitz in Washington to begin charting a change in course. They were fortunate to have with them former embassy political officer John Maisto, who was married to a Filipino woman, and well known and trusted by the opposition. To keep him from being transferred elsewhere at a crucial point, Wolfowitz arranged for his promotion from Philippine deputy desk officer to country director.

Armacost had followed up his symbolic attendance at the Aquino funeral with a speech before the Makati Rotary Club three months later that signaled the Reagan administration's effort to distance itself from the Marcos regime—an effort that had already begun with the cancellation of Reagan's planned stopover in the Philippines en route to China. Tackling head-on the increasingly shrill charges leveled daily in the Marcos-controlled "crony press" that America's active interest in the Aquino assassination constituted meddling, Armacost posed a rhetorical question: "Is the American reaction merely an expression of a national habit of intruding into the internal affairs of other countries?"

His answer neatly touched upon the historical and emotional aspects of the special relationship. Not only were there 1.5 million Filipino-Americans living in the U.S., who were troubled by the Aquino assassination, but there was also a Congress, which was threatening to cut assistance to the Philippines unless a fair investigation was launched. However, he reminded critics, these Americans did not form their opinions in a vacuum. They were heavily influenced by Filipinos' reaction to the events which were taking place in their country. Here Armacost deftly broached the sensitive, central issue of investor confidence.

The businessmen in Armacost's audience knew that as much as $5 million a day had been fleeing the Philippines since the assassination, compared to an already alarming $2 million during the weeks just prior to Aquino's return, when Marcos was reported ailing. A sizable portion of that money belonged to them. They had already made their decision about the stability of the regime—a negative one. They were not sure whether the Americans had. Armacost gave them their first strong clue. "I think it fair to say that the financial problems of this country have not been occasioned primarily by doubts about the soundness of the economy, nor second thoughts about the nation's long-term economic development prospects. They have been precipitated, rather, by questions concerning the social and political stability of the country."

What the businessmen heard encouraged their belief that pressure on Marcos for reforms would be forthcoming from the private creditors and international lenders outside the Philippines, who would be taking their cue from the Filipino business community. They interpreted the ambassador's speech as a signal of support from the sidelines by the State Department. Said Armacost simply, "Foreigners are unlikely to put new money into the Philippines if Filipinos are taking their money out. Restoring the confidence of the Philippine business community, I would submit, is the priority problem of the moment."

In a background interview not long after that speech, Armacost appeared heartened by public support for change in all areas of Filipino life, and particularly impressed by the lobbying efforts of the private business community, in conjunction with reformers in Marcos's own party, to force the president to set up a viable system of succession. "Those people favor political changes," Armacost explained, "so urging restraint of confidence is one means of strengthening their hands without getting ourselves in the line of fire."

He sounded a note of caution, against overt American intervention, that would guide the embassy and the policy-making establishment in Washington throughout the Philippine affair. "If we become identified with anything, it can be harmful, because of nationalist feelings," he said.

Even before the speech Armacost's once warm relationship with the First Couple had cooled. Al Croghan, the wry and rumpled U.S. embassy press attaché, told of a social encounter about one month after the assassination in which Mrs. Marcos, making snide reference to his boss, complained, "It's lonely around here. No one comes around anymore. It's just me and him here all alone." Croghan commented, "Mike could have gone over, but he did not, because the Aquino assassination really changed things." Pausing, he added, ". . . and after all, they had already signed a bases agreement."

In March 1984, news leaked that Armacost had been tapped to become under secretary of state for political affairs, replacing Lawrence Eagleburger, who was due to retire May 1. Imelda gleefully spread the story that it was her complaints to her friends in Washington about Armacost's bias that had led to his departure prior to the May 14 legislative elections.

About a month before Armacost left, I held my last interview with him. It was a backgrounder for a story assessing Marcos's prospects for political survival on the eve of the election campaign. Armacost's parting impressions offered valuable insight into the sensitivity with which he would handle the transition to a post-Marcos era, once he was back in Washington. The interview was conducted in the bleachers of a nearby athletic field, where his son was playing in a baseball tournament. Occasionally pausing to applaud his team, Armacost discussed the shrill tone of Marcos's American critics.

Some were calling for the withdrawal of American support from the regime. Others were proposing various forms of intervention to pressure Marcos to reform. Former U.S. Ambassador to Manila and Tehran William Sullivan had suggested that in order to avoid another Iran, the U.S. should encourage Marcos to make a deal with the moderate opposition to restore democracy. Armacost balked at the proposal. "He's talking about injecting the U.S. very directly into the politics of this country," he said. "I think that's a crazy idea."

What Armacost had in mind, however, was far from a passive role for the Reagan administration in Philippine affairs. While cautioning policymakers to "leave this to the Filipinos," he intended for the U.S. to work closely with the democratic forces in Philippine society to push Filipino priorities and to emulate the pace for change that Filipinos themselves set. This determination to keep the American government offstage was in sharp contrast to the policy the U.S. would pursue in its attempt to oust Panamanian strongman General Antonio Noriega several years later.

Armacost painted a portrait of a government that is "besieged on all sides." Its economic problems, he maintained, "are massive in their implications." Trying to keep a lid on political protests was a full-time job for a convalescing president, who had not yet regained all his former physical vigor. On top of all that, the ambassador observed, "They are having to cope with the buildup for a real election."

Given the number of fronts on which the president was being forced to fight simultaneously, said Armacost, "There are increasingly elements over which he does not assume any control as he once did." The economy, now largely under the control of foreign investment institutions, was no longer the only one. On the political front, he had also had to relinquish some of his power. "The game is much more even than it was. There is no doubt that the palace still has the upper hand, but if you look back over the last six months, you can see some devolution of power in the society and a number of additional constraints on the president. How durable it is is anyone's guess, but at least for the moment they cannot constrain criticism in the press or within their own party."

Armacost's departure came at an auspicious moment. Stories had begun appearing daily in the crony press, accusing the U.S. of covertly supporting opposition parties in the upcoming elections. Marcos himself was making snide innuendos about forcing the Americans off the bases, if Washington continued to interfere in domestic affairs. "It's probably time to send in a new ambassador who is not involved in any of this—a nobody," said an embassy officer. Fishing around for the name of Armacost's rumored replacement on his cluttered desk, he read from some notes: "Bosworth. Former ambassador to Tunisia. Career man. Never been out here before."

*   *   *

Stephen Bosworth, a veteran diplomat with a thatch of prematurely white hair, had retired from his post as chairman of the secretary of state's

Policy Planning Council on February 15, 1984, at the age of forty-four, to start a new career in the private sector and a second marriage. He had an understanding with Secretary of State George Shultz that he would stay on in his job until mid-year, when a successor would be in place. Two days later, Eagleburger made a sudden decision to leave his post, and Shultz decided almost as quickly to fill it with Armacost, thereby leaving a hole in Manila. Shultz promptly offered the post to Bosworth. "Although technically retired, I was still a Foreign Service officer," explained Bosworth, "and I knew what an opportunity this would be."

While he had no experience in Asia, Bosworth felt that his previous posts as principal deputy assistant secretary of state for inter-American affairs and deputy assistant secretary of state for international resources and food policy had exposed him to "situations tangentially similar to what was going on in the Philippines." His involvement in the planning of energy policy in 1978 and 1979 had brought him into the inner circle of policy-making on Iran at the time of the Iranian revolution. "It struck me that, given all we knew about the Philippines, at some point we would be in the midst of a transition crisis, because apparently there was no readily visible successor to Marcos, either within or without the government," he said later.

The embassy post also played into his personal plans. Like Bosworth, who had served in Panama, Madrid, and Paris, his second wife-to-be had spent a good part of her life overseas, while married to a Citibank executive. "Quite frankly, having done this sort of thing for over twenty-five years, I thought there was probably some lasting value in having my wife be part of this life," he said later. Bosworth gained quick Senate confirmation and arrived in Manila in April to prepare for the May 14 elections. Once the voting trend was clear, he returned to the U.S., married Chris, and moved into the ambassador's residence in the exclusive, walled, residential community of Forbes Park.

Bosworth's first priority was "to get to know as many people as I could." It was understood by all the parties involved that this meant people from one end of the political spectrum to the other, with the exception of the Communist front groups. "I had to deal effectively with President Marcos, so I had to have access there," he acknowledged, "but we had no interest in becoming a captive of the palace."

Bosworth was an immediate hit with the fifty-nine moderate oppositionists who were elected to the National Assembly in May. As soon as he returned to Manila following his remarriage, he set about acquainting himself with them and the rest of the democratic opposition leaders by hosting breakfasts and luncheons at the residence two to three times a week. After so many years out of power and out of grace with the Reagan administration, they were flattered by the ambassador's attention and spurred by his brief: to help ensure "an orderly transition to the next generation of responsible political leadership."

Although the opposition naturally assumed that it alone represented that next generation, Bosworth made sure that he invited equal numbers of ruling party members to his luncheons. He also encouraged his embassy's military attachés to scramble to get to know the young military officers who would figure in the various transition scenarios. Rumors of rumblings in the military were widespread within opposition circles, and as the Agrava Board drew nearer to drafting its report, the possibility of indictments against a number of soldiers made the question of military reaction far more urgent than it had been in the past.

"The American attachés and their deputies were everywhere, all over the country getting to know all of us," said Colonel Malajacan, about U.S. efforts to identify and cultivate reform-minded officers like himself. After General Ramos became acting chief of staff late in 1984, those contacts were encouraged by general headquarters, which methodically assigned officers who were members of the reform movement to escort visiting American congressmen and State and Pentagon officials. Those Americans in turn unfailingly promoted the cause of military reform, both in their meetings with Marcos, and later back home in debates over military assistance to the Philippines.

Bosworth also made it a point to cultivate one person who fit none of the categories of next-generation leadership—the widow of Ninoy Aquino. Bosworth had met Cory Aquino socially, and he had become acquainted with other members of the Aquino and Cojuangco families. By November 1984, however, he felt he needed the opportunity to get to know the most prominent family personality better. The Agrava Board had issued a majority report which recommended the indictments of sixteen men, including Generals Ver, Custodio, and Olivas. General Ver had taken a leave of absence that was to last at least as long as the legal proceedings in which he figured. Marcos had disappeared from public view once again, sparking rumors of a second kidney transplant, and sending diplomats and prospective candidates into a frenzy of activity in anticipation of a possible sudden or "snap" election, should he die. The post-Marcos transition suddenly seemed closer at hand.

Searching for the right environment—relaxed, friendly, discreet—Bosworth turned to a longtime Aquino family friend, who was also close to the embassy's naval attaché. Manuel ("Manoling") Morató had been a childhood friend of Ninoy, and had remained close to the Aquino family and to Cory throughout the martial law period and Ninoy's exile. Active in the fledgling Philippine Aerospace Association, with both young Filipino

Air Force officers and the diplomatic community, Morató also numbered among his friends a wide circle of opposition politicians, artists, entertainers, and even a number of Imelda's so-called "Blue Ladies," society matrons who had donned blue dresses to campaign for Marcos in the 1960s. Known as an impeccable host, Morató lived in an art-filled duplex atop a Manila apartment building owned by him, which had been the site of many such confidential meetings during martial law and after. Manoling would later arrange such a secret meeting there for me with the prosecutor in the Ver trial.

"When the ambassador told me who was coming to dinner," recounted Morató, well after the fact, "I asked if it was okay if I arranged for their cars to use a different entrance." He knew a sensitive guest list when he saw one—Cory, her mother-in-law, Doña Aurora, sister-in-law Maur, daughter Kris, speechwriter Teodoro ("Teddy Boy") Locsin, Jr., the U.S. ambassador, and the U.S. defense attaché. By using a secret entrance, he sought to protect both his guests and himself. Bosworth, however, told him, "I never act covertly." Given a flair for the dramatic, Morató jokingly claimed that he replied, "Easy for you to say, what about me and my business and my seven hundred employees?"

However, he respected the ambassador's wishes and opened the gates of his compound to the separate cars of his guests and their drivers and bodyguards. In Bosworth's case, Morató would learn later, "all ten security guards were from the Presidential Security Command—all Ver's men." From a diplomatic and political perspective, the evening appeared to the host to have gone well, although it brought him several seasons of harassment from Ver's men and the Blue Ladies.

"My feeling was that I could not possibly maintain confidential contact with anyone in this society," Bosworth explained later, referring to Manila's rampant rumor mill and the apparent inability of most Filipinos to keep secrets. Knowing that his security had been assigned to him by General Ver, he said, "I had to assume they were keeping track of me." He therefore proceeded to operate under the principle that "as the American ambassador, with long term interests in mind, it was entirely appropriate for me to be talking to everyone in the legitimate political arena."

Bosworth said he never raised the issue with Marcos, and he made a point of stressing that Marcos "never once raised the issue with me." Imelda was not so tolerant. "She did," he said, without further elaboration. Bosworth described his relationship with Marcos at that time as "correct" and "respectful." "He is a very smart man," said Bosworth. "He understood that times were changing."

The reverberations from Bosworth's meeting with Cory manifested themselves over the months that followed. "Steve was the first to have faith in Cory as a candidate," said a Filipino businessman, who became aware of her potential candidacy as early as June 1985 and quickly jumped on her bandwagon.

Bosworth's other priority in the months immediately after the May 1984 elections was to update and expand the embassy's analysis of the strength of the Communist insurgency. "When I arrived, I became concerned in the first couple of weeks we were here that we had not been giving enough focus to the insurgency in the countryside." He assigned political counselor Jim Nach, the man with the pinpricked wall map of NPA encounters, to do "a systematic study."

The impact of Nach's report in Washington, said Bosworth, "was great." Shortly after it was filed, it received valuable reinforcement from Admiral William Crowe, commander in chief of Pacific Forces (CINC-PAC), who visited the Philippines in June 1984 and, reported Bosworth, "became aware of how feeble the AFP was to counter it." Crowe, he said, "went back to Washington and energized the bureaucracy."

*　　　*　　　*

Admiral William Crowe was a rare soldier-intellectual, who was popular with subordinates at sea and impressive to his superiors in the Pentagon and his peers in the civilian bureaucracy, who remembered him from his days as the defense secretary's director of the East Asian and Pacific region. He had gone on to command the navy's Middle East Force in the Persian Gulf and the Mediterranean and Pacific fleets, before returning to Washington, where he became chairman of the Joint Chiefs of Staff. Born in Kentucky, and imbued with a heavy twang and a corn-pone sense of humor, which he never lost, Crowe graduated from Annapolis and earned a master's degree from Stanford and a doctorate in politics from Princeton. As a member of the influential Council on Foreign Relations, a bastion of Eastern establishmentarianism, he was as comfortable with the Rockefellers, Kissingers, and Bundys who held forth there as he was with his fellow officers.

Crowe also enjoyed a good rapport with Ronald Reagan. "He is a guy who can walk in on the president any time, a guy the president must listen to," said one security analyst who had witnessed the fallout from several of Crowe's forays into the Oval Office. "If Crowe says Ronald Reagan has to think about something, he does think about it."

Crowe did not enjoy a particularly good rapport with Ferdinand Marcos. During his two-year tour as CINCPAC, Crowe made five trips to the Philippines, meeting with U.S. base commanders and key Philippine government and embassy officials in Manila. Each time he had paid a call on President Marcos. He had been forced to postpone his first visit, due to the confusion that reigned in the immediate aftermath of the Aquino assassination. However, he had rescheduled it in December, thus becoming one of the first senior U.S. officials to see Marcos following his kidney surgery and the killing which threatened to bring down his regime.

Each time Crowe went to Malacañang, he left thinking that Marcos had understood the "guidelines" he had proposed "as to the kinds of things we wanted to get him to do, particularly in regard to the military and the way he was using it." Believing that Marcos's cooperation would be to the mutual benefit of both countries, and having been given no reason by Marcos himself to think that he was rejecting his proposals, Crowe assumed that results would be forthcoming by the time of his next visit. Invariably, however, the next visit would bring double-talk and no results.

Crowe's second visit took place June 12 to 15, 1984, six weeks after the arrival of Ambassador Bosworth, one month after the Philippine legislative elections, and one week after Enrile's trip to Mindanao. What few news reports later appeared about the unannounced visit described the admiral as "despondent" about the growth of the insurgency and Marcos's apparent indifference to the consequences.

Based on discussions he held with members of the U.S. "country team" in the Philippines, which included the U.S. base commanders, the ambassador, and the CIA station chief, plus talks with Filipino military and civilian officials, Crowe wrote a report on the spot, in longhand, and sent it to the Joint Chiefs, who forwarded a copy to President Reagan. "Reagan was so impressed," according to a security consultant who was privy to some of the discussions which followed, "that he ordered Crowe to Washington for a personal briefing."

Crowe's concern, according to the consultant, was the impact that the politicization of Marcos's military was likely to have on the security of America's premier defense facility in the Pacific, the Subic Bay Naval Base. "What Crowe was saying to Washington in that report," according to the consultant, "was 'There is no hope for my naval base with that guy as president of that country. Choose between Marcos and that base.' " Crowe did not express himself so bluntly.

"The insurgency was one of our main interests" at that time, acknowledged Crowe several years later, "but that was not the point. You could not associate with Marcos and the Philippine military and government very long without understanding that everything came together in his hands. Nothing major happened unless he manipulated it." This had long posed a problem to the U.S. military, which was the chief source of funding, arms, and supplies for Marcos's military, as well as its partner in the operation of the base facilities and its most important ally.

"We wanted the military to become more efficient and more responsive vis-à-vis the insurgency," Crowe continued, "and we had made a whole host of suggestions, but they were being ignored." The result, according to Crowe, was a lack of flexibility necessary on the part of the

AFP to effectively wage a counterinsurgency. Giving Marcos the benefit of the doubt, Crowe recounted, "I thought at first he did not understand how he had to respond." But eventually, he said, "I came to the conclusion that he had been given every chance."

One of Admiral Crowe's biggest beefs, according to other officers, was the regime's squandering of U.S. taxpayers' money on state-of-the-art military equipment that fed Marcos's vanity more than it contributed to the effectiveness of the soldiers who fought the NPA. Six weeks after Crowe's report began circulating in Washington, a tough, highly respected combat veteran, Brigadier General Teddy Allen, was dispatched to Manila to take command of the Joint U.S. Military Assistance Group (JUSMAG), which rides herd on the millions of dollars in U.S. military assistance that flows to the Philippines each year as part of a compensation package for the use of the bases. After years of official U.S. tolerance for Marcos's excesses in the management of his armed forces and the acquisition of expensive hardware that netted huge kickbacks to the president and his top brass, Washington had authorized General Allen to "play hardball with the Armed Forces of the Philippines."

After reviewing JUSMAG's books on past arms purchases, Allen delivered an ultimatum to General Ver. "Unless you change your way of doing business," Allen told the chief of staff, "I cannot do business with you." In a five-page letter to Ver, Allen outlined the practices that would no longer be acceptable. Foremost among them was the Philippine military's use of something called a "commercial direct contract," under which private U.S. arms dealers contracted directly with the Philippine embassy in Washington, and were then paid by the Pentagon, without JUSMAG's knowledge until after the fact. The scam was that Imelda's brother Kokoy was the Philippine ambassador to the U.S. and that agents' fees of up to $50,000 were permitted on every such contract negotiated with him. Among the scores of anomalies General Allen had found was a set of four contracts in one year—two on the same day—to the same company for identical pieces of radio equipment. Each contract had netted a Marcos crony a $50,000 commission.

Before Ver could respond to Allen, he was suspended from his post to undergo trial on charges of conspiring to assassinate Aquino. General Ramos, a good friend of Admiral Crowe and the West Point classmate of other ranking U.S. military officials, succeeded Ver as acting chief of staff. "We did more in twelve months under General Ramos than in the ten previous years," Allen explained later, citing the banning of the commercial direct contract, improved troop training and equipment maintenance procedures, and the growth of the reformist movement among the younger Philippine officers. However, the bottom line was that at the end of 1986 Ver was reinstated in his post and Marcos retained power over the course of the counterinsurgency and the negotiations that would determine the ultimate fate of the U.S. bases after the expiration of the agreement in 1991.

Mindful of Marcos's past attempts to play his "Russian card" by threatening to give Soviet ships docking rights near Subic, Crowe no longer trusted Marcos as a reliable partner. Looking back on the president's machinations during his last year in office, the admiral later told me, "I am convinced that if Marcos had remained in power, the next base negotiations would have been a shambles. If it were necessary to stay in power, he would have dumped us. The only thing that interested him was staying in power."

At that time, according to Crowe, "The big argument in U.S. government was 'Can we work this out under Marcos, or must we facilitate or encourage a change?' There were strong views on both sides. People were asking, 'Suppose you engineer a change, who will you get? It could be worse.' "

Crowe's response to that question and a main thrust of his report was, he said, the harsh reality that "no matter when we changed, there would be trauma." The admiral commented, "I was not so naive as to think everything could be wonderful." On the other hand, he believed, "When the time came—and it was going to come—the longer we allowed him to stay there, the more traumatic it would be." According to Crowe, President Reagan, quite understandably, counseled caution. "Obviously he felt that Marcos was a friend, and he was reluctant to do something precipitous unless we were on solid ground," said Crowe. "He did not just want to take somebody's word for it."

What most troubled Crowe about his report, he admitted later, "was that I did not pretend to know who would take his place." Crowe's only bureaucratic ally at that early date, former Ambassador Armacost, who was by then at the State Department, immediately ruled out any attempt to start betting on favorites. "We made the decision very early on that it was not our job to try and pick the successor," said Armacost. "You could not do it, because Marcos had been like a huge banyan tree, and nothing could grow in his shadow. Once we had a post-Marcos era, all those talented people would surface. Our job was not to try and supplant Filipinos, but to try and get behind those forces in the Philippines that would open up the process and institutionalize reforms."

The only nod that U.S. officials gave to specific leaders was a negative one to Mrs. Marcos, Danding Cojuangco, and General Ver. "They would have been disastrous," commented Armacost. The reasoning in some quarters of the state and defense departments at the time was that if the Armed Forces of the Philippines could be wrested from the absolute control of Marcos and Ver and restored to the command of a professional like

Ramos, who had Washington's confidence, a temporary vacuum of civilian authority in Manila could be tolerated.

*   *   *

Crowe's report triggered a demand for a redefinition of American policy in the Philippines. There had not been one since the imposition of martial law in 1972. "We needed a policy to use as a framework for congressional testimony," said Bosworth. "People wonder what is a policy, and how is it developed, and why? You do it because you have to explain to the Congress what you are about. You have to systematically frame your thoughts."

Bosworth had received an initial primer on the Philippines in September 1983, as head of Shultz's Policy Planning Council. He and Wolfowitz had, he said, "taken a quick look at the medium-term story in the Philippines, and with Mike's [Armacost] strong push, we decided that the National Assembly election offered a test, and we decided to pin ourselves to the revitalization of institutions."

"The goal of our policy was building up institutions that would have staying power beyond one individual," explained Wolfowitz. "We could be very confident that a professional military, a democratic system, and a nonmonopolistic economy would be good, but we would not be good at discerning who could successfully govern a country as deeply divided as the Philippines."

The secret policy directive, known as a National Security Decision Directive (NSDD), which incorporated this and other goals, emerged from the planning process shortly after the November 1984 American elections and was signed by President Reagan in January 1985. It did not please liberals like Congressman Solarz. He acknowledged that the new articulation of U.S. policy "indicates that the administration is far more disenchanted with Marcos than it is letting on." But he called it "naive" in its assumption that "you could pressure a man who was no slouch to undermine himself." Said Solarz, "You ask Marcos to hold honest elections and he would lose. You ask him to get rid of his cronies and he could not sleep well at night." Nor did it satisfy uniformed military men with more urgent agendas. When Crowe returned to the U.S. a year after his original report had set the policy process in motion, he was dismayed to find the debate "still in full heat, with the people who wanted to go with Marcos still thinking he would reform."

The authors of the directive, an interagency group of State Department and Pentagon officials, insisted that, far from being naive, they were being practical. "There were definitely influential people in government who thought that Marcos was hopeless and that U.S. policy should be to figure out how to get someone to replace him," said one. "But I never had much sympathy for that notion, partly because I did not think we could do it. Marcos was much too tough for that treatment. He would make sure that no American could pull a coup." Thus, the drafters, in outlining the reforms they wished to see, were buying time, hoping either that a viable successor would eventually appear, or that an act of God would intervene. "My own personal wish was that Marcos would drop dead," said one policymaker.

Given the president's uncertain health, said Assistant Secretary Wolfowitz, one goal of the policy was in fact "to set processes in motion that would assist the transition to something better in the event that Marcos died, and to head off the calamity that an Imelda-Ver takeover would represent." Wolfowitz stressed the pains taken by the drafters to ensure that in tightening the screws on Marcos they did not bring down the whole structure around him. "Basically we were delegitimizing Marcos, but not in a way that could destabilize the country," said Wolfowitz. "Our statements and actions constituted strong pressure on Marcos to change his ways, and by rejecting our advice, he transformed what we said into harsh criticism. But it was never in our interest—nor in the interest of the Filipino people—to further destabilize the terrible conditions in the Philippines. The 'levers' that so many people think we hold in our hands can wreak a great deal of damage, but chaos could only benefit the forces of extremism, left and right." Wolfowitz added, "Ironically, if Marcos had taken our advice, he might still be president, although that was not our goal either."

In fact, during the year it was operative, the National Security Directive on the Philippines served as a useful cover under which subtle but quite far-reaching intervention in Philippine affairs was able to go forward, cloaked in benign intentions to help a dictator foster a restoration of democracy. Designed to be all things to all people inside a divided foreign policy bureaucracy, it was sensitive to the many delicate nuances that were at play in a crisis which struck at the very heart of the sacrosanct Fil-Am "special relationship."

Striking the proper nuances was critical to the success of any policy involving the Philippines, where American energy and enthusiasm for quick solutions had rarely succeeded in moving a people whose metabolism and thought processes remained lethargically and ambiguously Malay. Accordingly, the directive recommended "a low-key approach" that would be exercised "in support of efforts that have already developed within the Philippines." Stressing that "in the Philippine cultural context the way we convey our policy messages is as important as the policy," it warned U.S. officials against "appearing too close to the Marcos regime."

Nuance was equally critical to the success of the policy in Ronald Reagan's Washington. Former United Nations Ambassador Jeane Kirkpatrick's articulation of America's interest in supporting "authoritarian" friends of the U.S. against the inroads of Communism had been embraced by the conservative president. The legacy of problems inherited by the Reagan administration as the result of the fall of dictators in Iran and Nicaragua to even more repressive regimes was constantly invoked as a justification for continued support of the few members of that endangered species who remained in power. If Reagan stood for anything, it was standing up for old, anti-Communist friends. Ferdinand Marcos was the epitome of such a friend.

Thus, the drafters of the directive were careful not to suggest Marcos's ouster as long as Imelda Marcos and General Ver or the Communists were positioned to seize power during the chaos that would inevitably follow his downfall. "While President Marcos at this stage is part of the problem, he is also necessarily part of the solution," said the NSDD. At the same time, the document was wise to Marcos's ways. "Marcos will try to use us to remain in power indefinitely," it warned.

The problem which the NSDD drafters chose to highlight was one on which all the policymakers could agree: the insurgency being waged across the archipelago by the Communist Party of the Philippines, together with its military and political wings, the New People's Army and the National Democratic Front. Containment of the insurgency, rather than human rights violations or other shortcomings of the Marcos regime, thus became the consistent justification for the political, economic, and military reforms which the U.S. government was pressing Marcos to make. "The NPA was one of the reasons we could clearly enunciate to the country," said Armitage.

A careful distinction was made by the policy planners between true Communist sympathizers and those anti-Marcos opposition leaders whom the president routinely accused of being subversives. To make that clear, the U.S. stepped up its public courtship of the latter.

Under the NSDD, increased aid would be forthcoming only if careful monitoring of the list of sixteen "high-priority changes"—ranging from reforms that would make the scheduled 1986 local and 1987 presidential elections relatively fair to an end to agricultural monopolies—showed progress in their implementation. If the regime failed to move in the right direction, the document implied that U.S. support would be withdrawn.

Although the final document was vague on details about this crucial option, those responsible for the initial draft were less so. One analyst privy to the drafting process revealed that its authors built into the NSDD "an escape clause which said, in effect, 'If this document fails, do the following: Get rid of Ferdinand Marcos.'" Naturally, such a sentence never appeared in print. However, a more diplomatically worded paragraph asserting the need to examine what the NSDD called a "no-sale option" of increased pressure on Marcos "from the public, opposition, business leaders, and even from his own close associates" if he refused to undertake the desired reforms, was inserted. The "no-sale option" was designed to serve as what this insider called "the mousetrap."

Its logic was impeccable. The U.S. would offer Marcos incentives to reform. The document drafters outlined what they considered his three likeliest responses to the proposal: (1) accept it and implement reforms; (2) accept it, take all the benefits offered, and then fail to make the promised reforms; (3) refuse the proposal out of hand. Those who knew Marcos best believed that, based on past performance, he would choose the second alternative. Thus, they reasoned, the NSDD had to be predicated on the assumption that Marcos would fail to comply with its conditions.

The document called for periodic reviews of Marcos's progress toward compliance, with funds being doled out, as one insider put it, "on the basis of performance, not promises, since the man in question is a chronic liar." In the event that noncompliance was established, the "mousetrap clause" would be baited and set.

14

Preliminary Justice

One month after the Agrava Board had completed its scheduled hearings, its members met in a Manila recording studio for a secret screening of videotapes of the Aquino assassination. They had viewed the three tapes shot in and around flight 811 that day many times before. Now record producer Jose-Mari Gonzalez had prepared a fourth composite tape, which he would play for them on a super-slow-motion machine, affording them a final opportunity to pinpoint previously unidentified witnesses. Justice Agrava had invited me to go along.

Mrs. Agrava and I arrived at the sound studio ahead of the others, so we had a bit of time to catch up on the events of the past month. I had not seen her since the day she had alienated much of her public by honoring Imelda Marcos with a chorus of "Happy Birthday" after her appearance as a witness before the board on July 2. Agrava pleaded with me not to read into her spontaneous serenade any more than an effort to be hospitable to a witness who had agreed to answer questions before a largely hostile audience on what happened to be her fifty-fifth birthday. "Wait until you see our report before you make up your mind," she begged me in her earnest way.

As soon as the rest of the group had assembled, the tapes were played, first at regular speed, then in increasingly slow motion, until they had been broken down into a series of video snapshots. Suddenly, a face that had been blank became that of an identifiable human being, standing inside the passenger jetway. Furthermore, he could be seen raising an automatic camera to his eye, stepping in front of Aquino, and snapping his picture with a flash. Comparing these video frames with two stills shot aboard the plane, the board was able to confirm that the man in question was Sergeant Prospero Bona, a member of the AVSECOM Special Operations squadron, who had previously sworn that he had never been inside the jetway. Fuming at yet another example of the deceit perpetrated by military witnesses under oath, Agrava instructed Narvasa to recall Bona to the stand.

Still in the process of reviewing the 20,377 pages of testimony, 1,472 photographs, and 480 exhibits put into evidence by 193 witnesses, the board had unanimously rejected the military scenario that it was Galman who had killed Aquino. The slow-motion tape had served to confirm its members in their resolve to stick to the evidence in making their judgment, despite heavy pressure from the regime to accept its version of the crime. "I'm glad we didn't have this machine earlier," said board member Luciano Salazar, "because you can never tell what pressure would have been exerted on us." Salazar's comment was greeted with nervous laughter by his fellow panelists and the board lawyers, all of whom knew whereof he spoke.

From the beginning Narvasa had come under pressure from people identified with the palace in an attempt to influence his presentation of witnesses. The palace had stepped up its campaign against the general counsel shortly after his damaging interrogation of General Ver. In a letter to the board, President Marcos had informed its members that he had amended their charter by secret decree, transferring prime responsibility for gathering evidence and preparing the findings from the general counsel to the board members themselves.

When Narvasa learned about the decree, he confronted the group, threatening to resign and go public unless he was given assurances that he would be able to continue his work unfettered as before. On May 15, all five members signed a secret resolution, reiterating the board's "confidence and trust in the general counsel and his decisions," and foreseeing "no change to be introduced in the procedure that will alter its present manner of investigation for presentation of evidence."

Board member Boy Herrera had been targeted by military men and toughs within the progovernment labor organization he headed, as soon as he began using his union contacts to gain information from Philippine Airlines workers about the shooting. "One morning during a board hearing," recalled Herrera, "I asked a witness if he had seen a black car near the scene of the crime, because the PAL workers had told me they were positive they had seen one." During the lunch break, Herrera received a call, "telling me to see someone at Malacañang."

After that he was almost never free from harassment by military officers, who hung around his office or called him up, openly trying to influence him to go easy on the military. "At first they wanted only Galman to be charged," said Herrera. "Later they admitted military involvement, but not to include Generals Custodio and Ver." One week before the board issued its report, Herrera later told me, those officers had signaled their willingness to sacrifice "everyone but General Ver." Hounded day and night by these men, yet unwilling to compromise himself, Herrera offered to resign. "But they were too smart to let me do that," he said, "they knew that would be worse for them." Finally, sighed Herrera, "I reached the point where I said, 'I leave it to God.' "

The palace and the military were not the only powerful entities trying to use their leverage to influence the Aquino case. The U.S. embassy, in its own discreet fashion, had also intervened. Early in the board's deliberations, Ambassador Armacost had hosted a small dinner for the board members, during which he and his aides subtly intimated that a report which named General Ver would be most welcome in Washington, where Congress was conditioning continued military assistance on an honest investigation and other reforms.

The board and its legal staff had weathered the nine months of hearings with what Mrs. Agrava liked to call their "precious oneness" intact. Although her motherly nagging at them and her overemphasis on group activities grated on the nerves of some board members, they had avoided major quarrels over their findings. They were in accord on their central contention that Aquino had been the victim of a military conspiracy. However, they had still not reached an agreement on how far up the chain of command to extend the guilt. The lawyers and two hard-line board members—Santos and Herrera—were prepared to take it as high as Ver. The two other board members remained to be persuaded by the legal evidence, which Narvasa would weigh in the report he was struggling to finish. The question mark in all of their minds was Chairman Agrava herself.

"At first there seemed to be a consensus that we were all in agreement up to the level of General Ver," said Herrera several years later. Sequestered in the Philippine Village Hotel, each board member was committing his own opinions to paper, which Agrava was to incorporate in a comprehensive report. Meanwhile, Narvasa, a championship typist, was at home on his porch tapping out his memorandum, which would provide the legal underpinnings for the board report. In frequent contact with board members, he was working to strengthen the case they had asked him to build against the Big Guy. He had requested more time, and Agrava had extended the deadline for the report's release from August 21 to late September.

The delay in the release of the report had heightened speculation that the board was preparing to indict the military. This in turn intensified the pressure on members from sources close to the palace and fueled their latent distrust of each other. In a matter of days the level of tension inside the suite of rooms occupied by board members had mounted to such a point that safety valves had to be sought. "Our first idea," Herrera later revealed, "was that we should brief President Marcos that our findings would include General Ver. We feared that our report might cause violence, so we thought the government should be prepared."

After discussing the proposal, however, the group decided it risked being compromised by going directly to the palace. Instead, said Herrera, "We appointed Justice Agrava and Attorney Salazar to talk to General Romulo." The aged former foreign minister Carlos P. Romulo was a man whom they felt they could trust with the sensitive information. They counted on him to pass it discreetly to Marcos. Before they were able to ascertain whether or not Romulo had in fact confided in Marcos, the two hard-liners decided to leak word of the board's consensus judgment to the press as a safeguard against palace pressure to limit the number of military indictments. "I leaked to the *Washington Post*, and Dante Santos leaked to the *San Jose Mercury*," Herrera admitted. The leaks, however, had the opposite effect from that which was intended. Threats from the palace intensified, and the consensus broke down when Agrava lost her nerve.

Herrera recounted how Marcos, through his legal advisor, Justice Manuel Lazaro, "conveyed the message to me and Dante that if we proceeded to include General Ver in our findings, the two of us would be 'his eternal enemy.' " As if the remark needed translation, Herrera added wryly, "That means 'Your days are numbered.' "

Meanwhile, in the extra three weeks which Agrava had given him, Narvasa was able to build what he deemed to be a strong case for including Ver within the conspiracy—strong enough to win over the two fence-sitting, male board members. But when he turned it over to Agrava, he said, "She acted as if I had betrayed her." By then she had completed her own report, which incorporated almost none of the other members' opinions. "It was all about a king [Marcos], whose errant knights [the lower-ranking military men] had done him a gross disservice," said Narvasa.

On September 29, following the return of two board members from private business trips abroad, the board held a heated meeting, in which the four men rejected the chairman's conclusion, that a limited military conspiracy existed, involving only six soldiers and General Luther Custodio, as too narrow in scope and too saccharine in tone to reflect their views. Instead, they accepted Narvasa's memo with its expanded portion on General Ver, subtitled "Twenty-one Questions for General Ver," as the basis for their own similar but more far-reaching set of conclusions, which they now began to draft.

Their plan was to present their report to Agrava, who would be given the option of signing it, proposing some sort of combined report in which her dissenting opinion on Ver would be recorded next to their majority opinion, or coming out with her own report separate from theirs. At that point, Marcos deployed a platoon of legal lieutenants, public opinion specialists, and fixers to try to limit the damage. "We understand that the board is split four to one against Ver," intoned the visiting Philippine ambassador to the Court of St. James, J. V. Cruz, from his customary chair in the Manila Hotel lobby lounge. Raising his vodka on the rocks, Marcos's favorite troubleshooter said sportingly, "We would prefer to see it split three to two."

It was not long before board members and lawyers were reporting increased pressures on them. As the divided board continued to vacillate, and the government increased the pressure on members and staff not to touch Ver, the Narvasas hosted a raucous party for the legal staff in their home. There, the Dean and his deputies, all of whom had been politicized by the ten-month ordeal, egged each other on to sing a few choruses of "Ninoy's homecoming song, 'Tie a Yellow Ribbon.'" Laughingly, they concluded, "We might as well go all the way up to Ver, since we'll get shot anyway."

On October 5, I was slipped a copy of the 479-page general counsel's report, which would form the spine of the board majority's report. The legal memorandum was tough and thorough. Not until page 371 was the subject of "the military conspiracy" finally broached. When it was, the weight of the evidence was behind it, and it was addressed in the hard-hitting language of someone whose intelligence had been insulted, someone whose good faith and even patriotism had been exploited, someone who knew that the opinion he expressed was shared by a majority of his colleagues and probably of his countrymen as well.

Narvasa exposed "at least forty circumstances which prove beyond doubt that, the claims of the military officers and men to the contrary, they knew well ahead of time the details of Senator Aquino's arrival at Manila International Airport, and therefore the elaborate plans ostensibly geared towards protecting the life of Senator Aquino were in fact designed to camouflage the taking of that life." The Narvasa report concluded, "The hard evidence proves beyond doubt that the military personnel at the tarmac, who claimed to have witnessed the shooting of Senator Aquino, were lying, concertedly and in conspiracy with one another."

The legal memorandum did not establish the identity of the trigger-man, although it concluded that it was one of the men who followed

Aquino down the stairs, and it recommended prosecuting all of them as coconspirators. What it did establish, through the testimony of witnesses and the audiovisual evidence, was that Galman was not in the right place at the right second to have killed Aquino in the manner that some fourteen soldiers described under oath.

In taking the conspiracy higher, Narvasa posed twenty-one questions about the credibility of Ver's testimony. So ingenuous did he find most of Ver's answers that he concurred with the board majority that Ver be charged as an "accessory after the fact to the conspiracy" for his role in the cover-up.

Fearful of filing such sensitive material from Manila, I flew to Hong Kong for the weekend and filed a cover story on the board's effective indictment of the president's men as the conspirators who killed Aquino. The first article to outline the extent of the findings on which the board members would base their own reports, it was on the newsstand several weeks before the actual reports were finally presented to the president and the public.

⁎   ⁎   ⁎

The stalemate between the board majority and Agrava continued for nearly one month. Meanwhile, the majority members, who were struggling to complete a draft on which all four could agree, were constantly reminded of the high stakes that were involved in their conclusions as to the role played by the armed forces chief of staff in the conspiracy. In hearings conducted by Congressman Stephen Solarz's House Subcommittee on Asian and Pacific Affairs, Assistant Secretary of Defense for International Security Affairs Richard Armitage questioned: "Do we write off the AFP as being hopelessly corrupt and ineffective, or do we provide adequate moral, material, and training support to a military institution that we established and nurtured—an armed forces that fought gallantly and honorably at our side during World War II, in Korea, and Vietnam?"

Coming as it did on the eve of a board report that was widely anticipated to indict General Ver, Armitage's message was interpreted in Manila for what it was—a warning to Marcos of a possible cutoff of U.S. military assistance, if Ver remained in his post. The impact of Armitage's particularly strong formulation of the alternatives was quick and powerful. "I had barely gotten back to my office after the hearing," Armitage commented later, "when I had a message from President Marcos. He was pissed off."

Two weeks later the board was no closer to a compromise, and Agrava, sensitive to accusations in the press that it was she who was delaying the release of the report, issued her colleagues an ultimatum. Her report, which had been completed for more than one month and was now being duplicated and bound, would be released by the following Monday, October 22, three days hence. If the four other members wished to present theirs at the same time, they should be ready to go by then.

In the end Agrava beat her male colleagues when she was speedily granted an appointment to present her report to the president on Tuesday, October 23. The majority, its own report still neither printed nor bound, had no recourse but to request its appointment at Malacañang the following day.

Agile tactician that he was, Marcos had been preparing for any eventuality. As early as two weeks before, the president had given heart to his more liberal advisors by requesting a copy of Israel's Kahane Commission Report on the Lebanese massacres, which had led to the ouster of that country's then defense minister, General Ariel Sharon. According to one palace insider, the president had been strongly lobbied by many of his own supporters and cabinet ministers to find a way to allow Ver to relinquish his command, if necessary, rather than further damage the president's credibility, should the Agrava report, like the leaked legal memorandum, implicate Ver. A group of ministers, which met regularly to make recommendations on the president's media image concluded that whatever the Agrava findings, Marcos must respond decisively and immediately. Although Marcos considered forcing Ver's resignation, close advisors confided that "the president is seeking every other alternative except that one."

Marcos jumped at Agrava's request for an appointment to deliver her report and promptly arranged for their meeting to be nationally televised. As soon as he had examined her findings, he returned to the airwaves to confirm that in response to the chairman's charges that AVSECOM Commander General Luther Custodio and six soldiers had conspired to murder Aquino, he was suspending all seven from duty and confining them to quarters. Meanwhile, he turned their cases over to the minister of justice for action by a civilian prosecutor in the special graft and corruption court, which was created to try government officials.

Neither in his brief expression of thanks to Justice Agrava nor in his later televised speech did the president refer to a second report still awaited from the board majority. The following morning when the four male board members weighed in with their report, the president was neither as prompt to meet them nor as cordial in his greeting as he had been the previous day. He kept them waiting outside for one hour. When they were finally shown into the presidential study, he confronted them. "I hope you can live with your conscience," he muttered. Then, without ceremony, he coldly and unsmilingly dismissed them. The meeting was not televised.

"I've never seen him as angry," said Herrera, who had observed Marcos under a variety of difficult circumstances. Yet, Marcos had little choice but to give equal treatment to the majority report, which recommended indictments against General Ver, twenty-four other soldiers, and one civilian. He therefore handed it over to the authorities and accepted letters from Ver and Olivas requesting permission to take a temporary "leave of absence." Shortly afterward, he named General Ramos to fill in for Ver as acting chief of staff. We would learn later that in granting Ver's leave, Marcos had promised the general his reinstatement if and when he was eventually acquitted.

As word spread that the majority report had named General Ver, the public responded first with incredulity, then joy. Agrava, once a heroine, was booed when she returned to the podium where she had presided for nine months to face reporters at a press conference. Fighting back tears, she defended her dissenting view. "Because I can face myself and in all conscience say that whatever I have placed in my report is what I believe in, I could hardly care whether you people who are booing out there should pelt me with tomatoes or slander me. I could care less. If my best does not satisfy you, I am sorry."

When I entered her twelfth-floor office for an interview the following day, accompanied by my editor from New York, whose scheduled visit just happened to coincide with the report's release, she greeted us, hugged me, tried to answer a few questions, but then broke down. We took our leave, rather than add to her pain.

By contrast, the four-man majority and the legal counsels were hailed as heroes when they presented their separate conclusions to the press. As Public Coordinator Benny Tan began reading the twenty-one findings regarding General Ver, the auditorium erupted with applause. Reporters strained to hear Tan's words above the din, while a jungle of TV cameras swiveled to catch the moist eyes of Filipino spectators in the back of the hall and the tired faces of those board members who had dared release a document that struck so close to the heart of the Marcos government.

Reaching the climactic point of his reading, Tan did his best to maintain an even tone. "In the light of all the foregoing considerations, we find the following to be indictable for the premeditated killing of Senator Benigno S. Aquino, Jr., and Rolando Galman at the Manila International Airport on August 21, 1983." Pandemonium broke out with the calling of the first name: "General Fabian C. Ver." It continued through number two, a general, number three, another general, two colonels, three captains, a second lieutenant, twelve sergeants, two police constables, two airmen, and the civilian who was charged with fetching Roland Galman on behalf of the military conspirators, who had set him up as the alleged assassin.

Nearly as remarkable as the majority's wide-ranging findings was its articulation of the broader significance of the board's mission. Chosen on the basis of their professional achievements and their nonpartisan political records, the board members had, during their year of public service, been at the center of the most explosive political issue in postwar Philippine history. The experience had obviously touched and toughened them, as evidenced by the epilogue of the report, with which Tan concluded his reading.

"More than any other event in contemporary Philippine history," they wrote,

> the killing of the late former Senator Aquino has brought into sharper focus the ills pervading Philippine society. It was the concretization of the horror that has been haunting this country for decades, routinely manifested by the breakdown of peace and order, economic instability, subversion, graft and corruption, and an increasing number of abusive elements in what are otherwise noble institutions in our country—the military and law enforcement agencies.

With the Agrava Board probe behind him and General Ver out of uniform, two of the main American complaints against the Marcos regime had become moot. Maybe now, his aides and allies were saying, Marcos could recover his momentum and finish out his term in a constructive manner. Less than a month later, however, the president suddenly vanished from public view once again, purportedly suffering from the flu.

The hysteria that accompanied his disappearance was an indication of the shallowness of the reforms that had been made since Aquino's death. It seemed hardly to matter that a National Assembly and an automatic process of succession now existed. The old specters of coups, countercoups, and the grabbing of power by Imelda and Ver had reappeared. I interviewed several Marcos ministers in an effort to verify rumors that Marcos had undergone a second kidney transplant. None believed the flu story, but none appeared close enough to the inner sanctum to know what in fact was ailing the president.

Enrile, who had received a phone call from Marcos five days after he entered his seclusion, told me, off the record, that Marcos had failed a stress test in October, after which he had been examined by a team of Filipino and American specialists and hospitalized. The minister did not know, however, whether his boss had subsequently undergone surgery. Marcos had told him he was calling from his yacht, a notion that brought a smile of disbelief to the face of the veteran defense minister. Marcos's staff had placed him, alternately, at home in the palace or in a nearby veterans hospital.

"Why such secrecy and deceit about where he is and what is wrong with him?" I asked Enrile. His cautious answer was reflective of the ongoing succession struggle, of which he was increasingly a part.

"The president probably felt that a confirmation of any serious medical problem might weaken his hold on the bureaucracy, the military organization, and the political situation in the country," he said. He paused, choosing his words carefully. "The moment there would be confirmation of an illness, then his possibilities would be limited."

No sooner had I returned from the Makati coffee shop where I interviewed Enrile, than I received a call from a Marcos aide, who just wanted to let me know that he was aware that we had been discussing Marcos's illness. With Ver on leave and Marcos dying, the spying and intrigues had escalated.

Much later I would learn the extent to which Marcos's recurrent illnesses triggered the reactions within the military to which Enrile had obliquely referred. General Ramos had established his own "crisis committee," which met daily during periods of presidential ill health to insure that the constitution would be followed if something happened to the president. According to Colonel Vic Batac, who served as the crisis committee's recorder, "We had men inside Malacañang who were supposed to inform us if Marcos died." Ramos's aim was to prevent a takeover by the First Lady, with the help of the Ver faction of the military, and to install in power instead Assembly Speaker Nicanor Yñiguez. Under the constitutional amendment passed shortly after the Aquino assassination, the Speaker had been designated to succeed Marcos and as head of a caretaker government preside over the election of a new president.

*   *   *

In March 1985, several months after General Ver went on leave and on trial, the Reform the Armed Forces Movement (RAM) burst into public view during PMA homecoming ceremonies at the academy in Baguio City.

"It was absolutely unheard of in the annals of the Philippines for anybody to be so blatant," said General Teddy Allen, who was there. "General Ramos was trooping the line, and a huge banner was unfurled in the front ranks. It was Alumni Day, and at first I thought it was a joke." When he saw the words "We Belong" printed on it, Allen realized that something serious was taking place on the parade ground.

General Allen's wife, Lynn, was watching the ceremonies with him. She noticed that when the procession of 300 uniformed PMA alumni, representing classes from 1971 to 1984, had completed its round of the field, the class of '84 kept on marching. Each of its members whipped out a sign and tore open his jacket to reveal a T-shirt bearing the same legend—"Unity Through Reforms."

To those alumni in the know, We Belong was the newly organized public manifestation of the underlying discontent of mid-level and junior officers with the corrupt, politicized upper echelons of the Armed Forces of the Philippines. Its members had first dared to speak out one month earlier in a mimeographed paper titled "Preliminary Statement of Aspirations," which was circulated within the ranks by anonymous PMA alumni. "We have earlier sought to ventilate our grievances and aspirations in conventional fora," it read, "but this too has been denied us mainly because of the prevailing military culture that has evolved in the 1980s, which rewards boot-licking incompetents and banishes independent-minded professionals and achievers." It called for an end to "incompetence and indiscipline" and warned, "We will no longer close our eyes to the graft and corruption happening in our midst."

Shortly afterward "A Statement of Common Aspirations" was issued. In addition to demanding a strong armed forces, capable of protecting the country, and a high standard of discipline, the anonymous reformists demanded that "the basis for promotions, assignments, schooling, and other related matters must be devoid of favoritism or *bata-bata* [protégés], the *Padrino* system [benefactor system], and other personal considerations." The statement concluded, "Loyalty must be directed to the constitution, not to any individual or group of persons."

As blatant as the alumni day demonstrators were, they refrained from duplicating their parade-ground performance the following day when the commander in chief, surrounded by a cluster of top brass, attended graduation ceremonies. On that occasion, acting Chief of Staff Ramos articulated his own similar version of aspirations in his speech to the graduating class of 1985. "We now strive for reform," said the professional general, in one of his first major speeches since replacing the political general. Pointedly, he stressed "professionalism instead of personalism, self-discipline to the point of self-sacrifice, cost-effectiveness instead of extravagance."

On April 20, General Ramos and a group of some forty reformist officers met for seven hours of dialogue. Several days later the group spent four hours with Enrile. After these talks, the acting chief of staff and the defense minister reported the movement's aspirations and complaints to President Marcos and recommended that he meet with its representatives himself.

Meanwhile, the press debut of a group of spokesmen for the reform movement was subtly choreographed by Enrile. Appearing as a guest speaker at a weekly coffee hour, which was heavily attended by the local and foreign press, he was accompanied by his usual, large security detail. In its ranks were several officers who stayed around after the forum to volunteer information to reporters about the new movement known as We Belong, or Reform the Armed Forces Movement (RAM), which also went by the acronym REFORM (Restore Ethics, Fairmindedness, Order, Righteousness, and Morale).

Although Enrile was quick to disclaim prior knowledge of or involvement in the organization, several of the officers acting as spokesmen for it were men whom I had met in his entourage during the Mindanao inspection tour. When questioned about it, the minister was deliberately low-key, but always positive. "These people are voicing an effort to unify the military organization further, a cohesion rather than fragmentation," he said. "They have a right to voice their opinions. They do not challenge the chain of command. We have to respect their suggestions and observations."

Conceived as a front organization for the secretive Core Group of Fourth Classmen, RAM served as a protective "lightning rod" for the spreading reform movement. While the Core Group plotted an eventual coup against General Ramos, RAM spokesmen spread the more palatable gospel of reform. As the Core Group began its search for sympathetic officers in key units around the country, it found the RAM membership roster a useful recruitment tool.

From its inception Marcos and Ver greeted the reform movement with suspicion and contempt. An assemblyman identified with Mrs. Marcos was the first to criticize RAM publicly, by branding it a CIA tool. "It was only after the Americans urged the military to reform itself that this reformist movement came about," said Rafael ("Raffy") Recto. "Any organization that is secret or underground is scary," he exclaimed. Speaking with greater prescience than we gave him credit for at the time, he questioned, "After they succeed in reforming themselves, will they be content and not try to reform the nonmilitary or civilian sector, which admittedly is perhaps just as corrupt?"

In an effort to dispel the twin notions that it was a subversive organization and a CIA front, RAM began lobbying for a meeting with Marcos. On May 21, a representative group of reformists was called to the palace. As navy Captain Rex Robles recalled, with tongue in cheek, "We were ready in our Sunday best, armed only with a copy of the president's latest book, *The Filipino Ideology*, for autographing." The officers had decided to flatter, rather than petition Marcos, because, explained Robles, "what we wanted was legitimization, not confrontation." They also knew that Ramos and Enrile had explained the aspirations and goals of the movement, and that there was no need for them to repeat all that.

As they were ushered into the presidential study, they were immediately aware of the paranoia which they had fostered. The small room was heavy with Presidential Security Command officers, including the PSC commanding general, and the president's son, Bong Bong, was packing a pistol under his barong.

A forty-five-minute monologue by Marcos ensued. "Our analysis," said Robles, "was that he was preparing for a confrontation, laying the groundwork for a debate." Instead of responding to his veiled challenge, however, the men simply surrendered. "Sir, you are the winner," said Robles, smiling, when Marcos finally stopped talking. Then he held up the book and asked for his autograph. "When he signed the book," said Robles, "the president used the phrase 'our reform movement,' which was important to us, because it meant that our mission to seek legitimacy for the movement had been accomplished."

*   *   *

Marcos was not fooled by the reformists at that point. The tone of his autograph aside, he never ceased referring to them as "my coup plotters." However, by meeting with them, Marcos hoped to win a few points with visiting American emissaries, who were pressing him to make military reforms. Chief among them was Assistant Secretary of Defense Armitage, whose provocative characterization of the Philippine Armed Forces had drawn his ire on the eve of the Agrava Board reports.

The harshness of Armitage's remarks and the correspondingly strong testimony by Wolfowitz before the same Solarz subcommittee in October 1984 had, Armitage acknowledged later, "caused a bit of consternation among our seniors. They knew we were going to be hard on Marcos, but not that hard." In an attempt to understand their thinking, Secretary of State Shultz and Secretary of Defense Weinberger invited their aggressive assistant secretaries to hold forth on America's still-evolving foreign policy in the Philippines at a luncheon meeting with President Reagan in the family dining room. In attendance were Vice-President Bush, CIA Director William Casey, Marcos's premier critic Admiral Crowe, and then Chairman of the Joint Chiefs of Staff General John Vessey.

"It was an extraordinary occasion," said Armitage, during which his seniors began to appreciate "the strategic angle" of the problem the U.S. would face in maintaining its bases there for the long term unless Marcos undertook serious social, political, and military reforms, which would allow him to overcome the threat represented by the insurgents.

"This was a very good think session," recalled Wolfowitz. "It was not intended to produce a policy decision, but to say, more or less, that we don't know what may break at any minute, but if it does, this group of players should have some common understanding of what is going on."

Subsequently, the Pentagon moved to encourage reformist elements in the military. However, care had to be taken not to provoke a backlash from the politicized senior officers so long favored by Marcos. "People Power in the Philippines was only embryonic at that point, and the military was not yet ready to change," said Armitage. "There was no leadership there. We wanted to push Marcos, but not so hard that the institution would blow up."

When Armitage visited the Philippines in January 1985, after Ver had gone on leave and during Marcos's convalescence from his second secret kidney transplant, he reported, "It was clear that Marcos was not moving, but the military was." During his stay there, he said, "officers kept coming up to me privately and telling me how bad things were." He carried with him on that trip a letter from Defense Secretary Weinberger to his counterpart, Minister Enrile, which expressed satisfaction with the recent public comments made by him and General Ramos about the need for reform. But the letter also included a strong statement aimed at President Marcos. "Without demonstrable progress, I am concerned that security relations between our countries may be strained," he said.

At that point, the succession crisis in the Philippines had catapulted the archipelago to the top of the U.S. foreign policymakers' crisis list. The ailing Marcos had become a virtual prisoner inside Malacañang of his wife, her brother, his cronies, and his doctors. Ver, although on leave, was still the man whom his commanders listened to. Ramos, therefore, had been unable to retire or transfer most of Ver's commanders. The democratic opposition remained weak, divided, and without leadership. The Communist insurgency continued to thrive.

Shortly after the Armitage visit, a Pentagon representative inside the U.S. embassy laid out the situation to me in the starkest terms I had yet heard. He said that in the course of his talks with Philippine government officials and opposition leaders, Armitage had called the Philippines "Washington's third-worst foreign policy problem, following the Soviet arms talks and Central America." He had appealed to the regime to take urgent measures to quell the flaring insurgency, which was feeding on the abuses of the Marcos regime and would prove just as destabilizing for a weak successor government.

"I see more scenarios for disorder than for order," said the diplomat. He touched on a number of issues, all inspiring dismal prognostications. He kept coming back to the bases. "You cannot maintain installations of that importance in a hostile environment," he said. "At Subic Bay nearly all the labor is Filipino, and if events deteriorate and you start seeing sabotage there, we would have to think of alternatives." His own preference in such a case would be to "cut our losses and get out." But, "this president," he noted, referring to Reagan, "is not one to run from an old ally." He admitted, "I feel very discouraged. We are clearly witnessing a watershed of Philippine history now."

The brightest prospect, he seemed to be saying, was military reform. There had been no hope for it while Ver was in charge. General Ramos still lacked the authority he needed to do the job. However, he said, wishfully, "If Ramos were given the authority, he could do what Magsaysay did in the nineteen fifties here."

*　　　　*　　　　*

The reform movement might have remained for me something of an abstract concept, ascribed to by an elite group of officers in Manila, and invoked by Pentagon officials, had I not stumbled upon a whole nest of reformists in the northern Mindanao city of Cagayan de Oro a few months later. I had been there for several days, working with photographer Robin Moyer on a story about the government's effort to battle the Communist insurgency.

As I was returning to the hotel one evening after a day of interviews with civilians, Robin was waiting for me with a message from one of these officers, Colonel Regino ("Jun") Calub. He wanted us to meet him at an address that he had scrawled on a piece of paper and handed surreptitiously to Robin. "He seemed insistent," was the way Robin put it. I remembered this particular colonel for his wiry crew cut and for his candid conversation the night before, during a dinner hosted for local journalists by the regional unified commander for the area, General Madriño Muñoz. Toward the end of the meal, Colonel Calub had switched seats with another military officer and sat down beside me. In no time, we were talking about General Ver.

I had become so accustomed to the loyalist military line that I did not expect much in the way of answers to my questions about whether conditions had changed during the ten months that Ver had been on leave. When Calub murmured that he thought Ver was "blackmailing" Marcos, I assumed that I had misunderstood him, and I asked him to repeat what he had just said. "Marcos has allowed himself to be cornered by Ver through his three sons, who are all in the military," he explained. The dinner had ended too soon for me to pursue the subject. I was glad we would have another chance to talk.

Robin and I flagged a tricycle and set out in a torrential downpour for a *pension* on the other side of town. The driver was having a hard time locating the address, and we started wondering just what we were getting ourselves into. For all we knew, this colonel was a Ver man, whom we should hesitate to meet in a dark alley like the ones we were riding through. When we finally arrived, the colonel was waiting downstairs with an umbrella. He led us upstairs into a cozy room, where his wife, Corazon ("Ching"), was waiting with beer, Cokes, and fresh roasted peanuts.

We traded small talk for a while before the colonel got to the point. He knew that I had accompanied Aquino on his last flight and testified before the Agrava Board. He had therefore assumed that I might be a safe person in whom to confide some things that had been on his mind since the assassination. He had also sat in on my interviews with General Muñoz, and he was concerned that, not knowing the general's background, I might give credence to the things he was telling me.

As he began talking, first about discrepancies in the military version of the Aquino assassination, and then about a plot by Ver and Army Commander General Josephus Ramas to crush the reform movement, I began to realize that he was one of the mid-level professional officers whom the reformists close to Enrile had said were seeded throughout the military, and who, at some crisis point, might refuse to obey "illegal orders" coming from Ver.

Calub had been assigned to military headquarters in Manila as chief of the Joint Operation Center at the time of the Aquino assassination. On the morning of August 21, he had called the duty officer of the Intelligence and Special Operations Division to ask what time Aquino's plane was due in. He was startled to learn that the officer did not know either his flight or his arrival time. When Calub insisted that he needed the information in case special forces had to be deployed to prevent trouble, he was even more startled to hear that General Ver and the Intelligence and Special Operations Division were handling everything. "I was surprised that we were cut out of it," he said. "It seemed to be highly compartmentalized."

The shock, which Calub felt on learning that afternoon that Aquino had been killed, turned to suspicion of military involvement when, a few hours later, he received the previous day's copy of the Daily Intelligence Operations Report (DIOR), which stated that Aquino would arrive aboard China Airlines Flight 811 on August 21. Later, when he heard Generals Custodio and Olivas state in public that the military did not know which plane Aquino was on, he knew that a cover-up was under way. When he tried to retrieve that particular DIOR as evidence that the military leadership did know, he could not find it. Not only had the August 21 issue disappeared, he discovered, but the bound volume of copies for the entire month of August 1983 had been removed from the shelf.

Since then, his faith in the top leadership of the AFP had been further shaken by the corruption which he and some of his fellow officers had unearthed within the command in their own headquarters here in Cagayan de Oro. An estimated $200,000 in funds, which had been appropriated to support tactical operations and medical care for soldiers fighting the Communist insurgents, had been siphoned off through the use of forged vouchers and, he suspected, handed over to General Ver to pay for his legal defense.

At that point, Calub admitted to us that he was a member of RAM. There was a large and active RAM group in this region, he said. It met secretly here in this *pension*. I mentioned my trip here with the press covering Minister Enrile's visit the year before. I observed that many of the officers I had gotten to know on that trip had turned out to be RAM members. He chuckled, as if to say there were many more of them than

I could imagine. Since then the movement had come out of the closet in Manila, but he feared that it would not be allowed to survive for long.

As the evening wore on, the colonel touched upon a number of ominous signs that the Ver group was plotting a takeover at the time of Marcos's death. He was concerned that Ver's commanders were trying to crush the reform movement and force the retirement of General Ramos. If Ramos went, army commander General Josephus Ramas would become chief of staff, he feared. He mentioned the suspicious stories that had leaked into the press about the training of a "countercoup" force under General Ramas. "My fear is that there are some people upstairs planning a worst-case scenario in which the transition of power is not going to be smooth," said the colonel. "In that event they would execute a countercoup attack. So as to make it appear that this was being done in reaction to a planned coup, they would arrest General Ramos and some members of the reform movement. That would give their story credibility."

I had heard some of these same scenarios spun by opposition politicians in the coffee shops, but I had not expected to hear them from a military officer. I had heard some of these same charges of corruption from RAM spokesmen in Manila. But they were far more cautious, speaking in almost clinical terms about the need for reform. That night in Cagayan de Oro, I was made privy to the pent-up anger and frustration felt by a professional officer in an increasingly unprofessional army. It was then that I began to contemplate for the first time the possibility of a split in the military so large that it might overwhelm even Marcos.

15

Political Passages

C ory came to Hong Kong the weekend of January 26, 1985, to escape. Accompanied by her children, she checked into the Marco Polo Hotel, leaving instructions that she was not receiving phone calls. She came to escape her growing responsibilities as the de facto spiritual leader of the anti-Marcos movement. She came to escape the petty jealousies of the professional opposition politicians and the ideological debates among the issue-oriented leaders of the grass-roots groups, whom it was her task to unify. She came to recapture the feeling of a long-ago life as a wife and mother, who had made occasional shopping trips to the British colony, ninety minutes by air from Manila, but worlds away, even then. She also came to escape celebrating her fifty-second birthday in Manila.

Birthdays were full, ceremonial occasions in the Philippines. A politician like Ninoy would be expected to hold an all-day, all-night open house for his legions of colleagues, followers, henchmen, friends, relatives, and constituents. In much the way that a state caucus or a party primary in the U.S. indicates the strength of a potential presidential candidate within his own party, the size and prestige of the crowd at a Filipino aspirant's birthday party was a gauge of his financial prowess and the strength of his patronage power.

With Ninoy gone, big birthdays had lost their sparkle. Last year she had been in mourning, so there had been no obligation to celebrate. This year, as a prominent personality in her own right, many of her friends and relatives had offered to give her parties or help her host one of her own. With rumors of her eventual candidacy for the presidency beginning to be bruited about, some had even suggested this would be the right time for a traditional, political coming-out party. But she was not seeking any office, she reiterated, as we met in the hotel lobby, nor was she a traditional politician.

"Ninoy thought it was necessary to meet a new person every day to justify his existence," said Cory. "He and his whole family loved a crowd." Thus, birthdays—those they hosted and the many others they attended as guests in the course of a year—were among the Aquino family's favorite occasions. "My family was different," she went on. "We were very close ourselves, but we were very insular. My father did not look rich, and we did not socialize that much." It had been, she reminisced, "a case of opposites meeting and attracting. But I would not have wanted to be married to anyone else. Life was never boring."

An important decision had to be made about where to eat. I had repeated each time that I had enjoyed the hospitality of Cory and her family in Manila that one day I was going to insist on returning it. While there, I had tried to invite her to lunch at a new restaurant or for afternoon *meriendas* at my hotel. But I understood her aversion to public socializing, and she had reminded me that she intended to boycott the government-owned Manila Hotel, where I generally stayed, until Marcos was out of power. More recently, when she had begun to fantasize about spending a long weekend in Hong Kong, she had promised to accept my open invitation.

So as not to lock her into anything too structured, we had agreed to meet at her hotel at the appointed hour and go somewhere within walking distance. No reservations were to be made, because she could not be sure how many children would go along. While she did her best to play down her importance, and seemed to feel most at ease in casual settings, I had felt a sudden desire, as well as a sense of responsibility, that afternoon to treat her to something special.

Not knowing what would appeal, I had protectively booked tables at the best French and Chinese restaurants along the waterfront. Without telling her about the reservations, I suggested the two possibilities, then deferred to thirteen-year-old Kris, who was with us. "Steak and baked potato," was her unequivocal choice. "She has become such an American," groaned Cory about the tastes her youngest daughter had developed during her formative years in exile in Boston. Fortunately, the best steak place in Hong Kong was only about a ten-minute walk away.

As we stepped out into the sultry night air, Cory was exuberant to be free. She had shopped all afternoon for fabric for the new clothes she needed, now that she was out of mourning and into a steady round of public appearances. Like most Manila matrons, she had her suits and dresses tailored for her by a dressmaker. Imported fabrics were frightfully expensive in financially hard-pressed Manila these days, and there was not much choice, so she was buying in bulk here. Kris made fun of her extravagance, and Cory retorted with a list of the brand-name clothing and accessories for which her style-conscious daughter had begged all day. It was a typical mother-daughter conversation, in which both seemed to revel.

The sidewalks were not crowded in the evening, but we passed about a dozen people en route, several of whom did a double take on seeing the bespectacled woman whose photograph frequently appeared in the international press. I called her attention to them. She had been more interested in the majority, she said, who had not betrayed even a flicker of recognition. That suited her just fine. "Ninoy's face was never as familiar all over the world as mine is now," she mused. "He would have loved this." For an instant the memories seemed to flood back into her mind. "Life is so unfair," she said.

The maître d' recognized her immediately, and showed us to a secluded table. Kris was pleased to note the large salad bar and immediately helped herself. We ordered aperitifs and traded political and personal *tsismis* (gossip in Tagalog), one of the few minor vices in which Cory seemed to indulge. An acknowledged prude about extramarital affairs, excessive drinking, and other human foibles, she nonetheless liked to keep abreast of the latest scandals. I was delighted to be able to offer one or two juicy tidbits, which she appeared not to have heard, but she outdid me by far, displaying a wonderful sense of humor and a relaxed spontaneity, which I had not witnessed before.

Neither of us being frivolous women, however, our talk eventually returned to the only subjects we had ever previously discussed: politics; Ninoy; and, only at my urging, herself. On October 27, 1984, she and two other perceived noncandidates, who were deemed acceptable to all opposition factions, had formed a Convener Group that would attempt to devise a mechanism for selecting a single candidate to run against Marcos or Imelda in a possible sudden "snap election." With her were former Senator Lorenzo ("Tany") Tañada, the eighty-seven-year-old dean of the opposition, who was chosen to represent the cause-oriented groups on the left of the opposition spectrum, and businessman Jaime ("Jimmy") Ongpin, representing the more conservative private sector.

The need for such a group had become more urgent after the suspension of General Ver in October and Marcos's hospitalization in mid-November. Although the president now appeared to be on the mend, both he and his regime were tottering. If he died, or, if he decided to install a successor before then by calling an election and running Imelda as the KBL candidate, the opposition had to be ready.

This was not an interview, so we did not go into campaign strategy and tactics. However, as she described the sorts of discussion that were going on within the Convener Group and the lesser-known circle of "facilitators," whose brainchild it had been, she revealed a greater political sophistication than I had given her credit for. I jotted down some of her most colorful observations after I got home.

In December the Convener Group had signed a "Declaration of Unity" and singled out eleven leaders, whom it considered qualified for eventual leadership, dubbing them "Potential Standard-Bearers" (PSBs). Representatives of the PSBs had met in January to begin designing a "Fast-Track System" of candidate selection. As they girded for possible electoral battle against Marcos, the discussion inside the group had naturally turned to money.

Cory, who had spent much of her time during the first few meetings listening to venerable opposition elders and the new breed of issue-oriented oppositionists expound on what it would take to win, now began to speak up. She had met most of these men through Ninoy. Her role in those days had been to serve them coffee and sandwiches when they came to the house to talk politics with him or, later, to draft his legal defense. She did not have the confidence they all did to discuss with authority subjects which some of them knew little about. But campaign fund-raising was something in which she was well versed, and she realized that what she was hearing from the nonpolitician newcomers was nonsense.

"These candidates today are so naive," said Cory. "They keep asking what we are going to do for money. They ask me who can give us money. I tell them that I won't give them any names, that what you have to do is just go to whomever you think will give and ask them and never tell anyone else who it was." After listening to them for a while, she had tried to conclude the discussion by telling them, "I don't want to know who gave you money, and it's better for you not to know who gave it to me."

So much for the naive housewife image, which many journalists, diplomats, and politicians continued to attribute to her, I thought. She was, after all, the daughter, sister, niece, and wife of politicians in a country where politics had traditionally been a dirty business. She was a crusader and a reformer, but she was also a realist. She grew easily impatient listening to people who seemed not to have answers to simple questions. She liked people who knew their trade and said what they had to say straightforwardly, even if what they said was repugnant to her. She seemed to apply this standard to everyone, from jail wardens to theologians. She took it for granted that the traditional party politicians, whom she knew and understood from past associations, would conform to it, but she seemed not so sure about some of the new breed.

"Some of them had an idea to have a campaign dinner with people paying so much a plate," she exclaimed in a tone of disbelief. "I said, 'Are you kidding? No one could afford to come.' " Friends of the opposition, like most other Filipinos, were still reeling from the effect of last year's peso devaluations and the numerous controls on credit and foreign exchange which had been slapped on the Philippine economy under pressure from the international creditors with whom the government was negotiating the rescheduling of its loans. More to the point, those people who were likely to contribute any meaningful amounts of money to the anti-Marcos opposition were not going to declare themselves publicly by attending a fund-raiser.

"How would the opposition finance a campaign?" I asked, fascinated by her preoccupation with such matters.

"The opposition's money has always come from the Chinese," she explained, "and that's fine, because they always do it quietly and never ask for recognition." She knew whereof she spoke. When Ninoy was preparing to campaign from his detention cell for a seat in the interim National Assembly in 1978, she related, "I would go get the money. It was always in cash, and I had to get it in the middle of the night. Usually they would wrap it in gift paper for me to carry it back." She generally made her midnight rounds accompanied by daughter Ballsy, then twenty-two. After that election was over, the entire opposition ticket having lost in one of the crookedest vote counts in history, Cory said, "I told Ninoy he'd better be free by the next election, because I was not going to do this anymore."

And now here she was, she sighed, back at it. Without directly crediting herself for any of it, she noted that Chinese donors, who always gave to both parties, had contributed 150 million pesos ($10 million) to the KBL and 1.5 million ($100,000) to the opposition during the recent National Assembly campaign. "But that's okay," she said. "The opposition does not need as much, because people know we are poor."

Kris lightened the conversation from time to time with her own considered political observations. Of the five Aquino children, Kris was the one in whom Ninoy's political genes were the most apparent. Her nurturing in and around her father's prison cell had reinforced whatever natural gifts she had inherited. Sensing that her mother was now drifting inexorably into politics, Kris saw no reason why she shouldn't shoot for the top. "I would like Mom to be president, so we could live in Malacañang," she said. Cory reacted in mock horror to her proposal, which she had obviously heard before.

She had a ready answer, which, interestingly enough, did not exclude the presidency, but merely the venue. She would stay in her own house and use the palace only for protocol functions. "That's what Ninoy always said he would do, and that's what I would do," she said. Kris reacted negatively, accusing her mother of being hopelessly old-fashioned. They sparred good-naturedly for a few moments, but Cory concluded the hypothetical discussion on a serious note. "I really think Filipinos are ready for someone who would show restraint," she said.

Over dessert, we slipped back into the past. On our first meeting, I had told Cory how much I wished I could have watched Ninoy in action in front of a crowd. She had laughed and exclaimed that it had indeed been something to behold. She liked to talk about their experiences on the campaign trail before martial law, and she knew I was an avid audience. "During campaigns we always flew from place to place in our light plane," she recalled. "Ninoy was such a male chauvinist that he wanted me to stay in the background and never say anything, to the extent that sometimes I did not even attend functions I was invited to."

One such occasion had been a Rotary Club meeting in the northern Mindanao city of Cagayan de Oro. The invitation had been extended to both husband and wife, and Cory had flown there with Ninoy. On welcoming the Aquinos to town, the club president had remarked that this would be the first time that a guest speaker's wife had ever attended a meeting. On the way to their hotel, Ninoy began to have second thoughts about Cory's presence there. Perhaps their hosts had not really intended for her to come. After checking in, said Cory, "Ninoy decided I had better stay in the room." She agreed. "I had my book, and I told him I would just have dinner with the pilot."

Making herself comfortable, she had curled up to read, when there was a knock on her door. "I thought it was the pilot," she said, "but it was the wives of the Rotarians, come to pick me up." Laughing now at what was clearly then a maddening experience, she recalled that when she arrived, "Ninoy pretended he was expecting me."

As we free-associated about Ninoy, the question of who ordered his assassination was, as always, evoked. I had not broached this subject since the Agrava Board reports had been released and a trial scheduled for General Ver and the twenty-five other accused conspirators. She continued to think that Marcos and Imelda had ordered Ver to arrange it, because Ninoy continued to be such an "irritant" to them. But on this evening, during her brief interlude of freedom in Hong Kong, some of the bitterness seemed to have disappeared, and she spoke of Marcos in a less accusatory manner than she had in the past.

Ninoy had spent most of his political life battling Marcos and had become a better person for it. Now Cory found herself following in his footsteps. In the course of her own voyage of self-discovery this past year, she realized that she had come to regard Marcos as more than just the cause of Ninoy's death. He had become a way of life for her as well. Setting her feelings aside, she offered a startlingly straightforward evaluation of the continuum in which all three of them had existed. "Ninoy would not have been Ninoy without Marcos," she said as we rose to leave.

*   *   *

Several days later in another restaurant, this one in Manila, I was finishing an interview with another person who would figure prominently in the post-Marcos era that everyone sensed was increasingly imminent. In the company of several of his ever-present "boys," Defense Minister Enrile and I had covered a lot of ground, ranging from the still-stalled counterinsurgency program he had urged the president to adopt, to the increasing "American paranoia" about the Communist threat. But we had spent much of the time between the entrée of grilled lapu-lapu and the dessert of mango and banana discussing the growing disunity within the ruling party.

Enrile had made it abundantly clear that the opposition was not the only political force suffering from fratricide. The KBL and the military were rife with dissension as well. His well-publicized confrontation with Imelda Marcos in the first party caucus of the new year, three weeks before, had been just the tip of the iceberg, he indicated. On that occasion, Marcos had asked his defense minister for a report on the insurgency. Enrile had spoken with a sense of urgency about the rapid spread of the NPA, and he had stated that latest military estimates put their number at 8,500 armed men—not as many as the Americans claimed, but twice as many as he had been willing to admit six months earlier, when Ver was still chief of staff and the NPA statistics deliberately underreported.

Enrile recounted, with considerable flair, ". . . and as I spoke, I saw the man in white [Imelda's brother Kokoy] get up and whisper in the First Lady's ear, and then she got up and called what I had been saying 'negative.' She said we should not end the caucus on a negative note, and that having been defense minister for fifteen years, if the insurgency was worse, I was a failure."

Enrile said that as she denounced him, he was trying to decide how to respond. Known to have a quick temper, he was holding himself in check. "At first I thought I would confront her with the facts and tell her they just came from the military and if we cannot believe the military, who can we believe?" Realizing, however, that the new, higher figures of guerrilla strength had come from General Ramos, whom Imelda distrusted as much as she did Enrile, he thought better of that idea. "I did not want to get into a fight, so I simply said, 'Mr. President, I have been very honored to serve as minister of national defense in your cabinet, and I thank you for the honor you have given me and my family. I offer this information because it has been presented to me, and I think you should know it. Sometimes the truth is painful.' "

There was a hush in the room, according to Enrile. "Everyone was amazed and reacting to having witnessed the knife being twisted in like that . . ." Making the diabolical gesture, he pronounced the word with a Castilian lisp: "the coup de grace." President Marcos, trying to change the subject to avoid open war in the caucus, had, said Enrile, begun talking about his hero Napoleon and *l'audace*. Enrile laughed heartily about the scene of disarray he had left behind him as he had departed the ornate palace hall that day.

Turning serious now, he confided that this contretemps had marked a turning point for him. "My loyalty is to the president," he said with the feeling that was always evident when he talked about Marcos. "He is a very remarkable man, whom I respect. I may not approve of everything he has done or that has happened, but I have been with him all these years, and I owe him everything that I and my family are. He brought me into his government and made me known."

However he said, in a stinging reference to Imelda, "My loyalty does not extend to her. I respect her as his wife, but if he is no longer here, I do not owe her my loyalty." I reminded him that he had said in the past that he would consider a run for the presidency if neither Marcos nor the First Lady decided to enter the race. "Yes, but that was politics," he chortled. "It would not be good for me to say publicly that I support him but not her. After all, she is his wife."

Enrile doubted that as long as Marcos were alive, he would call a special election to field Imelda. "Danding told him six months ago that Mrs. Marcos cannot win," he said. "So to go against the constitution and call an early election only to watch his candidate lose—Marcos would never do that." If he did, Enrile implied, the Marcoses might have the defense minister to contend with. He was, he confided, contemplating a run against her as a third-party candidate. It could be done, he said, and he believed he could beat her. "If Mrs. Marcos was running, the opposition would aim its fire at her, so a third-party candidate could run above it all, speaking about the issues. I think the people are ready for that."

There was a chance, he said in response to a question, that Marcos would support Enrile as his successor in a special election "if she was not in the picture." But he gave the impression that he thought the likeliest scenario would be an election called after Marcos's death, in which Imelda would almost certainly run. He would oppose her there. If she ran and managed to win, he said, "that would be the end. That would lead to a coup."

The military reform movement had not yet surfaced in public. But seated at the table with us were at least two of the young officers who would later figure in it. I had met and talked to others during the Mindanao trip. What Enrile said about the behavior of the military was based, to some extent, on the soundings these men had taken among their classmates on that and other recent outings. If the Ver clique of generals tried to install Mrs. Marcos in power, he predicted, "they could not count on more than two battalions to support him. Although people credit all the regional unified commanders to Ver," said Enrile, "they overlook the fact that those generals only give the orders. The soldiers must follow them, and there are plenty of young colonels who would not."

Enrile made an astute guess as to who the opposition candidate would be if an early election were called. "I think they might prevail upon Cory." He indicated that she would be the toughest to beat.

Such scenarios were, however, all hypothetical, he reminded me, because it was impossible to foresee how events would play upon Marcos's judgment. "The real question," he said, with the wisdom of experience and the insight of someone who was actively involved in planning contingencies for the future, "is not who can win the office, but who can run a government afterward, because that is what should concern us."

As the coffee was served, I switched my questioning from the presidency to the Ver trial. We were seated side by side on a banquette, and I was facing him, my back to the entrance to this particular dining room. As he talked, I noticed his eyes shift toward the entrance. He continued to speak, but a look of something akin to terror came over his face. Seconds later I understood why, as the First Lady swept past our table, trailing behind her an entourage of half a dozen people, including Cristina Ford and Filipino couturier Pitoy Moreno. Imelda looked at Enrile with a glare that gave way to a girlish look of vulnerability as he gave her a dazzling smile and his most respectful "Hello, Ma'am."

As soon as she and her party were seated at a large table next to ours, he motioned to his men, got up, gave her a sheepish "Good night, Ma'am," and guided us out of the restaurant. "Did she recognize you?" he asked me, nervously.

"She wasn't looking at anybody but you," I replied. However, Enrile's press secretary Jose ("Joe") Flores was certain she had. He chuckled as he reminded the minister that Mrs. Marcos would remember all the faces of witnesses before the Agrava Board. As we strode across the lobby of the Manila Peninsula Hotel, Enrile recovered his composure and suggested that we finish our conversation in the bar.

After another cup of coffee, we said good-night in the lobby, and Enrile headed back toward the dining room "to talk to her." "He feels guilty," observed one of Enrile's aides, indicating that his boss would not want to leave the impression he had snubbed the First Lady. Although Enrile joked about the encounter later, the message that it left in my mind was that, try as he might, breaking with his past would not be an easy thing for him to do.

The next morning I received an early call from Cory. "I hear you had dinner with Johnny Ponce Enrile," she said, trying to sound accusatory.

I was amazed that the news would travel so fast and in such an interesting direction. Aware of her disapproval of his reputation as a lady's man, I reacted defensively. "For heaven's sake, I was only interviewing him about the NPA," I said. But Cory's interest was broader than that.

"Is it true that he walked out of the restaurant when Imelda walked in?" she wanted to know.

The struggle for succession in the post-Marcos Philippines, to which I had referred so often in stories, was no longer an academic issue. Nor was it the impersonal political phenomenon I had described. It was taking place very close at hand, and it was, like everything else in Philippine politics, a very personal thing.

*   *   *

With the exception of a rare public encounter such as that between Enrile and the First Lady, the battle for succession within the ruling party took place behind the closed doors of palace caucuses, on the golf courses where ministers and cronies played, and in the mind of Ferdinand Marcos. From the moment Marcos went into seclusion in November 1984, preparatory to undergoing his second kidney transplant, until a special election took place on February 7, 1986, rumors that a so-called "snap election" either would or would not take place were constantly floated by members of his staff through the controlled crony press and the foreign media.

Marcos had used this technique successfully in 1971 and 1972 to lull his political opponents into a false sense of complacency about the imminence of martial law. Now he was using it to force today's opposition leaders to reveal in advance how united they could be and behind which candidate. Based on that evidence, he would decide how or whether to move.

The opposition's winnowing process, by contrast, was less tidy and more open. Fifteen political parties and as many as seventy of the so-called "cause-oriented" or non-party groups demanded a say in the selection of a common candidate. Almost weekly a new committee was established to study or arbitrate some element of the procedure that was slowly evolving by which the candidate would be chosen.

No matter how much progress might be made toward approving one set of procedures or another, however, two seemingly insoluble problems always loomed: how to unite the two main strands of the democratic opposition—the traditional political parties and the newer, more left-leaning cause-oriented groups—and how to overcome the fact that the front-running candidate, Doy Laurel, who controlled the party machinery that was essential to an opposition electoral victory, was unacceptable to important segments of the anti-Marcos forces.

Making the most determined effort to address these twin problems was a group of Jesuit-trained business and management people, working behind the scenes through contacts in both camps. The individuals involved liked to refer to themselves as "facilitators." Outsiders preferred the sobriquet "the Jesuit mafia." They came to light with the formation of their brainchild, the Convener Group, in November 1984. Their role in building the coalition that eventually brought Cory Aquino to power was a critical one.

The precursor to the Convener Group was an informal weekly gathering of like-minded friends, who had been jolted by the Aquino assassination and the resulting deterioration of the economy into putting their expertise in a number of professional areas at the disposal of the burgeoning anti-Marcos movement. Charter members of the so-called "Wednesday Group" were businessmen Jimmy Ongpin, Alfredo ("Alran") Bengzon, Ramon ("Mon") del Rosario, Emanuel ("Noel") Soriano, and educator Father Joaquin Bernas, president of the prestigious Ateneo de Manila.

"Noel Soriano was the thinker," said Narcisa ("Ching") Escaler, a frequenter of the Wednesday Group, who went on to become secretary to the Convener Group and later, appointments secretary to President Aquino. "He was asking the questions: 'What do we do if Ver is acquitted? What if he is not? How do we influence the public outrage?' " The group's bottom line, according to Escaler, was, "Whatever the answer, there has to be some science in it; homework must be done; plans are needed." When they began, there was little perceived need for their background papers. By the time snap elections were called, however, the demand for their services had soared, and with it their influence within the opposition.

In late October 1984, the biggest issue confronting the divided opposition was unity. People in both major camps were looking for some mechanism by which they could form at least a tactical alliance. Thus was born the idea of a group that could bring them together. In an initial "Concept Paper on a Sudden Presidential Election," the facilitators wrote that the possibility of a sudden, special election was "a matter of great concern, because various opposition groups are not addressing the new reality in the Philippine political situation: that there are very significant aggrupations [non-party groups] other than the political parties, which can have and which intend to have a significant influence in political developments in the Philippines."

The paper was a bid by the Jesuit mafia to include the issue-oriented, non-party groups, to which it was sympathetic, in the candidate selection process. Not incidentally their inclusion would dilute support for Laurel as the common candidate of the opposition.

The paper stated several key assumptions. First and foremost was that if a way could be found to minimize cheating on the part of Marcos, "it is better to participate rather than boycott the next presidential election." This marked a change in the thinking of issue-oriented activists, who had boycotted the 1984 National Assembly elections. The facilitators' paper continued: "Another KBL victory will be disastrous. It will just consolidate the power of the regime. If Marcos suddenly goes, there will be no need to resort to a coup, because the way the opposition is disunited, it will be easy for the KBL to win a sudden presidential election."

The Convener Group instantly attracted criticism. At its first meeting, two of the eleven proposed "Potential Standard-Bearers"—party leaders Salvador Laurel and former Senator Eva Kalaw—refused to sign the eight-point Declaration of Unity. Without them, the group became heavily weighted against the party politicians and toward the grass-roots activists. Kalaw had called the system outlined by the Convener Group for selecting a single opposition candidate "highly undemocratic." Laurel had objected to the provision in the declaration on the U.S. bases, which read: "Foreign military bases on Philippine territory must be removed, and no foreign military bases shall hereafter be allowed." His preference for dealing with the sensitive issue of the future of the bases was to put the issue to a plebiscite before the existing agreement expired in 1991.

The Convener Group had already modified the original bases provision in the declaration by eliminating from the original text of the clause the word "immediately," regarding the timetable for the dismantling of the bases. This had satisfied the other facilitators and PSBs, who supported the removal of the bases with varying degrees of zeal. I was never able to ascertain Cory's true feelings on the issue, although her acknowledged reaction to early probing by American officials had left me with the impression that she could agree to a conditional renewal of the bases agreement.

New to the game of international diplomacy, she and other oppositionists had taken offense at the manner in which visiting New York Republican Congressman Gerald Solomon had "asked us point-blank at a meeting: 'Anybody for the retention of the bases?' " Assemblyman Aquilino ("Nene") Pimentel had expressed her sentiments when he responded brusquely, "I am a politician. If you think I am stupid enough to say it right out . . ." Cory had been impressed at the way Solomon's Democratic counterpart, Stephen Solarz, had addressed them on the same issue, making clear the American position, but not subjecting them to a loyalty oath. Afterward Cory said she told Solarz, "I hope you understand the Filipino people and can leave it unsaid."

The next hurdle for the Conveners was their attempt to work out a delegate selection system for an opposition-wide nominating convention. Their proposal for a quota system that would give the non-party groups 30 percent of the nominating convention delegates provoked an uproar among the elected opposition members of the National Assembly, who had not been consulted. Cory was dispatched to pacify them and to persuade the leaders of the cause-oriented groups to participate, rather than boycott, the next election.

Her success in carrying out those twin missions enhanced her reputation as a unifying influence and a peacemaker. They also made her aware of the deep distrust which the two poles of the opposition felt toward each other. "The trouble with the Convener Group," she complained, referring to its strong non-party bias, "is that they know nothing about politics." Yet come an election, she warned them, "We need the politicians to do the campaigning for us. We cannot do it alone." She grew frustrated at the way "one group thinks it is so much more important than the other, when all are important."

As Marcos's health appeared to improve, and he grew feisty again, vowing to reinstate General Ver as chief of staff if and when he was acquitted, the urgency of selecting a common candidate lessened. Cory wanted to use the breathing spell to try to bring the two warring camps of the opposition together for direct talks, but she was vetoed by her male peers. Next she wanted to go to the March 10 convention of the National Unification Committee, which was meeting to agree on an alternate set of principles and a delegate selection system to be used by UNIDO and other parties. Again, her attendance at a function that was perceived to benefit the selection of Doy Laurel as a presidential candidate was vetoed.

Both times she had quietly accepted the decision of her peers. But she was determined not to tolerate it a third time. After that, according to Jimmy Ongpin, "Things changed very significantly within the Convener Group, because for the first time there was real disagreement." It sprang, he said, from pressure put on Cory by Laurel to attend the UNIDO convention in June that would nominate him as its candidate for the presidency. "She was very much inclined to go," recalled Ongpin, but by now relations between Laurel and the rest of the Convener Group had badly deteriorated, and they could see no benefit coming from Cory's lending of her name and prestige to UNIDO.

"That was the turning point," said Ongpin. "That was the first time I saw her driven to tears. She tried to control herself. She later said she was furious at herself for crying. But subsequent to that, she changed completely. She laid down the ground rules for the rest of us. She said, 'I let you have your way, but if you want me to be part of this exercise, I am going to do what my judgment tells me to do. I will not proceed against my judgment.'

"From then on people began to look up to her for leadership," said Ongpin approvingly. "Before that she had deferred to Tañada. She had been too coy, and her judgment had been trampled on. From then on she began to say exactly what she thought."

After her outburst, Cory not only accepted Laurel's invitation, but she began discussions with the chairman of the rival unification group, the National Unification Committee, Cecilia Muñoz Palma, a retired court justice and National Assembly member. The two women got on famously. With the help of a third—Judy Araneta Roxas, daughter of one of the country's leading families and widow of Liberal party president Gerry Roxas—they came up with the makings of a candidate selection formula designed to accommodate both traditional parties and cause-oriented groups.

By July 12, when Cory put in an appearance at the UNIDO convention that nominated Laurel, seven months had passed since Marcos's illness had plunged them into the fractious process of unification. They had not yet achieved it. UNIDO was the only party to have nominated a candidate, and other oppositionists were determined to oppose him. "These people are more anti-Laurel than they are anti-Marcos," she had said, with more than a slight bit of disgust at all the bickering.

Cory, more than most, was hoping that Marcos would give them a bit longer to put their house in order. If he did not die or call a snap presidential election until after the scheduled local elections in 1986, she reasoned, "it will be better for me, because then the potential leaders will emerge." What she meant was that one of the politicians who so badly wanted to become president would somehow capture the hearts of the people the way Ninoy's widow already had.

*   *   *

As Doy Laurel addressed the 10,000 UNIDO delegates and supporters who had come to Manila from all over the archipelago to nominate him for president, he looked back. "Exactly five years ago, we walked seventeen kilometers in Cebu to hold the first freedom rally under martial rule," he said. Implicit in that slice of history was the message that while other oppositionists had been in exile or committed to boycotting Marcos elections, he and his family had been waging a hard-fought campaign to put slates of non-KBL candidates in local offices.

More than any of the other things for which his fellow oppositionists resented him—his shifting loyalties, his transparent ambition, his playboy image, his perceived closeness to Washington—it was Laurel's willingness to play by Marcos's rules for so long that made them distrust him. In contrast to most of his rivals in the democratic opposition, Laurel had survived the martial law period without having caught any shrapnel in his body, without having spent any time behind bars, without having suffered serious financial reverses.

In their eyes he and his family were simply too close to Marcos. The dates he cited to signify his break with the president, the explanations he supplied for why he participated in two elections under the dictatorship before he finally joined the boycotters in 1981 did not alter their thinking. The president who succeeded Marcos, they insisted, had to have demonstrably shared the nation's pain, or all that had happened during that decade would signify nothing.

This political fact of life was especially painful for the Aquino family, because their friendship with the Laurels was an old and strong one, tested in politics and in war during two generations. Ninoy and Doy had remained friends, despite their rival party affiliations and contrasting martial law situations. They were preparing to mount a united opposition challenge to Marcos in the 1984 legislative elections, when Ninoy returned to the Philippines. It was Doy who, with Aquino family members, had organized Ninoy's homecoming celebration on August 21, 1983.

After the assassination, Doy had proceeded with the campaign, as he and Ninoy had planned it, refusing to be deterred by the barbs of the boycotters or the pessimism of many of his own followers. When the opposition wound up winning one third of the seats, his effort—and his claims to be a true oppositionist—seemed finally to have been vindicated. But once he set his sights on the presidency anew, his past came back to haunt him.

Calculating that the strength of UNIDO and its claim to accreditation as dominant opposition party would insure his nomination, even in the face of his detractors within the protest movement and rival parties, he plowed ahead, organizing in the provinces and lobbying for a National Unification Committee, which would be favorable to him, to supersede the pesky Convener Group.

However, he underestimated the groundswell of support that would build for the widow of his childhood friend, or, more surprising to him, failed to realize that she would ever accept to ride it. Although his relations with Cory continued to be outwardly friendly, I was startled during an interview in September 1985 to realize the depth of his resentment over Cory's failure to state her true intentions about whether or not she would accept the draft that had been organized in her behalf.

Over cups of the robust coffee grown in his native Batangas province, Doy talked about the imminent possibility of Marcos calling a snap election, and he outlined his prognostications, which were eerily similar to what eventually transpired in February 1986. He made a strong case that opposition unity could be achieved in the selection of a candidate. When, however, I posed the inevitable "What about Cory?" question, he asked to go off the record.

Speaking calmly and articulately, expert debater that he was, he could not hide his exasperation and, deeper than that, his disappointment at her coyness about her possible candidacy. "Assume they want Cory and not Laurel," he said. "She cannot just be a candidate unless she is nominated. To be a candidate, you must go through a convention as I did. I am bound by that. I cannot turn around and give it away like a piece of cake."

Continuing, he confided that before he had agreed to accept the draft of his party, he had consulted Cory about her own plans. "I don't want us colliding," he told her. "If the situation were reversed and I was the one who was killed, and if Ninoy was alive and Celia in your position, I am sure that Ninoy would have done what I am doing and come to consult you." According to Doy, her answer was "definitely a thousand percent no, negative, I am not interested, I like my privacy." He added, "I talked to her not once but three times. I had no reason to doubt her sincerity and that she was not interested and would campaign for me all over the country, so because of that, I went ahead and was nominated, based on the formula which she and Cecilia Muñoz Palma helped put together. The whole Aquino family was there, so they cannot say they did not know about it."

If, after all that, "she decides to change her mind and run," said Doy, "she should see me and tell me she has changed her mind, and we can talk about it." But, he said, "I cannot simply give her the nomination that was given to me." With a hard edge to his voice, he added, "And she will need the nomination of UNIDO."

Having talked to him at other difficult points in his battle to gain recognition as an opposition standard-bearer, I could feel the pain of someone who had come so far and suddenly perceived an unexpected obstacle in his path. "I am the most organized, I have done my homework. I have worked on this since 1980, and that is why I am ahead," he explained. "I have kept on working despite all of these things that are being said that I am the fly in the ointment. I am not stopping. I will not stop, even for this 'unite-behind-Cory movement.' "

It was not just Laurel who would have to change course, if Cory were to receive the nomination, he repeated. His supporters would have to go along. "I anticipate a great many people being so disgusted about this. Some of them don't know Cory. Some have risked their lives over the past five years, and they have sacrificed their funds. Loyalty cannot just be transferred."

What seemed to hurt most was the fact that so many people were talking behind his back, rather than leveling with him. He mentioned how

upset his friend Eva Kalaw had been when, during the rally commemo-
rating Ninoy's assassination the month before, Cory for President banners
had been hoisted in the crowd. "She felt it was improper, and she whispered
to me, 'Hurry up and speak so we can get out of here.' " He had tried to
be philosophical about it. "I've been subjected to worse things," he said.
"What bothers me the most is the moral aspect. A certain trust was imposed
on her to help choose the candidate. How will she explain how she became
the chosen one?"

*   *   *

On August 18 and 19, 1985, Admiral Crowe paid a farewell visit to
the Philippines as commander-in-chief of the Pacific fleet. As always, he
had requested a meeting with President Marcos. He had been prepped to
deliver some tough talk to Marcos about continued problems within his
armed forces. General Ver was still on leave, but that had not stopped
Ver and Marcos from trying to sabotage the reforms that acting chief of
staff General Ramos was attempting to make.

"The idea was for me to see Marcos and carry some messages to him,"
Crowe later explained, "but he outmaneuvered me." Instead of arranging
a private meeting between the two of them, Marcos had invited the admiral
and his wife to breakfast in the family quarters at Malacañang with Mrs.
Marcos and Defense Minister Enrile. "It was not appropriate for me to
talk business with him except one on one," said Crowe.

If the meeting was thus short on substance, it was nonetheless memorable. Crowe recalled with amusement how he had sat facing a large oil
painting of an idealized Marcos emerging Moses-like from a clump of
bulrushes. Mrs. Marcos had done most of the talking, he noted, "about
how dirty politics was, how little she knew about it, and how tough it was
for her as a housewife to deal with it." Enrile, on the other hand, "did
not say a thing," according to the admiral. "My wife certainly enjoyed
that breakfast," chortled Crowe.

There being no time during his short visit to see Marcos privately,
Crowe subsequently wrote the president what he described as "a very rough
and candid letter, telling him the things he should change." As Crowe
put it, "The thrust of the letter was 'you stop running the military.' "
Shortly after his return to Washington, Crowe was named chairman of
the Joint Chiefs of Staff.

16

Snap!

I t was the end of the long All Souls' Day weekend. After visiting the graves of their departed relatives, millions of Filipinos had returned home on Sunday night, November 3, 1985, and tuned in to an important, nationally televised, professional basketball game. At eight o'clock a bulletin flashed across the screen alerting sports fans to "watch for an important announcement" from Malacañang at 11:50 P.M.

Inside the palace, President Marcos was preparing for a live appearance, via satellite, on the American Sunday morning news program "This Week with David Brinkley." His media advisors had already alerted progovernment newspaper editors to hold open their front pages for a late-breaking announcement. At about 9:30 P.M. Manila time, Marcos received the phone call he had been expecting from Senator Paul Laxalt, who had paid him a visit in October as President Reagan's personal emissary. Laxalt was slated to appear with him, from Washington, on the Brinkley show.

Laxalt, whose October mission had been designed to convey White House concern about the crisis of confidence in the Marcos government, had "briefly discussed the idea of a snap presidential election" with the president while in Manila, as had CIA Director William Casey before him. However, he had concluded that the president "didn't entertain it

290

very seriously" at the time. Later, in phone conversations following Laxalt's return to the U.S., Marcos had reconsidered the possibility of an early election as a means of demonstrating the continued support of the Filipino people for his programs. Laxalt suggested supportively, "It would be very dramatic for you to make that announcement on the Brinkley show. That would be very effective for American consumption."

At around midnight the Filipino TV audience heard American columnist George Will broach the prearranged question about Marcos's declining credibility. "Some people here wonder if it would not be possible for you to call an early election to set a new mandate," Will suggested. Now Marcos adjusted his earphone, eyed his questioners on the TV screen before him, and stated, "I understand the opposition has been asking for an election. In answer to their request, I announce that I am ready to call a snap election." Responding to the excited barrage of questions that followed, Marcos elaborated, "If all these childish claims to popularity on both sides have to be settled, I think we had better settle it by calling an election right now." He proposed a sixty-day campaign, proclaiming, "I'm ready, I'm ready!"

Knowing that they had a breaking news story on their hands, the Washington correspondents moved in on the wily president to be sure he was not bluffing. Pressed about how he would get around a constitutional provision that appeared to call for the death or resignation of the sitting president before a new election could be called, Marcos indicated he could pass a bill in the National Assembly. "We control two thirds of the National Assembly," he reminded them. Questioned about whether he would permit outside observers to monitor the election to prevent fraud during the vote tabulation, Marcos impulsively agreed. "You are all invited to come," he told his audience.

After the program ended and the satellite link was cut, the president fielded more questions from a breathless palace press corps. What they saw and heard was a cocky Marcos, who proposed January 17—the anniversary of the lifting of martial law—as Snap Election Day, and who jokingly offered to help Cory Aquino gather the remainder of the 1 million signatures, which her supporters were seeking in order to draft her as the anti-Marcos candidate. He dismissed the notion of opening the election to vice-presidential candidates as well, reasoning, "The issue is Marcos." Not able to resist another jab at his opponents, he threw a snide parting shot. "I hope they are unified, so they have no excuse to lose the election."

*　　　*　　　*

Marcos had finally snapped under the ever-mounting pressure exerted on him by the Philippine opposition, the American government, and the international lending institutions. That was the only way many of his allies and supporters could explain his erratic behavior in recent months. "I've never seen the president panicked until now," reported a southern politician, following one pathological performance by Marcos during a hastily convened, late-night party caucus. For more than five hours, he had lectured his political lieutenants on the need for snap elections to counter opposition plots to impeach and even assassinate him. After the caucus was over, he had decided against advancing the elections. Now, only a few months later, desperate for funds that were being withheld pending reforms, and searching for a way to disarm his critics, he had reversed himself once again.

Imelda, never very stable, even in the best of times, had been in the Soviet Union when he made his announcement. Sensing, perhaps more acutely than he, the perilous situation into which his snap election gambit had thrust them, she reacted, on her return, like a threatened predator, lunging for the throat of the enemy she held responsible for this and other misfortunes. "Stupid America!" she ranted, as she emerged from a KBL caucus.

Most of the reporters in the palace that day belonged to the Malacañang press corps, which was free to witness, but not to write about, the indiscretions of the First Lady. TIME's Manila stringer, Nelly Sindayen, who was under no such obligation, recorded her catty, anti-American monologue, caustic excerpts of which were subsequently printed in TIME. "I cannot understand why America is pressing the Philippines so hard, while the Soviets don't," said Imelda for starters.

She had several theories to explain U.S. actions. "I was told there are actually four presidents in the U.S.," she said, knowingly. "One sits in the White House, another at the Senate, another at the House, and another in the media." Or perhaps it was pure sexism. "America cannot accept a woman's superiority," she said, "especially tall and beautiful Filipino women, who are smartly dressed like this." She added, "They go even crazier if you are wearing high heels and looking very smart. Just because you are a woman, they think you are frivolous. Just because you can sing a little, you are not to be taken seriously."

Imelda had always served as a lightning rod for Marcos. But at this particularly sensitive juncture in his relationship with the U.S., some of his advisors felt that neither of them could afford another storm, and they urged her to write a letter to the editor of TIME magazine to reassure American readers that the First Lady really loved America and Americans. She refused. She had meant what she said, she told them. In the end, the minister of information wrote the letter, and the Washington public relations firm, which the Marcoses had hired for a reported $950,000 to improve their image in the U.S., invited me to interview her in order to hear her true feelings.

The appointment was set for seven o'clock in the evening in one of the palace guest houses. I was picked up at the Manila Hotel by Mrs. Marcos's congenial nephew Babes Romualdez, in a small sports car, and shown upstairs to an empty table large enough to seat thirty people for dinner. The First Lady's assistant Ileana Maramag and a representative of the Washington public relations firm of Black, Manafort, Stone & Kelly greeted me. Shortly afterward, Mrs. Marcos made her entrance, accompanied by two security guards. She looked stunning, as usual, and she was as gracious and charming as one could imagine a First Lady to be. But there was no doubt that she was agitated.

With an air of vulnerability, which her critics claim is contrived, she began talking about how "completely misunderstood" she was. She spoke slowly, even demurely at first. But five minutes into her monologue, her voice took on a tone of desperation, and her mind began churning out half-formed thoughts at such speed that her concern for "poor Aquino" collided with her theories about the Communist insurgents and blew apart whatever it was she was trying to say about the "estrangement" between the U.S. and the Philippines.

She became clearer when she went into what journalists who had spent a lot of time with her humorously called "overdrive." Then, as if her mind had reached cruising altitude, she simply turned it off and coasted along, spilling out past legends that she knew by rote and spewing statistics that quantified her husband's achievements: "Fifteen thousand elected officials when he came to office, two hundred and fifty thousand elected officials now sharing power with him." While my mind tried to comprehend her point—that there was fifteen times as much democracy today as when Marcos took over—hers raced ahead. "Seventy-three governors, two hundred members of Parliament, sixteen hundred mayors, forty-two thousand *barangays*, each with seventeen brigades to deal with politics and disasters," she stated.

As the numbers mounted, even she needed to do some quick calculating. She crossed the room to a large classroom-style blackboard on wheels and hauled it over to the table. Mrs. Maramag, who appeared to have sat through this lecture countless times before, and who apparently knew better than either to try to stop her or to try to help, turned to me and explained gently, the way one would about someone with an impediment, "She was once a kindergarten teacher."

Interestingly, Imelda had not lost her train of thought while moving the blackboard. "Forty-two thousand *barangays* times seventeen brigades equals nine hundred thousand *barangay* brigades [her math was off], or twenty-seven million *barangay* brigade members to take care of fifty-four million Filipinos," she said proudly. My tape and her spiel ran out at about the same time. I inserted a new cassette into my recorder and tried to begin the interview. The questions were primarily political. The answers were invariably personal.

One of the purposes of this meeting was to give her a chance to clarify her thoughts about U.S.–Philippine relations. Although her initial sentiments were temperate, she could not hide her true emotions for long. "Stop beating up your friends," she pleaded. "You have very few allies left. You need friends, and we need each other badly."

Mischievously, she added a postscript about future bilateral relations. "The Filipino people are very generous, and they give a very warm welcome, especially to Americans, going all the way back to Magellan." Not sure whether I knew any Filipino history, she explained how when the Spanish explorer Ferdinand Magellan had landed in the Philippines, the famous tribal chief Lapu-Lapu had welcomed him warmly and generously feted him with wives and gifts. "It was only when he started intervening in tribal affairs that Magellan was killed," she said, laughing wickedly at her punch line.

High on her list of things she resented about the U.S. was its media, which portrayed her as a woman of extravagant tastes. "I'm so terrorized now that I don't shop in the U.S.," she claimed. "They said I had Bloomingdale's closed for my private shopping. The last time I was there was when we had promotions for Philippine products. Then they said I went to an antique shop and bought two and a half million dollars in knick-knacks. I did not even buy a toothpick."

A goodly portion of the retainer which Black, Manafort, Stone & Kelly was reportedly being paid for its services was no doubt spent by Marcos to try and shut Imelda up. Every time I tried to steer the conversation to the snap election campaign, she would giggle, turn to her public relations advisors, then make a motion as if to lock her lips. "We don't talk about the opposition in our campaign," she twittered. "When you are selling Pepsi, you don't talk about the others."

I allowed as how I could not very well publish an interview in which the First Lady did not even mention her husband's opponent. Again, she looked at her PR man, laughed, and said, "No comment." It was clear that she was bursting to say something malicious about Cory Aquino, but she stifled it. Describing how hard it was for her to keep her silence, she added, with a comic gasp, "There is little oxygen up here on the mountaintop." She was trying, she said, to learn to act as diplomats do: "No talk, no mistake."

As another tape ran out, I noted that we were into our second hour. It was now nine o'clock. I had not planned to be here this long. I had miscalculated, forgetting that hers was not a linear mind, and that it took a long time and many digressions to get answers to questions. I could not leave without a quote about Cory, although something told me that I would have to grovel for it. On the other hand, I had not eaten since lunchtime, and I was hungry. It was unusual for a Filipino to have talked this long without refueling. It was almost unheard of not to have offered a guest something to eat or drink. I had heard that Imelda, an insomniac, gained steam as the night wore on. The thought of hours more of this exercise left me weak. The strain must also have gotten to the PR man, who finally got up from the empty table to stretch and go to the bathroom.

As soon as he left the room, Imelda began talking about Cory. Taking advantage of his absence, I questioned her further. Did she not believe that Mrs. Aquino's emotional appeal would be hard to beat? "We have had three years of crying," she said [again, her math was wrong]. "Before we know it, the crying might shift to other issues. People are economically in need, they are getting hungrier. They are terrified by the insurgency. How much more do we have to cry until the Republic of the Philippines is gone?"

With a new burst of energy, she poured out her grievances against the opposition.

> Since Aquino died, General Ver, the poor man, has been so maligned. He was our number one Communist fighter. Unfortunately, it is the people who have gotten even with him. It was not even the Communists. This man has been crucified, went through Calvary and all of that. Did the government benefit by this? What is the result after three years? It succeeded in estranging us from America. We suffered an economic drought from four hundred and eighty-three banks for over three years, which has deprived us of funds, and an agricultural drought, which has robbed us of our agricultural products. We have had natural calamities. Even Marcos got sick. You name it and we have had it. Then our sugar, which is a political product, sank in price. Then they ask, "Why are you poor?" And they answer, "Because Marcos is corrupt and Mrs. Marcos has hidden wealth."

As her adrenalin rose, she returned to her blackboard and began scribbling lines of latitude and longitude. Her subject was the Marcoses' obligation to the free world, given the Philippines' strategic location. She dropped the first of many names. "Chairman Mao always said to me, 'You can change your ideology, but you cannot change your geography.'" Scrawling a mass of land representing the west coast of America, another to designate China, she asked, "Who is the center?" Her answer: "The

Republic of the Philippines." North of it were the rich nations, south of it the poor. In the vast Pacific spaces all around it were pockets of history and conflict.

Marking a dot here, an asterisk there, she filled in the spaces as she spoke. The click of her chalk on the board accompanied her stream of consciousness narrative: "Three hundred years of the Manila-Acapulco trade. . . . China with very shallow waters, so the transshipments were done in the Philippines. . . . when I go to China or Russia, it is to bring goodwill. We cannot fight them, so we befriend them." When one disjointed narrative was through, she reached for an eraser, wiped it away, and replaced it with another. "President Nixon asked me for a copy of this geopolitical map," she interjected at one point, as she erased a highly complex tangle of lines and shapes from the board.

I was feeling faint. My fingers were cramped from writing, I was running out of cassettes and pages. Yet she seemed to be gaining energy. "My advantage is my velocity," she remarked, stating the obvious. "I am not powerful, but I have boundless energy. I don't sleep too much—two or three hours a night. I don't eat."

I tried to hide my disappointment at that last remark, as she sped on. "It is an attitude that has helped me in my thirty-one years of public life. I always accentuate the positive. President Reagan was always my choice, eleven years before. He is so positive. That's my kind of guy. He's exactly like me. We accentuate the positive. I do so many things that I should look like a real old hag."

My head began to pound. Will this never stop? I wondered. I had tried to be polite and take her seriously. So had my colleagues at one time or another. Maybe that was one of the problems we all had in portraying her. Maybe we took her too seriously. People said awful things about her, but they were describing a rational woman, full of malice aforethought. The woman I was listening to could not be judged by normal standards. She was manic. Mad, perhaps. Touches of brilliance and insight here and there, but how was one to judge them in this tidal wave, this glut of diagrams, equations, and pop geostrategy?

Worn down by the fatigue of trying to follow her line of thought, if you could call it that, I dropped the veil of objectivity and professionalism I had been trying so hard to hold in place. I began to laugh and talk back to her. As she drew yet another diagram, I allowed as how I should have brought a video recorder rather than a tape recorder. She giggled. Mrs. Maramag laughed. The public relations man, who had returned to his place at the table, did not seem to see the humor. The board was again full of ideograms and equations. Trying to decipher it, I wisecracked: "Have you thought of advising the IMF?" The minute the words left my mouth, I knew I had made a mistake, because undoubtedly she had, and now she was going to tell me about it. She erased the board to clear space for new thoughts.

"My economic theory," she said, drawing as she lectured, "is that money was made round to go round [many circles]. Money was made to encircle man so that he would blossom with many flowers [a big circle drawn around the little circles with petals radiating outward]. The whole trouble is, the center is money [a black spot in the middle of all the circles]. All the heads of people thinking about money [more circles within circles]. All the hands of people reaching out for money [tentacles affixed to the circles]. All their poor little bodies working for money [stick figures at the end of the tentacles]. They are running in all directions for money."

After working feverishly to add diagonal lines, signifying motion, to each stick figure, she suddenly focused on the Rorschach she had created. Her mind returned to the image on the board, as opposed to the concept so recently in her head. She appeared confused as to which of the two realities she should react to. Then a switch seemed to go on in her head, and she zeroed in on the drawing. "It looks like . . . ," she said, haltingly, as if it were a totally alien form, rather than something she had just drawn herself. "It looks like . . . ," she stared at it again, still confused. Suddenly, there was a flash of recognition. "It looks like . . . a porcupine!" she exclaimed, with childish astonishment.

I let out a wild hoot. Then I convulsed in laughter. I didn't have the slightest idea what in the world she was talking about, yet I had been writing it all down, assuming that her tangled narrative would eventually lead to a point. "Porcupine" was not what I had expected. I didn't know which of us was more the fool. She looked dazed as she stood there watching me laugh, but seconds later she too whooped loudly at her own expense. At 10 P.M. a light and elegant supper was served. Imelda wheeled her blackboard back against the wall, and I put away my notebook, which was full of words but not of content. My interview with her was never published.

*   *   *

A snap presidential election was not something which the principal U.S. policymakers had called for. Nor did they welcome it when it was announced. They had been pressuring Marcos to make fundamental economic, political, and military reforms, among them election reforms that would keep the 1986 local and 1987 presidential elections clean. Their prognosis was that by 1987 Marcos would be either too sick or too politically weak to run again. On the other hand, a snap election, called at this point, when his popularity was still relatively high, and the opposition divided, would work to his advantage. He had the political machinery, he had the military, he could print the money.

What Marcos had done, with the unwitting encouragement of Senator Laxalt, was, quite simply, to call Washington's bluff. The professional diplomats and policymakers were quietly scornful of Laxalt for having encouraged Marcos to consider a snap election as an acceptable solution to the problems that plagued his relations with the U.S. The way they saw it, Laxalt, a foreign policy lightweight with presidential ambitions, had gotten in over his head.

"Laxalt did not even know what country he was in," huffed one irate diplomat. Laxalt, he charged, was taken in by Marcos, who blamed his bad reviews on his critics in Congress. "Ferdie bamboozled him," said this official. "Laxalt did not tell him to have an election; he just told him it was a good idea. Ferdie heard what he wanted to hear from Laxalt, which was, 'My president is concerned about you, but you are still our man.' "

Once presented with Marcos's fait accompli, U.S. officials had had to ask themselves some difficult questions. Would they simply stand aside and let Marcos engineer himself another six-year term? Or would they continue to lobby for free and fair elections? In that case, what would they do when the inevitable occurred and the elections were tainted with fraud? No one better understood the Americans' dilemma than the moderate Filipino opposition leaders, who had loudly advocated snap elections, but who knew they could not hope to win them without outside help.

Cory's campaign manager, Peping Cojuangco, posed the question most dramatically to me during an interview ten days after Marcos's announcement, and nearly a month before his sister became a candidate. "What will the Americans do?" he asked. Then he proceeded to speculate, in chillingly specific terms, almost the precise scenario of events that later came to pass. "Say the actual vote is sixty percent for Cory to forty percent for Marcos," said Peping, "but Marcos manipulates it, so that by the time it gets to COMELEC, it is almost fifty-fifty. If Cory only has a five-hundred-thousand-vote margin, the COMELEC will further manipulate it, and the National Assembly will refuse to declare Cory the winner. Then Marcos will say, 'I am still president. I won't resign.' " That, stated Peping in the baldest possible terms, "is the powder keg."

Peping stressed that in the 1978 legislative election, when Marcos had cheated Ninoy out of his Assembly seat, he and other Aquino campaign leaders had worked hard to defuse the angry protest demonstrations of his supporters, who had massed around COMELEC headquarters. He questioned whether he would choose to try to pacify Cory's supporters this time—or, more to the point, whether he would be able to do so.

Shades of the special relationship, I thought, as he posed questions for which I had no answers and was in fact asking myself. "It is important to find out how the American government feels about it," he repeated, "because in the event of a disputed election, we can surround the COM-

ELEC with one million people, but we need to know what will happen if we start the revolution there."

When pressed with that question by opposition leaders, Ambassador Bosworth was appropriately opaque. "Just have a go at it," he told Peping. "Life is full of uncertainties. There are no guarantees. We say we support the election process. Don't ask me a hypothetical question about what we do when we know the results. That becomes a new set of realities."

The American ambassador was more forthcoming when asked by a nonpolitician Filipino friend at a private dinner party, "What would America do if Marcos decides to stay in power and rams through his election?" Bosworth answered, according to two of the guests, "We will put so much pressure on him that within thirty days he will disintegrate."

*   *   *

Cory had tried to discourage talk of a draft candidacy months before by setting two conditions on her willingness to even talk about running. To her dismay, Marcos had met her first condition by calling for a special election. Her second condition—that her supporters gather 1 million signatures favoring her candidacy—was still about 980,000 signatures shy, but with an election in the wind, they would come easily.

During the week after Marcos's announcement, she was anxious and confused as she moved from one meeting to another. At the same time that she was searching for reasons not to run, she was also, unbeknownst to all but a few, undergoing a crash course in the art and issues of presidential campaigning under the tutelage of Peping and a selected group of advisors from business and academia. "I didn't know what I wanted to do or what I should do," she related. "I couldn't concentrate. The only way I could get all these things off my mind at night was to watch 'Dallas' and 'Falcon Crest.'"

Then suddenly on Friday morning, November 8, in the middle of a tedious meeting, she reported, "there came a little light." Joe Concepcion, chairman of NAMFREL (National Movement for Free Elections), the nongovernmental voter watchdog organization, had invited a University of the Philippines mass communications specialist to present the findings of a new electoral survey to her.

For more than hour, Cory sat listening to how highly Filipinos had rated Marcos's performance until the Aquino assassination, when it had plummeted from a 60 percent favorable rating to less than half that. "I thought to myself," said Cory, "I have to sit through all this when I have bigger problems." The professor went on to say that the decline in Marcos's popularity had, however, leveled off in 1984, as had the increase in the anti-Marcos ranks. Revealing a low threshold of tolerance for raw data, Cory asked him to "just give me the rough estimates of what people think now." His findings: 30 percent for Marcos, 30 percent against, and a high 40 percent undecided.

Once again demonstrating that she was far from being the political novice most people thought she was, Cory evaluated the statistics by drawing from the considerable store of information she had absorbed as Ninoy's wife. She quickly concluded that the numbers were not as bad as they sounded. "Ninoy always said that the administration has a captive thirty percent, the opposition a stable thirty percent, and that what elections are all about is how to bring over the forty percent."

Encouraged by the figures, she queried the professor about how to appeal to the undecideds. "Many people believe you, who are supposed to be the leadership of the opposition, have not asked them what they think about things," he responded. "You have neglected them."

Cory disagreed. Sharply opinionated on subjects about which she is knowledgeable, she retorted, "I am of the opinion that many Filipinos like to be told what to do. So many people come to me and ask." However, she was there to learn, not to pontificate, so she pressed him for answers to her many other questions about public opinion.

"Do the people understand abstract things like truth, justice, and freedom, which I always talk about?" she asked. "Or do they only understand material things, like enough food to eat, a roof over their heads, and school for their children?" He gave her an evasive answer, so she described a trip she had made as chairman of a fund-raising drive to benefit the economically depressed sugar-growing island of Negros. "The people welcomed me because I was bringing them a check, which meant rice for them," she said. "I am of the impression that if elections are held, we are lost, because it is only Marcos who can give them rice and pesos." Then, restless with so much inconclusive talk, she excused herself to go to a nearby church for mass. "If you have some answers, please let us know," she said curtly in parting.

Prayer was an important element in Cory's daily life and decision making. After querying a variety of family members, technocrats, and veteran politicians for suggestions on how to deal with any given problem, she would ask for heavenly guidance. Although waiting for inspiration might slow her down, it assured resolute action once she made up her mind.

On this occasion, she felt she had exhausted the advice of others without finding the answer. Certain confidantes had told her she had an obligation to run for president. Others had cautioned her that inevitable failure to beat Marcos might set back the opposition cause and even tarnish Ninoy's memory. Therefore, when she entered the sanctuary, she related, "I prayed as I had never prayed before, saying, 'Please, Lord, tell me what to do.' "

The following day supporters were pressing harder than ever for a commitment. By lunchtime she was so visibly agitated that her daughter Viel proposed a shopping trip as a diversion. But there was to be no escape. Entering a fabric store to buy material for dresses in her trademark yellow color, she encountered four members of a pro-Cory group called AWARE, that was preparing to back her candidacy. "What are you going to do?" they naturally wanted to know. She had no answer for them. Later in the day she sought respite in two home-video movies selected by her sister. "One," she said, "was about a widower who cannot forget about his wife—something nice and light with no complications. It made me happy."

In the evening she attended a wake. "When I walked in," she recalled, "everyone whispered." Showing that she had not lost her ability to laugh at herself, she added wryly that the thought crossed her mind as she sought out the widow in the funeral parlor that "she might think I was running for something." Cory shared with her some unsolicited advice on how to remain close to her departed husband. "I told her to put something belonging to her in his hand, then remove it from the coffin before burial, and keep it as her last material tie with him." Touched by the widow's appreciation, Cory had commented to her family afterward, "Somehow I think I was meant to console people, rather than to run for office."

On Sunday morning November 10, she went to Manila Memorial Cemetery to attend a mass for dead family members, as she had done on the tenth day of every month since her mother died. In the course of lunch afterwards with the celebrant, Monsignor Orlando Panlican, she repeated the critical, unanswered question: Could the opposition, if it put up a common candidate, win an election against Marcos?

"Monsignor, you have been dealing with the barrio people for so long," she said. "Can you enlighten me? Do you think they are aware that the main cause of their suffering is Marcos? Do they also realize and understand and believe that the opposition can give them a better life? Can they understand abstract concepts like truth, justice, and freedom?"

The priest's reply made a powerful impact. "Yes," he said, "in the same way they can understand abstractions connected with Marcos, because Marcos personifies evil and suffering." Then, she asked, "How do you personify truth, justice, and freedom?" He was unequivocal. "There are so many of you in the opposition," he said. "You must decide who among you will be that person." He added, "You must be certain that the person whom you assign is very different from Marcos. Then it will be a cinch."

There it was—the idea given flesh in a way that she intuitively understood and could translate to the Filipino electorate. By the end of the meal, she said, "I finally knew what I was going to do."

Nonetheless, she went ahead the next day with a spiritual retreat, which she had previously scheduled for herself in a convent of the Sisters of Perpetual Adoration just outside Manila. "I had one day free, and I wanted to spend it praying," she explained. She told her Jesuit spiritual advisor that she wanted to fast, but he balked at the request. "The nuns will be so disappointed if they cannot offer you food," he said. She insisted, adding that she would just bring some crackers.

By the time she arrived at the convent at nine o'clock on Monday morning, November 11, she had made up her mind to run and had formulated how she would break the news to Laurel. "It suddenly became very clear to me that I would have to tell Doy that the next election would be the first and last of a kind," she said, "and it would be such a unique situation that extraordinary things must be done if we hope to defeat Marcos."

She told her confessor that she felt "very confident" about what she wanted to do, so she would like to pray, not for herself, but for others.

"Pray for yourself," he instructed, and left her alone. By the time he returned, doubts had clouded her confidence.

"Father, I am sorry, but I think I am going to cry," she warned him. Dabbing her eyes with Kleenex, she questioned, "What bad thing have I done to deserve all this? Why is so much being asked of me?" He listened as she spilled out her contradictory feelings about running. Gradually, she returned to what she called a "state of peace."

"For the first time I am absolutely clear on what I want to do," she told the priest. Now she was ready to stop praying for herself and to direct her prayers toward others. He was not yet convinced. "Pray for yourself," he instructed her once more.

Later in the morning she was interrupted by the Mother Prioress, who wanted to take her lunch order. Cory repeated her desire to fast, which, she added, would serve the dual purpose of dieting. At 11:30 a nun brought her a tray with a cloth napkin, a cup of cream of mushroom soup, and a banana. Unable to refuse the sisters' hospitality, she sipped their soup with her crackers.

After confession and some readings that the priest had prepared for her, she was deemed ready to pray for others. "It was the most beautiful experience," she said later. "I even prayed for General Ver." Her spiritual advisor told her he thought that was going overboard. Cory tried to reassure him, "Don't ask me to shake hands with him, my forgiveness is not so complete. It will take time."

At seven o'clock she took her leave. Ten hours of meditation had confirmed her in her earlier decision. "We had to present somebody who is the complete opposite of Marcos, someone who has been a victim," she explained. She was modest but unflinching in her judgment of who that would be. "Looking around, I may not be the worst victim, but I am the best known."

*   *   *

There remained the problem of breaking the news of her decision to Laurel, who would return from a fund-raising trip to the U.S. on November 13, and then trying to hammer out a ticket with or without him on it. At the advice of her spiritual advisor, Cory made a preliminary appointment to see Cardinal Sin on Tuesday, November 12, before he left for Rome. The cardinal, whom many believe would have made a superb politician had he not had a religious calling, greeted her with a long recitation of the results of opinion surveys conducted by the Church, indicating she could win if she decided to become a candidate. He was pleased to hear her decision.

Then she confided to him, "I have a problem with Doy."

"No," said the cardinal, "the last time he was here, he said he would give in." She began to express her doubts about whether or not Laurel should be part of the ticket at all, given his past connections with Marcos and his perceived lack of suffering under martial law. The cardinal listened, but changed the subject. Her bigger problem at the moment, he said, was her security. She needed specially trained bodyguards, he told her. He said he would talk to Marcos about the matter.

As Cory set off for her meeting with Doy the next evening, her head was full of lines she had rehearsed in front of her children. "I pretended they were Doy," she told me later, "and I told them, 'We must present someone who has been a victim of Marcos.' " Once she had broken the news of her candidacy to Doy, she would go on to suggest that he should not only give up his presidential ambitions, but that he should forget about the vice-presidency as well this time around. "In choosing my running mate, I must enhance the suffering image," she would say. "I cannot choose someone who has been visibly connected with Marcos."

Her children had been dumbfounded by her candor. "You are going to tell Uncle Doy all that?" they had asked. "He will have a heart attack!" They questioned why he should heed her wishes. "What's in it for Doy?" they wanted to know.

Cory was ready with an answer that was typically more appropriate for the confessional than for the political arena. "I will tell him that I look upon this election as a cross I must bear. I will ask him to also take up the cross." Perhaps in so doing, she would suggest to him, he would finally convince his detractors that he was truly an oppositionist. But she never got that far.

They met, just the two of them, in her living room. Doy, overcome with jet lag, drank several brandies as they talked.

"How have you been?" he asked.

"Oh, my gosh," said Cory, "I must admit I did not think Marcos would call for elections. I never dreamed both my conditions would be met."

"So what have you decided?" he pressed.

"Well, Doy, they still don't have the million signatures, but I am really under terrific pressure to run." Describing her dilemma to him, she said, "I don't know if you believe this, but I really don't want it." She still hoped that Marcos would change his mind and was only floating the election proposal "in order to flush all of us out on our candidacies." She observed, "For all we know, elections will not be held until 1987, and by then people won't think of me any more."

He accepted her answer, then returned to the question of who was pressuring her. Some businessmen and the organizers of her signature campaign, she replied.

"What does your mother-in-law say?" he asked, valuing the judgment of Ninoy's mother, whom he knew had a soft spot for him.

"She does not want me to run," said Cory, who observed, "I could see Doy smile when I said that." Doy asked which one of them Mrs. Aquino thought could beat Marcos. "She does not think any of us can win," said Cory. "She tells me, 'Why go through with this useless exercise, when Marcos will not allow you to win?' I think she feels that if Ninoy were killed something just as drastic could happen to me."

Doña Aurora had asked her, Cory recounted, why she could not just give a categorical no to efforts to draft her. Cory answered with a quote from Ninoy, who said, "If there was something I could have done and did not do, I could never forgive myself."

Before they parted, Doy, professional politician that he was, wanted to agree on what they would tell the media. They arrived at a suitably bland summary. To Cory's amusement, Doy then suggested they adopt code names to be used in secret communication with each other in the coming days. "He wanted to be Dr. Avila," she said, giggling. "Could we please refrain from Doctor," joshed Cory, "it sounds so formal?" Doy finally settled for her idea to take their eldest daughters' names: Suzie and Ballsy. As she finished her account, she shook her head. "These men!" she exclaimed.

٭ ٭ ٭

Malacañang on the morning of December 3 was a microcosm of the many forces that had driven Marcos to call a snap election. The clusters of people waiting in the tastefully appointed reception hall to see the president on the morning after the Ver acquittal personified the divisions in the Philippine body politic on the eve of an historic election campaign.

On the left-hand side of the long, chandeliered hall, under the oil portraits of past presidents stood a group of twenty-two men in khaki uniforms. A shudder passed over me when I realized that they were the lower-ranking accused coconspirators in the Aquino case, who had won acquittal yesterday after a farcical trial in the Graft and Corruption Court. They had come to be reinstated by their commander in chief. They stared impassively at the portraits on the wall until they were summoned inside the music room. After a brief interval of quiet behind the closed doors, applause could be heard. Then out strode the diminutive figure of AV-SECOM lawyer Rudy Jimenez, followed by the soldiers whom he had defended. Gloating over his courtroom victory the day before, Jimenez said that he planned to write a book about "the case of the century," before taking on other legal clients.

Seated on a velvet sofa just outside the entrance to the president's study, U.S. Ambassador Stephen Bosworth sipped a cup of coffee while awaiting an appointment, which had been penciled in on Marcos's agenda following yesterday's verdict. Poker-faced, as usual, he said he was prepared to question the president on his intentions vis-à-vis the length of Ver's reinstatement and to read him Washington's highly critical line on that issue. It would then be up to Marcos whether he wished to "pay the cost" of keeping Ver on indefinitely, he commented.

Penciled into the appointment slot before Bosworth, it soon became clear, in much the manner that the hero of a restoration comedy discovers his rival behind the drapery, was Soviet Ambassador Yuri Sholmov. No sooner was Bosworth ushered through the main door than his Soviet counterpart was hustled out a back exit.

Occupying the cluster of Empire-style chairs and settees adjacent to the politicians were some three dozen top officers of the Philippine Armed Forces, summoned from command posts all over the country to attend the first session of the newly established "Board of Generals" that Marcos had tasked with reorganizing the AFP. Generals Ver, Olivas, and Custodio, back in uniform, had chosen to stand with this group, rather than with their fellow defendants.

Oozing good will, following his reinstatement as chief of staff, General Ver discussed the letter he had sent the president yesterday, minutes after his acquittal. Applying tactics that had never failed him in dealing with Marcos, he had confided that "certain security matters of a highly sensitive and extremely urgent nature" needed to be discussed. The president had, naturally, called for him at once. After hearing him out, Ver said, Marcos had handed back his letter, which bore a signed, handwritten notation in the upper-right corner, approving, as promised, his reinstatement "for such period as may be decided by me."

At first glance, the Board of Generals appeared to represent a good cross-section of the nation's largest and most powerful government institution. There were "his generals," "her generals," the cooly professional

General Ramos, newly demoted back to his post as vice-chief of staff, a representative from the reform officers movement, and combat veteran Colonel Biazon, who had flown in from Mindanao before dawn that morning. Their mission, as Biazon understood it, would be to work out a schedule for retiring the twenty-nine "overstaying generals" and replacing them with younger officers, whose upward mobility had been blocked long enough to have given rise to serious discontent. Ramos himself had warned that this might be "the last chance" for the military to reform itself. A spokesman for RAM, on the other hand, had called the proposed reorganization "all smoke and mirrors and distraction," as long as Ver remained in charge.

Adjacent to the generals, a group of politicians from the Visayan islands in the central Philippines waited to receive news from the president about their budget allocations prior to the February 7, 1986, election. All members of the ruling KBL party, they were talking about what every other politician in the country had on his mind that morning: the expected entry of Corazon Aquino into the political arena. They were, frankly, concerned about the upcoming election. All of them confessed to having sons, daughters, and in-laws on "the other side." The emergence of an appealing alternative to Marcos, like Mrs. Aquino, and the sobering possibility that she might be able to unite with a traditional pol who knew the KBL ropes as well as Marcos's former ally Laurel was giving them heartburn.

The president's choice of a running mate would be critical. They hoped it would be Arturo Tolentino, the feisty former senator and foreign minister, whom Marcos had sacked for talking back. The only KBL winner in Metro-Manila in 1984, he had a large popular base, and would, they thought, carry moral authority. "Tolentino has coattails which the president could ride," said one of the pols somewhat heretically. "If the opposition is united, the president may have to put a critic like Tolentino on the ticket to have credibility," said another.

By noon only the politicians and I were still waiting. Although this was an unusually event-filled day, Marcos was known to keep important cabinet officials and military commanders cooling their heels on these carpets for several hours even on quiet days. Day and night, people were kept in a sort of holding pattern in this hall, attended with unfailing politeness and served a succession of meals, drinks, and snacks by gentle, smiling ushers.

Ninety minutes later a valet summoned me to the presidential study. Marcos was running some three hours behind schedule. The Visayan politicians were still waiting outside, and he had not yet eaten lunch. Nevertheless, he settled back into the velvet-cushioned chair behind his desk, and under the glare of two violet-hued antiallergy lamps, talked for more than two hours about the coming election and the trial, which had just ended in the acquittal of his men. His comments on those subjects were largely predictable. Less so were his references to Ninoy.

Marcos spoke of his dead rival in the present tense, without visible emotion, but with the sense that the impending confrontation with the opposition was very much rooted in a past which he shared with Ninoy. He had avoided confronting the arrogant senator at the polls by jailing him. But he had not gotten rid of him or his unfinished agenda. In death both had loomed larger. He seemed eager for the drama to play itself out at last. He was counting on Cory to take on the role of Ninoy's surrogate.

"We are fraternity brothers, and we could always talk to each other pleasantly," Marcos began. Eerily, he recalled the same conversation which Ninoy had told me about in Taipei—the one held in the palace when Aquino was still a prisoner. Gesturing toward my chair, on the other side of the desk, Marcos observed, "He was seated right there, where you are seated." But Marcos's version was markedly different from Aquino's. Neither conformed to the transcript of the meeting, which I had unearthed from military archives. Being Filipino politicians, both were given to hyperbole.

"I asked him point-blank," said Marcos, " 'If I were to release you, what would you do right now?' As usual, he hemmed and hawed." Marcos explained in an aside, "Ninoy is the type who keeps his options. He does not say yes or no." By contrast, Marcos pointed out, "I say yes or no on critical matters."

Marcos had pressed Ninoy at that point to "answer categorically, so I can make my own decisions."

"It will depend on what you can offer me," replied Aquino.

"I offer you the future," said Marcos, quite obviously polishing his own words and tarnishing those of the departed in the telling.

"I never saw him again after that," said Marcos. However, he revealed that he had talked to Aquino by phone in April 1982. "He wanted to come back and join the government," the president claimed. "When he learned that I had confirmed the decision convicting him with the death penalty, he sent me a feeler, and then we talked by phone in the first quarter of 1983." Marcos said he had told Aquino, "You could be of help here. Your friends in the Communist party are acting up."

The role Marcos had in mind for Ninoy, had he joined the government, was as "a liaison with the opposition to prevent all these killings and terrorism, to convince the Communist party to turn legal by publicly vowing that they would not use violence to obtain political power." However, Ninoy had turned him down. "His answer was, 'You may have forgotten that I may have more enemies in the Communist party than in your administration.' "

Marcos claimed, as had Imelda, that Ninoy had "promised the First Lady he would not go home without informing her." I asked Marcos if he had been aware that one of the reasons Ninoy had rushed back, without a passport, and in defiance of the warnings against his life, was his fear that Marcos was about to die. He let out a hearty laugh. "I was going to die in December," he reminded me, still chuckling.

Marcos refused to admit that he had ever undergone a transplant or was even seriously ill at the time of Aquino's homecoming. He seemed oblivious to the fact that most analysts of the crime exempted him from direct involvement in the assassination only on the grounds that he was presumed to have been near death on the days just prior to the shooting. Spelling out details of his illness, Marcos claimed that he had been treated with drugs for an asthma attack that had made him prey to "a new virus," which his doctors described as "probably connected with lupus." However, he insisted, "I never lost consciousness, and I never slept in the hospital."

Although I got nowhere trying to debate the merits of the case against the military in the shooting of Aquino, I could tell from his arguments how closely he had studied the testimony of all the witnesses. As a lawyer himself, he intimated, he could have presented a better case against the military than the prosecutor did, but he thought better of discussing that with a witness for the prosecution. "It's all a war game, as far as I am concerned," he said, referring to the just concluded trial with more than a bit of world-weariness.

Then Marcos offered a rare glimpse into his private life. "I have a table for a war game with a little computer," he said. "My son is pretty good at these things." Impudently, I asked him if he always won. "More often than not," he replied matter-of-factly. "The war games are set battle pieces, which I have gone through repeatedly," he explained. Returning to the subject of politics, he added, "It is different in a nonconventional game, where anything can happen."

With yesterday's acquittals, Marcos deemed the assassination finally behind him. His task now was to beat Ninoy's widow, whose candidacy had been confirmed to him, even as we talked, by an aide, who interrupted the interview to hand him a Philippine News Service bulletin about her announcement. After reading the wire, Marcos asked me to turn off my tape recorder for a moment, although his own continued to run. Off the record, he made a prognosis, which would turn out to be correct. Despite their "bitter rivalry," he predicted, Cory and Doy would manage to compromise and form a joint ticket. He would select his own running mate on that premise.

"Doesn't the issue of the acquittals give the opposition—and especially the widow of the assassinated opposition leader—a very good issue to run on?" I asked.

"The issue was always there," replied Marcos, "whether the decision came out or not, and the issue was already being used by them." Instead of continuing in a philosophical mode, Marcos seemed unable to resist venting the pettiness, which had always colored his public remarks on his political opponents. "She goes into a crying binge and then asks for the support of the people. You can read the issue: 'We cannot obtain justice under the Marcos administration. Therefore we must depose Marcos in order that there be justice throughout our land.' That's the line. We don't care what qualifications she has. We don't care if she cannot answer your questions about what her platform is. The most important thing is justice."

He did not think that line would win her the election. "Filipinos are not exactly dull," he observed. "They will ask the question 'What is she going to do?' " Marcos's guess was that the people would "cry with her," but vote for him.

"Look, let's admit it. She's being used," Marcos said finally, tired of talking about a candidate whom he rightly felt could not be analyzed in traditional political terms. He questioned, "Who is financing her?" When asked if he knew who, he answered, "I hope the Americans are not," and then proceeded to quote from Joseph Smith's book *The Cold Warrior*, which detailed CIA funding of Filipino politicians before martial law. While stressing that he had no evidence of such support to Mrs. Aquino, he said, "The CIA is all over here apparently. There are some people who are new faces to us."

Like his wife, Marcos perceived the U.S. government, rather than Mrs. Aquino, as his primary adversary. He took offense at the way Americans were using the issue of Ver's reinstatement as a litmus test of Marcos's intentions regarding military reform. "General Ver is just an excuse," he said. "There will be others." Presciently, he added, "What I am feeling is that slowly we are losing our credibility with the U.S. government."

If that were the case, he warned, he was preparing the necessary contingency plans for survival without U.S. support. In the past, when U.S. pressure had gotten too much for him, he had resorted to veiled threats that he would play the Soviet card. He did not go so far as to say that now. He did not have to. Imelda had done that for him by traveling to the USSR and denigrating the U.S. on her return.

Congressman Solarz, Marcos noted, had issued a public warning that if General Ver's reinstatement proved to be more than a token expression of loyalty, Marcos could forget about more military aid. Barely controlling his anger, Marcos explained that the military reorganization meeting, which I had seen going on in the palace dining room, had as its aim "to strengthen the combat capability of the entire armed forces, preferably on the basis of there being no military aid from the U.S."

"What is the saying of Cervantes?" Marcos asked. Then he repeated a favorite quotation: "The old woman, seeing the Muslim king crying before crossing the bridge in withdrawal, said, 'Don't cry like a woman over the kingdom that you lost because you did not defend it like a man.' " He left no doubt that he would do what was necessary to defend his kingdom, which meant, in his lexicon, to survive in power. The snap election had been his first move in that direction. He had called it, he said, because "I was so irritated by all this talk on the impeachment question and the failure of the insurgency program. Sometime back I had decided that if I was going to be put to the post with questions like this, whether in the Philippines or in the U.S., I was going to say, 'All right, let's call a snap election.' I got fed up with all this harassment."

"Can you contemplate losing?" I asked.

"No, I cannot," said Marcos flatly. He stressed that at the time he announced a special election, he had in his possession professional surveys, which justified his confidence. He was looking to the election to demonstrate to his critics that he retained the mandate of the Filipino people. Some Americans, he complained, called him "the unwanted dictator" and compared him to the Shah of Iran. Railing at such comparisons, he implied that he was no more of a "dictator" than the late French President General Charles de Gaulle. "They call me dictator because of Amendment Number Six [which gave him emergency decree-making powers]," he said, reminding me that he had simply borrowed that from de Gaulle.

As a reporter who had lived and worked in France, I had steeped myself in the memoirs and the lore of General de Gaulle. I retorted that de Gaulle, too, had been called a dictator by those who found his emergency powers excessive in a purported democratic republic. Only when he resigned as president after French voters had rejected a referendum on which he had staked his prestige, were many of his critics able to perceive de Gaulle as a democrat.

"Can you picture yourself doing that?" I asked Marcos, mindful of opposition hopes that he could be pressured to resign. I found his answer fascinating. He too had read de Gaulle's memoirs and other works about him. Unlike me, who appreciated them in an abstract way, Marcos had read them in the way a mechanic would read a how-to manual. Unlike me, Marcos saw nothing noble in defeat.

"If the referendum was that important, he himself should have campaigned for it," he said. But de Gaulle had done nothing of the kind. "He wanted out," said Marcos. "He stayed away. He was so proud that he did not want to campaign. He was supposed to have said, 'If they don't like me, then they should not have me.' "

That was not Marcos's attitude at all. "Every election or referendum, I always run scared. I am not going to call an election to prove my egoistic wish," he declared. On the other hand, he admired de Gaulle and emulated his style of decision making. Paraphrasing the French president, Marcos said, "You cannot run a government with if's and but's. It's either yes or no." Another sentiment of de Gaulle's which he had taken to heart, he said, was "When you make a decision, you wager everything in your life. If you cannot do so, don't be a leader." Marcos concluded, "I buy that. When you make a decision, you have got to be able to put your neck on the chopping block if necessary."

17

Saint Vs. Sinner

Marcos never took Cory seriously. Although he prided himself on "running scared" during his last campaign, as he had in all his previous races, he placed too much of the responsibility for victory on his machine and directed too little of his intellect toward responding to the moral challenge she had sounded. In what was meant as a lighthearted reference to his opponent, one week before the election, he correctly articulated what the contest had been all about. "The man who stands before you today is the true and real Ferdinand Marcos," he said to the combined Rotary Clubs of Manila. "Last week, when a certain lady visited with you, you heard a caricature of the impostor Marcos—a combination of Darth Vader, Machiavelli, Nero, Stalin, Pol Pot, and maybe even Satan himself."

However, Marcos sensed no need to counter that image. Instead, he did what came naturally and added another accusation to the long list he had already brought against her. "My opponent grossly oversimplifies when she reduces the complex world of politics into a Manichaean battle between good and evil," he railed, forgetting that oversimplification was his specialty.

The fact was that the strategy Cory Aquino followed to fight Marcos was virtually preordained by the way he had, over the sixteen years since he had last faced a serious rival at the polls, closed off all other options. It was Ninoy, she said, who had devised that strategy. Reaching into her desk drawer and pulling out a loose-leaf notebook containing some of his speeches and letters, she quoted him: "We cannot fight Marcos with arms, because he has so many. We cannot fight him with money, because we do not have any. The only way we can fight him is with morality."

Fortunately, she and her advisors had enough sense to know that morality alone would not do the job. It would take cunning, compromise, obstinacy, theater, and even a bit of deceit, not to mention money and powerful allies. But morality would be the metaphor.

* * *

"It's done." Doy handed the pen back to the COMELEC clerk and moved toward the tiny clearing in the crowd. He had just signed away the presidential ambitions he had harbored since 1949, when he had watched his father become the graceful loser of another presidential bid. With only ninety minutes to spare before the midnight, December 11 deadline for filing their certificates of candidacy, Doy had withdrawn the document he had filed to run for president and had refiled for the office of vice-president. Exhausted and resigned, he too was gracious in defeat. "I feel right about it," he said. "It was necessary to unite to topple the dictator. Someone had to make the sacrifice. I did it."

That was more than could be said for some of his supporters. One of them, Rene Espina, had just taken a punch at UNIDO Assemblyman Alberto ("Bert") Romulo, who had switched his allegiance from Laurel to Aquino when Cory became a candidate. "Traitor!" yelled Espina, as mutual friends rushed to separate the two men before a melee broke out.

The pack of photographers and cameramen nudged Doy into place beside Cory, then stepped back to frame a photo of opposition unity. Cory in yellow. Doy in green. A decade and a half of the suppressed aspirations of the political opposition embodied in the widow and the boyhood friend of Ninoy Aquino. "We owe it to the Filipino people to present them with just one ticket," said Cory. Then, in an effort to overcome whatever sentimentality she felt, she looked at her running mate and said, "Last Sunday, my friends told me you looked better than me, but now I think we are even in having such heavy eye bags."

No one in the room, on either side of the cameras, had slept since last Sunday, December 8, when the two candidates' efforts to hammer out a joint ticket had broken down within hours of the press conference that was supposed to have announced success. Doy had finally agreed to sacrifice his presidential ambitions to become Cory's vice-president, if she would run on the ticket of his UNIDO, thereby making it the ruling party, should they win. Cory, however, had been unable to sell such an agreement to the newly formed coalition named after Ninoy's Laban party, which was backing her candidacy.

Although the candidates themselves both held centrist views that were not far apart, their supporters on the right and left were divided by a fundamental ideological rift. As one UNIDO leader put it, "There are two diverse groupings behind Cory—one is capitalist in nature and one is pink, and I don't see how both can get along."

Both sides knew unity was essential if they were to hope to beat Marcos, yet neither could overcome its own prejudices or rise above its petty interests to compromise. The concept that "no man is an island" was not one that Filipinos readily conceded, perhaps because they belonged to an archipelagic culture. Not until they found themselves poised on the brink of disaster, could obstinate individuals finally be convinced to consider the collective good. At that point the two institutions which enjoyed the most power in their society, the Church and the family, would begin to act on them.

On this occasion, once failure was apparent, feelers immediately went out between the Aquino and Laurel families. The cardinal, who had just returned from Rome, readied himself for some intensive politico-spiritual counseling. He was well briefed. In his absence his political advisor had been working with the indefatigable NAMFREL chairman Joe Concepcion and the businessmen behind the Cory Aquino for President Movement to lay the groundwork for the cardinal's intervention in the delicate negotiations between the two warring camps. "As a face-saving device, never try to force a decision in front of the two of them," the businessmen had advised the prelate in a memo on mediating techniques. "Discuss realities such as reimbursement of expenses if compromise is reached."

The businessmen had also furnished the churchmen with a chart listing the pros and cons of each candidate, according to a survey of leading opposition politicians and business community supporters. On the negative side, Cory's capacity to win was "questioned by chauvinists and traditional politicians." Her "sentiment/emotional factor" read, "All sentiment and no intellect. Massive info campaign needed to correct people's perceptions." Laurel's weightier list of negatives included "political turncoat, tainted with Marcos connection, plastic personality, very uninspiring."

The day before the filing deadline, it was time for the cardinal and Concepcion to go to work. During a private dinner he had arranged with the Laurel family, the cardinal lobbied for a joint ticket. Early the next morning Concepcion followed up with a call on Doy at home to discuss the mechanics of unity. With a list of Doy's demands, including 25 percent of the cabinet positions and mayoralties, in hand, Concepcion went to see Cory. "She was not in agreement with some," he reported, "but others she accepted." He radioed the cardinal, who resumed his own negotiations with the two parties.

First he called Cory to the Spanish-style archbishop's palace. No sooner had she and the cardinal begun to talk than his secretary brought word that General Ver had stopped by to deliver his annual Christmas gift of fruit. Lest he betray his mediating role in opposition politics, the cardinal told Cory to duck into the dining hall while he exchanged greetings with Marcos's chief of staff. When Ver was gone, they resumed their discussion, chuckling over the bipartisan nature of the cardinal's ministry.

"Why are you running?" asked the cardinal.

"To win," Cory replied.

"There is no reason to run if you are not going to win," he agreed. "Between you and Doy, you are more attractive and stronger, but you cannot win without a political party."

The cardinal proposed to talk to Doy. "I think I can convince him to be your vice," he said. Without consulting her Laban partners, whom she knew would argue against it, Cory relented and agreed to run under the UNIDO banner. "The people would have blamed me if I had not agreed with Doy," she rationalized. Cardinal Sin opined, "She decided because there is no other way. She is the only one who can unite." He promptly called Laurel to tell him he had a deal.

Two hours later Doy, accompanied by Ernie Maceda, a politician with feet in both camps, discussed the situation with the cardinal and Concepcion over lunch. "Doy lamented that all his posters were ready, and that he had been campaigning for more than a year," said the cardinal.

"If you run and she runs, you both will lose," said Sin. "Between the two of you, Mrs. Aquino has the charisma, because of what happened to her husband, and because of the verdict acquitting General Ver. The people are mad that you are not together. Make some sacrifices. This is an act of humility. The deadline for submission of the certificates of candidacy is midnight." As the cardinal finished speaking, he said he noticed that "a little tear rolled down Senator Laurel's cheek."

At five o'clock Doy called Cory and asked to see her at seven. Meeting for dinner in the spacious home of Cory's sister-in-law, Maur Lichauco, a traditional site of family powwows, Cory, with her brother Peping and his wife, Ting-Ting, the Lichaucos, and Doña Aurora, sat down with Doy and his brothers. Doy asked Cory if she was agreed on UNIDO. She responded affirmatively, then asked about the demands he had conveyed through Concepcion. "Let's forget about those," he said gallantly. His older brother Jose Jr. ("Pepito"), godfather of the Laurel clan and minority leader in the National Assembly, had decided that there was no need for a written agreement on such things between friends. The verbal agreements already made would suffice. Cory assured Doy that he would receive "a meaningful post," that he would not be a "mere figurehead."

"This is what I call supernatural enlightenment," commented Cory Aquino for President member Victor Sison, after receiving a call at 9:30 P.M. that night, confirming the formation of a joint ticket. A delegation of opposition assemblymen reacted to the message with relief. "We had told them if they failed to file the necessary papers by ten o'clock, we would withdraw our support, because it would amount to an exercise in futility," recounted Assemblyman Marcelo Fernan.

After midnight, Cory capped an already arduous day with several interviews in the living room of the Times Street house. Looking back on the grueling experience of unification, she had, as usual, managed to sift through the straw and come up with at least one nugget. "All of these problems had to happen so that we could get the support of more people," she said. "I really think of this as something we had to undergo to convince everybody how necessary it was to unite, because before we reached the eleventh hour, people were still thinking of the possibility of two candidates. But as the days went by and the people were besieging us to do something, then many more forces came into play and the cooler heads prevailed."

Many questions would be raised and many speculative words written in the course of the campaign and afterward about Cory's style of leadership. From what I saw over that nine-day period, it was democratic to the point of being messy, bold only when threatened with failure, and harrowing to watch. But it had accomplished the impossible: unity of the long-divided opposition forces.

❋   ❋   ❋

The race was on. Only hours before the leading oppositionists finally agreed to join hands, 8,000 delegates to a KBL nominating convention had unanimously proclaimed Marcos as their candidate. He in turn had named Arturo ("Turing") Tolentino as his running mate. Marcos's choice of his most outspoken ally to be his vice-president came as a shock to most of the delegates. It was premised on his hunch that he would be facing a united opposition.

The wiry, seventy-five-year-old former senator and foreign minister was the closest thing to a public conscience that the KBL could claim. It was he who had pressured the president to create the Agrava Board and to restore the vice-presidency. He had joined the opposition in calling for the abolition of the president's decree-making powers under Amendment 6, once martial law had been lifted.

Largely on the basis of his perceived understanding of the need for change in the wake of the assassination, he had been the only KBL survivor of the opposition landslide in Metro-Manila in the 1984 National Assembly elections. The mathematics of that race—a big win in the vote-rich opposition bailiwick of Manila—had clearly figured in Tolentino's selection this year.

In his acceptance speech Tolentino stressed the moral aspect of his selection over the mathematical. "Once more President Marcos has shown the highest degree of statesmanship," declared Tolentino, "when he overlooked our differences of opinion on some public issues and considered that these differences are healthy signs that democracy prevails within the KBL." Tolentino concluded, with questionable logic but catchy rhetoric, "There is no more need for the opposition to be in government, because I'll be the opposition in the government."

Marcos had taken the offensive against Cory, even before she had become a declared candidate, hitting her inexperience. As soon as she declared, he let loose a barrage of accusations that she and her leftist advisors were soft on Communism and prepared to "dismember" the republic by making a deal with Muslim secessionists. His aim was to prevent the contest from becoming the morality play that her Jesuit advisors had scripted.

He drew blood almost immediately. Her inexperience and fatigue and the confusion that reigned within the jerry-built opposition camp during the initial weeks of the campaign made Marcos's job easy. She had entered the race, not as the leader of a strong party with a clear-cut platform, but as the unifying force within an uneasy coalition. As a nonpolitician, she was guided, not by a set of publicly identifiable positions, but by a body of privately held beliefs that made her morally strong in arguing right and wrong, but weak in arguing the fine points of world affairs. Not until a seventeen-point "minimum program" was finally approved by the various opposition factions, three weeks into the race, did she have the tools she needed to counter Marcos's charges on such sensitive issues as the insurgency and Muslim autonomy. By then, her fledgling campaign seemed in danger of self-destruction.

A New York Times article, published the day after the campaign opened, had implicitly questioned Cory's competence to be president. It reflected the initial chaos in the opposition camp, as well as her own naiveté in dealing with the press after her status had changed from housewife to candidate. According to the Times, she had referred her interviewers to a Jesuit priest for information on the Communist insurgency, had said she was for the removal of the U.S. bases, and could not remember the specific platform planks on which she and her running mate disagreed.

When I interviewed her ten days earlier myself, I had found her in far better form than the Times described. The next time I saw her, I asked her what happened. While not trying to excuse herself for a performance that she realized had not been exemplary, she could not hide her anger at the way in which what had been scheduled as "a social call" in her home by *Times* executive editor Abe Rosenthal and foreign editor Warren Hoge and their spouses had turned into a verbatim interview. It was the second day of the campaign, and she had been on the road all day, returning home to dress for a golden anniversary party and to receive the visiting editors.

The discussion had taken place in a casual atmosphere, unlike most of the official interviews she had given. While she had seen the *Times* Manila bureau chief Seth Mydans place his tape recorder before her midway through the conversation and had not objected, she had not taken care to switch from the conversational mode in which the exchange had begun to the more statesmanlike manner called for by the weight of the subjects discussed.

It was typical of Cory in talking to reporters, when she was not on camera or speaking directly into a microphone, to say too much—to surround cogent observations with light conversation, self-deprecating comments, and references to friends who knew more about a given subject than she. Until she became a presidential candidate, few reporters had quoted her verbatim, and most had protected her.

"Some people have been telling me the problem is that I am too honest," she said, "but I don't want to be dishonest." All she would say about the experience for the record was that "it was good that it happened early enough." She was learning what most other politicians had learned early in their careers—to be on guard.

What appeared to upset her most about the article was its negative portrayal of her remarks about the U.S. bases. No opposition politician, in principle, wanted U.S. bases on Philippine soil. Some were simply more practical than others about the cost, both economic and geopolitical, of expelling them. She was among the more practical. "Doy had his own position and I had mine," she explained.

After she had agreed to run on the UNIDO ticket, a unified position had to be hammered out between the centrist supporters of UNIDO president Laurel and the left-leaning Laban ng Bayan coalition that also backed Cory's candidacy. The very week that the *Times* interview took place, Laban leader Jovy Salonga, Ninoy's former lawyer and fellow Liberal party member, had drafted a compromise position, which he had presented to Aquino and other opposition leaders. It was softer than previous opposition positions, which had called for the immediate removal of U.S. bases from the Philippines. It pledged to respect the bases agreement up to its expiration in 1991, but urged a U.S. military pullout at an unspecified date after that.

Salonga claimed that his wording incorporated Cory's position, which was to respect the bases agreement until its expiration in 1991 and to keep her options open regarding what to do after that. She disagreed. "Maybe for you lawyers that's okay," she had told him, "but my people will think yours is a much harder line." Salonga grumbled about all the problems that had been caused by entering into an alliance with UNIDO. He warned that yet another revision of the text would delay publication of the joint opposition "minimum program," which was already overdue. To save time, he proposed putting an asterisk after the minimum program statement on the bases, referring to a footnote, which would contain Cory's position.

On hearing that, she said, "I took a deep breath." Then she announced with barely controlled anger to her Laban partners, who had gathered to review the platform, "Since I am a presidential candidate, I think I am entitled to more than an asterisk." Salonga was overridden, and Cory's more accommodating position became the general opposition position.

Largely in response to the concern caused in U.S. officialdom by the *Times* article, Aquino supporters there hurried to the rescue. A prime mover in Cory's behalf was Robert Trent Jones, Jr., who had met the Aquinos in the 1960s, when he built a championship golf course at the Cojuangco family's estate, Hacienda Luisita, and had lobbied to get Ninoy out of prison in the 1970s. Jones had seen a lot of Ninoy and Cory after they moved to the U.S., and he had become a strong friend of both. When Peping first began gearing up a campaign for Cory, he enlisted Jones to help with what they called "the second campaign."

"If she lost the election, it would not matter," explained Jones, who premised his remark on inevitable cheating by Marcos, "as long as she won the second campaign." As he explained it, the first campaign was that in which Cory would seek to win a majority of Filipinos' votes against Marcos.

If the results were clouded by fraud, the second campaign would click into action to win her the presidency by convincing the world that she was the victor. It would be waged on several fronts in both the U.S. and the Philippines. Jones's role was to mobilize U.S. public opinion to pressure Marcos to step down if Cory was perceived to have won the election. He lobbied U.S. policymakers in her behalf and engaged former *Economist* correspondent Mark Malloch Brown and John Scanlon, a New York public relations consultant, to enhance Cory's image in the U.S. media.

One week after the *Times* article appeared, Jones took it upon himself to reassure Secretary of State George Shultz, who was spending the Christmas holidays at his home in Palo Alto and golfing at a club to which Jones belonged. "I wrote him a long note," said Jones, "and waited for him to come off the golf course." In the letter Jones explained why he was supporting Cory and the purpose of the "second campaign." They agreed to keep in touch as the election neared. Jones used the same approach with his friend Democratic Senator Sam Nunn of Georgia and others. He reported on his progress in daily phone conversations with Peping.

Not leaving anything to chance, Jones went to see a numerologist in December. Jones knew that the superstitious President Marcos consulted his own numerologist in the palace, and he figured that he could get the same reading in San Francisco that Marcos himself was getting in Manila. In January he communicated what he had learned to Cory. "I told her that the reading I had had done on Marcos indicated that his really bad time would start on February 21." Her response: "The election will be on February the seventh, do I have to wait that long?" From then on "numerologist" became their code word for the "second campaign."

Although the U.S. constituency was important in any Philippine election, Cory was, she reminded her worried media advisors, running for president of the Philippines, and the people whose opinions she really valued were Filipinos. She chafed under the unsolicited advice which poured in from Americans, who had concluded from reading the *Times* story that her attitude toward Marcos was overly vindictive and her appreciation for the importance of the American bases weak. "Some of these people still think we are a colony of the U.S.," she complained.

The U.S. embassy had sent word to her through four different people to put more stress on strengthening Philippine-American relations. She was irritated enough to tell me how my government was behaving. "Very clearly, I would much rather have the Americans here than the Russians or the Chinese," she said, "but I wish people would give me the respect I am entitled to. I am a presidential candidate now, I am no longer your friend." There she touched upon the dilemma of any presidential candidate in a country with as important an American presence as the Philippines.

"Ninoy used to say the Americans would like somebody who is not too popular, but someone who would need their help," she recalled. That was how the opposition viewed Marcos, and that was one of the reasons why oppositionists opposed the bases so vehemently. "America has supported him so long, because it needed those bases," Cory declared. Again invoking her late husband, she observed, "Ninoy used to say that it was only when Marcos's health failed that the U.S. would back away from him."

If that time had come, she surmised that the U.S. was looking for a new surrogate. She did not feel that she fit that description, which she thought more aptly characterized Doy. On the other hand, she correctly believed that she was the only candidate popular enough to win this race. She had concluded that therein lay her strength and her freedom. In the indirect way she had of making assertive statements, she confided, "Since the *New York Times* story, I have felt so much pressure on me to say so many other things, that finally I asked one of my close friends, 'Does America have some other choice besides me?' "

If she had problems communicating her positions to Americans through a free press, she had many more communicating them to Filipinos through a controlled press. As the result of a misstatement she made in a January 3 press conference in the mountain resort city of Baguio, local reporters had jumped to headline-making conclusions that she would accept Communists in her cabinet. For weeks thereafter, Marcos exploited her faux pas outrageously in the crony press and on government-controlled broadcasting networks. Initial attempts by her spokesmen to deny that she had made any such remarks sent all of us scurrying to listen to the tapes of the few reporters who had been present. On establishing that her tone and her words had indeed left the impression that she would entertain a coalition government if the Communists would renounce violence, we sought explanations or clarification. None was forthcoming.

By the time Cory addressed the issue during an appearance before the Makati Business Club and the prestigious Management Association of the Philippines, on January 6, the issue of "Reds" in the cabinet had eclipsed all others, and she was primed to tackle it. "I would like to assure everybody here that I will not appoint a Communist to my cabinet," she stated forcefully, in response to a question. Then, encouraged by thunderous applause, she went further. She looked her audience straight in the eye and prevaricated: "I do not know where Mr. Marcos gets his information." After thirty seconds of elaboration on what Marcos said she had said, she lowered her voice half an octave from what many found to be an irritatingly prissy, female register and bellowed, "Mr. Marcos, either you put up or you shut up." With that, the crowd of 700 businessmen rose to its feet for the third time.

In retrospect, that speech marked a turning point in the making of the president of the Philippines. She may not have been a politician when she launched her campaign the month before, but she showed an audience that was already prepared to love her that she was learning quickly. Not only did she take the offensive against Marcos, but she delivered her first public white lie.

Twelve advisors had contributed to the toughening of Cory's words and image. Marcos had maintained the offensive for three weeks. He would never fully regain it. Although Cory had held her own, prior to the Makati speech, opposition polls had shown that Marcos's red-scare tactics were having an impact on strongly anti-Communist Filipinos. "You hear businessmen saying they talked to the janitor in the office, and he expressed fear and concern about the Communists," acknowledged Jimmy Ongpin, Cory's leading businessman-advisor.

It was decided that she had to hit back hard on that issue, and at the same time demonstrate that she had the mettle to handle tough problems which would confront the next president. Her media advisors began staging mock press conferences, during which they helped solidify her thinking on how to handle the CPP-NPA. Concise policy formulations were extracted from those sessions and printed on index cards for the candidate to refer to before interviews and press conferences, which she was advised to conduct only in the mornings, when she was "refreshed."

Among the policy positions produced in that manner was her call for a six-month ceasefire between the armed forces and the NPA. Although it would become a highly controversial issue early in her presidency, it was popular with voters and reflective of the view shared by all opposition leaders at the time, that most of the NPA guerrillas and their civilian supporters were not Communist ideologues, but poor, persecuted people, who would surrender to a just government. Mindanao Assemblyman Homobono ("Bono") Adaza, who claimed credit for the initial proposal, was among those who would later accuse Cory of being soft on Communism for having kept her promise of a ceasefire.

A major problem of the opposition was that it lacked the means to quickly correct misstatements or counter false charges nationwide since it did not have free access to the mass media or to the mass circulation "crony press." As a result, said Ongpin, "We decided that the most effective solution would be for her to write a letter to all the priests in the country, appealing for their help." The point of the message which Cory was asking the Church to communicate was that a woman as devoutly Catholic as she could not possibly sympathize with godless Communism. Immediately, the tide began to turn.

*　　　*　　　*

"The old Marcos is not there," observed opposition columnist Kit Tatad midway through the campaign. Marcos's former information minister was referring not only to the president's deteriorating health, but to his campaign tactics as well. Indeed, the Marcos who was carried into his rallies on the shoulders of security guards and, visibly flinching with pain, lowered to the stage, during his initial rallies, was but a shadow of his once robust self. His face was alternately drawn and wan or puffed up in reaction to the drugs he took to control his advancing kidney disease. His voice cracked and rasped in the course of his long, rambling addresses. On at least one occasion, his mind appeared to go blank in the middle of a speech.

Everywhere he went on the campaign trail, a large van with darkened windows followed in his caravan. It was reported to contain a portable dialysis unit. A nurse was always with him onstage to daub a sudden spurt of blood from a vein in his needle-pocked arm or hand, or to rewrap one of his bandaged fingers. Because of his frequent need to urinate, a portable toilet was installed backstage at every stop.

Given his physical condition, it was not altogether surprising that his campaign had thus far not taken shape, except as a series of attacks against his opponent in the government-controlled media. "What wins Philippine elections is not rallies but machinery," said a Marcos aide confidently, in response to questions about why the president had campaigned in only six provinces, compared to Cory and Doy's blitz of twenty-two during the first month of the campaign. Yet the political machine was not being lubricated with the kind of cash that had gotten out the vote in previous, less difficult elections.

Speculation as to why the flow of campaign cash had been so restricted was rife in the coffee shops. Some observers believed that Marcos was not serious about going through with the election. He was, they said, counting on the Supreme Court to rule a snap election unconstitutional unless there was a vacancy in the office of the president. That strategy failed, however, when the court—taking its cue from oppositionists, who argued that the decision should be a political, rather than a legal one—voted not to rule on the constitutionality of the snap election.

Still the rush of funds was withheld, leading observers like opposition businessman Ongpin to conclude that Marcos did not want the cash to fall prematurely into the pockets of provincial officials, who, sensing a Cory landslide, might save it for their own local election campaigns several months hence. Marcos would, predicted Tatad, "go on a buying spree and flood the market in the last two days."

Buying elections was nothing new in the Philippines, but what worried some of Marcos's lieutenants was that their candidate had so little to sell this year. Thus far, Marcos had not offered any agenda for the future to counter the vision of hope projected by Cory. His campaign had been largely negative. In addition to painting Cory and her supporters red, he had retained General Ver and had allowed rumors of martial law in the event of an opposition victory to fester.

Once his health improved in late January, those who were urging the president to switch gears and pursue the high road took heart. As a host of postponed southern rallies was put back on the calendar, his aides predicted a transformation in the campaign persona of their boss from the "not-quite-like-old Marcos" to a visionary and conciliatory "new Marcos," prepared to use the next six-year mandate he was confident of winning to correct past mistakes and assure himself an honorable place in his country's history.

"A new Marcos will emerge from the cocoon of the old," predicted his often-critical minister of labor, Blas Ople, who even went so far as to talk about "a national unity government," in which leaders of the opposition would be invited to participate. A few other perceptive men had been similarly encouraged by Marcos to believe that major changes were just around the corner.

Makati businessman Enrique Zobel, who had managed to remain publicly apolitical throughout Marcos's two decades in power, stunned the business community several weeks before the election by expressing qualified support for the president in an interview in the influential financial daily *Business Day*. "I can only use my own experience as a businessman," explained Zobel shortly afterward. "If I have to take over a bankrupt corporation with corrupt managers, I have to calculate how long it will take to turn it around. By the time a housewife and her twenty business advisors get to know what is what and whom to weed out, two to three years will have passed. Meanwhile, the people in the provinces will still only be eating one meal a day." As Zobel saw it, "Marcos put these corrupt managers in place, so he knows who is who." Newly chastened by the strong appeal that Cory had demonstrated, Marcos would at last be forced to reform. "If he is a true student of history," said Zobel, "he will realize that he has to change, and he knows how to do it."

But Marcos did not change. When he resumed his travel schedule on January 27, addressing an enormous rally in the provincial capital of Negros Occidental, an area of intense NPA activity fueled by the depressed sugar industry, he did not depart an iota from the old Marcos script. His message was the same one of doom and paranoia, not about the real crisis that gripped the country, but about the motives of his opponents. There was almost nothing in it to tug at the heartstrings of one of the world's most sentimental peoples.

The centerpiece of Marcos's speech was a cleverly staged "giveaway," wherein local leaders joined him on the podium, as he signed stacks of freshly printed presidential decrees calling for the release of billions of pesos in aid and benefits to local people. "I have been blamed for the problem in the sugar industry," said Marcos to his constituents in "Sugarlandia." To help growers survive the depression in world sugar prices, he ordered a cornucopia of guarantees, loans, and other benefits worth 1.25 billion pesos ($62.5 million).

It was the cynical solution of a leader with little energy, imagination, or idealism left to draw on. The fact that his government lacked the financial resources to back up his promises made it all the more shameful. To increasingly deafening applause and cheers, he ordered that interest rates on loans to growers be lowered from 42 percent to 16 percent, that electricity rates be brought down, and that the price of sugar be subsidized above the present floor price.

Hitting his stride as the crowd grew more enthusiastic, Marcos returned to the subject of his opponent and the recurring theme of death. Summoning up whatever latent fears lurked in the minds of the people, whom he sensed liked the idea of change, but were not sure about Cory, Marcos built to a bizarre climax. "Many times I have faced death, and when some guardian angel told me, 'You are in danger,' I took precautions." Concluded Marcos, "That is what I am feeling now. You must warn your fellow Filipinos. Wake them up while it is still early and tell them Marcos and Tolentino are ready to die for the Philippines."

While the emptiness of the electoral spectacle staged by the Marcoses over the next two days repelled me, my last memories of them were strangely benign. I have wondered since then how that could be, just as I had wondered earlier how Ninoy could have portrayed the president as a failed hero rather than a grand villain.

In retrospect, I have concluded that it had something to do with the obvious intellect of the man, which managed to shine through even the pettiest of his speeches, reminding the listener of the unfulfilled potential of both Marcos and the Filipino people. It also had a lot to do with the legend that he and his wife had created for themselves. Even as that legend was being eroded by revelations about fake medals and hidden wealth, so it grew larger and more fascinating in its perversity. But what I found most intriguing about this couple was the power of their gall, their orneriness, their lack of shame. Never had I seen those qualities writ so large in two people.

Those were not attractive qualities, but they had merit in a third-world country as geographically and culturally fragmented, as poor, and as confused about its collective identity as the Philippines. For a time Marcos had put those qualities to good use, persuading international bankers and foreign governments to invest vast sums to build an infrastructure of roads, bridges, airports, irrigation canals, electricity and telephone lines to link the 7,100 islands together into something that might eventually behave more like a country than a collection of vindictive tribes. Initially, his orneriness had proved effective in helping him keep overbearing friends, like the U.S., and enemies, like the private armies of his rivals, in check. His lack of shame had allowed him to turn a deaf ear to critics of martial law.

But several years into the so-called "New Society," he had lost the point of it all and settled for the personal gains. Law and order had become synonymous with repression, development with theft, the state with himself.

By the time I met the Marcoses, all of their energy and enterprise was being put to the narrow purpose of survival. There was little positive to report about them, except the tenacity with which they were hanging on, and what I wrote about them was largely negative. And yet, curiously, they still agreed to interviews. Ninoy's friend Teodoro M. Locsin, the editor of the *Philippines Free Press*, had told me that his most lingering souvenir of the Marcoses was their persistence in trying to win him back to their side after jailing him during martial law. "They never gave up on me, they never stopped trying to win me over. They were always pushing. Imelda was always sending limousines for me."

My last souvenir was a similar one. It had been raining for days in Mindanao, and at each rally the mud and water on the playing fields, where the reporters and the masses stood, grew deeper. At the last rally, I had sunk so far into the muck that I had lost one of my black espadrilles. Afraid to bend down and search for it, lest I be trampled by a huge, restless crowd, I had gratefully accepted an abandoned, white, plastic shoe, which a Filipino woman standing next to me had found underfoot.

Halfway through the rally, one of Marcos's security men had spotted me, shin-deep in the mud. He nudged Marcos to look at the plight of a member of the "meddling foreign press." I assumed they would conclude that it served me right and simply gloat over my predicament. Instead, the president signaled a bodyguard to fetch me and help me up onto the dry stage. Once there, others gave me a towel and helped me wipe off my legs and feet. On seeing that I was wearing a mismatched set of shoes, they all had a good laugh.

After the rally, the First Lady found that she had one empty seat on the jet that would carry her and Tolentino back to Manila. She offered me a ride. During the hour-long flight, while Tolentino slept, Imelda munched on butter cookies and bantered about campaign strategy and the recent American newspaper exposés on Marcos's medals. "Timing is everything in a campaign," she said, crediting Marcos with the decision to delay his trip to Mindanao until now. "Our strategy was to fix up Manila first," she said. "By now we know more or less what the opposition is saying, so we just come back to the places where they have already been and counter them." As for the suspiciously timed reports that the president's claims to have led a guerrilla unit were fraudulent, Imelda smiled a distant smile. "Marcos can flaunt his war record," she said. "The shrapnel in his body is his proof." As imprecise as always about her facts, she added, "Filipinos know that at the time he was fighting for his country, Doy and Ninoy were sitting in the imperial palace in Japan."

She appeared relaxed and confident that Marcos and Tolentino would win, and that these last several days had been well spent. She concluded the conversation by invoking one of her favorite brand names. "Like riding a Rolls-Royce," she said, "I like campaigning only for the best."

Her Lincoln Continental limousine was waiting for her at the entrance to the Villamor Air Force Base terminal. She insisted on giving me a ride. I tried to stamp the rest of the mud off my shoes before I climbed into the richly carpeted backseat with its organdy-covered footrests. She laughed and told me not to bother. It was then that I first noticed what would soon become the legacy of her years in office—her shoes. She was wearing a pair of Valentino espadrilles that were by far the most attractive and stylish of that genre of canvas-and-straw footwear I had ever seen. I complimented her. She giggled and thanked me, explaining that she had enough identical sets to see her through the rigors of the campaign. I allowed as how I should have thought of that myself.

When the eight-car caravan, preceded by police cars with lights flashing, pulled up to the entrance of the Manila Hotel, attendants dashed to open the door for the First Lady. She gestured to my side of the car and giggled again as I was helped out and escorted to the front door, wearing one black espadrille and one white flat, caked with mud.

*   *   *

There was abroad in the land an undocumentable, unquantifiable force that had welled up from sources deep within the Filipino populace. For want of a better name, it had been dubbed "People Power." Untapped since martial law, it had been divined by Ninoy, but it had not burst to the surface until after his assassination. In search of a medium since then, it had found one in the candidacy of Cory Aquino.

I witnessed it one day during the final week of the campaign in the neglected region of Southern Luzon known as the Bicol peninsula, where Cory would win her greatest margins. In the half-hour before the two candidates' private planes appeared over the dune-bordered beach at the end of the runway at Bagasbas Airport, a massive traffic jam formed, almost imperceptively, on the airport tarmac. At first kids on bikes, yellow and green balloons bobbing from their handlebars, peddled in. Next, horse-drawn *calesas* began to arrive, followed by motorized tricycles with Bible verses stenciled on their mudguards. Then came crowded passenger jeepneys, draped with green and yellow bunting, and finally trucks, vans, and even a limousine.

At the heart of the Aquino-Laurel campaign here, as elsewhere, was a core group of middle-class, nonpolitician doctors and lawyers, who had volunteered their services to the opposition candidates or to the citizen watchdog group NAMFREL, rather than to any party. Some 30,000 residents had pledged their availability on election day to form a "Vigilante Brigade" that would station itself throughout the province to patrol the 480 polling places and to accompany the ballots from precinct to provincial capital.

Mingling with the nonpolitician volunteers were numerous traditional politicians, who suddenly sensed the return to power by the opposition and were eager to share the limelight with the popular party standard-bearers. "I call Cory Aquino Marcos's greatest miscalculation," said former

Congressman Pedro Venida. But like most other Filipinos, he was worried about what would happen after the votes were cast. If Marcos won, the people would protest the election results. If Marcos lost, he would refuse to surrender power.

Given the circumstances, Venida and his colleagues welcomed the well-publicized arrival at Subic Bay of ships from the U.S. Seventh Fleet. "The presence of the Seventh Fleet gives Filipinos the message that the Americans want clean elections," explained Venida. "The mere appearance of the Seventh Fleet Band on TV the other night gave a message of calm, a message designed to prevent the possibility of a military takeover." Contrary to Marcos's portrayal of the opposition as opponents of the U.S. bases, who would kick them out, leaving the country open to invasion by the Soviets, observed Venida, "If there were a contest between the Philippine military and the American military, we still prefer the imported." Only half-jokingly, he added, "As a people we are still willing to pay extra for the American brand name."

As the Aquino-Laurel motorcade of some 1,000 supporters inched its bumpy way along the four-kilometer route into the provincial capital of Daet, it multiplied itself by twenty, into a solid mass of chanting, cheering evangelists. Mothers holding children freshly dressed in yellow waited on the front stoops of their modest *nipa* huts to wave a yellow handkerchief or towel at the yellow pickup truck carrying Cory and Doy. Men with faces wrinkled from the sun and backs stooped by years of labor in the fields stood along the roadside and followed her with eyes suddenly alive to the prospect of light at the end of a long, dark tunnel.

As rural huts gave way to houses, the roadside crowds thickened. More jeepneys stationed themselves on the shoulders so passengers inside and on top could catch a glimpse of the small, bespectacled woman who dared challenge the dictator. "Co-ry, Co-ry," they chanted, returning the "L" (for Laban) sign that she flashed at them with both hands. A mobile sound system wafted opposition songs and campaign hype across rice paddies glistening in the morning sun.

By the time the caravan reached the outskirts of town, people were standing ten-deep to greet her, pelting her with flowers and confetti or running alongside her vehicle, trying to prolong their encounter. Down the main street of town they moved, past small businesses with names reflecting their faith and the distant horizons of their dreams: Angel Hardware, Electrical and Construction Supply . . . California Bakery . . . Celestial Memorial Life Plan. From storefronts, sidewalks, windows, and rooftops people cheered.

Kids on stilts stretched to get a better look, old men fought to hold back tears, and dozens of brown hands sought to clasp the pale palm of the candidate. Filipino Life . . . J & H Rice Dealer . . . Mercury Drug

. . . Bumblebee Pizza Parlor. Welcome Cory & Doy streamers competed with store signs and marquees for prominence, while yellow confetti made from shredded yellow pages rained down from office windows, and cries of "*tama na! sobre na!*" (enough! too much!) rose up from shop floors as she passed. Our Nation's Hope for a Meaningful Change read one storefront streamer. "She is our liberator, God Almighty has sent her to us," blared the mobile public address system.

I was overcome. Ninoy's funeral had been this big and this emotional, but people's attitudes then had been tentative. Now they were determined. These people lining the streets had waited years to make a commitment. They were pragmatists. They were not inclined toward tilting at windmills. They did not want more violence than they already had. And yet, they were allowing themselves once more to dream the impossible dream of peaceful deliverance from poverty and abusive authority to an ideal of democracy, which four decades of American influence had inculcated in them.

Aquino and Laurel seemed to point a way out of the impasse with a plan for nonviolent change, which they articulated at rallies such as this one, spelling out each citizen's role and responsibility in the days ahead. The opposition ticket enjoyed the implicit support of the U.S. government, which was sending observers to monitor the polls on election day, and of the Roman Catholic Church, which was encouraging citizen participation in NAMFREL. With both heads and hearts, the multitudes here today were responding to Cory's call and awaiting her instructions.

It was Laurel's role to fire up the audience and exhort the people to protect themselves and their ballots. With humor and brimstone, he led them in chants of "Laban" and listed the provisions they should carry with them to the polls when they voted on Friday morning: food, water, flashlights for the all-night vigil that would be necessary to prevent cheating in the vote tabulation process, and *dos por dos* (two by two's) for self-defense.

There followed another presentation designed to educate voters to the blandishments that might be offered by the KBL on election day and to remind them that the bishops of the Church had said in a recent pastoral letter that it was permissible for those in need to accept the money offered to them, but to vote the way their consciences directed them.

Last on the program was Cory, whose basic campaign speech relating the life and death of her martyred husband had by now been expanded to include references to other, more recent victims of Marcos. As tears appeared in the eyes of her listeners, she assumed a more aggressive tone, signaling them to be courageous. "In Basilan," she related, "someone wrote on the wall, 'Cory Aquino, you are only one bullet.'" But she added, "Don't worry, I am not afraid of Marcos."

Cory listed the problems faced by the country on every front, problems that these people knew firsthand: a corrupt government, poverty, unemployment, military abuses. She did not promise to solve their problems for them, she promised only to help them to help themselves. "I am not only asking for your votes, but for sacrifices, so our country will work better," she said. To mounting applause, she vowed to form a committee to investigate Marcos's hidden wealth and not to allow the Muslim areas to secede from the Philippines. She concluded her brief remarks by refuting Marcos's charges against her. "I am not a Communist, I have never been a Communist, and I will never be a Communist," she declared. "I am a Catholic. After twenty years of Marcos misrule, we have more or less sixteen thousand Communists in this country, and Mr. Marcos is the number one recruiter."

An hour later Cory boarded her plane, accompanied by several family members and close friends. The cordon of burly security guards from her home province of Tarlac, who once protected Ninoy, preceded her in one small plane, running mate Laurel and his party in another. Once aloft, I asked her to turn her thoughts to election day and after.

"I know that during my first few months I need to have one project that will have a dramatic impact on the poor," she began. Although she had been opposed to the hypocrisy of the Marcoses' so-called "impact projects," she had learned from her campaigning that the people still remembered populist President Magsaysay's program of more than three decades ago to install an artesian well in every town. She had been shocked to find that a local supply of potable water was still a luxury in many parts of the Philippines. "Water must be the number one priority," she said. She would also need to do "something very dramatic" on the peace front.

Sensing, correctly, that I was skeptical about her chances for victory, she goaded me to have more faith. "I am so convinced I am going to win," she said, sounding as though she really believed it. I agreed that today's emotional high could leave that impression, but I still could not imagine Marcos or the military allowing that to happen. While on the subject of the military, I turned off my tape recorder and asked her if she had heard anything more from some "friendly colonels" she had mentioned the week before.

She had relayed word to me through Ballsy that some reformist military officers, who had offered her their support, were preparing to disguise themselves as NPAs and to ambush a truck carrying a shipment of fake ballots, which the KBL had ordered, to provincial capitals just before election day. The officers had asked Doy to provide them with dynamite to do the job. Cory was to see that sympathetic journalists would be on the spot, ready to record the incident, which would expose fraud in the Marcos camp even before the voting took place. I was asked if I would stand by to cover the event.

I had thought about it and had relayed word back that this sounded like a harebrained scheme that could easily backfire on her. While I, as a reporter, might be obliged to go anywhere for a possible story, even under compromising circumstances, it frightened me to think that her name might be linked to something like this after the fact. I even suspected that the soldiers who proposed it might be pro-Marcos men trying to frame her, or CIA plants who might themselves be exposed. She did not comment on my expressed fears, nor did she indicate whether or not she had communicated further with the soldiers, although in the end nothing came of the proposal.

However, she confided that she had had an even more interesting conversation with a group of RAM officers, who had indicated that they were planning to stage some kind of operation and had sought her support. Off the record, she said that these men had claimed during a secret meeting with her that they had the support of 1,000 out of 30,000 AFP officers and felt that others would join them "when they finally stage whatever they will." Although she acted vague about their plans, she added, "I think they realize they cannot do this without the backing of a political figure or a national figure, and this is where I come into the picture."

Concerned that the military might be antagonized by her cease-fire proposal, she said she had asked the reformists for their opinions. She was heartened by their response. "They said that even Marcos asked for one with the Muslims in 1973, under heavy pressure from the Arab countries. They remembered their fellow soldiers being killed by the Moro National Liberation Front. It hurt them to see the Muslims go free, but they did not object. They said they are all for me calling a cease-fire. They appreciate the value of human life."

During their discussion, she said, the reformists had told her how they were asked by some American military people why they supported her. Their response was that on the night Ninoy was buried, all Cory would have had to do was give the word, and a mob could have stormed the gates of Malacañang and killed Marcos. They had praised her restraint.

She had reaffirmed to the officers her desire for peaceful change, but she had described how during a recent twelve-day campaign sortie, many people had told her they were prepared to die for her. "I said, 'I am convinced that if these people shouting for me are prepared to die for me, whether it's all drama or not, some of them mean it, and if I am cheated in the elections, I can get these people to demonstrate in the streets to pressure Marcos to bring about certain reforms, if not to install me as president.' "

She was not anxious to exploit that charisma however. She was concerned that protests against anticipated election fraud might lead to more violence, but, she admitted, "I cannot just say, 'Okay,' if I lose. Nobody will believe I lost." She wished that more Filipinos had been trained in the art of nonviolence, because then a campaign of civil disobedience could be effective. But, she acknowledged, nonviolence "really requires a high degree of sanctity." Her best alternative, if she should lose through cheating, she suggested, would probably be to "say we will demonstrate, but emphasize that nobody will win if Filipino lives are sacrificed in the process."

Still, she predicted, "I think the military will come into the picture if they perceive gross irregularities will be committed." She said some Americans had asked her, "Do you realize that all these generals will be against you?" She had impressed them with her Machiavellian response. "All of the colonels are aspiring to be generals," she said.

*   *   *

The colonels and captains of RAM had confided far more to Cory than they had to me and other journalists. What I did not know until well after the fact was that by August 1985, three months before Marcos suddenly decided to call an election, the RAM Core Group had revised their original strategy of girding for a post-Marcos grab for power by their superiors and were instead planning a coup against Marcos himself.

As the Graft and Corruption Court had moved inexorably toward acquitting General Ver and the other accused soldiers of guilt in the Aquino conspiracy, the reform officers felt time running out on their movement. Those who were publicly identified with RAM would surely find themselves in trouble once Ver was reinstated as chief of staff. Nor did Marcos's death any longer appear imminent. "The point had always been that we thought President Marcos was going to die," said Vic Batac, one of the founders of the reform officers' Core Group. "His death was supposed to trigger our move. We really could not legitimate a move if the president did not die."

Several events and two diverse personalities had, however, conspired to change their minds. One was Enrile, who by mid-1985 was sounding increasingly like a presidential candidate pursuing his own agenda. Marcos had responded to his defense minister's increasing air of independence by further reducing his already diminished responsibilities. In July he removed the Integrated National Police from Enrile's ministry and placed it under direct presidential control. After Enrile endorsed the abolition of Amendment Number 6, which granted Marcos his decree-making powers, Marcos warned him, "If you are going to injure my interests, we know how to take care of you."

Enrile's political frustration had reinforced the Core Group's own growing restiveness over the inability of the reform movement to make an impact, as long as Ver still enjoyed Marcos's confidence. Its leaders began talking to the minister about moving against Marcos himself. "We realized you cannot really reform the AFP if you don't reform the society," said Batac. Enrile, who had entertained notions of a coup on previous occasions, but had always changed his mind, gave them his blessing this time. The officers set several timetables for their planned move against the palace, the firmest being December 26, 1985.

Unbeknownst to Enrile, Colonel Jose Almonte, a fifty-four-year-old former Marcos ally with a lively intellect and considerable charisma, had been preaching the virtues of a coup to some of Enrile's boys. Almonte, who had been relieved of his post as director of Marcos's think tank, the Philippine Center for Strategic Studies, in 1979 but had remained on the intelligence roster, had been "floating" ever since. Shortly after the reform movement came out of the closet in early 1985, he had expressed an interest in RAM to Gringo Honasan, who had introduced him to some of the other involved officers.

Before very long Almonte had insinuated himself informally into the ranks of the Core Group as sort of an "an elder brother." Having fought his own battles within the Marcos military well before the consciousness of the young RAM officers had been raised to the inherent corruption and politicization in the ranks, Almonte was enormously supportive of their efforts to implement reforms, and he quickly won the confidence of many of them. Some, however, remained wary of his close connection to Alejandro Melchor, Marcos's sacked former executive secretary, who was widely perceived as an "American boy." Among the wariest, when he learned of Almonte's involvement, was Enrile.

By his own admission, Almonte had, in August 1985, listened to the Core Group's initial plans to force a bloodless change of leadership in the military, through psychological warfare, and told them flatly, "Peaceful means will not work." He also made it clear that President Marcos, not Ver or General Ramas, must be their target. At first he was shouted down by the group, which had imbibed well its American-inspired indoctrination on the sanctity of civilian supremacy. Later, however, three key officers, Honasan, Kapunan, and Batac, had confided to Almonte that they too had come to believe that a more far-reaching action than they had been preparing for would be necessary. They asked him for advice.

"I told them," said Almonte, " 'We are talking about revolutionary politics, and that is like a cobra. You never play with it below the head. If you cannot strike the head, forget it, for the cobra will strike you.' " Playing the role of guru, Almonte engaged in a long series of dialogues with the young officers in order to help prepare them for the mission that was beginning to take shape in their minds.

"Will we succeed?" one of them asked him at the start.

"This enterprise is not measured by success," Almonte answered. "This is a social action. We do it if it is our conviction that it is right. Once we have decided to do it and die for it, then it is a success."

"Sir, we will all die," declared one officer, as the realization struck him for the first time.

Almonte, a military romantic, replied, "It is precisely in dying that we will be successful." Moved by the moment, the four men rose and embraced each other. "It is very rare that a group of young men like you is given the right to die for your country," said Almonte. "We should be grateful to Marcos for having given us this privilege."

Almonte, because of his age, offered to lead the palace attack, but the younger men would not hear of it. He then made one request: that a Soviet-made AK-47 machine gun, which he had brought back from the war in Vietnam as a gift to the president, but had never presented to him, be used now to assassinate him.

During that encounter the men committed themselves to two principles, which their fellow officers would similarly accept as they too were drawn into the plot. If they succeeded in acquiring power, they would "return to barracks," turning the government over to a group of qualified civilian and military leaders. Once back in the barracks, they would seek "no rewards, promotions, or positions" in return for their act. "If we ask for anything," vowed Almonte, "it is a hope that the government that will be installed will seek to actualize the yearnings of our people."

Marcos's snap election announcement caused chaos in the ranks of the Core Group, which was forced to postpone its coup plans, lest its motives appear undemocratic. "We did not want to deny the opposition the opportunity to ascend to power peacefully," said Batac. However, on the assumption that a fair election would not be allowed to take place, the officers continued to organize support for an eventual coup. Meanwhile, RAM members worked at building "linkages" with political and business leaders, whose trust they would need at the appointed hour. Cory Aquino was such a leader.

18

The First Campaign

Had the Philippines been a democracy, and had a "new Marcos" emerged in the course of the campaign, I might have covered the 1986 presidential race as I would have a Western election: spending time in each camp, talking to voters, and reporting who won on election day. But the Philippines had not been a democracy for the past fourteen years. Even before martial law, although power had alternated with regularity from one party to the other, the concept of a loyal opposition had not existed the way it did in Western democracies. With martial law, the opposition had become the mortal enemy of the regime, and a huge army had been established, in large part, to keep it in check.

There was no "new Marcos," willing to disappear, de Gaulle-like, into retirement if the people rejected him. In that event Filipinos feared that the "old Marcos," threatened with defeat, would call on his armed forces to prevent Cory from taking office. Nor was the burden of guilt entirely on Marcos. As Cory herself had observed, hopes for victory were now running so high among opposition supporters that they would never believe an honest defeat possible. If she lost, they would take to the streets claiming fraud. Their protests would most certainly be exploited by the Communists.

In such a context, the idea of a democratic election being allowed to proceed to its logical conclusion was inconceivable to most analysts and observers. Thus, while the major players on both sides continued their charade of doing everything possible to insure that one took place, all of them were girding for the inevitable showdown that would follow the vote. What form it would take—whether it could be something as benign as the "second campaign" that Peping Cojuangco and Robert Trent Jones, Jr., were preparing, or whether a loyalist military coup, a RAM "exercise," a civil war, or a revolution was more to be feared—would depend largely on who moved first and what sanction their actions received from the U.S.

Journalistic coverage of the February 7 election therefore required keeping a close watch on the machinations, not only of the politicians, but of the power brokers on the sidelines. Most menacing was the Armed Forces of the Philippines, the bulwark of Marcos's authoritarian government, which remained under the command of General Ver, for whom defending the nation had become synonymous with defending Marcos. The emergence of RAM as an alternate power group within the AFP, with bridges to church, liberal business, and opposition political groups, was an encouraging development, although it was difficult at the time for outsiders to gauge its potential strength or what its real plans were.

The only Philippine institution with influence comparable to the AFP was the Roman Catholic Church. While struggling to remain above politics by exhorting its flock to vote its conscience and channeling its support through officially neutral organizations like NAMFREL, it felt a moral obligation to help the fragile, unarmed, democratic opposition.

The perceived arbiter of the postelection process was the U.S. government. It was the only force powerful enough to prevent Marcos and the AFP from prevailing, if they prevented the voters' will from being manifested, either through fraud or an outright coup. No one expected that the Americans would intervene through the use of force—the presence of the Seventh Fleet was merely a symbolic deterrent. Rather, they hoped the U.S. would use its power over the purse strings of the AFP and its influence with the international lending agencies to pressure Marcos to step down.

While it was tempting to assume that the Reagan administration would not have supported a "snap election" if it did not have some blueprint for bringing the process to a successful conclusion, the reality was that Laxalt had departed from the prepared script when he encouraged Marcos to seek a new mandate, and the contingency planners had barely been able to keep up with events, much less anticipate what would happen once the votes were counted. When the postelectoral storm broke, American policymakers would be forced to fly by the seats of their pants, hoping that by the time they could see the ground, the "constitutionalists" whose campaigns they had simultaneously encouraged—Aquino-Laurel and RAM—would be occupying it. It was fortunate to have in the cockpit a crew of experienced diplomats, blessed with calm nerves and a steady fix on the political center, who would be determining where and when to land.

*   *   *

Tension within the Armed Forces of the Philippines had reached a flashpoint by election day, as Marcos's generals awaited his orders, and the reform officers anticipated their consequences. Since his reinstatement in November, Ver was back with a vengeance. The much-publicized "reorganization," which Marcos had set in motion as a justification for returning Ver to the top command, had turned out to be the sham which RAM members had predicted. Relations between Ver and General Ramos were brittle. What modest progress had been made toward reform during Ramos's brief incumbency was threatened by Ver, who had maintained control over major promotions and assignments throughout the period of his leave. As for RAM, it was certain to be targeted by Ver and Marcos, once the snap election period was over.

In fact, the Fourth Classmen, as the members of the Core Group were also known, had received information that Marcos had already furnished Ver with warrants for their arrest. Without revealing their own evolving coup plans, the officers turned to the new assistant U.S. defense attaché, Lieutenant Colonel Victor Raphael, for advice. During the period when RAM was emerging into the public eye and receiving its first good reviews from Pentagon officials, they had become close to Raphael's predecessor. When he had been transferred one month ago, he had told Raphael, "These are my boys, take good care of them." Raphael had been able to confirm their suspicions that secret, undated arrest warrants had been issued in September 1985 for those officers who had become publicly identified with RAM.

"That was a turning point," observed Batac. "They were suspecting, correctly, that we were planning to do something against them." Feeling cornered, the Fourth Classmen began looking for ways to defend themselves. Once again Raphael was able to be helpful. He invited his friend Dr. Jeffrey Race, an independent financial risk consultant with close Pentagon contacts, to meet them. Race, who was in Manila at the time on business, had written articles critical of the Marcos regime and an insightful book about America's ill-fated counterinsurgency campaign in Vietnam, which some of the officers had read.

"His insights were fantastic," said Captain Robles later. "He talked about how to deal with the insurgency and Marcos, and how to protect a mass movement within the military by making alliances with the retired generals and with the Church. We understood that this was a game of alliances, but we were poor at it." From the American perspective, such linkages with civilian organizations and the private business community represented a form of life insurance for the officers, as well as a source of private funds, which would help lessen their dependency on the military or on individuals like Enrile. "The worst way to go about moral regeneration," one American visitor advised the Core Group leaders, "would be to ally yourselves with a political party."

Cruder subjects were not discussed in the presence of the Americans. "We were not talking about coups and weapons," said one of those present during the discussion. "We were talking about the corruption of the AFP and doing the right thing professionally and morally in a murky situation."

Among the greatest concerns of the Fourth Classmen were the growth of the Communist insurgency and the Marcos government's failure to mount a coherent political, economic, and military offensive against it. "How can we hope to put up a respectable counterinsurgency, if we cannot get the word through to the commander in chief?" asked Gringo Honasan. "Every time the minister or General Ramos is in the mood to talk about it, General Ver places a derogatory report about the reform movement on the top of the presidential pile."

That was exactly the complaint the Americans made against Ver. It was a key reason why more and more American policymakers had given up hope of mounting an effective counterinsurgency as long as Ver and Marcos were in command. It was another reason why the Americans liked what RAM was saying. "We certainly encouraged the ideals they were espousing," said Assistant Secretary of Defense Armitage, "the need to get rid of insurgency, combat corruption, return to being an apolitical army. Those are things like motherhood or apple pie that we could support, and we were sending a very loud and clear signal through our testimony in Congress that very much coincided with what we were telling them."

The election campaign offered the Core Group, through its public front organization, RAM, a golden opportunity to promote the apple-pie aspects of the reform movement all over the country. The reform officers had no trouble financing *Kamalayan* 86 (Consciousness 86), the campaign of prayer meetings in support of free elections, which they mounted. If anything, the money came too easily from anti-Marcos sources, who were looking to buy their own protection from General Ver's forces. Businessman Jimmy Ongpin, who had become publicly identified with the Aquino campaign, was open in his support of RAM, telling a group of visiting American executives in October, "The military reform movement is one of the most important developments in the Philippines today."

"Jimmy was so excited about it that he wanted to give it a lot of publicity," Robles recalled with a smile. RAM encouraged him to dampen his public enthusiasm and point them to private support. In no time, so much money was coming in that Almonte had to caution his colleagues against accepting contributions of more than 1,000 pesos, "in order to keep yourselves broad-based."

Under the benign public cover of Kamalayan 86, RAM officers were able to extend their network of support for the secret operation they were planning. During visits to military camps, they recruited more of their classmates. In speeches to community groups, they propagated their image as the "good guys" in uniform, hoping that by the time the coup came, Filipinos would be able to make a distinction between the reform-minded officers and the jaded commanders of General Ver.

Meanwhile, the Core Group was preoccupied with drafting tactical plans for capturing or killing Marcos and Ver, an operation which still had not drawn the unanimous agreement required for the implementation of any action. "It was a very difficult thing for us to involve ourselves in something political, because that has never been the role of the Philippine military," stressed Colonel Malajacan. "So while we had the forces available to do it, how to utilize them was something else."

Colonel Almonte played an influential role in winning over the hold-outs by proffering an ideology which justified a soldier's right "to question the unquestionable Marcos." As the election campaign unfolded, even the most reluctant officers concluded that Marcos, by his refusal to resign his office in order to run for reelection, and by his stonewalling of vital election reforms, had every intention of blocking, rather than furthering, prospects for peaceful change. That made a coup against him easier for them to justify. "We had been trying to look to the point where there was no other alternative but to topple Marcos," said Malajacan. That point was reached when the snap election became official. By late November 1985, he related, "the tactical commanders were just waiting for the signal. We had laid out our plans. We would take over Malacañang."

A potentially greater problem than getting rid of Marcos was deciding whom to put in his place. "We were simply after change, and we wanted to make it clear that we were not after power," said Malajacan. However, plenty of politicians were, and they were already seeking to align themselves with the officers who might grab or share power after Marcos. The particular bone of contention between Enrile and Almonte and their respective Core-Group supporters was Almonte's political ally, Alex Melchor.

"It was Almonte who was floating the names of people who would be on the National Reconciliation Council [NRC]," said Enrile, referring to the body which the Core Group planned to invite to take power. "What I heard was that Melchor was coming into the picture." Having tangled with Melchor during martial law, when the then executive secretary almost succeeded in getting Enrile fired, the defense minister harbored little sympathy for him. "Don't trust Melchor," he warned his "boys," who regarded Melchor as a Trojan horse for the Americans.

If she had not been considered for membership on the NRC before she became a candidate, Cory Aquino became a prime nominee once the campaign began. It was Almonte who initiated RAM's contact with her. Well before Cory decided to run for president, some of her supporters had been put in touch with Almonte. A mutual friend had subsequently tried to get the colonel and Cory's brother together for a meeting, but Cojuangco had not been anxious to meet the former Marcos man. "I thought he might be a mole," said Peping. In an effort to check out Almonte, Peping had asked Ambassador Bosworth what he knew about him. When Bosworth rendered a credible assessment, Cojuangco agreed to talk to him.

By the time Cojuangco and Almonte got together for a serious discussion, the snap election campaign was already under way. Almonte told him that the reform officers were planning to stage a coup against Marcos. "They were asking for assurance that Cory would publicly support them if ever they made their move," said Peping, "because they felt they could never succeed without it."

Other obvious choices for membership on the NRC were Enrile and Ramos, as well as a prominent businessman. It was roundly agreed that General Ramos, who was represented in the Core Group by two officers, would hold the military seat on the council. Although many officers had been disappointed at the "lack of vinegar" he had displayed as acting chief of staff, all of them acknowledged his moral leadership. "Because of his own interests, he was providing us with the moral support we needed to do what was right for the AFP," said Malajacan. The Americans were solidly behind Ramos, but decidedly cold toward Enrile.

No one was to be informed of his selection to the council until the coup was a fait accompli. "Our joke," said Malajacan, "was that we would haul them into one room and tell them, 'Okay, we will give you five minutes to connive, and then tell us whether you accept the invitation or not.' "

RAM officers held meetings with numerous other oppositionists as well. One Core-Group member reported, "The opposition has said that RAM asked for their support, but it was the opposite. They were begging us to move against Marcos. They were offering arms and money if we would move." Among the requests which RAM officers made of oppositionists in advance of the rebellion was a mobilization of people in the streets to deter the loyalist military.

Almonte made just such a request of Peping Cojuangco and his stunning wife, Ting-Ting. In an effort to block loyalist troop reinforcements, which Ver could be anticipated to call down from the "solid North" when the action broke out in Manila, Almonte asked the Cojuangcos to organize their people in their own province of Tarlac, which was centrally located between Manila and Ilocos Norte, to "steal trucks and block the roads." In compliance, Peping recruited a number of truck drivers to serve as campaign leaders in Tarlac. When the need arose, they were there to create a blockade. Other Cojuangco allies saw to it that Manila hospitals were well stocked with blood supplies in advance of the reformists' move. Ting-Ting, a former model who had cut a fine figure when she donned fatigues to join the ranks of the street demonstrators following Ninoy's assassination, earnestly organized a "flower brigade," which would attempt to disarm loyalist soldiers, if and when they were ordered to fire on civilians.

The reformists' hyperactivity naturally deepened the suspicions of Ver and his men that they were up to no good. Several of the officers were called to account for their actions. When Ver tried to cancel their final climactic prayer meeting, which was to be held in a Manila sports coliseum owned by a well-known opposition family, RAM called on one of its strongest supporters to reason with the chief of staff—retired General Jesus Vargas, Ver's counterpart during the Magsaysay presidency and head of a group of respected retired officers, who had formed a RAM auxiliary group wryly known as SCRAM. Said Vargas to Ver, "All they are saying is that we should have clean and honest elections. What is wrong with saying that now? That is what the president says." Ver had no recourse but to stand down.

*   *   *

"I am staying out of politics," said Cardinal Sin, with a twinkle of the eye. In fact, the jovial, joke-telling Archbishop of Manila was as important a player as there was in these elections. He had come only gradually to his reputation as a major critic of the Marcos regime and protector of the struggling democratic opposition, and even now many of his parishioners thought he was too conciliatory. However, no one was more comically candid about where he stood than the cardinal himself. Chuckling over his much-criticized embrace of President Marcos during a mass of reconciliation on the dictator's sixty-eighth birthday, and the release of two white doves, Sin recalled, "The president's dove soared into the sky, but my dove went straight to Ambassador Bosworth, awaiting instructions from Washington!"

Several weeks after he had helped to broker the Aquino-Laurel ticket, Sin had been invited to say the traditional New Year's Eve mass at the palace. He had looked forward to a dialogue with the president, but had found him in extremely poor health, forced repeatedly to be helped to the bathroom. "He could not even walk, and his fingers were so swollen he did not shake hands, because it was so painful," said the cardinal. In Marcos's absence, Imelda berated the prelate, asking, "Why are you always against us?"

Before leaving, the cardinal asked Marcos, "Why did you call for the snap election instead of filling out your term?" The president, observed Sin, "could not answer me, because he was caught now in this tragicomedy." Sin believed that Marcos had called the election to bluff his opponents, never intending to follow it through, but that events had forced his hand. The cardinal asked Marcos if he had been pressured by the U.S. to try for a new mandate. Marcos indicated that he had acted on his own, believing that he would win. "Mr. President, there is a great danger you will lose, because the people are mad," warned the cardinal. That was the last time the two men saw each other.

Since then, reflecting what he believed to be the will of the people, the cardinal had actively engaged the Church in the task of assuring free and honest elections. "I am only giving guidance to my people, because they are asking for guidance," explained Sin, who was a master at cloaking controversial actions in euphemisms and parables. "My role is to see to it that harmony is maintained, because this opposition is very healthy for the country."

Thus far, his guidance had had a calming influence on his people. Fearing violence, he had counseled activist churchmen against civil disobedience. "Some of them wanted to pray inside the polling places," he chuckled, "but I said, 'How can they vote if you are there praying?'" Instead, he had worked to channel the energies of laymen and religious alike into the NAMFREL effort to protect the balloting process.

"I think it will be very hard for them to commit mistakes," said the cardinal, referring to Marcos's henchmen in the most neutral of language, "because the people are now very aware. Especially the women, who will not sleep, so how can the men sleep?" He had encouraged the women to volunteer as poll watchers. "I even told all the contemplative nuns to get out of the monasteries. They should vote and fast, and I think God will help us." Joking again, he said, "If it was allowed, I would tell them, 'You vote for this woman under pain of excommunication,' like they did in the sixteenth century."

Sin acknowledged his concern about what would happen after the voting. He said he would be meeting daily with his bishops until well after the election in an effort to ward off violence. Having activated his institution, he confided the hope that the U.S. would become similarly engaged. "They should not be watching like this," he said, his arms folded. What was needed to see the opposition through to victory, he confided, was money to pay, not only for their campaign travel and posters, but also for their poll watchers. "No one wins here without the help of America," he stated flatly.

When I expressed doubt that even money could win an election against the Marcos machine, the cardinal appealed to me to have more faith. "If it is a clean and honest election, Cory will win," he said. "I feel the people are really running after her." As if to cheer me up, he made a not-so-subtle reference to the fact that a good deal of campaign money was in fact passing through his hands. "The money just comes in addressed to me, but none of it is for the president," he said, holding up his palms in mock surrender. "Fifty thousand pesos from a parishioner for Cory, and I am bound to pass it on." He noted that most of it was flowing into the Philippines from the U.S., entrusted to him by Filipino-Americans, who wanted to be sure it went into the proper coffers.

The cardinal would soon have another reason to be optimistic about Cory's prospects. Immediately after the fraud-marred election, as RAM was finalizing its plans to oust Marcos, Colonel Almonte paid a call on the cardinal in his palace. The meeting had been arranged by Alex Melchor's wife. Without going into detail, Almonte told Sin that he had come as a representative of RAM to tell him the reformists were "ready to bring down Marcos." He was asking for the support of the cardinal "and the people," he said. Almonte recounted how, following the delivery of his message, "the cardinal embraced me for almost three minutes." His leave-taking was full of emotion. "This is the last time I will talk to you," said the colonel. Sin replied, "Please do your duty for God."

*   *   *

When Marcos called for a snap election, the U.S. suddenly found itself in the uncomfortable position of championing free and fair elections, while publicly and privately expressing support for a reform movement within the Philippine military, which was planning a coup to forcibly replace Marcos with a military-civilian junta. U.S. officials insist that they had not been able to foresee either the snap election or the coup when they had begun to court the political opposition, after the 1984 legislative elections, and to offer moral support to the RAM officers, after their organization came out of the closet in March 1985.

Indeed, both the opposition and RAM deserved to be cultivated on their separate merits. Both were non-Communist and prodemocratic, and both were forces to be reckoned with in the post-Marcos era. Meanwhile, since both had indicated a determination to press Marcos for badly needed reforms, each fit perfectly into the evolving U.S. strategy of "a long, slow separation from Marcos," as one Pentagon official described it.

"It was a game of shadows," said a U.S. official familiar with the subtle maneuvering that was necessary to withdraw support from Ferdinand

Marcos and transfer it to a new government, whose composition could not be precisely detailed very much in advance. "We knew Marcos had to go, but how do you get someone to go, when you have a treaty between your two countries which says you respect their government? What do you do? Drop the Hundred and First Airborne on Malacañang? We used to kill them when I was a boy, but we don't do that any more."

As time had passed, without any improvement in the state of affairs in the Philippines, more policymakers had expressed their readiness to avail themselves of the "other options" referred to in the National Security Directive "mousetrap clause." However, the choices were limited, not only by law and failed precedent, but by the openness of Philippine society, Filipinos' passion for gossip, and their tendency to accept rumors as fact. "We learned in the Philippines that doing business there is a very overt affair," said one official. "Everyone knows what you are doing."

Looking at it in retrospect, the policy which evolved was artfully tailored to exploit that very openness, and to play upon the assumptions and perceptions held by both Filipinos and Americans of the "special relationship." By withholding funds to the regime, prodding the opposition to organize and unify, and pressuring for military and political reforms, Washington had fenced Marcos in. Now the plan was, as one policy analyst articulated it, "to simply let nature take its course." The idea was clean and simple. "We will not do anything. We will not help Marcos. We will just say there have to be honest elections, an honest counting of the ballots, full media access. We would not have to let the CIA in. We would just have to let the Filipinos speak. All the supersecret documents would say was that the U.S. was supporting an honest election."

The elections to which he was referring, however, were the regularly scheduled local elections in May 1986 and the presidential election in June 1987, not an earlier "snap election." Had nature taken its course in those later contests, the ruling party was expected to fare poorly enough that Marcos would be forced by his own party mates to retire at the end of his term, or even before. By speeding up the scenario and calling a snap election, Marcos had gained a decided advantage over his opposition, which could only be countered by a bit of extra U.S. intervention to help Mother Nature.

The "extras" became discreetly available in record time. In addition to the $6-million campaign war chest which Filipino businessmen and other private contributors were able to raise for the opposition, the U.S. Agency for International Development channeled $369,000 to the Asia Foundation and a similar amount to NAMFREL for election-related projects, which were destined primarily to help the anti-Marcos forces. An opposition campaign official, who sought funds from the Asia Foundation for the printing of RAM's clean-election propaganda, was referred to NAM-

FREL, where the money was quickly made available. The Asia Foundation, meanwhile, came up with an almost instant grant to the Federation of Catholic Broadcasters, to set up a nineteen-station alternative to the crony radio networks for use during the campaign.

In November nature's course threatened to become a collision course, as U.S. State Department and Pentagon officials became aware that the reform officers were planning a coup, even as the snap election campaign was getting under way. Before election day, they were forced to make some critical, last-minute adjustments. "You don't stage a coup to win an election" is the way one U.S. policymaker summed up his feelings, on learning one week before the snap election that the RAM officers were indeed planning to move against Marcos.

The Pentagon had been officially in touch with RAM since May 1985, when it had dispatched a representative to Manila to personally meet the reformists, whom U.S. officials were already praising in their congressional appeals for more military assistance. The Pentagon representative had been impressed by their professionalism and their distress over the strength of the insurgency and the politicization and corruption from top to bottom in the military. "They saw the U.S. holding its nose and dealing with the military on the one hand and blanket disapproval of the AFP by Filipinos on the other," he related, "and they basically said, 'We cannot stand this.'"

As a token of Pentagon support, following that visit, said Armitage, "We sent them some things—not TOWS or Hawks, but copies of Colonel Harry Somers's analysis of the Vietnam war, *On Strategy*, which I paid for myself." The reformists were avid students of counterinsurgencies beyond the Philippines, and some of them were anxious to read this book.

When the Pentagon representative made a follow-up visit to Manila in November 1985, however, he sensed that the Core Group's attention had shifted from counterinsurgency theory to the nitty-gritty of plotting a coup. The reformists had learned about the warrants that had been issued for their arrests, and they were preoccupied with protecting themselves. As a military man himself, he said, "I feared the worst." By the time he returned to Washington, said the emissary, "I could not say that something would take place on February twenty-second, but I did know that these people believed they were at risk, and that their ability to withstand it was limited. They felt cornered."

No action was taken to try to rein in the reformists until the end of January 1986, however, when their coup-planning reached a point where it set off alarms in Washington. Admiral Crowe, who was by now chairman of the Joint Chiefs of Staff, indicated that while Washington had been privy to rumors of coup plotting for some time, it had been hard to take them seriously. "There were so many scheduled," he said, indicating he himself knew of ten or twelve. "Successful plotters do not share what they are going to do, yet these people were certainly very busy sharing what they had in mind." Moreover, the officers involved did not appear "very aggressive," leading U.S. military officials to surmise that the Filipino officers were having trouble getting a civilian leader to front for them.

On January 30, 1986, however, Armitage received reports, which he took seriously, that the leaders of RAM "planned to run a military event to try and change the government." Neither the date nor the time had been divulged, nor could the Americans' informants be certain about which of several targets would be chosen for initial attack. The information had come from an American operative, who had been approached by a RAM officer asking for antitank weapons. The agent had squeezed the Filipino for information in return. On January 31, Armitage and his aides met to discuss this development and draft a reply.

Armitage's reaction to the news, according to someone present at the meeting, was to say, "That is the wrong way to change a government. You cannot have a single military coup. After you have had one, it becomes a license for instability." By now, he indicated, Filipinos were deeply involved in the election campaign. "Marcos was clearly through. Whether Mrs. Aquino succeeded or not was a question. So the Defense Department's point was that events were moving toward a bloodless change, and it would be foolish as well as contrary to the proper role of the military to accelerate change through violent means."

Other U.S. military analysts, who had been more kindly disposed toward the notion of a coup, had, after studying the situation, added their objections on the separate ground that Ver's commanders controlled most of the troops and the armor, and that a RAM-initiated coup was therefore likely to fail, leading to civil war, "with the NPA watching happily from the sidelines." One officer commented, "I looked at their plan and said, 'Jeez.' First there was no way to keep this secure, especially in the Philippines, where the notion of security is a joke, and second, there was a big question militarily of whether they could put sufficient pressure on the loyalist forces to stop them rolling."

The information was shared with State Department officials, who, a Pentagon man suggested, "were surprised, knowing Armitage, that he said no way would he support it." A message was duly communicated to the embassy in Manila instructing the defense attaché to contact the RAM officers in question and pass the word that "the U.S. would not support under any circumstances a military coup." It was Colonel Raphael, by now a trusted confidant of key Core-Group leaders, who verbally relayed a message, which had been worked out over the phone between Washington and Manila.

There was relief on the State Department side of the embassy when it learned of Washington's response. The diplomats had been privy to numerous reports of coup plans, "which kept slipping," in the words of one political officer. They appeared to take it for granted that a coup would be among the contingencies for which their military counterparts would be prepared. But, said Bosworth, "We did not look kindly on a coup."

A year after Marcos's ouster—and several anti-Aquino coup attempts later—Bosworth observed that U.S. caution had proven well advised. "I had been staunchly resisting any temptation to stage a coup for many of the reasons we still see at play in the society," he said. He opined that the divisions, which had become evident within the AFP with each successive coup attempt against the Aquino government in 1986 and 1987, "are not as exaggerated as they would have been had we supported one faction." He added, "What I have always been suspicious of is the strain of moral absolutism in the reformist movement. There were many different people involved, not all of whom were motivated by professional concerns. Some of them raised the hair on the back of my neck. They were zealots, and they were not incorruptible."

Like his Pentagon counterparts, Bosworth discounted the possibility of success of any of RAM's coup plans, due to the transparency of their operations in general. "Ver had agents within the reform group," he said. He added acerbically, "Those guys had about as much operational security as Little Bo-peep. They held their meetings in the lobby of the Manila Peninsula."

However, the Pentagon message did not stop the RAM plotting. All that stopped was further traffic between Manila and Washington on the subject. "Maybe they got the impression in Manila that we did not want to be told," said a Washington official. That was the prevailing view inside the Core Group as they puzzled out the meaning of the verbal communiqué.

"Vic Raphael had memorized the message," reported Colonel Batac, "four crisp sentences in very diplomatic language." The first three warned against the coup. It was the fourth sentence which most of the reformists would later quote, because it seemed to add an important qualification. According to Batac, it indicated that the U.S. would understand if the Filipino officers found it necessary to act in the interests of their "enlightened self-defense." Said Batac, "On hearing that last sentence, we saw no problem with what we were planning."

"Frankly," said a Philippine intelligence officer and RAM member, "we were encouraged by the Americans. They could not interfere officially, but they agreed with our assessment of the situation."

Whatever the proportion of official American complicity, there came a time when there was nothing more to do but wait for February 7 and be prepared to deal with whatever came afterward. "To have a plan is a good idea," said Admiral Crowe, "but it is sort of a futile drill. When the time comes, you have to just hang on as the roller coaster goes down the hill."

*   *   *

Before dawn on election day, I headed for Ninoy and Cory's province of Tarlac, which was notorious for election fraud attributable to the forces of Marcos crony Danding Cojuangco. "Danding will try to embarrass me in Tarlac," Cory had predicted. Indeed, the coffee-shop consensus was that if Marcos could skew the vote enough to defeat her in her home province, which had become largely the fiefdom of her hostile cousin since Ninoy's imprisonment, he could more easily convince the country that she had lost elsewhere.

Cruising down the empty highway, past water buffalo in the rice paddies at sunrise, I wished that a relatively fraudless election might take place and surprise us all. What I feared, however, was a form of cheating so sophisticated that perhaps none of the hundreds of foreign observers standing at the required fifty-meter distance outside polling places all over the archipelago would be able to detect it. I recalled how little cheating I had been physically able to document during the 1984 election. Much more was riding on the conduct of this one.

I needn't have worried. Vote fraud, as carried out in the Philippines, was not a subtle art. The closer the election result was expected to be, the more brutal the attempts to fix it. The grossness of the fraud that was carried out in this election would reflect the further breakdown of the regime. Pretense, pride, secrecy were gone—behavior which desperate men could not afford. Orders were still being obeyed, but they were being executed crudely by gangs of mercenaries, who were without accountability or concern for the consequences to the president who issued them.

Doña Aurora was in residence in the Aquino ancestral home in Concepcion, as she had been for all the premartial-law elections since her marriage to Ninoy's father. She was overseeing meals for the Aquino campaign workers and fielding calls for reinforcements, first aid, and worse. The polls had opened at seven o'clock. At 8 A.M., one of her men reported a pro-Cory barrio councilman clubbed. At 8:30, a courier brought news of an Aquino poll watcher's arrest. Leaving the further serving of the eggs and sausages to her help, the seventy-five-year-old matriarch, dressed in yellow, summoned a Jeep and driver, climbed in, and was off for a day of election monitoring.

I took my leave of her and spent the rest of the day hitching rides with a variety of people from one *barangay* to another, along roads that were no more than the dry beds of rivers, a testimony to years of deliberate deprivation of public funds to the half of the province that remained loyal to Marcos's chief rival.

On reaching the humble *barangay* of Balutu, in the company of several other foreign journalists, I decided to go no further. Only four kilometers outside Concepcion and under the flight path of Clark Air Base, it seemed decades away from the mainstream and targeted for trouble. Four men with long arms, one wearing a constabulary uniform, blocked the road as we approached. Silently, three of them took aim at our windows as the fourth looked inside, then motioned us on.

Violence had already occurred in Balutu on election eve, said a young Filipino NAMFREL volunteer, who welcomed our arrival. About one o'clock in the morning, barrio counselor Carlito Garcia and his family were rudely awakened by the breaking of windows in their small, bamboo-frame house on stilts. When Garcia opened his bedroom shutter to see who was outside, he found the barrel of an Armalite pointed at him. Two men, whom he recognized but later feared to identify, ordered him to come down.

Carrying his lamp, Garcia descended to the yard, where his two visitors extinguished the flame, then beat him with the barrels of their M-16s, as three more men watched from a waiting Jeep. When they had finished their dirty business, they roared off, leaving Garcia with a crushed right cheek and other injuries. His family helped him inside and nursed him until daybreak, when he was taken into Concepcion to a doctor, who bandaged his face. The NAMFREL volunteer, Jun DeLeon, a native of Balutu, who had emigrated to the U.S. and was now serving in the U.S. Navy, insisted that I interview Garcia.

When Garcia heard that a foreign correspondent was at his door, he said he felt as if his prayers were being answered. Seated at a table before a crucifix inside the spotlessly clean though humbly decorated house, Garcia related his story, while his wife brought out refreshments. Using the jargon of Tarlaqueños, he said he believed his attackers had wanted to "make a sample" of him for voters on election day. Garcia explained, "I am identified as opposition here, and a lot of young people drop by to see me." All of his fellow barrio counselors and the *barangay* captain were members of the KBL, he said, beholden to Danding Cojuangco.

Garcia had not always been with the opposition. As recently as the 1984 legislative election campaign, he had remained "on the fence," afraid to express the sympathy he felt for the opposition candidate. Since then he had been emboldened by the courage of other Filipinos, who had been demonstrating in the streets of Manila and circulating in the barrios here, encouraging people to join the opposition campaign or volunteer for NAM-FREL. "People really want some change," he said, "and I feel a certain form of security in this atmosphere." It was an ironic comment coming from a man wrapped in bandages, sitting inside a house made of bamboo and palm fronds.

Garcia had been told that there would be foreign observers at each polling place and NAMFREL volunteers to protect the rights of the voters. He had believed what he heard. But there had been no protection last night, and when he went to the polls this morning, no outside observers were keeping watch. Now I was here. He begged me to stay, at least until the polls closed at 3 P.M. Citing precedent, he predicted that just about the time the ballots were ready for counting, "goons" would arrive to snatch them.

All such mercenary gunmen in these parts were in the employ of Cojuangco, he said, as were the government law enforcement officers. He explained that that was how this *barangay*, which he characterized as 80 percent pro-opposition, had managed to wind up with a vote count of zero for the opposition in May 1984. "They did the counting themselves, and there was no NAMFREL or UNIDO there to stop them," said Garcia. The only hope for reversing that trend this time, he said, was for foreigners like myself to bolster the resistance of the locals.

Within sight of the gunmen manning the checkpoint, several hundred voters waited in a schoolyard for a turn to cast their ballots. A NAMFREL volunteer and a poll watcher, representing the opposition party UNIDO, urged residents to stay near the school after they had voted, as a deterrent to the goons. "We are asking all the people to stay here with us," said UNIDO poll watcher Gloria Valdez, "because with People Power and God's help, maybe the things that happened last time here will not happen again." All afternoon she checked the voter registration list provided by the Marcos-dominated Commission on Elections for the names of registered voters.

To her dismay and that of many young *barangay* residents, who had registered to vote for the first time, 20 to 30 percent of the 1,000 eligible voters were not listed. "Some people are even crying," she said, "because they waited so long for a presidential election to be held, and now they cannot vote." Valdez filed a complaint with the local registrar's office, but she expressed faint hope of receiving any reply. "They made it hard for new voters to register, because they know that the young generation is not for the people in power," she said.

At 2:25 P.M., thirty-five minutes before the polls were officially to close, several dozen people were still in line waiting to vote. The schoolyard was full of some 100 watchful men. Suddenly, just as Garcia had predicted, goons struck. A red Jeep, trimmed in chrome with Marcos-Tolentino stickers on its bumper, pulled up behind the school. Six men, wearing white straw hats and carrying M-16s with Marcos decals on their barrels, jumped out and ran to meet eight armed, resident Civilian Home Defense Force members, who had been lolling in the shade across the road from the school all day.

After a brief exchange, two of the resident CHDF gunmen headed for the schoolyard, weapons raised and ready to fire. The *barangay* captain, Patricio Samson, preceded them, entering all three polling centers, each located in a different classroom, to urge the poll supervisors to "hurry up" and finish the voting, so the counting could begin.

Voters panicked at the prospect of a replay of 1984. They began to scatter. The poll watchers inside the classrooms clustered around the ballot boxes to protect them from the intruders. A woman fainted. A man carried her away. Like the murder at the airport, the violent assault, which was taking place right before my eyes, was all the more horrifying for the mundanity of the setting, the sunny calm of the afternoon, and the fact that the villains were wearing boaters and looking for all the world like they had just stepped off a vaudeville stage. It occurred to me that Greg Jones of the *Washington Post* and I, the only two foreigners in the town at that moment, were miles from anyone who knew us, without communication, and outnumbered by armed gunmen. However, the foreign press cards, dangling from strings around our necks, carried the protective powers of amulets here.

Still full of regret that none of us reporters on Ninoy's plane had questioned the soldiers who were taking him away, I ran after the *barangay* captain, obnoxiously demanding to know what was going on. "It's time!" shouted Samson, cryptically, repeating the phrase. "It's time!" Jones approached him from another direction. As we reminded him that it was against the law for armed men to enter the polling places, Samson glowered at the two of us and warned us to stay away from him. When asked to explain his sudden presence here at this school, one of the straw-hatted goons with the Marcos decals on his gun barrel gave us a malevolent smirk and said, "I'm for Cory."

As the goons reconnoitered with Samson and the CHDF members in a nearby bamboo grove, the voters and poll watchers banded together in the schoolrooms, preparing to sit on the ballot boxes, as they had been instructed by their NAMFREL representatives. Their terror was palpable as they waited for the men to come back to snatch the boxes.

Suddenly, from over the bluff, just like the cavalry in a western, came a caravan of brightly colored, passenger jeepneys full of UNIDO workers from Concepcion. As they approached the checkpoint, the constabulary officer and the CHDF men waved their guns in warning at the vehicles not to advance. Down from the lead jeepney leaped Jose Feliciano, former secretary of agriculture under the Macapagal government, now head of UNIDO in Tarlac. He strode up to the gunmen, made his case, and was allowed passage. As he and his followers entered the schoolyard, cheers erupted from the rescued poll watchers and voters.

Within minutes Feliciano and the poll chairmen had agreed among themselves that in view of the terrorism in the *barangay*, the counting should not take place in this isolated setting. They decided to seal the ballot boxes and carry them into Concepcion for counting. Three of the aluminum boxes, one from each precinct, were duly hoisted aboard the jeepneys by the appropriate election chairmen and bipartisan poll watchers, who accompanied them into town. About 100 people followed on foot.

No sooner had the group left, than a baby blue Land Rover full of uniformed constabulary officers entered town, like Keystone Kops, from the opposite direction. They said they were responding to a report of stolen ballots. Four officers holding walkie-talkies rushed through the *barangay* looking for the election chairmen. On the butts of the revolvers in their holsters were tiny I Love Marcos stickers. They refused to answer our questions about the identity of the "goons," whom we described as having terrorized the voters. Feliciano would later describe them as "Danding's men." "No one can act here without the approval and sanction of Cojuangco," he said. "He controls everything in the province, especially the Philippine Constabulary."

Toward dusk, as jeepneys full of embattled, citizen poll watchers pulled up before the municipal office in Concepcion, they were greeted with wild ovations from a gathering crowd for simply having survived the ordeal. As they escorted the ballot boxes from their respective *barangays* into the office of the municipal treasurer, the cheering spectators made way for them. It was clear that the preaching of the opposition candidates and the NAMFREL volunteers to stay with the ballots through their transport and counting had sunk in. Those who had made it all the way here, boxes and ballots intact, glowed with pride.

Others wept over their failure to protect the ballots in their custody. As volunteers who had been posted in *Barangay* San Antonio, just up the river from Balutu, began returning to Concepcion, their tale was excitedly circulated. The same red Jeep full of the same goons in straw hats had arrived there en route from Balutu. Finding no foreign correspondents and no jeepneys full of UNIDO volunteers to deter them, the goons, joined by the local CHDF, had scared the poll watchers away and stolen the ballots. Rose Alday, a twenty-three-year-old University of the Philippines Law School student, who had been serving as a poll watcher, sobbed, "What hurts is that we left the ballots there. All the while I was explaining the law to these people. I am a law student. You know, the law here means nothing."

As I recorded her story, I tried to console her. All democratic elections did not demand such sacrifices from voters and poll watchers, I said. Filipinos often wrote themselves off as "cowards." But the anonymous displays of courage I had witnessed today in the face of brazen military excess proved otherwise. These people knew what it was to lose their freedom, and they had turned out by the millions today, all over the

Philippines, to try to win it back. Although many of them lacked enough food to eat or proper shelter, they had shown themselves willing to risk their lives for a concept of liberty and justice that we, perhaps too blithely, had encouraged them to seek through the ballot.

They had believed the Americans would stand by them and bolster their cause. The presence of American observers in several hundred of the 86,000 precincts would prove to have made a great difference. But election day was not the last chapter. Having gone this far, how could we stop here? The questions raised by Peping and the cardinal, among others, still swirled in my mind. What were we Americans prepared to do when the hopes of these people were dashed and they took to the streets?

19

Countdown to "Operation Boodlefight"

February 8, 1986, Manila:
"President-Elect Corazon Aquino has a statement . . ." With that straightforward introduction, Cory claimed victory. At the urging of her security force, she was, for the first time in months, dressed in something other than her highly visible campaign yellow. But the nervousness of her bodyguards and her supporters about hotly contested returns, which were still being tallied, appeared to have had no effect on her. She radiated calm and confidence. She also managed to act as though she had won yesterday's election, although the outcome at this early stage was far from certain.

While both the unofficial NAMFREL count and the official COM-ELEC tally showed her running ahead of Marcos, only 10 percent of the vote had been tallied, most of it from urban centers, where she would be expected to run stronger than Marcos. Even then, the margin was not as great as the 12 to 15 percent that her own tacticians had confided she would need, at a minimum, to counter anticipated cheating by the KBL.

A NAMFREL officer, who had originally reported to the U.S. embassy political counselor that Cory would lose her lead as the counting proceeded, had reversed himself this morning, informing the embassy that

354

she "might actually be able to hold on to a slight lead." Based on his latest data, he estimated that the election "could end up in a dead heat, plus or minus two hundred thousand votes." Peping was already blaming himself for not having foreseen the way Marcos would manipulate the registration lists in Manila—as he had in Tarlac and many other places—so as to deny as many as 20 percent of all registered voters a ballot. He had been counting on Manila to provide much of Cory's margin.

Just as ominous, the ballot counting had slowed appreciably since midnight in heavily pro-Marcos regions like his "solid north." By tradition, Marcos suspended the count in secure areas to give his operatives time to pad the vote to compensate for shortfalls that might crop up elsewhere around the country.

Demonstrating that she could bluff with the best of the professional pols, Cory called on Marcos to concede early "in the best tradition of democratic politics." Cheekily, she expressed her hope that "it will be possible to meet with Mr. Marcos to make arrangements for a smooth transition of power." She made note of the fraud which had "severely reduced" her vote, but she did not dwell on it, lest Marcos be tempted to void an election that he had not yet won. She concluded her brief statement with a reminder of why she was here today and why she would see this race through to the end. "I am almost able to realize Ninoy's fight," she said.

We were gentle in our questions—much gentler than we would be with Marcos in a few hours. Not until nine easy ones had been lobbed her way did a reporter ask where she got her figures. "We have people all over the country getting results for me," she said. Indeed, a secret network had been mounted by her "Jesuit mafia," drawing on academic polling and programming expertise, and the computers, phones, and telex lines of the supportive Bank of the Philippine Islands. Having foreseen a contested election and a discredited official tally, these advisors knew they would need their own numbers, not just to gauge how they were doing, but also to provide them the ammunition to fire up their sometimes reluctant candidate to assert herself against Marcos in what was bound to be a long contest over the count.

Their strategy was working well. When asked what she would do if Marcos simply went ahead and declared himself the winner, she vowed, "I will lead daily demonstrations—peaceful demonstrations."

*　　　*　　　*

Across town at the palace, Marcos was much windier. "In this serious hour of our history, as we await the verdict of our countrymen, I want to appeal to all to join together in exercising the utmost prudence," he said. Rambling on in that vein for nearly half an hour, Marcos easily outbluffed Cory. "This was one of the most peaceful elections ever held in our country," he said, with a straight face. Then he proceeded to offer us his own region-by-region rundown, which showed him winning by 1.5 million in "a worst-case scenario," 2.5 million in all likelihood.

Like picadors, we lined up at the microphones in the Ceremonial Hall to prod him about the electoral fraud which nearly all of us had witnessed yesterday. Marcos feigned ignorance of most of it, urging people with complaints to "bring them before the COMELEC," where they could be investigated. But he was startlingly specific about one instance of fraud, which he claimed had been perpetrated by the opposition. "She is not even winning in her own region," he said, as Cory had predicted he would. "In her own hometown Feliciano seized three ballot boxes," added Marcos, to my astonishment, "and he has been charged."

I knew, from having witnessed the event in Balutu, that it was UNIDO leader Feliciano who had rescued the ballot boxes there from the gun-toting Marcos goons in straw hats. Typically, Marcos had crossed the line between normal campaign bluster and a perversion of the facts, as if there were no distinction between the two. Lacking for so long a critical press or an opposition free to voice its views, he had become utterly unaccountable for his words or actions.

*　　*　　*

February 9, Manila:
I returned to the hotel after dinner to find the lobby full of opposition supporters, passing the word to foreign correspondents that "something is up" at Baclaran Church. When I arrived there, the church was teeming with TV cameras and opposition personalities. Highly visible in the crowd were several U.S. embassy staffers and members of the official team of U.S. election observers. Holed up in a room behind the altar was a group of thirty computer operators, who had walked out of the COMELEC vote tabulation center at 10:30 P.M., protesting that the vote counts posted in public by the government Commission on Elections did not correspond to the data on their screens.

"I think these are the most damning comments that I've ever heard," exclaimed U.S. Senator John Kerry, one of the U.S. observers, who had been summoned to the church by concerned oppositionists, "and the most dramatic event that I've witnessed in the course of my being in the Philippines." Joker Arroyo, Aquino's campaign lawyer, declared, "This is a smoking gun." He quickly denied that the opposition had any advance knowledge of the walkout, although oppositionists had assisted the group in taking refuge at Baclaran.

It was after midnight by the time the frightened operators, most of them women, appeared before the altar to give a press conference. "We could no longer, in conscience, continue to do the things they were ordering us to do," said one of their spokesmen. The operators had begun noticing irregularities at about midnight on Friday, February 7, she said, when the input of new vote counts began to slow down, and discrepancies developed between the computer-generated reports and the tallies that were displayed on the COMELEC board. When the slowdown occurred, Aquino had been leading. By the time of the walkout, some forty-eight hours later, Marcos was ahead by some 150,000 votes, according to the official COM-ELEC count, although the unofficial, citizens' NAMFREL count, which had been proceeding much more quickly, showed Aquino leading by more than 770,000.

University of the Philippines political science professor Francisco Nemenzo could not resist drawing a lesson from Marx: "As he said in the *Communist Manifesto*, when the revolutionary process reaches the advanced stage, a portion of the ruling class will drop out and join the revolution." The computer operators were but the latest defectors from the establishment.

After the press conference, the group was escorted into the parish hall, by a cordon of priests and oppositionists. Before dawn a squadron of RAM officers transported the operators to a safe house inside a military camp, where the cardinal later visited and blessed them. The most senior of the computer technicians in the group, Linda Kapunan, was the wife of a leading RAM Core-Group member, Colonel Eduardo ("Red") Kapunan.

"That event was really heaven-sent," commented Cory the following day. "The timing was just right." Later I asked her when she had learned about their defection. She smiled sheepishly, and uncharacteristically for her, she answered: "No comment."

*   *   *

February 10, Manila:

After hours of bickering and nit-picking procedural squabbles, the official counting of the votes by the National Assembly began. After each specially sealed and marked envelope was drawn from the official, aluminum ballot box and ceremoniously slashed with a silver letter opener by the Assembly speaker, the provincial or city count, which he called out, was challenged by representatives of either the opposition or the ruling party, or both.

The counting was interrupted on numerous occasions by opposition MPs, seeking to delay the tally until all 147 provincial, city, and district canvasing centers around the country were in hand. When the speaker ruled that the tally could begin before all the certificates had arrived, the opposition appealed his ruling. When a vote was finally taken, the opposition was, predictably, defeated three to one by the ruling party's three to one majority.

"We are a nation of lawyers," sighed Marcos's acerbic spokesman

Adrian Cristobal, as he watched the proceedings. "This is a heritage from the Americans, who urged the Filipinos to fight for their independence via the law, not the gun." He predicted that the assemblymen would cite "precedents dating back to one million B.C." in challenging the contested results in the debate that would follow the tally.

According to the bill governing the snap election, the count had to be completed and a winner proclaimed within fifteen days of its start, and a president inaugurated ten days later. Among those to whom the date of the inauguration of a new president was a critical issue were members of the Core Group of RAM, who by now were secretly ready to stage their coup. Having seen the lengths to which Marcos had already gone to pervert the election, they felt sure that he would not stop until he had had himself proclaimed for another term. They had decided to schedule their "exercise" after Marcos's proclamation. Otherwise, said Captain Robles, "He could claim that we did it because Cory was losing."

*   *   *

February 11, San Jose, Antique:

The news was tragic and explosive. Evelio Javier, a forty-three-year-old former governor, whom optimists liked to believe was the prototype for the post-Marcos politician, had just been assassinated. As chairman of the Cory Aquino for President Movement in his home province of Antique, Javier had received numerous threats from the henchmen of a provincial warlord named Arturo Pacificador, who derived his power from Marcos. "Every time I move around Antique, I have to play cat and mouse with the goons of Pacificador," Javier had said in a taped interview only a few days before.

The two men were longtime rivals. A lawyer, former provincial governor, and outspoken Marcos critic, Javier had been defeated by Pacificador, fifty-five, in the 1984 National Assembly elections, after seven of his men were killed in an election-eve shootout with Pacificador and his followers. The incumbent assemblyman had been investigated, but never charged with that crime, and had gone on to become assistant majority leader. Javier had left the country for a while after his defeat to study at Harvard University's Kennedy School of Government. He could have stayed on in the U.S. or moved back to Manila to practice law. Instead, he had chosen to return home to help rejuvenate the opposition in his province.

In the capital of San Jose, Pacificador's name was on everyone's lips. Outside the capitol building, where the gangland-style execution had occurred, dazed government workers talked about the horror they had witnessed right there in the main plaza.

The votes were being counted on the second floor, and Cory was leading, they related, when Evelio was summoned by phone to discuss a contested tally sheet. At about the same time, Pacificador's man on the canvasing committee was heard placing a call to the provincial constabulary commander. Settling his business quickly, Evelio had ambled out onto the front lawn with several friends at 10:30 A.M., and sat down under a tree to talk. In a matter of minutes, two Nissan Jeeps, which witnesses later identified as belonging to Pacificador's men, pulled out of a side street and into the driveway of the capitol. Suddenly the clip of a baby Armalite was emptied in the direction of the group, which dispersed in all directions.

Evelio, the obvious target of the attack, took off across the broad cement plaza in front of the building, zigging and zagging to elude the spray of bullets. His assailant was a masked man, who had leaped out of the Jeep and was pursuing him on foot. Some seventy-five yards from the capitol, already dripping blood from a large crater in his shoulder, Evelio tried to jump a small fish pond, but stumbled and fell into it.

As terrified spectators in nearby buildings focused on the chilling chase and yelled supportively to the popular politician, he picked himself up and staggered on across a street. By then, more gunshots were coming from two men on foot to his left, and another, with a .45 pistol, in front of him. Self-interested merchants rushed to shutter their shops. Finding the first door he came to already locked, Evelio ducked into an alley and sought refuge behind the galvanized-steel-and-wood door of a backyard latrine. But his killer, following the trail of his blood, stalked him there and finished him off with a last burst of automatic fire that left two dozen bullet holes in the four-inch-thick door and adjacent concrete wall. Police later recovered fifty shells from the scene.

That afternoon, outside the morgue, a copper bullet casing wrapped in white paper was passed to TIME's photographer by a man in the crowd. On the paper, written in Tagalog, was a message, "I heard the police commander say, 'Seek cover because there will be firing.' " Implicit in that note from a citizen who was afraid to speak openly was the close working relationship between local law enforcement officers and the warlord, which was common in many areas of the still-feudal Philippines. "We cannot distinguish between goons and the military here," said one provincial official, who was also afraid to have his name published. "Pacificador controls them all."

Several arrests were made, but Pacificador was never touched. Cockily denying any role in the killing of the man who challenged his suzerainty over the province, he continued to appear daily in the National Assembly, assisting in the official vote-tallying process.

RAM officer Robles viewed the Evelio Javier murder with particular interest. One of Enrile's "boys," Robles had been privy to confidential information that the president had asked Pacificador to give him a 100,000-vote margin of victory in Antique, just as he had called upon Minister

Enrile to give him 350,000 votes in his region. As Enrile would later admit, he had fulfilled the president's quota before leading the rebellion against him. Due to the zeal of Javier and his followers in protecting the ballots, Pacificador had evidently had to go to greater extremes to comply with the president's order. "After they killed Javier," said Robles, "they stuffed the ballot boxes." Marcos was declared the winner in Antique.

*   *   *

February 11, Washington, D.C.:

It was jarring to return to Manila, intensely aware of the means Marcos was using to win this election, and read the news from Washington. The White House appeared to be proposing that Aquino and Marcos forget their quarrels and form a coalition government. As if he were talking about a Western democracy in which the ruling party accepts the need for a "loyal opposition," White House spokesman Larry Speakes was urging the losers in the Philippines "not to have demonstrations just because you did not like an election; get on the team and work to form a government." Philippine oppositionists were understandably offended by the implication that by refusing to accept the outcome of a patently fraudulent election, they would be acting like sore losers.

Marcos wasted no time in picking up that strand of White House thought and running with it. He offered the opposition an invitation to join a council of presidential advisors, which he proposed to form after his inauguration. Cory shot his balloon down the minute it hove into view. It was a delusion, she retorted, "to believe that the opposition, whose leaders and followers have been and are being killed, can suddenly settle down to a Western-style, two-party system. Too many would be dead the moment the world's head is turned."

As soon as he heard the Speakes statement, Peping Cojuangco called Ambassador Bosworth. "We met and had lunch together," he recounted, "and Steve said, 'Don't worry about it, Ronald Reagan is going to have a press conference.' " However, Bosworth cautioned Cojuangco not to expect too much from the president's early remarks on the subject, since he could not appear to prejudge the election results.

Bosworth had had input into the twenty-one sample questions and answers that the State Department's East Asia and Philippine desk staff had prepared and passed to Reagan's national security advisor, Vice-Admiral John Poindexter, for the president's perusal before the press conference. The proposed answers to reporters' questions about the election were studiously neutral, emphasizing the positive aspects of the election, such as "the emergence of a large and popular moderate party in addition to the government party." They de-emphasized the importance of the bases as an election issue. On the sensitive subject of fraud, they offered Reagan a subtle way of signaling that the blame lay with the ruling party, without at the same time appearing to interfere in the election: "The evidence suggests that it was the opposition's electoral chances which were most affected by incidents of fraud and violence."

Bosworth also knew that Senator Richard Lugar, Republican head of the official delegation of U.S. election observers, who was scheduled to brief Reagan just prior to the presidential press conference, had been outraged by the reports of fraud he had received in the course of his mission. Lugar could be expected to tell the president, as he had told Bosworth on his departure from Manila only the day before, "We are at the end of the Marcos era. The only question is the how and the when of his leaving power."

Bosworth and Lugar both assumed that Reagan would follow the script written by the foreign-policy makers who had spent the past two and one-half years preparing for the post-Marcos era. However, when Reagan stood before the press and began addressing the reporters' actual questions about the Philippines, his answers ranged far afield of his briefing material. When prodded as to the impact of a fraudulent election on U.S. interests in the Philippines, he fell back on his own parochial assumptions about the workings of democratic systems and his partiality for his old friend Ferdinand Marcos. "Well, I think that we're concerned about the violence that was evident there and the possibility of fraud," said Reagan, "although it could have been that all of that was occurring on both sides . . ."

As for the bases, his briefers' ambiguity was not for him. "One cannot minimize the importance of those bases," he declared, "not only to us but to the Western world and to the Philippines themselves. I don't know of anything more important than those bases."

Diplomats on both sides of the Pacific, who were familiar with the way every nuance of an American president's commentary on their country is weighed by Filipinos, winced at Reagan's sledgehammer answers. Reagan seemed to believe his own propaganda that an election would solve the Philippine problem. He appeared to know nothing about the "mousetrap clause," which assumed that Marcos was incapable of reform, or about "the second campaign," which was premised on the belief that the election would resolve nothing. Nor did he appear aware of U.S. knowledge of the plotting by RAM against Marcos and his top commanders. Scrambling to try and control the immediate damage caused by the press conference, the White House issued a second statement, which was not much different from the first.

Bosworth did not wait for Cojuangco to call him after it appeared on the wires in Manila. "He called me and wanted to see Cory," said Peping. When they got together the following day, Bosworth was unable to explain Reagan's remarks, said her brother, "because he did not expect them."

Initially Bosworth met with Cory alone. After a polite interval, Cojuangco and opposition Assemblyman Ramon Mitra entered the room. They found the ambassador and the candidate sitting there in silence. "I don't know what Ambassador Dobrynin looked like when he was talking to Kennedy while the Russians were moving the missiles to Cuba, or what the Japanese ambassador looked like when they were bombing Pearl Harbor," observed Mitra about the meeting with Bosworth, "but I imagine they looked like Steve. I have never seen him inarticulate, but there was a moment of absolute silence in the room." All three had enormous respect for the American ambassador, who now found himself in the uncomfortable position of having to mouth a line with which he did not agree and about which he had received no forewarning. Good soldier that he was, Bosworth went through the motions of trying to reassure them about U.S. intentions. However, his audience of three remained unconvinced, and their discussion more muted than usual.

"Ronald Reagan must think he is still in Hollywood," said Cojuangco several days later, in exasperation, as he discussed what he viewed as a negative shift in U.S. policy, on which the opposition had banked much of its hopes. "After all that assurance we received that the U.S. will exact all pressure to make this a clean and honest election, to force the retirement of General Ver, to revamp the COMELEC," he said. "What happened? Ver is still there, the COMELEC did not revamp, we never had equal access to the media, and the elections were not clean and honest."

*　　　*　　　*

February 12, Washington, D.C.:
American editorial and congressional reaction to Reagan's press conference remarks was equally stinging. By the day after, most of the influential opinion makers had weighed in with their thoughts on the consequences of trying to conduct business as usual with Marcos after a discredited election. If Reagan were going to support Marcos, he would have a lonely fight on his hands. In the ensuing battle for Reagan's mind, Lugar let it be known that the sentiments expressed by the president did not reflect the report he had conveyed about the election results. "The president was misinformed," he said at a high school convocation in his home state of Indiana. "The predominance of fraud is on the government's side." Meanwhile, House and Senate committees drafted resolutions condemning the fraud and seeking to penalize the Marcos government by withholding assistance.

It was Secretary Shultz in his own discreet way who forced the president to reckon with the reality that the election, far from giving Marcos a new mandate, had sounded the death knell for his regime. In order to impress upon him the scale of the fraud which Marcos had perpetrated, Reagan was made privy to a damning recording of conversations between Marcos and his henchmen shortly after the election. "There was one instance where Marcos was meeting with key lieutenants, including Ali Dimaporo [an important Muslim ally in Mindanao, who was famous for manufacturing votes], and referring to how many votes needed to be changed," acknowledged a high-ranking U.S. official.

The president was told that events had already moved beyond the point where the U.S. could continue to defend Marcos. The Philippine political opposition refused to deal with him; several of his cabinet ministers were ready to resign; and elements of his military were ready to overthrow him. What would happen once a divided army was ordered to fire on an angry citizenry was too gruesome to contemplate. In short, if the U.S. chose to side with Marcos, it would be opposing the very Filipinos on whose long-term support it would depend for the maintenance of its bases in the Philippines: the professional military, the middle class, and the private business community.

*   *   *

February 14, Manila:

The Church added its weight to the case against Marcos, following a two-day meeting of the Catholic Bishops Conference of the Philippines, which produced a letter of thunderous moral eloquence. "According to moral principles, a government that assumes or retains power through fraudulent means has no moral basis," pronounced the bishops.

The country's two most eminent women had, separately, figured in the bishops' deliberations. Imelda had gate-crashed. Cory had done it by invitation. Cardinal Sin had been in constant contact with the opposition candidate throughout the campaign. In the wake of the fraudulent outcome, both she and Sin had agonized over how best to channel the anger of her supporters. The cardinal had urged her to hold prayer rallies in lieu of protest rallies, and a number of bishops had joined her for two of them. But the people were clamoring for more than prayers. Cory had to make good on her promise to lead daily demonstrations, something which she did not wish to do without the support of the Church.

In a meeting with the bishops, she spoke of her fears that she and her moderate supporters would be preempted by the extreme left, which, although it had boycotted the election, was preparing to take to the streets to protest the Marcos-perpetrated fraud. She had refused to meet with representatives of the leftist Partido ng Bayan, who had wished to unite their cause with hers. But she would not be able to hold her supporters back from the siren song of the left much longer. As soon as Marcos had himself proclaimed, she would be forced to move. In the end, the churchmen and the politicians agreed on a policy of "nonviolent resistance," and introduced a set of moderate measures designed to exert gradually escalating pressure on Marcos to step down.

As Imelda's informants inside the Church began to feed her information on the drift of the pastoral letter the bishops were drafting, she appealed to the longtime papal nuncio in Manila, her most faithful ally in the Church, to help persuade them to withdraw or dilute it. With the nuncio, she went to the cardinal's palace—which the cardinal jokingly referred to as "the house of Sin," when he retold the story—late on the night of February 13. For two hours they discussed issues of Church and state, and the First Lady alternately badgered and pleaded with the cardinal not to issue the letter. When he insisted that it was his duty to do so, she resorted to a technique that had worked for her in the past: she threw a tantrum. It did not work for her this time.

✻ ✻ ✻

February 15, Santa Barbara, California:

As veteran American diplomat and negotiator Philip Habib landed in Manila, events were building toward a climax within each of the disparate camps that had a stake in the outcome of the contested election.

President Reagan, sobered by the revelations of Marcos's attempts to vastly alter the election results and newly aware of the irreversibility of events in the Philippines, had agreed to issue a new version of his statement, which would place the burden of the cheating on the ruling party and position the U.S. to further distance itself from Marcos. The text was drafted by State Department and National Security Council officials and relayed to the president's staff in Santa Barbara, where Reagan was vacationing.

"It has already become evident, sadly, that the elections were marred by widespread fraud and violence perpetrated largely by the ruling party," the revised statement read. "It was so extreme that the election's credibility has been called into question, both within the Philippines and the United States." Reagan approved it without revision.

Shortly afterward, a message was relayed to diplomatic posts around the world from the office of Secretary Shultz, containing a summary of U.S. policy toward the Marcos administration "which may be shared on a confidential basis with friendly governments." Far more than the public statement issued under President Reagan's name, this text indicated that the Marcos regime was rapidly coming to an end, and that the U.S. would no longer act to prop it up.

"The election has not given President Marcos the clear popular mandate he had sought," said the cable. It sketched the possibilities for violence from both right and left, once Marcos had been proclaimed president and Aquino's moderate supporters took to the streets in protest.

Reasoning that "the government's energies may be primarily devoted to dealing with the question of public order over the short term," which would render it ineffectual in dealing with either the Communist insurgency or major economic reforms, the State Department drew a devastating conclusion, which it passed along to the other governments that provided the Philippines' much-needed foreign aid. "These circumstances will make it difficult for the Philippine government to elicit external support for economic recovery," stated the communiqué.

* * *

February 15, Manila:

At about the same time that the White House was preparing to issue its amended assessment of the election, Marcos's lieutenants in the National Assembly were rushing to proclaim his victory before Saturday midnight, Manila time. The assembly had two more days to name a winner, but it was of critical importance to Marcos that when he met Ambassador Habib on Monday morning, he would do so as the legally proclaimed president of the Philippines for a new six-year term.

Marcos had even gone so far as to ask his aides to arrange for him to be secretly sworn in as president before he met with Habib. The chief justice of the Supreme Court had been summoned to the palace, prepared to spend the night, so that he would be on hand to administer the oath of office at whatever hour the assembly might complete its tally. However, Marcos's legal advisors had intervened, pointing to a provision in the election code that stipulated that the inauguration of the new president must follow his proclamation by ten days.

When it came time to vote on the proclamation, KBL Assemblyman Rene Cayetano felt that he could not in good conscience vote Marcos the winner of a stolen election. He told his law partner and political mentor Minister Enrile, "Johnny, as your good friend, I want out. I don't want to be counted."

Fearful of tipping his hand prematurely to either Cayetano or Marcos, Enrile urged his colleague to be patient. "I must tell you as a friend that the president did not win," Enrile acknowledged, "but we must raise our hands to say 'Amen.' " Doing his best to reassure his protégé that he had not sold out, Enrile added, "Don't worry, later on this grievous error will somehow be rectified." A puzzled Cayetano grudgingly followed Enrile's instructions.

At 11:45 P.M. on February 15 the National Assembly proclaimed Ferdinand Marcos the winner of the 1986 election. The official count was 10,807,197 votes for Marcos to 9,291,716 for Aquino. The opposition had already walked out on the charade.

NAMFREL's count, which was based on the 69 percent of the vote which its own inspectors were able to monitor and thus verify, showed Cory winning by 7.5 million to Marcos's 6.8 million votes. A CIA projection, which was leaked to the press, indicated that Cory should have gotten 58 percent of the vote if the count had been fair. Marcos's victory, such as it was, was forged in those rabidly pro-Marcos areas which NAMFREL inspectors had been unable to penetrate.

In the palace the Marcos and Romualdez families, together with a tight circle of friends, celebrated the president's fourth electoral victory in two decades and saw nothing to stop them from enjoying another six years in power.

*　　　　*　　　　*

RAM was intent on stopping them. On that very night, Core-Group members were meeting with Minister Enrile at his home in Dasmariñas Village to fix the final details of their move against the Marcoses and Ver. They felt secure there. Not only was the house, which bristled with antennae, surrounded by a wall and located within a well-guarded enclave, but tonight's guest list had been carefully screened. Colonel Almonte, who some feared was leaking information to the Americans, had not been invited.

"Our plan was to do it when Cory's nationwide boycott was being felt and morale was low. At that point there would be a political rationale for it," said Captain Robles. However, the plotters were mindful of the need for American support, once their move against Marcos had provoked large-scale fighting between rebels and loyalists, so they waited for propitious signs from Washington.

"The condemnation of the election by Ronald Reagan was a 'go' signal for us," confided Colonel Hernani ("Nani") Figueroa. "It made us more confident that if we did our thing, we would not be abandoned." Stressing that RAM was not at that point prepared to support Cory Aquino for President, Figueroa explained that Reagan's revised statement that the election was marred by fraud was viewed by the reform officers as an acknowledgment that "there was no legally elected President." They read Reagan's message as "a signal to do something and let the people decide who is the winner." Preparations had been made to implement any one of three plans, which had been drawn up several months before. The most dramatic and clean-cut was the one to storm the seat of power, kill Ver and force Marcos to resign, then invite a military-civilian junta to rule. "Greg and Red were just in love with that palace plan," said Batac. He himself liked it, because it de-emphasized their negatives. "It was a natural for a group without armor," he observed.

"There would be no fallback for the men who took the palace," said Colonel Malajacan, "because, even if we failed, we would have driven home a point. Things would never be the same again, and that was our primary objective." They would either succeed in breaking through the cordon of 3,629 armed men who protected the palace and forestalling the entry of others, or they would themselves be killed.

"It was feasible," said one officer. "We had timed it, and we had tested the security by smuggling cars filled with empty boxes. No one had even bothered to open them. We had explosives and timing devices prepared, as well as frogmen. They did not realize that the river was their soft underbelly."

Colonel Malajacan was equally optimistic, given the Core Group's operatives inside the palace and the highway patrol. His plan was to await a call from a reformist mole inside the Presidential Security Command, asking for reinforcements. As if acting under orders, Malajacan would then move a company of armor—light tanks and armored personnel carriers—across town under escort by the highway patrol. He calculated that the trip from army headquarters at Fort Bonifacio to the palace at two o'clock in the morning would take only about fifteen minutes.

If the troops that stormed Malacañang failed to accomplish their mission there, another group would already have embarked on a separate plan to capture and secure Villamor Air Base in Metro-Manila, which would become the point of entry for troop reinforcements from Mindanao. Well before the storming of the palace, RAM officers in Mindanao would be assembling men and weapons at a pickup point for transport to Manila.

The third option would be to work from the outside in, by declaring "liberated zones" in two outlying provinces and amassing military and civilian support in the countryside, to the point that Marcos would be forced to resign in favor of a junta. The sites targeted would be Enrile's Cagayan Valley, which was already under the command of friendly forces, and northern Mindanao, where RAM was exceptionally strong, thanks in large part to the grievances of officers against the regional unified commander.

As the men finalized their tactical plans, they began reminiscing about their days together at PMA. They marveled at the fact that they had remained idealists, despite the greed and the corrupt politics to which they had been exposed during their careers. They talked about their hopes and their dreams for their country and about the new problems that would face them if they were successful.

"We were quite romantic about it," admitted Malajacan. "That was understandable, considering the common experience we had at the academy and the way the Ver forces had been pitted against us. We were even talking about holding a 'Masada' in Malacañang," he said, referring to the ancient Jewish fortress near the Dead Sea, whose defenders committed mass suicide, rather than allow themselves to be captured by the Romans after a prolonged siege. "We thought that could be a symbol, because we wanted to give maximum impact to what we were doing."

Honasan, in particular, was bothered by the fact that "the AFP had not established any tradition or value that it could be proud of," recalled Colonel Calub. Drawn to danger and fantasy, Honasan had proposed to skydive over Malacañang, landing on the roof "like a gypsy moth," but he had been hooted down by his fellow officers.

Toward dawn, Robles, a latecomer to the Core Group, who played the roles of court jester and devil's advocate, posed a question that would come back to haunt the men in the room that morning. "Failure is something a soldier can cope with," said Robles, "his own death being the ultimate failure. But how many militaries can cope with success?"

In response, Enrile, who had become something of a father figure to these "boys" over the years, was moved to make a pledge about how they would handle success. "We will form a group, we will draw up a list of moral guidelines. We will go back to our old houses, no new cars, no change in life-style, no change in personalities, no heroes, just the NRC." If he disappointed them in his actions, once Marcos was gone and he was part of the ruling junta, Enrile invited them to "put a knife in the back of my throat."

Not prone to taking themselves so seriously, the group convulsed in laughter when Robles interrupted the minister's oath to say, "Does that mean we can call you Johnny?"

They parted company without having set a date for their exercise. "The date was a tactical decision," explained Malajacan. In recent days in order to test Ver's defenses, Core Group leaders had deliberately leaked information that indicated they were planning some kind of action against the palace. However, they had been careful not to divulge when it would occur. "We had to keep them guessing," said Robles, "and the only way to do that would be to make a final decision with only twenty-four hours notice."

*   *   *

February 16, Manila:

Before an estimated half-million yellow-clad supporters in Manila's Rizal Park, Cory kicked off the continuation of her election campaign with a massive "People's Victory" rally. Although she never used the phrase "civil disobedience," she announced a seven-point program of boycotts of government-controlled businesses, including popular San Miguel beer, news media, and banks, and delayed payments of water and light bills, which amounted to the first elementary stage of such a strategy.

She explained that the first seven points were "deliberately" limited, but that each week she planned to hold more rallies in different parts of the country and to add "more protest measures," culminating in a nationwide general strike scheduled for the day after Marcos's inauguration, February 26. She said she would give the boycott three months to show results. Among the tougher, second-stage measures under discussion by her advisors was the withholding by businesses of their corporate income taxes, a major source of government revenues.

Cory's chief advisors were candid about their limited expectations for this campaign alone to force Marcos to budge. What continued to worry them most—as it worried the U.S. embassy and the reform officers—was the prospect that the left would exploit the general strike for its own ends. "If the moderates do not bring Marcos down," warned Peping Cojuangco, "then a vacuum will be formed. If the moderates lose out there, the Reds will take over, I am sorry to say." Cory was still keeping them at bay by refusing to combine forces with their front groups to protest the fraudulent election, as they had hoped she would. So far, she had been successful in drawing huge crowds on her own, without need to engage their well-known mobilization abilities. But, questioned her brother, "How long will the people listen to Cory when they are getting killed?"

As February 26 approached, the prospect of violence sparked by leftists and leading to a military crackdown made people in the center increasingly nervous. Reports circulated that the left was buying up gasoline for Molotov cocktails to be used once the situation began to come apart. Security arrangements were said to have been strengthened inside Malacañang, and two to three helicopters had been placed on twenty-four-hour alert to fly Marcos out of Manila to his northern palace in Laoag, if necessary. A growing "siege mentality" had taken over the palace, one informant told the U.S. embassy, as machine guns had been readied for use inside the grounds, and even more tanks and armor deployed there than usual.

*　　*　　*

As Cory was outlining her boycott measures, Marcos was preparing to make the one announcement that might have prolonged his presidency—that General Ver was retiring. Fifteen minutes before the event one of his aides thought to call his friend Ver to wish him well and ask him why he was resigning at this particular moment. Ver's response surprised him. "It's just a courtesy resignation," said the chief of staff, referring to the routine submission of resignations by all top officials after the president's reelection was proclaimed. "Are you sure?" questioned the aide, who added, "You better check with the president." Ver laughed and dismissed him.

Half an hour later, Marcos was sparring with the press, which greeted his announcement of Ver's retirement with well-founded suspicion that this was but another example of Marcos *moro-moro*, or play-acting, mounted to impress Ambassador Philip Habib, who was scheduled to hold his first meeting with Marcos tomorrow. In his answers to reporters Marcos was vague as to the date of Ver's retirement, whether he would surrender his intelligence commands as well as his military commands to Ramos, and whether he would receive another official post.

The following day the Malacañang Office of Media Affairs slipped press releases under the doors of foreign correspondents at the Manila

Hotel, noting that Ver's retirement would not be effective until March 1. However, the president had apparently neglected to give either Ver or Ramos such specific information.

Several days after the press release had gone out, the long-suffering General Ramos had still not been officially informed by the president of his appointment to the top command. Anxious to know his status, he called one of Marcos's civilian advisors to ask if he knew where things stood. The advisor was stunned by the question.

"Why does he humble himself so low as to call me to find out when he is supposed to take over command of the military?" he asked himself. When the aide next saw the president, he remarked to him about the curious call from Ramos.

Marcos laughed and said, "You should have asked him why he is in such a hurry." Then, added the president, with a touch of malice, "Don't make me change my mind."

Yet it appeared that Marcos already had changed his mind. Palace insiders had seen Ver accost the president not long after the retirement announcement, and some of them deduced that he did then what he had done following his acquittal—pulled a document from his bottomless intelligence portfolio, which convinced the president that yet another plot against his life was afoot. "He told the president he was in a position to crush it," said one source, who surmised that that pledge, together with Marcos's anxiety about the contested election, had bought Ver a few more months in his old job.

Later Ramos would reveal that Marcos had signed a secret order to keep Ver in the post indefinitely. A favorite subject of speculation among RAM officers for quite a time afterward was how different things might have been for the president, had the West Pointer been confirmed immediately.

                    ☆   ☆   ☆

February 17, Manila:
Philip Habib had had other tough assignments in the course of his thirty-six years in the Foreign Service. He had been involved in the Paris peace talks that led to the end of the Vietnam war, and he had shuttled back and forth, to little avail, among the Syrians, Israelis, and Lebanese as President Reagan's special envoy to the Middle East. Now he was in Manila, buying time for the Reagan administration, as it sought to reconcile a president's instinct to protect a longtime ally and personal friend and the inevitability of events, which favored the advice of almost his entire foreign-policy bureaucracy: Marcos must go.

Given the paranoia bred by the "special relationship" and compounded by the uncertainty of the postelection situation, Filipino oppositionists assumed Habib was there to force them to compromise with Marcos. The coup-plotting reform officers believed his mission was to see that Fidel Ramos was finally installed as chief of staff.

During a dinner party at the end of his second visit to Manila, Habib indicated that the first assumption was erroneous. Sipping a Château Lafite-Rothschild, 1971, which had been deliberately selected by his host, opposition businessman Jorge Araneta, for its premartial-law bouquet, the visiting envoy raised his glass to the newly inaugurated President Aquino's brother Peping and recalled aloud how he had relayed a message to him by way of their mutual friend Bobby Trent Jones, Jr. "I told Bobby to assure you that I was a good guy, who had no intention of suggesting that your sister should form a coalition with Mr. Marcos," he said. Peping smiled and nodded, and both men agreed that many people had jumped to the erroneous conclusion that the U.S. position in the immediate aftermath of the February 7 election was the pro-Marcos line that President Reagan had first articulated.

On Monday, February 17, Habib spent two and one-half hours with Marcos, leaving the palace with a sober mien and a large album of exhibits documenting instances of election fraud allegedly committed by the opposition. They had met, not in the president's study, where he usually receives official visitors, but in an inner sanctum which was unwired for recording.

That afternoon Habib, accompanied by Bosworth and State Department Philippine country director John Maisto, paid a call on Cory Aquino in the Makati office building owned by her family. Her press statement on the meeting was notably combative. However, she told me later that their discussion had been cordial and full of humor. She recounted how he began by telling her, "I understand you thought I would ask you to cooperate with Marcos." She had confessed to Habib that she had been "terribly upset about the first Reagan statement." "Unfortunately my face shows all that I feel," she added. "I will have to learn to have a poker face." Everyone had laughed at that remark, she said, especially the poker-faced Bosworth. Another chuckle had resulted from Aquino's prescription for her much-noted energy and serenity throughout the election ordeal and its aftermath: "American vitamins." Both Habib and Maisto had made note of her brand.

Meanwhile, Habib's traveling companion, Allen Weinstein, a member of the U.S. election observer team, who had returned to Manila for follow-up discussions, had had a sobering meeting with an important advisor to Marcos, who had predicted a crackdown by Ver as soon as the election protests faded. The advisor, Ronaldo Zamora, anticipated "something worse than martial law—a form of dictatorship in which there is no room for opposition politics." Zamora urged the follow-up group to talk to some military reformists. The embassy subsequently arranged such a meeting.

✳   ✳   ✳

February 18, Washington:

A Pentagon official lunched with an intelligence attaché from the Philippine embassy, who asked, "Is there anything we could do? Would it help if Ver resigned?" The American, reflecting the thinking of his seniors, replied, "My personal opinion is that there is nothing you could do. The situation has gone too far to be retrieved."

✳   ✳   ✳

February 20, Manila:

The time had come to inform General Ramos of the Core Group's plans for an imminent coup, and formally to request his leadership. "Ramos is the only one who can mobilize the AFP for the wrong reasons," quipped Colonel Almonte. Although two of Ramos's men were Core-Group members, and he himself was close to both Almonte and Enrile, he had managed to keep all of them in suspense as to how much he knew about what they were plotting and whether or not he would agree to join them. Cool, discreet, and Protestant, Ramos was a most un-Filipino-like Filipino.

The younger officers were hesitant to approach him, so Almonte had volunteered his services. Their association went back a long way. They had been together in Vietnam. Later, when Almonte was heading Marcos's think tank, Ramos had frequently stopped by to solicit his ideas and observations.

"We talked for maybe two hours," Almonte recalled. "I tried to describe the crisis the nation was in, which he shared fully. My feeling is that I was just repeating what he already knew." Almonte told him that the Core Group had decided to resolve the situation by force. "We look up to you to lead us," he said. "We cannot mobilize the soldiers. You are the only one who can."

Not a flicker of emotion had crossed Ramos's impassive face, but, said Almonte, "I could feel what was in his heart. My impression was that he himself was thinking the same way and had no doubts about what should be done." For most of the conversation, said Almonte, "we talked in parables. I gave him the plan in general. I didn't need to tell him the tactical details. To him that was clear."

Almonte did, however, provide Ramos the details about the National Reconciliation Council to whom the military would turn over power. "It was to be a civilian junta with one military representative—General Ramos," said Almonte. Its task would be to restore democracy and preside over elections after an eighteen-month transition period. As Almonte portrayed it, the military would wield power disproportionate to its member-ship in the junta by way of a military committee, which would also be chaired by Ramos. "People might say this military committee is a hidden junta," observed Almonte, "but we anticipated a difficult military situation that might last a long time."

As the conversation drew to a close, Ramos took a box of his favorite Cuban cigars, Romeo & Juliets, from his desk. He handed two to Almonte and lit one for himself. "Joe," he said, as he ushered his visitor out of his office, "whatever you are planning, just don't make it very bloody."

*   *   *

February 21, Manila:

During the week following their last meeting, members of the RAM Core Group waited for the final "go" signal from their leaders. "The PMA Alumni Association was playing soccer at that time," recalled Malajacan, "so we used those games on Tuesday and Thursday to get in touch with each other." It was during a soccer game on Tuesday, February 18, that Malajacan was told RAM would move at two o'clock on a Sunday morning—the hour of the changing of the guard at Malacañang, "when normally a soldier would be at his lowest effectiveness, either sleepy or bored." He was not, however, told which Sunday morning it would be.

The very next day, he was alarmed to learn that the palace guards had been put on "red alert," their highest state of readiness. He also discovered from a source inside the palace that Ver was seeking to learn the identity of a general on active duty, whom he had been informed was a RAM member. The fact that the Core Group numbered a general in its ranks was a highly confidential piece of information—one that had not been the product of any deliberate leak to Ver. Clearly, Malajacan con-cluded, there had been a serious breach of security within RAM itself. Gringo and Red needed to be informed. Unable to get away from his own duties inside Fort Bonifacio that evening, he sent his friend and fellow Core-Group member Major Saulito Aromin, commanding officer of an-other army division, to relay the message.

The word came back to him that another Core-Group meeting would be held on Friday night at Enrile's residence, for the purpose of recon-sidering their plans. Meanwhile, in need of another man inside the palace, Gringo had approached Major Edgardo Doromal, an officer in the Pres-idential Security Command, to join them. Doromal had agreed, but had immediately suffered pangs of guilt over consenting to betray superiors to whom he felt he owed such a debt of gratitude. Almost immediately, he had broken down and told Irwin Ver what he had learned about the nature of the RAM plot and the officers whom he had been told would be involved.

Thus, by Friday night, when RAM met—again at Enrile's house, again without Almonte—to assign a date to its action, General Ver had heard from at least two inside sources who were not among those authorized to leak details of RAM's plot to attack the palace. At that time RAM did not know the identity of either informer. However, a last predawn inspection of the palace vicinity had convinced Honasan and Kapunan that their plot had been exposed. In addition to the troop buildup about which Malajacan had already warned them, they saw that a marine battalion had been moved in to guard one of their planned entry points.

The scouting party returned to Enrile's house and informed the group that it was calling off the palace operation, dubbed "Operation Boodlefight" (PMA jargon for "food fight"). In its place, the Core Group was tentatively rescheduling the "liberated zones" scenario to coincide with Aquino's general strike.

Unbeknownst to them, some of their sympathizers were already in custody. For the first time since election eve, Malajacan had gone home to his wife and children, rather than to his detachment. He had not had the nerve to tell his wife what he was up to, for fear of frightening her. She was the nervous type. Worse, she had also been actively campaigning for Ferdinand Marcos's reelection. Military wives were expected to do their part for the commander in chief, and Malajacan had not objected, lest he call attention to his own loyalties and jeopardize his family's well-being.

While the plotters slept, Ver was closing in on them. Doromal had spilled the names of the major conspirators, including Malajacan and Aromin. Malajacan was located at home at 11 A.M. on Saturday morning and told that his commanding officer was waiting for him inside Fort Bonifacio. Dazed from too little sleep and the letdown of the aborted coup, he did not sense that a trap had been laid for him. When confronted with information about his participation in the coup, his main concern was to convince his superior, General Roland Pattugalan, whom he revered, that his actions were in no way directed against him, but at the top of the chain of command. That afternoon Malajacan and Aromin were placed under technical arrest along with two other officers.

Knowing that the palace plot had been called off and the "liberated areas" plot substituted for it, the captured soldiers answered questions about the former, with which Ver was already quite familiar. Asked to write statements, they did not know until the television lights went on and the cameras were set up that they were to be exhibit "A" at a Marcos press conference. Nor were they aware that while they had been under interrogation, their fellow plotters, together with Minister Enrile and General Ramos, had learned that they, too, were marked for arrest and had withdrawn into Camp Aguinaldo, where they had just announced in a press conference that they no longer recognized Marcos as the legal president of the Philippines.

20

People Power

The dramatic decision by Ramos, Enrile, and their men to withdraw from the regime into their own armed enclave broke the postelection stalemate. Few could have predicted the form the struggle would assume or that it would last only four days and remain essentially bloodless.

In its aftermath, definitions of the process that had taken place would vary. Filipinos would call it a "bloodless revolution." Noting that it only overthrew one particular family and its cronies, not a social class, nor even the dictator's entire support system, Westerners would describe it in more technical terms as a "popularly supported military rebellion." A general, who did not officially take sides during the revolt, speculated that military historians might term it a "passive coup." A sardonic American embassy official called it "part two of the election: getting the count right."

Whatever the proper terminology, during the four days in which a dictatorship collapsed and a fragile, new government was installed in its place, the warring social and political forces that had blocked peaceful change so often in the past came together in a brief, harmonious moment of mutual interest and inspiration. As a result, the events which came to pass along the highway that was appropriately named *Epifanio de los Santos*

(EDSA) transcended, for once, the individual claims and factional rivalries of the people involved.

It is that transcendent happening which deserves to be remembered. However, to understand how those individuals and factions managed to function, if only fleetingly, as a synchronous whole is to understand why they would come apart just as suddenly when the common focus of their rage had been sent into exile in Hawaii, and they were forced to confront the deeper roots of their discontent.

✱   ✱   ✱

Day One, February 22:

At 12:45 P.M., Philip Habib was taking his leave of President Marcos. He was due to depart the Philippines at two o'clock to return to Washington. While he and Marcos had been closeted in the president's study, a noticeably nervous General Ver had been cooling his heels next door in the music room. Marcos's personable military aide Colonel Arturo Aruiza had dropped by to keep him company during his wait. Habib had barely been ushered out the front door of Marcos's study when Ver slipped in a side door to give him urgent news. His men were in the process of grilling four officers, whom Major Doromal had exposed as plotters of a plan to storm the palace and oust Marcos.

Already the captured men had spilled the names of some of those involved. Prominent among them were a number of Enrile's boys, the RAM officers whom Marcos, in his snide wisdom, had referred to as "my coup plotters." Ver had sent an emissary to arrange a meeting for him with Gringo Honasan, and he had called Vic Batac's father, a retired general, and instructed him to tell his son, "Whatever you are planning, desist from it."

✱   ✱   ✱

After a few hours sleep, Minister Enrile, accompanied by his daughter Katrina, paid a routine Saturday morning visit to a Makati coffee shop. With rumors of his resignation on the front pages of the morning newspapers, and his boys' still-secret coup plan in limbo, it was important to keep up appearances. While there, he was called away to the telephone. Trade Minister Roberto ("Bobby") Ongpin was on the line, reporting that his security guards had been arrested last night. He assumed Enrile would know what was going on, since the men had been assigned to Ongpin through the Ministry of National Defense. That was the first Enrile had heard about the incident. He said he would check it out.

Just before lunchtime Enrile headed home. His wife, Cristina, was entertaining some friends. The minister joined them at the table, still looking unruffled. During lunch there was another call for him. "When he came back to the table, his whole attitude had changed," reported one of the guests. "He was very serious. He had changed his clothes. He told his wife, 'I think I am going to be arrested. If I am, please call these journalists.' " He handed her a list, and left the house with several of the boys. He had made arrangements earlier in the week for the protection of his family in this event.

That call had come from Colonels Honasan and Batac, who had warned the minister that the crackdown they had anticipated was under way. Since the Core Group's decision in the predawn hours this morning to postpone the coup, its leaders had become privy to information that made them fear for Enrile's safety. Following the arrests of nineteen of Ongpin's twenty-man security force, Colonel Victor ("Vito") Paredes, a marine commander, whose men were among those protecting Cory Aquino, had also been detained. Had the coup plan gone ahead, Paredes was to have played the important role of leading marines sympathetic to RAM to take over Fort Bonifacio. The wife of a presidential security guard had just confided that Ver's men were mining the grounds of Malacañang. Meanwhile, another palace insider had reported that Ver was finally issuing the warrants of arrest Marcos had signed last September.

"It all fit into a scenario that Ver was arresting a group of soldiers who were linking us to a plot of moving against the palace," recounted Captain Robles. Ever since the election, the two sides had been playing a waiting game. "We were waiting for them to move to give us justification for moving," said Robles. Both sides had been warned by the U.S., which financed most of the country's arsenal, that violence would not be condoned. As long as Habib was in town, neither side could afford trouble. No sooner had his plane lifted off than both took aggressively defensive positions.

Justifying his actions with the confessions of reformist officers, Ver ordered his men to begin rounding up soldiers and politicians identified with RAM. Justifying their actions with the threat of arrest by Ver, Enrile and his boys moved to salvage as much of their plot as possible by arming themselves and holing up inside Defense Ministry headquarters at Camp Aguinaldo, then daring Marcos and Ver to come after them.

The Aguinaldo option had not been among the plotters' early contingency plans. "We told the minister there was no time to explain there in his house," said Robles. "We flew him to Aguinaldo by helicopter and did our talking there, where we could protect him." For two hours chaos reigned. "Everyone was volunteering to die first," said Robles. Colonel Tibursio ("Tirso") Gador, constabulary commander in Enrile's province of Cagayan, was contemplating flying him home and making his region the first "liberated zone." Another alternative was to fly everyone to Mindanao and hold out there. When Robles left the camp at 3 P.M. to begin work on his mission—getting the story to the press—he assumed that his companions would soon be leaving for the provinces.

*   *   *

Before he left home, after learning of his imminent arrest, Enrile had placed a call to his old friend and colleague Lieutenant General Fidel Ramos. The two men were a study in contrasts. Where Enrile was voluble, quick to anger, and prone to wear his heart on his sleeve, Ramos measured his words and checked his emotions, showing little of his inner self to the public, or even to his friends. While Enrile had been tainted by charges of corruption and hidden wealth, Ramos's image had remained clean to a fault. While Enrile was instinctively a political animal, one of Ramos's failings was perceived to be his inability to play politics inside the AFP.

And yet, to survive for more than a decade as chief of a bureaucracy with as fetid a reputation as the Philippine Constabulary enjoyed and to emerge with his own personal integrity intact obviously required a certain degree of political sophistication. Thus, there was about Ramos an air of perfidy that added intrigue to his Calvinist image. "That's what makes Ramos so dangerous," said another Filipino known for his integrity. "Ramos was the one who drew up the plans to arrest Ninoy, and yet the next morning there he was inside the detention center, the picture of suavity and humanity, explaining it all and yet seeming detached from it."

Even the Americans, who were among his greatest boosters, found Ramos impenetrable. A U.S. official, who was familiar with Ambassador Habib's recent discussions with both Enrile and Ramos, noted marked differences in the exchanges between the two men and the visiting emissary. "Enrile told Habib, 'This election has ripped things apart.' " When asked about the possibilities of putting it back together, Enrile had given the Americans an answer laden with implications as to his future course of action. Said he: "I love my president, but I love my country more." Ramos, on the other hand, in a meeting with Habib that same morning, "did not lead us to believe anything would happen. He is the inscrutable Oriental. You really don't get much out of him."

Enrile's phone call assumed that Ramos already knew what he was talking about from previous conversations. "I said, 'Eddie, I am in this predicament. My "boys" are in this predicament. I am with them. I would like to find out whether you will join us or not.' " According to Enrile, Ramos answered, "I am with you all the way, but we cannot speak over this phone."

In fact, Ramos later acknowledged, he had been kept closely informed about the coup plans all along. Stressing that the roots of his grievances against the politicization of the military ran every bit as deep as those of the young reformist officers, Ramos explained how, during his many years on the job, he had visited soldiers in all seventy-four provinces. "I was not just talking to these men, but doing the things they were doing: eating the chow, getting up to join them in reveille and running, staying up late at night to socialize and drink a little with them. That was my way of trying to generate support for what I was trying to preach—professionalism and dedication to duty."

Ramos was frank about his pique over what he called Marcos's "flip-flops" on his promotion to replace General Ver. "I had been announced as incoming chief of staff," said Ramos, "but I saw key positions of the AFP being filled by orders of General Ver or President Marcos at that same time. I became alarmed by this obvious move to put me further into the freezer, and to severely limit my freedom of action in a position of major responsibility, so I wrote to President Marcos to establish if he really intended for me to take over the AFP." Ramos never received a reply. "Events overtook all of that," he said.

Prior to the week of February 22, when he expected the move against Marcos to be made, Ramos had, on his own, begun pulling the 400 men of the constabulary's antiterrorist Special Action Force in from the provinces, where they had been deployed, on the pretext that there were indications of possible massive civil disobedience in Manila.

The reform officers' coup plot, he said, had been conceived as "a form of deception, meaning there would be some moves or plans that would leak out as part of the psychological preparatory plan." The reformists had been waiting for a response to those leaks, but Ver's reaction had been slow. "The thing that clinched it for me in believing that Mr. Marcos was making a move," said Ramos, "was the report of Minister Bobby Ongpin." Like Enrile, Ramos had received a call from Marcos's trade minister, questioning him about the arrests of his bodyguards.

Before Enrile phoned him, Ramos had been alerted to his plight by his friend newspaper publisher Betty Go Belmonte. By the time Enrile himself called, Ramos was, ironically, in the midst of a debate with a group of Cory's Crusaders, who had picketed his house to protest his "indecisiveness" in opposing Marcos. The women were impatient with Ramos for not following the example set by his sister, U.N. Under Secretary Leticia Ramos Shahani, who had burned her diplomatic-career bridges behind her, by announcing her support for Cory on December 20, 1986. "Why didn't you do what your sister did?" the women asked Ramos.

"Somebody has to be in the middle to try to keep things stable and to prevent anarchy," he told them. "I am like the boy in the story, trying to put his fingers in all those holes in the dike."

After the revolution, Ramos explained to me his reasons for taking so long to turn on Marcos. "I had on my shoulders the future of ninety thousand people, members of the constabulary as well as many others in the armed forces, whom I knew were with me. I had to make sure I did not compromise their well-being by making a decision that was poorly timed. If I had to make a great move, I had to be sure that it would be for some useful purpose that would contribute to the accomplishment of what we were trying to do."

Ramos's failure to report to Camp Aguinaldo for three hours after Enrile's first phone call raised speculation within the Core Group that he had not yet firmly decided to support the rebellion, which, due to circumstances beyond any of their control, was being mounted prematurely and according to an improvised script under the leadership of Enrile. As Ramos would soon learn, Colonel Almonte, who had been excluded from the final RAM planning sessions, was unaware until several hours later that the defense minister and his boys had made a move.

"Ramos checked first what his people were doing," said one Core-Group member, "and only when he realized that most of his key personnel were part of the plan, did he join. He was not a risk taker." An American consultant with close ties to the AFP made a similar observation about Ramos. "He is a very, very cautious guy," he said. "He was saving himself for his wedding night, and he might have died a virgin, but in the end he had to make his choices."

Some sources close to Ramos believe that that choice was finalized only after he had assured himself and such vital supporters as Cardinal Sin that the actions of the rebel forces would be directed toward restoring constitutional authority. "The amount of time it took for Cardinal Sin to go on the air to appeal to the people," said one, "leads me to believe that he waited for assurance that this coup would be for Cory. The person who would have been able to convince Enrile of that would have been Ramos."

As usual, Ramos was discreet in his revelations. "Let me just say that timing to me was very important," he remarked. "I felt there should be popular support and a political anchor, because military action that would become just a plain coup would not last." Quoting one of his younger officers, Ramos added, "Anything like that without the people's support would just self-destruct."

If he did exercise his leverage to draw commitments from Enrile and his boys as to who would be the political beneficiaries of their move, should it succeed, he left as few tracks on that ground as he had during the months leading up to the revolt. Few people even realized that Ramos had been represented inside the reform officers' Core Group. Typically, noted an American official, "Ramos's men routinely left halfway through the meetings." He added, "That's probably how Ramos wanted it—to give himself deniability."

Ramos was, after all, an expert in psychological warfare. He had studied it and practiced it throughout his career, and his expressionless face and boundless credibility had added to his success in the discipline. He was the right man, both temperamentally and militarily, to lead the revolt, which Enrile's defensive move had precipitated. A cousin to Marcos, as was Ver, Ramos had been judged too loyal and too weak ever to react to Marcos's mistreatment of him. His retaliation, though a long time in coming, was impeccable in its strategy and its implementation. "I have to give Eddie Ramos credit," said an American official after it was all over. "He played a brilliant psy-ops game. He was in command of a very unprofessional military, but he managed it beautifully. Much of what they said and did was bogus, but it worked, and it kept his opponents offside."

Ramos's delayed arrival at Camp Aguinaldo held up a press conference, which Enrile had been promising the rapidly growing press corps that had assembled inside the Ministry of National Defense. Once it got under way, a principal question of the reporters was whether Aquino would reap the benefits of their mutiny if they succeeded in ousting Marcos. Enrile was reluctant to link his actions to Mrs. Aquino, but after repeated hammering from the media, he stated, "I am morally convinced that it was Mrs. Aquino who was elected by the Filipino people. Yes, we are committed to support her."

✳   ✳   ✳

Although she knew that the reform officers were planning to strike and that she would be a beneficiary of their action, Cory was not about to entrust her fate to the military. Among the lessons she had drawn from her life with Ninoy was to be dogged in her pursuit of even an impossible dream. Her determination to complete his mission would serve her much as blinders served a horse—it would keep her eyes narrowly focused on the finishing line, and render her blissfully oblivious to both the dangers and the opportunities which might otherwise have destroyed or diverted her along the way.

"Peping told me in January 1986," she later confided, "that the military said there was no way for me to win, because Marcos would manipulate the returns, so maybe it would be better for me to be part of their group, which would take over and set me up as president." Her response to her brother, she told me, had been unambiguous. "I am not here for the power. I want to know if the people really support me, so we must go through with this election."

The test of her will power came on Friday night, February 21, when she was scheduled to take her boycott campaign on the road, seeking the support of the people to help her claim the victory she felt was hers. As she prepared to leave for the island of Cebu, accompanied by Laurel and Peping, her godson Captain Jose Honrado, who was also the head of her inner security, tried to convince her not to leave town.

"If I don't show up there," she told him, "my people will not believe me anymore." With that, he confided the cause of his anxiety. "He was in tears," she recounted. "He told me he had strong rumors that there would be a coup Sunday morning." Cory replied, "I believe you, but suppose what you are telling me does not take place, and in the meantime I cancel my rallies?" The officer pushed no further. "What could he do?" said the determined candidate. "I had already said, 'We're going.' "

Laurel had called Manila between rallies and learned what was going on there. Later he got through to Enrile, who told him, "Submerge yourselves, your lives may be in danger."

Laurel said, "He said he was fighting to give the people their mandate. His thinking was that the four of us—Cory, myself, Enrile, and Ramos —would have a coalition government." By late afternoon some of the campaign reporters had picked up rumors about the developments in Manila. Word was passed to the speakers on the platform, "Make your speeches short." Immediately after the rally Laurel left the stage and flew home.

The rest of the party went to the residence of a Cebu supporter, and turned on the radio, eager for news. Around nine o'clock Cory received a call from a mutual friend, saying, "Johnny wants to talk to you." She had not spoken to Enrile since her husband's imprisonment. She didn't know him well, but she had misgivings about him. Some of the people close to her strongly distrusted him. She could not help but wonder why he had waited so long to split from Marcos. When Peping had first been informed by Almonte and his group of RAM's plan to oust Marcos and form a junta, he had asked point-blank where Enrile fit in. The officers had assured him they were acting as independent agents. It now looked as if RAM was no more of a monolith than the armed forces in general.

When she finally got through to Camp Aguinaldo, however, she was full of compassion for the defense minister. "I am really worried about you," she told him. "All I can offer you for the moment are my prayers."

Enrile replied, "That's all we need." Their conversation was brief and formal. Neither talked about anything so crass as politics.

"I hope this will be the beginning of better times," she said in parting.

"She put down the phone and walked back to listen to the radio," recounted Cebu Assemblyman John ("Sonny") Osmeña. "She looked very sullen. She said Enrile asked her to pray for him. 'I guess he expects the worst,' she said."

Although no one in the room was any particular friend to Enrile, Osmeña acknowledged that "at that moment he was a welcome ally. We had gone through an episode where we had been cheated out of our victory, and we did not expect much from the boycott. Then suddenly Enrile comes into the picture. We were expecting that at any moment Marcos would send in troops. Then Ramos goes over. Now the ballgame was tied. Many people felt that Ramos and Enrile together would be a counterpart to Ver."

As their thoughts turned to finding secure places in which to spend the night, into the house strode Blaine Porter, the U.S. consul in Cebu

City. "We could hear the 'Star Spangled Banner' playing," said Osmeña. He joshed Porter, "I know you Americans knew the whole thing." Porter retorted playfully that he had wandered into the house "by chance." He had been instructed by Bosworth to offer Cory the use of a U.S. navy frigate for her security.

Everyone appeared more worried about Cory's security than she. She declined to board the American ship "for reasons of image," said Osmeña later, although it was kept as a possible option for the following day, should events warrant. Her first priority was finding her daughter Kris, who had gone out to dinner and the movies before anyone was aware of events in Manila. While waiting for Kris to return, the politicians in the room began spinning scenarios. "We talked of setting up a rebel government in Cebu or Davao," said Osmeña.

Once mother and daughter were finally reunited, they slipped out to a Carmelite monastery, where Cory had decided to spend the night. "I got to the monastery," she related, "which was like *The Sound of Music,* and these nuns welcomed me. They said, 'Cory, you will be very safe here, because they will have to kill all of us before they do anything to you.' I slept very well, considering that they had no mattress."

Despite the fears of her advisors, she left by private plane for Manila the following day, escorted to the airport by reformist troops.

*　　　*　　　*

One and one-half hours after Enrile and his "boys" had occupied Defense Ministry headquarters, Captain Roger Diaz, a RAM leader based in the northern Mindanao city of Cagayan de Oro, received orders from Manila via Colonel Tibursio ("Tiboy") Fusilero. "Yazdi, are the logs ready for transport to Butuan?" Fusilero asked, in a phone call. That was code for "Can we do it now?"

Diaz replied, "Sir, any time."

Fusilero ordered, "Meet me at the airport."

Diaz had met with Gringo, Red, and other leaders three days before in Manila, and had sensed that D-Day was imminent. But he had expected notification twenty-four hours in advance to give him time to finish stocking weapons. He got to the airport just as a Cessna belonging to the Ministry of National Defense landed.

"What's happened?" asked Diaz.

"The 'boodlefight' is now," said Fusilero.

Diaz's mission was to mobilize reinforcements for the men carrying out the assault on the palace and the taking of Villamor Air Base. Throughout the night tonight he would fly and motor to the various military regions of Mindanao, signaling rebel sympathizers to begin sneaking weapons and armored personnel carriers out of their camps to a prearranged rendezvous point for pickup by transport plane at dawn.

His first stop was brigade headquarters in Butuan City, an area of heavy NPA activity, where First Lieutenant Allen Martin controlled all the armor for the area. Martin was an active RAM member. He was prepared to carry out his orders, but he was also surprised by the lack of advance notice. He would have to wait until after dark to sneak the three V-150 commando vehicles needed by RAM out of the camp, which was under the control of a loyalist colonel.

Diaz proceeded next to nearby Butuan Logging Inc. (BLINC), where he informed the manager, an Enrile man, that he was occupying his area to use as a tactical operations center. After a quick dinner, he briefed sympathetic mayors and citizens, who had been cultivated as part of RAM's outreach to the civilian community—a force which, within a matter of hours, would come to be known to all the world as People Power. Diaz and Martin then mounted motorcycles and made the rounds of all the camps in the region, alerting sympathetic brigade commanders, whose men were needed for the operation, to head for the logging camp.

Arriving back in Butuan City before dawn, they radioed Fusilero to find out if the C-130, which would transport the men and materiel, had landed. "No" was Fusilero's reply. Calculating that they would have time to mobilize one more company while waiting for the plane, they returned to the road.

When Diaz and Martin reached their final destination at six o'clock on Sunday morning, they were greeted with bad news. Their RAM counterparts handed them a transistor radio tuned to Radio Veritas in Manila. They heard the recorded voice of President Marcos announcing to a news conference late on Saturday night the arrests of RAM officers, who had confessed their roles in a plot to assassinate him. "I realized the 'boodlefight' was a failure," said Diaz. Lieutenant Martin slumped onto a bench, drained of all his energy.

Gradually the consequences of the plot's failure dawned on them. Exposed now as part of the conspiracy, it was only a matter of hours before they would be missed and hunted down. All over northern Mindanao, men and vehicles were moving toward the Butuan logging camp, where they would be trapped. "I was gazing at the mountains," recalled Diaz, "and thinking, By God, I will be staying in these hills for a long time. When shall I see my family?"

＊ ＊ ＊

American officials in Washington were as taken aback by the sudden events as the Filipinos had been. "Oh shit, they've done it," said a Pentagon official, who was awakened on Saturday morning before dawn in Washington by a reporter wanting to know what was going on. "I felt absolutely sick to my stomach," said a State Department man, "thinking maybe our advocacy of military reform had caused a fracture." Richard Armitage was outside the country on a trip to the Middle East. President Reagan was spending the weekend at Camp David.

In the Philippines, Ambassador Bosworth had just seen off Habib, and was back at the embassy conducting a follow-up briefing on the special envoy's trip. With him were his entire country team, including CIA station chief and base commanders. JUSMAG chief General Teddy Allen, recalled that about 3:15, Bosworth got a phone call. "He came back and said, 'That was Enrile on the phone, wanting to advise me that he was holed up in Aguinaldo with a warrant out for his arrest.' " Bosworth was "very noncommittal," said Allen. "We did not want to get involved."

Yet the U.S. was already deeply involved in the unfolding events. Despite the strong, official statement from the Pentagon to the RAM officers the week before the election that the U.S. would not condone a military coup, the plotting had intensified, with the knowledge of U.S. defense attachés and the CIA. Enterprising as the American agents were, much of what they knew had been deliberately fed to them by the Philippine plotters themselves. The officer who had approached an American operative in an effort to obtain antitank weapons had done so with the knowledge of Enrile himself. Another Filipino had confided the entire list of Core-Group members to an American agent, from whom he had solicited protection for the families, should the officers be killed in the process of storming the palace.

In no case, said RAM, were any officers actively discouraged by the Americans in whom they confided. On the contrary, said one Core-Group officer, "Some people in the U.S. embassy said we were a third force. They did not trust the opposition, and we were strong enough to fight Marcos." He claimed that one American told him, "If we back up Cory, we are actually backing up the leftists, and if Cory cannot cope, we have a problem, whereas your political platform is based on morality." This agent, however, cautioned the Filipino, "We cannot condone anything violent, unless it is done in self-defense."

The week of the rebellion, in response to mounting evidence that RAM was still planning to move, several embassy officers had met again with Core-Group members to issue another warning. One official with knowledge of that meeting said, "Our policy was not to condone a military coup, but whether there was some other understanding they gleaned from it with a wink and a nod, I don't know." He added, "We ended up condoning everything that happened. It worked out well."

"We were correct," said Admiral Crowe.

*   *   *

Marcos lost the war that first afternoon and night, when he did not attack his mutinous defense minister and vice-chief of staff. For at least nine hours there were no crowds outside Camp Aguinaldo, and no more than 300 military men and several dozen journalists inside. Some blood would have been shed, but tactically it would not have been difficult to quell the rebellion at the start. Why did Marcos hesitate at the opportune moment?

Some speculated that the president, mindful of his place in history, was not willing to take responsibility for the casualties that would have ensued, including those of his two longtime allies, Ramos and Enrile. The reformists suggested that Marcos sounded the orders, but that there were not enough loyalist soldiers to carry them out. A palace aide had a more poetic response. Quoting some favorite lines of the president, he bemoaned the irony that the "old man" had ignored their teaching during this greatest crisis of his long career:

On the beaches of hesitation
Bleach the bones of those,
Who, on the dawn of victory
Tarried.

None of those answers was by itself satisfactory. One night later, Marcos issued orders that would have resulted in far more bloodshed, because by then the streets were crowded with Filipinos, who had assembled to defend the besieged reformists. By the same token, nonreformist officers insisted that there were plenty of professional soldiers to have carried out an order to attack a thinly defended Camp Aguinaldo that Saturday night, had one been issued. They claimed, however, that Ver, a political rather than a professional general, had panicked. Instead of thinking offensively, he diverted more and more crack troops to defend the palace, which the captured plotters had confessed was to be attacked at 2:30 A.M.

Marcos had a simpler answer for his behavior when I asked him, in an interview several months later in Honolulu, why he had not retaliated at once. "I had talked them out of it before," he said. Then he added, "I did not want to kill Ramos and Enrile. I still hoped to be able to reconcile with them. Perhaps that was my error."

Enrile was all too aware of Marcos's ability to talk him out of his opposition to any number of past policies. That was why he refused to negotiate with Marcos that first night. "The president tried to reach us," Enrile told me during a phone interview in the early hours of Sunday morning, "but we did not want to talk to him. I know his game."

Shortly after the 7:15 P.M. press conference in which Enrile and Ramos had publicly withdrawn their support from Marcos and implicitly pledged it to Aquino, Enrile had agreed to talk to Ver. The chief of staff, still spooked by his discovery of the scope of the palace plot earlier in the day, had pleaded with Enrile, "You must tell your men not to attack the palace." Enrile only too happily agreed. He knew full well that he did not have the troops to counter the palace defenses called in by Ver. He was impressed at how much psychological damage RAM's widely leaked and ultimately aborted plot had inflicted on his opponent.

"Just don't allow your men to approach our area," he said, bluffing about the strength of his defenses. After Ver had agreed, Enrile added, "Why don't we talk in the morning?"

A Scout Ranger officer later observed, "If a coup lasts for more than twenty-four hours, it is already won."

*   *   *

People Power began as a rather pitiful little display. As Ramos and Enrile ended their defiant press conference inside Defense Ministry headquarters at Camp Aguinaldo, and General Ramos jogged back across the highway known as EDSA to organize the defense of his own constabulary headquarters inside Camp Crame, the area was void of people. Ramos told his deputies they were going to need some protection. The daughter of General Hermilio Ahorro, deputy director general of the Philippine Constabulary, had called her father to volunteer the services of some activist friends. When Ahorro informed Ramos of her offer, the general had asked, "How many?" He frowned at the answer. "About sixty, sir." Exclaimed Ramos, "I need a million!" But he did not refuse. "Bring them over," he said.

Those who arrived first were drawn to the gates of Camp Aguinaldo, instead of Crame, having heard about all the activity there on the radio. "I went to the front gate and saw a few honking cars," General Ahorro recalled, "but they were all protecting Aguinaldo, which already had protection from Enrile's security force. So I crossed the street, went up to the first person who looked like a leader, and told him, 'You are guarding the wrong side of the street.' "

As more people arrived, they were sent a short distance away to a third camp, where Metropolitan Police Commander General Prospero Olivas had just been named by Marcos to replace General Ramos as chief of the constabulary. These volunteers were told to block the gates of that camp with their cars to prevent Olivas from moving troops and vehicles out in an attempt to take over Camp Crame. Their presence was not needed for long, however, for Olivas secretly sided with Ramos and managed to fall sick for the rest of the revolution.

Among the first oppositionists to visit the defenders of the military camps was Butz Aquino, whose ability to mobilize anti-Marcos demonstrations was well known to the military men who had often faced him across the barricades. The RAM officers had made "linkages" to Aquino and his supporters before the election. Now they were asking him to rally people to help defend the camps. He did not think twice about trying to help them, even though a number of his fellow leaders in the Parliament of the Streets refused. "They did not trust Enrile and Ramos," said Aquino. "Their feeling was 'Let the military kill each other.' "

It had been difficult to locate political leaders on Saturday night, so Aquino had contacted some friendly journalists to spread the word. When he showed up at the designated assembly point at 11 P.M., he was embarrassed to find only six people waiting there. "How do we conduct a revolution with six people?" he wailed. Gradually, however, as the news circulated through the opposition community, cars full of opposition supporters arrived. After the cardinal went on Radio Veritas to appeal for support for the rebel soldiers, people streamed toward military headquarters.

At 1:30 A.M., when General Ramos went out to the gate to give them their orders, he was greeted with what one marcher called "a deafening roar" from some 20,000 people who had answered the rebels' call. Ramos was appreciative, but made no secret of his greater expectations. "We would like one million people in the same manner as you did it before," he told Aquino, referring to Ninoy's funeral procession. Ramos explained, "We are in a defensive posture, because we are not waging an offensive. We are not taking power. We need People's Power."

*   *   *

Marcos was also appealing to the people, in his way, by calling a televised news conference at which he displayed two of the four captured plotters. Clearly believing that exposure of a coup plot against him would discredit the rebel cause, Marcos denied that he had planned to arrest Ramos and Enrile. He claimed that the palace had simply uncovered the reform officers' coup plot and had subsequently seized four ringleaders and "neutralized without force" the three battalions under their control. There would be no need, he stressed, for the use of his emergency powers to deal with the situation. All that was called for was to file rebellion and sedition charges against the conspirators. What remained, the president said, was a "political problem."

The reporters present at the press conference and others, like myself, who were watching it on television, listened to Marcos, weighed his charges of a coup against the explanation we had heard earlier from Ramos and Enrile about their imminent arrests, and simply disbelieved the president. The fact that Marcos, for once, was telling something approximating the truth was irrelevant.

The battle we were now witnessing was being waged largely in an arena of perceptions, the two sides challenging each other with threats and claims, rather than deadly weapons. Filipinos excelled in such exercises. In this war of imagery, there was ultimately no way Marcos could win.

All the public knew was that the reformists had defected from Marcos and Ver, and for that they would be greeted as heroes.

If Marcos seemed confident during the press conference, he appeared troubled afterward, as he spent an hour talking to the captured plotters. The first question Marcos had asked the officers, once the cameras stopped rolling, was if Enrile, Aquino, and Laurel were involved. That had been the object of Malajacan's interrogators as well. "They wanted to link those people to the plot," said the colonel.

Malajacan told the president they were not involved. In his mind he believed what he said. He explained that rationale to me later. "Enrile gave us his blessing to plan things," said Malajacan. "He told us, 'I will take care of the political side of whatever you guys are thinking of doing. But as far as the military side of it, that is your business.'"

As for Aquino, in Malajacan's view the reformists' association with her was simply "an offer of security assistance, because we were concerned about her life before the election." She would have become a member of the National Reconciliation Council, not because she was any favorite of the military, but "because during the election you could see the popular support she had."

When Marcos protested that this plot was "just a small thing of Gringo and Red," Malajacan interjected. "No, sir," he said, "this is more serious than your advisors are telling you. Yes, you have the generals, but seventy percent of the officer corps cannot follow your generals. Without them, your generals are nothing." Marcos listened and did not appear to resent the men for their straight talk, even when Colonel Aromin told him, "Sir, if you love this country, you should step down."

✻   ✻   ✻

Day 2, February 23:

The only front on which Marcos's commanders had fought during the last decade was the political front. When it came to plotting a military strategy against the rebels, they were over their heads.

Having made good on his promise not to attack on Saturday night, Ver had spent most of the hours before dawn in command conferences, preparing to attack on Sunday. There was bitter division among the brass. General Josephus Ramas, the ambitious army commander, who had been designated head of operations, had already infuriated Marine Commandant Brigadier General Artemio Tadiar by ordering his marines, some of whom were all the way across town guarding the palace, to make the first strike against the rebels. "Ramas was conserving the army for his own use later, after the smoke died down, while asking the marines to fight," opined rebel Colonel Malajacan. "Our assessment was that this was a post-Marcos move." Tadiar had argued for a strategy that would isolate the rebels without firing a shot: cutting off electricity into their camps. Ramas had ignored him.

Before the battle could begin, however, all the loyalist generals were summoned by the president to join him on the propaganda front, flanking him at another televised news conference, which was designed to convey the illusion of military unity behind Marcos, and to prepare public opinion for an attack against the rebels. Marcos, his hands swollen like two crab claws, his face bearing the peculiar butterfly-shaped mark that is symptomatic of lupus erythematosus, made another appeal to Ramos and Enrile to surrender, assuring them that there had been no warrants out for their arrests, and thus there was no reason to defend themselves inside their headquarters. Although he was charging some of their men with conspiracy to assassinate him, he was not accusing them of being involved.

He presented two more captive plotters to reporters in a press conference. Unlike the others, Colonel Malajacan did not read from a prepared affidavit. He ad-libbed. After confessing to being part of the plot to attack the palace, he veered off into what sounded more and more like a candid account of his motives. "If we were to die in that confrontation, it would be better than our people dying in the streets," he said. As he spoke, we journalists began nudging each other to express our astonishment at his statements.

"Our intention was to capture the president, talk to him, and force him to resign or send him into exile, and invite some people credible to the Philippine nation to lead," continued Malajacan. He was indicting the regime right there on government television. "To win our battles against the insurgency," he said, "we have to win back the respect of the people." The generals seated behind the president began to squirm uncomfortably, as the colonel expressed his fellow plotters' preference for their commanding officer, General Roland Pattugalan, to replace General Ver as chief of staff. Marcos, by now realizing that such statements were not part of the script, moved to cut him off. Malajacan yielded, and everyone on the podium tried to act as if nothing had happened. The fact was, however, that Marcos had lost control even of his own press conference.

Returning to his men and his tanks after the press conference, Tadiar shouted at Ramas, "This is insane." Then he headed off on a mission, which he did not want to undertake. It was mid-afternoon before his six tanks, ten armored personnel carriers, and 3,000 men got on the road to Camp Aguinaldo, where they had orders to disperse the crowds, force their way into the camp, position their tanks, and bombard Camp Crame across the street.

*　　　*　　　*

By Sunday afternoon, the repeated appeals of Cardinal Sin, Butz Aquino, Ramos, and Enrile on the radio, and the escalation of accusations against the rebels by Marcos on television had drawn at least 1 million people to the area between the two military camps. One look at the sight of the four-lane highway, transformed by the crowd into a stage for a political-spiritual happening, and the most wary citizen felt this was where he belonged. It was a typically Filipino mixture of the sacred and the profane. A statue of the Virgin Mary stood on a pedestal above the entrance to Camp Crame. The grillwork over the gate was festooned with banners of support for the men inside, printed pleas for Nonviolence, Ave Maria, and the first of a series of demands that would be made to whatever new government might emerge: Free All Political Prisoners.

Overnight, the morality play that had pitted Cory against Marcos had been recast into a vast pageant, offering roles to hundreds of thousands of Filipinos, who had participated by proxy when they voted, but who had ached for physical involvement as well. Now they felt needed.

Since the first campaign, a new element had been added: the break-away elements of the military. However that had not upset the balance between good and evil in the eyes of the people. It had merely tilted the scale further against Marcos. Now, they sensed, the people finally had force behind them. Miracles transpired in strange forms and mys-terious ways, they believed. This one came clothed in military cam-ouflage. But it was a source of no less ecstasy than if it had assumed the form of a less-despised institution. Suddenly these rebel soldiers, identified by the inverted Philippine-flag patches pinned to their uni-forms, were their saviors. The moment they heard the confessions of Ramos and Enrile for their actions in the past and the blessing conferred on them by the cardinal, the people extended their trust to these once-feared men.

The predominance of yellow in the crowd was clear evidence that the people perceived the reformist forces as supporting Cory. But their primary role at EDSA, the highway separating Camp Aguinaldo from Camp Crame, was to feed and protect the soldiers, and that they were doing with such joyous efficiency that even Filipinos were led to wonder why they were so much better at improvising solutions to deal with crises than at getting the job done in ordinary times.

When Enrile and his 320 men crossed the Epifanio de los Santos in the afternoon to consolidate forces with the 450 men of Ramos in the better-defended Camp Crame, they were greeted with adoration for the first time in their careers by a grateful people. "John-ny! John-ny!" they chanted, as the crowd parted to make way for the former defense minister, wearing jeans and a khaki jacket, an Uzi slung around his neck.

"I was very scared as we walked toward Camp Crame," said Colonel Honasan, whose nickname "Gringo" would be known nationwide by the end of the week. "But when we reached the first row of people, they started wiping our brows, giving us food, and thanking us. I knew then that we had won."

*   *   *

As Tadiar's tanks rolled toward their target, Enrile phoned Ambassador Bosworth, noting that many foreign journalists were inside the camp. Bosworth did not need to be told. The U.S. had already urged Marcos not to fire on the camp, and General Teddy Allen had worked out a plan for evacuating rebel leaders and the diplomats and journalists inside with them from a besieged Camp Crame by helicopter, if necessary.

When the tanks became visible from the upper stories of Philippine Constabulary Headquarters, Enrile was finally persuaded to return the president's calls. He asked Marcos to order the tanks to retreat. "Johnny, I am not going to harm your men," said Marcos, seeking a compromise whereby he could end the mutiny without bloodshed, yet show that he was enforcing the law. Enrile stalled for time by telling Marcos he could make no decisions about surrendering without first consulting his men, "because we now have a committee on a one-man-one-vote basis." He repeated his plea that the tanks be withdrawn. Marcos, also stalling, assured Enrile he would order the tanks not to fire, but said he could not prevent them from moving into position.

The people could, however, and that is what they did. A call went out for People Power from a military man with a microphone. Like a school of fish, the huge mass simply turned around and began moving in the direction of the tanks. Half an hour later the armor approached the intersection where the crowd had relocated itself. "Turn back!" shouted the people. Many had never seen an armored personnel carrier at such close range. Some stared, full of curiosity at the sight. Others knelt to pray and say the rosary.

Seeking an alternate route, the lead tank crashed through a concrete wall and attempted to bypass the sea of humanity. But the people massed to cut it off. General Ramas radioed orders to Commander Tadiar to move ahead. "I don't want to hurt these people," the marine answered. "I'm also human like you." While Ramas's men scouted possible detours from a helicopter hovering overhead, Tadiar waited. An opposition politician arrived to negotiate with the marine commander. When an intermediary relayed the general's message to give way to his armor, the crowd booed and jeered. Buoyed by a newfound sense of self-confidence and determination, they began to chant: "Co-ry! Co-ry!"

Butz Aquino arrived and, megaphone in hand, climbed up onto an APC to explain to the soldiers that the purpose of People Power was to prevent bloodshed. The pressure built. A soldier turned on the engine. Others motioned Aquino to jump off.

Screenwriter Amado Lacuesta, who was among the people blocking the tanks, later recounted his impressions in an anthology of recollections by Filipino participants in the four-day struggle. "Panic sweeps over us all," wrote Lacuesta. "Unthinking, I drop to my knees. Looking up I see only the general and his marines, disciplined, hard-eyed." As the armored vehicles lurched forward, Lacuesta described his emotions:

> I shout and raise my hands, daring them: "Go on, kill us!" I am only dimly aware of angry booing and hissing, from the thousands on the streets, walls and buses, of cameras clicking, motor-winders whirring furiously. The metal mountain jerks forward. Defiant, nervous shouts all around. The praying voices rise another key. I wonder what it is like to be crushed under tons of metal. Then the engine stops. There is an astounding split second of silence. The crowd erupts into wild cheers and applause.

After several more attempts to move ahead had been frustrated by praying nuns and chanting civilians, the tank column finally received permission to withdraw and return to nearby Fort Bonifacio. Now, swelled with pride, the people who had stood in their path moved aside. They had come as close as anyone can to the dark, steel heart of the dictatorship that had cowed them for so many years, and they had stared it down. That was already a victory.

✳　　　✳　　　✳

Shortly after the tanks had been repulsed without physical force, Enrile adopted a tougher line toward Marcos. He responded to the president's earlier request for surrender with a message delivered by two KBL intermediaries: "The situation has changed, and the bottom line demand—which is nonnegotiable—is for him to step down!"

Enraged, Marcos called a midnight press conference to respond to Enrile, who had wasted no time in publicly airing the message he had sent the president. All constraints now loosed, Marcos charged Ramos and Enrile with committing "an act of rebellion" for which they would have to stand trial. He accused Enrile of being "out to grab power and rule the country through a junta," and he counseled Mrs. Aquino "not to delude herself into thinking that she is being supported by Enrile, because she will be a mere member of the junta."

That thought had been very much on Cory's mind when she returned to Manila from Cebu that morning. The cardinal later revealed that she had called him to say, "We have a big problem, there is a third force." He had told her: "No, I am sure they are staging this because they want you to be president. Go there and thank them. Without this, you could be demonstrating every day and you will still not be president. But now, you will be. You can see the hand of God. This is the answer to our prayers."

American policymakers had not yet publicly pronounced themselves on the politics of the rebellion, and so well played was their appearance of neutrality that many spectators were confused. Among them was Lynn Allen, wife of the JUSMAG chief. "We did not know whether the Americans were supporting the loyalists or the rebels," she recalled of the four days she spent at home, tuned to the radio and television news and talking to other wives of U.S. officials. The women, however, knew which side they favored—embassy wives organized a sandwich brigade to help feed the rebels.

On Sunday night in Manila a ranking embassy official indirectly tipped his hand to the rebels, when he met with Colonel Edelberto Yap, an officer who had been publicly critical of Ver's leadership, but who was closer to Cory than to RAM. Yap was seeking permission from the Americans to land and refuel rebel planes at Clark Air Base. The rebels, who were already confident that they controlled the pilots of the Philippine Air Force planes and helicopters, which were parked at Philippine bases throughout the area, did not yet control those bases. They would need a place to set down the aircraft before the defections could go forward.

"It's your base," said the American official to the Filipino, choosing to interpret the Military Bases Agreement between the two countries more literally than was generally the case. "Just get in touch with your people there, and be sure it's understood that it's between you." After recounting the episode to me, the diplomat added an aside, "We did not want to get in the middle of it."

Not many officers on either the American or the Philippine side, however, were made privy to that conversation, as Colonel Romeo David, deputy base commander at Clark, discovered on Monday morning when the first four Philippine Air Force defectors landed. Shortly after their takeoff, David had received an order from the loyalist chief of staff of the air force to capture the pilots, if they landed at Clark. Unbeknownst to his superiors, David had already pledged his loyalty to General Ramos. He therefore disobeyed his orders and instructed the tower to let the planes land. He was startled when he arrived on the landing strip, however, to see American military base personnel pointing guns at the rebel pilots as if they were prisoners. "Treat them with respect, they are officers!" barked David, who identified himself to the Americans, and exercised his right to claim responsibility for the defecting Filipino officers and planes.

* * *

From the moment they woke up on Saturday morning in Washington (already Saturday night in Manila), U.S. policymakers had known that the Marcos regime was finished. What was not clear was how much damage it would wreak in its final death throes. "None of us has experience with implosion, when things pick up a momentum of their own," said Armitage. He confessed that "in Vietnam, at the moment of evacuation, I thought we had another week."

Gentle pressure had been exerted on Marcos in a message from President Reagan on Saturday, accompanied by an even softer public statement urging that force not be used. The fact that the first night of the rebellion had passed without attack was viewed as an encouraging sign.

However, the attempt to position loyalist tanks in front of rebel headquarters on Sunday afternoon had changed the equation. It was the middle of the night, by then, in Washington, but both the embassy and the White House were quick to urge restraint and threaten a cutoff of U.S. military assistance if heavy weapons were used against the rebels.

Habib had arrived back in Washington late Saturday night, and top Pentagon, State, National Security Council, and CIA officials gathered at Secretary Shultz's house in Bethesda, Maryland, for a Sunday breakfast and briefing from the special envoy. "Waiting for Habib was like waiting for Godot," said Assistant Secretary of State Wolfowitz. "It bought us time." Until the president's White House advisors heard from Habib, they had continued to believe that Marcos could get away with another term, despite the fraud-marred election. Habib was able to put the revolt of Ramos and Enrile in a context which convinced the president's men that the faction of the military that Marcos still controlled would not be strong enough to save him.

A sneer in his voice, Presidential Chief of Staff Don Regan questioned whether anyone could be sure that what would follow Marcos would not be worse. Habib, at his bombastic best, argued that Aquino and her supporters were "not a Khomeini gang," but were straight from the mainstream. He noted that the private business community backed her. "Who will her finance minister be?" asked Regan. The several names which Habib threw out stopped him cold. They were respectable men, whom Regan had encountered in his former life in the private sector. Observed one official, "I couldn't tell if he was convinced or if he had just lost his best argument."

Given the rapid flow of developments in Manila, and a growing consensus that Marcos's time on the stage was over, it was decided that a meeting with the president, which had been scheduled for Monday, was necessary today. The breakfast group moved to the White House, where Reagan and additional members of the National Security Planning Group joined them at 3 P.M. for another wide-ranging discussion.

As the portrait of a president who could no longer govern was once again sketched by Shultz and Habib, the secretary of state presented what several colleagues would later describe as a "brilliant" proposal to offer Marcos refuge in the U.S., rather than leave him to wander the earth in search of asylum, as the Shah had been forced to do. It was, in the words of one official, "important to our image and respectability in dealing with some other leaders some other time." More important in the short term was the psychological appeal of Shultz's suggestion to President Reagan. It helped ease the pain of letting an old friend go. By the end of the meeting, the president and the other holdouts, Defense Secretary Weinberger and CIA Director Casey, had come around.

Immediately a secret cable, titled "Landing Instructions—Marcos," went out from the State Department to the U.S. military command in the Pacific, instructing air bases in the region to "honor any landing request from Philippine President Marcos and/or members of his family."

The press release issued by the White House immediately after the meeting revealed nothing of the decision to persuade Marcos to step down. It merely served as a public warning to Marcos to avoid an attack against the rebel elements of his armed forces, lest he invite a cutoff of U.S. military aid.

The bad news was communicated to him privately in Malacañang through three different channels. A message from Reagan, which was described by one official as "full of diplomatic gobbledygook," was relayed to the U.S. embassy in Manila for delivery to Marcos by Ambassador Bosworth. Meanwhile, Marcos's longtime labor minister, Blas Ople, who had been dispatched to the U.S. to rally support for the president's new mandate, was recruited by Shultz and Armacost to deliver a tougher verbal message informing Marcos that Reagan's missive was final. Marcos's onetime chief assistant, Alejandro Melchor, who, curiously enough, also happened to be in Washington at the time, was asked by National Security Council director, Vice-Admiral John Poindexter, to voice a similar message to his former boss.

*   *   *

Day 3, February 24:

At 3 A.M. a caravan of black Mercedes with tinted windows attracted the attention of residents near the palace gates, through which it passed. Its speedy passage past the U.S. embassy in the direction of the airport was reported to General Allen. "We thought it was the president making a run for it," he said. A short while later, however, Allen was informed by the tower at Clark that the cars had carried, not the Marcoses, but all the presidential pilots, who had defected en masse in several private planes which had been waiting for them at the airport. They were requesting permission to land at Clark. Marcos was now truly a captive in his palace. While he had executive jets and choppers at his disposal, he had no one to fly them.

Across town the marines had finally been able to position themselves and some of their armor inside Camp Aguinaldo. By leaving Fort Bonifacio at 4 A.M. and dispersing the thin crowds camped out around rebel headquarters with tear gas, they had averted casualties. Recognizing the danger the rebels were now under from a desperate General Ver, Ramos summoned the journalists inside the camp and took to the airwaves in alarm. "Overwhelming military force has been directed to move against us. Please tell the world it is Mr. Marcos who is now able to inflict violence, terror, and vengeance upon our people here in Camp Crame."

As the marines under Colonel Braulio Balbas, deputy commandant of the corps, set up their 81-mm and 60-mm mortars on the elevated lawn of the Camp Aguinaldo golf course across the street, tension inside Camp Crame mounted. It had taken Ver a long time, but now his superior arsenal was beginning to make an impact. If his men fired, Camp Crame would fall. "We thought we were going to die," said Core-Group member navy Captain Felix Turingan. "We said our good-byes, embraced each other, even cried a little and sang our alma mater."

Ver had ordered Colonel Antonio Sotelo and his Fifteenth Strike Wing to provide air support for the marine assault at dawn. The rebels knew that Sotelo and his men were with them, but could not defect until they had an order to take off. Ramos could only hope that would occur before the bombardment from Aguinaldo commenced. At 6 A.M. Sotelo's order came. His men, piloting nine helicopters, flew low over an awakening city, hovered briefly over the two camps in the transparent light of dawn, then dived down onto the parade ground at Crame.

To those who knew which side Sotelo was on, his helicopters were a glorious sight. To the people cowering near the gates, they were engines of terror. As they landed in quick succession, the pilots jumped out, waving white handkerchiefs and flashing the Laban sign, to be embraced by fellow rebels. The anti-Marcos forces now controlled the skies.

*   *   *

In the confusion a mysterious message had been relayed from reformist intelligence sources to rebel headquarters and from there to rebel Radio Bandito. The report claimed that Marcos had fled the palace. It was greeted with jubilation when it was received inside Camp Crame. Actually believing the battle to be won, Ramos and Enrile left their headquarters at 7:45 A.M. to confirm the news to the crowds outside. Surrounded by a phalanx of weary men and flanked by a statue of the Virgin Mary, which they had kept in their midst since the beginning of their siege, they waded into an exuberant crowd.

It was a jubilant reunion of survivors. It had happened so quickly that it lacked the fanfare I had fantasized would accompany the fall of Marcos. But it was no less emotional. Ramos and Enrile were hoisted onto a concrete podium, where they proclaimed February 24, 1986, the birth of a free Philippines.

Enrile, his craggy face sagging with fatigue, began to speak. Only three weeks before, he had put his considerable oratorical talents to work in his northern region campaigning for Marcos. Now, just as easily, he began speaking the language of the opposition, invoking its martyrs, Ninoy Aquino and Evelio Javier. Suddenly the crowd was no longer chanting "Cory, Cory," but "Johnny, Johnny." Enrile was a politician to whom words came easily, but it sounded as though these were coming from the heart. They were solemn and strong.

"Never again in the history of this republic will there be a tyrant sitting in Malacañang," he intoned. The rhetoric did not stop with commemorative phrases. "We must remember what happened in the last few days," said Enrile, "and we must always count on the Armed Forces of the Philippines to be the guardian of the freedom and the welfare of the Filipino people."

"Where is Cory?" I wondered. She had remained in hiding since her return to Manila. Neither her name nor her campaign platform to free all political prisoners and call a six-month ceasefire with the Communist insurgents crept into the agenda which Enrile was presenting for a post-Marcos Philippines. "I am warning the Communist Party," he said, "that they must not test the resolution of this group of the Armed Forces of the Philippines. All of the freedom fighters who joined us in this noble enterprise made a solemn and moral commitment that we shall see to it that freedom and democracy will always be in this land."

The usually bland Ramos followed Enrile on the podium. Today he was absolutely ebullient, raising his clenched fist in the air and invoking People Power like a civilian politician. However, he limited his statement to the military matters at hand. He sounded a warning to "any armed elements still remaining to challenge the Armed Forces of the Philippines" to lay down their arms, or "we will assault you and we will not spare you."

When a man in the crowd yelled, "Down with Marcos," everybody cheered. Ramos shot back with a grin, "He's left!" and the cheers intensified. At the end of his speech the general, displaying a dash of uncharacteristic frivolity, did a frog jump into the air, which drew squeals of delight from the crowd.

Ramos closed by paying homage to "the young man whose action in defending ourselves in Camp Aguinaldo precipitated our revolution, Colonel Gregorio Honasan," and "the dedicated young men" of RAM. "I'm proud to be a soldier again," a young enlisted man in fatigues told me. Overhead two F-5 fighter jets, loyal to the rebels, circled protectively.

But Marcos was not gone. As we filed back inside constabulary headquarters, we could see him on television, presiding over what was billed as a live press conference, and threatening to blast the rebels out of their camp. Sobered about the quality of their intelligence and their exposure to the enemy in place across the street, the rebels ordered all civilians out of their operations room. Then they launched an offensive that was made possible by their newly won control of the air.

What the reformists lacked in intelligence capability, they had more than made up for in the propaganda value of their premature proclamation of victory. It had spread the impression to the remaining military holdouts and civilian fence sitters that the Marcos era was indeed over. It had also shaken Aquino supporters, who saw in Enrile's curious performance a preview of a power grab by the military once Marcos was gone. "That day at lunchtime," Cory told me, "I met with Tanada and others, who advised me to take my oath now. Many of us were thinking Johnny was in it for himself. They thought his speech was scary." Determined not to allow events to pass them by, the opposition political leaders dispatched a delegation to Camp Crame to seek the support of Ramos and Enrile for a civilian government led by Cory Aquino.

*   *   *

Once Washington had taken steps to pressure Marcos to abdicate, the process of transition to a new government moved along quickly. Bowing to the popular will, as well as to signals from the Americans, Enrile greeted Aquino and Laurel with a proposal that was similar to theirs. All he asked was that he serve as defense minister and Ramos as chief of staff in their administration. Defensively, he said, as he recounted the incident months later, "We did not want a junta or to create a situation where the country will become the operation of one military government after another. At that point we had eighty-five percent of the military under our control, and if we were hungry for power, it would have been easy for me, but we did not want to start a precedent that would be regretted later by all of us." Shrewd as he was, however, it could not have escaped Enrile that as long as fighting continued between rebels and loyalists, or, after that, between government forces and the Communists, it was the defense minister, on behalf of the military, who would wield the real power within an Aquino cabinet.

On the night they decided to topple Marcos, the rebel military leaders had pledged not to take power themselves nor ask for rewards. They had kept their word. However, they had been led to believe they would get something in return. "Enrile said he and General Ramos would have full rein over the military and the counterinsurgency," said Colonel Batac later. "He was supposed to be consulted by the government on those matters." Others believed he had gotten more than that. "He was talking about a tacit coalition," said a Core-Group member.

In the immediate aftermath of the revolution the rebels were too busy trying to consolidate their forces to hold Enrile and Ramos accountable for the deal that had been struck. Only later would they look back and question how they had ended up with so little authority over affairs in their own domain. "Before February, we decided we would turn the government over to a civilian-military council," said a dejected Malajacan, "but at some point in those four days, the decision was made to give it all to Cory."

*   *   *

The rebels had so far been unable to force Marcos to step down from power, but there was little to stop them from forcing him off the air. They seized Channel 4, and pulled the plug on the president in mid press conference. Viewers had just witnessed another bit of play-acting, or *moro-moro*, between Marcos and Ver, which seemed intended to impress upon his official U.S. audience the president's concern for preventing bloodshed, even as the Americans' sensitive communications devices were intercepting his generals' orders to fire on rebel headquarters.

Marcos had just repeated assurances that he was doing his best to avoid violence, when Ver stepped over to him and whispered, within range of the TV cameras and microphones, "Sir, we cannot keep retreating all the time. They are massing civilians against our troops. They are engaged in a massive disinformation campaign. We came here to show you that we are strong, we are organized, and we are ready to annihilate them." Hyperventilating again, Ver grew more and more excited. "Just give me the order, sir, and we will hit them."

Marcos, looking reasonable, compared to his bellicose chief of staff, refused. Yet even as he spoke, his generals were ordering Colonel Balbas to stop making excuses and fire the mortars he had positioned early that morning on the golf course inside Camp Aguinaldo.

As Balbas continued to procrastinate, Colonel Sotelo's rebel helicopter pilots went on the offensive. One swooped low over Villamor Air Base, warned loyalist soldiers to get out of the way, made another circle and strafed five helicopters which, they had learned through intercepted communications, were being readied for an attack on Crame. Another buzzed Malacañang, letting fly six rockets, which blasted holes in the palace gardens and destroyed the Mercedes Benz of one of Marcos's sons-in-law, Gregorio ("Greggy") Araneta.

That attack so terrified the First Family that Marcos called Washington in alarm. Richard Childress, the National Security Council's Asian expert, in turn called Prime Minister Virata to enlist his help in "deescalating" the level of the rebels' attacks. Virata had resigned his post as finance minister and gone into hiding, but had not transferred his support to Ramos and Enrile.

"The White House is saying that even if your group wins, you will have a hard time with military assistance if you keep fighting," Virata told Enrile, when he finally reached him on Tuesday morning, February 25. Enrile's indifference to Virata's message led the prime minister to suspect that the politically ambitious Enrile "was ready to declare himself chairman of something."

Virata found Ramos more receptive to Washington's implicit threat of withholding aid from any government that took power by force. In a telephone conversation with Ambassador Bosworth later on Tuesday, Virata learned why the Americans were so insistent that the rebels hold their fire: U.S. officials in Washington and Manila were already making arrangements for the imminent departure of President Marcos and his family from the Philippines.

Enrile's spokesman Sylvestre ("Yong Yong") Afable swore that the attack on the palace was not meant to harm anyone or to take power. "It was just an attempt to show the soldiers there that we control a good number of air assets, so that they would not fire at our troops," he said. It was also a clever bit of psy war that was part of RAM's strategy to spook the Marcoses.

"We floated information to Malacañang that the U.S. Marines were on their way, and that we had the palace surrounded," said rebel Colonel Nani Figueroa. "All we had to do to scare them was fire in the air every hour in the vicinity of Malacañang. Since they never moved away from the palace, they couldn't tell what was out there." What it all came down to, said a rebel sympathizer, was that "this is a war of nerves and words, so whoever will be able to maintain and sustain that will be the winner."

The scare tactics were effective. Colonel Balbas was finally granted permission to pack up his mortars and retreat, rather than risk an air attack against his men. And the First Family was finally forced to view its future in power as subject to limits.

*　　　*　　　*

The Marcoses spent what would be their last night in the palace cowering in fear at the nearby sounds of gunfire. Children and grandchildren huddled together in Imelda's windowless bedroom, engaged in melancholy conversation. When I talked to Marcos several months later in Hawaii, he claimed that helicopters had continued to buzz the palace late into the night, causing his security force to decide that the family must leave. Marcos, according to his aides, had lost confidence in General Ver's ability to protect him. Chastising his chief of staff for not having warned them about the approach of the rebel helicopters earlier in the day, the ailing president himself took control of palace security.

He remained obsessed by a message which he said had been sent by a duty officer at the U.S. embassy to a minor official at the palace Office of Media Affairs, warning that if street violence broke out, U.S. marines stationed in the Philippines would be fielded "to prevent a slaughter." His old paranoia welled up in him, as he accused the U.S. of "rearming and refueling" the planes that the rebels had landed at Clark. "Our intelligence shows [the rebellion] was planned way back with the help of some Americans," he told me later.

Officials in Washington, worried about reports that disaffected loyalists under Ver might try something desperate, decided to preempt them and to increase the pressure on Marcos by going public with President Reagan's message to step down. They woke the president up to approve it, and they released it before the morning news shows in the U.S. It was evening in Manila when the embassy delivered the statement to Marcos. "Attempts to prolong the life of the present regime by violence are futile," it read.

An aide who saw Marcos shortly after news of the public statement had begun to circulate in Manila was full of pain for his longtime idol and foreboding for himself. "The old man looked sick and terrible," he said. "He is rapidly disintegrating. He is the color of a skeleton." Not having slept since the rebellion began, Marcos was rambling and incoherent when he appeared later that evening, obviously made-up, on the only television channel not commandeered by the rebels. He conducted a ghostly press conference. Marcos's questioners were on camera in a heavily guarded studio across town, which they could not leave, while the president appeared alone in an empty room in the palace, responding to their voices.

It was a pathetic performance. Marcos continued to play the role of absolute ruler, as if he still had a kingdom. Hopelessly isolated from the reality of the revolt, which was now all but over, he announced that he was accepting the resignation of Ramos and declaring a state of emergency. Parodying his martial law proclamation of fifteen years before, he announced that he was taking over all public utilities. Broadcasting stations, he said, would have to "confirm all news with the minister of information." Then, as if by reflex, he began to bark orders over the screen. "To all the commanders in the field, you are now free to use small arms to defend your installations." Asked one of his unseen questioners, "Are you imposing a curfew?" Replied Marcos, "Now that you mention it, I am hereby declaring that a curfew be observed from six o'clock to six o'clock."

The pressure inside the palace was taking its toll on the sleepless First Family. After the press conference, Bong Bong Marcos pulled a gun on a presidential aide whom he accused of mishandling his father's television appearance.

Marcos was on the phone most of the night. He phoned Bosworth, proposing the sort of power-sharing arrangement that Aquino had refused to discuss with Habib. Imelda phoned Nancy Reagan, who tried to avoid speaking to her but finally did. The Marcoses had never accepted rejection, and they were not doing so now.

Unless he heard it from Reagan himself, Marcos seemed likely not to believe that the Americans had withdrawn their support. Yet Reagan's advisors had insisted that it would be unseemly for the president of the U.S. to discuss such an issue on unsecured telephone lines. And there was always the danger that Marcos, his shrewd lawyer's mind dulled from lack of sleep and anxiety, but still treacherous, might come up with a loophole that could cause the kindly Reagan to soften his stance.

"They are treating me like the Shah," Marcos complained to Ople, who finally reached him to pass along the tough message from Washington. After so many contentious years together, Ople was known for his ability to tell the president things he did not want to hear, clothed in flowery language and delivered in a deep, mellifluous voice. "No," Ople assured him, soothingly, "you will be treated as an honored guest." In the indirect, face-saving Asian manner, Ople let his boss know what he had to do.

*   *   *

Day 4, February 25:

At 2:45 A.M. Manila time, Marcos placed a call to Senator Laxalt. It was afternoon in Washington, and Laxalt was meeting in a Capitol Hill office with Armacost and Habib. Marcos had received not only President Reagan's personal message offering him asylum and the stronger verbal message relayed by Blas Ople, but the blunt public statement from the White House as well. Yet he was not ready to concede defeat. "They are telling me not to use force, how do they expect me to govern?" a belligerent Marcos asked Reagan's friend.

"He was blinking," said Armacost, "proposing a coalition government where he could be a counselor in the government." It was the irrepressible compromiser at work. Armacost smiled just a bit as he said, "You could see the lawyer in him: give a little, retain a little." He was asking Laxalt what he thought the president would say to that idea. Laxalt said he would have to ask Reagan. Marcos also expressed a desire to go up north to his Ilocos home for a while. Laxalt asked Armacost afterward, "What would be the matter with that?"

Armacost replied laconically, "For one thing, he would become the symbol for the disaffected elements of the military, and you would have a civil war."

After conferring with the president, Laxalt called Marcos back. By now it was 5:30 in the morning in Manila. The senator told him that power sharing would be impractical and undignified. He repeated the president's invitation to the Marcoses to move to the U.S. His considerable reserves of determination and defiance now practically depleted, Marcos turned to Laxalt for advice. What should he do? he asked. Laxalt put it to him straight. "I think you should cut and cut cleanly. I think the time has come."

The silence at the other end of the phone was so pronounced, so profound that Laxalt finally had to ask if Marcos was still there. He was, but his persona had changed. He had no brash comeback with which to respond to Laxalt's recommendation. No counterproposal. For once, he was honest in showing his emotions. "I am so very, very disappointed," he said.

Half an hour later he canceled the still-standing orders to loyalists to fire on Camp Crame. Then he joined his family. His children had been urging him to leave, to no avail. Imelda had resisted the idea for a time, but now she too was resigned to the prospect. He had continued to insist that he would stay and fight, but had urged the family to go. Now, however, something in his demeanor told them to proceed with arrangements for all of them to leave. Son-in-law Tommy Manotoc called a friend at the U.S. embassy and gave him the "go" signal he had been waiting for since Sunday night.

*   *   *

Apparently having second thoughts about accepting Laxalt's advice, Marcos called Enrile early Tuesday morning before the swearing-in of Mrs. Aquino. "How can we settle this gracefully?" he asked the man most responsible for his dilemma. Enrile, who had tried but failed to separate himself from Marcos so many times in the past, felt he had been through all this before.

"I don't know," he said. Marcos, as usual, had several proposals.

"Maybe I can remain as honorary president," Marcos suggested. "I will concede the election and form a provisional government, and I will serve as honorary president until 1987, and you will run the government."

Late for the inauguration of the new president, Enrile was too weary to bargain with the old one. "I told him, 'Mr. President, I am not interested in having a government. Our effort was not really to grab power to form a junta or any kind of revolutionary government, but to see the will of the people respected.'" Besides, he said, more to the point, "It's too late for this discussion, because my group has agreed upon my suggestion that we must now support Mrs. Aquino."

But Marcos wasn't finished. "Do you think I can safely live in the country?" Enrile promised him that as far as he was concerned, "we have no aggressive intentions against you. You have been our superior for the last twenty years." Having won at least that concession, Marcos pressed for another, as if mindless of Enrile's sensitivities and what finally drove him to rebel.

"What about General Ver?" Marcos asked.

"I cannot answer that," snapped Enrile. Marcos asked his former defense minister to please talk to the new government about the matter. Enrile said he would do so and would get back to him in "a couple of days."

General Ramos, who had been present in the office during their conversation, asked Enrile to let him have a word with Marcos—his first since the rebellion. "*Manong* Andy, this is Eddie," said his cousin, addressing him as one would an older brother in the Ilocano dialect. In an effort to convince him that the battle was lost and that he should step down, Ramos read him the roster of commanders and units who had now pledged loyalty to the rebels. "Can you please believe what I am trying to tell you?" pleaded the general. "You no longer have the support of the armed forces." According to Ramos, Marcos answered him in the manner of an older brother. "He just said, 'Shut up, you guy, that's neither here nor there.'"

*　　　*　　　*

Two inaugurations took place within one hour of each other. One was positive and full of hope, the other vengeful and tinged with pathos.

At 11 A.M. Corazon Aquino took her oath as the seventh president of the republic. The simple ceremony was symbolically important, in that it took place in daylight in the private Club Filipino, rather than at night inside Camp Crame, as Enrile and Aquino's security force had proposed. It was her first assertion of independence from the men who had helped put her in the office to which the people felt she had been elected. "We must remember what Crame means to me and to the people," she had told them. "Camp Crame was the first place where Ninoy, where every political detainee was brought during martial law." She had also refused to arrive by military helicopter, as Enrile and Ramos did. Instead, she insisted on riding in her Chevrolet and stopping at traffic lights rather than zipping through, Imelda-style with sirens blazing. The significance of her gestures was not lost on the adoring crowds that greeted her.

Nor was it lost on the reform officers. "There was a shouting bout inside Camp Crame early in the morning," recounted Enrile, "because the officers wanted Mrs. Aquino to take the oath at Crame instead of Club Filipino." Enrile pleaded with his "boys" to forget it. "Let's unify the group and support the one who went through this election," he said. One Core-Group member, a key Enrile ally, boycotted the event. However, those officers who attended were greeted like conquering heroes by their new political bedfellows and by the spectators outside in the street.

While there was an air of euphoria among the stylishly dressed, mostly affluent guests at the inaugural ceremony, the occasion was a poignant one. Dressed in lacy yellow and sporting her now famous yellow-framed glasses, Cory swore on a Bible held by Ninoy's mother, Doña Aurora. Her brief inaugural address was studded with poignant references to her late husband's past and the nation's future.

"It is fitting and proper that, as the rights and liberties of our people were taken away at midnight twenty years ago, the people should firmly recover those lost rights and liberties in the full light of day," she said. "And now, I would like to appeal to everybody to work for national reconciliation, which is what Ninoy came back home for."

Across town Marcos was inaugurated at high noon, not before the people on an open stage, as he had been three times before, but behind the heavily secured walls of Malacañang. Outside the palace a raucous crowd of some 4,000 loyalists, which would become a vindictive mob after nightfall, chanted, "Hang Enrile and Ramos!" Inside, cabinet and diplomatic representation was notably thin. Former Prime Minister Virata, who had been replaced by Laurel as prime minister that morning, did not attend. Even Marcos's vice-presidential running mate, Arturo Tolentino, failed to show up.

"Whatever we have before us, we will overcome," said Marcos, who urged his followers to "defend not only the democratic process, but the freedom and dignity we love so much."

Secret negotiations on the Marcoses' departure had been completed by 8 A.M. on Tuesday morning, before the oath taking. "It's all over," said one of the few informed Marcos ministers to an unsuspecting aide. The president, however, never let on that he was leaving, so there was no way for those who knew to say good-bye to the man most of them had served for the better part of their adult lives. He was a father figure to some, a towering influence on all. It had been a truism among them that he would leave Malacañang only feet first. That it was ending this way was unbearably sad.

It was also a frightening experience for those who would be left behind. They feared reprisals from a new regime, which they expected to be as vindictive as any that had preceded it. Worse, unless they had been farsighted, they would find themselves without patronage in a society which was dependent on it. All appointments were political. Favors, not merit, were what counted. As the prime dispensers of such patronage for two decades, they could foresee, better than the idealistic oppositionists, how brutal this transition was likely to be.

Since Marcos had refused to consider leaving until the last minute, his settling of accounts was uneven. Some aides left with fat envelopes of newly minted pesos in their pockets. Others left with IOUs. Only a few were favored with a seat on the airplane that would carry him into exile. Among the disappointed was presidential legal advisor Justice Manuel Lazaro, to whom had fallen much of the dirty work that had helped win the acquittal of the president's men for the murder of Aquino. Lazaro had not known that the president would be departing. He had not made special preparations to attend the swearing-in. Thus, when he arrived at the palace, he had not been allowed inside. "Suddenly the checkpoints were manned by different people," explained one of his colleagues.

As the official guests took their leave of the palace, supporters in the garden below the Ceremonial Hall called for the First Couple to address them. Imelda, clad in white and fighting back tears, led Marcos out onto a balcony, where he expressed thanks to his followers "for the twenty years you've given me." They closed with a duet of their favorite, "Because of You."

*   *   *

At seven o'clock Tuesday morning Bosworth, who had been on the phone all night to Washington and Malacañang, gave General Teddy Allen the order to arrange the evacuation of President Marcos from the palace. A tentative agreement for his departure had been reached. Marcos did not want to leave the country under the protection of rebel soldiers. It was thought, however, that he would accept a proper American escort. "I want you to lay on transportation to bring Marcos and thirty people out of the palace, take them wherever they want to go, and assure their safety," said Bosworth. He stipulated that he needed the option of transport by air, land, and sea, and that he wanted it available within one hour from the time Marcos notified the Americans he was ready to go.

Everything on that checklist except the potential passengers was routine for a combat veteran like Allen. By 8:30 A.M. he had four helicopters and crews standing by at Clark Air Base "on a one-hour string," a C-130 transport plane ready to fly from Clark into Manila International Airport, should they leave the palace by car, and four boats embarked on the six-hour journey from Subic to Manila Bay, where they would remain "in orbit" until directed to make the short trip up the Pasig River to the palace.

By Tuesday afternoon Bosworth became concerned that the embassy had been unable to make contact with anyone at the palace all morning. "They haven't returned our phone calls," he told Allen. He asked the general to leave a message for Tommy Manotoc. Allen had never met Imee Marcos's husband, the basketball coach, but like everyone else, he had heard plenty about Imelda's disapproval of the couple's secret marriage. In the days ahead he would come to appreciate the Manotocs' abilities as referees in family quarrels.

All afternoon Marcos had lain on his bed, hot with fever. Gunshots continued to punctuate the air, giving those inside the impression that they were under siege. General Ver was across the river in his headquarters, unable to defend them. Colonel Aruiza, painfully taking stock of the situation, finally did what duty commanded. "It was I who had to decide, according to standard operating procedure, that it was beyond our control to protect the president," he said. "Tommy Manotoc had some friends at the American embassy, and he suggested we call them."

Manotoc returned General Allen's call half an hour after receiving his message, and the two talked frequently after that about logistics, though never about destination. "Each time I would say, 'Where do you want to go,' he would say, 'I cannot tell you.'" In their first few calls the decision to evacuate by helicopter from the grounds of Malacañang Park had been made. However, as the afternoon wore on, the number of passengers kept increasing. It doubled from thirty to sixty, when Marcos asked to take his personal medical staff and security guards along. When it ballooned to 100, Allen, juggling figures in his head, decided he could fit fifteen in each helicopter and bring the rest out by boat. When it climbed to 120, he told Manotoc, "That's all the transportation I have."

At 6:30 P.M., as Allen and Manotoc were in the process of finalizing details for the lift-off, Marcos picked up the phone and repeated certain of the instructions Manotoc had already relayed. "Obviously he had taken the bait and was going to go," said Allen. "I asked him, 'Where do you want to go, Mr. Marcos?' He said, 'Clark Air Force Base.' I asked, 'Where from there?' He said, 'Ilocos Norte.' I said, 'Where from there?' He said, 'I'll tell you when we get there.' I asked, 'When do you want to go?' He said, 'We are ready to go now.'"

Darkness had already fallen. When Allen contacted General Gordon Williams at Clark, he learned that although the runway in Marcos's home province had been constructed to land the large aircraft that had carried Imelda's jet-setting friends from Rome and the U.S. to the wedding of their younger daughter, Irene, in 1983, it had no landing lights. Thus, the evacuees would have to spend the night at Clark. After checking the readiness of his modest armada of helicopters and ships, Allen told Manotoc to have the family out of the palace and across the river in Malacañang Park—where General Ver's headquarters and the presidential golf course were located—by 8:30 P.M.

The only treeless area inside the palace ground, even the park could only accommodate two choppers at a time. Allen had decided to put the thirty family members, General Ver, and close staff on the first two. As soon as they had lifted off, two more would land. Meanwhile, the boats would be loading the rest of the passengers, together with the luggage and crates, which the staff had been packing for days.

"We went into a black hellhole with night-vision goggles," said Allen, who rode the lead helicopter. "My interest was in getting them aboard as quickly as possible and getting them out of there." Although the silhouettes of the giant machines were barely visible, flying without lights, the shudder of steel descending was unmistakable to the thousands of anti-Marcos demonstrators massed in the streets bordering the palace compound, and the hundreds of loyalists who had remained inside the gates since the inauguration "to protect the president." It would not take long for these people to deduce what was going on.

"Teddy Allen at your service," snapped the general, stepping down from the chopper to greet Marcos. Old soldier that he was, Marcos might have been expected to return the salute. But he was so exhausted, after four days without sleep, that he could not even lift his arm. "He was being carried by his bodyguards," said Allen. "I had to pick him up and physically lay him in the belly of the helicopter."

So eager were household and medical staff members to get away from the chanting mobs, that twenty-one people clambered aboard the lead helicopter—six more than planned. As the first two lifted off and headed out over the bay, the second two homed in. Minutes after they too were airborne, demonstrators stormed through the gates and into the park.

Meanwhile, on the other side of the river, the navy had run into some problems with its boats. One of the four carried an antenna that was too high to allow it to pass under the five bridges that lay between the mouth of the Pasig and the palace. There was not enough room on the remaining three to hold all of the luggage and the remaining forty-five passengers. As the first boat docked, forty-five people, many of them guards from the elite Presidential Security Command, jumped aboard, while other guards who had not been invited, began firing at it. The captain was forced to pull away from the landing without the luggage.

*　　　*　　　*

With several other reporters, I followed the sound of the second pair of helicopters to the palace, arriving just as they lifted off, carrying the last of their passengers. The surrounding streets, which had been closed to traffic and secured by soldiers for almost as long as the Marcoses had lived in Malacañang, were suddenly deserted. Wary at first, we tested the un-manned, barbed-wire barricades at Mendiola Bridge, that landmark of the long and bloody civilian protest against the Marcos regime. Encountering no armed resistance, we pushed them aside and marched up to the iron gates.

It would take several hours for the reality to register that Marcos was gone. "He would not abandon us," insisted the crazed Marcos loyalists, who had taken it upon themselves to protect the palace after the truckloads of soldiers, who usually did the job, had vanished. As we tried to negotiate our way into the grounds, shots sounded, and men ran toward us under a blaze of gunfire. It was the last of the palace guard, shooting into the air as they fled an oncoming phalanx of anti-Marcos demonstrators, come to storm the citadel.

In a matter of minutes, the demonstrators had climbed the gates and opened them. Once inside the walls, some ransacked the executive office buildings, throwing official papers out the windows, while others broke into the presidential residence.

Most of those who entered the mansion did so more out of curiosity about how the Marcoses had lived than a desire to vandalize. Inside, the First Family's presence was still palpable in the food left out on tables and counters, the boxes and wrappings of items stuffed hastily into suitcases, the tangle of toys and costume jewelry pulled out of drawers and cupboards, and then not taken.

Marcos's bedroom was that of the afflicted man he was. Beside the hospital bed, to which he had been frequently confined, were three phones and two oxygen tanks. Imelda's chamber was the morbid inner sanctum of an insomniac: dark, carved-wood ceilings, no windows, a piano, which she had played into the morning hours, and a tank of oxygen next to her regal bed, from which she was said to inhale a rejuvenating whiff each morning. Her dressing room was more inviting, with its glass closets full of gowns and shoes, movie-star mirrors, and jewelry vault.

The library had been converted into a war room these past four days. A detailed map of Camp Crame had been drawn with chalk on a blackboard, and charts littered the reading table and its Roman-style chairs. In the dispensary was the incriminating evidence of the disease Marcos had always denied he had: a kidney-dialysis machine and a *Handbook for Renal Transplant Outpatients*.

Only when Cory's Crusaders were cataloging the contents of the palace, prior to turning it into a museum, would the basement storeroom containing Imelda's gowns, her carefully labeled stocks of underwear and hosiery, shelves of gift-wrapped boxes, and her vast collection of 1,060 pairs of shoes be discovered.

Outside on the lawn celebrants continued to arrive by the thousands, most of them content to simply stand and stare in amazement at the seat of power, which was finally theirs after twenty years. A banker, who had become politically active for the first time during the election campaign which had just ended, brought his family to see the spectacle. "So this is what a revolution looks like," he said, full of wonder, as we watched a group defacing portraits of the deposed ruler. Elsewhere across the archipelago, joyfully, with horns honking and bells chiming, the populations of whole towns and cities streamed into the streets again, in numbers unmatched since the day Ninoy was buried.

21

Exeunt

A tragic cycle was complete. Ninoy's death had been vindicated. Marcos had been banished. A new leader had been christened. Tonight the people, whose victory this was, were celebrating. Tomorrow the hard part would begin.

That was how the story should have ended. But nothing was ever so unambiguous in the Philippines. Marcos would not disappear so easily. The twisted tale of intrigue that he managed to weave during his final hours in the Philippines was almost a parable of the sensitive problems that would confront the new president, as she attempted to lead the country through a harsh and bitter transition.

Around midnight, while the rest of the nation was thrilling to news of Marcos's departure, President Aquino learned that the former president was still inside the country, reportedly spending the night at Clark Air Base. Having been on the phone repeatedly in the course of the day, participating in negotiations for the exodus of both Marcos and Ver, she had been under the impression that everything had been settled and that all parties would be beyond her borders by now. She called Ambassador Bosworth to inquire what had gone wrong. The ambassador, who was wondering about that himself, relayed her message to General Allen at the base.

It was fitting that her first major decision in office should concern the fate of the man who had held such power over her own for so many years. Marcos had finally succumbed to the pressure from his family and the U.S. government to leave the country. But, always pressing for maximum concessions from his opponents, he had attached a last condition: a day and one-half in his native Paoay, in Ilocos Norte, to "rest" and "to assure my friends and relatives that I am not deserting them, that I will be back."

When first confronted with this request, Bosworth had phoned President Aquino for guidance. Desirous of being "magnanimous in victory," she had been inclined to consent. "I thought maybe he wanted to die in his own country," she told me. Remembering Ninoy's gratitude to Marcos and Imelda for releasing him from jail to go to the U.S. for heart surgery in 1980, she felt obligated to do as much. Bosworth said he did not believe Marcos was near death. Aquino asked for time to consult her advisors.

Less quick to forgive than she, they sketched for her the likely consequences of her generosity. Although General Ramos denied having been consulted on the matter, sources close to the negotiations claimed not only that he was consulted, but that he was particularly strong in urging that Marcos be given no more leash. While he could identify with the good and decent instincts of his new commander in chief, he had learned the hard way that Marcos would never stop exploiting such virtues. He explained that loyalist generals still controlled much of the north. Once Marcos returned to his province, he would be protected, and he was likely to become a magnet for hundreds of thousands of discontented supporters. "Get him out of there" is the way one of the parties to the negotiation described Ramos's advice to Aquino.

Accordingly, she had called Ambassador Bosworth back to deny Marcos's request. Before he could relay her message, however, he learned that the Marcoses had already been airlifted from the palace. "Marcos has left," said the president after hanging up the phone. The friends and relatives who were with her in her sister's home cheered. Curiously, noted Cecilia Muñoz Palma, "Cory did not." Her failure to take pleasure in Marcos's misfortune was not surprising. The sudden responsibility that had been thrust upon her to govern all the people of her divided country had already had an impact on her thinking. "By making it so difficult for me and the opposition to get there," she had told me several days before, "God wants to impress upon us the great danger of being vindictive."

What she did not know at that time was that Marcos was still holding out for Paoay, and that his request had not been vetoed by General Allen, who had secured rooms for the exhausted party at Clark, and set departure time for 10 A.M. the next morning.

The bizarre events of the next several hours would make an appropriate finale for this extraordinary tale. "We had been up for so many days and nights," said Colonel Arturo Aruiza, the handsome military aide who was never far from Marcos. "I looked forward to a good night's sleep and a chance to wash my underwear and my socks," he recounted later. Having showered and put his clothes on a chair to dry, the colonel climbed into bed.

Most of the other weary travelers did likewise. But Marcos, ailing, defeated, and having gone without sleep for five nights, was still not ready to lie down. He got on the phone and began calling former ministers and supporters, squeezing them for face-saving favors and complaining that the Americans seemed to be wavering about allowing him to return to Paoay. Some of these supporters in turn reported his calls to Ramos and Enrile, who began questioning Aquino and Bosworth about what Marcos was up to now.

Newly aware of the political pressures to get the ex-president out of the country soon, and worried about Marcos's security inside the base, which was in rebel hands, General Allen sought permission from Washington to leave for Guam as soon as possible. "I told the head of U.S. intelligence inside Clark that I could not guarantee the safety of Marcos," said Colonel David, the Philippine base commander. "If our people saw the president, they might shoot him." Just as threatening, said Allen, "word went out in the province to mobilize People Power around the base, and I had visions of 1 million people converging on the gate by morning."

At 2:30 A.M. Allen contacted Tommy Manotoc and Bong Bong Marcos and informed them of the necessity of leaving before daybreak for Guam, where he could guarantee the family's safety until it could decide upon a final destination.

One hour later, recounted Aruiza, "someone banged on my door, yelling, 'Get up! Get up! We are being attacked by the NPA!' " As a military man, Aruiza knew that made no sense. Clark Air Base was probably the best-defended installation in the country. Penetration by the NPA, especially given the extra security precautions taken tonight, was out of the question.

Still groggy and annoyed at the untimely commotion, Aruiza put on his damp undergarments and went out to confront the American base commander, General Williams. "As one military man to another, I asked him, 'How can we be under attack by the NPA inside Clark?' " Williams, he said, "admitted they were rousing us quickly because they had received orders to take us to Guam."

Angered by the evident deceit of the Americans, Aruiza was tempted to take issue with them. "My men were carrying long arms," he noted, "and it was my understanding that our destination was Laoag." A proud and respected soldier, he winced as he told of the final humiliation to which he was then subjected. "At that moment," he said, "General Williams disarmed us."

The memory hurt. It hurt that his president now found himself in such a circumstance. It hurt that his PMA classmates and friends were the heroes of this chapter of history, while he was about to leave his country under a cloud, rather than desert the man who had been like a father to him. Most of all, it hurt him to hand over his gun to a foreigner in his own land. But Aruiza was a professional soldier, so he told the story fairly. "The general did it courteously," he said. "I understood. He had his orders."

As the group prepared to board the U.S. Air Force C-9 medical evacuation plane for Guam, it fell to General Allen to ask Marcos and his men for their guns. "I told them that the price of admission on U.S. Air Force aircraft is no guns," said Allen. No one moved to turn over his weapon. It was Marcos who finally broke the deadlock by handing the general his own .357 Magnum. Like Aruiza, Allen understood the feelings of his Filipino counterparts. "It signified that they were no longer in control," he said.

Such were the divided loyalties, the fierce feelings of pride, and the wounds of the unfinished revolution, which had swept a new president into power without at the same time wiping out the underpinnings which had for so long supported the old. The problems of governing under such circumstances would be enormous. Ninoy, with all his confidence, had been cowed by the prospect, when he was the one contemplating the presidency after Marcos. "Even Saint Peter could not solve our problems," he had said.

His widow was humble enough to try.

Epilogue:
The Unfinished
Revolution

The complex set of circumstances under which Cory became President Aquino all but guaranteed a power struggle between the civilian and military leadership. The mutual suspicions that would flare periodically into coup attempts throughout her first two years in office were painfully apparent from the start.

"How could I possibly think that at some point in my life Minister Ponce Enrile and I would be working together?" she asked, incredulous, when I interviewed her four days after her oath taking. Questioned whether she considered Enrile's role in the ouster of Marcos positive or negative, she weighed her words carefully. "It is difficult for us to explain him," she said coldly. "And yet," she added, "how much longer we would have had to go through the exercise of the boycott if he had not done what he did."

Had the largely psychological war that Ramos and Enrile waged against the Marcos loyalists lasted longer than four days, they might well have assumed a dominant role in the transitional government that they urged Cory to establish. But the game changed when Marcos was airlifted out of his besieged palace only hours after she was inaugurated.

While the military was preoccupied with removing booby traps from the grounds of a deserted Malacañang and neutralizing the remaining pockets of pro-Marcos resistance, the civilian leadership moved quickly and shrewdly to begin fulfilling its campaign promises to release political prisoners, including a number of top Communist leaders, and to restore the writ of habeas corpus—hardly top priorities of the New Armed Forces of the Philippines.

Before objections could be raised, President Aquino took charge and named a cabinet. Although it was primarily moderate in composition, important portfolios were given to several left-leaning human rights lawyers who had supported and defended Ninoy when he was Marcos's most prominent political prisoner, and Ramos and Enrile were the prime enforcers of martial law.

Serious strains between the civilian leadership and the reform officers were already evident by April 1986, when I accompanied Enrile on his first public speaking engagement since February. Basking in the glow of his newfound popularity as a hero of the revolution, he was not yet prepared to openly criticize as beloved a figure as President Aquino. Yet his message to civilian and military audiences in the provinces to "continue the revolution" against the Communists was decidedly different from her standard message of reconciliation and peace.

In a speech in Cebu City, he warned against the dangers of entering into a cease-fire agreement with the Communists that would most likely be conditioned on a coalition government. "If they can accomplish that," he said, "there should be no need to continue the armed struggle—they could take us from within." After a pause, he added, "I have no doubt that our lady president is aware of this threat, and that she moves with utmost caution in approaching this area of our security." His tone of voice led the U.S. consul general, who was seated next to me, to lean over and ask whether I thought that Enrile was speaking facetiously about Aquino.

Later that evening, I concluded that he was. Discreetly, in his car en route to a dinner speech, Enrile voiced doubt that Aquino was aware of much of what was going on in the country or even within her own narrow circle of advisors. Two known leftists were among the president's speechwriters, he claimed. Patronizingly, he remarked, "Poor girl, she might not know what words they are putting in her mouth." As an afterthought, he snapped, "That's off the record."

Back in Manila, Enrile's boys spoke more candidly about the minister's dissatisfaction with the new regime, which mirrored their own. In contrast to the many people who would criticize the president for not doing enough, they scored her for doing too many things too quickly. Her initial moves to dissolve the National Assembly and abolish the constitution were, they believed, instigated by her left-leaning advisors, while her decision to sack local government officials across the archipelago and appoint pro-Aquino replacements was a response to the territorial imperatives of the traditional politicians who surrounded her. In neither case had the military had any input. "Most of the pillars she shook had security consequences," said Captain Robles, reviewing her first months in office. "She undermined all those pillars at the same time, but without consulting the defense establishment."

What gnawed at the young officers even more than the new administration's overly ambitious political initiatives were its attempts to play politics inside the military, by going over the heads of Ramos and Enrile, just as Marcos had done, to make appointments and promotions on the basis of past favors and personal loyalty, rather than seniority and professional merit. The president's men had offered money-making concessions and promotions to some of the reformists. In keeping with the pledges they had made during the planning of their revolt against Marcos and Ver to restore professionalism to the ranks, Colonel Honasan and other Core-Group members politely declined. Had they accepted promotions, they explained, they would have had to "leapfrog" over older officers, much as General Ver's son had once done to them.

Relations between the reformist officers and the palace froze after what Enrile's boys regarded as attempts by the president's staff to preempt the military leadership on the highly sensitive issue of Aquino's campaign promise to negotiate a cease-fire with the New People's Army. Presidential spokesman and speechwriter Teodoro ("Teddy Boy") Locsin, Jr., had asked Robles to submit a position paper on the pros and cons of a negotiated truce, prior to an important speech he was writing for the president to deliver at the University of the Philippines graduation exercises.

Robles prepared a two-page summary on "the insurgency situation" that accepted a six-month cessation of hostilities as being "of immense use to the New Armed Forces of the Philippines in preparing for the inevitable resumption of hostilities." When he heard the actual speech, Robles felt betrayed. It implied that the armed forces had approved the cease-fire on its merits, rather than for the strictly tactical reasons, which Robles had outlined, of allowing the army more time to prepare for war.

Having failed to co-opt Enrile's boys, the palace offered similar perks and promotions to others, who accepted them more readily. This resulted, Robles claimed, in "the creation of a counter group to our minority group, which became another favored minority." The reformists did not personally blame the president for exercising her prerogative as commander-in-chief to make her own appointments and promotions. They resented the fact that leftist civilian advisors had more influence over the promotion process and other aspects of policy affecting the national security than did the military. "If she is just a figurehead, why shouldn't she be a figurehead of the right rather than a figurehead of the left?" questioned Robles.

Aquino's chief advisor, Joker Arroyo, as much as confirmed the military's misgivings in the course of a remarkably candid explanation to me and two other journalists of the strategy he had designed to facilitate Cory's consolidation of control over the military. "Whom can we trust in the military?" he asked rhetorically, then answered his own question. "Until four months ago these people were fighting us. She cannot choose her security guards from among these people. Neither can she count on their loyalty until she establishes herself as commander-in-chief." In order to do this, Arroyo and Locsin had proposed that she employ "the moist-eyed technique."

Speaking cynically about a leader whose credibility rested on her perceived lack of guile, Arroyo described how she would invite each of the officers due for promotion, together with his wife, to watch her pin the star on his chest. "They are so imbued with the tradition of obeying the civilian commander-in-chief," he said, "that they immediately put themselves at her service. The presence of the wife, with whom Cory can easily deal, is what clinches things." From then on, he concluded smugly, "that officer is hers for life."

The president's executive secretary did not stop there, but went on to explain that the power base that she would build by these means would serve to "buffer" the influence of General Ramos, whom he saw as her greatest long-term threat. "Enrile we can handle," said Arroyo of his fraternity brother, "but Ramos is very powerful. He controls the military, and he has ambitions of his own." Even more threatening, in Arroyo's view, was "the American imprimatur" that Ramos carried, because, he said, "he would assure the Americans of their bases."

Arroyo's game, Locsin later acknowledged, was "power—not for himself, but for the president." According to Locsin, who worked hand in glove with the executive secretary, "Joker's job was to get rid of all other possible power centers, and he succeeded—from Enrile to Jimmy Ongpin."

           *   *   *

Enrile was the first to go, but only after nine months of largely public wrangling that was played out on the front pages of the newly unfettered press. Besides exposing the deep divisions within the governing coalition over the conduct of peace talks with the Communists, the jockeying for influence between the military and civilian leadership drained energy and diverted attention that might have been focused more constructively on trying to ameliorate the poverty that was the root cause of the insurgency. Furthermore, the publicity given to rumors of a coup, which were deliberately floated by Enrile's boys as part of a psychological war campaign against Aquino's advisors, frightened investors away from channeling badly needed foreign exchange into the ravaged economy.

The coup talk built toward a climax in late October 1986, shortly before the president's state visit to Japan, when Enrile delivered a speech that was strongly critical of the Aquino government's stalled efforts to bring about a cease-fire with the New People's Army. Before leaving the country on November 10, Aquino threatened to call her supporters into the streets in a second display of People Power, if necessary to prevent a military move during her absence.

In an effort to defuse an incipient crisis, General Ramos urged disgruntled officers to present their grievances to the president in writing and to give her an appropriate period of time after her trip to respond. That action, one reform officer would later admit, effectively saved Cory from overthrow by allowing cooler heads within the military to prevail. "Between November eighth and tenth," the officer revealed, "General Ramos agreed with Minister Enrile that a military action might have to be undertaken to restore military influence over the peace process, but he asked for sixty days."

When the president arrived home from Tokyo, Ramos forwarded her a respectful but pointed "bill of particulars" calling for replacement of certain ministers judged to be excessively left-leaning or corrupt, restoration of a central role to the military in drafting the strategy to be used against the Communists, and the setting of deadlines for cease-fire talks with the rebels. With coup rumors by now accepted as fact by coffee shop habitués and headline writers, Aquino treaded cautiously. First, she met privately with each of the service commanders to try to gauge the depth of their discontent and to discuss what should be done. Then on November 21, she summoned General Ramos for a long meeting.

"In the past we had talked, but I had never been as frank as I was that Friday night," she told me later. "From the outset it was easy for me to relate to General Ramos, unlike Ponce Enrile." The president and her chief of staff apparently agreed on measures to pacify the military and bring an end to the infighting so that the government could speak with one voice as it prepared to begin peace talks with the rebels.

The following evening, Ramos acted on the pretext that Enrile was planning to lead a group of former pro-Marcos assemblymen to occupy the National Assembly and declare the Aquino government illegitimate. He set up roadblocks around the National Assembly building in a remote area of the capital and ordered troops to ignore any commands that might be issued by Enrile.

In fact, no coup was under way that evening. General Ramos had simply chosen to call the bluff of Enrile and his boys, by preempting their oft-threatened coup before it materialized. "It was not a coup by the traditional definition of a coup as men taking up arms against a government, although Enrile's men had threatened to destabilize it," said General Eduardo Ermita, who had worked closely during his career with both Enrile and Ramos.

Months after the fact, Aquino's spokesman Locsin was even more candid. "I spent the whole night checking out the coup reports," he said, "but the only troops I ran into were our own." The high visibility of those troops was enough to convince Manila's newly liberated press to make Enrile's purported coup attempt a reality in the next morning's headlines. By then Aquino had called an emergency cabinet meeting for the purpose of requesting the resignations of all her ministers. She would accept five: four of the names that had been on the military's "hit list," and Enrile.

It is a sad comment on the deterioration of relations between the president and one of the men most responsible for clearing her path to power that as Aquino prepared to summon Enrile to her office, she also took precautions to protect herself from him. "Don't you need someone else in the room?" her friend and political ally Aquilino ("Nene") Pimentel asked her. Startled by the suggestion that her defense minister might harm her, yet sufficiently distrustful of him to heed Pimentel's advice, she asked her daughter Ballsy, who serves as her private secretary, to be on hand, out of sight but within earshot, in the room behind her office.

"Johnny, I cannot continue to work like this, where everything I do is being dictated by these boys," said the president, leaving no room between her sentences for objections.

Aquino's handling of Enrile won praise from her dispirited supporters and from the international community, which had begun to doubt that she had what it took to survive in the cutthroat world of Philippine politics. On hearing the news, the editors of TIME firmed up previously tentative plans to name her the magazine's "Woman of the Year."

Although her slowness in confronting Enrile was costly in terms of energy diverted from other pressing problems, it was shrewdly calculated on her part. "It was not a question of just thinking of doing something and thinking of doing it right away without weighing the possible consequences," she explained to me later, exhibiting the innate caution with which she undertook all her major decisions. "I sincerely believed that I could still win him over, so I tried to have more patience." More important was her second reason for going slow. "I was not sure how far Eddie Ramos would go," she confided. "I was not about to go into a confrontation where I would be a clear loser." Only when she felt she could count on the backing of Ramos, would she openly turn against Enrile.

Enrile's political ambitions and his premonitions that official commissions established to investigate Marcos's "hidden wealth" and military abuses were targeted at him and his boys had impelled him to take an unacceptably aggressive stance against a president whom most Filipinos, not to mention an adoring public in the world outside, judged to be making an admirable attempt to solve the seventeen-year-old insurgency. Although Enrile's pique over the exclusion of the military from the planning for the truce talks was widely shared within the military, many officers were justifiably suspicious of his motives for launching a frontal attack on Aquino. They felt more comfortable with General Ramos's behind-the-scenes efforts to exert pressure on the civilian leadership.

Indeed, Ramos proved to be a better reader of the political pulse than Enrile. "General Ramos realized that you cannot dispense with a popular leader like Cory," observed University of the Philippines President Edgardo Angara, who functioned as an intermediary in attempts to reconcile the president and her defense minister. From the start he had therefore insisted on direct access to her, and had spent time getting to know her and cultivating her trust.

*   *   *

With Enrile no longer a dissenting voice in the cabinet, and with Ramos and her new defense minister, Rafael Ileto, behind her, Aquino was free to honor her campaign promise to conclude a cease-fire agreement with the Communist rebels. On November 27, 1986—four days after the sacking of the defense minister—government negotiators and representatives of the Communist Party of the Philippines announced a sixty-day truce with the New People's Army that would run through the Christmas holidays, when Filipino Catholics traditionally take a break from politics and wars. It would end just after the referendum on the country's new constitution.

Enrile, who had automatically become the leader of the political opposition on leaving government, promptly launched a campaign to oppose ratification of the constitution and the full six-year term it would give President Aquino. He portrayed Aquino as naive and subject to manipulation by the Communists, who would try to prolong the peace negotiations in order to consolidate their forces. Once again, he misjudged both the president and the public mood.

True, she longed for peace, and believed, erroneously, as did the other leaders of the anti-Marcos opposition, that as soon as a "just government" was in place, up to 90 percent of the guerrillas, who were purported to be simple farmers, would come down from the hills and surrender their arms. At that point, she reasoned, the army would find a reservoir of public support for its subsequent drive against the 10 percent, who could be presumed to be hard-core ideologues.

However, as her life history demonstrated, she was not one to settle for peace at any price. Once the talks got under way and the Communists proved intractable in their demands for an active role in the government and the removal of U.S. military bases, she began to lower her expectations.

By then the people were with her. The constant media exposure given the rebel negotiators on TV talk shows and in newspaper interviews had worked against them. Their evasive answers to questions about their policies of taxing peasants and collecting "blood debts" from enemies aroused deep skepticism on the part of ordinary Filipinos, whose religion and American acculturation had made them fearful of Communism.

When I talked to Aquino in mid-December 1986, less than two weeks after the cease-fire began, she seemed prepared for the failure of the talks. As usual, however, she accentuated the positive. She feared neither the influence of the military nor the seductive powers of the Communists, because she had faith that the Filipino people were sophisticated enough to make the right choices. "I am so convinced that this country of ours has become so conservative," she said, referring not only to its aversion to Communism, but to military coups as well. "Anything in the extreme is very upsetting to a great number. We have gone through so much controversy and division that people would like officials who won't divide them." Her greatest strength lay in her ability to sashay from left to right and back again on major issues, seeking to disarm the extremists, without straying too far from her natural constituency at the political center.

On January 22, Philippine marines opened fire on leftist peasants who were demonstrating for land reform at Mendiola bridge, site of two bloody anti-Marcos protests in the past. What would come to be known as "the Mendiola massacre" effectively put an end to the president's search for an accommodation with the Communists before the cease-fire had even expired.

That incident was "the president's lowest point," according to Aquino's former appointments secretary, Ching Escaler. "She almost broke down," Escaler recalled, when confronted by members of her human rights constituency, whose hopes for social justice had been dashed by an attack on unarmed demonstrators that was more brazen than any that occurred under Marcos. Imploring them to recognize her delicate position as arbiter between the military and the various social groups seeking redress of their long-suppressed grievances, she argued, "I am still convinced that I am the only one who can handle the situation." Observed Escaler, "There was silence in the room when she finished speaking." Many of the old friends in attendance had concluded sorrowfully that she had become a prisoner of the military.

On the eve of the referendum on the new constitution, fate intervened in Aquino's behalf. Not even agnostics could explain it otherwise. Right-wing, pro-Marcos elements of the armed forces exploited their last opportunity to oust the Aquino government before it was legitimized by the new constitution. They attacked two military bases and occupied the headquarters of Channel 7 television in Manila. The coup attempt helped assure the largest voter turnout in Philippine history and a massive victory for the president against the forces of violence on both the left and the right.

Had Aquino been bold enough to follow up that decisive vote of confidence in her centrist government by unleashing the military against the guerrillas, setting up facilities designed to help relocate surrendered rebels, and speeding economic aid to the rebel-infested areas, she might finally have convinced foreign investors that stability was a high priority of her administration. However, elections for the new congress were coming up, and such an initiative was sure to be both bloody and costly. Thus, as threats to her authority appeared to recede and her popularity peaked, she listened to the politicians who were preparing to ride her coattails and played it safe.

In order to spend the maximum amount of time possible on the campaign trail, she turned over even more of the day-to-day operation of government to her inner circle of advisors. The resulting policy drift began to alarm even Aquino's most ardent supporters, who were reluctantly drawing the same conclusion that Enrile's boys had reached months before: the president had become overly dependent on her executive secretary, Joker Arroyo. According to her longtime booster Finance Secretary Jimmy Ongpin, she had inexplicably "abdicated her presidential prerogatives" to Arroyo.

It was not so much Joker's left-of-center views that bothered these issue-oriented people. Rather, it was his lack of administrative skills and his perceived bitterness toward all of the interest groups that competed for Cory's attention. "Joker and Cory reinforce the weaknesses in each other," observed Ongpin. "Both have a desire to retreat from all the critics and an instinct to put off dealing with problems." Added a disillusioned staffer, "Cory cries a lot."

Although the president had discreetly indicated in the wake of Enrile's ouster that Joker's "resignation" would soon be accepted as well, he was, months later, still in control of the flow of information and visitors to the president. In exasperation, Ongpin leaked a five-page letter he had written to the president in which he claimed that one item that required quick presidential approval languished in Joker's "in" box for 149 days before being acted upon. Ongpin's letter drew instant fire from Arroyo, who attacked the influential minister's decisions to seek foreign loans to finance land reform, and accused him of "giving in" to the World Bank and International Monetary Fund. Hitting the headlines as it did when Ongpin was in the U.S. negotiating a rescheduling of the country's loans, the open feud only worsened investor confidence in the Aquino government.

Among the most egregious examples of Joker's mismanagement of state affairs was his handling of the long-anticipated rebel rehabilitation program, which was to have been launched shortly after the end of the cease-fire. A special committee had spent months drafting it, the cabinet had approved it, and it was scheduled to be announced to the press, when suddenly Joker commented to reporters that it was too reminiscent of Marcos's efforts to co-opt the rebels to be a good program. Startled and upset, its authors demanded that Joker be more specific about his objections. Revealed a member of the presidential staff: "It turned out that Joker had read the wrong draft."

Even after he got around to reading and approving the right draft, the program was never fully implemented. Worse, American auditors reported that more than one billion dollars in American aid was bottled up in the bowels of the Philippine bureaucracy, unappropriated and unspent.

By then the president's own family was questioning Joker's hold over her. "It's scary," remarked one in-law, who was anxious to disabuse people of the widely accepted notion that Cory continued to tolerate Joker because she owed him a debt of gratitude for his defense of Ninoy. "Ninoy had seventeen lawyers, and Joker was always on the periphery. He was only a gofer."

Had her political opposition been stronger, the president might have been forced to account for such negligence on the part of her administration. However, another phenomenal electoral victory deflected criticism from her performance. Twenty-two of the twenty-four Senate candidates whom she had endorsed were elected, and she commanded an overwhelming majority in the House as well. Many of the new legislators had, like Ninoy, served in the premartial-law congress. They recalled its padlocking by Marcos's military as a moment of deep national shame. For them, as for most Filipinos, its reopening would be the crowning achievement of Ninoy's widow's eighteen months in office. For the president, it would mark the completion of the second stage of the mission she had undertaken in his memory. Only the election of seventeen thousand local officials on January 18, 1988, remained to make the restoration of democracy complete.

*   *   *

In the early morning hours of August 28, 1987, Colonel Gringo Honasan and some 1,200 officers and men attempted a coup against Aquino and Ramos, which illustrated, more graphically than any of their verbal warnings had, the vulnerability of the new democracy to determined men with guns, whether from the right or the left. As Gringo and his men stormed Armed Forces Headquarters, Senator Rene Saguisag, one of the issue-oriented "new politicians" whom Aquino had persuaded to run for office, stood on the floor of a Senate deserted by even its military guards, who had joined the rebels. "I think we have become irrelevant," he said to his colleagues.

Indeed, the legislators would have been irrelevant, had not a majority of the military remained loyal to the constitution and once again followed the orders of General Ramos to defend the Aquino government. More than the five previous documented coup attempts and the several other feints at usurping power, Honasan's truly threatened the survival of the civilian leadership. Not only had it targeted the actual seats of power—first the presidential residence and then Camp Aguinaldo—but it enjoyed an aura of moral authority that the others, tainted by the participants' ties to Marcos, had not.

Yet when Honasan's men appeared on television, after commandeering the TV studio, they offered no alternative to Aquino's handling of the nation's problems, other than a return to the authoritarianism of the recent past. There would be no vast outpouring of People Power in their behalf this time. Quelling this revolt would be purely a military matter, and a difficult one, given the divided loyalties of the rank and file.

However, the president's men were not content to simply acknowledge the government's dependence on Ramos and leave him alone to counter the coup. They engaged, instead, in a charade to demonstrate that civilian authority remained supreme. Installing himself just outside the office from which the chief of staff was directing his counterattack, Locsin began barking orders and summoning generals to the phone to speak with Arroyo and the president. The arrogance of the young speechwriter aroused in the long-suffering commanders, who were preparing to defend the constitution one more time, a degree of hostility akin to that which had motivated Gringo to resort to extra-legal measures.

"Here was a group of civilian advisors dipping their fingers into something they knew nothing about," said General Ermita, who, along with a handful of other ranking officers, spent most of that day defending the besieged headquarters building from occupation by Gringo's men. Ramos himself made no effort to either apologize or explain. He was too busy working the phones inside his inner sanctum, assessing the number of loyal troops who would obey his orders to fire on their fellow officers for the first time and deploying them to the various theaters of rebel activity.

When rebel officers seized Channel 13 and began broadcasting their propaganda, Locsin excitedly directed Ramos to "smash" the Channel 13 transmitter. The general's explanation that too many civilians would be injured by such action did not sit well with Locsin, who promptly went over his head and ordered the Presidential Security Group to "knock off Channel 13." Receiving no more satisfaction from the palace guard than he had from military headquarters, the presidential aide ranted, "Somebody will get demoted for this!" At the height of Locsin's tantrum, an army chaplain muttered to his colleagues under his breath: "If anyone among you wants to slap this guy, I will grant him instant absolution."

Some nine hours after the attack began, the forces of General Ramos finally opened fire on rebel bunkers inside Camp Aguinaldo. Honasan had gambled that before Ramos was able to mount a counterattack, his own men would have captured enough key installations to draw fence-sitting soldiers to their side. Like Enrile, he had underestimated Ramos. Although the general's grip on the fractious military had weakened with each successive coup attempt, he remained the commander to whom the most men owed the greatest loyalty.

When defeat became inevitable, Honasan escaped by helicopter. As a fugitive who taunted the government in clandestine interviews until his capture in December 1987, and then succeeded in making a daring getaway on Easter weekend in 1988, Gringo became a national folk hero. But the mantle of moral leadership that had fallen to him and his fellow Fourth Classmen after their successful ouster of Marcos now belonged to Ramos alone. In the eyes of most Filipinos and the world outside, Cory was the legitimate leader of the republic. In rescuing her, General Ramos had taken on a new role in the public perception: that of leader of the "constitutionalist" elements of the armed forces.

To the great relief of the Philippines' international creditors and diplomats and businessmen with security interests and investments to protect, Ramos was finally in a position to influence, if not veto, the making of security-related policy. Blind to this new reality, Cory's advisors counseled her to speed Ramos's retirement as chief of staff by offering him patronage-rich cabinet posts as secretary of public works or local governments. That mistake would be their final undoing. "He would rather resign and plow the fields," sniffed the general's sister, Leticia Ramos Shahani, a newly elected senator who had run on the pro-Cory ticket.

Ever correct, Ramos did not reject the posts outright. Rather, he communicated through Senate President Salonga and others that the only civilian post that interested him was secretary of defense. He reminded Aquino of her previous pledge to replace Joker. "Ramos will quit on his own terms," predicted a U.S. military official. Cory would have little choice but to concede, he added, because she had finally come around to "seeing him as part of her means of continuing as president."

*   *   *

Like the earthquakes that frequently shake Manila and other parts of the archipelago, the Honasan coup attempt jolted the government into confronting some painful truths about itself. When I returned to Manila one month later, I found Aquino's allies in disarray and despair. Interviews with them turned into something akin to therapy sessions, as they tried to analyze what had gone wrong.

Speaker Pro Tempore Antonio ("Tony") Cuenco, who was filling in for hospitalized Speaker Monching Mitra, was almost morbid. "The coup has shaken us badly," he confessed. "We were supposed to do something for the country, but now I feel helpless." A veteran member of the anti-Marcos political opposition, Cuenco was now openly questioning whether the Filipino people had the will to overcome their problems on their own, without the goading of an authoritarian figure. "If the Cory approach fails," he ventured, "perhaps we will have to look to a benevolent dictator like Lee Kuan Yew."

I found their Senate counterpart, Jovy Salonga, similarly discouraged. Known widely as one of the most eloquent opponents of martial law, Salonga had nonetheless been among the first legislators to publicly acknowledge the critical role played by the "Ramos faction" of the military in defending the Aquino government. He mused aloud as to whether the commitment of the civilian sector would prove as strong. "Cory may no longer have the kind of civilian support that we know as 'People Power,' because the expectations of the people were too high to be sustained and her capability to meet them limited by our foreign debt, our prostrate economy, and the attacks from the extreme left and the extreme right," he said.

"Our democratic space is getting narrower and narrower," mourned Salonga. A proponent of land reform, he worried aloud about the consequences of trying to implement one. "You cannot have meaningful land reform in an atmosphere of such instability."

Salonga had put his finger on the central dilemma that the Aquino government faced. For eighteen months it had pursued a policy of reform at the expense of stability. It had continued to deny the military a voice in policy-making. Now, with a significant portion of the armed forces in rebellion against it, and debate over its most controversial reform measure heating up, the administration was under pressure to reverse its priorities and put stability first. The president had announced that she would reshuffle her cabinet. Then, as was her wont, she retreated from public view. "She will take her own sweet time to make sure the choices are right this time," her brother Peping confided.

Aquino's subsequent hesitation to formally acknowledge Ramos as the guarantor of her administration and to give him a voice in policy-making debates exasperated the officers who were close to him. "The armed forces are weary," said a Ramos intimate. "They are weary of Cory. Even General Ramos is weary of her. He is like a prizefighter being told to go for the championship with one arm tied behind his back."

Others stated the case more bluntly. "She needs the military, and General Ramos is the only commander with the moral stature to hold the country together," explained a Ramos ally. "If that is power-sharing, she should be grateful it is with a man like him. She should stop acting as if she had a choice. All this adulation has given her the impression she has one."

When no word of Joker's resignation or Ramos's future had emanated from Malacañang more than two weeks after the Honasan coup, alarms began to sound within and without the government. Vice-President Laurel, who had been dispatched by the president to the military camps to survey the attitudes of soldiers about their conditions and their support for government policy, climaxed his tour by resigning his cabinet post as foreign minister and openly expressing solidarity with the restless troops in their quest for pay raises and a coordinated campaign against the insurgents. Never content with being a neglected number two, the opportunistic Laurel was clearly positioning himself to take over the government, should the military manage to oust Aquino.

Meanwhile, reports that the American intelligence community in Manila was sending to Washington were full of dire predictions about the continued viability of a civilian leadership at war with its military. "President Aquino was getting advice from everybody to get rid of Joker and reach out to the military," admitted Bosworth's successor, U.S. Ambassador Nicholas Platt, several weeks later. While expressing his own confidence that "she has what it takes to make it," he confirmed the fact that in the immediate aftermath of the Honasan coup attempt, "certain circles" in Washington were of the opinion that "she might not last."

Aquino was, however, able to traverse that particularly dangerous juncture, and she has survived to celebrate a second tumultuous year in office. She has done it, for the most part, the way experienced politicians do: by mastering the art of the possible. She went as far as she could go in implementing the reforms that she and her political coalition had promised voters, provoking opposition from the armed forces all along the way. When hostile elements of the military would tolerate it no more, she was faced with what one Ramos ally had euphemistically called "the limits of her situation." She had no choice but to reach an accommodation with the man who had saved her on several occasions from overthrow. So she did.

First, she called on congress to pass the 60 percent military pay hike for which Ramos had been lobbying. Next, she honored Ramos's long-standing demand for the replacement of Arroyo. Joker did not part gracefully. He insisted that his nemesis inside the cabinet, Jimmy Ongpin, precede him. The president agreed, and steeled herself to accept the resignation of the man who had been her mentor and most prominent booster back when the search for a credible opposition candidate had just begun.

Not long after he left government, Ongpin mused aloud to me about the paucity of alternatives that faced the still-dithering Aquino. "If she is going to make it, she's going to have to change her attitudes and her decision-making style radically," he said. "She is going to have to make the tough decisions rather than avoiding them."

Ongpin wondered whether she would be able to overcome the flawed advice she had been fed as she struggled to learn how to govern. "At the heart of the problem is that very early on they kept telling her, 'your popularity is the most precious thing you have, and it should not be put at risk,'" he related. "Yet the opposite is true. She must put it at risk to get something done." If she did not move ahead with land reform and a coordinated military and economic offensive against the rebels in the countryside, he cautioned, "She will force the hand of the military to do something dramatic to fill the vacuum."

When I saw the president several days later, it was obvious that the internecine strife and the mounting pressure on her had taken their toll. I found her in an agitated state. It was the first time in our four-year acquaintance that I had seen her that way. She looked exhausted, and there were blemishes on her normally glowing complexion.

I never got a word in edgewise, as she sought to justify her recent actions. "If I had clamped down early on, people would not have supported me," she said, referring to the harder line toward social disorder and a licentious press that she had been taking of late. "So many people are trying to destroy me," she went on, speaking in disjointed sentences. In an elliptical reference to the many rumors about her attachment to Arroyo, she snapped, "It is not as if I needed someone to hang on to. If I am going to look for someone, it would have to be a king."

As we parted, she assured me that she was not about to be defeated by her recent travails. She was in the process of preparing a speech in which she would confront her critics. The anger in her voice told me that she had reached a new plateau in her education about how to exercise power. She was prepared to admit that she had made mistakes. She was prepared to make compromises. But she would do so at her own speed and on her own terms. Her support came from the people, she reminded me, and she would answer only to them.

I left feeling, as I always did after talking to her, that somehow she would figure out a way to surmount the latest political and military obstacles to her pursuit of Ninoy's impossible dream. Her vision of a democratic space in which differences could be reconciled and problems solved remained ill-defined and elusive. Yet her continuing faith that it was attainable was what kept her going in the dark moments, and her ability to convince her quarrelsome constituents that it was within their grasp was the essential element of her leadership. No one else could have presumed to attempt such a feat, much less carry it off.

As a journalist, I knew that her allies in Camp Aguinaldo and Washington were actively considering alternatives to her continued service as president. As a person, I could not imagine any of them enjoying a better chance of success than Aquino. Her exasperating slowness in reaching decisions was balanced by the soundness of the major ones she made. She was the only public figure whose self-interest was perceived to be synonymous with the national interest. Her fearlessness under fire was impressive. "There is nothing they can do to hurt me," she had once told me, "except to harm my children." Honasan's men had nearly killed her only son in the course of their assault on the presidential residence, and she would never forgive them for that. Neither would most Filipinos. To undermine her now would be entirely self-defeating.

Her speech several days later to an influential gathering of businessmen was exactly the right mixture of contrition and obstinacy. She addressed her audience defiantly. "The question you all really want to ask is, 'Can she hack it? Isn't she weak?' " Her own answer was that she was strong. After setting the agenda for the restoration of democratic institutions, she had hoped to leave the details of governing to others. However, public response to the "hands off" policy that she had adopted as an antithesis to Marcos's manner of governance had been negative. Therefore, she would change her style. "Henceforth, I shall rule directly as president," she stated.

She then proceeded to tell this conservative audience what it wanted to hear. She announced that she had ordered the police to break up illegal union strikes that had closed down many factories, and she put an end to dovish rumors by stating flatly that no new peace negotiations would be considered with the Communists. When the government and the rebels had failed to arrive at a peaceful settlement in February 1987, she said, "it was time to fight." Today, she added, "It is still fighting time."

*   *   *

On December 7, 1987, Jimmy Ongpin, who was only forty-nine years old, committed suicide. His widow confided to me later in a letter that he had been plunged into depression toward the end of his embattled finance ministry tenure by the warfare within the cabinet that had paralyzed the government and by "the disappointment that after all there was really no revolution."

It pained me to read that phrase. In fact, it was Ongpin, and other moderate, middle-class Filipinos like him, whose reaction to Ninoy's assassination had snapped the country out of its lethargy and eventually triggered a revolution. It was, however, an unfinished revolution. If the moderates failed to harness its energy to legislate the radical reforms that were necessary to give meaning to democracy in a poor country like the Philippines, they would miss their chance. They would leave to the authoritarian left a monopoly on the issues of social and economic justice.

Although the Communists were not yet strong enough to overthrow the government militarily, they were well-positioned to profit politically from the absence of progress in correcting the inequities of Filipino society.

Ninoy had convinced me that moderates could prevail in the Philippines and that that heretofore moribund slice of the ideological spectrum—the political center—could be infused with new dynamism. His death had pointed the way. His widow had used her popularity to buy the time and create the institutions that were necessary to set the process of change in motion. But that time could not be squandered simply expecting results. It was imperative to convince the people that democracy meant, not only the freedom to protest injustice and inequity, but also the capability to correct it.

Shortly after Marcos's departure, an American diplomat had aptly characterized the dilemma facing the Aquino government. "This country had a 'white revolution,' which is better than a 'red revolution,' if it sorts things out," he said. "The problem of this government will be to translate what happened at EDSA for the man in the rice paddies."

As I write this epilogue, the Aquino government has not yet succeeded in that task. Since the August 28 coup attempt, President Aquino has continued to pursue a policy of restoring stability before undertaking further reforms. In January 1988 she took the necessary steps to consolidate relations with the mainstream military by retiring General Ramos from uniform, naming him to the civilian cabinet post of secretary of national defense, which he desired, and appointing his protégé to replace him as chief of staff.

Ramos, Aquino, and their policy of restoring stability will be put to the test in 1988, as the administration prepares to finance and enforce the new land reform law and to renegotiate the last automatic renewal of the Military Bases Agreement before its expiration in 1991. If reform is not possible without stability, the reverse is also true. By the time congress passed a land reform bill, a consensus had built, both inside and outside the Philippines, that a program of redistribution of acreage from owners to tillers was a prerequisite to the establishment of social peace and economic growth, without which full recovery could not be expected. Yet many landowners—some of the biggest of whom are Marcos loyalists with strong claims on dissident factions of the military—have warned that they will employ mercenary troops, if necessary, to avoid losing their haciendas.

It will take a firm hand and more cash than the government has to make the program a success. There Aquino, whose family is among the largest of the country's landowners, confronts a cruel double bind. Even with a praiseworthy economic growth rate of 5.1 percent last year and a projected 6.1 percent in 1988, the government cannot afford to pay out one-third of its annual export earnings in interest on the bloated $29 billion debt that Marcos left and still foot the bill for the $2.6 billion that the land reform program is estimated to cost over a six-year period. It will have to solicit at least half that amount from sources outside the country in the form of foreign assistance from governments, which will naturally expect something in return.

A bipartisan group of U.S. legislators headed by Democratic Congressman Stephen Solarz has proposed a five-year, ten-billion-dollar Marshall Plan for the Philippines to enable it to revive and expand its economic development. Singapore Prime Minister Lee Kuan Yew has endorsed the idea of making the program a multilateral effort, with countries from the European Economic Community and the Asia-Pacific region building on seed money put up by the U.S. government. Support for such a plan would be the best contribution American taxpayers could make to the survival of a system modeled on our own in a part of the world that shares our democratic aspirations. To the considerable resentment of Filipino nationalists, it also represents Washington's best hope of retaining access to its military bases in the Philippines. The carrot of massive aid dangled before a beleaguered government and an electorate that may be called upon to vote for or against the bases in a national referendum could prove decisive.

The Communist Party of the Philippines is banking on the failure of U.S. resolve to pay the price. The party was badly beaten on the political front when the popular Aquino succeeded Marcos, who had been labeled as "the Communists' best recruiter." Since the breakdown of peace talks, it has resorted to a strategy of escalating violence. The base negotiations, which officially opened in March 1988, offer the Communist rebels and their political allies their best opportunity to exploit the bona fide nationalist sentiment that exists in the islands against a continued American military presence there.

That strategy is premised on the belief that eventually Aquino's centrist position will be undermined by its own inherent contradictions. She entered office as the president of peace, but at some point she will have to preside over more violence, if she is to eliminate the threat posed by the insurgents. The Communists question whether she will have the stomach to do so. If she does, they point out, she will incur the wrath of the masses, which will inevitably be caught in the cross fire, and of her liberal constituents in the Philippines and abroad. If she does not, they predict that her armed forces will move against her as a prelude to declaring all-out war on the guerrillas and their politifcal allies.

"Who will do the dirty work in the Philippines?" asked Mark, a ranking member of the National Democratic Front, whom I had interviewed in different places, at different times, and under different noms de guerre over the years since the Aquino assassination. In the past, I had had to meet him clandestinely in remote places. Now, however, the insurgents were boosting their forces in the cities, where they were so well integrated into the general populations that Mark had no trouble meeting me in my hotel.

As a student of Central American revolutionary politics, he was aware that President Aquino enjoyed a far stronger popular base than any of the elected leaders of that region. However, he pointed out, they had one great advantage over her. By the time elections were held, the dirtiest phases of the counterinsurgencies in their countries had already been completed. That was not the case in the Philippines.

Aquino, who pursued a strategy of peaceful negotiations until forced to do otherwise, still hesitates to unleash the Philippine Armed Forces. Yet already her endorsement of anti-Communist vigilante groups set up under military supervision to provide intelligence and bolster village security forces has made her a target of the international human rights lobby. In order to defeat the New People's Army on the military front, Mark wagered she would have to authorize far more sweeping measures, which would inevitably incur greater involvement of American trainers, advisors, and suppliers. Therein lay her dilemma and her enemies' opportunity.

"I would not be surprised if in the next year or two, there would be one or two American casualties," Mark volunteered. After that, the "Vietnam syndrome" would take over, he forecast, and the U.S., which would not be willing to become mired in another guerrilla war, would pull out. His threatening words seemed at odds with his smiling face and delicate physique, but then, this was the Philippines. Two weeks later three American servicemen were shot dead by gunmen just outside the gates of Clark Air Base. I drew the obvious conclusion.

✳   ✳   ✳

"Welcome to Ninoy Aquino Airport," said the stewardess as I landed in Manila on my last visit to the Philippines early in 1988. I had been away since the airport had been officially renamed by an act of the new congress. The announcement startled me. Yet at the same time, I found it consoling. It seemed to be telling me that I had come full circle, and that it was finally time to move on.

I had wanted to stay around long enough to see the revolution reach the rice paddies, but that was clearly going to take more time than I had. In the future, I would have to agonize about the Philippines from afar. I had no doubt that the news from Manila would continue to be alarming. The base negotiations would be savage. I sympathized with those who wanted to rid the country of foreign influence, but I found their wish naive, given the presence of the rival superpower at nearby Cam Ranh Bay in Vietnam. I remembered Enrile relating anecdotes about how during the Marcos era, base renewal agreements were worked out on cocktail napkins by surrogates who answered only to the president, and I wondered if Washington would come to regret its support for the restoration of democracy and the marketplace of diverse opinions it champions. I hoped not.

In any case, I hoped I would remember how to read between the lines of the many dispatches that would be published before the debate was over for the signs of compromise and accommodation to reality that had saved the place from exploding many times before. Filipinos had the greatest tolerance for chaos of any people I had ever met. In that sense, more than in others, they seemed suited to democracy. In President Aquino they had a leader who truly believed that democracy could produce results in a poor and polarized country. But I would try to keep my expectations about its success on this volcanic soil within the bounds of realism.

For their sakes, I hoped that a workable system—whatever it might be —would one day evolve in the Philippines. For mine, I hoped that I would find another people whose aspirations would touch me as much as the Filipinos' had.

Reference Notes

This book is based largely on my interviews with the leading characters in the Philippine drama from 1983 to 1988. As a correspondent for TIME, I first talked to them when the news was breaking. Later I went back to many of them to ask their help in viewing those events in the broader perspective of a book. Unless otherwise footnoted, quoted remarks were made to me in the course of such interviews. In most cases the approximate date of the interview is obvious, given the context in which quotations appear. When that is not the case, I have specified the precise date of the interview in the reference notes. A number of sources, who preferred anonymity, are quoted without attribution in the text and, when relevant, footnoted to that effect.

PROLOGUE

PAGE

2 *"Ningas cogon"*: George M. Guthrie, "The Philippine Temperament," in *Six Perspectives on the Philippines,* ed. George M. Guthrie (The Bookmark, Manila, 1968), p. 79.

"Optimistic fatalism": Guthrie, p. 68.

1: MEETING NINOY

Wherever possible, I checked dates and details cited by Ninoy Aquino in our long, August 20, 1983, interview with sources who were in a position to confirm them. Ferdinand and Imelda Marcos confirmed certain elements of their longtime rival's account, but, as had been true throughout their careers, their interpretations of events and motives were vastly different from his. The majority report issued by the Fact-Finding Board, which was established to investigate the Aquino assassination, was particularly helpful as a source of confirmation of what Ninoy told me about his exchange of messages with Manila. Here and in future chapters, I will refer to transcripts of its proceedings (FFB transcript) or to the report of its General Counsel (GC report), published by Mr. & Ms. Publishing Company, Manila.

Other references:

8 "In mid-July": GC report 5.9.0; July 19, 1983, coded telex from President Marcos to Philippine consul general in New York for Aquino and his attorney Ernesto Maceda.

"On July 31": The *Metro Manila Times* revealed that a military court had affirmed the death sentence imposed in November 1977 and still presumed to be under appeal.

12 "Imelda later told": GC report 5.7.0; FFB transcript, July 2, 1984, A.M., p. 21.

15 "While at Harvard": Ninoy's friend Dr. Steve Agular, head of the Ninoy Aquino Movement in Boston, provided me with the tape of an April 14, 1983, lecture by Ninoy at MIT in which he elaborated further on his research.

21 "One was told him": Retired General Manuel Salientes confirmed to the author on August 18, 1986, his telling of this anecdote.

2: "HE WOULD BE LONELY WITHOUT ME"

The first three sections of this chapter are a continuation of my interview with Aquino en route to Manila. The last section is a more opinionated version of the testimony that I gave before the Fact-Finding Board on March 20, 28, and April 11, 1984; before the Marcos-appointed *Sandiganbayan* (graft and corruption court) on March 14, 1985; and before the Aquino-appointed *Sandiganbayan* on January 26, 27, 1988. It is based on my tape recording of the assassination, my memory of that event, and what I learned subsequently about how politics was played in the Philippines.

Other references:

23 "Ninoy was late": Cory read from the Jerusalem version of the Bible.

3: FERDINAND AND IMELDA, NINOY AND CORY

In addition to numerous interviews, I have relied upon the following four biographies for general information about the lives of the four main characters. Unless otherwise footnoted, primary information about their early lives comes from: Nick Joaquin, *The Aquinos of Tarlac: An Essay on History as Three Generations* (Cacho Hermanos, Inc., Manila, 1983); Lucy Komisar, *Corazon Aquino: The Story of a Revolution* (George Braziller, New York, 1987); Carmen Navarro Pedrosa, *Imelda Marcos* (St. Martin's Press, New York, 1987); Hartzell Spence, *Marcos of the Philippines* (The Marcos Foundation Inc., Manila, 1979).

I also found three other biographies helpful for corroborating details: Isabelo T. Chrisostomo, *Cory: Profile of a President* (J. Kriz Publishing, Quezon City, 1986); Isabelo T. Crisostomo, *Imelda Romualdez Marcos: Heart of the Revolution* (J. Kriz Publishing, Quezon City, 1980); Alfonso P. Policarpio,, Jr., *Ninoy the Willing Martyr* (Isaiah Books Inc, Manila, 1986)

In order to sketch the historical backdrop against which the leading characters and their ancestors played their roles, I relied on the following works: Teodoro Agoncillo, *A Short History of the Philippines* (New American Library, New York, 1969); David Howard Bain, *Sitting in Darkness: Americans in the Philippines* (Houghton Mifflin, Boston, 1984); Renato and Letizia Constantino, *The Philippines; The Continuing Past* (Foundation for Nationalist Studies, Quezon City, 1978); Benedict J. Kerkvliet, *The Huk Rebellion: A Study of Peasant Revolt in the Philippines* (University of California Press, Los Angeles, 1977); William Manchester, *American Caesar* (Little, Brown and Co., Boston, 1978); Stuart Creighton Miller, *Benevolent Assimilation: The American Conquest of the Philippines, 1899–1903* (Yale University Press, New Haven, 1982)

My attempt to capture the mood of the Philippines in each period was greatly aided by three books on the psychology and sociology of the people and the place: Alfred McCoy, and Ed C. de Jesus, eds., *Philippine Social History, Global Trade and Local Transformations* (Ateneo de Manila University Press, Manila, 1982); David Joel Steinberg, *The Philippines: A Singular and a Plural Place* (Westview Press Inc., Boulder, 1982).

Other references:

37 "To his opponents": My summation of the two schools of thought on the question of whether or not Marcos murdered his father's political rival is based on interviews with anti-Marcos opposition leader Raul Manglapus and a Marcos advisor who wished to remain anonymous.

38 "On December 7, 1938": Circumstances of Marcos's arrest: Benjamin Cray, *Rendezvous with Destiny* (Philippine Educational Co., Manila, 1968) pp. 34–35; *Manila Times*, Dec. 7, 1938, p. 1.

39 "In the trial": Vicente Francisco, *Was Ferdinand Marcos Responsible for the Death of Nalundasan?* (East Publishing, Manila); Senator Ambrosio Padilla, *Philippines Free Press*, October 9, 1965.

40 "Two weeks later": The People vs. Mariano Marcos et. al., No. 47388, October 22, 1940, case contained in *Philippine Reports* 70, p. 468; *Philippines Free Press*, November 12, 1940.

42 "Yet the thirty or so": Charles C. McDougald, *The Marcos File* (San Francisco Publishers, 1987).

"While most citations": Author's interview with Congressman Bonifacio Gillego (1987).

"On the eve": Jeff Gerth and Joel Brinkley, *New York Times*, January 23, 1986, p. 1.

"Reexamined in the more neutral": Marcos's claims: communiqué from "Maharlika Commanding" to U.S. Forces in the Philippines, July 26, 1944 (National Archives, Washington, D.C.).

"Contained in the same": Affidavit by Narciso Ramos, Minister Counselor, Philippine embassy, Washington, D.C. November 25, 1947 (National Archives, Washington, D.C.)

43 "In response": Letter to Major Marcos from Assistant Adjutant General Thomas J. Brown, HQ, Philippines-Ryukyus Command, Office of the Commanding General, June 6, 1947 (National Archives, Washington D.C.).

"Marcos retorted": Letter to Commanding General, HQ, Philrycom, December 2, 1947 (National Archives, Washington, D.C.).

"Escolta guerrillas": McDougald, p. 97.

"Rated one": Marcos's common law marriage: Beth Day Romulo, *Inside the Palace: The Rise and Fall of Ferdinand and Imelda Marcos* (G.P. Putnam's Sons, New York, 1987), p. 47; Pedrosa, p. 78.

44 "It was not out of character": Cover story, TIME, June 7, 1976.

"In those days": Author's interview with Araneta (September 2, 1986).

45 "The official wedding": Crisostomo, *Imelda Romualdez Marcos: Heart of The Revolution*, p. 70.

47 "Pacing Gueco": Author's interview with Doña Aurora Aquino (September 5, 1986).

48 "Ninoy was quite talkative": Author's interview with Laurel (March 2, 1987).

"Ninoy's eldest sister": Author's interew with Lichauco (September 5, 1986).

"The Conjuangco family": Author's interview with Zobel (August 5, 1986).

49 "Ninoy always called her": Author's interview with Moreno (March 15, 1987).

"Having viewed Ninoy's": Authors interview with Celia Diaz Laurel (March 6, 1987).

51 "When we went to school": Author's interview with Lichauco (September 5, 1986).

"I was nine years old": Transcript of meeting between President Marcos and Benigno Aquino at Malacañang, June 21, 1977, obtained from Philippine military archives.

52 "Ninoy, with the help": Author's interview with Antonio Aquino, Manila (1984).

54 "Three generations ago": Benedict Anderson, *London Review of Books*, February 5, 1987, p. 3; press material prepared by Office of Philippine Press Secretary for President Aquino's state visit to China (1988); and William Stewart, November 28, 1986, files to TIME (Time Inc., Editorial Reference Library).

"Demetria's father": Agoncillo, p. 196.

55 "Profiting from": *London Review of Books*, February 5, 1987, p. 3.

"Warball": *Philippines Sunday Inquirer*, March 9, 1986.

"The elder Conjuangcos": Crisostomo, *Cory: Profile of a President*, p. 17.

"Distilling alcohol": Stewart, files to *Time*.

56 "What impressed Ninoy": Napoleon Rama, in *Hero: A Collection of Incidents in the Life of Ninoy Aquino*, ed. Cynthia Y. Sycip (unpublished, 1984).

"I was a Junior Republican": Author's interview with Cory Aquino (April 24, 1984).

"I was interested in law": Ibid.

57 "My husband wanted to be": Stewart, files to TIME.

58 "Everyone knew": Stewart, Sindayen, interview with President Aquino, TIME, January 5, 1987.

"My husband": Author's interview with Doña Aurora Aquino, (September 5, 1986).

4: INTO THE VORTEX OF MARTIAL LAW

In order to chronicle the rivalry between Marcos and Aquino and the events that culminated in Marcos's imposition of martial law, I relied upon interviews and the following additional works: Reuben R. Canoy, *The Counterfeit Revolution: The Uncensored Story of the Marcos Regime in the Philippines* (Canoy, Manila, 1980); Manuel F. Martinez, *The Grand Collision: Aquino vs. Marcos* (Manila, 1986); and Primitivo Mijares, *The Conjugal Dictatorship of Ferdinand and Imelda Marcos* (Union Square Publications, San Francisco, 1976). Also, the weekly reporting of *Far Eastern Economic Review* (FEER) and *Philippines Free Press* (*Free Press*).

Other references:

59 "From the outset": Author's interview with Tatad (February 26, 1987).

"A student of Napoleon": Mijares, p. 132.

60 "Enrique Zobel recalls": Author's interview with Zobel (August 5, 1986).

"*Utang na loob*," "compadre system": Guthrie, pp. 62–63.

61 "Retired editor": Author's interview with Locsin (August 12, 1986).

"It was a handsome": Author's interview with Salonga (March 3, 1987).

"He was a brilliant tactician": Freedom of Information Act (FOIA) case no. 8501129 (November 19, 1965, airgram from Am Embassy to DOS: "Philippine Presidential Elections of November 9, 1965: Post-Election Analysis") notes that Marcos's lock on a bloc of 400,000 Ilocano voters gave him an automatic lead in a national election.

"An American embassy report": FOIA case no. 8501129 (July 4, 1965, memorandum of conversation with unnamed source, from Am Embassy to DOS, by William Owen: "Forthcoming Philippine Elections").

62 "She was not allowed": *Free Press*, January 23, 1965; Chrisostomo, *Imelda Romualdez Marcos: Heart of the Revolution*, p. 72; Spence, pp. 243–44.

"She began to suffer:" Quijano de Manila, *Free Press*, January 23, 1965; author's interview with Imelda Marcos (December 19, 1985).

"When Filipino doctors": Chrisostomo, *Imelda Romualdez Marcos: Heart of the Revolution*, p. 76, refers to New York Presbyterian Hospital.

"Everybody knew then": Author's interview with Imelda Marcos (December 19, 1985).

63 "In order to buttonhole": Pedrosa, p. 97.

"While Marcos worked": Canoy, p. 214.

"Thereafter the superstitious": Canoy, p. 216.

64 "The Nalundasan murder": Jose Nolledo, *The Life of Ferdinand Edralin Marcos: An Analysis* (Filipino Publishing Company, Quezon City, 1965), p. 5.

"Her ingenuous comments": Napoleon Rama, *Free Press*, November 20, 1965, p. 83.

"Marcos was determined": Joaquin, p. 350; Mijares, pp. 129–35; Bernardino Ronquillo, *FEER*, August 6, 20, 1970; author's interviews with Ninoy Aquino, Diokno, Laurel, Salonga.

65 "He made them laugh": Policarpio, p. 54.

"Persuaded that": Author's interview with Doña Aurora Aquino (September 5, 1986).

"By virtue of the fact": Peter Stanley, *Harvard Magazine*, May 1976, p. 43.

"As soon as Marcos took over": Joaquin, pp. 289–91.

"He struck at the very": Martinez, p. 181.

"Aquino's private army": Joaquin, p. 303.

"I personally": Author's interview with President Aquino (March 13, 1987).

66 "If a landlord refused": Teodoro Locsin, Jr., *Free Press*, March 29, 1971.

"He acknowledged": Ibid.

"Columnist Luis Beltran": Beltran, in *Hero*, p. 75.

67 "Culatingan Massacre": Joaquin, p. 309; *Manila Bulletin*, July 1, 1966; *Free Press*, July 9, September 10, 1966.

"He was thus forced": Joaquin, 309–10; transcript of June 21, 1977, Marcos-Aquino meeting.

68 "Having been a reporter": Author's interview with Salonga (March 3, 1987).

69 "He became very aggressive": Author's interview with Manglapus (August 20, 1986).

"It is the observation": Gene Garcia, *The Weekly Nation*, February 2, 1968.

"When Ninoy got": Author's interview with Lopa (March 10, 1987).

"There was that same romance": Author's interview, Manila (1986).

70 "Ninoy and Marcos": Author's interview, Manila (August 1987).

"An American political": Author's interview, Washington, D.C. (November 1986).

"The rhetorical question": Joaquin, p. 323.

"Titled": Benigno S. Aquino, Jr., *A Garrison State in the Make and Other Speeches* (Benigno S. Aquino, Jr. Foundation, Manila, 1985), pp. 11–26.

71 "Jabidah was what turned": Author's interview with Tatad (February 26, 1987).

"In a Senate privilege": "A Pantheon for Imelda," in *Garrison State*, pp. 215–30.

"Marcos once said": Author's interview with Cristobal (April 28, 1987).

72 "Plagued by rising": "A Pantheon for Imelda," in *Garrison State*, pp. 215–30.

"In my administration": Author's interview with Imelda Marcos (December 19, 1985).

"The answer was love": Ibid.

"When I became First Lady": Ibid.

73 "I became a beggar": Quijano de Manila, *Free Press*, February 22, 1969.

"There will always be poor": Jose F. Lacaba, *Free Press*, November 8, 1969.

"Rockefeller could not": Author's interview with Imelda Marcos (December 19, 1985).

74 "She came out": Lacaba, *Free Press*, November 8, 1969.

"Perhaps the most outrageous": FOIA case no. 8501128 (May 20, 1969, report from Am Embassy to DOS: "Marcos Campaign") Notes that the elevation of Archbishop Rosales of Cebu "provided a fortuitous opportunity for the Marcoses to demonstrate their devotion. The subsequent scramble of both Marcos and Osmena supporters to get on the plane to Rome quickly reached ludicrous proportions. But through control of the press only Mrs. Marcos and her two daughters got publicity as the devoted and devout sponsors of the new cardinal."

"She hit front pages": Quijano de Manila, *Free Press*, May 24, 1969.

"Since no Filipino": FOIA case no 8501128 (May 20, 1969) (cited above).

75 "Marcos succeeded in": FOIA case no 8501128 (October 11, 1969, report from Am Embassy to DOS: "Philippine Democracy at Work").

"Even before": Joaquin, p. 342.

76 "Former Marcos spokesman": Author's interview with Cristobal (April 28, 1987).

77 "His preliminary analysis": Joaquin, p. 348.

"Finally on February 2": Martinez, pp. 84–90.

"In time, nervous residents": Frances Starner, *FEER*, October 17, 1970.

78 "Then as the president": *FEER*, January 23, 1971.

"More humiliation": Author's interview, Manila (1985).

79 "Rumors had swept": A.B. Colayco, *Asia Philippine Leader*, September 10, 1971; *Free Press*, August 29, 1971.

80 "Ninoy took to the press": A.B. Colayco, *Asia Philippine Leader*, September 10, 1971; *Free Press*, September 11, 1971.

"An opinion poll": A.B. Colayco, *Asia Philippine Leader*, September 10, 1971.

81 "This one presented him": Ronquillo, *FEER*, January 15, 1972; Bruce Nussbaum, *FEER*, May 13, 1972; Locsin, Jr., *Free Press*, July 22, 1972; TIME, April 12, 1971; Mijares, pp. 161–64; Canoy, p. 150.

"Signs of a marital spat": Roquillo, *FEER*, April 29, 1972.

"On May 19, Delegate Quintero": Canoy, pp. 150–51.

82 "A U.S. National Security": FOIA case no. F85-800 (August 28, 1972, National Security Study Memorandum no. 155, Annex on Martial Law: "Philippine Policy"), p. 1.

"It was widely believed": FOIA case no 8504183 (October 6, 1972, INR document: "Philippines: Marcos Gambles on Martial Law"), p. 2.

"In a cable": FOIA case no. 8501907 (September 15, 1972, telegram from Ambassador Byroade to Sec State).

"The following day": "Operation Sagittarius," in *Garrison State*, pp. 345–52.

83 "Playing to the galleries": FOIA case no. 8501907 (September 22, 1972, cable from Am Emb to Sec State: "Marcos-Aquino Feud Contributes to Public Unease"; *Manila Bulletin*, September 21, 1972.

"He had been warned": In the June 21, 1977, transcript of the Marcos-Aquino meeting, the president asked his prisoner why he had not heeded the warnings he sent and thereby escaped arrest. Aquino indicated that he had not taken them seriously.

84 "Ninoy's sister Guadalupe": Author's interview with Kashiwahara (March 10, 1987).

"In response": Author's interview with Ninoy's cellmate, Max Soliven, (March 10, 1987).

"Summing up Ninoy's": Cesar Aguila, *Free Press*, September 30, 1972.

"Years later": On the night of February 22, 1986, during a press conference inside the Ministry of National Defense.

"If the charges and countercharges": Aguila, *Free Press*, September 30, 1972.

85 "Six years after": Ferdinand E. Marcos, *Revolution from the Center* (Raya Books, Hong Kong, 1978), p. 16. The book was ghosted by his spokesman Adrian Cristobal.

"There was a tremendous": Transcript of Marcos-Aquino meeting, June 21, 1977.

86 "Politics was in our minds": Ibid.

5: THE WILLING SACRIFICE

In chronicling the actions of the Marcoses and the Aquinos during the martial-law years, I am indebted to the following additional works: Raymond Bonner, *Waltzing with a Dictator: The Marcoses and the Making of American Policy* (Times Books, New York, 1987); Raul Manglapus, *The Silenced Democracy* (Orbis Books, Maryknoll, N.Y., 1976); David A. Rosenberg, ed., *Marcos and Martial Law in the Philippines* (Cornell University Press, Ithaca, 1979); *Ninoy Aquino: Testimony from a Prison Cell* (Benigno S. Aquino Foundation, Makati, 1984); David Maramba Asuncion, ed., *Ninoy Aquino: The Man, The Legend* (Cacho Hermanos Inc., Manila, 1984); Psinakis, Steve, *Two Terrorists Meet* (Superprint Lithographers, Naga City, 1981).

Other references:

87 "At one o'clock": Policarpio, p. 124.

"He had even contacted": June 21, 1977, transcript of Marcos-Aquino meeting.

"Cory balked": Author's interview with President Aquino (March 13, 1987).

88 "It was journalist": Author's interview with Soliven (March 10, 1987).

"Across town": Canoy, p. 21.

"Welcome to the club": Jose Mari Velez, in *Ninoy Aquino, The Man, The Legend*, p. 83.

"It was, at least": TIME, October 9, 1972.

89 "In the days": My summary of the achievements of martial law is largely derived from Jose Veloso Abueva, in *Marcos and Martial Law*, pp. 32–36.

"American businessmen": Robert B. Stauffer, "The Political Economy of Refeudalization," in *Marcos and Martial Law*, p. 188.

90 "Nixon White House": Bonner, pp. 3–7.

"Ninoy felt": Corazon Aquino, "Life with Ninoy," in *The Fookien Times 1986–87 Philippines Yearbook* (Fookien Times Publishing Co., Inc., Manila, 1987).

"I told her": Author's interview with Gonzales (March 6, 1987).

"Ninoy's cellmate": Author's interview with Soliven (March 10, 1987).

"In January 1973": Author's interview with Maria Elena ("Ballsy") Aquino Cruz (March 13, 1987).

91 "There, they were stripped": Policarpio, pp. 127–29.

"In a long letter": June 19, 1973, letter to Rodrigo, in *Letters from Prison and Exile* (Aquino Family, Manila, 1983), pp. 14–15, 130.

92 "One day": Author's interview with Len and Tessie Oreta, Hong Kong (June 1985).

"I thought he was going": Author's interview with Cory Aquino (September 27, 1983).

94 "On August 27": Policarpio, pp. 130–31.

"An exuberant Ninoy": Author's interview with Salonga (March 3, 1987).

"I cannot remember": Corazon Aquino, in *Fookien Times Yearbook*.

95 "She worried about": Corazon Aquino, *Mr. & Ms.* December 27, 1983.

"Look, we're married": Diane Sawyer interview, *60 Minutes*, September 14, 1986.

"Magic slate": Author's interview with Cruz (March 13, 1987).

"Ramas became disturbed": Transcript of August 20, 1974, conversation monitored in Aquino's cell, obtained from Philippine military archives.

"Although he was denied": Transcript of August 30, 1974, monitored conversation (cited above).

96 "In July 1974": Transcript of July 3, 1974, conversation monitored in Aquino's cell.

"By the time": Author's interview with Ninoy Aquino (August 21, 1983).

Letter to Cory: Martinez, p. 335.

97 "In the course of": Author's conversation with Butler at Council on Foreign Relations, New York (June 30, 1987).

"On the thirty-seventh": Author's interview with Locsin (August 12, 1986).

98 "Pact with Lord": Martinez, p. 334.

"One of his responses": Rodney Tasker, *FEER*, July 8, 1977.

"On June 21, 1977": Martinez, p. 338.

"As the conversation meandered": Transcript of Marcos-Aquino meeting, June 21, 1977.

99 "The legal proceedings": November 25, 1977, hearing: Tasker, *FEER*, December 9, 1977.

"Continuing his strategy": Policarpio, p. 134.

"The hearing was abrubtly": Circumstances recounted in letter to Supreme Court, in *Testimony from a Prison Cell*, appendix A., pp. 104–10.

101 "December 5": Tasker, *FEER*, December 16, 1977.

"Where lies my duty": Text of speech, in *Testimony from a Prison Cell*, pp. 97–102.

"In response he articulated": It was the analysis of Ninoy's fellow opposition leader Raul Manglapus that Ninoy's political philosophy was evolving in that direction. Author's interview with Manglapus, August 20, 1986.

102 "You are really strongest": Author's dinner conversation with Cory Aquino (January 27, 1985).

"In April 1978": Information on political situation at that point derived from Kit Machado, "The Philippines 1978: Authorization Consolidation Continues," *Asian Survey*, February 1979.

"Ninoy's subsequent entry": Tasker, *FEER*, March 3, 1978; *Asiaweek*, April 19, 1978.

"Should his enemies": Jose DeVera, *Manila Bulletin*, March 4, 1978.

"Ninoy's surrogate campaigners": Author's interview with Philippine military intelligence officer (August 25, 1986).

103 "An effort was therefore": Ibid.

"But when the counting": Tasker, *FEER*, April 21, 1978; ibid., May 19, 1978; *Asiaweek*, April 21, 1978.

104 "In growing numbers": Author's interviews with Alvarez (June 21, 1987), Maceda (August 20, 1986), Zobel (March 2, 1987).

"Before the 1978": Author's interview with President Aquino (March 13, 1987).

"Further complicating": Tasker, *FEER*, January 6, 21, 1978.

"After five months": Copy of Tañada letter furnished author by Vice-President Salvador Laurel.

105 "In fact": Tasker, *FEER*, July 21, 1978; *Asiaweek*, June 23, 1978; Clark Neher, "The Philippines 1979; Cracks in the Fortress," *Asian Survey*, February 1980; Sheilah Ocampo, *FEER*, April 13, 1979; Richard Vokey, *FEER*, October 5, 1979; Ocampo, *FEER*, January 11, 1980; ibid., January 18, 1980.

"After conferring with Marcos": Author's interview with Laurel (March 2, 1987).

"On March 8": Copies of documents furnished author by Vice-President Salvador Laurel.

"On June 30, 1979": Copy of letter furnished author by Minister of Tourism Antonio Gonzalez.

"On January 7, 1980": Aquino to Zobel: Copy furnished author by Enrique Zobel.

106 "When his mother": Author's interview with Doña Aurora Aquino (December 10, 1986).

"Among the first": Account of Barbero's conversations with the Marcoses related to author by Doña Aurora Aquino, (December 10, 1986).

"Covenants": Policarpio, p. 169.

"He later summarized": Ocampo, FEER, May 2, 16, 1980.

"Before Aquino left": Near the end of the 1986 presidential campaign, Imelda told me that President Marcos had confided Ninoy's rosary to Cardinal Sin with instructions to pass it on to Cory, who was preparing to announce her candidacy. "We thought that as a widow, she would want something he had cherished," said Imelda. She said she had received no reply from Mrs. Aquino.

107 "I myself": Author's interview with Doña Aurora Aquino (December 10, 1986).

"When Imelda": Author's interview with Laurel (March 2, 1987).

"While Ninoy": Author's interview with Huntington (January 23, 1987).

"Tony Gonzalez": Author's interview with Gonzalez (January 15, 1987).

108 "Heherson ("Sonny") Alvarez": Author's interview with Alvarez (June 21, 1987).

"Among the violent groups": Author's interview with Maceda (August 20, 1986).

"As a preview": Ocampo, FEER, August 15, 1980.

"Assistant Secretary of State": August 27, 1980, memo from Assistant Minister of National Defense Barbero describing Ninoy's attempt to prove to Holbrooke that he did not espouse violence. Furnished author by a friend.

"Several days later": Ibid.

109 "In correspondence": Copy of November 4, 1980, letter furnished author.

"He saw the logic": Author's interview with Benigno (March 13, 1987).

"Imelda was among those": Author's interviews with Alvarez (June 21, 1987), Maceda (August 20, 1986).

"You must act differently": Psinakis, pp. 24–29.

"The FBI": Author's interview with Gonzalez (January 15, 1987).

110 "Ninoy had dispatched Maceda": Author's interview with Maceda (August 20, 1986).

"The one thing": Author's interview with Benigno (March 13, 1987).

"The king": Author's interview with Maceda (August 20, 1986).

"Immediately after his return": Policarpio, p. 173; Jose Mari Velez, in Hero, p. 59.

111 "At first Ninoy": Author's interview with Cory Aquino (March 13, 1987).

"Nearly a decade": Ocampo, *FEER*, August 15, 1980.

"More and more, he looked": Author's interviews with Agular (January 22, 1987), Alvarez (June 21, 1987), Pelaez (August 25, 1983).

"The people on the left": Author's interview with Alvarez (June 21, 1987).

112 "In December 1982": Author's interview with Maceda (August 20, 1986).

"On February 3, 1983": Author's interview with Pelaez (August 25, 1983).

"His favorite poker player": Author's interview with Agular (January 22, 1987).

113 "Ninoy and his party": Singapore incidents related in interviews with Ninoy Aquino (August 21, 1983), Cory Aquino (September 27, 1983), Abul Khayr Alonto (June 13, 1986), Oreta (August 15, 1986), Zobel (February 25, 1984), Mahmood Iskandar, then Sultan of Johore, and his daughter (February 25, 1984).

"During a brief stopover": Hong Kong incidents recounted in interviews with Oreta (August 15, 1986), Hong Kong and Manila Immigration sources (September 1985), and Jun Rivera, former director, Philippine Aviation Administration (August 26, 1986).

114 "On August 20": Author's interview with Colonel Regino Calub (September 27, 1985).

"Dear Padre": Ninoy's last note furnished author by Vice-President Salvador Laurel.

6: <u>THE COVER-UP</u>

118 "Accordingly, Filipino photographers": GC report 9.2.1.

"In return": Ibid. 23.0.0

"She was Rebecca": Excerpts from her testimony drawn from GC report 16.1.0; author's notes of her testimony on May 2, June 6, 1985; Greenwald, Burton, Sindayen, TIME, May 13, 1985; Wright, Burton, Sindayen, TIME, June 17, 1985.

"When I first saw": Author's interview with Quijano (May 1, 1985).

120 "As soon as they": Ibid.

"Outside the terminal"; Nielson, Burton, Munro, TIME, September 5, 1983.

121 "The so-called "findings": Rosales, Foz, *Bulletin Today*, August 22, 1983; Olivas press briefings, August 22, 1983.

122 "The call": Author's interviews with Ken and Lupita Kashiwahara (March 8, 1986) and Grant (August 14, 1986).

123 "On reaching the gates: Author's interview with Laurel (August 22, 1983).

"I saw the feet": Author's conversation with Butz Aquino (June 1985).

124 "Maur maintained a vigil": Author's interview with Lichauco (September 5, 1986).

"A young photographer": Affidavit of Alexander Loinaz, sworn before Ombudsman in Graft and Corruption Court, November 10, 1986.

"At about the time": Imelda's activities recounted in conversation with J.V. Cruz (April 17, 1984).

125 Kidney transplant: Author's interviews in Washington, D.C. (1987) and with Enrile (April 13, 1986).

"Even before Ninoy": Ninoy had told Teddy Benigno during his Christmas furlough in 1978 that he had received "A-1" information from the CIA that Marcos had lupus (author's interview with Benigno, March 13, 1987).

"On August 5,": Author's interview with Ninoy Aquino (August 21, 1983).

126 "By the time": Ibid.

"The president had complained": Author's interview with Armacost (July 8, 1987).

"He would flash": Author's interview with President Marcos (December 3, 1985).

"When Enrile": Author's interview with Enrile (November 21, 1984).

127 "He looked like": Author's interview with Armacost (July 8, 1987).

"It was in that context": Author's interview with Solarz (October 26, 1986).

"Those two had": Author's interviews with Pelaez (August 25, 1983; November 17, 1987).

128 "Aquino's death had sent": U.S. tracking of Aquino recounted by Alvarez in interview with author (June 21, 1987).

Intelligence through Ver: Author's interview, Washington, D.C. (1986).

129 "A few days before": Author's interview with Armacost (July 8, 1987).

"Congressman Solarz": Author's interview with Solarz (October 26, 1986).

131 "Meanwhile, bank runs": *Philippines Daily Express, Times-Journal, Business Day,* August 23, 1983.

133 "When he was in prison": Author's interview with President Aquino (March 13, 1987).

134 "Ninoy compared": Author's interview with Cory Aquino (February 1, 1986).

136 "In Ninoy, the martyr": A.R. Magno, "Autumn of the Opposition," *Diliman Review,* July–August 1983, vol. 31, No. 4, pp. 1–8.

137 "Intuitively, Cory": *Asiaweek,* September 9, 1983.

138 "Once home": Cory Aquino to TIME News Tour, October 29, 1985.

139 "Suddenly out of the blue": Lupita Kashiwahara speech to San Francisco Organization of Women, in Manila *Sunday Magazine,* January 15, 1986.

"She set out": Author's interview with Grant (August 14, 1986).

145 "When darkness fell": Russell, Burton, Sindayen, TIME, September 12, 1983; Lito Catapusan, *Bulletin Today,* September 2, 1983.

8: INTERMEZZO

147 "Exactly one month": Willie Ng, *Bulletin Today,* August 28, 1983; *Times-Journal,* August 30, 1983.

149 "Former Vice-President Pelaez": Author's interview with Pelaez (Novermber 17, 1986).

152 "Part of the solution": National Security Study Directive, "U.S. Policy Towards the Philippines, Executive Summary" (released by Philippine Support Committee), p. 2.

"Not only did Armacost": Donner, p. 353.

"I was never invited": Author's interview (1987).

153 "He had relayed": On a 1982 visit to Manila, Senator Daniel Inouye left behind a report indicating that the Philippines was already in serious economic trouble. Author's interview, Washington (1987).

"In October they invited": FOIA case no. 8600329 (October 30, 1982, telegram from Ambassador Armacost to Sec State: "A Voyage with the First Family"); author's interview with Armacost (July 8, 1987).

"The Reagan administration promised": June 1, 1983, memorandum of agreement, amending the agreement of March 14, 1947.

155 "Although the rally's ": Author's interview with TIME photographer Sandro Tucci (September 23, 1983); Guy Sacerdoti, FEER, Ocotber 6, 1983; Palmer, Burton, Sindayen, TIME, October 3, 1983.

156 "Marcos is a man": Asiaweek, October 7, 1983.

"Marcos had earlier": Asiaweek, October 7, 1983.

9: SEE NO EVIL

161 "Dear Mrs. Aquino": Letter written September 4, 1983; first meeting on September 20, 1983.

163 "From the start": Author's interview with Solarz (October 26, 1986).

"Peping Cojuangco": Author's interview with Cojuangco (September 29, 1983).

"When a TIME correspondent": Los Angeles correspondent Joseph Kane's discussion with source who claimed to know nothing (October 6, 1983).

164 "Crime reporter Ruther Batuigas": Tempo, August 30, 1983.

165 "Other publications": Asiaweek, September 9, 1983; Rogal, Vokey, Clifton, Newsweek, September 26, 1983.

"From the start": Asiaweek, September 23, 1983.

166 "Cawigan took full": Asiaweek, October 14, 1983.

"Later, when he was": GC report 41.1.4.; FFB transcript, December 20, 1983, A.M., pp. 81, 82.

"He died": Reported by Philippine News Service, July 13, 1984, although Asiaweek expressed skepticism, July 27, 1984.

167 "Meanwhile, Seno summarized": GC report 25.0.0, 29.0.0, 30.0.0, 31.0.0; FFB exhibit 436; TIME, October 24, 1983.

"The seedy office": Author's interview with Seno (October 1, 1983).

170 "Dr. Nieto Salvado": Asiaweek, September 23, December 16, 1983.

171 "The new, more autonomous": Asiaweek, November 18, 25, 1983.

172 "When the corpse": In initial court hearings, state officials had testified that Galman was 175 cm. tall and Aquino, 169 cm.

"Shortly thereafter": *Asiaweek*, December 2, 1983.

173 "Board Chairman Corazon": *Reports of the Fact-Finding Board on the Assassination of Senator Benigno Aquino* (Mr. and Ms. Publishing Co., Manila, 1984), p.27; *Asiaweek*, November 21, 1983; author's interviews with other board members

"Dante Santos": *Reports of the Fact-Finding Board*, p. 29; interviews with other board members.
"Luciano ("Sally") Salazar": *Reports of the Fact-Finding Board*, pp. 30–31; interviews with other board members.
"Ernesto ("Boy") Herrera": *Reports of the Fact-Finding Board*, p. 30; interviews with other board members.

174 "No one seemed to": p. 29.

"In taking a leave": author's interview with Narvasa (October 27, 1984).

"Narvasa assigned": *Reports*, p. 27; *Asiaweek*, November 21, 1983.

175 "First on the stand": FFB transcript, November 17, 1983, A.M. p.29; *Asiaweek*, December 2, 1983.

176 "Sergeant de Guzman": FFB transcript, November 25, 1983, A.M. p.35; *Asiaweek*, December 9, 1983.

178 "When the session reopened": FFB transcript, November 25, 1983, P.M. p. 23.

179 "As soon as Sergeant Ernest Mateo": FFB transcript, November 29, 1983, A.M. pp. 25–27.

180 "Deployed around the nose": Kavinta testimony, FFB transcript, December 5, 1983, A.M. p. 85, P.M. p.33; *Asiaweek*, December 16, 1983.

"Kavinta sounded aggressive": Valerio testimony, FFB transcript, December 12, 1983, A.M. p. 89; *Asiaweek*, December 16, 1983.

181 "I might as well": Author's interview with a fellow soldier (August 1986).

"It had observed": GC report 42.0.0.

"At the end": Estelo testimony, in *Asiaweek*, December 16, 1983.

182 "It was four o'clock": Author's notes and tape of this impromptu session; Hoyle, Burton, TIME, January 9, 1984.

10: HEARING FROM THE BAD GUY

This chapter relies upon my own experiences with the Fact-Finding Board and my coverage of the three days of testimony by General Ver, as well as interviews with Andres Narvasa (August 2,6, 1984, October 8, 1987).

Other references:

186 "Justice Agrava was in": March 28, 1984.

Author's testimony: FFB transcript, March 28, 1984, A.M.

"Not until one": March 19, 1984.

187 "The first time": FFB transcript, March 20, 1984, A.M.

189 "It was but one": *Free Press*, March 29, 1971. Aquino declared he would block Ramos's promotion until he revealed what he knew about the infamous Jabidah Massacre. The resulting setback to Ramos allowed Ver to gain seniority, as he explained in FFB transcript, April 10, 1984, A.M., p.75.

190 "In July 1983": Author's interview with Enrile (February 17, 1986).

191 "He had quite obviously": FFB transcript, April 6, 1984, A.M., p.3; Johnson, Burton, TIME, April 6, 1984.

"Tan's sister Christine": Author's interview with Sister Christine Tan, April 6, 1984.

192 "Project Four Flowers": FFB transcript, April 6, 1984, A.M., pp. 33–73.

"Deftly, he then attempted: Ibid., pp.49, 63,66.

193 "Astonishingly, he claimed": Ibid., p.68.

194 "Ver finally conceded": FFB transcript, April 6, 1984, P.M. p.7.

"His men had, he said": FFB transcript, April 10, 1984, A.M., p.109.

195 "He was shocked": FFB transcript, April 6, 1984, P.M., p.35.

"I am a loyal soldier": FFB transcript, April 10, 1984, A.M., pp. 78–84.

196 "Thus I was surprised": April 24, 1984.

11: <u>THE BALLOT VS. THE BULLET</u>

The last section of this chapter relies heavily on a trip I made (April 16–18, 1984) to interview members of the Communist New People's Army. The following works on the Philippine Communist movement were useful to my understanding of the NPA: William Chapman, *Inside the Philippine Revolution: The NPA and Its Struggle for Power* (W.W. Norton & Co., New York, 1987); Amado Guerrero, *Philippine Society and Revolution* (International Association of Filipino Patriots, Oakland, 1979); Kerkvliet, Francisco Nemenzo "The Millenarian-Populist Aspects of Philippine Marxism," in *Marxism in the Philippines*, Marx Centennial Lecture (Third World Studies Center, University of the Philippines, Manila 1984); David A. Rosenberg, "Communism in the Philippines," in *Problems of Communism*," September–October 1984, Vol. 33, No. 5, pp. 24–26. *The Communist Insurgency in the Philippines*, (reported by Ministry of National Defense, Office of Media Affairs, Presidential Center for Special Studies, Manila, May 11, 1985); Sacerdoti, Tasker, *FEER*, November 21, 1985; Alfredo Tiamson and Assolinda Caneda, "Overview of Violence: The Philippine Case" (Paper presented before Second Group on Peace and Conflict Research (Philippine Center for Peace Research, December 9–10, 1984).

Other references:

197 "Watching Cory Aquino": April 24, 1984

199 "Her most painful lesson": Nelly Sindayen, February 15, 1984, file to TIME.

"Not surprisingly, Marcos": *Bulletin Today*, January 25, 1984.

200 "I said to Butz": Author's interview with Cory Aquino (March 2, 1984).

"When the people see": Author's interview with Cojuangco (April 23, 1984).

201 "One week later": *Asiaweek*, March 16, 1984.

"When I saw her": Author's interview with Cory Aquino (April 24, 1984).

202 "It's difficult to accept": Ibid.

"There is no talk": Author's interview with Laurel (April 4, 1984).

"Before you had to provide": Author's interview with Cory Aquino (April 4, 1984).

204 "If this election": Author's interview with Cardinal Sin (April 24, 1984).

"His greatest asset": *Asiaweek*, February 24, April 20, 1984; Sacerdoti, FEER, April 26, 1984; Robert Manning, *International Herald Tribune*, May 4, 1984; Nielsen, Burton, Sindayen, Munro, TIME, April 9, May 14, 1984.

"In addition to new money": Estimate of Bernardo Villegas, Vice-President, Center for Research and Communication, in interview with author (April 27, 1984).

205 "$28.5 million": *Asiaweek*, May 18, 1984.

Author's trip with NPA: Nielsen, Burton, TIME, May 14, 1984.

206 "The major ingredients": According to a study by the Rand Corporation, 5 percent of the population controls 95 percent of the country's wealth. Cited by Bonner, p. 120.

208 "Not only were the guerrillas": Sacerdoti FEER June 28, 1984.

"Meanwhile, Democratic": Nayan Chanda, Robert Manning, FEER, March 15, 1984 *Asiaweek*, March 16, 1984.

214 "Another had just returned": Author's interview (March 26, 1984).

12: THE MILITARY ALTERNATIVE

The focal point of this chapter is a military inspection tour of Mindanao, the largest theater of NPA activity, made by Defense Minister Enrile June 1–6, 1984. The narrative is based on my notes from that trip, plus interviews with a number of officers and civilians who would become central figures in the military reform movement, which was already organizing, unbeknownst to me at the time. Also covering that trip was Cecilio Arillo, a reporter with close ties to Enrile, whose subsequent books *Breakway: The Inside Story of the Four Day Revolution in the Philippines* (J.A. and Associates, Manda Luyong, 1986) I found useful.

The following books and papers were helpful in summarizing the other insurgency in the southern Philippines—that of separatist Muslims: T.J.S. George, *Revolt in Mindanao: The Rise of Islam in Philippine Politics* (Oxford University Press, 1980); "The 400 Year War—The Moro Struggle in the Philippines," *Southeast Asia Chronicle* (Southeast Asia Resource Center, Berkeley) (no. 82, Februrary 1982).

Other references:

221 "I had spent several days": Author's interview with Enrile (May 3, 1984); Enrile campaign trip: May 6–8, 1984.

223 "Some 50,000": "The 400 Year War;" Tasker, *FEER,* August 9, 1984.

226 "Six weeks before": Author's interview with Enrile (May 3, 1984).

"He had confirmed": Author's interview with Enrile (December 10, 1986).

227 "We could not contradict": Ibid.

"Eventually Marcos was persuaded": Enrile testimony on CAP program before National Assembly, February 5, 1985; Palmer, Burton, TIME, March 18, 1985.

"However, Enrile admitted later": Author's interview with Enrile, (December 10, 1986).

228 "The cover for the trip": Ibid.

"I had been coasting": Author's interview with Enrile (February 27, 1986).

"Relations between the two": Arillo, p. 128.

Three years later": Ibid. p. 131.

"Still the combative loner": Author's interview with Enrile (May 8, 1984).

"Following a shoot-out": Arillo, pp. 135–36.

"I could be the only": Arillo, p. 136.

"As early as 1979": Author's interview with Benigno (March 13, 1987). See note for Chapter 6, p. 125.

229 "In a meeting in Houston": July 13, 1981, notes on meeting with Ninoy Aquino in Houston, furnished to authors by Aquino supporter.

"Enrile vehemently denies": Author's interview with Enrile (October 24, 1987).

"By then the officers": Interviews with Robles (February 26, 1986), Honasan (February 27, 1986).

230 "Their concerns were": Author's interview with Enrile (February 27, 1986)

"So exercised": Author's interview with Malajacan (August 8, 1987).

231 "There was no room": Tifft, Burton, TIME, December 16, 1985.

"These are soldiers": Author's interview with Ahorro (February 25, 1986).

"It is no coincidence": Author's interview with Salientes (August 7, 1985).

"My mission": Author's interview with military officer, 1985; TIME, December 16, 1985.

232 "The people were not": Author's interview with Batac (October 10, 1987).

More power to Ver: Arillo, p. 142; Sacerdoti, *FEER,* October 13, 1983.

"Colonel Ver and his father": Author's interview with Robles (February 26, 1986).

233 "Some military people": Author's interview with Hernandez (August 6, 1987).

"As Enrile viewed": Author's interview with Enrile (February 27, 1986).

"We knew that from a military viewpoint": Author's interview with Honasan (February 27, 1986).

"Not long afterward": Author's interview with Enrile (February 27, 1986).

"Within forty-eight hours": Author's interview (February 1986).

234 "Now the war": Author's interview with Robles (February 26, 1986).

"Our assessment": Author's interview with Malajacan (August 7, 1987).

13 THE SPECIAL RELATIONSHIP

The following works were particularly useful in understanding the change in U.S. policy toward the Philippines: Agoncillo; Bonner; Jeane Kirkpatrick, "Dictators and Double Standards," *Commentary*, November 1979; National Security Study Document: "U.S. Policy Towards the Philippines," Executive summary released by Walden Bello (March 12, 1985; Robert Pringle, *Indonesia and the Philippines: American Interests in Island Southeast Asia* (Columbia University Press, New York, 1980).

Other references:

237 "Among the first": U.S. Senate Report on the Situation in the Philippines".

238 "With the Soviet occuption": Alva M. Bowen, "Philippine Bases: U.S. Redeployment Options," document published by Congressional Research Service, Library of Congress, February 20, 1986, pp. 6,8.

239 "Robert Pringle": Pringle, p.52.

"It was the latter": Agoncillo, p.11.

"Either we 'meddle' ": Author's interview (1986).

"Marcos was as good": Author's interview with Armitage (July 6, 1987).

240 "This is a people": Bosworth to TIME News Tour, October 29, 1985.

241 "He and Imelda bragged": Notes of a meeting in Houston on July 13, 1981, between a convalescing Ninoy Aquino and several supporters include a reference to Imelda Marcos having "boasted" to Ninoy that the Marcoses have "quite a lot of influence with [Vice President George] Bush" by virtue of the fact that Ronnie Velasco, Philippine energy minister, was channelling "all the proceeds of Philippines oil transactions" into the First National Bank of Texas, where Bush was said to have clout.

242 "Armacost had followed up": "U.S. Policy Toward Recent Developments in the Philippines", November 17, 1983.

"The businessmen in Armacost's": Sacerdoti, FEER, October 13, 1983.

243 "In a background interview": Author's interview with Armacost (December 1, 1983).

"About a month before": March 2, 1984.

245 "Although technically": Author's interview with Bosworth (December 11, 1986).

"It struck me": Author's interview with Bosworth (December 11, 1986); Kai Bird, *Foreign Service Journal*, September 1984.

246 "The American attaches": Author's interview with Malajacan (August 7, 1987).

"The Agrava Board": *Reports*, pp. 354–84.

"Marcos had disappeared": Francisco Tatad, *Business Day*, November 19,20, 1984; Sacerdoti, *FEER*, November 29, December 6, 1984; editorial, *Malaya*, November 20, 1984.

247 "When the ambassador": Author's interview's with Morato (January 1985, October 19, 1987).

"Steve was the first": Author's interview (October 1987).

248 "When I arrived": Author's interview with Bosworth (December 11, 1986).

"He is a guy": Author's interview (1987).

249 "What few news reports": Chanda, *FEER*, August 30, 1984.

"Based on discussions": Author's interview (October 1986).

"Reagan was so impressed": Ibid.

"What Crowe was saying": Ibid.

"The insurgency was one": Author's interview with Crowe (July 16, 1987).

250 "After years of": Author's interview with Allen (August 25, 1987).

251 "Looking back": Author's interview with Crowe (July 16, 1987).

"We made the decision very early on": Author's interview with Armacost (July 8, 1987).

252 "We needed a policy": Author's interview with Bosworth (December 11, 1986).

"The goal of our policy": Author's interview with Wolfowitz (October 28, 1987).

"The secret policy directive": Bonner, p. 362.

"It did not please": TIME, March 25, 1985.

"There were definitely": Author's interview (1987).

253 "Drop dead": Author's interview (1987).

"In fact, during the year": "U.S. Policy Towards the Philippines;" Chanda, *FEER*, January 31, March 21, 1985.

254 "The problem": Author's interviews with several people knowledgeable about the NSDD draft.

"The NPA was one": Author's interview with Armitage (July 6, 1987).

"One analyst privy": Author's interview (January 1987).

255 "The document called for:" Author's interview (January 1987).

14: <u>PRELIMINARY JUSTICE</u>

256 "One month after": August 6, 1984.

257 "When Narvasa learned": Author's interview with Narvasa (September 30, 1984).

"Board member Boy Herrera": Author's interview with Herrera (October 16, 1987).

258 "The U.S. embassy": Confirmed by a board member.

259 "She acted as if": Author's interview with Narvasa (September 30, 1984).

261 "The first article to outline": Iyer, Burton, TIME, October 22, 1984.

"In hearings": October 4, 1984.

"I had barely gotten back": Author's interview with Armitage (July 6, 1987).

262 "As early as two weeks": Author's interview with Marcos's labor minister, Blas Ople (March 9, 1984).

"I hope you can live": Nelly Sindayen, October 25, 1984, file to TIME.

263 "We would learn later": At a press conference five months later, Marcos revealed his agreement with Ver. Iyer, Burton, Sindayen, TIME, March 11, 1985.

"Fighting back tears": October 23, 1984. *Mr. and Ms.*, "Extra Edition," October 24, 1984.

"When I entered": October 25, 1984.

264 "Enrile, who had received": Author's interview with Enrile (November 5, 1984).

265 "It was absolutely unheard": It took the media longer than it did General Allen to understand the significance of the reformists' demonstration on March 21, 1985. Only after Enrile and some of his boys began publicizing the new movement in Manila and a Pentagon official urged the *Washington Post* to assign a correspondent to write about it did articles begin to appear: *Asiaweek*, May 24, June 14, 1985; *Bulletin Today*, May 30, 1985 (reprint of speech by Commodore Brillante Ochoco); Sacerdoti, *FEER*, June 13, 1985; Tasker, *FEER*, August 1, 1985; William Branigan, *Washington Post* (carried by *International Herald Tribune*, June 4, 1985).

"Its members had first": "Preliminary Statement of Aspirations" initially presented during meeting of PMA Core Group on February 15, 1985.

266 "Shortly afterward": "A Statement of Common Aspirations," composed by eighty officers, was circulated March 15, 1985.

"We now strive": Tifft, Burton, TIME, December 16, 1985.

"On April 20": Author's interview with Batac, Honasan, and Robles (November 19, 1985); Tifft, Burton, TIME, December 16, 1985.

"Meanwhile, the press debut": May 6, 8, 1985. Nelly Sindayen, May 17, 1985, file to TIME.

267 "Conceived as a front": Author's interview with Robles (February 26, 1986).

"While the Core Group plotted": Author's interviews with numerous RAM and Core-Group members (1985–87).

"It was only after": Nelly Sindayen, May 17, November 28, 1985, files to TIME.

"In an effort": Author's interview with Batac, Honasan and Robles (November 19, 1985).

268 "The harshness of Armitage's": Author's interview with Armitage (July 6, 1987).

"This was a very good": Author's interview with Wolfowitz (October 28, 1987).

269 "He carried with him": The letter from Weinberger was dated January 2, 1985.

"At that point": *Asiaweek*, March 22, 1985.

"Ver, although on leave": Author's interview with Philippine military officers (October 1984, October 1985).

270 "The reform movement might": Author's interview with Calub (September 27, 1985).

15: **POLITICAL PASSAGES**

Interviews with Marcos's likeliest heirs—Cory Aquino (January 27, 1985), Juan Ponce Enrile (January 31, 1985), and Doy Laurel (August 28, 1985)—are the basis for this chapter. A campaign biography by Nick Joaquin, titled *Doy Laurel In Profile* (Times Publishing Co., Inc, Makah, 1985) provided most of the biographical material on Laurel.

Other references

273 "Birthdays were full": Sacerdoti, *FEER*, November 28, 1983.

275 "On October 27, 1984": *Asiaweek*, January 11, 25, March 22, 1985; Sacerdoti, *FEER*, January 24, 31, 1985.

276 "In December": "Declaration of Unity" signed December 26, 1984. *Asiaweek*, January 11, 1985.

"Fast-Track System": Sacerdoti, Tasker, *FEER*, April 4, 1985; Belinda Olivares-Cunanan, *Mr. and Ms.*, January 4–10, February 15–21, 1985.

279 "His well-published confrontation": *Asiaweek*, January 25, 1985.

282 "From the moment Marcos": Second kidney transplant confirmed in author's interviews, Washington, D.C., (1987) and with Enrile (April 13, 1986).

"Snap election" rumors: *Asiaweek*, May 31, 1985; Vokey, *Newsweek*, May 27, 1985.

283 "Noel Soriano was the thinker": Author's interview with Escaler (February 28, 1987).

"In an initial 'Concept Paper' ": Minutes of October 27, 1984, meeting (Convener Group Archives).

284 "At its first meeting": *Asiaweek*, January 11, 1985; Belinda Olivares-Cunanan, *Mr. and Ms.*, February 15–21, 1985.

"The Convener Group had already": Author's interview with Cory Aquino (January 21, 1985).

"Cory had been impressed": Author's interview with Cory Aquino (September 4, 1985).

285 "Cory was dispatched": Author's interview with Cory Aquino (June 8, 1985).

"The trouble with": Ibid.

"After that": Author's interview with Ongpin (January 13, 1986).

286 "After her outburst": Olivares-Cunanan, *Mr. and Ms.*, April 12–18, 1985.

"These people": Author's interview with Cory Aquino (June 8, 1985).

289 "The idea was for me": Author's interview with Crowe (July 16, 1987).

16: SNAP!

In the immediate aftermath of Marcos's call for a snap election, I interviewed Cory Aquino (November 7, 14, December 5, 1985, January 7, 1986), Doy Laurel (November 13, 1985), President Marcos (December 3, 1985), and Imelda Marcos (December 19, 1985). This chapter is about their reactions to the new political landscape in which they suddenly found themselves.

Other references:

290 "Inside the palace": Author's interviews with presidential aides and Sol Vanzi, who was then ABC-TV's Manila stringer (November 5, 1985).

"Laxalt, whose October": Paul Laxalt, "My conversations with Ferdinand Marcos," *Policy Review* (Summer 1986, No. 37), pp. 2–5.

292 "Stupid America!": Nelly Sindayen, November 11, 13, 1985, files to TIME; TIME, November 25, 1985.

"$950,000": Bonner, p. 383.

293 "She became clearer": The journalists who coined the description were Lin Neumann, of *San Francisco Examiner*, and Guy Sacerdoti, then correspondent for *FEER*.

298 "Laxalt did not even": Author's interview with diplomat (August 25, 1986).

"Cory's campaign manager": Author's interview with Cojuangco (November 13, 1985).

299 "Bosworth answered": Author's interviews with two guests (August 1986).

"During the week": Author's interviews with Cory Aquino (November 7, 14, December 5, 1985); Burton, TIME, January 7, 1987.

303 "The Cardinal . . . greeted her": Author's interview with Cory Aquino (November 14, 1985).

" 'No,' said the cardinal": Author's interview with Cardinal Sin (December 11, 1986).

304 "Some businessmen": Some among them were preparing to do battle with Goliath by circulating, October 30, 1985, an anti-Laurel campaign document known as "A Gathering of Davids."

305 "Oozing good will": To my astonishment, Ver had phoned me the day before to read me his December 2, 1985, letter to Marcos and the marginal notations from the president reinstating him, as well as to tell me he would be too busy for the interview I had repeatedly requested.

307 "He was seated": Ninoy's seat during June 21, 1977, meeting with Marcos in Malacañang.

309 "What I am feeling": Author's interview with Marcos; TIME, December 16, 1985.

17: SAINT VS. SINNER

312 "Last week, when a certain lady": *Asiaweek*, February 9, 1986.

313 "Reaching into her": Author's interview with Cory Aquino (November 7, 1985).

"No one in the room": *FEER*, December 26, 1986; TIME, December 16, 1985.

314 "As one UNIDO leader": Author's telephone interview with Susan De Los Reyes (December 12, 1985).

"As a face-saving": Copies of memos furnished the author by businessman Victor Sison.

"With a list of Doy's demands": Author's interview with Concepcion (October 24, 1987).

315 "No sooner had she and the cardinal": Author's interview with Cardinal Sin (January 13, 1986).

"Without consulting her Laban": Author's interview with Cory Aquino (January 30, 1986).

Aquino-Laurel dinner: Aquino's version of events, author's interview (December 12, 1985).

316 "After midnight": Author's interview with Cory Aquino (December 12, 1985)

"The mathematics of that race": Author's interview with KBL Assemblyman Narciso Monfort on convention floor (December 11, 1985).

317 "As soon as she": *Asiaweek*, January 19, 1986; *FEER*, January 16, 1986.

"A *New York Times* article": December 16, 1985.

"When I interviewed": Author's interview with Cory Aquino (December 5, 1985).

318 "What appeared to upset": Author's interview with Cory Aquino (January 30, 1986).

"Salonga claimed": Author's interview with Cory Aquino (January 30, 1986).

319 "Since I am a": Author's interview with Cory Aquino (January 30, 1986).

"If she lost": Author's interview with Jones (September 22, 1986).

321 "As the result of a misstatement": *Asiaweek*, January 19, 1986; *FEER*, January 16, 1986.

"Twelve advisors": *Asiaweek*, January 9, 1986.

322 "Concise policy formulations": Author's interview with Adaza (January 13, 1986).

"Indeed, the Marcos who": Sacerdoti, *FEER*, January 30, 1986; eyewitness accounts of TIME photographers Robin Moyer, James Nachtwey, and Sandro Tucci; TIME, January 27, 1986.

323 "That strategy failed": Author's interview with Pelaez (November 17, 1986); Lewis M. Simons, *Worth Dying For* (William Morrow & Co., New York, 1987), p. 22.

"A new Marcos will emerge": Author's interview with Ople (January 12, 1986).

324 "Makati businessman Enrique Zobel": Author's interview with Zobel (January 27, 1986).

326 "My last souvenir": January 29, 1986.

327 "I witnessed it one day": January 21, 1986.

330 "An hour later": Author's interview with Cory Aquino (January 31, 1986).

332 "After Enrile endorsed": Author's interview with Enrile (December 8, 1986).

333 "We realized you cannot": Author's interview with Batac (October 10, 1987).

"Among the wariest": Author's interview with Enrile (October 24, 1987).

"By his own admission": Author's interview with Almonte (October 13, 1987).

18: THE FIRST CAMPAIGN

337 "In fact, the Fourth Classmen": Author's interview with American official in Washington (July 1986); FOIA case no. 8701496 (October 30, 1985, message from Ambassador Bosworth to Sec State, "AFP Reform movement, A Glimpse Beneath the Surface").

"These are my boys": Author's interview with newsman Cecilio Arillo (August 12, 1986).

"Insightful book": Race, Jeffrey, *War Comes to Long An: Revolutionary Conflict in a Vietnamese Province* (University of California Press, Berkeley, 1972).

"His insights": Author's interview with Robles (February 26, 1986).

338 "The worst way": Author's interview (1987).

"Cruder subjects": Author's interview, Washington, D.C., (1986).

"How can we": Author's interview with Honasan (February 27, 1986).

"We certainly encouraged": Author's interview with Armitage (July 6, 1987).

"Businessman Jimmy Ongpin": Address to TIME News Tour, October 30, 1985; TIME (Pacific edition), December 16, 1985.

"Jimmy was so excited": Author's interview with Robles (February 26, 1986).

339 "Meanwhile the Core Group": Author's interview with Malajacan (August 7, 1987).

"Colonel Almonte played": Author's interview with Almonte (October 13, 1987).

"It was Almonte": Author's interview with Enrile (October 24, 1987).

340 "It was Almonte": Author's interview with Peping Conjuangco, December 10, 1986, who said that the mutual friend who put him in touch with Almonte was Dr. Fernando Carrascoso, whom he described as a one time ally of Peping's pro-Marcos cousin Danding.

"The Americans were solidly": Author's conversations with American officials from both State Department and Pentagon in Washington and Manila.

"One Core-Group member": Author's interview (1986).

341 "When Ver tried to cancel": Author's interviews with Vargas and Robles (February 4, 1986).

"I am staying out": Author's interview with Cardinal Sin (February 5, 1986).

343 "Without going into detail": Author's interview with Almonte (October 13, 1987).

"A long, slow separation": Author's interview (1987).

"It was a game": Author's interview (1987).

344 "We learned": Author's interview (1986).

"Now the plan was": Author's interview (1986).

"The 'extras' became": Author's interviews with Americans in charge of funds (August 1986).

345 "You don't stage a coup": Author's interview (1987).

"One week before the Snap election": according to an October 30, 1985 message from Ambassador Bosworth to the State Department (FOIA case no. 8701496), "It is clear that some elements in the movement have begun to talk of a military coup."

"They saw the U.S.": Author's interview, Washington, D.C., (1987).

"We sent them": Author's interview with Armitage (July 6, 1987).

"I feared the worst": Author's interview (1987).

"There were so many": Author's interview with Crowe, (July 16, 1987).

346 "Armitage's reaction": Author's interview (1987).

"Other U.S. military": Author's interview, Manila (1986).

"One officer commented": Author's interview, Washington, D.C., (1987).

"It was Colonel Raphael": Author's interviews in Manila and Washington, D.C., (1987).

347 "But, said Bosworth": Author's interview with Bosworth (December 11, 1986).

"Maybe they got": Author's interview (1987).

"Vic Raphael had memorized": Author's interview with Batac (October 10, 1987).

"Frankly . . . we were": Author's interview (1987).

348 "On reaching the humble *barangay*": Burton, TIME (Pacific edition), February 17, 1986.

19: COUNTDOWN TO "OPERATION BOODLEFIGHT"

In addition to my own firsthand observations and interviews, my reconstruction of the events leading up to the military rebellion against Marcos also draws from several earlier works on the events of February 1986: Arillo; Bryan Johnson, *Four Days of Courage: The Untold Story of the Fall of Ferdinand Marcos* (McClelland & Stewart, Toronto, 1987); Alfred McCoy, Gwen Robinson, Marion Wilkinson, "The Last Days of Marcos," *National Times of Australia on Sunday*, October 5, 12, 1986; Simons.

Other references:

354 "Even then the margin": Author's interview with Cojuangco (January 9, 1986).

"A NAMFREL officer": FOIA case no. 8601724, parts 3, 4 (February 10, 1986, cable 4365 from Am Embassy to Sec State.)

355 "Indeed, a secret network": Author's interview with Philippine political analyst (July 1987).

356 Joker Arroyo: Comments reported to TIME by Nelly Sindayen.

"It was after midnight": FOIA 8601724, parts 3, 4 (February 13, 1986, cable from Bosworth to Sec State: "COMELEC Computer Operators Walkout Updater").

357 "No comment": Author's interview with Cory Aquino (February 10, 1986).

"We are a nation of lawyers": Comments reported to TIME by Barry Hillenbrand.

358 "According to the bill": RP Philippines, 1st Batasan Pambansa, 2nd session, July 22, 1985, BP No. 883, Sections (2) and (10).

"Otherwise, said Captain Robles": Author's interview with Robles (December 3, 1986).

"Javier had said": TIME, February 24, 1986.

360 "It was jarring": UPI dispatch, February 10, 1986.

"He offered the opposition": *Economist*, February 15, 1986; Sacerdoti, *FEER*, February 20, 1986; FOIA case no. 8601724 February 11, 1986, cable from Am Embassy to Sec State: "Election Observers Sitrep Eleven").

"As soon as he heard": Author's interview with Conjuangco (February 13, 1986).

"Bosworth had had input": FOIA case no. 8601724, part 3 (February 11, 1986; for Vadm John M. Poindexter: "Q & A concerning the Philippines").

361 "Bosworth also knew": FOIA case no. 8601724, parts 3, 4 (February 10, 1986, briefing memorandum from Will Ball to Sec Shultz: "Your meeting with the President, Senator Lugar and Congressman Murtha," February 11, 1986, 9:45 A.M.).

362 "I don't know what": Author's interview with Mitra (February 19, 1986).

"Ronald Reagan must think": Author's interview with Cojuangco (February 12, 1986).

"The President was misinformed": FOIA case no. 8601724 (February 13, 1986), memo to Wolfowitz from Mike Privitera titled "Dole/Lugar/Nunn Action on Philippines").

"It was Secretary Shultz": Three sources confirmed to author that this recording was instrumental in making the president realize Marcos's involvement in massive election fraud.

363 Bishops Conference letter: Moody, Burton, Sindayen, TIME February 24, 1986.

"Cory had done it by invitation": Author's interview with source close to Cory Aquino (February 10, 1986).

"She had refused": Author's interviews with campaign advisors Aquilino, Pimentel, and Mitra (February 13, 1986).

"As Imelda's informants": Johnson, p. 61.

364 "When he insisted": According to Pedrosa (pp. 100–101), Imelda was assigned to persuade the influential Fernando Lopez to accept the nomination as Marcos's vice-president in 1965. Hoping to overcome his reluctance, the new First Lady paid a visit to his hotel suite. When her charm and entreaties did not move him, she turned on the tears. Unable to bear her sobbing, he asked what she wanted. "Sign this," she said, handing him a document in which he agreed to take the post.

"The text was drafted": David Beckwith, February 28, 1986, filed to TIME. Take 15.

"It has already": FOIA case no. 8601724 (February 15, 1986) telegraph from Sec State to Am Embassy: "White House Statement Concerning Philippine Presidential Election").

"Shortly afterward": FOIA case no. 8601724 (February 15, 1986, cable from Sec State to all depts and consular posts: "Philippine Election").

365 "The assembly had two more days": Author's interview with source close to Marcos (February 15, 1988).

"Marcos had even gone so far": Ibid.

"When it came time": Author's interview with Cayetano (February 25, 1986).

NAMFREL count: Joe Concepcion, press conference, February 18, 1986.

" A CIA projection": Sacerdoti, Tasker, *FEER*, February 27, 1986.

366 "In the palace": Author's interview with source close to Marcos (February 16, 1986).

"On that very night": I called Enrile's home that night to try and confirm rampant rumors that he would resign from the cabinet. He insisted that he had only submitted a "courtesy resignation," and told me I would be "unwise" to play it up in my story that week. He promised to explain everything "on Monday." Core-Group members later confirmed they had gathered together to complete plans for their coup.

"Our plan was to do it": Author's interview with Robles (August 24, 1986).

"The condemnation": Author's interview with Figueroa (October 25, 1987).

367 "It was feasible": Author's interview (February 26, 1986).

"Honasan, in particular": Author's interview with Calub (August 22, 1986).

368 "In recent days": Author's interviews with four sources.

369 "Reports circulated": FOIA case no. 8601724 (telegram no. 00503, February 13, 1986: "Conversation with Unnamed Source").

"Security arrangments were": FOIA case no. 8601724 (telegraph no. 05294, February 14, 1986; from Amb Manil to Sec State: "Conversation with Unnamed Informant").

"A growing 'siege mentality' ": Ibid.

370 "Why does he humble": Ibid.

"He told the president": Ibid.

"Later Ramos": Author's interview with Ramos (August 19, 1986).

371 "The coup-plotting": Author's interviews with two officers.

"During a dinner party": February 28, 1986, at the home of Jorge and Stella Araneta, also attended by Ambassador and Mrs. Bosworth, Peping and Ting-Ting Cojuangco, and the author.

Habib meeting with Marcos: Author's interview with Marcos aide (February 17, 1986); Sacerdoti, Tasker, FEER, February 27, 1986.

"That afternoon Habib": Author's conversation with Cory Aquino (February 18, 1986).

"The advisor, Ronaldo Zamora": FOIA case no. 8601724 (February 17, 1986, cable from DOS to Poindexter: "Philippine Election Update No. 17").

372 "The embassy subsequently": Author's interview with U.S. embassy official (October 24, 1987).

"A Pentagon official": Author's interview with U.S. Government official, Washington (1987).

"We talked for maybe": Author's interview with Almonte, (October 24, 1987).

373 "The PMA Alumni": Author's interview with Malajacan, (August 7, 1987).

"Meanwhile, in need": Among those who identified Major Edgardo Doromal as the source of one leak were Marcos, Malajacan, and Robles.

"Thus, by Friday night": Figueroa, Malajacan, Robles, and others confirmed that Ver had learned of the plot from at least two unauthorized leakers with RAM.

374 "Operation Boodlefight": Author's interview with Captain Roger Diaz (August 14, 1986).

"Knowing that the palace": Author's interview with Malajacan, (August 7, 1987).

20: PEOPLE POWER

The following works were helpful in reconstructing the so-called "four day revolution": Arillo; John Bresnan, ed., Crisis in the Philippines—The Ferdinand Marcos Era and Beyond (Princeton University Press, 1986); Johnson; National Times of Australia on Sunday; Patricio Mamot, People Power: Profiles of Filipino Heroism (New Day Publishers, Quezon City, 1986); People Power—An Eyewitness History, (SJ Foundation, Manila, 1986); Simons.

Other references:

375 "A general": Author's interview with General Dionisio Tan-Gatue (August 21, 1986).

376 "While he and Marcos": Recounted to author by Aruiza and other Marcos aides, and by Honasan and Batac.

"Ver had sent": Author's interview with Batac (October 10, 1987).

377 "Following the arrests of": Author's interviews with Robles (February 26, 1986) and Malajacan (August 7, 1987).

"It all fit": Author's interview with Robles (August 24, 1986).

"We told the minister": Author's interview with Robles (February 26, 1986).

"When Robles left": Ibid.

378 "That's what makes Ramos": Author's interview (November 1984).

"A U.S. official": Author's interview (August 1986).

"Enrile's phone call": Recounted by Enrile in phone conversation with author from Camp Aguinaldo before dawn on February 23, 1986.

"In fact, Ramos later": Author's interview with Ramos (August 19, 1986).

379 "Before Enrile phoned him": Author's interview with Belmonte (October 5, 1987).

"Somebody has to be": Author's interview with Ramos (August 19, 1986).

380 "An American consultant": Author's interview, U.S. (February 1987).

"Some sources close to Ramos": Author's interviews, Manila (October 5, 1987).

"As usual, Ramos": Author's interview with Ramos (August 19, 1986).

381 "I have to give Eddie": Author's interview, Manila (August 25, 1986).

"Enrile was reluctant": Nelly Sindayen (February 23, 1986) file to TIME.

"Peping told me": Author's interview with President Aquino (December 9, 1986).

382 "Laurel had called": Author's interview with Laurel (March 2, 1987).

"When she finally got through": Author's interviews with President Aquino (February 28, 1986), Osmeña (August 8, 1986), Enrile (February 23, 1986); Burton, TIME, March 3, 1986.

"As their thoughts turned": Author's interview with Osmeña (August 8, 1986).

383 "I got to the monastery": Author's interview with President Aquino (February 28, 1986); Burton, TIME, March 10, 1986.

"One and one-half hours": Author's interview with Diaz (August 14, 1986).

384 "American officials": Author's interviews, Washington, D.C., (August 1987).

385 "In the Philippines": Author's interview with Allen (August 25, 1987).

"The officer who": Author's interview with Enrile (October 24, 1987).

"Another Filipino had confided": Author's interview, Manila (October 16, 1987).

"On the contrary": Author's interviews with two officers (February 26, 1986, October 25, 1987).

"Our policy": Author's interview (October 1987).

"We were correct": Author's interview with Crowe, (July 16, 1987).

386 "Marcos had a simpler": Author's interview with Marcos, Honolulu (April 16, 1986).

"The chief of staff": Arillo, p. 19.

387 "A Scout Ranger": Author's interview (August 6, 1986).

"When Ahorro": Author's interview with Ahorro (February 25, 1986).

"Their presence was not": Arillo, pp. 42–43.

"Among the first": Author's interview with Butz Aquino (October 13, 1983).

388 "At 1:30 A.M.": Ibid.

389 "The first question": Author's interview with Malajacan (August 7, 1987).

"General Josephus Ramas": Arillo, p. 60.

390 "This is insane": *National Times of Australia on Sunday* October 12, 1986.

391 "I was very scared": Arillo, p. 121.

392 "As Tadiar's tanks": Johnson, p. 111.

"When the tanks": Arillo, p. 60; *National Times of Australia on Sunday* October 12, 1986.

"Seeking an alternate": Arillo, pp. 60, 61.

393 'Screenwriter Amado Lacuesta": *People Power*, pp. 125–29.

"Shortly after the tanks": Arillo, p. 66.

"The cardinal later revealed": *People Power*, p. 119.

394 "On Sunday night": Author's interview with U.S. embassy official (August 1986).

"Not many officers": Author's interview with David (October 19, 1987).

395 "Waiting for Habib": Author's interview with Wolfowitz, Jakarta (October 28, 1987).

"A sneer in his voice": Scene recounted to author by participants (1987).

"As the portrait": Ibid.

396 "Immediately a secret cable": FOIA no. 8601724 (February 23, 1986, cable from Monjo to JCS Washington, Sec Def, CINCPAC: "Landing Instructions, Marcos").

"A message from Reagan": Author's interview with Ople (May 12, 1986).

397 "Across town": Arillo, p. 71.

"As the marines": *National Times of Australia on Sunday* October 12, 1986.

"In the confusion": Johnson, pp. 188–89.

399 "That day at lunchtime": Author's interview with President Aquino (December 9, 1986).

"We did not want a junta": Author's interview with Enrile (February 27, 1986).

"He was talking about": Author's interview with Malajacan (August 7, 1987).

400 "As Balbas continued to procrastinate": Arillo, pp. 84–85.

"That attack so terrified": Author's interview with Virata (March 3, 1987).

401 "We floated information": Author's interview with Figueroa.

"Colonel Balbas was finally": Arillo, p. 86.

"The Marcoses spent": Author's interviews with Marcoses and Aruiza, Honolulu (April 16, 1986).

"He remained obsessed": Author's interview with Marcos, Honolulu (April 16, 1986).

402 "Officials in Washington": Alessandra Stanely, February 27, 1986, file to TIME.

"Bong Bong Marcos pulled": Author's interview with witness (February 24, 1986).

403 "They are treating me": Author's interview with Ople (May 12, 1986).

"They are telling me": Author's interview with Armacost (July 8, 1987).

404 "I think you should": Smith, Burton, McGeary, Stewart, TIME, March 10, 1986.

"Half an hour later": Arillo, p. 108.

"Son-in-law": Author's interview with source close to Marcos (May 1986).

"Apparently having second": Author's interview with Enrile (February 27, 1986).

405 "*Manong* Andy": Author's interview with Ramas, (August 19, 1986).

"Two inaugurations": Nelly Sindayen (February 27, 1986) file to TIME; Tifft, Burton, Sindayen, TIME, March 10, 1986.

"There was a shouting bout": Author's interview with Enrile (October 24, 1987).

"One Core-Group member": Author's interview with Enrile (October 24, 1987).

406 "Secret negotiations": Author's interviews with Allen (August 25, 1987) and palace aides.

407 "At seven o'clock": Author's interview with Allen (August 25, 1987).

"All afternoon Marcos": Author's conversation with Aruiza, Honolulu (April 16, 1986).

410 "Inside, the First Family's presence": Author's interview with TIME photographer Robin Moyer (February 26, 1986).

"1,060 pairs of shoes": Seth Mydans, *New York Times*, February 9, 1987.

21: <u>EXEUNT</u>

412 "But, always pressing": Author's interview with Allen (August 25, 1987).

"Desirous of being": Author's interview with President Aquino (February 28, 1986).

"Bosworth said": Author's interview with Bosworth (December 11, 1986).

"Although General Ramos denied": Author's interview with Ramos (August 19, 1986).

"Get him out": Author's interview (December 1986).

"Marcos has left": Author's conversation with Cecilia Munoz Palma (October 5, 1987).

"By making it so": Author's interview with Cory Aquino (February 10, 1986).

"What she did not know": Author's interview with Allen (August 25, 1987).

413 "We had been up": Author's interview with Aruiza (April 17, 1986).

"He got on the phone": Johnson, p. 268.

"Newly aware": Author's interview with Allen (August 25, 1987).

"I told the head": Author's interview with David (October 19, 1987).

"One hour later": Author's interview with Aruiza (April 16, 1986).

414 "Even Saint Peter": Author's interview with Ninoy Aquino (August 21, 1983).

EPILOGUE: THE UNFINISHED REVOLUTION

415 "How could I possibly": Author's interview with President Aquino (February 28, 1986).

"Had the largely psychological": Sandra Burton, "Aquino's Philippines: The Center Holds," *Foreign Affairs* 65 (Nov. 3, 1987).

416 "Yet his message": Enrile speech, Ilo Ilo, April 13, 1986.

"In a speech in Cebu City": April 13, 1986.

417 "Most of the pillars she shook": Author's interview with Robles (May 9, 1986).

"In keeping with": Author's interviews with several officers.

"Presidential spokesman": Author's conversation with Locsin (January 27, 1988).

"Robles prepared": Author's conversation with Robles (January 28, 1988).

"If she is just a figurehead": Author's interview with Robles (December 3, 1986).

"Aquino's chief advisor": Author's interview with Arroyo (June 1986).

418 "Arroyo's game": Author's conversation with Locsin (January 27, 1988).

419 "The coup talk built": Enrile's October 26, 1986, speech before an anti-Communist rally in Manila; *Business Day*, October 27, 1986.

"That action": Author's interviews (December 3, 1986).

"Bill of particulars": Ibid.

"In the past we had talked": Author's interview with President Aquino (December 9, 1986).

"It was not a coup": Author's interview with Ermita (December 8, 1986).

420 "It is a sad comment": Author's interview with President Aquino (December 9, 1986).

"It was not a question": Author's interview with President Aquino (December 9, 1986).

421 "General Ramos realized": Author's interview with Angara (February 23, 1987).

422 "When I talked to Aquino": December 9, 1986.

"That incident was": Author's interview with Escaler (October 8, 1987).

423 "According to her longtime": Author's interview with Ongpin (October 12, 1987).

"In exasperation": Author's conversation with Arroyo (June 26, 1986).

"Among the most egregious examples": Author's interview with a cabinet member (October 17, 1987).

424 "Worse, American auditors": Author's interview with Platt (October 24, 1987).

425 "Locsin began barking": Account of ranking officers who were present (December 8, 1986).

426 "Honasan had gambled": Author's interviews with fellow officers.

"He would rather": Author's interview with Shahani (Novemer 14, 1987).

"Ramos will quit": Author's interviews (October 1987).

427 "Speaker Pro Tempore": Author's interview with Cuenco (October 22, 1987).

"I found their Senate": Author's interview with Salonga (October 20, 1987).

"She will not take her own": Author's phone conversation with Cojuangco (Second week in September 1987).

"The armed forces are weary": Author's interview (November 1987).

"Others stated the case": Author's interviews (November 1987).

428 "President Aquino was getting": Author's interview with Platt (October 24, 1987).

"He insisted that his nemesis": Author's interview with source close to President Aquino (October 8, 1987).

"Not long after": Author's interview with Ongpin (October 12, 1987).

429 "When I saw the president": October 19, 1987.

430 "His widow confided to me later": Letter from Maribel Ongpin, January 26, 1988.

431 "Even with a praiseworthy": Xinhua news service quoting Central Bank Governor Fernandez, April 4, 1988.

"Annual export earnings": Galang, FEER, August 13, 1987.

432 "The land reform program": Chanda, FEER, July 2, 1987, citing a World Bank review of the Philippine government's land reform plans.

"Singapore President Lee Kuan Yew": Associated Press, April 16, 1988.

"The Communist Party": Analysis based on author's interviews with two party officials in Manila, November 1987.

Index